The Postclassic Mesoamerican World

The Postclassic
Mesoamerican
World

Edited by
Michael E. Smith
and
Frances F. Berdan

The University of Utah Press

Salt Lake City

First paperback printing 2010

14 13 12 11 10   1 2 3 4 5

 The Defiance House Man colophon is a registered
trademark of The University of Utah Press. It is
based upon a four-foot-tall, Ancient Puebloan
pictograph (late PIII) near Glen Canyon, Utah.

LIBRARY OF CONGRESS CATALOGING-IN-PUBLICATION DATA

The postclassic Mesoamerican world / edited by Michael E. Smith and
Frances F. Berdan.
        p.   cm.
Based on a conference held April 1999 at the Kellogg Center at Michigan
State University.
Includes bibliographical references and index.
    ISBN 978-1-60781-024-7 (alk. paper)
    1. Indians of Mexico—Antiquities—Congresses. 2. Indians of Central
America—Antiquities—Congresses. 3. Social systems—Congresses. 4.
Indians of Mexico—Commerce—Congresses. 5. Indians of Central
America—Commerce—Congresses. 6. Mexico—Antiquities—Congresses. 7.
Central America—Antiquities—Congresses. I. Smith, Michael Ernest,
1953– II. Berdan, Frances.
    F1219 .P733 2003
    972'.0009'021--dc21   2002013834

Contents

Figures

Tables

Preface

The past two decades have seen an explosion of research on Postclassic Mesoamerica by archaeologists, ethnohistorians, and art historians, and the chapters in this book seek to make sense out of the results of this work by applying a world-systems approach tailored to the setting. This project had its seeds in a symposium organized by Janine Gasco and John Pohl at the 1996 Annual Meeting of the American Anthropological Association in San Francisco. The session, titled "Ideological and Socioeconomic Transformation in Postclassic Mesoamerica," brought together scholars actively working on new data and new approaches. At the end of the session, it was clear to a number of participants that we were on the verge of a new understanding of Postclassic Mesoamerica. What was needed was a working conference where scholars representing diverse regions and distinct methods could interact to develop that new understanding.

The editors agreed to organize such a conference, which was held at the Kellogg Center at Michigan State University in April 1999 with funding from the Wenner-Gren Foundation for Anthropological Research. (Our home universities—the University at Albany, SUNY, and California State University, San Bernardino—also provided limited funding.) Most of the contributors to this volume attended the conference and presented papers. Nikolai Grube attended the conference but was unable to prepare a chapter for this book. The conference was very productive and intellectually challenging, and the participants agreed that important progress had been made toward generating a new understanding of Postclassic Mesoamerica.

Rather than simply editing our original conference papers to produce a book, we decided that our new insights on Postclassic Mesoamerica could be better communicated by constructing a book from scratch. On the final day of the session, we designed a table of contents that contained a large number of short contributions, and we divided up the work of preparing the chapters, many of them coauthored. As writing progressed, Phil Kohl added Evgenij N. Chernykh as a coauthor for chapter 37, which compares Postclassic Mesoamerica to Bronze Age west Asia. There has been considerable communication among the various contributors during the writing of these chapters, and this book is a joint project of all of the authors; many of the chapters contain insights and information from individuals in addition to those listed as the authors.

A fundamental point of discussion at the conference, and in this book as well, concerns the role of world-systems theory in our model of Postclassic Mesoamerica. Archaeologists today run the gamut from born-again world-systems theorists who see this approach as the salvation of archaeology, to staunch opponents who see world-systems approaches as fundamentally flawed and misguided. Although neither extreme was represented at our conference, this group of authors does include a range of opinions on the subject.

As we describe in a preliminary report on the conference (Smith and Berdan 2000) and in more detail here (chapters 2, 3, 37 and 38), no single world-systems theory or approach—neither Wallerstein's original formulation nor the various versions published by archaeologists and historians—seems adequate to model the dynamics of Postclassic Mesoamerica. Nevertheless, the body of literature on world-systems approaches provides insightful ways of looking at the data from Mesoamerica, and we think many concepts derived from that literature are essential to understanding the nature of Postclassic changes and dynamics. There was some tension at the 1999 conference on this issue, and that tension finds expression in several of the chapters in this book. We see this as a creative tension that contributes to a fuller picture of the setting described in this book. To those opponents of world-systems approaches who view our enterprise with suspicion, and to those world-systems partisans who think we are too loose with the concepts, we invite critique and dialogue. This is a book about Mesoamerica using concepts from world-systems approaches, not a book about world systems using Mesoamerican data as illustrations. Readers can judge for themselves whether our use of world-systems concepts helps or hinders an understanding of Postclassic Mesoamerica; the proof is in the pudding.

We would like to thank the Wenner-Gren Foundation for Anthropological Research for providing the major funding for the conference. The University at Albany, SUNY, and California State University, San Bernardino, contributed additional funds for conference costs. Helen Pollard was very helpful as our local host for the conference in East Lansing, and we also thank her students for helping out in various ways. The staff of the Kellogg

Center provided excellent facilities and support for the conference. Timothy S. Hare produced helpful maps used at the conference, and he later generated the base maps used to produce the maps in chapter 3. We thank Lisa Montiel for compiling the bibliography and helping with various tasks. In preparing the manuscript, Mary Flynn, Elizabeth Hoag, Cynthia Heath-Smith, and Tiffany Kenny helped in numerous ways.

Part I

An Ancient World System

I

Postclassic Mesoamerica

Michael E. Smith

Frances F. Berdan

The first meeting between European and Mesoamerican peoples occurred during Christopher Columbus's fourth voyage to the New World, when he came upon a trading expedition of Maya merchants paddling a large dugout canoe off the Bay Islands. These merchants were carrying goods from all over Mesoamerica, including obsidian knives and swords from a highland source; cacao beans from the tropical lowlands; bronze axes and bells most likely from the Tarascan realm of west Mexico; crucibles for smelting copper; and fancy cotton textiles (Columbus 1959; see also Blom 1932:533–34; Edwards 1978; Sauer 1966:128).[1] The diversity of products carried by these merchants exemplifies the fact that during the final preconquest period, the entire area of Mesoamerica, from the Aztec highlands to the Maya lowlands and beyond, constituted a single economic and cultural zone integrated by commercial exchange and a variety of other types of social interaction.

The high degree of long-distance integration shown by the Maya trade canoe is one of the remarkable features of Mesoamerica during this Late Postclassic time period. Although trade and interaction over long distances had characterized Mesoamerican societies for millennia, these processes reached new heights of intensity and importance in the centuries prior to the Spanish conquest in the early sixteenth century. The volume of exchange expanded greatly during this interval, and economic networks became increasingly commercialized with the widespread use of money, marketplaces, and merchants. Stylistic interaction—the spread of graphic styles and the standardization of iconography and symbolism across broad areas—also reached new levels of intensity in the Late Postclassic period. These processes of economic and stylistic interaction had major impacts on Mesoamerican societies. As people throughout this large area were drawn into macroregional exchange networks, the economic and social lives of households and communities were transformed in myriad ways.

Although long-distance trade and stylistic interaction both have long histories of research in Mesoamerica, only recently have scholars begun to appreciate the magnitude of macroregional networks and their effects on peoples throughout Mesoamerica in Postclassic times. Scholars in the early twentieth century, lacking firm archaeological data, invoked migrations of peoples and vague processes of long-distance "diffusion" to explain the course of cultural development in different regions (Bernal 1979; Willey and Sabloff 1993). By the 1960s archaeologists had begun to accumulate large bodies of reliable information about early Mesoamerican societies. Many of these scholars applied an ecological perspective (linked to the "new archaeology" approach) that sought the causes of social changes in the local environment, not in the vague long-distance influences of the diffusionists (e.g., Sanders and Price 1968). Although trade was a topic of analysis by these and later archaeologists (e.g., Parsons and Price 1971; Tourtellot and Sabloff 1972), the predominant focus of Mesoamericanists on local areas and environmental adaptations prevented scholars from appreciating the full extent and significance of long-distance exchange and interaction (Feinman and Nicholas 1991; see discussion below).

It is only recently that empirical and theoretical advances have revealed the nature of Postclassic innovations in long-distance trade and stylistic interaction, and the extent to which these processes permeated life in societies from western Mexico to Yucatán. Empirical advances include new results from the chemical sourcing of ceramic, obsidian, and metal artifacts; expanded regional surveys and household excavations; new analyses of texts and documents; and more-systematic studies of Postclassic art and iconography. The new data resulting from these advances can best be interpreted within the broad theoretical approach called "the world-systems perspective." Postclassic Mesoamerica is an example of a pre-capitalist world system in that it was a large-scale zone of economic and social interactions that tied together independent polities, and these interactions had significant impacts on the participating societies (see chapter 2).

The authors of this book use a modified world-systems approach to describe and interpret new evidence—archaeological, ethnohistoric, and art historical—on Postclassic Mesoamerica. Regions traditionally conceived as relatively separate units are treated here as part and parcel of a larger, integrated world system and as sharing in common historical and cultural processes. This perspective helps in the identification of the factors that generated the distinctive characteristics of Postclassic Mesoamerica. In chapter 2 Kepecs and Kohl review archaeological approaches to world-systems theory and set the theoretical context for this book. Then, in chapter 3, Smith and Berdan detail the modifications of the world-systems approach that this group of authors has found helpful for understanding Postclassic Mesoamerica.

THE DEVELOPMENT OF THE POSTCLASSIC WORLD SYSTEM

Our consideration of the Postclassic Mesoamerican world system begins in the aftermath of the collapse of the major Classic-period civilizations. The centuries between these events and the Spanish conquest of the early 1500s saw two broad cycles of expansion and diversification of long-distance trade and communication that engulfed the entire area of Mesoamerica. The destruction of the central district of Teotihuacan during the seventh century A.D. (Millon 1988) was followed by the first economic cycle, a major reorientation of long-distance trade and communication throughout much of Mesoamerica.

The Epiclassic period—as the seventh through tenth centuries A.D. are called in most of Mesoamerica outside the Maya area—saw new patterns of connections among regions. Unlike long-distance trade during the Classic period, which focused primarily on large centers such as Teotihuacan, Monte Albán, and the major Maya capitals, Epiclassic trade was more decentralized, flourishing in coastal and peripheral zones (Pollard 1997; Smith and Heath-Smith 1980; Webb 1978). A set of common symbols painted and incised on ceramics (including geometric designs such as the step-fret and stylized serpents) spread along the coastal trade routes at this time. Sometimes inappropriately labeled as the Mixteca-Puebla style (see Smith and Heath-Smith 1980), we refer to these symbols as the Early Postclassic international symbol set (see chapters 3, 23, and 24). The iconography of these symbols has recently been interpreted as marking the spread

of a new international religion focusing on Quetzalcoatl, the feathered serpent (Ringle et al. 1998). Whether or not one accepts that argument, it is clear that many parts of Mesoamerica were drawn into close economic and symbolic contact during the Epiclassic period.

These processes of trade and communication continued in the Early Postclassic period (ca. A.D. 950–1150) after the ninth-century collapse of the southern lowland Maya cities. Much of west Mexico was drawn into the Mesoamerican economic and religious orbit at this time. Major cities with considerable international influence arose at Tula in central Mexico and Chichén Itzá in Yucatán (Andrews 1990b; Diehl 1983, 1993; Healan 1989; Tozzer 1957). These two cities were clearly in contact with one another, but the nature of their interactions has remained unclear.

The collapse of Tula and Chichén Itzá in the twelfth century signaled the start of the second great cycle of Postclassic change. All over Mesoamerica, local populations grew and regional systems of city-states arose. The small size and limited political power of these polities were particularly conducive to an expansion of both commercial exchange and stylistic communication. This second cycle of Postclassic development is our primary focus in this book. Although the dynamic economies of the Epiclassic and Early Postclassic periods can be analyzed usefully from a world-systems perspective (e.g., Kepecs et al. 1994), it is more difficult to provide a comprehensive, Mesoamerica-wide framework for that time period, due to the smaller number of excavated sites and some serious gaps in archaeological knowledge. The available information on the second Postclassic cycle—archaeological, ethnohistorical, and art historical—is much richer, and we focus most of our attention on events in the final three to four centuries of the Prehispanic epoch, encompassing the Middle and Late Postclassic periods.

POSTCLASSIC CHRONOLOGY

In most regions of Mesoamerica, archaeologists have neglected the Postclassic period in favor of earlier epochs. They have preferred to work on the first agricultural societies of the Early Formative period, the Olmec and other early complex societies of the Middle and Late Formative periods, or the spectacular civilizations of the Classic period. One result of the neglect of Postclassic archaeology is that the chronological control in many regions is much rougher than for earlier periods. The most striking example of this phenomenon is the Valley of Oaxaca, where a refined sequence of century-long Formative ceramic phases contrasts with a single, massive Postclassic period (Monte Albán V) six centuries in length (Flannery and Marcus 1983). Needless to say, it is difficult if not impossible to study change within the Postclassic epoch with such a rough chronological sequence.

Table 1.1
Postclassic chronologies

Year (A.D.)	Periods	Lake Pátzcuaro Basin	Basin of Mexico	Morelos	Cholula	Mixteca	Valley of Oaxaca	Yucatán	Highland Guatemala
1500	Late Postclassic	Tariacuri	Late Aztec	Late Postclassic, B					
1450					Late Cholollan	Late Postclassic		Late Postclassic	Late Postclassic
1400				Late Postclassic, A					
1350									
1300	Middle Postclassic	Late Urichu	Early Aztec	Middle Postclassic	Early Cholollan		Monte Albán V		
1250								Early Postclassic	
1200					Late Tlachihualtepetl				
1150	Early Postclassic	Early Urichu	Toltec (Mazapan)	Early Postclassic		Early Postclassic			Early Postclassic
1100									
1050					Middle Tlachihualtepetl			Epiclassic	
1000	Epiclassic	Lupe	Coyotlatelco	Epiclassic					
950							Monte Albán IV		
900									
850									
		Pollard 1997	Sanders et al. 1979	Smith 2002	McCafferty 1996b	Lind 1987	Flannery and Marcus 1983	Masson 2000a	Fox 1987

Although most areas of Mesoamerica have Postclassic archaeological chronologies more refined than that for the Valley of Oaxaca, the degree of temporal refinement varies considerably from region to region. Table 1.1 presents Postclassic archaeological chronologies for some of the better-known areas of Mesoamerica. In most areas, the interval between A.D. 900 and the Spanish conquest is divided into either three periods (labeled Early, Middle, and Late Postclassic) or two (labeled Early and Late Postclassic); in a few areas—parts of the state of Morelos and the site of Cholula—there are four periods (on Postclassic regional chronologies, see the sources cited in table 1.1, and also Fowler 1996; MacNeish et al. 1970; Masson 2000a; Pollard 1997; Smith 1992b, 2003). In spite of these regional differences in chronological refinement nearly all areas have transitions between phases during or at the end of the twelfth century. Furthermore, this twelfth-century transition was a time of major social, political, and economic change in almost all regions, setting off the second Postclassic cycle of change mentioned above. These processes and their continuing dynamics are the major foci of this book, although of necessity earlier time periods must be considered to document the twelfth-century changes and to understand changing sociocultural dynamics over the entire Postclassic epoch.

POSTCLASSIC CHANGES

By the twelfth century a significant constellation of processes was underway in Mesoamerica that distinguishes this period from earlier ones. These processes include an unprecedented population growth, a proliferation of small polities, an increased volume of long-distance exchange, an increase in the diversity of trade goods, commercialization of the economy, new forms of writing and iconography, and new patterns of stylistic interaction. Together, these processes stimulated the integration of the diverse regions of Mesoamerica into a single world system.

POPULATION GROWTH

In several parts of Mesoamerica, the Postclassic period was a time of major population growth. In highland central Mexico, where demographic patterns are well documented from settlement-pattern research, the Middle and Late Postclassic periods witnessed a dramatic growth of population (Hare et al. n.d.; Sanders et al. 1979). It is probably not coincidental that this occurred during a time of increased highland rainfall that ended a period of drought that had lasted from the sixth through eleventh centuries (e.g., Metcalfe et al. 1989; O'Hara and Metcalfe 1997; O'Hara et al. 1994). This episode of population growth was accompanied by massive investments in intensive agriculture, including irrigation systems, chi-

nampas (raised fields), and terracing (Sanders et al. 1979; Smith and Price 1994). Similarly, in the Tarascan core area around Lake Pátzcuaro, Late Postclassic population growth coupled with rising lake levels led to population pressure and the need to import food from outside of the Pátzcuaro Basin (chapter 29).

We see these data as supporting Netting's (1993) Boserupian model in which population pressure leads to household-level agricultural intensification, but we reject the extension of Boserup's model by Sanders and others in which population pressure and intensification in turn necessarily cause political centralization and cultural evolution generally. Recent quantitative reconstructions in the Basin of Mexico suggest that agricultural intensification may not have kept up with population growth, leading to periodic famines and food shortages (Whitmore and Williams 1998).

PROLIFERATION OF SMALL POLITIES

The larger regional populations of Postclassic Mesoamerica were carved up into numerous relatively small political units. Generally called city-states or sometimes kingdoms (by us), they went by various names in the native world (e.g., altepetl among the Nahuas, sina yya among the Mixtecs). These city-states combined hereditary political rule, territorial control, specific flamboyant rituals, and specialized economic interests. They were the basic building blocks of political organization throughout the Late Postclassic period. Prominence could be based on military might, hereditary claims, or symbolic stature. Some city-states developed recognized specializations or particularly noteworthy qualities: Texcoco was a center for law, the arts, and learning in general; Cholula was a pilgrimage destination; Acalan was known for its cacao resources. These centers and their characteristics were not only known locally, but also renowned throughout the broader area. There were additional complexities. In some areas (such as in present-day Morelos and Oaxaca) regional conquest states engulfed nearby city-states, while in others vast empires spread a stratified veneer over these long-standing city-state entities. These polities—whether regional conquest states, a hegemonic empire (Aztec), or a more centralized empire (Tarascan)—were hierarchical in demanding services and surpluses from their conquered polities.

The prevalence of small polities at the time of Spanish conquest, and the widespread development of these polities around the twelfth century, are two of the remarkable features of the Postclassic Mesoamerican world system. The chapters in part 2 explore the similarities and differences among these small polities, and the innovations and continuities of the powerful Tarascan and Aztec empires that also developed in Late Postclassic times.

INCREASED VOLUME OF LONG-DISTANCE EXCHANGE

Long-distance exchange was important to all of the ancient cultures of Mesoamerica, from the first inhabitants up through the Spanish conquest (Smith 2001a). The Postclassic period, however, witnessed the largest numbers and greatest diversity of trade goods, the greatest volumes of exchange, and the greatest access to imported goods by communities of all sizes in all areas (chapter 16). The nature and dynamics of small polities of Postclassic Mesoamerica were conducive to the expansion of commercial exchange (Blanton et al. 1993: 208–217; Mann 1986:7–10). The archaeological record reveals higher quantities of imported goods in Postclassic contexts than in earlier ones (see part 3), and ethnohistoric accounts describe marketplaces, professional merchants, and the use of money throughout Mesoamerica at the time of Spanish conquest (chapter 16).

GREATER DIVERSITY OF TRADE GOODS

An important key to Postclassic Mesoamerica is provided by the role of commodities, or goods intended for exchange. The number of different commodities in circulation appears to have been higher in Postclassic times than in earlier eras. This is a difficult hypothesis to prove because our information is clearly biased by the documentary lists of hundreds of trade goods available for the Late Postclassic period (which include many perishable items that cannot be identified archaeologically for earlier periods). Nevertheless, several informal comparisons suggest that there was greater diversity of imports at many Postclassic sites compared to equivalent Classic or Formative sites. In the Yautepec Valley of Morelos, for example, Late Postclassic sites yield imported ceramics from a larger number of areas than Formative or Classic sites, and Late Postclassic sites have obsidian from a larger number of sources than Classic sites (Smith, unpublished data). Also, there seem to be imported goods from a larger number of areas at the Aztec Templo Mayor of Tenochtitlan than at comparable deposits at Teotihuacan or Tikal.

One of the interesting processes in the Postclassic world system was the conversion of former prestige goods into commercial luxury goods. Whereas the production and exchange of high-value goods—such as feathers and exotic jewelry of greenstone and other materials—had previously been under the control or direction of elites, in Postclassic times these goods became commodities available for sale in the marketplace. Although they were still used more heavily by elites, commoners who could afford such goods often purchased them in markets (see chapters 16, 32, and 34). Bulk luxuries such as fine salt (chapter 19), cacao, and decorated textiles (chapter 18) played particularly important roles in the Postclassic economy. The production and exchange of

obsidian reached new heights in the Postclassic period. Shaft mines were used at a number of extraction zones, and the amount of obsidian in circulation increased greatly (chapter 20). New research on copper-bronze metallurgy helps document technological and exchange processes, and highlights the importance of west Mexico (Michoacán and Jalisco) within the overall world system (chapter 21).

COMMERCIALIZATION OF THE ECONOMY

The Postclassic economy was more highly commercialized than earlier Mesoamerican economic systems. Carol Smith (1976c) divides economies into three categories, and we find these distinctions useful here: (1) *uncommercialized*, where distribution systems are based on direct or nonmarket exchange; (2) *partially commercialized*, where distribution systems are based on noncompetitive or controlled market exchange (solar and dendritic market systems); and (3) *fully commercialized*, where distribution systems are based on broadly articulated competitive market exchange (complex interlocking market systems). These three levels are differentiated not only by amount of commercial integration or division of labor, but by the spatial range of the economic system and the degree to which a price-making market allocates commodities and the factors of production (Smith 1976c: 314; see also Neale 1971 on commercialization).

A number of authors have proposed that commercial exchange based in marketplaces was pervasive in Late Postclassic Mesoamerica (e.g., Blanton et al. 1993), whereas others do not agree. Fernández Tejedo (1996), for example, argues that there were few markets in Postclassic Maya settlements and that most long-distance exchange was noncommercial in nature. We believe that the archaeological and ethnohistoric data from most areas of Mesoamerica support the arguments of Blanton et al. (1993) for a high level of commercialization of the Postclassic economy (e.g., Freidel 1981b; Piña Chán 1978; Rathje 1975; Sabloff and Rathje 1975a, 1975b; Smith 1999). Mesoamericanists have been slow to adopt this model partly because of their traditional reliance upon the substantivist economic anthropology of Karl Polanyi (Polanyi et al. 1957; Chapman 1957), in which the very existence of precapitalist markets and market systems is denied (see discussion below). Blanton (1983:52) points out some of the problems created by the application of Polanyi's "anti-market mentality" to the archaeological record.

NEW FORMS OF WRITING AND ICONOGRAPHY

In contrast to earlier phonetic Mesoamerican writing systems—Epi-Olmec, Classic Maya, and Zapotec—the Mixtec and Aztec systems of writing that developed in Postclassic times contained far fewer phonetic glyphs

(Justeson and Broadwell 1996; Marcus 1992a). Although this had the disadvantage of severely limiting the range of ideas that could be communicated, it did have the benefit of uncoupling written texts from particular languages. Postclassic pictorial texts could thus be "read" or interpreted by speakers of diverse languages (Boone 1994; Pohl 1994b; Jansen 1988), and the distinction between "writing" and iconography was reduced. These new "international" systems of pictorial representations made ample use of color, and they flourished in a variety of media in Postclassic times—codices, polychrome ceramics, and mural paintings (see the chapters in part 4). The portability of codices and ceramics was a particularly important feature, allowing written texts and iconography to be exchanged over great distances.

The best-known example of the new Postclassic iconography/writing systems is the Mixteca-Puebla style (Nicholson 1960; Nicholson and Quiñones Keber 1994a). This representational art style was widely adopted in central and southern Mexico during the Middle Postclassic period. It was composed of highly conventionalized symbols painted in vivid, colorful imagery. As discussed in part 4, the Mixteca-Puebla style became a crucial component in the systems of regional and long-distance communication and exchange among diverse polities and languages in Mesoamerica.

NEW PATTERNS OF STYLISTIC INTERACTION

When the codices and painted ceramics containing new forms of writing and iconography entered the expanding commercial networks of the Postclassic period, the result was an unprecedented spread of graphic styles and symbols throughout Mesoamerica. Several pictorial art styles achieved distributions over large areas; these include the Aztec style, the Mixteca-Puebla style, the coastal Maya mural style, and the highland Maya style. These styles shared many formal traits that link them together under the banner of what has been called the Postclassic international style (Robertson 1970). These art styles can be distinguished from a set of standardized religious motifs—an iconography—we call the Late Postclassic international symbol set. These symbols had their origin in an Early Postclassic symbol set that spread over much of Mesoamerica in the Epiclassic and Early Postclassic periods (chapters 23 and 24).

The relationship between the spread of these symbols and styles on one hand, and commercial exchange networks on the other, was complex and mutually reinforcing. Whereas active commercial networks contributed to the spread of the styles and symbols, the meaning and social significance of the pictorial art were in turn important in stimulating trade and communication. These representations had significance to elites, priests, and other individuals in diverse parts of Mesoamerica (see chapters 22, 26, and 27), and they helped forge long-distance social bonds that provided a basis for continuing trade and other forms of interaction.

A number of authors have suggested that the cultural unity of Mesoamerica reached its greatest height in the Postclassic period. Borhegyi (1980), for example, contrasts the greater uniformity of the ballgame and ball courts in Postclassic times with the greater regional differences in the Classic period. Ringle et al. (1998) posit the spread of the Quetzalcoatl cult throughout Mesoamerica in the Epiclassic period, another example of greater religious integration of Mesoamerica in Postclassic times relative to earlier periods. These and other examples of increased cultural integration and uniformity in the Postclassic period were the products of the new patterns of stylistic interaction described above.

TYPES OF MACROREGIONAL LINKAGES

In their comprehensive treatment of preindustrial world systems, Chase-Dunn and Hall (1997:28) define world systems as "intersocietal networks in which the interactions (e.g., trade, warfare, intermarriage, information) are important for the reproduction of the internal structures of the composite units and importantly affect changes that occur in these local structures" (see chapter 2). The sorts of interactions at play in world systems, therefore, are not superficial but rather have substantive effects on the internal workings of the system's components. These same authors (1997:52) identify four basic types of networks that we find useful: the bulk-goods, prestige-goods, political/military, and information networks. Each serves to bound the constituent units of the system differently. A world system, then, can be viewed as composed of all these networks working at the same time but in different ways to integrate the system as a whole. This also means that the system's various constituent units may not have easily defined boundaries. While we may readily identify a city-state's political boundary, it may encompass quite different economic boundaries (for bulk and prestige goods), a different military sphere of influence, and a yet different information network.

Chase-Dunn and Hall's (1997) concept of the *bulk-goods network* refers to the area in which most exchanges of foodstuffs and other heavy, bulky goods take place. In ancient societies with rudimentary transport the bulk-goods network is typically localized, and it is usually the smallest of the world-systems networks. Bulk goods in Mesoamerica moved from producers to consumers along lines of tribute and through long-distance and regional commerce, and local exchange. The *political/military network* describes the area in which regularized political and military interactions take place. For the city-states of Postclassic Mesoamerica, the political/military network sometimes coincided with the bulk-goods network, whereas larger, expansionistic polities produced networks that included more than one bulk-goods network. An interesting feature of the Postclassic world system was the permeability of political borders to trade, even heavily fortified military borders such as that between the Aztec and Tarascan empires (see chapter 14).

Chase-Dunn and Hall (1997) use the concept of a *prestige-goods network* to describe the long-distance exchange of luxury goods that characterized ancient civilizations. As discussed in the next chapter, an explicit appreciation of the systemic importance of luxury goods sets current archaeological world-systems approaches (e.g., Blanton and Feinman 1984) apart from Wallerstein's (1974) initial formulation. Among the major luxury goods traded over long distances in Mesoamerica were textiles, metal, jade, turquoise, feathers, and codices (see chapter 18). This notion of a prestige-goods network must be distinguished from the concept of a prestige-goods "economy." In the latter model, elites control the production, exchange, and consumption of luxuries, and they derive much of their power and status from such goods (see chapter 18). Although the prestige-goods economy model has been applied to Mesoamerican states (e.g., Blanton and Feinman 1984; Schortman and Urban 1996), it is in fact more applicable to chiefdoms than to states. As noted above, the commercialization of the Postclassic economy turned prestige goods into commercial luxuries available to the most humble peasant as well as the highest lord (see chapter 16). It is possible to acknowledge the economic and social importance of luxury goods without invoking the prestige-goods economy model. Many luxury goods carried significant symbolic information, and they were important mechanisms for the construction and maintenance of the information network.

The *information network* was particularly important in the operation of the Postclassic Mesoamerican world system. Much of the information that was exchanged was esoteric religious knowledge that was the purview of elites: calendrical information, rituals, myths, accounts of dynastic history, and the iconography that encompassed these themes. Three media played crucial roles in the establishment and maintenance of the Postclassic Mesoamerican information network: codices, mural paintings, and polychrome ceramics. The information network pertained mostly to elites because the information exchanged tended to be esoteric knowledge (often religious) that required literacy in codex-reading. This network is especially important since it linked high-status persons from various polities and regions, and was probably accompanied by increased bilingualism, marriage alliances, and luxury gift exchanges between elites. Many

analyses of past world systems focus almost exclusively on economic and political processes, and our inclusion of art-historical perspectives on information exchange is one of this study's innovative features. It is simply not possible to understand the complex dynamics of Postclassic Mesoamerica without emphasizing both the commercial and information networks.

CHANGING VIEWS OF POSTCLASSIC MESOAMERICA

The very label "Postclassic" suggests negative value judgments about the quality or condition of the cultures of this time period compared to the "Classic" cultures that preceded them. These terms were proposed by Willey and Phillips (1955, 1958), who used them to represent stages of cultural development. For them, "the Postclassic stage in the New World is defined by the features of, or tendencies toward, urbanism, secularism, and militarism" (1955:784). Rowe (1962) pointed out several problems that arise from using cultural stages to compare regions, and argued strongly for the superiority of chronological periods over stages. Because periods lack the developmental implications of stages, comparisons among regions can be more empirical and direct. Today, Mesoamericanists still use the terms "Classic" and "Postclassic," but they are almost universally interpreted as periods, not stages.

Nevertheless, remnants of the original negative connotations of "Postclassic" as a cultural stage continued in print by recognized scholars until quite recently (e.g., Andrews 1968). More important to Postclassic scholarship today than this antiquated bias has been variation in the theoretical orientations of scholars toward the Postclassic economy. Two broad views can be identified: one emphasizing state control of the economy, and another emphasizing the importance of commercial exchange. The study of Postclassic Mesoamerica has long been dominated by the former view, which in our opinion has slowed acceptance of the archaeological and ethnohistorical evidence for the pervasive role of market systems and long-distance exchange. This section briefly reviews the historical development of ideas about Postclassic Mesoamerica in reference to these themes of decadent decay and state versus market.

THE POSTCLASSIC MAYA:
DECADENT SURVIVORS OR DYNAMIC ENTREPRENEURS?
The use of denigrating labels for Postclassic cultures has been more common in the Maya area than in other parts of Mesoamerica. Ever since Stephens and Catherwood first revealed the splendors of Classic Maya cities to a European audience in the 1830s, the cities of the Postclassic period have been deemed of lower quality, as pale reflections or poor imitations of the great achievements of the

Classic period. The changes between the Classic and Postclassic periods were discussed in terms of decline and decay, and a series of dichotomies was developed to contrast the Classic and Postclassic Maya, including dynamic/decadent, peaceful/warlike, and religious/secular.

This negative view of the Postclassic Maya as decadent survivors was expressed quite explicitly by the archaeologists associated with the Carnegie Institution of Washington who excavated at Mayapán in the 1950s (Pollock et al. 1962). For example, A. Ledyard Smith (1962:269) described the architecture of Mayapán in these terms: "There seems to have been little striving for permanence, just window dressing and false fronts." In 1968, E. Wyllys Andrews IV (1968:46) stated, "The era of Mayapán was a decadent one in all of its arts except perhaps those of politics and war." As late as the 1980s, the term "Decadent Period" was regularly used to denote the Postclassic period in eastern Yucatán (Freidel and Sabloff 1984). Some writers continue to use terms such as "decline" and "decadence" for the Postclassic Maya (Solís 2001: 21, 24).

Challenges to the "decadent survivors" view of the Postclassic Maya came from several directions. Charles Erasmus (1968), in a critique of Sabloff and Willey (1967), suggested that by overemphasizing the severity of the Classic Maya collapse, these and other archaeologists were reinforcing the inappropriate decadent view of the Postclassic Maya. Instead, Erasmus noted, archaeologists should recognize Postclassic Maya society as different than, but not lesser than, Classic society. He suggested that the Postclassic Maya may have been more highly stratified than the Classic Maya, and were just as religious and not any more warlike. This theme was later taken up by Richard Leventhal (1983), who showed that the old contrast between a powerful state religion in the Classic period and a secularized, household-based religion in the Postclassic period was based on preconceptions deriving from the types of structures excavated by early archaeologists: huge urban pyramids at Classic sites, and small domestic shrines at Mayapán.

The most significant challenge to the decadent view of the Postclassic Maya was mounted by William Rathje, Jeremy Sabloff, and David Freidel, who developed a "mercantile model" for the Postclassic period in the 1970s and 1980s (Freidel 1981b; Freidel and Sabloff 1984; Rathje 1975; Sabloff and Rathje 1975a, 1975b).[2] In the most explicit statement of this model and its contrasts with the prior view, Sabloff and Rathje ask, "Can a period of history that witnesses the rise of a merchant class, the development of a new ethic and a substantial increase in economic complexity (including such events as the introduction of mass manufacture and an improvement in the general standard of living) be fairly considered the decadent last gasp of a dying civilization?" (Sabloff and Rathje 1975a:82).

Although some details of their model have been modified or discarded (see chapter 16), the period since 1975 has seen an unprecedented level of research demonstrating that trade and exchange were indeed important and extensive among Postclassic Maya polities (e.g., Andrews 1983, 1990a; Andrews et al. 1989; Kepecs 1999; Mac-Kinnon 1989; McKillop and Healy 1989; Masson 2000a; Schortman et al. 1986; Sidrys 1977b). The chapters in this book, especially chapters 5, 33 and 34, continue this tradition and help provide a broader theoretical framework for Postclassic Maya society through our application of a world-systems approach.

THE AZTEC ECONOMY:
STATE CONTROL OR INDEPENDENT MARKETS?

In central Mexico, the "decadence" of Postclassic cultures was never as prominent an issue as it had been in Yucatán. The many achievements of Aztec civilization were well known from early historical sources, and their Classic-period ancestors at Teotihuacan were only recognized as such relatively recently, in the mid-twentieth century (Bernal 1979). Nevertheless, the same dichotomies applied to Classic and Postclassic cultures in the Maya area (dynamic/decadent, peaceful/warlike, religious/secular) occasionally turn up in descriptions of central Mexico. The more important issue for our overall understanding of Postclassic central Mexico, however, has been the characterization of the Aztec economy.

A useful framework for approaching the diversity of views on the Aztec economy is provided by Brumfiel and Earle's (1987) classification of three theoretical positions, which they term adaptationist, political, and commercial. Although originally proposed for the domain of craft specialization, this scheme is more widely applicable to theoretical orientations on ancient political economy in general.

The Adaptationist Approach

In this approach, elites manage craft production for the benefit of society. This functionalist viewpoint has been applied to the Postclassic economy by William Sanders and some of his associates and students (Evans 1980; Sanders 1956; Sanders and Nichols 1988; Sanders et al. 1979; Sanders and Price 1968; Sanders and Santley 1983). In this approach, the state is assumed to control both production and exchange, and marketplace trade is seen as limited to small local areas (except for the huge market in Tlatelolco, whose size is attributed to the effects of imperial expansion).

The Political Approach

This approach resembles the adaptationist approach in positing strong state control over the economy, but differs in emphasizing the exploitative nature of that control. Elites are seen as selfish agents who exert control to benefit themselves at the expense of commoners, rather than altruistic representatives who assume the burden of control to benefit the entire society. Two varieties of the political approach have been influential in Aztec studies. The first, represented by Pedro Carrasco and others (including Angel Palerm and Pedro Armillas), classifies the Aztec state as an example of Marx's "Asiatic Mode of Production" type. Based in part on Wittfogel's (1957) classification of the Aztecs as a "hydraulic civilization," scholars viewed the Aztec state as a dominant and exploitative institution that strove to control all of the economy, from agriculture to craft production to markets (P. Carrasco 1978, 1981, 1996a, 1999; see also Bartra 1975; Boehm de Lameiras 1986). In the most extreme statement of this view, Carrasco (1982) suggested that the Aztec state was similar to the Inca state, one of the most strongly centralized redistributive economies of the ancient world. We find it hard to imagine two ancient political economies more different than the Aztec and Inca empires, and it is difficult to take Carrasco's comparison seriously. (For criticisms of Carrasco and other applications of the Asiatic Mode of Production model to Postclassic Mesoamerica, see Gándara V. 1986; Isaac 1993a; and Offner 1981.)

The second variety of the political approach, less extreme than Carrasco's statist views, is exemplified by the work of Elizabeth Brumfiel (1980, 1983, 1987a, 1987b, 1991, 1996a). Although Brumfiel does not deny the existence of market systems as institutions that operated independently of the state, she accords them only a minor significance in the economy and chooses instead to focus on state exploitation of commoners through the institution of tribute. Thus when archaeological data reveal an increase in domestic textile production concurrent with the expansion of the Aztec empire, Brumfiel (1996a) simply assumes that this must relate to tribute demands without considering the possibility that textile production may have increased because of greater marketplace involvement (textiles served as media of exchange in Aztec markets; see chapter 16). Similarly, in his analysis of the Late Postclassic obsidian industry at Pachuca, Alejandro Pastrana (1998) simply asserts that mining, tool production, and exchange were controlled by the Aztec state without considering the role of market systems. Pastrana can provide no concrete archaeological or documentary evidence for the supposed state control of obsidian, a view that runs counter to most analyses of the industry (see chapter 19).[3]

The Commercial Approach

In this approach, craft specialization (and, by extension, other sectors of the economy) is viewed as organized commercially, and changes must be explained by the actions of markets and merchants, not the controlling hand of the state. Scholars who have applied this approach to the Aztec economy include Frances Berdan (1977, 1985, 1988), Richard Blanton (1982, 1985), Blanton and Feinman (1984), and Michael Smith (1979, 1980, 1987a, 1996a, 2001c). This book can be classified under Brumfiel and Earle's (1987) commercial approach, although we do not neglect the often overwhelming role of the state and elites in controlling some sectors of the economy (e.g., land tenure, labor arrangements, and the tribute system). To introduce our approach more fully, it will help to place it within the context of archaeological applications of economic anthropology.

ECONOMIC ANTHROPOLOGY AND THE POSTCLASSIC WORLD SYSTEM

The substantivist model in economic anthropology—associated with the work of Karl Polanyi—has exerted a powerful influence on views of ancient Mesoamerica (chapter 2). The scholars mentioned above under both the adaptationist and political approaches have all been influenced to some degree by Polanyi, either directly (Polanyi et al. 1957; Polanyi 1977) or indirectly through Anne Chapman's (1957) application of Polanyi's model to Mesoamerica. Although Polanyi made many valuable contributions to economic anthropology, we feel that reliance upon his model has held back progress in understanding the dynamic nature of the Postclassic economy.

The Influence of Karl Polanyi

Polanyi never acknowledged the existence of precapitalist commercial economies (such as that of Postclassic Mesoamerica), nor did he understand peasant marketing systems that are only weakly connected to modern capitalist national economies. Such noncapitalist commercialized economies, whether rural or urban, find no place in Polanyi's famous trilogy of exchange types: reciprocity, redistribution, and exchange. This scheme jumps directly from preindustrial redistribution to modern capitalism. In order to force ancient commercial economies, from Assyria to Rome, into his framework, Polanyi distorted historical evidence and made numerous inappropriate and artificial interpretations. For example, he claimed that there were no true "prices" in the ancient world (that is, exchange values that rose and fell in response to changes in supply and demand), but rather "equivalencies" that allowed disparate goods to be exchanged. These equivalencies, according to Polanyi, were set by the king and did not change except by royal decree. Subsequent scholarship showed that this was a serious distortion of the evidence, and that prices were indeed present in many ancient economies (e.g., Harris 1993; Snell 1997).

Polanyi's concept of equivalencies was just one of many errors of scholarship that have been pointed out by more than a generation of scholars of the ancient world. For the Near East, Adams (1974) and Larsen (1976)

showed that the merchants of Ashur in the Isin-Larsa period engaged in what is clearly highly commercialized exchange with agents in Kanesh (in Anatolia). Subsequent
studies (e.g., Dandamayev 1996; Gledhill and Larsen
1982; Kuhrt 1998; Snell 1997) have pointed out numerous problems with Polanyi's interpretations of Assyrian
and other ancient Near Eastern economies.[4] Likewise,
scholars have also criticized Polanyi's use of sources and
his interpretations of the Greek (Figueira 1984) and Roman economies (Harris 1993; Storey 1999) as well as the
economies of India and precapitalist Europe (Subrahmanyam 1990). Even Polanyi's analysis of early capitalism (Polanyi 1957), generally acknowledged as his major
contribution to economic history, has been heavily criticized by subsequent scholars (Swaney 2002).

Polanyi's famous "port of trade" model (Polanyi et al.
1957; Polanyi 1963) is particularly problematic for ancient commercial economies. In this model, applied by
Chapman (1957) to Mesoamerica in an influential paper,
all merchants are portrayed as sponsored by the state,
prices are said to be set by the king rather than respond-
ing to supply and demand, and long-distance trade is
seen as divorced from local and regional exchange systems (see chapter 2). In line with criticisms of the model's
use in the Old World (e.g., Figueira 1984; Pearson
1991:73–74), Kepecs and Kohl (chapter 2) and Gasco
and Berdan (chapter 17) show the limitations of this
model for Postclassic Mesoamerica. The latter authors
describe an alternative concept—the international trade
center—that better fits the Mesoamerican data. The authors of the chapters in part 3 show that the Postclassic
economy was far more open and commercialized than
posited by the Polanyi/Chapman model (or by the adaptationist and political approaches).

Our Approach
The world-systems approach followed in this book is described in chapters 2 and 3. At this point, however, we
should relate our views of the Postclassic economy to the
various models described above. The degree of state control over the economy clearly varied both by region and
by the sector of the economy. The Tarascan empire, for
example, maintained tighter control over production and
exchange than did the Aztec empire (chapters 11, 13, 29,
and 30); similarly, craft production and trade were more
closely linked to the state among the polities of the
Mixteca-Puebla region than among their counterparts in
Yucatán (chapters 5, 10, 31, 33, and 24).

Perhaps more fundamental than this regional variation, however, was variation by economic sector. In all
Mesoamerican states, rulers and other elites maintained
strict control over land, labor, and tribute, the primary
bases of political power. As discussed above, however,
one of the greatest innovations of the Postclassic period
was the development of commercial exchange systems

only loosely linked to state institutions. The archaeological and documentary evidence for the pervasive role and
influence of merchants, markets, and money in all parts
of Postclassic Mesoamerica is incontrovertible (chapter
16). We see no contradiction in suggesting that the state
control of land, labor, and tribute coexisted with an autonomous commercialized exchange system; in fact, this
general pattern characterized many past agrarian states,
from China to Rome to precapitalist Europe to the Islamic world (Abu-Lughod 1989; Braudel 1982, 1984;
Elvin 1973; Garnsey and Saller 1987; Hosseini 1995).

When we turn to the realm of craft production and
specialization, however, there was great variation in the
extent to which elites and states exerted influence. Some
craft industries, particularly those producing luxury
goods in Tenochtitlan and in the city-states of the
Mixteca-Puebla area, were closely supervised by elites; in
the latter area, nobles may even have been the artisans
(chapter 22). Other crafts were produced by part-time
and full-time artisans working independently for the
market. Brumfiel's paper (1987b) describing two contrasting forms of craft production in the Aztec economy—rural, part-time artisans producing utilitarian
goods for the market, and urban, full-time specialists
producing luxury goods for elite patrons—is particularly
important in describing this variation in elite control over
economic activity.

One of the reasons we have adopted a world-systems
perspective for Postclassic Mesoamerica is that it is one
of the few approaches capable of encompassing an area
as large as Mesoamerica while accommodating a wide
range of variation in the economic and political organization of the constituent societies. Although commercialized trade and information exchange were two of the
major forces in Postclassic Mesoamerica, they are not the
whole story. The chapters that follow will reveal the true
complexity and dynamics of Postclassic Mesoamerica,
free from biases about decadent survivors and free from
the restricting influence of Polanyi's substantivist economic anthropology.

A NEW APPROACH TO THE POSTCLASSIC MESOAMERICAN WORLD

With this conceptual framework in mind, the contributors to this book examine and unravel the nature and
extent of long-distance and regional interactions in Postclassic Mesoamerica. With a dozen contributors and a
multitude of topics involved, the 38 chapters are necessarily focused and concise. More extensive information
on these topics is available in the works listed in the composite bibliography.

We have divided the chapters into six parts. Part 1 (of
which this is the initial chapter) presents the theoretical
and conceptual framework on which the remaining chap-

ters hang. In the following chapter Kepecs and Kohl present a review of world-systems theory and its applicability to Postclassic Mesoamerica. The final chapter of part 1, by Smith and Berdan, analyzes the spatial components of the Postclassic Mesoamerican world system, explicating our customized version of a world-systems perspective.

Part 2 examines the essential political building blocks of this world system. The eleven chapters in this section begin with a general overview that highlights the importance of city-states and other small polities in Postclassic Mesoamerica. Case studies of small polities from highland Guatemala to west Mexico reveal a variety of forms and processes, which are contrasted to the two extensive empires that developed in the final century before Spanish conquest, the Tarascan and Aztec.

Economic networks are treated in part 3 in eight chapters. A general framework of Postclassic economic institutions is provided in chapter 16, followed by more-specific chapters on international trade centers and key commodities. Then follow chapters on three of the most important commodities in the Postclassic world system: salt, obsidian, and metal. A final chapter examines the political and religious dimensions of commerce in the Mixteca-Puebla area.

Part 4 highlights information networks as significant components of the Postclassic Mesoamerican world system. Key concepts here are international styles—pictorial art styles found over large areas and not clearly linked to a single point of origin—and international symbol sets—iconographic elements that similarly covered large parts of Postclassic Mesoamerica. Three chapters cover the crucial material bearers of these styles and symbols: murals, codices, and polychrome ceramics.

While parts 1–4 address the Postclassic Mesoamerican world system conceptually and topically, the case studies in part 5 take a regional perspective. Although not every part of Mesoamerica is covered here, we do include case studies from many of the areas where there is sufficient evidence to evaluate world-systems processes at Postclassic communities. Part 6, the final section of the book, offers, predictably, a set of conclusions. Non-Mesoamericanists Kohl and Chernykh revealingly compare and contrast this world system with that of Bronze Age west Asia as a stimulus for further worldwide comparisons of such systems, and the final chapter closes the book with a synthesis of our most important results.

Overall, this book, in content and scope, is designed to direct the reader's attention to Mesoamerica not as a collection of separate regional cultures and polities, but as a complex integrated network—a world system—featuring intricate and dynamic linkages of political, economic, and symbolic processes.

2

Conceptualizing Macroregional Interaction

World-Systems Theory and the

Archaeological Record

Susan Kepecs

Philip Kohl

In the 1970s, historical sociologist Immanuel Wallerstein (1974, 1976, 1979, 1982) developed a theoretical framework for studies of the rise and persistence of capitalism. He named this model "world-systems theory." Although the theory deals with the history of today's global economy, many prehistorians are attracted to its macroscale perspective. Yet the relevance of Wallerstein's ideas for premodern cases is open to question.

Since its basis is economic, world-systems theory is subject to the oft-cited "formalist/substantivist debate." Formalists (in the manner of Adam Smith) see the difference between premodern and modern economies as one of degree, while substantivists (following Karl Polanyi) view this distinction as one of kind (Cook 1966; Isaac 1993b).

To grapple with this debate, we need to compare premodern macroregional systems with today's world. Toward this end sociologists, historians, cultural anthropologists, and archaeologists have developed several kinds of world-systems approaches (as distinguished from world-systems theory proper). "World" in premodern terms refers to macroregions in which differentiated social groups were linked through regular interactions involving broad segments of participating populations. Today we have both formalist and substantivist perspectives on premodern world systems. Thus there are theoretical differences among researchers who use this framework. There also are investigators who question whether it should be used at all in archaeological or precapitalist cases.

The authors of this chapter agree that the empirical evidence presented in this book supports a formalist interpretation of Postclassic Mesoamerica (see chapter 1), but we diverge when it comes to the question of whether the world-systems perspective is an appropriate lens through which to examine precapitalist societies. Thus

this chapter was written in two parts. The first begins with an overview of Wallerstein's model and points to where it fails vis-à-vis premodern case studies. This discussion continues with a look at current world-systems approaches, and finally draws from this body of theoretical work several comparative concepts that Kepecs (chapter 33) finds useful in approaching the Postclassic Mesoamerican world. The second part of the chapter (written by Kohl) is a counterpoint, raising important questions about differences between the modern world and premodern interaction systems.

WORLD-SYSTEMS THEORY

Wallerstein (1976) launched his world-systems paradigm against the prevailing developmentalist perspective that spread across the social sciences after World War II. Developmentalists defined the basic unit of analysis as the single society and cast social change in terms of regional shifts in the balance between population and environment. World-systems research took a distinct point of departure: instead of single units, world systems are composed of multiple sociocultural systems bound through a single division of labor that transcends cultural and political boundaries.

The division of labor in the modern world system is tied to dependency theory, brought to the fore (at least in English-language literature [see Stern 1993:27–28]) by Andre Gunder Frank (1966). Dependency refers to the "development of underdevelopment" in which a hegemonic "first world" core exploits an undercapitalized "third world" periphery. The spatial channels through which this core/periphery hierarchy operates are very complex. The core is an economic "world metropolis" that encompasses multiple, competitive, "developed" centers. Each center extracts capital and surplus from the peripheries of its own political sphere, but on a broader scale the world metropolis drains a technologically underdeveloped third world that also consists of multiple nations. For example, the single division of labor in today's world system allows elites in the United States to enjoy part of the high-tech surplus produced by their counterparts in western Europe and Japan, and vice versa, but these highly industrialized countries also extract resources from Latin America and Africa (e.g., Wallerstein 1982:92; Hopkins et al. 1982:45–46).

Although Wallerstein challenged the developmentalist approach, he retained an eco-determinist perspective, arguing (1974:42–45) that the modern world economy was built on the production and transport of bulk goods (food and fuel), driven by increasing population in western Europe. The drive to increase food supply gave rise to technological innovations that created a single division of labor across more territory than ever before.

Wallerstein hypothesized that prior to this expansion the globe was dotted with smaller world systems. Among these were little mini-kin systems and larger-scale but short-lived economic liaisons. Yet Wallerstein, following Polanyi (1957), framed premodern macroscale connections in political rather than economic terms. Given the limits of premodern production and transportation technology, successful large-scale world systems were "world empires" in which cores extracted surplus bulk necessities from their peripheries for redistribution. These politically bound systems were not isolates, but trade among them was external (nonsystemic), involving the diplomatic transfer of high-value, low-weight luxuries between heads of state. In contrast, the modern (capitalist) world economy lacks an overarching political structure. Since there is no mechanism for political redistribution, interacting polities are linked economically rather than politically—through profit-making markets (Wallerstein 1976:348).

WORLD-SYSTEMS THEORY IN PRECAPITALIST CONTEXTS
In the 1980s Wallerstein's ideas spread to other social science disciplines, where they met with mixed success. World-systems ideas were attractive to historians of the "third world," since they could not escape the empirical impact of core/periphery relations on their particular areas of study. Yet they objected to Wallerstein's emphasis on the "world" as the unit of analysis, along with his emphasis on capitalism as the mode of production in the modern world system. Both assumptions failed to account for macroregional interactions among groups using diverse economic strategies at local or regional scales (see Wolf 1982; Stern 1993a, 1993b; Cooper 1993; Mallon 1993).

The historians had an ally in anthropologist Eric Wolf (1982:23), who noted that by focusing on how the core subjugated the periphery, Wallerstein and Frank overlooked the range and variety of "peripheral" societies and their responses to capitalist globalizing processes. Wolf's (1982) landmark book, *Europe and the People Without History,* examines the role of nonwestern groups in the process of capitalist development.

The literature on the "use and abuse" of world-systems theory in history and cultural anthropology is substantial, but our focus here is on prehistory—the realm of archaeology, history, and iconography—since we are interested in finding what is relevant for Postclassic Mesoamerica. A number of archaeologists (e.g., Blanton and Feinman 1984; Kohl 1989) turned to world-systems ideas as an antidote for the developmentalist or cultural ecology perspective championed by Lewis Binford (1962, 1968, 1983). Despite the impact of Binford's approach (e.g., Sanders and Price 1968), empirical evidence of macroregional interactions among premodern societies is common (Blanton and Feinman 1984). World-systems theory offered a systematic new perspective on this evidence—a way out of static diffusion/migration models (e.g., Feinman 1994; Feinman and Nicholas 1991; Trigger 1989:194–195). Yet, as in history and cultural anthropology, the results of archaeological world-systems research often did not fit the model.

The model failed in the realm of core/periphery hierarchy. No one would deny that within regions some ancient centers reached higher levels of ideological, economic, or political achievement than others, but empirical patterns often fail to fit theoretical expectations of a dominant core with an underdeveloped periphery. Various researchers (e.g., Feinman and Nicholas 1991, 1992; Schortman and Urban 1992, 1994; Kohl 1992; Stein 1998; Webster 1994) cite empirical evidence that premodern peripheries were not necessarily underdeveloped vis-à-vis the core, and that core/periphery links were not one-way streets. Ancient peripheries sometimes possessed technologies on which cores depended (Feinman and Nicholas 1992; Kohl 1992; Schortman and Urban 1992b:247). Far from being static receivers of core influences, fringe areas often are hotbeds of activity in which challenges to "the establishment" are generated (Chase-Dunn and Hall 1997:79; Blanton and Feinman 1984; Blanton et al. 1992). This evidence led some researchers to question not only the notion of core/periphery hierarchy, but the utility of world-systems models in ancient contexts in general (e.g., Webster 1994; Stein 1998).

Another stumbling block was Wallerstein's emphasis on bulk goods and his rejection of luxury goods as dynamic factors in world-systems processes. Anthropologist Jane Schneider (1977) argued early on that the search for luxuries—gold, silk, and spices—drove the European age of exploration. Demand for exotic prestige goods is not "extra-systemic"—it can cause drastic shifts in the organization of resource extraction and production (Schneider 1977; see also Adams 1974). Further, the transfer of exotics fostered macroregional interdependence, since in traditional societies these items were critical for elite social reproduction (e.g., Flannery 1968; Blanton and Feinman 1984; Schneider 1991; Helms 1993; Feinman and Nicholas 1991; Kepecs et al. 1994). In this context power-laden exotics were used by core elites to signal their identity, and as gifts to create patron/client chains that bound subordinate elites and middle-level groups in webs of reciprocal obligations. Through this mechanism class enemies were co-opted, political loyalty was promoted in the peripheries, and energy was captured in the form of labor and tribute.

Schneider's (1977) redefinition of the role of luxury goods in macroregional exchange facilitated the discovery that premodern world systems were not necessarily world empires. Instead, several researchers reported evidence of systemic exchange across political boundaries. In these cases some bulk products may have been traded, but in general luxury goods were more important to interaction and integration than "food and fuel." Kohl (1989:227) described the systemic effects of the transfer of metals and textiles among autonomous city-states in Bronze Age Anatolia and Mesopotamia. Similarly, Blanton and Feinman (1984) and Carmack (1996) documented a multicentric world economy in Postclassic Mesoamerica. Centers and routes changed through time, but the Mesoamerican world system always involved multiple cores bound through economic relations (chapter 33). And the best-documented case of a premodern world economy is found in the medieval Old World, where systemic exchange linked oriental empires and feudal European kingdoms (Abu-Lughod 1989:3).

WORLD-SYSTEMS APPROACHES

To paraphrase the great French historian Fernand Braudel (1980:45), models are like ships—gratifying when they float, but the true test is whether new information can make them sink. Much of Wallerstein's framework capsized in the rough empirical waters of premodern political economies, but these failures informed the design of new craft, and the process of exploration was renewed. For reasons that will become apparent, the substantivists focused on the issue of core/periphery hierarchy, while the formalists zeroed in on the world-scale division of labor.

CORE/PERIPHERY HIERARCHY
The modern core/periphery hierarchy is based on unequal exchange. Yet empirical data often contradict the notion of underdeveloped peripheries in the premodern era. Sociologists Christopher Chase-Dunn and Tom Hall see this distinction as a key to developing a diachronic

theory of change in world systems. Toward that end they redefine world systems as core/periphery structures (Hall and Chase-Dunn 1996:19) and ask how these differ empirically through time and space.

Chase-Dunn and Hall's emphasis on core/periphery relations over the other key tenet of world-systems theory—the macroregional division of labor—stems from their basically substantivist perspective (Hall and Chase-Dunn 1996:13). Economy essentially was embedded in polity; thus complex premodern world systems generally were world empires, in which accumulation was monopolized by rulers for redistribution. Chase-Dunn and Hall's notion of world empires is not absolute; they emphasize that empires exercised a high degree of control over sometimes larger world systems. Like Wallerstein, they agree (Chase-Dunn and Hall 1997:210) that multistate systems sometimes existed. Yet in their view world economies were neither successful nor predominant before the sixteenth century. This notion, which evidently overlooks the empirical studies on premodern multistate world systems cited above, is linked to their belief that only the modern capitalist system is driven by competition and profit motives—and competition thrives best in the absence of overarching political control (Chase-Dunn and Hall 1997:33–35).

Thus a key question for Chase-Dunn and Hall is the nature of core/periphery relations within essentially political units. In this context some researchers (e.g., Bairoch 1986, cited in Chase-Dunn and Hall 1997:35) hold that core/periphery hierarchies were relatively unimportant, since technological and developmental gaps were minimal until the industrial era. Yet Chase-Dunn and Hall (1991:18–19, 1997:35–36) argue that all world systems have cores and peripheries based on important differences in social structure. However, premodern core/periphery structures were not necessarily hierarchical. Instead, while some premodern systems were arranged hierarchically (a relationship based on political domination and unequal exchange), others were simply differentiated—that is, lacking underdevelopment (Chase-Dunn and Hall 1997:36).[1]

The addition of core/periphery differentiation to the world-systems framework is a positive advance for research on premodern cases—but we are left with a problem. As Mesoamericanists we cannot relegate the idea of premodern multistate world economies to near-irrelevance. How do we apply core/periphery concepts to Mesoamerica, or, for that matter, to the Bronze-Age Middle East or the medieval Old World? We return to this issue below, in the section on our approach to Postclassic Mesoamerica.

INTERPENETRATING ACCUMULATION
Barry Gills and Andre Gunder Frank (1991; Frank and Gills 1993a) offer a contrasting and essentially formalist

model that emphasizes and expands theoretical concepts of the division of labor in precapitalist world economies. In their opinion, "there has been a widespread underappreciation or underestimation of the role of capital accumulation, markets, the profit motive, 'entrepreneurial elements,' and of long-distance trade for most of world history" (Frank and Gills 1993b:301). By "most of world history" they mean the long-term development of what they see as a single, economically based world system that began with the rise of Egypt and Mesopotamia and culminated in today's global economy. In this context they argue (Gills and Frank 1991:75) that accumulation is the major incentive for, and the ultimate cause of, world-systems linkages and expansion. Elite accumulation is based on surplus extraction, and at the world scale, the accumulation of surplus is shared across political boundaries (Gills and Frank 1991:84–85, 90–93). In other words, world systems are based on interpenetrating accumulation, which is the process through which elites in one zone capture part of the surplus exacted by their counterparts in another. Interpenetrating accumulation is systemic: it engages people from multiple social strata, creating a complex political economy that shifts some labor (formerly invested in domestic production) to surplus production for exchange. As more workers are tied up in production for long-distance trade, more surplus in essential domestic goods also is needed to meet local and regional demands.

There are two modes of accumulation (Gills and Frank 1991:92). In one, private entrepreneurial forces predominate (in most cases with some assistance from the state). In the other, state accumulation prevails (usually with some help from the private sector). These two forces create antagonistic factions; thus over time and space there is a pattern of oscillation between powerful, state-based hegemonies (empires) and weaker political structures in which private entrepreneurs thrive. Under precapitalist conditions, the formation of multistate arrangements is associated with the decline and fragmentation of hegemonies (Abu-Lughod 1989:18; Blanton et al. 1992; Gills and Frank 1991:96, 1993:100; Hansen 2000b). Centralized control is weak on the boundaries of empires, and tensions between powerful core elites and hinterland entrepreneurs are important factors in these shifts (Blanton et al. 1992).[2] Thus Europe, which had been somewhat peripheral (not in a political sense, but in terms of development) to the hegemonies of China and the Middle East, rose in the late fifteenth century to economic dominance. This change was driven by collaborations between rulers and merchants that took advantage of deteriorating conditions in the old empires (Abu-Lughod 1989; Wolf 1982).

Modes of accumulation, like modes of production, need not be uniform throughout the world system (Gills and Frank 1993:98). Today multinational entrepreneurs (primarily private accumulators) trade with communist China (where state accumulation is predominant). In precapitalist times tributary empires (China, the Aztecs) engaged in systemic long-distance trade with smaller, weaker polities (Europe, the Late Postclassic Maya) in which competition among private entrepreneurs flourished (Blanton 1985; Kepecs 1999; see also Abu-Lughod 1989). Accumulation rests on investment in infrastructure and technological development in diverse areas, including agriculture, manufacturing, communications, transportation, trade routes, international nexuses or markets for surplus transfer, and nationalist or religious cults (Gills and Frank 1991:81). When these structures of accumulation are shared regularly across political boundaries, they create macroregional interdependence, and as a result of this joint usage the structures of each independent component merge to some degree (Gills and Frank 1991:84–85).

Since interpenetrating accumulation is shared and systemic, change in any of the component units should reverberate throughout the macroregion (Gills and Frank 1991:85). As Gills and Frank (1991:79) put it, "the rise and fall of great regional metropolitan centers reflects extra-regional changes in which they participate." For example, system-wide restructuring can occur as the result of conflict between state and private forces of accumulation, or from improved transport technology (Gills and Frank 1991:85, 93). World systems generally decline and then (after a period of disorganization) restructure. Through time, world-systems organization is somewhat cumulative, since older patterns tend to persist even though the roles and locations of routes and centers change. And finally, given cumulative technological change, world systems tend to increase in terms of overall size and integration through time (Abu-Lughod 1989: 366–368, cited in Frank and Gills 1993c:9; Chase-Dunn and Hall 1991:16).

DEVELOPING A WORLD-SYSTEMS APPROACH FOR POSTCLASSIC MESOAMERICA

Anne Chapman (1957), a Polanyi substantivist, wrote the original study of macroregional exchange in Mesoamerica. She could not overlook the documentary evidence for markets in the late Prehispanic Mesoamerican world, but she took pains to separate "democratic exchanges of home market places, at which anyone with a few cacao beans to spend was welcome" from long-distance trade—a political event divorced from the direct concerns of common people (chapter 1).

Chapman's notions prevailed in Mesoamerican studies until challenged on two fronts. First, authors such as Berdan (1978), Freidel and Sabloff (1984), and Voorhies (1989b) pointed out empirical difficulties with her port of trade model (chapter 17). Second, in a separate approach

Schneider (1977) underscored the systemic properties of prestige goods, which in turn spurred Blanton and Feinman's (1984) original paper on Mesoamerica's multicentric world economy (see also Blanton et al. 1992). Later research, following this lead, deals with diachronic empirical evidence of large-scale production and exchange across political boundaries, described in terms of interpenetrating accumulation (chapter 33). Various household-level studies (chapter 32) reveal the presence of nonlocal goods in "commoner" contexts. In the Aztec case we even know what people produced for exchange (e.g., Smith 1997a; Brumfiel 1980, 1987b; Blanton and Hodge 1996). And both ethnohistoric and settlement-pattern research (e.g., Berdan 1975, 1985; Blanton 1996) indicates that markets were the mechanism through which Aztec commoners were integrated into far-flung exchange systems (chapter 16).

All of this research depicts Postclassic Mesoamerica as a multicentric and increasingly profit oriented (commercialized) world economy. In this sense the difference between our example and the modern world system is one of degree, rather than one of kind. Yet the Mesoamerican world also differed from the modern case in significant ways. Cores drained resources from their own hinterlands, but there was no "world metropolis," or the development of underdevelopment at the world-system scale. We consider "hinterlands" to belong to political units rather than to the broader structure of world systems. Thus we agree with Chase-Dunn and Hall that underdevelopment is less important at the world scale in premodern systems than in the modern one. Yet we depart from their scheme since it fails to account for long-term multicentric precapitalist world systems.

In Mesoamerica, there is no core/periphery hierarchy at the world-system scale. There are what we decided to call "unspecialized peripheries" and "resource-extraction zones" (chapter 3), but these areas were peripheral because they simply were not involved in highly systemic contacts with the Mesoamerican heartland, rather than being peripheries in a political sense.[3] Nevertheless there was no single, all-encompassing world system in the Prehispanic Americas. At the north and south ends of Mesoamerica were "contact peripheries" (see chapter 3); these regions participated more actively in different Prehispanic world systems: the realm of the desert Southwest, or lower Central America.

Within Mesoamerica we discern several distinct but not unequal kinds of subsystems (chapter 3). In taking this approach we follow the empirical example set by sociologist Janet Abu-Lughod, whose landmark book, *Before European Hegemony: The World System* A.D. *1250–1350*, lays bare the macroregional interconnections that bound the far corners of the medieval Old World. Abu-Lughod is well-versed in the rugged terrain of world-systems theory, but her approach is free of jargon and avoids the theoretical labyrinths of Chase-Dunn and Hall or Gills and Frank.

Abu-Lughod (1989:32–33) simply divides the Old World into a nested arrangement of eight subsystems grouped within three large circuits—Europe, the Middle East, and the Far East. Contacts were mediated through trade emporia without hinterlands, and people and goods moved across the various parts of the world system via sea lanes, rivers, and overland routes. Some of these subsystems (Europe, the Islamic world of the Persian Gulf/Arabian sea) were characterized by multiple city-states; in others (Mamluk Egypt, the Mongolian empire of Central Asia, and especially China), cities were bound hierarchically in imperial domains (Abu-Lughod 1989:39, n. 9). Prior to the thirteenth century, Europe was peripheral (in the sense of our "unspecialized" category) to the Orient, and later (in the fifteenth century) it became dominant. But in the thirteenth century each of the Old World subsystems participated, at the world scale, in equal exchange (Abu-Lughod 1989:37).

The Mesoamerican world system differs from the Old World case by orders of magnitude, yet similar processes were in effect (chapter 33). Mesoamerican subsystems, like those of the medieval Old World, were linked by sea, riverine, and overland routes—and as in the Old World, no single subsystem prevailed. Like Abu-Lughod, the authors represented in this volume are interested in the empirical aspects of this systemic trade. Thus 50 years after Chapman's description of trade as acts of elite diplomacy, we are documenting the ways in which long-distance trade meshed with regional and local markets, and how production for exchange was organized. We want to trace corridors and nexuses, to describe how transport systems worked, and to show how a symbolic lingua franca facilitated macroregional communications. The chapters in this volume address these and other issues.

MODELING THE WORLD SYSTEM: *CAVEAT LECTOR*

The perspective sketched above emphasizes basic structural similarities between the final premodern world system of the Old World and that of Postclassic Mesoamerica. In both cases, significant quantities of commodities were being produced and moved across political boundaries, and what many people did within their own polities depended on this international movement of goods; that is, basic divisions of labor also extended across these political boundaries. The substantivist model championed by Polanyi and adopted uncritically by many archaeologists romanticizes Precolumbian Mesoamerica and does not fit well with the bulk of evidence reviewed here. The Postclassic Mesoamerican economy was much more commercialized than the Polanyi model allows. Although substantial tributes were extracted by centralized states and aspirant empires, many materials also responded to supply and demand forces operating under competitive market conditions; to paraphrase Gills and Frank (1991), these latter movements, which were often directed by entrepreneurs in search of gain, have been widely underappreciated and underestimated. In its most basic sense, the world-systems model postulates that the connections between areas or polities were sufficiently and systemically integrated that significant developments or changes in one region affected developments throughout the entire interconnected system; interdependency characterized the component parts of the system, and such interdependencies clearly can be reconstructed for the Postclassic Mesoamerican world.

What problems or difficulties beset the adoption of this world-systems model? Certainly one always runs the risk of applying it anachronistically, naturalizing characteristics of the modern era as if they operated universally in the past; reciprocal and redistributive means of exchange are everywhere supplanted by the greedy, acquisitive activities of *Homo economicus*. Are the observed similarities between one "world system" and another more interesting and informative than the differences that distinguish them? Abu-Lughod's world system "before European hegemony" in the thirteenth and fourteenth centuries A.D., discussed above, can usefully be contrasted with the Postclassic Mesoamerican world. There are striking differences in scale or spatial extent (the entire Old World—save for parts of Africa and Australia—compared with a very circumscribed region of the New), monetization of the economy, development of credit institutions, and the like. Only an extended and detailed analysis could reveal other differences such as, say, the significance and pervasiveness of non-economic/ideological or technological factors in these terminal premodern world systems. In many cases the comparison or contrast would resist definitive analysis; the cup would be half empty or half full depending upon the interests of the investigator and the features selected for analysis. It can also be argued that the lack of correspondence between ancient and modern world systems or between different preindustrial world systems is itself interesting and worthy of analysis. Why, for example, was "the development of underdevelopment" itself underdeveloped or constrained in premodern times? Why did significant technological innovations or specialized practices often occur in less developed, if not peripheral, areas under premodern conditions? Answers to such questions inform us not only about the past, but also potentially about what actually distinguishes human history during the last 500 years from previous times.

If the Postclassic Mesoamerican world system only imperfectly resembles other world systems, is it useful or confusing to use the same term or model to apply to all cases? If there are no peripheries or semi-peripheries, few or only exceptional cases of deliberate underdevelopment, and characteristic innovations occur repeatedly in less developed, non-core areas, then does the term "world system" even apply, or is its invocation unnecessarily confusing and misleading? One can only modify a model so far before it is best to scrap it and start anew. Ptolemaic astronomers ultimately had to abandon postulating additional epicycles to explain observed celestial phenomena; at a certain point the simplicity (and accuracy) of Copernicus's system won out. Have we reached that point with the modification of the world-systems model for Postclassic Mesoamerica presented here? *Caveat lector*. There is also another problem always to be guarded against: the dangers of reifying the model, ascribing a reality to it that it actually does not possess. This danger is evident in some of Wallerstein's later studies where the world system is repeatedly invoked as a convenient *deus ex machina* to explain away differences in developments throughout the system.

Ultimately, a pragmatic question must be asked in this adoption of the world-systems model to Postclassic Mesoamerica or, more generally, in any model-building applied to the human past: Is the use of the model illuminating? Does its application enhance our understanding of the past, or does it distort that past by trying to make it conform to a preexisting and, in some important respects, poorly fitting model, which in this case was initially developed to explain features of the modern post-fifteenth century A.D. world? The authors of this chapter disagree on the answer to that question. One of us (Kepecs) believes that the model functions as a valuable corrective to past misconceptions of Precolumbian Mesoamerica, such as those following the Polanyi model; its emphasis on the integration of various interlocked spheres of activities resulting in the specialized production and exchange of commodities throughout the system works well with the Postclassic Mesoamerican evidence. The other author (Kohl) worries more about the lack of correspondence between the model and reality, and its possibly misleading or overstated application. To Kohl, some scholars spend too much time consulting an increasingly opaque corpus of literature devoted to world-systems theory and expend too little effort trying to understand the data in their own terms. If the data only poorly conform to the model, it is time to build a new model, not distort the data for purposes of making it fit. In the following chapter, Smith and Berdan begin this task of constructing a new model for Postclassic Mesoamerica.

Each perspective has merit, and reasonable people can reasonably differ in terms of the utility of applying the world-systems model to the Postclassic Mesoamerican world. Ultimately, the reader must decide for herself/ himself whether the empirically grounded search for interconnections throughout Postclassic Mesoamerica is facilitated or impeded by recourse to world-systems approaches.

3

Spatial Structure of the Mesoamerican World System

Michael E. Smith

Frances F. Berdan

The spatial extent of the Postclassic Mesoamerican world system corresponds closely to the traditional Mesoamerican culture area as defined long ago by Paul Kirchhoff and others from a specific list of traits (Kirchhoff 1943, 1952). Postclassic Mesoamerican societies interacted with peoples to the north and south, obtaining turquoise from the American Southwest, and bronze technology and perhaps other items from South America and lower Central America. Although this might suggest that the relevant world system included these distant areas, the intensity of economic and stylistic interaction was far higher within Mesoamerica than between Mesoamerican societies and these other groups, suggesting that Mesoamerica is indeed a useful scale of analysis for the Postclassic period. In this chapter we discuss the spatial and functional organization of the Postclassic Mesoamerican world system at a large scale. Aspects of this model will be clarified and extended in the remaining chapters in the book.

BOUNDING THE POSTCLASSIC WORLD SYSTEM

Mesoamerica traditionally has been interpreted as a culture area, meaning a large geographical area whose cultures exhibit numerous similarities. Although in ancient times Mesoamerica was the home of many diverse peoples, cultures, and languages (e.g., Justeson and Broadwell 1996), they all shared a number of traits. Paul Kirchhoff (1943, 1952) was the first scholar to provide a systematic definition of "Mesoamerica" as a meaningful spatial unit. He compiled lists of traits that Mesoamerican cultures shared with other New World cultures, and traits that differentiated Mesoamerican cultures from their neighbors to the north and south. Although Kirchhoff's list was a mixed bag of economic, religious, and social traits, many of the features pertain to elite cul-

ture. But, in the words of Rosemary Joyce, "the vast majority of [Kirchhoff's] traits diagnostic of Mesoamerican civilization can be seen as expressions of a common high culture propagated by social elites: exclusive practices in cuisine, costume, and building; exclusive and expensive ceremonies; and the creation of historical documents" (Joyce 2000b:66).

Kirchhoff did not provide a map of Mesoamerica, but his spatial definition—a sharp but shifting northern boundary signaled by the limits of maize cultivation, coupled with a southern boundary of more gradual cultural transition—has continued to be followed up to the present day by most scholars (e.g., Blanton et al. 1993; Sanders and Price 1968; Weaver 1993). Although Kirchhoff (1952:19) noted explicitly that his study developed out of the culture-area approach popular in early twentieth-century North American anthropology (Kroeber 1931, 1939; Wissler 1914, 1927), he did not apply the diffusionist explanations for trait distributions that were at the heart of culture-area research (Harris 1968:373–379). In fact, Kirchhoff avoided any kind of explanatory model to account for the distribution of Mesoamerican traits. Other authors did apply diffusionist models to explain the widespread distribution of styles and symbols at certain points in the Mesoamerican past. For the Postclassic period, for example, George Vaillant (1940) defined a "Mixteca-Puebla culture" that diffused, he claimed, from central Mexico to the rest of Mesoamerica. Nicholson (1960) refined Vaillant's model, recasting the Mixteca-Puebla phenomenon as an art style that diffused out from central Mexico in successive waves of influence. Some authors (e.g., Smith and Heath-Smith 1980; see also chapters 23, 24) rejected the diffusionist model for the Mixteca-Puebla phenomenon as part of a more general trend emphasizing the role of exchanges of goods and information in linking the diverse

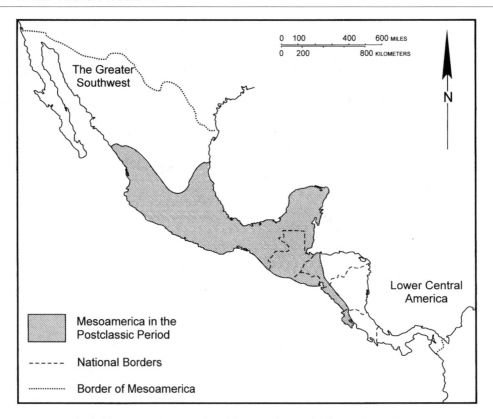

Figure 3.1 Map of Mesoamerica. (Produced by Pamela Headrick.)

regions of Mesoamerica (e.g., Blanton and Feinman 1984; Flannery 1968; Hirth 1984; Schortman et al. 1986; Zeitlin 1982).

During the 1960s and 1970s, as archaeologists focused primarily on local adaptations, there was little research on the definition and nature of Mesoamerica as a unit. With the rise of the world-systems approach in the 1980s (see chapter 2), many scholars redefined Mesoamerica as a zone of economic and stylistic interaction—that is, a world system (Blanton and Feinman 1984; Blanton et al. 1993:219–224; Feinman and Nicholas 1991; Whitecotton and Pailes 1986). We believe that Kirchhoff's initial definition of Mesoamerica is still valid as a descriptive construct (Guzmán and Martínez 1990), but the world-system approach now provides a more adequate explanation for why Mesoamerica looked the way it did in different time periods.

NEIGHBORS TO THE NORTH AND SOUTH

During the Postclassic period, a number of Mesoamerican polities traded and exchanged ideas with their far distant neighbors to the north and south (figure 3.1). As noted in chapter 1, the Epiclassic and Early Postclassic periods were a time of intensive long-distance interactions throughout Mesoamerica, particularly in coastal regions. A variety of goods were exchanged, and the standardized symbols of the Early Postclassic International symbol set reached a wide area (Foster 1999; Smith and Heath-Smith 1980). This was the time when metallurgy was introduced to west Mexico from South America (Hosler 1988b, 1994; see chapter 21), and at this time Southwestern archaeological sites (the Pueblo II period) contained noticeable quantities of Mesoamerican trade items such as copper bells, macaws, and other goods that may have been Mesoamerican imports (McGuire 1989; Meighan 1999). Plumbate pottery, one of the key commodities of the Early Postclassic exchange system, was distributed to all parts of Mesoamerica, reaching as far north as Tepic in Nayarit (Kelley 1995) and south into Costa Rica.

After A.D. 1200, interaction between Mesoamerican polities and the peoples of the American Southwest and lower Central America increased dramatically. Not surprisingly, this expansion of exchange and contact with distant areas accompanied the processes of economic and stylistic expansion outlined in chapter 1. Although these long-distance networks might suggest the inclusion of the American Southwest and lower Central America within the Mesoamerican world system (e.g., McGuire 1989; Pailes and Whitecotton 1979), we prefer to view them as examples of extra-systemic exchanges. The bounding of interaction-based units like world systems is never precise and unequivocal, and the much higher volumes of commercial and information exchanges within Mesoamerica (as traditionally defined) compared to the external links justifies our model of the spatial extent of the Postclassic Mesoamerican world system. As Kohl and Chernykh note in chapter 37, the integration and boundedness of Postclassic Mesoamerica were far greater than was the case in the central Asian Bronze Age world system.

Mesoamerica and the American Southwest
In contrast to earlier speculations that Mesoamerican traits were introduced to the Southwest by Toltec merchants (e.g., DiPeso 1974) most authorities now see these connections running through west Mexico (Foster 1999; Mathien and McGuire 1986; McGuire 1989; Schaafsma and Riley 1999b). This view is strengthened by the fact that the Epiclassic/Early Postclassic period was a time of extensive trade and interaction within west Mexico (Darling 1998; Pollard 1997; Williams and Weigand 1996). Various other explanations have also been offered for long-distance interactions at this time, including small-scale military activities (Nelson n.d.) and the spread of a new religion focused on Quetzalcoatl (Ringle et al. 1998). Whatever the nature of world-system processes before the twelfth century, these patterns of interaction set the stage for continued exchange between Mesoamerican peoples and their distant neighbors during the Middle and Late Postclassic periods under consideration here.

The emergence of the Postclassic Mesoamerican world system in the twelfth century was marked by an expansion of trade and stylistic interaction between Mesoamerican polities and those of north Mexico. Sites on the Pacific coast as far north as Guasave in Sinaloa established links to west Mexico and even central Mexico through both trade and stylistic interaction as part of what Foster (1999) calls the Late Aztatlan tradition, dating to A.D. 1200–1400 (figure 3.2). The impressive urban center of Casas Grandes (Paquimé) reached its maximum size and regional importance at this time, known locally as the Medio period, now dated to A.D. 1200–1400 (Bradley 2000; Ravesloot et al. 1995). Mesoamerican imports at Casas Grandes include worked copper/bronze, macaws, and perhaps worked shell, conch shell trumpets, and pyrite mosaic plaques (Kelley 1995); these and other goods from west Mexico are also found at Hohokam and other sites in the American Southwest (Cobb et al. 1999; Meighan 1999). Turquoise from areas to the north was also abundant at Casas Grandes, which is generally interpreted as a center for exchange between the American Southwest and Mesoamerica (DiPeso 1974; Kelley 1995; Schaafsma and Riley 1999a). A number of Mesoamerican religious concepts may have been present at Casas Grandes, but the evidence is not unequivocal; in any case, the elements of the Late Postclassic international symbol set are not found at this site.

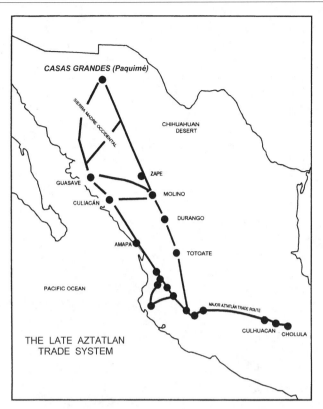

Figure 3.2 Map of the extension of the Postclassic world system into northern Mexico. (From Foster 1999: figure 11.3.)

Foster's map of what he calls the "Late Aztatlan Trade System" (figure 3.2) shows the likely network of exchange reaching from west Mexico up to Casas Grandes (Paquimé). This entire area can be considered a distant periphery of the Mesoamerican world system after the twelfth century. McGuire (1989) argues that the U.S. Southwest had been a periphery of Mesoamerica during the Early Postclassic period, but this label does not fit well after A.D. 1200. Importation of turquoise from the Southwest was important in Postclassic Mesoamerica (Weigand and Harbottle 1993; Harbottle and Weigand 1992), but this is best viewed as extra-systemic exchange rather than core/periphery exchange because of the great distances and low quantities involved, and because of the seeming lack of additional linkages (such as information and bulk-goods networks).[1]

Mesoamerica and Lower Central America
The polities of lower Central America engaged in active exchange with Mesoamerican polities throughout the Postclassic epoch. Prior to A.D. 1200 (during the Epiclassic and Early Postclassic periods), polychrome ceramics from Honduras to Costa Rica exhibited the symbols of the Early Postclassic international symbol set, suggesting symbolic interaction with many areas of Mesoamerica (Smith and Heath-Smith 1980). These symbols have been particularly well documented in the Middle

Polychrome period ceramics of the Nicoya region of Costa Rica (Lange 1988; Lothrop 1926). Several authors describe evidence for direct commercial and stylistic contacts between the Nicoya area and west Mexico at this time (Smith and Heath-Smith 1980:28–29; Sweetman 1974).

The two distinctive Mesoamerican ceramic trade wares of this period—Fine Orange from the Gulf Coast and Plumbate from coastal Guatemala—are common at Central American sites (Fahmel Beyer 1988; Neff and Bishop 1988; Rands et al. 1982; Shepard 1948; R. Smith 1958). Other trade wares such as obsidian tools and copper bells are also found at Central American sites (Fowler 1989; Healy et al. 1996; Lange 1986; Sharer 1984). Trade in the opposite direction is indicated by numerous objects of gold from Panama (and perhaps other areas of lower Central America) recovered from Early Postclassic deposits at the Great Cenote at Chichén Itzá (Coggins and Shane 1984; Graham 1996; Lothrop 1952). Several groups of Nahua speakers—including the Pipil and Nicarao—migrated to the Mesoamerican frontier zone of El Salvador during Epiclassic/Early Postclassic times, and Fowler (1989:272–276) suggests that the Pipil engaged in an active trade with Toltec merchants. On the other hand, Smith and Heath-Smith (1980) emphasize that the overall spatial configuration of Mesoamerican exchange at this time points to active coastal trade not strongly controlled by Tula or any other single polity.

The processes of commercial and stylistic interaction between Mesoamerican and Central American polities continued in a modified fashion after A.D. 1200. Whereas lower Central America below Nicoya was less involved with Mesoamerican trade networks, polities from El Salvador to Nicoya showed stronger links to Mesoamerica. The symbols of the Late Postclassic international symbol set continue to be found on the Late Polychrome–period ceramics of Nicoya (Day 1994; Lothrop 1926), and some Central American symbols, including images of gold frogs, were incorporated into the Mixteca-Puebla style, including the Codex Nuttall and Mixtec gold jewelry (Day 1994; Graham 1996; Lange 1986).

Fewer specific Mesoamerican imports have been reported from Late Postclassic sites in Central America (Late Period VI in the chronology presented in Lange and Stone 1984). Nevertheless, most authors see this as a time of active commercial exchange networks linking Mesoamerica and Central America (Fowler 1989; Lange 1984, 1986; Stone 1982). Fowler (1989:275), for example, emphasizes the role of cacao production for export in El Salvador, and Sharer (1984) points to the large trade canoe encountered by Columbus off the Bay Islands (Edwards 1978; see chapter 1) as exemplifying the long-distance trade that linked the Maya with peoples of the Caribbean coast of Central America. The Pipil of El Salvador maintained their tradition of exchange with

Mesoamerican polities in Late Postclassic times (Fowler 1989:272–276), and documentary sources mention a colony of late Nahuatl-speaking immigrants as far away as Atlantic Panama who maintained an active trade with "Indians from Mexico" (Lothrop 1942). As in the case of the American Southwest, we acknowledge these links between Mesoamerica and Central America as important processes that had impacts on larger world-system dynamics, but prefer to view them as extra-systemic exchanges between the Mesoamerican world system proper and the external polities of Central America because the mutual impact of these exchanges appears to have been relatively small.

SPATIAL COMPONENTS OF THE WORLD SYSTEM

As noted in chapter 2, the traditional units of world-system theory—cores, peripheries, and semi-peripheries—do not adequately model the spatial organization or the dynamic processes of the Postclassic Mesoamerican world system. Compared to prior models of ancient and modern world systems, we see a greater diversity of interactions among regions (including stylistic and well as economic exchange) and a greater diversity of functional roles for the individual regions that composed the Postclassic world system. In order to address this diversity, we employ the following set of functional and spatial concepts. *Core zones* correspond to some prior definitions of world-systems cores (see chapter 2), but without the connotation that cores must dominate peripheries. Our concept of core zones emphasizes high populations, concentrated political power, and urbanization. We introduce the new concept *affluent production zone* to describe areas of high economic production and the generation and accumulation of wealth, but without the same level of political centralization and urbanization as cores. Functionally these areas are closer to cores than to peripheries in traditional world-systems models, and the areas we designate as affluent production zones have been variously included as cores, peripheries, and semi-peripheries in past studies (Blanton et al. 1992; Carmack 1996; Schortman and Urban 1996; Whitecotton and Pailes 1986).

We divide other areas traditionally classified as peripheries (or semi-peripheries) into three categories. *Resource-extraction zones* are areas where important raw materials were mined or obtained, whether by local residents or foreigners. *Unspecialized peripheral zones* were areas whose inhabitants participated in the processes of the world system, but at lower levels of economic and political activity; these include many of the sparsely populated, rugged mountainous regions of Mesoamerica. *Contact peripheries* describe distant areas—such as Casas Grandes and the American Southwest, and lower Central America—that exchanged goods

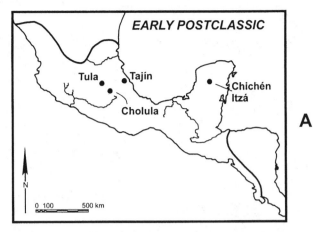

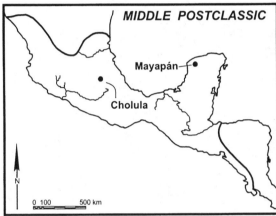

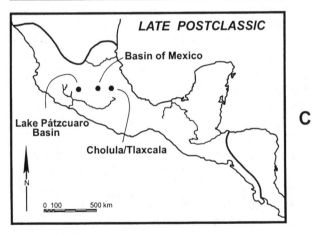

Figure 3.3 Map of Postclassic core zones through time. (Produced by Pamela Headrick.)

and information with the polities of Mesoamerica, but were outside of that world system proper.

We also consider a larger spatial scale and define *exchange circuits*. These are large systems within which the movement of goods and ideas was particularly frequent and intensive; they correspond to Abu-Lughod's (1989) use of the term "subsystem." *International trade centers* were cities or towns heavily involved in long-distance exchanges. One of their primary roles was as entrepôts or

gateways linking various exchange circuits with other parts of the world system. Finally, *style zones* describe large areas characterized by distinctive Postclassic art styles; these tend to crosscut the economic units defined above. The rest of this chapter is devoted to a discussion of these concepts and their distributions in Postclassic Mesoamerica. Additional details can be found in the succeeding chapters of the book.

CORE ZONES

As discussed in chapter 2, our notion of core zone is somewhat different from the various definitions found in the world-systems literature. In our usage, cores are areas of high populations and concentrated political power. These features lead to urbanization (typically including major investments in monumental architecture) and to a high demand for luxury goods by core-zone elites. It is important to note that levels of economic and intellectual production are not necessarily higher in cores than in other areas, although artistic production of large public objects such as architecture and sculpture is often concentrated in cores. We have identified several core zones for the Early, Middle, and Late Postclassic periods (figure 3.3).

Early Postclassic

Although our focus is on the Middle and Late Postclassic periods, it is important to understand the Early Postclassic situation out of which the Late Postclassic world system evolved. Early Postclassic core zones include Chichén Itzá, El Tajín, Cholula, and Tula. Chichén Itzá was the center of a powerful polity, probably a small empire, and its monumental architecture is among the most impressive in ancient Mesoamerica (Andrews 1990b; Kepecs et al. 1994; Schele and Mathews 1998; Tozzer 1957). El Tajín was an impressive urban center in the Epiclassic and Early Postclassic periods whose artistic style was highly influential over large parts of Mesoamerica (Brüggemann 1994a, 1994b; Castillo Peña 1995). Cholula was a major political capital in central Mexico during the Classic and Postclassic periods, but its interval of maximum power was probably the Early Postclassic period, when its huge pyramid, the largest in Mesoamerica, was built (Marquina 1964; McCafferty 1996a, 1996b). Tula was another large central Mexican urban center with impressive architecture (Fuente et al. 1988; Diehl 1983; Healan 1989; Matos Moctezuma 1974). Although not the capital of an empire, as some have claimed (see Smith and Montiel 2001), Tula ruled a powerful regional state just north of the Basin of Mexico.

Middle Postclassic

We have identified only two core zones for the Middle Postclassic period. In Yucatán, Mayapán took over from Chichén Itzá as the major political capital. Although a

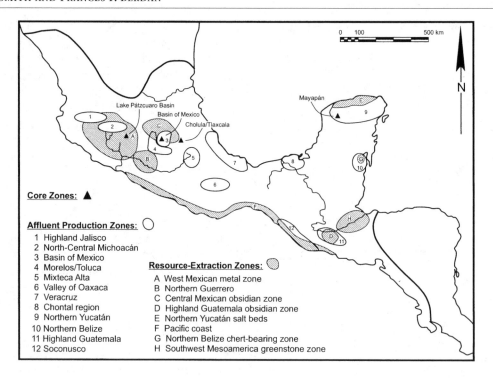

Figure 3.4 Map of affluent production zones, resource-extraction zones, and unspecialized peripheries in the Late Postclassic period. The Basin of Mexico was transformed from an affluent production zone in the Middle Postclassic period to a core zone in the Late Postclassic period. (Produced by Pamela Headrick, from base maps compiled by Timothy S. Hare.)

more modest city and polity than its predecessor, Mayapán was large and powerful enough to qualify as a core zone (Pollock 1962; Roys 1972; Masson 2000a; see chapter 5). In central Mexico, the Cholula/Tlaxcala region can be considered a dispersed core zone. Cholula remained an important urban center, and a number of new and powerful Nahua polities emerged nearby. These polities were based in relatively small and dispersed urban centers compared to most other core zones (see chapters 10 and 22). Although the Aztec city-states in the Basin of Mexico and Morelos were growing in size and strength at this time, we feel that they were not yet sufficiently powerful to warrant calling those areas core zones.

Late Postclassic
Mayapán continued to thrive into the first part of the Late Postclassic period, but after its fall around 1450, no comparable core zone developed in Yucatán (Masson 2000a). Cholula/Tlaxcala remained a core zone, and the Basin of Mexico emerged as a new and powerful core at this time. As the seat of the Tepanec empire (ca. 1370–1428), followed by the Aztec empire (1428–1519), the Basin of Mexico contained the largest cities and most powerful polities of Late Postclassic Mesoamerica (see chapters 9 and 30). The Lake Pátzcuaro Basin of Michoacán, the heart of the Tarascan empire, was another Late Postclassic core zone (see chapters 13 and 29). An-

other possible Late Postclassic core zone is the Mixteca/ Valley of Oaxaca region, but we feel that the small size of the urban centers and polities argues against core status for this area.

AFFLUENT PRODUCTION ZONES
We are introducing the concept of the affluent production zone to describe areas of high populations and intensive economic activity (both production and exchange) that lacked the powerful polities and large urban centers found in core zones. Core zones were not the only areas with busy commercial economies; in fact, the dispersion of commercialization across the Mesoamerican landscape was one of the notable features of the Postclassic world system (see chapters 1, 16), and the small polities of the affluent production zones were conducive to this growth of commercial exchange.

Scholarly attention has traditionally focused on core zones because they were politically powerful, they had large urban centers with impressive monuments, and they left a disproportionate amount of material behind. Nevertheless, the affluent production zones also played crucial roles in the world system. There were a greater number of these zones than cores, and they contained a larger proportion of the population, and thus were the scenes for high levels of production and exchange activities. The key economic role played by these zones may have been one of the features that differentiated the Post-

Table 3.1
Functional zones in the Postclassic world system

Type of Zone	Area	
Core Zones	1	Lake Pátzcuaro Basin
	2	Basin of Mexico
	3	Tlaxcala/Cholula
	4	Mayapán
Affluent Production Zones	1	Highland Jalisco
	2	North-central Michoacán
	3	Basin of Mexico
	4	Morelos/Toluca
	5	Mixteca Alta
	6	Valley of Oaxaca
	7	Veracruz
	8	Chontal region
	9	Northern Yucatán
	10	Northern Belize
	11	Highland Guatemala
	12	Soconusco
Resource-Extraction Zones	1	West Mexican metal zone
	2	Northern Guerrero
	3	Central Mexican obsidian zone
	4	Highland Guatemala obsidian zone
	5	Northern Yucatán salt beds
	6	Pacific coast
	7	Northern Belize chert-bearing zone
	8	Southwest Mesoamerica greenstone zone
Exchange Circuits	1	West Mexico
	2	The Aztec empire
	3	The Maya zone
	4	Southern Pacific coastal plain
Style Zones	1	Aztec style
	2	Mixteca-Puebla style
	3	Coastal Maya mural style
	4	Southwest Maya style

classic world system from earlier Mesoamerican economies. These zones are called "affluent" because their inhabitants were economically successful due to some combination of highly productive intensive agriculture, active craft industries, and/or specialized extraction industries (Rathje 1975; Sabloff and Rathje 1975b). Following is a list of areas we have classified as affluent production zones. It is likely that additional fieldwork and archival research will permit the addition of other areas to this list (table 3.1, figure 3.4).

1. *Highland Jalisco.* This lake region was rich in agricultural and lacustrine resources, some of which were exported. Craft industries such as basketmaking and ceramics also flourished using local raw materials (Pollard 1997; Valdez et al. 1996; see chapter 8).

2. *North-Central Michoacán.* Well-endowed for high agricultural productivity, this region also was known for its abundant fish resources and for salt and obsidian. The manufacture of a variety of products—ceramics, reed baskets and mats, and metal objects—

also contributed to the region's affluent economy (Pollard 1997; chapter 29).

3. *Basin of Mexico.* As an affluent production zone in the Middle Postclassic period, the Basin of Mexico produced salt, obsidian tools, and decorated ceramic vessels for export (Sanders et al. 1979). Highly productive agricultural systems, including the chinampas and canal irrigation, were developed at this time (Parsons 1991), setting the scene for the transformation of the basin into a core zone in the Late Postclassic period (see chapters 9 and 30).

4. *Morelos/Toluca.* The productive irrigated agriculture of the Morelos and Toluca valleys supported dense, economically active populations in the Middle and Late Postclassic periods. Polities in both areas paid tribute in grains and textiles to the Aztec empire; Morelos also produced paper for tribute and trade (Smith 1994a, 1994b; see chapter 32).

5. *Mixteca Alta.* This region of competitive city-states exhibited a varied economy based first and foremost on agriculture. Elite artisans produced luxury goods including decorated cotton textiles, feather adornments, polished greenstones, gold and other metal jewelry, painted codices, and polychrome ceramics (chapters 22, 31). By the Late Postclassic, towns in the region were paying tribute to the Aztec empire in many of these goods, plus cochineal (a red dye) and gold dust. These small polities (chapter 10) were among the most affluent in Postclassic Mesoamerica (Berdan and Anawalt 1992:4: f. 43r; Byland and Pohl 1994a; Spores 1967, 1984).

6. *Valley of Oaxaca.* The agricultural importance of this area during Late Postclassic times is highlighted by Aztec imperial tribute demands in staple foodstuffs; no other conquered province at such a distance from the imperial capitals paid tribute in such foodstuffs. Towns in this area also paid tribute in cochineal and gold disks, emphasizing the local availability of these raw materials and manufacturing in, at least, gold objects. The valley was known for its metallurgical craftsmanship throughout the Postclassic (Berdan and Anawalt 1992:4: f. 44r; Blanton et al. 1993; Flannery and Marcus 1983; Pohl 1999; see chapters 22, 31).

7. *Veracruz.* Coastal Veracruz, from Tabasco to the Huaxteca, was a rich agricultural region that produced large quantities of cotton (in several varieties) as well as reliable yields of foodstuffs. Tropical feathers, cacao, rubber, and liquidambar were also prominent resources in this region (Curet et al. 1994; Medellín Zeñil 1960; Stark et al. 1998).

8. *Chontal region.* This region is a humid lowland coastal zone between the Laguna de Términos and the Río Usumacinta. Its rich agricultural and natural products—cotton, cacao, rubber, and tropical feathers (Izquierdo 1997; Scholes and Roys 1968)—paralleled those of Veracruz. Three international trade centers (Xicalanco, Potonchan, and Itzamkanak) were located in

this region, which we classify as an international trade center as well as an affluent production zone (see chapter 17).

9. *Northern Yucatán.* With the exception of the area around Mayapán, northern Yucatán was an affluent production zone from the fall of the large Early Postclassic polities (including Chichén Itzá) until the advent of Spanish administration. These small polities, often ruled by merchant lineages, engaged in competitive production and exchange on regional and macroregional scales. High-grade salt was especially important (Freidel and Sabloff 1984; Kepecs 1997, 1999; Quezada 1993; Roys 1972). See chapters 5, 19, and 33.

10. *Northern Belize.* The Postclassic populations of northern Belize produced cacao, honey, wax, cotton, and textiles, and extracted a variety of animal products such as pelts and feathers. Exports from this area included forest products such as dyes, paints, vanilla and *achiote* seasonings, copal, canoes and paddles (Jones 1989; Masson 2000a; Piña Chán 1978), as well as high-quality chert from the Colha area (see chapter 34).

11. *Highland Guatemala.* Excellent soil and rainfall conditions combined to make this a highly productive agricultural region where irrigation enhanced crop yields. In addition, the highlands were endowed with valuable resources such as obsidian, copper and some gold, jade, and clay for pottery making (Carmack 1981; Fox 1987; see chapters 6, 12).

12. *Soconusco.* This region, along the Pacific coast of present-day Chiapas and Guatemala, was noted especially for its cacao cultivation. However, the economy was diversified, as Aztec imperial tribute demands included large quantities of tropical feathers, amber and amber adornments, jaguar pelts, and greenstone beads. The region also served as an important international trade center (Berdan and Anawalt 1992:4: f. 47r; Gasco 1996b; Voorhies 1989b; see chapters 17, 35).

All of these zones exhibit features of affluence: they contained substantial populations supported by a relatively rich and reliable resource foundation. Furthermore, they augmented this economic base with a diversity of additional production activities drawing on local resource availabilities. Many of the resulting products were exported to other regions, linking these zones to nearby and distant cores, international trading centers, and other affluent production zones.

RESOURCE-EXTRACTION ZONES

A resource-extraction zone is a peripheral area (in world-systems terms) where important nonagricultural raw materials were mined or obtained. Many resource-extraction zones are regions with several individual mines or extraction loci, and thus not every locale within the larger area was necessarily involved in the extraction of the particular resources. "Important" raw materials were those used to manufacture key commodities (defined in chapter 18) and other products that were distributed widely through Mesoamerica. These areas are mapped in figure 3.4 (table 3.1).

1. *West Mexican metal zone*. Michoacán and Guerrero are heavily mineralized, with extensive occurrences of copper, silver, and arsenical copper ores found throughout both areas. Local documentary sources from the sixteenth century mention many copper deposits and mines. Most were probably small-scale local operations, with a few of the larger mines under the control of the Tarascan state (Hosler 1994; Hosler and Macfarlane 1996; Pollard 1987, 1993; see chapter 21).

2. *Northern Guerrero*. This mountainous zone had copper and many other resources sought by the Tarascan and Aztec empires (Berdan et al. 1996; Brand 1943; Litvak King 1971).

3. *Central Mexican obsidian zone*. Numerous obsidian sources are known from the northern Basin of Mexico and areas to the north and east, and this obsidian was traded over much of Mesoamerica (Charlton and Spence 1982; Cobean 1991; Pastrana 1991, 1998; see chapter 20).

4. *Highland Guatemala obsidian zone*. This zone covers the three major obsidian sources in highland western Guatemala (Braswell 1998a; Braswell and Glascock 1998; see chapter 20).

5. *Northern Yucatán salt beds*. Throughout the Prehispanic sequence and up to modern times, the northern Yucatán salt beds have been the most productive salt resource in Mesoamerica (Andrews 1983; Ewald 1985; Kepecs 1999; see chapters 19 and 33).

6. *Pacific coast*. Several marine and other resources were harvested along the Pacific coast of Mexico, including *Spondylus* and other shells for jewelry (Feinman and Nicholas 1993), purpura dyes (Turok et al. 1988; Turok 96), feathers, cacao, and other products.

7. *Northern Belize chert-bearing zone*. Specialists at the settlement of Colha had exploited the high-quality chert from this zone since Preclassic times. Early Postclassic household-based artisans at Colha produced a series of distinctive tools that were traded throughout Belize and perhaps as far as Mayapán (Dockall and Shafer 1993; Hester and Shafer 1991; Michaels 1987). Although Late Postclassic production has yet to be documented extensively at Colha, Postclassic tool types characteristic of Colha have been recovered in Late Postclassic contexts at Laguna de On and Caye Coco (Masson 2000a; Oland 1999), suggesting that production continued unabated.

8. *Southwest Mesoamerican greenstone zone*. The precise sources of jadeite and other forms of greenstone are not known, but many authorities think that these crucial materials came from the Motagua Valley or parts of Honduras (Lange 1993; Thouvenot 1982). Costa Rica

is another source of greenstone used in Mesoamerica (Graham et al. 1998).

UNSPECIALIZED PERIPHERAL ZONES

This is a residual category that covers areas within the Mesoamerican world system that do not fall into one of the previous categories. Most of these areas were mountainous, had poor soils, or were remote and isolated, and as a result they had relatively low populations without large cities. These features also led to lower levels of historical documentation and archaeological fieldwork, and it is possible that some of the areas classified as unspecialized peripheral zones were in fact affluent production zones or resource-extraction zones, but we lack the research to establish this. Unspecialized peripheral zones in the Postclassic world system include parts of the lowland Maya area (Demarest 1997), many areas in Guerrero (Harvey 1971; Vega Sosa and Cervantes-Delgado 1986), west Mexico (Michelet 1995; Pollard 1997), and the northern rim of Mesoamerica.

CONTACT PERIPHERIES

"Contact periphery" is Chase-Dunn and Hall's (1997: 61) term for areas that had only slight contact with a world system. These areas, discussed above, include the Greater Southwest area of Casas Grandes and the American Southwest, and lower Central America (see figure 3.1). We do not discuss these areas further, apart from the goods they provided to the polities of Postclassic Mesoamerica. Of these, turquoise was by far the most important (chapter 17).

EXCHANGE CIRCUITS

Exchanges of goods and information were not uniform throughout Mesoamerica during the Postclassic period. Instead, most exchange took place within smaller areas or subsystems that we call *exchange circuits* (see Abu-Lughod 1989). We have identified four such circuits for the Late Postclassic period: west Mexico, the Aztec empire, the Maya zone, and the southern Pacific coastal zone. If there were abundant data on imported goods and styles from numerous sites, lines connecting exchange partners would cluster within these subsystems, with fewer lines extending outside of them (as in the maps produced by interaction studies in the field of geography). Although we do not have that level of coverage, the available archaeological and ethnohistoric data do support our identification of exchange circuits for the Late Postclassic period (figure 3.5; table 3.1).

We refrain from formal identification of exchange circuits in the Early and Middle Postclassic periods because of the smaller amounts of relevant data. We can make a few suggestions, however. In Early Postclassic times the main exchange circuit linked central Mexico, the Gulf Coast, and northern Yucatán; this included the four Early Postclassic core zones identified above

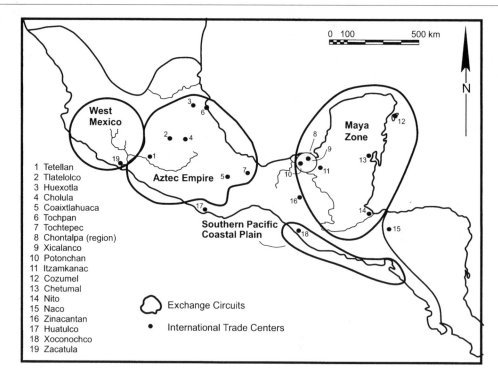

Figure 3.5 Map of exchange circuits and international trade centers. The Chontalpa region, trade center no. 8, had many trade centers, including Xicalanco and Potonchan. (Map produced by Pamela Headrick, from base maps compiled by Timothy S. Hare.)

(Kepecs et al. 1994; Kepecs 1999). A second, smaller system may have existed on the southern Pacific coast centered on the city of Cotzumalhuapa (Parsons 1967–1969; Thompson 1948). Iconographic similarities between inscriptions at Cotzumalhuapa and El Tajín suggest connections between these two exchange circuits. In the Middle Postclassic period, the larger exchange circuit contracted to include just central Mexico. For the Late Postclassic period, we see four significant exchange circuits.

1. *West Mexico*. This exchange circuit included the Tarascan empire and adjacent areas of Jalisco and Nayarit. The exchange of obsidian, ceramics, copper-bronze objects, and other goods was particularly extensive in this area in Postclassic times (Foster 1999; Hosler 1994; Pollard 1997). As discussed above, the polities in this area were in contact with Casas Grandes and other settlements in northern Mexico and the American Southwest. Turquoise from the latter area passed through the west Mexico exchange circuit on its way to the rest of Mesoamerica.

2. *The Aztec empire*. This circuit corresponds to the territory of the Aztec empire. In addition to the flow of tribute from the Aztec provinces to Tenochtitlan, processes of commercial exchange and elite interaction were particularly prominent within the Aztec empire (Berdan et al. 1996; Smith 1990; Umberger and Klein 1993; see chapters 11 and 27).

3. *The Maya zone*. This exchange circuit includes the Maya area from Yucatán south to the highlands of Guatemala and Chiapas. During the Postclassic period, exchange and stylistic interaction, particularly along coastal routes, linked this whole area into a single circuit or subsystem of intensive interaction (Chase and Rice 1985; Masson 2000a; Scholes and Roys 1968).

4. *Southern Pacific coastal plain*. This area, among the more poorly known of Postclassic Mesoamerica, was the setting for a variety of active trade networks involving cacao, tropical feathers, and other goods (Voorhies 1989b; Edwards 1978; Feldman 1985). Contact with lower Central America and even South America passed through this exchange circuit.

Exchange circuits were of fundamental importance to the construction and dynamics of the Mesoamerican Postclassic world system. These "mini-world systems" are the largest subunits within the system, and highlight the intensity of interactions among polities within each unit. While we subsume them under one category, they nonetheless exhibited considerable variability: two subsystems—west Mexico and the Aztec empire—essentially encompassed the territories of empires, while the others included many polities of differing sizes. The empires emphasized integration through political and economic means, with more political emphasis in the Tarascan empire, and more economic emphasis in the Aztec empire. Polities in the Mayan zone were primarily linked through economic and symbolic exchanges, while those in the southern Pacific coastal zone emphasized maritime trade and commercial interactions. Each of these subsystems, therefore, developed its own workable strategy for large-scale regional integration.

INTERNATIONAL TRADE CENTERS

We propose this category as a replacement for the Polanyi/Chapman "port of trade" model traditionally used for centers of long-distance trade in Late Postclassic Mesoamerica. International trade centers have several or all of the following characteristics: they engage in trade with distant areas; they trade with many different areas; they have a high volume of trade; and they exhibit a great diversity of trade goods (figure 3.5). These centers are discussed in greater detail in chapter 17.

STYLE ZONES

We are using the term *style zone* to depict large areas characterized by distinctive Late Postclassic art styles. We have identified a single Postclassic international style that divides into four substyles: the Aztec style, the Mixteca-Puebla style, the coastal Maya mural style, and the southwest Maya style (figure 3.5). The existence of these zones, which cut across polity boundaries and economic regions, implies high levels of interaction among artists or patrons within each zone.

1. The *Aztec style* corresponds to most of the Aztec empire, whose scattered provincial and core-zone elites engaged in numerous types of intensive communication and interaction (Berdan et al. 1996; see chapter 27).

2. In our usage, the *Mixteca-Puebla style* is a pictorial style found in the codices, murals, and polychrome ceramics of the Mixteca-Puebla area (from Tlaxcala through Cholula and central Puebla into the Valley of Oaxaca and down the Río Verde Valley to the Pacific Coast). The distribution of this style includes areas both outside of and within the Aztec empire, where it overlaps with the Aztec style (chapters 26, 27).

3. The *coastal Maya mural style* describes Postclassic mural paintings from Tulum, Santa Rita, Mayapán, and other sites in northern and eastern Yucatán (chapter 25).

4. The *southwest Maya style* is a poorly documented but distinctive style found in the highland Maya region. These styles, their distributions, and their implications are discussed in greater detail in chapters 23 and 24.

SYNTHESIS

The fundamental spatial building blocks of the Postclassic Mesoamerican world system were individual small polities or city-states. Some of these polities (singly or in concert) emerged in different times as focal points in the system as cores, affluent production centers, international trading centers, or resource-extraction zones. These and other city-states, discussed in greater depth in the chapters in part 2, established and maintained significant links with other city-states on a variety of intertwined dimensions: economic, political, social, and religious. It is the nature of these linkages that gives this world system its special texture, and it is to the small polities of Postclassic Mesoamerica that we now turn.

Part 2

Polities

4

Small Polities in
Postclassic Mesoamerica

Michael E. Smith

When Hernando Cortés and his invading army marched through eastern Mesoamerica on their way to Tenochtitlan, they found themselves facing one small army after another. Each of them fought for a separate small polity ruled by its own king. Although many of these polities paid tribute to the Aztec empire, each maintained a significant measure of control over its internal affairs. The chapters in this section show that this pattern of small polities characterized almost the entire area of Mesoamerica in Late Postclassic times. This politically fragmented landscape did not arise by accident. The world-systems processes outlined in chapter 1—population growth, economic expansion, and information exchange—contributed to the expansion of small polities across Mesoamerica and were, in turn, stimulated by the dynamics and institutions of these polities. One of the remarkable features of the Postclassic political situation is that the city-states and other small polities emerged in most areas almost simultaneously—in the thirteenth century A.D. This fact alone provides strong evidence for the pervasive influence of the Postclassic world system in linking together the diverse regions of Mesoamerica.

THE CITY-STATE MODEL

The small polities of the Postclassic period in most parts of Mesoamerica are examples of the broader category of city-states, and recent cross-cultural research on city-states can help illuminate features of the Mesoamerican polities. Mogens Herman Hansen (2000b) has developed a comparative cross-cultural model that emphasizes the occurrence of city-states in regional groups of interacting polities that he calls "city-state cultures." In Hansen's approach, city-states are small polities consisting of a single capital city or town and a surrounding territory of farmland and smaller settlements. They are almost never self-

sufficient, typically engaging in trade with both nearby and distant states. Although self-governing, city-states are not necessarily politically autonomous; they may be subject to another polity yet retain their own government and internal autonomy.

More important than the definition of the city-state, however, is Hansen's concept of "city-state culture," which is a group of interacting city-states in a region characterized by a common language and culture. The constituent polities interact with one another through means both friendly (e.g., commercial exchange and diplomatic relations) and antagonistic (warfare and conquest). Some polities in a city-state culture are typically more powerful than the others, and they sometimes manage to defeat their neighbors and impose various political and economic sanctions. Nevertheless, the subject city-states usually maintain a degree of self-government, and the existence of hierarchies among city-states does not destroy the patterns of the city-state culture. Political relations in city-state cultures are typically highly dynamic and fluid as individual polities establish alliances, wage war, and break apart alliances. City-state cultures often come to an end through conquest by an outside power.

Hansen's (2000b) model fits many cases cross-culturally, but it allows for significant variation among the cases.[1] He has identified more than 30 city-state cultures in world history, of which the best-known cases are the Sumerian, Palestinian, Phoenecian, Greek, Etruscan, Early Roman, northern Italian, Spring-and-Autumn-period China, Southeast Asian maritime, Hausa, and Yoruba. Within Mesoamerica, he includes the Aztec (Smith 2000), Mixtec (Lind 2000), and Classic Maya (Grube 2000) among his 29 well-documented cases. Beyond the Aztec and Mixtec cases (chapters 9 and 10), most of the polities conquered by the Aztec empire appear to represent city-states organized into regional city-state cultures (Berdan et al. 1996:115–150) and Late Postclassic Yucatán also fits the model well (chapter 5).

OTHER KINDS OF POSTCLASSIC POLITIES

In addition to the various city-state cultures, three large, powerful states flourished in Middle-to-Late Postclassic Mesoamerica. Mayapán rose to power and later collapsed within a context of small Maya polities in Yucatán (chapter 5). The Aztec empire arose out of a system of competing city-states (chapters 9, 10, and 11), but its expansion did little to disturb the underlying foundation of city-states. The Tarascan empire was the biggest exception to the pattern of small Postclassic polities. This state was more centrally organized than most Mesoamerican empires, relying to a greater extent on direct control of its provinces (chapter 13). Between the levels of the city-state and the empire were confederations of city-states that acted to promote the interests of their constituent polities. Hodge (1984) has described the role of confederations among Aztec city-states in the Valley of Mexico, and in chapter 10 Pohl documents confederations involving Nahua, Mixtec, and Zapotec polities in the eastern Aztec empire. The latter situation provides a fascinating variant on Hansen's model of city-state culture. Whereas most city-state cultures are integrated culturally by the use of a common language, in the eastern Aztec empire confederations, origin myths and elite interactions provided a common cultural background for an extensive city-state culture that linked speakers of three languages. The role of commercial exchanges in this city-state culture is explored in chapter 22.

Not all of the non-imperial polities of Postclassic Mesoamerica conform to Hansen's city-state model. One of the most interesting (and controversial) cases is highland Guatemala, for which the nature of Postclassic societies has been debated for many years (e.g., Carmack 1981; Fox 1978; Fox et al. 1996; Fox et al. 1992; Braswell 2001a, 2001b). In chapter 6 Braswell provides a fresh look at these polities and concludes that the "house society" model (Carsten and Hugh-Jones 1995; Chance 2000; Gillespie 2000a, 2000b; Lévi-Strauss 1987; Joyce and Gillespie 2000) provides a more apt description than prior discussions of states, empires, and lineages (e.g., Carmack 1981; Fox 1987). In addition to polities that do not fit within the city-state model, there was considerable variation among the city-states of Postclassic Mesoamerica. Yucatán (chapter 5), Aztec central Mexico (chapter 9), and the Mixteca-Puebla region (chapter 10) are all areas where Postclassic city-states are well documented, and each region had its own set of distinctive institutions and political processes. The polities of Soconusco (chapter 7) and highland west Mexico (chapter 8) are among the most poorly documented in Mesoamerica, and it is not clear just how to categorize these.

Despite the variation among Postclassic polities, they shared an important characteristic beyond their generally small size: their extent was defined by affiliation with a ruler rather than by territory. In other words, people belonged to a particular polity not because they lived in a particular place, but because they were subject to the polity's ruler. In the case of Aztec city-states (chapter 9), for example, the villages subject to adjacent polities were sometimes interspersed with one another, making it impossible to draw discrete polity territories on a map. This would be an intolerable situation for modern nation-states, with their territorial principles of affiliation, but for Postclassic polities this is not unusual. Braswell (chapter 6) discusses this principle for the great houses of highland Guatemala, and Grube (2000) has even identified it among the Classic Maya polities, calling it a "place-specific" principle of political organization. This may in fact be an ancient and fundamental principle of Mesoamerican political organization.

THE RISE OF POSTCLASSIC POLITIES

As noted in chapter 1, the twelfth century A.D. was a time of far-reaching change in most parts of Mesoamerica. One of those changes was the development of city-state cultures in many areas. Table 4.1 is a very rough outline of the political histories of the areas for which we have the best data; these cases are discussed in the chapters that follow. The data in the table illustrate three distinct developmental trajectories for city-states. In the first pattern, city-states or small polities appear to have been the norm for the entire Postclassic epoch, from the Epiclassic through Late Postclassic periods. Some of these areas are not well documented, however (chapters 7, 8).

In a second pattern—found in Yucatán and perhaps the Cholula area—city-state cultures developed out of the collapse of earlier large-scale states. Although Marcus (1989, 1998) claims that this pattern characterized all past city-state cultures, the annals of world history (Hansen 2000a; Nichols and Charlton 1997) include many cases of city-state cultures that developed by other paths (see also Adams 2000), and our data support this latter view. A third pattern found in Postclassic Mesoamerica describes city-state cultures that were formed in central Mexico in the wake of the Aztlan migrations. In these cases—the Basin of Mexico, Morelos, and parts of Puebla and Tlaxcala—the newly arrived Nahuatl speakers established new polities that flourished through the time of the Spanish conquest. Although the Nahua dynasties traced their descent back to the Toltec kings, this was a new city-state culture only marginally related to the earlier Toltec state.

Although each region had its own rhythm of change and development, the twelfth-century transition from the Early to the Middle Postclassic periods was particularly

Table 4.1
Chronology of polities in Postclassic Mesoamerica

Area	Chapter	Epiclassic	Early Postclassic	Middle Postclassic	Late Postclassic
Basin of Mexico	9	Teotihuacan	Tula		Aztec empire
Morelos	9	Xochicalco	??		
Puebla/Tlaxcala	10	Cacaxtla	Cholula		
Mixteca	10				
Tarascan Zone	13				Tarascan empire
Highland Jalisco	8				
Western Yucatán	5	Puuc States		Mayapán	
Eastern Yucatán	5	Chichén Itzá, Cobá, Ek Balam			
Belize	5	Late Classic			
Highland Guatemala	6				
Soconusco	7				

KEY:

Polity name	Large state(s)
	Small polities
Polity name	Coexistence of large state and small polities

significant in Mesoamerican political evolution (table 4.1). The Aztec city-states originated at that time; in Yucatán the large polities of the Early Postclassic period collapsed to usher in a period of both city-states and the more powerful Mayapán state; and other areas underwent a number of changes not easily depicted in the simplified scheme of this table (see the following chapters). The near-simultaneous occurrence of these political changes, and their linkages to economic and other social changes at the same time, suggests that they cannot be explained at a purely local or even a regional scale. Instead, the twelfth-century political transformations were part of the dynamics of the Mesoamerican world system's expansion in that century. These small states were crucial for developing processes of commercialized trade and information exchange that characterized the Postclassic Mesoamerican world system.

SMALL POLITIES IN THE POSTCLASSIC WORLD SYSTEM

The development of small polities throughout Mesoamerica in Postclassic times was closely linked to the other world-systems processes identified in chapter 1. The central Mexican population surge in the Middle and Late Postclassic periods (Smith 1996a:60–64) led to the dispersion of settlements across the landscape, a process accompanied by the formation of city-states (chapter 9). The competitive dynamics of Aztec (and probably other) city-states may have in turn stimulated further population growth along the lines suggested by Cowgill's (1979) comparative research.

The cross-cultural association between small polity size and commercial exchange is well known (e.g., Blanton et al. 1993:210–217; Braudel 1984; Hansen 2000c; Pearson 1991). Indeed, Mogens Hansen notes that "one of the major results of the present investigation [Hansen 2000b] has been to demonstrate the close connection between city-states and trade" (Hansen 2000c:615). Blanton et al. (1993:212–214) suggest that during the Classic period in Mesoamerica, trade and markets were politically controlled by large, powerful states. After their collapse—most notably, that of the lowland Maya states, Teotihuacan, and Monte Albán—commercial institutions and practices developed along more-autonomous lines (see, for example, Hirth 1998, 2000). By the Middle and Late Postclassic period, their argument goes, the commercial economy was sufficiently strong and autonomous that it acted against the development of powerful centralized states (chapter 5).

Just as the existence of an autonomous commercial economy favored smaller polities, so too did Postclassic city-states actively promote commercial exchange. It is no accident that one of the most remarkable systems of commercial exchange in the ancient world—the Near Eastern trade between Ashur and Kanesh during the Isin-Larsa period—flourished during a decentralized epoch of city-states rather than under the empires that preceded and followed this period (Larsen 1987; Kuhrt 1998). As M. N. Pearson notes, "Controllers of small political units typically have to take much more interest, for better or worse, in overseas trade than do rulers with large peasant populations that can be taxed relatively easily" (Pearson 1991:69). Following this logic, the promotion of trade was probably a strategy used by Postclassic rulers to pursue their own advantages (see especially chapters 5 7, and 10). These developments led to the three observed Postclassic economic trends: an increased volume of exchange, a greater diversity of trade goods, and a growing commercialization of the economy. These processes are discussed in greater detail in the chapters in part 3.

The proliferation of small polities in Postclassic Meso-america—with their high levels of political and commercial volatility—was at least partially responsible for the two trends in information exchange noted in chapter 1: the introduction of new forms of iconography and writing, and the development of new patterns of stylistic interaction. Increased interaction among ethnically distinct elites in Postclassic times favored the widespread use of the Aztec and Mixtec scripts, each of which was more international in character and less phonetic in emphasis than the Classic-period Maya and Zapotec scripts. These patterns of elite interaction across polity lines also contributed to the extensive use of international styles and symbols in the Postclassic period (chapter 10).

THE ROLE OF WARFARE

One process whose political (and other) implications are difficult to assess for Postclassic times is warfare. On one hand, there is abundant documentary evidence for warfare in all parts of Postclassic Mesoamerica. On the other, few Postclassic cities and towns had defenses, and the predominance of commercial exchange and elite visiting among polities indicates that warfare could not have been too disruptive to regional social and economic dynamics. The ethnohistoric evidence for conquest-era warfare is abundant, and it is clear that in most regions city-states were constantly at war with one another (Fox 1978; Lind 2000; Roys 1957; Smith 2000). The tactics and methods of Aztec warfare were highly developed (Hassig 1988; Isaac 1983), and the Aztec empire raised the ideology and practice of warfare to a cosmic level (D. Carrasco 1999). Several impressive Postclassic fortresses—for example, Oztuma, Tepexi el Viejo, and Guiengola—have been studied archaeologically (Gorenstein 1973; Peterson and MacDougall 1974; Silverstein 2000), and the Aztec/Tarascan border was marked by parallel lines of local and imperial fortresses (Berdan et al. 1996: chapter 6; chapter 14).

Yet despite these clear indications for widespread violent warfare, only some regions exhibited fortified Post-

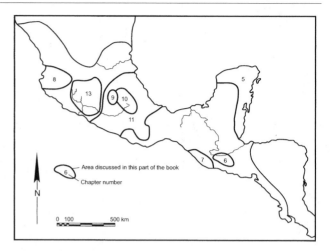

Figure 4.1 Map showing locations of the polity case studies in this section of the book. Areas are labeled with their corresponding chapter numbers. (Produced by Pamela Headrick.)

classic urban centers. Mayapán in Yucatán is a well-known example of a large fortified city (chapter 5), and many Postclassic towns in the Petén and highland Guatemala were protected by both natural topographic features (islands, ravines, cliffs) and constructed walls (e.g., Wurster 2000; Fox 1978). But for urban centers in the rest of Mesoamerica, the lack of perimeter walls and defensive settings is striking. The undefended nature of Aztec towns, for example, contrasts sharply with the ethnohistoric record of Aztec warfare.

It seems that trade and other processes of interaction were allowed to operate despite widespread warfare. We know that the heavily fortified and frequently attacked Aztec/Tarascan border was permeable to trade (chapter 14), and such situations were not uncommon in other parts of the world where commercial exchange coexisted with continual warfare. For example, Chaudhuri (1991) quotes Ibn Jubayr, a Moorish diplomat of the twelfth century, on warfare and commerce in Iberia at that time: "Likewise, in Muslim territory, none of the Christian merchants is forbidden entrance or is molested. The Christians impose a tax on the Muslims in their land, which gives them utmost security, while the Christian merchants also pay customs for their goods in the land of the Muslims. Reciprocity prevails and equal treatment in all respects. The warriors are engaged in their wars, while the people are at ease" (Chaudhuri 1991:435).

THE DIVERSITY OF POSTCLASSIC POLITIES

The chapters in this section provide brief descriptions of Postclassic polities and political dynamics in most parts of Mesoamerica (figure 4.1). In the first case study Kepecs and Masson (chapter 5) describe the spatial and temporal variation among small polities in Postclassic Yucatán. In the next chapter (6) Braswell presents an innovative and perhaps controversial new view of polities in highland Guatemala based on the "house society" model. The next two chapters—Gasco (chapter 7) and Pollard (chapter 8)—treat poorly documented areas (Soconusco and west Mexico) that appear to have been the settings for small polities throughout the Postclassic period. In chapter 9 Smith summarizes city-state organization in the Basin of Mexico and Morelos, areas where Hansen's model fits particularly well (see Smith 2000). Next, Pohl (chapter 10) explores the dynamics of confederations in the Mixteca-Puebla area, stressing the linkages between politics and information. The final four papers in this section cover the two major Late Postclassic empires—the Aztec (chapters 11 and 12) and Tarascan (chapter 13). The interactions across the border between these two empires (chapter 14) were important components of Postclassic world-systems dynamics.

Most of the case studies that follow describe polities located in affluent production zones (chapters 5, 6, 7, 9, 10, 12) and/or core zones (chapter 9, 10, 11, 13). Only one resource-extraction zone is included (chapter 8). This coverage reflects the availability of documentary sources and archaeological fieldwork, which tend to center on cores and affluent production zones. Nevertheless, some key areas are not included, most notably the Gulf Coast, most parts of Oaxaca, the Petén, and southeastern Mesoamerica. For the Postclassic political situation in these areas the reader is referred to the following works: Berdan et al. 1996; P. Carrasco 1999; Flannery and Marcus 1983; Gerhard 1993a; Jones 1999; Scholes and Roys 1968; Stark et al. 1998; and Wonderly 1985, 1986. Although we lack political case studies for these regions, economic patterns in many of these areas are discussed in the chapters in part 3.

5

Political Organization in Yucatán and Belize

Susan Kepecs

Marilyn Masson

Lowland Maya political organization in Yucatán and Belize—important affluent production zones in the Post-classic world system—was particularly dynamic. Regional political organization cycled from city-states to hierarchical regional states and back again (chapter 4). Yet the northern and southern Maya lowlands followed different organizational paths to the city-state culture of the Late Postclassic. We pick up these trajectories at mid-point—the end of the Mesoamerican Classic period, defined at the world scale by the demise of Teotihuacan. Below we outline Postclassic political shifts in both areas and provide brief case studies from Chikinchel (in the northern lowlands) and Chetumal (in the southern zone). Both were affluent production zones that played important economic roles in the Postclassic world system.

THE ERA OF LARGE REGIONAL STATES

Information on Yucatán's Classic-period political organization is limited, but available studies indicate a prevailing pattern of single-center polities or city-states of various sizes (Andrews 1990b; Kepecs 1999; Kepecs et al. 1994). This pattern was transformed during the post-Teotihuacan (Epiclassic/Early Postclassic) era, when large regional polities crystallized in several parts of the peninsula. Chichén Itzá gained prominence on the northern plains, becoming one of three key centers in the Meso-american world system along with El Tajín on the Gulf coast and Tula in the central Mexican highlands. At the regional scale Chichén Itzá was the core of a powerful new hierarchical state (chapter 33). Other large regional polities (with less influence in the world system) emerged in the Puuc region and at Ek Balam and Cobá (figure 5.1).

Each of these states was organized differently. The Itzá set up a system of secondary administrative centers linking the core to key coastal outposts at regular days' round-trip intervals—roughly 20 km each way. Through this network they gained tight control over fertile inland plains and coastal enterprises (Andrews 1978, 1983, 1993; Andrews et al. 1988; Kepecs 1999, 2000; Kepecs et al. 1994). During much of this period the Puuc centers probably were politically independent, but at the end of the Epiclassic these towns evidently were subsumed in a political hierarchy centered at Uxmal and allied with Chichén (Dunning and Kowalski 1994; Kowalski and Dunning 1999). Cobá was an immense settlement covering some 70 km², with a large sustaining area and a dendritic string of smaller centers stretched west along a 100 km causeway to Yaxuná, on Chichén's frontier (Robles and Andrews 1986; Suhler and Freidel 1998).

In contrast to the north's increasing political complexity, the southern lowlands became fragmented when the hierarchical Classic-period states of the Petén failed. This collapse sparked new developments in Belize. Refugees from the old Petén cores joined local coastal populations, and new polities and alliances were established. In the absence of signs of substantial hierarchical development at most political centers and smaller sites, it is likely that the settlements in northern Belize were highly autonomous and loosely integrated into regional polities (Masson 2000a).

MAYAPÁN AND THE CITY-STATE CULTURE OF THE MIDDLE AND LATE POSTCLASSIC

After several hundred years Yucatán's regional states declined, along with the Epiclassic/Early Postclassic world system. Factors in this reorganization include interelite conflicts at multiple levels, as well as shifts in technology

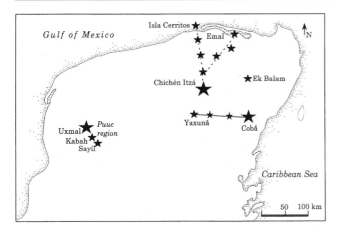

Figure 5.1 Regional polities of the Epiclassic/Early Postclassic period

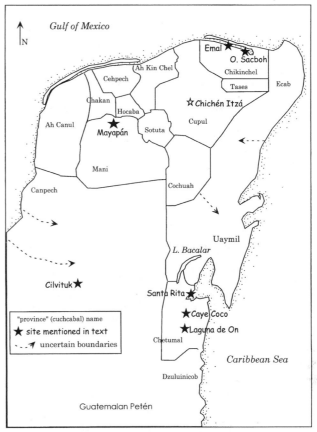

Figure 5.2 Yucatán provinces as identified by Ralph Roys (after Andrews 1984; Jones 1989; Roys 1957), and key sites mentioned in the text

and the organization of labor (chapter 33). Mayapán, a large nucleated center and the seat of a much-debated joint government (*multepal*), arose on the flatlands 75 km west of Chichén (figure 5.2). From the Middle Postclassic through the middle of the Late Postclassic, Mayapán flourished as part of the Mesoamerican world system. Copper bells, obsidian, and shared art styles link Mayapán with central Mexico and Central America (Proskouriakoff 1962b; Peraza Lope et al. 1998; Root 1962).

Mayapán, an international city, was the core of a large regional polity. The written record on the organization of this unit is relatively well developed, since the grandsons of its leaders were key informants to colonial administrators. Mayapán was a voluntary confederation (multepal) of prominent lineages—a sharp contrast to the Itzá administrative infrastructure or the Aztecs' tributary hegemony (chapter 11). Mayapán's governors and their retainers lived in the center, from which they evidently ruled their own towns (Landa, in Tozzer 1941:26). Yet these towns and their territories probably were held under core authority (Roys 1943:58; Tozzer 1941:35 n. 172); colonial descendents of prominent confederate leaders claimed heritage to lands granted when the League of Mayapán dissolved in the 1440s (Restall 1998:26; cf. Roys 1957:3). Landholdings were disputed, and settlement patterns probably shifted somewhat during the 60 years between Mayapán's decline and the Spaniards' arrival, but 16th-century descendents of multepal leaders still lived in the general vicinity—a day or three on foot from the old confederate capital.

Farther east, independent city-states coexisted with the Mayapán confederacy. Trade, marriage alliances, and religious codes connected these small polities to one another and to Mayapán in various ways and to varying degrees. In the following short case studies, we describe Late Postclassic city-state culture in Chikinchel and Chetumal, beyond Mayapán's administrative reach. In our longer case studies (chapters 33 and 34) we offer empirical evidence for the vital role of commercial activities in these city-state contexts.

The Mayapán confederacy folded in the face of increasing economic competition at various scales. Internally, at least two multepal families, the Cocom and Xiu, were mercantile rivals whose enmities finally split the great league into smaller teams (e.g., Edmonson 1982: xvi–xvii, 1986:2–3; Landa, in Tozzer 1941:37; Restall 1998). Macroregionally, Mayapán's collapse occurred only two decades after the consolidation of the Aztec Triple Alliance (Smith and Berdan 1996a:2). Concurrent expansion of the Aztec empire placed new demands on the world system (e.g., Smith 2001c; Stark et al. 1998), and at the level of the Yucatán Peninsula, Mayapán's merchant kings evidently were unable to compete with independent traders in the east (Kepecs 1999).

THE BATABILS OF THE LATER LATE POSTCLASSIC

After Mayapán's decline the city-state culture of the Maya lowlands stretched from Campeche (Williams-Beck 1998) to Belize (Masson 2000a) and into the Petén

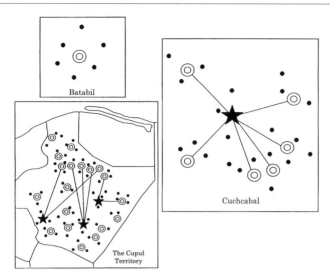

Figure 5.3 The small polities of Late Postclassic Yucatán, as reconfigured by Quezada (1993) and Okoshi (1994, 1995): Batabils sometimes formed hierarchical alliances, or cuchcabals. Both kinds of polities coexisted within the bounds of the territories.

(D. Rice 1986; P. Rice 1986; Rice et al. 1998). Yet regions not linked to the failed confederacy had a head start in the period's economy, since commercial competition thrives best in the absence of centralized political authority (chapter 32). There were populous small polities in the old confederate lands of western Yucatán (Roys 1957; Williams-Beck 1998), but key trade and production centers were east and south—and distant from Mayapán. The most active territories, including Chikinchel and Chetumal (see below), were situated in areas with coastal access and fertile inland support strips (see also Andrews 1993).

Until recently our model of Yucatán's political organization on the eve of the Spanish invasion was based on Ralph Roys's (1957) pioneering map, which divides the peninsula into some 16 petty provinces (*cuchcabals*) of three types (figure 5.2). The first was a hierarchical arrangement in which towns governed by local leaders (*batabs*) were centralized at the top under a single ruler (*halach uinic*). This king resided in the capital, for which the province was named. The second type of polity lacked centralization at the top, but primary towns were governed by batabs of the same lineage. These were kinship confederacies, although the degree of cooperation among principals varied. Organization of the remaining territories, which Roys hesitated to call polities, consisted of regions in which independent towns formed shifting alliances.

Today many researchers (e.g., Alexander n.d.; Restall 1997, 1998; Kepecs 1999; Williams-Beck 1998) prefer a radical revision of the Roysian scheme developed by historians Sergio Quezada and Tsubasa Okoshi (Okoshi 1994, 1995; Okoshi and Quezada 1988; Quezada 1993).

Based on their own advanced documentary and linguistic research, Quezada and Okoshi propose that native polities were not box-shaped, Euro-style polities; instead, they resembled amoebas with boundaries that fluctuated as lands between towns were contested. Further, the basic unit was not cuchcabal, but *batabil* (figure 5.3)—a single central place (with its dependents, or *cuchteels*) governed by a batab (see Quezada 1993:42, 63). The term "cuchcabal" applies only to hierarchical polities consisting of multiple batabils centralized under halach uinics. Administrative ties were fluid (Marcus 1993:118; Quezada 1993:37; Roys 1957:114). Batabils formed alliances for marriage, trade, or defense—and ended them over territorial disputes.

Finally (contra Roys), lineage and polity did not necessarily overlap. Towns ruled by related batabs did not always belong to the same political unit, nor did they invariably occupy contiguous areas, although they often did. The territory Roys called the Cupul cuchcabal, for example, included a number of independent polities, all ruled by Cupuls. Quezada (1993: map 3) indicates that some of these units were batabils, while others were cuchcabals. The overall scene was unstable. Cupul-ruled polities reportedly fought with each other (see Roys 1957; Marcus 1993; Quezada 1993). Yet related batabs often maintained ties extending far beyond administrative or territorial boundaries. The native name for these lineage-based confederations was *tzucub* (Quezada 1993:47–48). These little "mafias" had various functions. Some were landholding units (e.g., Restall 1998), but others served commercial interests (see below).

In addition to Yucatán's well-established city-state culture, Rani Alexander (n.d.), following Kopytoff (1987), proposes that the southern base of the peninsula was an interior frontier. Throughout the Postclassic, Alexander holds, small factions splitting off from more-centralized polities formed new communities on the Maya lowlands fringes. Internal frontier settlements—exemplified by Alexander's empirical case at Cilvituk, in southern Campeche (see figure 5.2)—may have been organized as weak *batabils*, but there is little evidence of well-developed political authority. Settlement founders used prestige goods to create patron-client relations, but the local economy essentially was subsistence-based. Cilvituk contrasts notably with northern batabils like those in Chikinchel, which are characterized by large centers with numerous satellites, regional marketing systems, specialized production, and a working class (chapter 33).

CASE STUDIES

The variety of Maya city-state arrangements is too great to address in a short chapter, but below we offer two brief case studies that provide some insights into how different regions were organized. The first is written by Kepecs, the second by Masson.

CHIKINCHEL

Chikinchel—one of the territories Roys (1957) hesitated to call a "polity"—was administratively integrated into the Itzá polity in the previous epoch (chapter 33). With the fall of Chichén Itzá, Chikinchel was liberated from the forces of political centralization. Some old centers declined, but new towns were established. There is some variability among these settlements, but none stands out archaeologically or in the documentary record as a regional capital. Thus I assume that each first-order site was the center of an independent polity or batabil. At times several of these polities may have united through alliance or conquest, but these little hierarchies were too fleeting to crystallize in the archaeological record. In one case the town of Chauaca was said to control Sinsimato, about a day's trip away. This arrangement probably was short-lived, since other Spanish papers record wars between these towns (Kepecs 1999).

Archaeological and documentary information allow the identification of first-order centers within the bounds of Roys's Chikinchel territory. Among 70 sites with Late Postclassic components, nine stood out (chapter 33). Eight of these towns were represented in both records; the ninth, Sacboh, lies in the undocumented east, beyond the Spanish fringe. The documents contain no information on the remaining 61 sites. Archaeologically there is a lot of variation among them, but all have at least some public architecture as well as surrounding house remains. Many of these sites cluster around coastal support towns, but farther inland some smaller Late Postclassic settlements lie beyond a day's range of any key center.

Opportunities for work and rewards on the populous coastal tier were linked to long-distance exchange routes circling the peninsula (Kepecs 1999; also Andrews 1993; Freidel and Sabloff 1984; Sabloff and Rathje 1975b; Rathje and Sabloff 1975). Under politically decentralized conditions, production and economic competition increased. The Itzá maintained a single, centralized salt operation at Emal, but in the Late Postclassic a second solar evaporation facility (Otro Sacboh) was built farther east (see figure 5.2). The documents record battles between batabils of inland support towns near these *salinas*; independent salt producers probably were competing for regional and macroregional markets. Economic ties were extended, in part, through tzucub. The Chans, who controlled Emal in the Late Postclassic, had strong ties with Chans in Uaymil, who built canoes (chapter 33).

CHETUMAL

Northern Belize represents the southern half of a territory known as Chetumal at the time of Spanish contact (Roys 1957; Jones 1989: map 2). The archaeological evidence for the organization of small, autonomous Late Postclassic polities in northern Belize consists of community analyses performed at the centers of Santa Rita (Chase and Chase 1988), Lamanai (Pendergast 1981, 1985, 1986), Caye Coco (Masson and Rosenswig 1998, 1999), and a host of smaller sites including Colha (Michaels 1987, 1994; Hester and Schafer 1991), Laguna de On (Masson 1997, 2000a), and Cerros (Walker 1990). All of these sites are within the estimated boundaries of the Chetumal territory, with the exception of Lamanai, which may have been the capital of a territory known as Dzuluinicob in the Colonial period (Jones 1989: map 2).

During the latter half of the Postclassic period (A.D. 1250–1500), five centers can be identified in the Chetumal territory, based on settlement size or the size or elaboration of architecture (Sidrys 1983; Masson 2000a). These include the sites of Santa Rita (Wilson's Beach), Ichpaatun, Caye Coco, Sarteneja, and Bandera. Although the functional relationships among these sites are poorly understood, it appears that multiple centers existed during the latter half of the Postclassic period in northern Belize. The trappings of authority are variable at each site, including elaborate murals (Santa Rita), colonnaded halls and walled centers (Ichpaatun), large elite residential platforms (Santa Rita and Caye Coco), stone monuments (Ichpaatun, Caye Coco, and Sarteneja), and elaborate caches (Santa Rita).

Ethnohistoric documents describe friendly ties with Mayapán and groups along the east coast, though no evidence of direct control is implied (Pollock 1962; Roys 1962). At contact, the Chetumal territory was governed by a halach uinic, Nachan Kan, who resided at a primate center also called Chetumal. This was a territory with a probable three-tier hierarchy; other such provinces with halach uinic authorities studied by Roys (1957) were supported by secondary centers with local administrators (batabs) and a host of other subordinate offices. Sites like Caye Coco were probable seats of secondary batabs, under the leadership of the territory capital of Chetumal. It is doubtful that relationships between small centers were always peaceful, and it is not known whether such multiple centers enjoyed primarily complementary relationships or whether their history was punctuated by conflict and competition.

Economic evidence from third-tier supporting agrarian communities such as Laguna de On suggests that if conflict and competition existed, it rarely disrupted local community patterns of production (Masson 2000a). The archaeological record of Laguna de On suggests long-term economic stability from A.D. 1000 to 1500, and the same has been suggested for Lamanai (Pendergast 1981; Graham 1987) and Santa Rita (Chase and Chase 1988). Indirectly, these stable community patterns suggest that elite activities in this region, whether amiable or contradictory, promoted lengthy economic prosperity and social affluence (Masson 2000a).

CONCLUSIONS

City-state culture prevailed in the Maya lowlands from the Middle Postclassic through the Late Postclassic, although during part of this period towns in western Yucatán were centralized under the Mayapán confederacy. Mayapán's political authority could not, however, withstand increasing macroregional commercialization. Sixteenth-century Spanish chronicles describe trade canoes and enterprising professional merchants who hustled goods and slaves in international markets (e.g., Díaz del Castillo 1984:29–31; Landa, in Tozzer 1941:94–96). In chapters 33 and 34 we discuss archaeological evidence for this flourishing economy in the context of our own empirical research.

6

Highland
Maya
Polities

Geoffrey E. Braswell

My view is that the lineage model, its predecessors and its analogs, have no value for anthropological analysis. Two reasons above all support this conclusion. First, the model does not represent folk models which actors anywhere have of their own societies. Secondly, there do not appear to be any societies in which vital political or economic activities are organized by a repetitive series of descent groups. (Kuper 1982:92)

Highland Guatemala, an area rich in resources, was the setting of a number of dynamic and competitive polities during Late Postclassic times. These polities have been characterized by a variety of scholars as empires, segmentary states (Fox 1987, 1994), or segmentary chiefdoms (Brown, in Fox et al. 1992). These disparate views are rooted in the contradictory assumptions that K'iche'an polities were similar to—but not quite as complex as—centralized states, and that social organization was based on elementary principles described by traditional kinship studies. To resolve these seemingly opposing reconstructions, and at the same time move toward a more accurate view of political structure, it is necessary to reexamine the nature of K'iche'an social structure.

TRADITIONAL VIEWS OF K'ICHE'AN SOCIETY: KINSHIP VERSUS TERRITORY

The predominant view is that the fundamental unit of K'iche'an society was the patrilineal descent group. In fact, the lineage concept has become so central to Maya studies that many archaeologists, ethnohistorians, and epigraphers do not even consider alternative social "types." To a great degree, this perspective is derived from the pioneering work of Miles (1957), Carrasco (1964), Carmack (1977, 1981), Fox (1987), and other ethnohistorians of the Guatemalan highlands. Carmack

(1981) proposes that K'iche'an society was arranged in a nested hierarchy of strictly exogamous patrilineages, with larger groups (called, in ascending order, "major lineages," "moieties",[1] and "groups") formed out of "principal lineages" and "minimal lineages." According to this scheme, the K'iche' *Ajpop* (king) came from the Ajpop principal lineage, the *Ajpop K'amja* (king receiving-house) from the Ajpop K'amja principal lineage, and lesser titled lords from inferior principal lineages. The rank and priority of different titles were reflected in the rank of competing lineages. Moreover, each principal lineage had its own titled positions, which often replicated titles used in the greater political structure. According to Carmack (1981:157), segmentation and the proliferation of lineages occurred as a natural result of political expansion and the competition for new titled offices. Principal lineages were closely identified with the structures in which they conducted their affairs, called *nimja* (big houses).

Although Carmack considers the patrilineal descent group the basis for K'iche'an social structure, he also argues for the existence of "castes" and "classes" (1981: 148–156). Lords (*ajawab*), commoners (*alk'ajol*), and slaves (*munib*) formed endogamous strata in society, but classes such as warriors (pigeonholed within the ajawab stratum) contained both lords and social-climbing vassals (Carmack 1981:152–153). Thus, K'iche'an society also is depicted as stratified, but containing the potential for mobility among classes. Finally, a lord could have a walled-in country estate, called a *chinamit*, that housed both commoners and slaves (Carmack 1977:12–13).

A very different perspective is offered by Hill and Monaghan. They consider kinship to be unimportant to K'iche'an social structure (Hill 1984, 1996; Hill and Monaghan 1987). According to Hill (1984), the basic unit of K'iche'an society was the *chinamit*, which he interprets as a closed corporate group defined by territorial concerns. Hill and Monaghan (1987) elaborate on this idea, and discuss the similarities between the chinamit and Aztec *calpolli*. In this model, *chinamita'* were largely endogamous communities that shared a group identity defined by localized settlement and the common ownership of land and other resources (Hill 1984:314–316). Members of the chinamit shared responsibilities such as the cost of marriage feasts, the upkeep of temples and shrines, and the maintenance of law and order. Certain individuals within the chinamit held titled offices, some of which became fixed within certain families (Braswell 2001a). Economic specialization could focus on natural resources, such as salt (Hill and Monaghan 1987), located within the chinamit's territory. Finally, group membership could be expressed through the use of a common surname, borrowed from the leading officeholder, but not determined by kinship or marriage ties (Hill 1984).

Hill (1996; Hill and Monaghan 1987) further argues that larger social units, such as the *amaq'*, were forged through alliances between chinamita'. Such alliances could be formed through exogamy practiced by chinamit leaders, but also through common economic or military concerns, often related to territorial contiguity. Capitals such as Kaqchikel Iximche' and Chajoma' Saqikajol Nimakaqajpek may have been established to further cement even larger confederacies comprised of distinct *amaq'i'*. Thus, in this model, K'iche'an polities were fragile alliances between factions and superfactions formed of corporate groups.

A NEW MODEL OF K'ICHE'AN SOCIAL STRUCTURE

These apparently contradictory perspectives have less to do with K'iche'an society than with traditional taxonomic approaches to kinship and social structure. Many contemporary scholars (e.g., Bourdieu 1977; Kuper 1982; Leach 1961; Schneider 1984) have argued that the unilineal descent group is an ideal analytical type that does not, in fact, exist. Similarly, others view the division of society into mutually exclusive economic units based on residence or localized settlement ("corporate communities") as an artificial construct of Anglo-American anthropology (Lévi-Strauss 1987:153–154). Thus, the dichotomies of kinship versus residence, and lineage versus territory may be more important to some anthropologists and ethnohistorians than they were to K'iche'an peoples. Moreover, both theoretical positions tend to give priority to deterministic rules and normative behavior at the expense of agency and practice.

An alternative approach to K'iche'an society is to consider indigenous terms for basic social units and to try to understand their characteristics. Important structures of

highland Maya society include the *molab*, chinamit, amaq', and nimja. *Molab*, the Poqomam equivalent of the chinamit (Hill 1984), is derived from the common highland root <mol>, which means "together." It does not imply anything more than a group or community of people, though it may suggest common residence within a single territory. The remaining three terms, however, all share one thing in common: they refer to physical structures, buildings, or households. *Chinamit*, borrowed from Nahua, seems to mean a "fenced-in place," leading Carmack (1977:12–13) to interpret it as a feudal estate. But it also may refer to the corn-stalk enclosures built around many highland Maya houselots.

In Kaqchikel, *amaq'*, most often translated as "tribe," has numerous meanings that combine ethnic connotations with a sense of otherness. Coto (1983:LXXXV) gives "place" as one definition, suggesting that it is a kind of territorial unit. The morpheme can be combined to form a verb meaning "to settle as a neighbor," which has the sense of both place and otherness. It is often used to describe something lasting or permanent. Most interestingly, in Colonial times *amaq'* could be combined to form *amaq'ib'äl*, meaning "old or former household." Finally, *nimja* has only one literal translation: "big house." I suggest, therefore, that the predominant metaphor used by the Postclassic Maya for social order was the house (i.e., a physical structure) and the household. Membership in a household is determined not only by kinship, but also by marriage and alliance, so it is likely that affiliation was as important as kinship in determining membership in K'iche'an social groups. In addition, *molab* and *amaq'* suggest neighborly residence, supporting the notion that social structure was derived at least in part from a sense of community that was not rooted in kinship (Hill 1984; Hill and Monaghan 1987). Despite Hill's (1996) cogent arguments, I remain unconvinced that the amaq' always differed in scale and kind from the chinamit. To me, the hierarchical and qualitative distinctions between amaq' and chinamit/molab/nimja are not particularly clear (Braswell 2000b).

Analysis of kinship terms employed by the Kaqchikel and K'iche' does indeed support the assertion that the building blocks of social structure "sound like lineages" (Tedlock 1989:498). K'iche'an kinship is weakly patrilineal, but it is difficult to see how a structure as fragile and prone to conflict as the patrilineal descent group could have grown to be as large as some K'iche'an nimja or chinamita', which contained thousands of members. Thus, it is more likely that kinship provided the *language* used by large-scale social groups to interpret their integration, but did not serve as the sole principle defining group membership. In other words, kinship may have been more "practical" than "official" (Bourdieu 1977:37). The use of kinship as a metaphor rather than as a social principle also resolves Carmack's (1981) seemingly contradictory assertion that K'iche'an society was both class- and kinship-based.

Social units such as the chinamit did control property. Such property included territory, resources, shrines and temples, and the physical buildings (nimja) where leaders of the chinamit conducted their affairs. The chinamit also controlled intangible possessions, including titles. Such titles described roles not only within the chinamit itself, but also in the greater political system. Hence, they were the subjects of competition both within and among chinamita'.

K'iche'an social units were both endogamous (Hill 1984) and exogamous (Carmack 1981). I argue that endogamous marriage was a strategy designed to maintain the wealth of the chinamit within the group, and that exogamous marriage was practiced in order to increase the property of the social unit. In other words, marriage practices were pragmatic rather than normative, and complex rather than elementary. Finally, the basic unit of K'iche'an social structure persisted over time, a fact reflected in the term *amaq'*. It existed as an organic being, and engaged with similar units in agency-based strategies designed to increase group property and to prolong group survival.

Together, these characteristics satisfy Lévi-Strauss's (1987) definition of the *maison* (house), an organizational institution that he intended as a classificatory type characteristic of certain societies. According to his formulation, a social house is: "a moral person holding an estate made up of both material and immaterial wealth, which perpetuates itself through the transmission of its name, its goods, and its titles down a real or imaginary descent line, considered legitimate as long as this continuity can express itself in the language of descent or of alliance or, most often, of both" (Lévi-Strauss 1987:174). *Sociétés à maisons*, or "house societies," may be composed of just one such social house, but their full expression is manifest only when more than one house interacts. This is because the relationships maintained between groups are more important than the criteria used to establish group membership. In fact, the house is a "dynamic formation that cannot be defined in itself, but only in relation to others of the same kind, situated in their historical context" (Lévi-Strauss 1987:178).[2] In this sense, a house society with numerous social houses may be consistent with the concept of city-state culture described in chapter 4.

TOWARD A NEW MODEL OF K'ICHE'AN POLITIES

House societies do not correlate well with standard political models. They range from the egalitarian societies of Australia, to the ranked societies of northwest North America, to the highly stratified societies of medieval Europe and feudal Japan (Lévi-Strauss 1987). Most important, they span the analytical gap between the preliterate "primitive" societies usually studied by anthropologists, and the literate civilizations that are the focus of historians. Thus, the recognition that Postclassic highland Guatemala was organized in a large number of great houses will not enable us to resolve the question of whether or not K'iche'an political organization had crossed the essentialist rubicon between the "chiefdom" and the "state." On the other hand, the house society model does allow us to understand certain aspects of the structure and dynamics of K'iche'an polities, because the great houses were the building blocks that formed these polities and the agents of political action.

First, K'iche'an great houses are best viewed as localized groups that competed for property and prestige. Since land and natural resources were controlled by great houses, competition often was manifest in territorial warfare. Boundary maintenance was a common concern of all great houses, and the maps and geographical descriptions that frequently make up indigenous *títulos* attest to the continuation of long-standing competition well into the Colonial period.

Second, the desire to generate more wealth and prestige within great houses led to the formation of alliances. This cooperative strategy created greater concentrations of force and hence led to the emergence of factions. Marriage alliances commonly were used to cement ties within factions such as the Kaqchikel Tuquche', Sotz'il, or Xajil, and also helped hold together even larger alliances between factions. Still, the principle that provided the basis for alliance was mutual interest rather than kinship. Power-sharing strategies between great houses and larger factions developed in order to ensure that no particular group would emerge as the single dominant power. Thus, K'iche'an polities are correctly depicted as segmented, but the units of segmentation were the great house and faction (an alliance of great houses) rather than the lineage.

Third, although the greatest concentration of coercive force was controlled by the leading alliances of great houses, the mandate to use force was not restricted to these factions. Numerous powerful groups, such as the Kaqchikel Xpantzay and the K'iche' Tamub' and Ilokab', lived outside of the political capitals and engaged in aggressive competition designed to increase their wealth and prestige. Coercive force, then, seems to have been the right of whoever could control it, rather than a monopoly held by a state. Indeed, since each great house within a given faction was responsible for enforcing codes of conduct, it was imperative that each exert at least enough coercive force to control its members and defend its property.

Fourth, the notion that highland Maya groups such as the Kaqchikel of Iximche' or the K'iche' of Q'umarkaj controlled "kingdoms" with meaningful territorial boundaries is erroneous. These regions also were home to other factions—including the Xpantzay, Tamub', and Ilokab'—that sometimes supported and sometimes struggled against the great houses centered at regional capitals. Again, the meaningful territorial unit was not the polity, but the land controlled by each great house or alliance of houses (see chapter 4 for a discussion of the lack of territory-based principles in Postclassic Mesoamerican polities).

Fifth, K'iche'an capitals are best interpreted as sites where allied great houses maintained important residential and administrative buildings. They were little more than palace complexes, whose locations were determined more by administrative and military necessity than by central-place economic concerns. Capitals also served as defensive military strongholds (Borhegyi 1965) and offensive bastions from which punitive raids could be launched (Braswell 1996:329–330). Their locations changed as alliances between great houses or among factions coalesced and disintegrated, and as interests in controlling particular resources shifted.

Sixth, given the desire of different great houses to increase their wealth and the concomitant intensity of between- and within-group competition, it is not surprising that inheritance was based as much on capability as on kinship. K'iche' and Kaqchikel titles sometimes were passed from father to son (especially if a father was a strong leader), but often went to more-able kinsmen, in-laws, or even rivals within the great house. Although kinship principles *did* play a role in determining who inherited particular titles, affiliation and ability also were important factors. Rigid models focused on lineage and descent fail to account for the pragmatic manner in which power and position were negotiated in K'iche'an society.

Seventh, factionalism often was manifested through warfare. Rebellions were not uncommon, and factions sometimes were expelled from alliances. The Kaqchikel Tuquche' faction, for example, was ousted from Iximche' and was "annihilated" in battle (Arana X. and Díaz X. 1573–1605:49–50). Constant factional struggle caused K'iche'an society to become militarized to a surprising degree. Occasionally, powerful rulers emerged, such as Kikab' of the K'iche'. Such rulers are accurately depicted as military despots. But during most of K'iche'an history, power within the major polities was much more fragmented. We may characterize such times as periods of factional balkanism. In Marcus's (1993, 1998) dynamic model, these are the "valleys" rather than the "peaks."

Eighth, the local resources that supported the power bases of the K'iche'an great houses were augmented by goods extracted from territories beyond their direct political control. The desire to tap distant sources of wealth played a key role in the formation and maintenance of alliance groups. In most cases, distant territories were not directly integrated into K'iche'an polities, and access to resources was maintained through the threat of force. Thus, beyond the immediate territory of the chinamit, K'iche'an great houses jointly commanded access to the "means of destruction" (Goody 1971) and did not directly control the means of production. Wealth acquired by this piratical strategy could be received in the form of gifts or tribute. Joint rulership and the complex system of aristocratic authority allowed equitable distribution of these resources to individual factions and great houses.

CONCLUSIONS: THE SMALL POLITIES OF THE K'ICHE'AN HIGHLANDS

K'iche'an society was based as much on affiliation or alliance as on kinship. As such, it cannot be described using elementary terms of social structure. Moreover, the notion that social units were closed corporate communities seems somewhat in error. Instead, the best model for K'iche'an social structure is Lévi-Strauss's house society. The fact that terms for K'iche'an social units refer to houses or households is strong evidence for this identification.

K'iche'an polities were formed of alliances of great houses, where the pragmatic concerns of the maintenance and increase of great-house prestige and wealth were the overriding factors determining membership. The factions formed even larger alliances out of which coalesced the various "kingdoms" of the K'iche', Kaqchikel, Tz'utujil, and Chajoma'. Within the polity, balance was maintained through elaborate strategies of power sharing that, along with marriage ties, served to diffuse rivalries between individual great houses and among factions comprised of great houses.

K'iche'an polities should not be considered as controlling large territories of the sort that are easily represented on maps, because the basic territorial unit was the chinamit or great house. Capitals were built at strategic, defensible locations and served as "power centers" out of which punitive raids could be made on recalcitrant neighbors. K'iche'an polities, therefore, were poorly integrated territories held together by the threat of military destruction.

The Late Postclassic K'iche'an polities—including those of the K'iche', Kaqchikel, Chajoma', and Tz'utujil—fit well with the definition of small polities adopted in this volume (chapter 4), though none are rightly called city-states. Instead, they were networks of great houses linked by alliance. At their largest, they were hierarchically organized, and demanded services and extracted surpluses from conquered (or at least intimidated) territories. At their smallest, K'iche'an polities consisted of the territories, resources, and titles controlled by one or a few great houses. As the Postclassic period progressed, there was a tendency for these small polities to proliferate as rival factions coalesced in the central and western highlands. What is not clear is when this process of balkanization began. Little is known about the Early Postclassic period, largely because the methodological tools needed to distinguish Early Postclassic occupations from Late Classic and Late Postclassic components have not been developed (Braswell 1993, 1996). In fact, settlement hierarchy studies suggest that the highlands west of the Valley of Guatemala may have been divided into small polities since the beginning of the Early Classic period, when K'iche'an peoples first spread into the departments of Sololá, Chimaltenango, and Sacatepéquez.

ACKNOWLEDGMENTS

I thank Susan Gillespie and Rosemary Joyce for sharing critical unpublished manuscripts with me in 1999, when this chapter was written.

7

The Polities of Xoconochco

Janine Gasco

Xoconochco (or Soconusco, the Hispanicized name in use today), was one of the leading producers of cacao in Mesoamerica and a major affluent production zone in the Postclassic world system. Compared to most of the other regions discussed in this volume, this area (figure 4.1) remains poorly understood for the Postclassic period, and most of the available information dates to the Late Postclassic period. No known codices exist from this region, and early Spanish accounts from the area have been lost (De Vos 1994:22–24). The only written/pictorial records that pertain to Postclassic Xoconochco were created not by local scribes but by the region's conquerors. In the Early Colonial period, there were no friars—no Sahagún, no Landa—to record ethnographic information about the region. A second problem is that archaeological research on the Postclassic period in Soconusco has lagged behind interest in earlier time periods (Voorhies and Gasco 2002). The first archaeological research project to focus specifically on the Postclassic period was begun only in 1997 (Gasco 1998a, 1998b), although valuable data from Postclassic sites come from earlier archaeological projects that had broader goals (e.g., Lowe et al 1982; Voorhies 1989a, 1989b; Voorhies and Gasco 2002). Despite the data's many shortcomings, however, it is possible to sketch out the broad outlines of political organization in Late Postclassic Soconusco based on the available documentary and archaeological evidence.

As was the case throughout most of Mesoamerica, numerous small polities dotted the landscape in the Soconusco region during the Late Postclassic period. In the following pages I review what we know about these polities. While it is possible to identify some of them, to speculate about their territorial extent and makeup, and to consider relationships between and among them, their internal organization is more difficult to discern. We do not

know how they were ruled or who were the rulers, nor can we determine with any confidence whether the Late Postclassic polities are best characterized as city-states, *cacicazgos* (political rulerships), kingdoms, or great houses.

In the last decades of the Late Postclassic period the Soconusco region was besieged by forces from neighboring and distant polities, and documents describing these events list what must have been important Soconusco towns, or at least the towns targeted by foreign powers. The K'iche', under the leadership of Q'uik'ab, successfully raided four Soconusco towns in the mid-fifteenth century (Recinos 1957). Central Mexican documents describe the conquest and subjugation of several Soconusco towns by forces of the Triple Alliance sometime after 1486 and list their subsequent tribute obligations (Alvarado Tezozomoc 1944:370 ff.; Anales de Cuauhtitlan 1945:67; Anales de Tlatelolco 1948:17–18; Berdan and Anawalt 1992:2:22–25; P. Carrasco 1999:343–351; Durán 1967:2:387 ff.; Hassig 1988:215 ff.; Sahagún 1950–1982, book 9:3). Finally, the earliest Spanish record of tribute collection from Soconusco towns lists the major towns and their tribute obligations in 1530.[1] In all, 13 Soconusco towns appear in one or more of these documents (table 7.1 and figure 7.1).

We know from early Spanish colonial documents that many more than 13 towns existed in the Soconusco region in the early sixteenth century. Early Colonial town lists mention more than 40 towns (CDIU 1885–1932: 17:169), and these documents suggest that a three-tiered political hierarchy existed during most of the Colonial period. This arrangement was, at least in part, adopted from the organization in place when Soconusco was under Aztec domination. The highest-ranking town was the provincial capital, Soconusco, from which the entire province was administered. The province was subdivided

Table 7.1
Soconusco towns mentioned in documents relating to Prehispanic or Early Colonial events

Town	1	2	3	4	5	6	7	8	9	10
						Sources				
Mapastepec				X	X	X			X	
Xoconochco				X	X		X	X	X	X
Acapetahua				X				X	X	
Huixtla		X	X	X	X				X	X
Huehuetan		X	X	X	X				X	X
Mazatan	X	X	X	X	X		X	X	X	X
Tapachula	X									
Coyoacan				X					X	X
Tuxtla										X
Ayutla	X			X		X	X	X	X	X
Naguatlan	X									
Acacoyagua				X						
Xolotlan		X	X	X			X	X		

Note: Numbers refer to the following sources:
 1 Títulos de la Casa Ixquin-Nehaib (Recinos 1957).
 2 Anales de Tlatelolco (1948).
 3 Anales de Cuauhtitlan (1945).
 4 Memorial de Tlacopan (Paso y Troncoso 1940:14:121–122).
 5 Codex Mendoza, part 1, conquest list (Berdan and Anawalt 1992).
 6 Sahagún 1950–82, book 9.
 7 Durán 1967.
 8 Alvarado Tezozomoc 1944.
 9 Codex Mendoza, part 2, tribute list (Berdan and Anawalt 1992).
10 Tribute to Spaniards, 1530–1531 (AGI-Contaduria 657).

into *partidos* (districts) or parishes (usually six to eight during the Colonial period) that were administered from *cabeceras* (head towns). Finally, within each partido or parish were smaller *sujetos* or *anexos* (subject towns).

The Matrícula de Tributos (Castillo Farreras 1974: 280–281) and part 2 of the Codex Mendoza (Berdan and Anawalt 1992), both of which record tribute payments made to the Aztecs by Soconusco towns, clearly indicate that the town of Xoconochco was the provincial capital and that the other seven named towns were of lower rank. Both documents also depict two high-ranking Aztec officials, a *tezcacoacatl* and a *tlillancalqui*, who were stationed in the town of Xoconochco (P. Carrasco 1999:394; Castillo Farreras 1974:234–235; Berdan and Anawalt 1992:3:18r). The first Spanish document to list tribute payments in 1530 also notes that Xoconochco was the provincial cabecera, and other towns (table 7.2) were called sujetos. None of these documents, however, reveal whether this form of political hierarchy existed prior to Aztec conquest of the region, nor do they explain how the town of Xoconochco came to be designated the provincial capital. The earlier K'iche' documents do not clearly indicate whether or not Xoconochco—or some

other community—dominated the region earlier in the Late Postclassic period.

Archaeological data provide another view of relations between and among Late Postclassic Soconusco communities. Survey and excavation within a 755 km² area in the vicinity of Escuintla, Mexico, were conducted as part of the Proyecto Soconusco directed by Barbara Voorhies (see Gasco, chapter 35). Within the study area, 29 habitational sites were located that date to the Late Postclassic period. Taking into account the size of the Late Postclassic period occupations, the amount of construction activity, and ceramic data, the evidence suggests that a three-tiered settlement hierarchy existed in the Late Postclassic period within the study area (Voorhies 1989c; Voorhies and Gasco 2002). In this scheme, the largest community in the area, Acapetahua, is the highest-ranking town. Acapetahua also happens to be one of the towns listed in the Matrícula de Tributos and the Codex Mendoza, and we assume that it was the administrative center of a small polity. Below this primary center are five secondary centers and twenty-three tertiary communities (none of which appear in Early Colonial documents).[2] Most of these communities presumably belonged to the

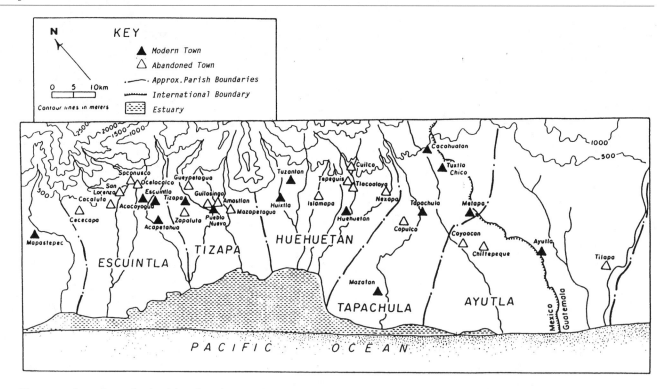

Figure 7.1 Locations of colonial and modern towns in Soconusco

Acapetahua polity, although a few towns in the eastern or western portion of the study area may have belonged to neighboring polities.

The view of the political landscape provided by the documentary data and the scheme devised from archaeological data both indicate a hierarchy of settlements in Late Postclassic Soconusco. The archaeological data from the Proyecto Soconusco cannot be used to address the question of whether or not there was a higher-ranking provincial capital to which Acapetahua was subject. At the lower end of the hierarchy, the documentary evidence lists only the category of "sujeto," which included all of the communities that were subject to the cabecera. The archaeological data suggest that there were two kinds of lower-ranking communities, here called "secondary" and "tertiary" communities. There are clear differences between the sites designated secondary and tertiary, but it seems likely that under Spanish colonial rule, all of the lower-ranking towns were simply lumped into a single category.

In sum, both the archaeological and documentary data suggest that across the Soconusco region there were several small polities in the Late Postclassic period. These polities consisted of administrative centers such as Acapetahua, which often became cabeceras in the Colonial period,[3] and lower-ranking communities in their hinterlands: secondary and tertiary communities that became sujetos under Spanish rule. The clearest picture of this arrangement comes from the Matrícula de Tributos

and the Codex Mendoza, which appears to reflect the situation ca. 1517 (Berdan 1992b:65). At that time, there appear to have been eight polities within the Soconusco region, represented in the documents by the glyphs for the administrative centers (Mapastepec, Xoconochco, Acaptehaua, Huixtla, Huehuetan, Mazatan, Coyoacan, and Ayutla). These eight centers are distributed fairly evenly across the landscape, each within a different river valley. It seems likely that each of these polities controlled the territory within the various river valleys that crosscut the Soconusco region. The five other towns mentioned in the K'iche' or Aztec documents may have served as administrative centers at some earlier time.

The lack of consistency in lists of administrative centers may reflect the shifting of these small polities' boundaries in response to the changing fortunes of particular centers. The most puzzling case is that of Xolotlan, a town mentioned in several documents related to Late Postclassic events (table 7.1). Although it is listed among conquered Soconusco towns, it is absent from the tribute lists and does not appear in a single Colonial-period document. None of the documents provide reliable clues about its location.

One question that remains is whether, prior to Aztec domination, there was any political unification across the Soconusco region. Were the eight centers named in the Matrícula de Tributos and Codex Mendoza the highest ranking towns for eight independent polities, or did one polity have dominance over the others? Although the

Table 7.2
Towns in the Colonial province of Soconusco, 1573–1581

Parish/cabecera	Sujetos/visitas	Parish/cabecera	Sujetos/visitas
Ayutla	Apatzapa	Tianguiztlan	Amastlan
	Chacalapa		Cahuala
	Chiltepeque		Gueypetahua
	Cuyoacan		Mazapetahua
	Naguatlan		Olotzingo (Guilocingo)
	Tilapan		Tatahuitla
	Tonalapa		Tizapa
			Zapaluta
Tuxtla	Cacahuatan		
	Copulco	Soconusco	Acacoyagua
	Mazatlán		Acapetahua
	Tacalapa [may be the		Cacaluta
	same as Chacalapa]		Cececapa
	Tlapachula		Escuintla
	Ylamapa (del Mar)		Ocelocalco
			San Lorenzo
Huehuetan	Cuylco		Zacapulco
	Huiztla		
	Nejapa	Mapastepec	Pixixiapan
	Talibe		Quezalapa
	Tepeguistin		Tiltepeque
	Tlacoloya		Tonalá
	Tuzantan		
	Ylamapa		

Sources: Veblen and Gutierrez-Witt 1983; AGI-Guatemala 10, Tasaciones de pueblos de indios, 1578–1581; AGI, Escribanía de Cámara, Investigación de Alonzo Rodríguez Vizcayno, cura y vicario de Ayutla; AGI-Contaduría 972A, Cuentas de Milpas, Tasación de la provincia de Soconusco 157, from Relación de los Caciques y numero de yndios que hay en guatemala, 21 abril 1572 (published in Mesoamérica 5:212–235, ed. Thomas T. Veblen and Laura Gutierrez-Witt, 1983).

town of Xoconochco was designated as the provincial capital when the region fell to the Aztecs, the reason for its selection is unknown. It may have been selected because it was already the highest-ranking town in the region, or it may have been chosen for some other reason. The documentary data do not provide a clear picture about intercommunity relationships before the arrival of the Aztecs. Durán does state that Mazatan was subject to Xoconochco (1967:2:387), and Alvarado Tezozomoc notes that Xoconochco's leaders cried, "Por nosotros ha muerto multitud de gente" (many people have died for us) as they surrendered to the Aztecs (1944:374). This statement might be interpreted to mean that Xoconochco occupied some position of authority.

The archaeological evidence is not particularly helpful in resolving this issue. The site known locally as Soconusco Viejo, and presumed to be the location of Postclassic Xoconochco, is singularly unimpressive, consisting of 15 low mounds and a large residential area with no mounds. Less than half a kilometer to the east is another Late Postclassic site called Las Gradas. The ceramics from test excavations at these two sites indicate that they are roughly contemporary; that is, they both date to the Late Postclassic period. But the precise relationship between the two sites is not yet fully understood, and it is possible that one or the other was established after the Aztec conquest. Until more research is conducted at these two sites, it is difficult to conclude with any certainty the sizes of the pre-Aztec town of Xoconochco (chapter 35). From a strictly archaeological perspective the site of Acapetahua is larger, and it has many more mounds and a larger area of occupation, suggesting that it was more important than Xoconochco. So why did Xoconochco become the provincial capital? It is possible that the

Aztecs purposefully elevated the town's status for some strategic purpose, or perhaps Xoconochco leaders cooperated with their conquerors in some way and were rewarded; as noted above, one account does state that Xoconochco surrendered.

It is interesting to note that Xoconochco was unable to retain its position as provincial capital into the Colonial period. By 1561 Huehuetan had become the provincial capital (CDIU 1885–1932:17:167).[4] Xoconochco's position had slipped even further by 1611, when it lost its cabecera status within its own parish.[5] From the early seventeenth century until the town was abandoned in the early 1800s, Xoconochco was reduced to the status of sujeto. Perhaps this rapid decline in political status came about because Xoconochco had not served as a provincial capital prior to the Aztec conquest and was not seen as a legitimate capital. Future archaeological research at this site will help to clarify some of these issues.

Unfortunately, because of the absence of written documents noted earlier, we do not know how the polities of Soconusco were governed in the Postclassic period. We don't know what title the leaders held, or how they acquired their positions. It seems likely that leadership positions were inherited, as they were elsewhere in Mesoamerica, and there are individuals who appear in Early Colonial documents with titles (e.g., *gobernador*) that might indicate noble status. Archaeological data can be useful to explore intracommunity sociopolitical relationships. We have not yet excavated in Postclassic houses, although future work will focus more specifically on residential structures, which presumably will lead to the identification of differences between elite and commoner households. A more in-depth discussion of related issues can be found in chapter 35 of this volume. Attention now turns to the area of west Mexico.

8

West Mexico beyond the Tarascan Frontier

Helen Perlstein Pollard

West Mexico beyond the Tarascan empire includes the highland lake district of Jalisco and Nayarit, the expanding Caxcan states to the northeast, and the Pacific coastal valleys from Michoacán to Nayarit (figure 8.1). Sometimes referred to as the Trans-Tarascan zone, it includes the Zapotlan and Sayula basins on the south, much of the Chapala Basin, the Magdalena Basin, and goes north to the Santiago River (Río Grande de Santiago). In the early sixteenth century this region was dominated by city-states and small polities. Some of these were the product of the collapse of the Classic-period Teuchitlan tradition, some were the descendant polities of the collapse of the Early Postclassic Aztatlan trade network, and others were the product of reaction to expanding Tarascan military aggression.

Most of our understanding of this region during the Postclassic period comes from ethnohistoric sources recorded in the sixteenth century through the eyes of conquering Tarascans or Spaniards (Relación de Michoacán 1956; Weigand and Weigand 1996). More recently, this has been supplemented by archaeological research at a few large sites, and excavation and survey in coastal valleys and in the Sayula Basin (see below).

RESOURCES, SETTLEMENTS AND REGIONAL ECONOMIES

The heartland of this region was in the lake basins of the volcanic highlands of Jalisco, in the western extension of the central Mexican Mesa Central (Weigand 1985; Weigand and Weigand 1996). In and near these lake basins are major deposits of obsidian (especially the Tequila flows), salt (the Sayula Basin), copper, silver, gold, and quartz; associated with these are smaller deposits of malachite, azurite, chrysacola, hematite, pyrite,

and opal. The northern coast has large areas of lagoons and estuaries, while the central and southern coast has shallow to deep bays with significant coastal salt deposits and shell, and easy access to mountain and foothill resources.

During the Early Postclassic period, there was widespread nucleation of populations into defensible locations, often away from riverine and lacustrine shores. This shift is commonly associated with population migrations from the northern boundaries of the zone (e.g., Zacatecas and Guanajuato) as indicated in the legendary histories of sixteenth-century states of Jalisco (Baus Czitrom 1985; Brand 1971; Michelet 1995; Weigand and Weigand 1996). During the Epiclassic and Early Postclassic in the lowland and coastal region of Jalisco and Nayarit, to the west of the highland lake district, there was a series of centers whose elites were associated with a characteristic set of artifacts also found in adjacent highland zones. The wide areal distribution of these artifacts, from coastal Jalisco to coastal Sinaloa and highland northwest Michoacán to Durango, has been referred to as the Aztatlan Trade System, the Aztatlan Mercantile System, and an Aztatlan Horizon (see Kelley 2000; Michelet 1995; Mountjoy 2000).

From the initial excavations of Aztatlan sites in Sinaloa during the 1930s the polychrome ceramics and figurine types were seen to be related to central Mexico, especially the Mixteca-Puebla region (Bell 1971; Kelley 2000; Michelet 1995; Mountjoy 2000). Suggestions have been made that these similarities reflect a population movement from central Mexico to the west, but most archaeologists now view the similarities as reflecting either a trading relationship bringing goods and "influence" from central Mexico to the west along the Lerma-Santiago river system (through the Bajío of southern

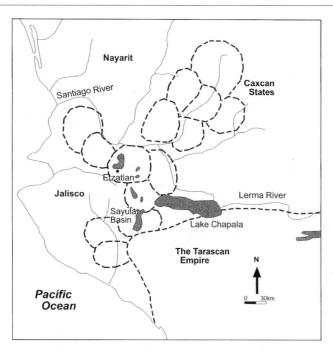

Figure 8.1 Map of highland polities west of the Tarascan empire. (After Weigand 1993.)

Guanajuato), or from coastal Oaxaca by Pacific canoe trade, or, alternatively, the spread of goods and ideas from west Mexico to central Mexico.

Goods produced in the coastal valleys and found in the highlands include a distinctive polychrome pottery with a "codex style," shell jewelry, cotton textiles, and salt. In the northern end of the network (Durango, Zacatecas), the coastal valley centers may have also provided copper artifacts. In return the highland centers of Jalisco provided fine-quality obsidian, especially prismatic blades, and other rare stone. The highland centers farther north may have provided turquoise, malachite, peyote, and animal hides. In addition, plumbate pottery and Mazapan figurines are occasionally found in both coastal and highland Aztatlan sites. Kelley and Weigand believe that by A.D. 1200 the trading network had expanded to include northwestern Mexico and even the American Southwest, delivering turquoise into west and central Mexico, and copper artifacts manufactured in west Mexico (especially bells) into the Southwest (Kelley 2000; Weigand and Weigand 1996).

After A.D. 1200, communities in the coastal valleys and highlands include small to medium-size towns (5,000–15,000 people) with religious, political, and marketing functions; large and small villages; hamlets; and specialized settlements associated with the mining and processing of obsidian, salt, copper, and with marine (especially shell jewelry), forest, and other localized resources; fortifications; and isolated shrines (Weigand 1993; Mountjoy 2000).

Early ethnohistoric documents refer to centers with 10 to 15 tributary communities, leading Weigand (1993) to propose that at least two, and possibly eight, of the lake basins contained small states. However, Brand (1971) considered these to be chiefdoms, based on the documentary evidence. Surface survey of the larger communities indicates that they had planned plaza/pyramid/elite-residential compounds, some with multiple plazas and ball courts, occasionally oriented to the cardinal directions (Weigand and Weigand 1996). Clustered residential mounds/plaza groups suggest larger communities were often organized by lineage into *barrios*. Most residential units were single-room rectangular or square dwellings with stone foundations and clay floors. Walls were constructed of wattle-and-daub, adobe, or uncut stone, with thatched roofs. Higher-status dwellings had multiple rooms facing or enclosing a sunken patio with banquets and plastered floors; walls were made of adobe and/or cut stone, and stairways flanked by columns are found at the largest centers. Many parts of Jalisco reveal significant population increases beginning around A.D. 900, although other regions reflect not an increase but reorganization, as populations nucleated in defensible sites. After A.D. 1300 there are indications of major population increases in the limited areas that have been well surveyed, such as the Sayula Basin (Valdez, Liot, and Schondube 1996) and the Magdalena Basin (Weigand 1993).

Highland Jaliscan agriculture included several forms of intensification, including terracing and floodwater and permanent canal irrigation. Communities specialized in salt production, obsidian tool production, cotton production, fishing, the processing of forest products, and the production of manufactured goods, all of which were regionally traded or produced for tribute (Valdez, Liot, and Schondube 1996; Weigand 1993; Weigand and Weigand 1996). Tributary and trade networks linked production of both subsistence and luxury goods.

TARASCAN–WEST MEXICAN INTERACTION

Compared to groups in other regions, the Tarascans were not as successful in incorporating the uncentralized polities to the north and west of their frontier. During the 1460s major campaigns were launched into the Lake Chapala basin and to the southwest to Zacatula. In the following two decades, much of the territory gained from what is now Jalisco and Colima was lost due to (1) the politically factioned nature of the region, where rebellion was a constant threat; (2) the diversion of the Tarascan military to the eastern frontier to fight the Aztecs; and (3) the general difficulties of any Prehispanic empire attempting to hold hostile territory more than five to six days' distance from their capitals. In those areas successfully incorporated into the empire, such as the Sayula

Basin, documents indicating the placement of Tarascan administrators have been confirmed by the excavation of burials with Tarascan elite goods such as pottery and metal artifacts (Valdez and Liot 1994).

The western Tarascan expansion was motivated by desire to control specific raw materials, including silver, gold, copper, and salt, which were acquired through the tribute system (Hosler and Macfarlane 1996; Pollard 1993). Other materials originally from Jalisco, Nayarit, and Zacatecas were probably acquired by the state through long-distance merchants. These materials included tin, marine shell, chrysacola, malachite, azurite, cinnabar, pyrite, lead, specular iron, opal, quartz crystals, and peyote. Tarascan merchants may have also obtained turquoise, originally from New Mexico, through trade networks with polities in the west and northwest.

NATURE OF THE WESTERN POLITIES

All societies within this region were either ranked or stratified. Weigand documents four- and five-tier settlement hierarchies for the Magdalena and Ahualulco basins, and suggests the likelihood that similar hierarchies existed in the Zacoalco, Atemajác, and Sayula basins (Weigand 1993). Based on this, he proposes that up to eight states emerged in highland Jalisco during the two centuries prior to Spanish conquest. These states emerged from the confederation of local chiefdoms in response to the territorial aggression of the Tarascan empire to the east and the Caxcan states to the north and northeast (Brand 1971; Relación de Michoacán 1956; Weigand 1985, 1993; Weigand and Weigand 1996). The centers of these states contain evidence of palace-like residences, specialized ritual structures, and large, specialized craft workshops. Early Spanish documents refer to their leaders as *señores* or *caciques,* terms used interchangeably in such documents for both kings and chiefs, and give little additional information about the structure of these societies. At least one leader was a female (referred to as a *cacica*), but it is not known whether this was a regular practice or whether the high death rates in the early sixteenth century left widows/daughters in a po-

sition to assume leadership positions previously unavailable to them.

Throughout this region there were high levels of military competition, expressed by defensive placement of settlements, palisaded settlements, and documentary records of aggression and loss. The goals of warfare were to secure strategic resources such as obsidian, copper, gold, and silver; to acquire military captives to sacrifice; and to enrich the elite class, who depended on the tribute system for much of their income. Much warfare was defensive, in response to the active Tarascan and Caxcan military frontier. Portions of this territory were held by the Tarascans for brief periods (the western Chapala Basin), while others were incorporated into the Tarascan empire.

The active participation of these polities in the Postclassic world system is signaled by the widespread distribution of structures and artifacts associated with Mesoamerican religion, including ball courts, ceramic incense burners, copper bells and tweezers, ceramic figurines, skull racks, and sweat baths (Bell 1971; Hosler 1994; Weigand and Weigand 1996). The primary languages spoken in this region were Uto-Aztecan (Cora, Huichol, Nahuat), and historical documents of the mid-sixteenth century refer to a Tezcatlipoca-like deity (called El Diablo) associated with the Indian rebellion led by the Caxcans. Peoples of the highland lake district did participate in the rebellion, but it is not clear if they also worshipped El Diablo (Weigand and Weigand 1996). While Caxcan religion is thought to be similar to that practiced by the migrant ancestors of the Aztecs, if highland Jaliscan lake district beliefs were ancestral to those of the modern Cora and Huichol, they may have been quite different from the hunting/sun/human sacrifice Caxcan complex, with instead a primary focus on agricultural fertility, shamanism, and the ancestors. One product of the Early Postclassic Aztatlan trade network was the widespread use of the Postclassic international symbol set and a marked increase in the quantities of goods flowing between the Pacific Coast, these polities, and those to the east, including copper and bronze, shell, turquoise, cotton and cloth, salt, semiprecious stones, and peyote.

9

Aztec City-States in the Basin of Mexico and Morelos

Michael E. Smith

Compared to the polities described in the last few chapters, Aztec city-states (*altepetl* in Nahuatl) in the Basin of Mexico and Morelos are among the most extensively documented polities of ancient Mesoamerica. Aztec native historical traditions contain accounts of dynasties and their accomplishments over time (Davies 1973); Spanish administrative documents illuminate many aspects of the structure and operation of city-states (Gerhard 1970; Gibson 1964; Hodge 1984); Nahuatl-language administrative documents fill in details of local customs and practices (Cline 1986; Lockhart 1992); and archaeological surveys and excavations have examined the territories and capital towns of city-states (Brumfiel 1987a; Charlton et al. 1991; Hodge 1994, 1997). In this chapter I describe briefly Aztec city-states and city-state culture in the Basin of Mexico and Morelos; more extensive treatment can be found in Smith 2000. Discussion of the most heavily documented Aztec polity—imperial Tenochtitlan—is left for chapter 11.

Most Aztec city-states were founded in the twelfth century in the wake of the Nahua migrations from Aztlan (Smith 1984). The immigrants set up a number of localized petty kingdoms whose new rulers endeavored to establish genealogical links with the renowned kings of the Early Postclassic Toltec state. The Middle Postclassic period saw the spread of these city-states throughout highland central Mexico and the creation of the Aztec city-state culture (chapter 4). Several towns rose to political prominence through military success, although none was able to forge a polity sufficiently large or complex to be called an empire. Some of these powerful towns—notably Tenayuca and Cuauhnahuac—contained monumental twin-stair temple-pyramids that still survive. Archaeological evidence on exchange suggests that the Basin of Mexico and Morelos were each the setting for several regional market systems that linked neighboring

groups of city-states (Minc et al. 1994; Smith 2000); as described in chapter 30, Aztec central Mexico at this time can be described as an affluent production zone.

The Late Postclassic period was marked by two cycles of empire formation in the Basin of Mexico (Davies 1973). The processes of political competition and economic interaction established in Middle Postclassic times continued to operate, and populations grew at a rapid pace as the Basin of Mexico became a core zone in the world system; Morelos, however, remained an affluent production zone. By the early fifteenth century two polities—Azcapotzalco in the west and Texcoco in the east—had carved the Basin of Mexico into small-scale empires. The Tepanec war of 1428 brought about the downfall of Azcapotzalco and the rise of Tenochtitlan as the region's dominant power. Tenochtitlan's imperial expansion is discussed in chapter 11.

LATE POSTCLASSIC CITY-STATES

The size of Aztec city-states varied with political hierarchy and region. Table 9.1 shows average data for a sample of city-states whose sizes have been estimated from documentary and archaeological data. In this table Texcoco is the major polity in the eastern Valley of Mexico (Tenochtitlan is not included here); for Morelos, the major polities included are Cuauhnahuac, Yautepec, Huaxtepec, and Yacapitztlan. Other city-states are placed in the "regular city-state" category. Regular city-states in the Basin of Mexico were larger in area and population than those in Morelos, whereas major polities in Morelos had higher rural population densities and larger overall populations than Texcoco.

The sizes of polity capitals also varied with political hierarchy and region (table 9.2). Most city-state centers were quite modest settlements probably more accurately

Table 9.1
Mean sizes of Aztec city-states

	N	Population	Area (km²)	Density (pop./km²)
Eastern Valley of Mexico				
Major polity	1	40,400	120	340
Regular city-state	10	13,500	90	150
Morelos				
Major polity	4	56,100	90	620
Regular city-state	11	7,200	70	100

Sources: Hodge 1997; Smith 1994.

Table 9.2
Mean sizes of Aztec cities

	N	Population	Area (km²)	Density (pop./km²)
Valley of Mexico				
Tenochtitlan	1	212,500	1,350	160
Texcoco	1	24,000	450	50
City-state centers	13	9,100	200	60
Morelos				
Major capitals	4	18,400	—	—
City-state centers	6	2,900	13	118

Sources: Hodge 1997; Smith 1994.

categorized as towns than cities. These small urban centers were typically laid out around a central public plaza with a modest temple-pyramid on the east side and other civic buildings (such as the royal palace, ball courts, or schools) on the other sides of the plaza. The central precincts of a few city-state centers (e.g., Huexotla) may have been surrounded by walls as in Tenochtitlan, but most lacked these walls. Outside of the central area, the houses in city-state centers were scattered without evidence of planning or central organization (Smith 1997b).

The Nahuatl term for these small polities was *altepetl* (this discussion is based on the following sources: Gibson 1964; Hodge 1984, 1997; Lockhart 1992; Smith 2000). Each altepetl was governed by a *tlatoani*, or king, who was assisted by a council composed of high-ranking nobles. The total population ruled by the king (i.e., the people—both noble and commoner—who paid tribute to the king) made up the altepetl. Since this population did not always inhabit a discrete territory, the houses and villages belonging to nearby city-states were sometimes interspersed. Thus city-states were not defined in terms of territory but in terms of social relations, and it is sometimes impossible to draw simple contiguous maps of the territorial extent of individual polities because of the interspersed nature of dependent settlements (Gibson 1964:44–47).

This principle—polities defined by relations of domination rather than by territorial extent—also worked on higher levels. For example, the Yautepec conquest-state, consisting of city-states subject to the king of Yautepec, included one polity, Huitzillan, that was separated from the rest of the area by an intervening city-state not subject to Yautepec (Smith 1994b). And at the highest level, the towns and polities subject to the Aztec empire did not constitute a single contiguous territory (chapter 11). Aztec altepetl maintained their identities and most of their functions even after they were conquered and incorporated into the Aztec empire (see chapter 11). They also continued into the Spanish colonial period with much of their internal organization intact (Lockhart 1992), and their legacies are still visible today in the names, locations, and even the extent of modern *municipios* in some parts of central Mexico.

AZTEC CITY-STATE CULTURE

The Aztec altepetl of the Basin of Mexico, Morelos, and several other regions of central Mexico were part of the larger Aztec city-state culture (Hansen 2000a). Individual polities were linked through linguistic and other cultural ties, economic exchange, elite interactions, and various political connections. Nahuatl was the dominant language in these city-states, although speakers of Otomí and other languages were also present in many polities. The domestic material culture of this area exhibited a basic uniformity in spite of local production of goods and localized stylistic traditions, pointing to common cultural practices and beliefs (chapter 16).

All documented city-states had at least one marketplace, and these markets were linked into several large regional marketing systems, which in turn were tied together by regular long-distance commercial exchange of a large number of goods (see chapter 30). The role of regional and local marketing systems in the economic integration of Aztec city-states is shown by the presence of abundant imported goods in both the capitals and the rural hinterlands of city-states (see also chapter 32). These city-state market systems provided one of the major channels by which the residents of Aztec city-states were tied into the wider exchange circuits of the world system. The relative weakness of Aztec tlatoani fostered the growth of commercial trade as the dominant means of exchange in Aztec central Mexico. As was the case in many ancient city-state systems around the world (Hansen 2000b), Aztec city-states were far from self-sufficient in the economic sphere.

In addition to regional marketing systems that integrated nearby city-states, various types of social and political interactions bound the elites of Aztec city-states into a single, large regional elite class (Smith 1986). Elites in separate city-states shared a number of social and ritual attributes that distinguished them from their commoner subjects. Elite intermarriage across polity borders was the norm. Such marriages between royal families were an important component of the political process (Carrasco 1984), and among lower-ranking nobles such marriages were also common. Elites visited one another for important state occasions and major ritual events, and these were the settings for much feasting and gift giving. Finally, by 1519 Aztec city-states were also tied together by their common subjection to Tenochtitlan. In sum, the numerous autonomous Aztec city-states interacted heavily with one another in the cultural, economic, political, and social realms, producing the best-documented example of a city-state culture in Postclassic Mesoamerica.

Below the level of the altepetl, scholars have identified significant differences in political and social organization between the western Nahua area (the Basin of Mexico, Morelos, and Toluca) and the eastern Nahua area (Puebla and Tlaxcala). In the former area, the topic of this chapter, the *calpolli* was the dominant institution below the altepetl, whereas in the eastern area the *teccalli*, or noble house, was more important (Lockhart 1992:105–108). Chance (2000) has recently applied the house society model (chapter 6) to the teccalli of Puebla, commenting on this east/west distinction. These regional differences had important implications for the organization and interactions of city-states in the two areas, some of which are explored by Pohl in chapters 10, 22, and 26.

10

Creation Stories, Hero Cults, and Alliance Building

Confederacies of Central and Southern Mexico

John M. D. Pohl

In A.D. 1458, an Aztec imperial army marched 500 miles south from the Basin of Mexico and attacked the Mixtec-Chocho kingdom of Coixtlahuaca, Oaxaca. According to various Colonial-era histories, the expedition was organized by Motecuhzoma Ilhuicamina to avenge the murder of 160 merchants by Coixtlahuaca's Lord Atonal. However, at 300,000, the invasion force was clearly intended as more than simply a punitive expedition. Atonal immediately summoned the help of numerous Mixtec kingdoms, including Teposcolula, Tilantongo, and Tlaxiaco, as well as the Eastern Nahua city-states of Cholula, Huexotzinco, and Tlaxcala, with whom Coixtlahuaca was "confederated." But the plea was sent too late, and Coixtlahuaca was overrun before relief could arrive (Durán 1994:182–187; Torquemada 1986:159–160). According to Spanish Colonial–era histories, Atonal was garroted, and many of his men were captured and later sacrificed at the Great Temple of Tenochtitlan. Scores of city-states and kingdoms throughout Puebla and Oaxaca were stunned by the defeat. It was the beginning of the end of an era of unprecedented independence and prosperity in Mesoamerica.

Both written and pictographic histories recorded in books, lienzos, and codices suggest that Coixtlahuaca's confederacy was not a single-instance response to a mutual threat, but rather was rooted in shared religious, political, and economic institutions. Confederacies have received little serious attention from scholars (see Blanton 1998 for an exception) for a variety of reasons. "Confederacy" implies social agendas that were shared between multiple political units of generally equal size and influence, a phenomenon that is difficult if not impossible to evaluate on any broad regional basis through archaeological study alone.[1] This chapter examines a field of common ideological values established through shared religious traditions that enabled the multiethnic kingdoms of Tlaxcala, Puebla, and Oaxaca to establish systems of exchange and mutual support, thereby unifying much of Mexico's central and southern highlands for more than 250 years prior to the intrusion of the empire of the Triple Alliance. These ideological linkages among independent polities were key components of the Postclassic Mesoamerican world system (see the chapters in part 4).

CREATION STORIES AND HEROIC HISTORIES

Mesoamerican creation stories seldom describe events through any natural perception of the world; in fact, their recounting of supernatural origins is what made them so highly sacred and the focus of religious cults (Bierhorst 1990; Caso 1958; Carrasco 1990; Florescano 1993; López Austin 1993, 1994; Nicholson 1971). By and large, creation stories described the origins of the universe and in so doing accounted for the movements of peoples and their claims to land and property, as well as prescribing rituals and establishing codes for cooperative behavior. Heroic histories, on the other hand, were typically placed in post-creation times and blended factual accounts with mythic traditions. They were recounted in multiple, often conflicting variations but were always filled with enough detail to suggest that they could be based on historical events (López Austin 1993, 1994; Nicholson 2001).[2]

It was through these creation stories that religion bound together both the human and divine inhabitants of a place. We learn from analyzing the sagas of heroes such as Quetzalcoatl, Camaxtli-Mixcoatl, 8 Deer, and 9 Wind that creation stories and hero cults played a significant ideological role when a number of independent communities desired to incorporate themselves into larger reciprocal entities in Postclassic Mexico. The goal of sharing

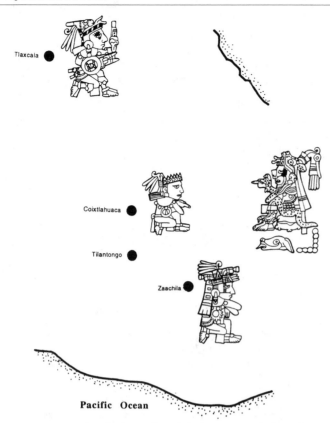

Figure 10.1 The ideology of confederacy as encoded in religious stories such as the Mixtec 8 Deer saga. Codex Zouche-Nuttall depicts 8 Deer (on the right) forming an alliance with Tlaxcalan (top), Chocho-Popoloca (middle), and Zapotec (bottom) kings.

Figure 10.2 The cult shrine dedicated to the culture hero Quetzalcoatl at Cholula, as depicted in the *Historia Tolteca-Chichimeca.*

myth and heroic history was to elevate the ideology of an elite group to a point above and beyond the petty disputes of individuals that would divide others from the mutual benefits of coalition. Over time, heroes and ancestors became symbolic expressions of relationship and interdependence apart from their historical basis in fact. If there was no established tradition, a hero could even be invented and patterned to reflect newly adopted ideals. Since they were sanctified by religious ritual, they could be used to incite patriotic sentiments. As a consequence, the spiritual connection to gods, heroes, and ancestors maintained through their cults could be comparable to the claims of nationality and language that contemporary societies use to define a state (figure 10.1).

THE EASTERN NAHUA

During the Postclassic period, the most widespread creation stories and heroic histories revolved around a hero called Quetzalcoatl, son of the Chichimec warlord Camaxtli-Mixcoatl and a priest of the Toltec capital of Tula, located about 70 kilometers north of Mexico City (Nicholson 2001). Here the Toltecs prospered until a rift

developed between two opposing factions. When Quetzalcoatl's rivals Tezcatlipoca and Huitzilopochtli incited the hero to drunkenness and incest, he was shamed before his followers and left the city to spend the remainder of his life wandering from kingdom to kingdom. By most accounts he established a new cult center at Cholula. Some report that he then traveled through Oaxaca, where he even constructed the palaces at Mitla. Others state that Quetzalcoatl reached the Atlantic Gulf coast, where he either died and was resurrected as the Morning Star, or boarded a raft of serpents bound for the east, promising to return one day to reclaim his kingdom.

The odyssey of Quetzalcoatl was revered by more than a dozen different ethnic groups who claimed that the penitent hero had traveled through their kingdoms to establish his cult. These peoples marked the surrounding landscape with pictographs and other signs to commemorate his journey (Sahagún 1950–1982, book 3:33–36). At the time of the conquest, the principal seat of Quetzalcoatl's cult was at Cholula (Durán 1971:128–139). Ethnohistorical studies combined with an urban archaeological survey have confirmed the location of the great temple of Quetzalcoatl at what is today the convent of San Gabriel in Cholula's main *zócalo* (figure 10.2). Between 1200 and 1520, confederations of kingdoms throughout the central and southern highlands venerated Cholula as a major market and pilgrimage center, and even submitted to the authority of its priests in matters of alliance and factional dispute (Lind n.d.).

The foundation of this theocratic authority was a religious ceremony dedicated to Quetzalcoatl whereby a prince was required to journey to Cholula to meet with two high priests called the *Tlalchiach* and the *Aquiach* (Rojas 1927). After several days of prayer and penitence, the ears, nose, and lips of the initiate were pierced with sharpened eagle and jaguar bones, and an ornament was

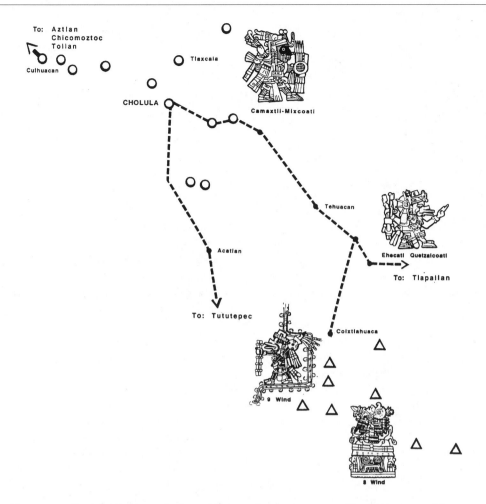

Figure 10.3 Shared religious cults featuring legendary conquests and heroic journeys. The Eastern Nahua city-states (circles) claimed Camaxtli-Mixcoatl as their principal deity. The triangles indicate the Mixtec and Zapotec places of ancestral emergence, and the dashed line represents the migration route of Quetzalcoatl and other "sons" of Camaxtli-Mixcoatl.

inserted according to the custom of the kingdom from which the petitioner came. In this way the prince was declared a *tecuhtli,* or lineage head, and was thereby granted, through Quetzalcoatl's divine authority, the rulership of a royal estate, or teccalli. The appeal of the cult of Quetzalcoatl and the tecuhtli ceremony was that it transcended all local religious customs and bound ethnically diverse peoples into similar social and political units, thereby facilitating elite alliance and economic exchange throughout the central and southern Mexican highlands.

The epic of Quetzalcoatl—with its emphasis on supernatural feats, moral dilemmas, and codes of elite behavior—was joined to more-historical accounts of actual Tolteca-Chichimeca migrations through the legacy of a patriarch called Camaxtli-Mixcoatl (Davies 1977:423–440). According to legend, Camaxtli-Mixcoatl entered the Valley of Mexico in the twelfth century at the head of a band of nomadic Chichimecs from the northwestern desert. After killing the demon Itzpapalotl, he led his

people to the southern shore of Lake Texcoco, married two Toltec women named Ilanque and Chimalma, and founded the city-state of Culhuacan. A variant of the archetypal warlord embodied by the Mexica's Huitzilopochtli and the Acolhua's Xolotl, Camaxtli-Mixcoatl was particularly revered by Nahua peoples who settled around the southern Basin of Mexico, Tlaxcala, and Puebla, but also by those as far south as Oaxaca and even Central America (Pohl 1994c:83–108).[3]

Camaxtli-Mixcoatl was said to have had seven sons, the ancestors of the principal ethnic groups that dominated central and southern Mexico at the time of the conquest (Torquemada 1986:1:32). In many cases the journeys of the lesser sons replicate the odyssey of their half-brother Quetzalcoatl. Mixtecatl and Xelhua, were the leaders of migrations of the Tolteca-Chichimeca into southern Puebla and Oaxaca. According to the *Relación de Acatlan,* Mixtecatl led a faction of Tolteca-Chichimeca from Cholula to Acatlan in the Mixteca Baja

(Acuña 1985:35–36). From there Mixtecatl's descendants claimed to rule all the land between Acatlan and Tututepec. He thereby became the eponymous ancestor of the "Mixtecs" (figure 10.3).

The *Historia Tolteca-Chichimeca* and the *Relación de Coxcatlan* state that Xelhua was among the first to leave Tula after its destruction (Kirchhoff et al. 1976:135–136; Acuña 1985:94; Pohl 1994c:83–108). If not actually a member of Quetzalcoatl's party, Xelhua's journey overlapped the same route as he led his people around Lake Texcoco to Cholula, where they lived for a short time before migrating south and founding the kingdoms of Tehuacan, Coxcatlan, and Teotitlan del Camino. The *Mapas de Cuahtinchan* (Bittmann Simons 1968; Reyes 1977; Yoneda 1981) further elaborate on the *Historia Tolteca-Chichimeca*. Cuauhtinchan Map 1, portrays the journey from Cuauhtinchan to Coxcatlan, symbolized by a hill qualified by a shell jewelry collar. Cuauhtinchan Map 2, on the other hand, indicates a route taken directly to Coixtlahuaca in the Mixteca Alta (Reyes 1977: 60). The Coixtlahuaca place sign is depicted as a mat of serpents upon which are seated two couples, among whom is Atonal, a Tolteca-Chichimeca lord named in both the *Anales de Cuauhtitlan* and Mixtec-Chocho lienzos as the direct ancestor of the king of the same name executed in 1458 (Reyes 1977:60; Pohl 1994c; see figure 10.3).

How true are the Tolteca-Chichimeca migration stories as history? By the Late Postclassic, the odyssey of Quetzalcoatl and the Tolteca-Chichimeca had become a myth complicated by numerous regional accounts that continue to defy any easy synthesis (Davies 1977). Nevertheless, the abandonment of Tula by the middle of the twelfth century has been confirmed archaeologically (Sanders et al. 1979; Matos Moctezuma 1974; Cobean and Mastache 1989). Archaeological and linguistic studies show that the Basin of Mexico subsequently experienced a major reorganization in settlement patterns at the same time that large populations of Nahuatl speakers entered the region (Smith 1984; Parsons 1970; Knab 1983).

Settlement-pattern studies for the Tehuacan Valley indicate that not only did the Tolteca-Chichimeca population reputedly led by Xelhua subsequently leave the Basin of Mexico, but that they in fact "arrived" at Tehuacan, Coxcatlan, and Teotitlan shortly afterward (Pohl 1994c: 104). Mixtecatl's migration is more problematical because so little is known of Acatlan archaeologically, but linguists have documented an intrusive Nahuatl language corridor extending through the Mixteca Baja to the Mixteca Costa (Smith 1998:159–162). Although our knowledge of Tututepec is little better, two of its coastal subjects—Pochutla and Huatulco—claimed to be of "Chichimec" heritage, spoke a Nahuatl dialect, and

venerated as their goddess Itzpapalotl, the monster who was defeated by Camaxtli-Mixcoatl (Acuña 1984:2:188–193). We may never prove that Quetzalcoatl, Mixtecatl, and Xelhua existed as historical individuals, but that should hardly impede our use of these sources in interpreting past events. Their legends were primarily intended to encapsulate the essence of social history through allegory and highly dramatic performance for an elite class that clearly is archaeologically verifiable.

THE MIXTECS AND ZAPOTECS

While some Mixtec kings affiliated themselves with the Eastern Nahuas by declaring a Tolteca-Chichimeca heritage through their connection with Atonal, Mixtecatl, Xelhua, or some other Aztlan/Chicomoztoc migration-history hero, others centered around the Nochixtlan Valley (as well as the Zapotecs of the Valley of Oaxaca) emphasized a different kind of creation story. Believing that their ancestors were born from trees, stones, rivers, the sky, and other natural phenomena, the kings of Yanhuitlan, Tilantongo, Jaltepec, Achiutla, Teposcolula, Tlaxiaco, Cuilapan, and Zaachila claimed that they had always been the stewards of the land (Furst 1977; Jansen 1982). Metaphorically speaking this was true. Archaeological surveys have demonstrated that many of these sacred birth shrines were located on or near major Classic-period sites, including Monte Albán, Yucuñudahui, Yucuita, Cerro Jasmín, and Mogote del Cacique, to name a few (Byland and Pohl 1994a). The stories were composed to break with the old social order through a miraculous act of renewal, without giving up claims to territory itself. Attributing multiple sources of ancestral power also bolstered claims of autonomy by the much smaller political units that characterized Oaxacan realms, which in some cases were more like great houses than city-states.

References to differing creation places are found in many Colonial writings. According to the chronicler Francisco de Burgoa, three were located at Apoala, Achiutla, and Sosola, but many more are depicted in the Mixtec codices as the sources for the numerous ancestors that integrally linked Mixtec and Zapotec royal lines (Burgoa 1934b:25:274–276; Pohl 1995:58–65). Contrasting with legends of the fall of Tula and the subsequent Tolteca-Chichimeca migrations, Mixtec heroes participated in more-localized cosmic struggles such as the War of Heaven and the 8 Deer saga. Nevertheless, some gods and heroes were clearly modeled on Tolteca-Chichimeca prototypes through indigenous processes of syncretism.

Nine Wind appears in the Mixtec codices as the iconographic counterpart of Quetzalcoatl, but his biography is uniquely Mixtec (Nicholson 1978). According to the Codex Vindobonensis, prior to the first sunrise, 9 Wind was born from a stone and journeyed to the Place of Heaven, where he was given the ritual dress and sacred objects of his cult by two Mixtec gods. The hero then traveled to the ancient Classic citadel of Yucuñudahui in the northern Nochixtlan Valley, where he lifted the sky from the rivers and the earth, and introduced a set of core religious rituals dedicated to his cult. Another figure appearing in the codices named 4 Jaguar is comparable to Camaxtli-Mixcoatl or one of his sons and followers. Multiple variants of 4 Jaguar appear in both the Coixtlahuaca group lienzos and the Mixtec codices behaving very much like a priest-impersonator of the Tolteca-Chichimeca warlord (Smith 1973a:71–75; Pohl 1994c: 83–108). He even introduced Mixtecs to a ceremony equivalent to the tecuhtli ritual performed at Cholula. In this way Oaxacan kings shared many Tolteca-Chichimeca cult beliefs and rituals in principle, but were careful to reconfigure them as locally inspired phenomena.[4]

Other gods, or their priestly impersonators, appear as oracles presiding over funerary cults. Unlike the Tolteca-Chichimeca, who preferred to cremate their dead, Mixtecs and Zapotecs mummified the dead at sacred shrines such as Chalcatongo and Mitla. Mummy bundles served as physical proof of the ranking lines of succession upon which Mixtec and Zapotec social order was defined. The maintenance of a funerary cult that focused on the grouping of the remains of the royal dead in central places was ingenious. In societies like those of the Mixtec and Zapotec, rank was traced through one's familial relationship with the oldest royal lineages. By controlling access to the divine dead and managing their cult, oracles were actually manipulating the affairs of the living descendants, as kings and queens were forced to use them as mediators in their lineage disputes. Funerary cults thereby provided a source of corporate identity, ensuring political stability among various members of the competitive royal kin groups in the absence of any overarching governmental capital in Postclassic Oaxaca (Pohl 1994c: 69–82, 1999).

For the Mixtecs and Zapotecs, heroes as both gods and ancestors were a reflection of the importance of family as a pervasive social model: men and women who held property together because they advocated a common descent. For the Eastern Nahua and other peoples who appropriated Tolteca-Chichimeca migration legends, creation stories and heroic histories justified expansion into new lands and impressed upon dominated peoples the divine sanction of their claims.

FACTIONALISM AND THE RISE OF THE AZTEC EMPIRE

At times, various members of the Eastern Nahua, Mixtec, and Zapotec confederacies attempted to expand their political control over neighbors by force. Local-level disputes involving land and inheritance are frequently portrayed in the Mixtec codices (Caso 1960; Byland and Pohl 1994a:231–264, 1994b). Multiple marriages allowed Oaxacan kings and queens to consolidate control over vast estates that nonetheless were redivided among their children when they died. Competing heirs numbering in the dozens seldom had little recourse but violence.

Codices Zouche-Nuttall and Colombino-Becker feature the rise to power of the twelfth-century usurper 8 Deer, who battled a formidable assortment of close relatives to achieve the throne of Tilantongo. Eventually he was murdered by Lord 4 Wind, whose mother, Lady 6 Monkey, had previously been executed by 8 Deer. Codex Bodley tells us that in A.D. 1206, 8 Deer's great-great-grandson, Lord 2 Motion, became embroiled in a successional dispute between his sons from two different marriages that ended with his own exile. By 1353, 8 Deer's line at Tilantongo had failed, and the throne was usurped by a relative from Teozacoalco named Lord 9 House (Byland and Pohl 1994a). Lord 9 House was a formidable conqueror who not only waged war against rivals throughout the Mixteca Alta, but may have even attacked Cuauhtinchan in league with Lord 9 Lizard of Jaltepec (Jansen 1989:73–74).[5]

The politics of the Eastern Nahua kingdoms were equally divisive (see Davies 1980:157–176, for summary). Cuauhtinchan fought with its neighbors over the centuries, climaxing with a major confrontation with Tepeacac that led to the displacement of a large Cuauhtinchan population. Tlaxcalan histories record numerous examples of assassination and internal strife among its ruling families (Pohl 1998a). Confrontations between Tlaxcala and Huexotzinco date to as early as 1300 in the historical annals (Pohl 1998a; Davies 1980:167–176). In 1352, Huexotzinco and Cholula attacked Tlaxcala. Shortly thereafter, Huexotzinco turned on its former ally, defeating Cholula in 1358 and causing near starvation among its population.

Despite this seemingly volatile atmosphere of alliance, economic competition, and warfare, it is clear that confederacy members also provided mutual support to one another when faced with any major outside threat to their existing social order, such as it was at any given time. After the overthrow of the Tepanecs by a Mexica-Texcocan–led coalition in 1428, a triple alliance was formulated between Tenochtitlan, Texcoco, and Tlacopan that posed a major threat to the Tolteca-Chichimeca-Mixtec-Zapotec alliance system. Preliminary expansion into Morelos brought Triple Alliance armies alongside the principal social and economic arteries linking Puebla and Oaxaca. Izucar, located on the frontier with both the Mixteca Baja and the Puebla Valley, became a perfect staging area (Hassig 1988:166). By 1458, the Triple

Alliance was ready to attempt its first protracted long-distance campaign into southern Mexico, and the rich kingdom of Coixtlahuaca was its first target.

Having severed the primary alliance corridor controlled by the Eastern Nahuas, Mixtecs, and Zapotecs at its most critical link, the Aztecs then turned on other confederacy members by continuing to destabilize the internal relationships that bound royal houses into systems of mutual obligation, and then providing military support to the faction that best served their interests (Hicks 1994b). By 1500 only Tlaxcala remained autonomous under the rule of a council of four *tlatoque*, while the Mixtecs and Zapotecs reoriented their interests to the Pacific Coast, establishing new centers of power at Tututepec and Tehuantepec, respectively (Davies 1968; Spores 1993; Marcus 1983d, 1983e; Whitecotton 1977: 124–132). The following chapter describes the Aztec empire and its wider role in the Postclassic world system.

11

The Aztec Empire

Frances F. Berdan

Michael E. Smith

The Aztec empire emerged in A.D. 1428 out of the regional system of competing city-states described in chapter 9. Prior to that time, Aztec city-state culture resembled the other Postclassic Mesoamerican city-state cultures described in the previous chapters. Once the empire was formed, however, Aztec city-states did not cease to exist, nor did they lose their importance in local administration (Berdan et al. 1996; Hodge 1984, 1997; also see chapter 9). Instead, city-states formed the building blocks for the empire, and in many respects Aztec city-state culture continued to flourish as a system of small interacting polities under the overall domination of the Aztec empire (chapter 10).

The Aztec empire was one of the four extensive exchange circuits of Postclassic Mesoamerica (along with west Mexico, the Maya zone, and the southern Pacific coastal plain; see chapter 3). Resembling Abu-Lughod's (1989) "subsystems," these exchange circuits define regions of relatively intense interaction, especially economic. In the case of the Aztec empire, the exchange circuit was also strongly shaped by political criteria: the extension of hegemonic imperial control over vast and diverse territories. Some studies of the Postclassic Mesoamerican world system (e.g., Blanton and Feinman 1984) have conflated the processes and institutions of the Aztec empire with those of the larger world system (for discussion, see Smith 2001c). Although imperial tribute in tropical luxury goods can be seen as an important process in the world system, it is important to distinguish economic channels that were part of imperial organization and policy from those that existed independently of the empire. In this chapter we focus on the nature of the Aztec empire and imperialism, showing how the empire was both influenced by broader world-system dynamics and in turn contributed to those dynamics.

THE GROWTH OF EMPIRE

Over a brief 93-year period the combined forces of Tenochtitlan, Texcoco, and Tlacopan conquered and controlled a large number of city-states throughout central and southern Mexico. The Postclassic demographic explosion in central Mexico (chapters 30 and 32), part of the first world-system process identified in chapter 1, was one of the prime factors generating imperial expansion. Growing populations needed greater supplies of staple foodstuffs, and growing elite populations in particular desired a greater supply of exotic luxury goods. Beginning in 1428, these three allied powers first succeeded in conquering powerful city-states (most notably Chalco) in the Basin of Mexico. During the aggressive reign of Motecuhzoma Ilhuicamina (1440–1468), this Triple Alliance expanded beyond the Basin of Mexico into far distant regions; these regions provided the imperial rulers with control over status-linked luxuries such as fine stones, valuable metals, and shimmering tropical feathers. The imperial enterprise was firmly in motion by the end of Motecuhzoma Ilhuicamina's reign: warfare was idealized and unremitting, long-range military ventures became commonplace, ever-increasing tributes were expected, urban imperial centers demonstrated increased elite standards of living and expanded ceremonial and public architecture, and human sacrifice increased in scale and frequency.

The subsequent Mexica rulers, accompanied by their Texcocan and Tlacopan counterparts, intensified these trends and expanded the bounds of empire. This was achieved through a tripartite political structure that entailed the sharing of risks and rewards in military undertakings and diplomatic ventures (P. Carrasco 1999). It should be emphasized, however, that the Aztec military

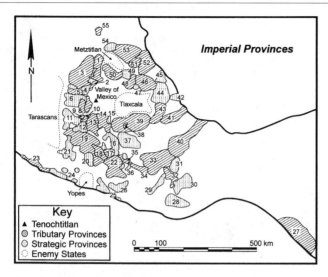

Figure 11.1 Map of the Aztec empire. (After Berdan et al. 1996.) Numbers indicate imperial provinces as identified by Berdan et al. (1996). (For lists of provinces, see Berdan et al. 1996:112.)

machine was not invincible, as it suffered an especially severe defeat at the hands of the Tarascans in the west and was never capable of subduing the indomitable Tlaxcalans and their on-again, off-again allies, Huexotzinco and Cholula. Neither did life always proceed smoothly in the Aztec core. During the reign of Motecuhzoma Ilhuicamina alone, the Basin of Mexico was visited with a locust plague, a devastating flood, and a disastrous four-year famine (Berdan and Anawalt 1992:2:17). Such events highlighted a certain precariousness, and imperial growth assured an enlarged resource base for these internally expanding, competitive societies.

As the empire extended its control over more-distant and more diverse city-states and regions, control became more tenuous. Imperial administrative policies were based on a general hands-off approach. If military conquest was involved, local rulers were allowed to retain their traditional rulerships as long as they delivered prescribed tributes to their conquerors on schedule. Aztec tribute collectors were forever roaming about in conquered areas, but the installation of governors or garrisons was relatively uncommon. If a client relationship was established with an outlying city-state, a friendlier, reciprocal bond was established with no perceived need for imperial administrators.

While this hegemonic approach (Hassig 1985, 1988) was relatively inexpensive for the imperial rulers, it did leave considerable room for mischief in the provinces. Imperial enemies spent considerable effort fomenting rebellions among dissatisfied Aztec subjects, such as Tlaxcalan "diplomatic incursions" in rich Gulf Coast provinces (chapter 12). At the empire's twilight, during Motecuhzoma Xocoyotzin's rule (1502–1520), a great deal of military effort was expended on quelling rebel-

lions and reconquering upstart city-states. Figure 11.1 shows the extent of the empire on the eve of Spanish conquest.

STRATEGIES OF EMPIRE BUILDING

As the empire expanded, the Aztec rulers employed a set of diverse strategies to achieve a variety of political and economic goals. Many of these goals and strategies can be seen as responses to the seven dynamic processes of the Postclassic world system as outlined in chapter 1, but they were also parts of a series of deliberate efforts to further promote and take advantage of those processes. The strategies of the imperial kings can be summarized under four headings: economic, political, frontier, and elite. The employment of these strategies in individual cases depended to a great extent on several features of conquered or incorporated polities. Among the most important of these features were: (1) the time of conquest or incorporation in the history of Aztec expansion; (2) patterns of regional political geography (e.g., location near or far from the imperial capitals, on an active trade route, or along a hostile military frontier); (3) locally available resources; and (4) the local ruler's response to Aztec overtures of imperial incorporation.

Equally important in the development of patterns of local control were the needs of the imperial rulers and cities; as their needs changed (and expanded), so did their demands for specific types of goods and labor obtained through imperial activities. The four generalized strategies (economic, political, frontier, and elite) provided the Aztec empire with flexibility in establishing and maintaining control in diverse outlying regions, at the same time fulfilling the changing needs of those in power. While they overlapped somewhat, each strategy was geared toward specific expansionist goals. These four strategies were first described in Berdan et al. 1996; here we summarize that discussion and emphasize the relationships among the imperial strategies and world-system processes.

THE ECONOMIC STRATEGY

The economic strategy emphasized goals of production and exchange. The imperial rulers pursued actions designed to increase the amount of trade and the diversity of goods traded (the third and fourth processes discussed in chapter 1), and these actions emphasized both commercial exchange (the fifth process) and political tribute. During the empire's brief history, the Basin of Mexico core zone grew rapidly in both size and complexity. Also accelerating were the subsistence and utilitarian demands of the basin's burgeoning urban centers (especially Tenochtitlan), and the prestige and luxury needs of increasing numbers of elite. These changes influenced the empire's economic strategy. As Aztec control extended to more and more distant areas, for example, the tribute demanded was increasingly in the form of luxury elite goods. This is partially a function of the costs involved in moving bulky goods (such as maize and beans) over long distances, and also a function of the increasing luxury-consumption levels of a burgeoning urban elite.

Conquered city-states were grouped into regionally contiguous provinces for purposes of tribute administration, collection, and record keeping. These provinces, which we call *tributary provinces* (Berdan et al. 1996), served as domains for imperial *calpixque*, who were responsible for collecting tributes (and sometimes haranguing the local populations, if local complaints are considered). The concept of province, however, probably had little or no meaning for the individual city-states so grouped, who may even have been warring with one another (chapter 12).

The economic strategy first and foremost entailed the imposition of tribute on conquered city-states (Berdan and Anawalt 1992; Matrícula de Tributos 1980). Tribute was a scheduled, repetitive, and relatively predictable way of assuring the delivery of economic resources to the imperial centers of power. The goods delivered in annual, semiannual, or quarterly payments included large quantities of staple foodstuffs (maize, beans, chia, amaranth, and chiles), raw materials (such as cotton, cochineal, lime, canes, feathers, and gold dust), and manufactured goods (such as feathered warrior costumes and shields, elaborately decorated clothing, greenstone beads, and amber lip plugs).

While some of the tribute rendered was unworked (like the raw materials mentioned above), most of the tribute involved fashioning and manufacturing procedures before being delivered to the imperial core. This included, for instance, weaving and decorating clothing, fabricating complicated feathered warrior devices, fashioning and polishing fine stones (*chalchihuitl*), manufacturing copper axes and bells, creating turquoise masks, and building carrying frames (*cacaxtli*). Some of these products derived from affluent production zones (such as cotton from Morelos and coastal Veracruz, and cacao from Xoconochco; chapter 35), but many were paid by areas defined as unspecialized peripheries. People in these areas, often lacking immediate access to the raw materials for specialized manufacture, were required by the very act of tribute to interact with producers in other polities to obtain these materials. Most commonly, this involved the acquisition of lowland cotton and tropical feathers by highland city-states for the manufacture of cotton clothing and elaborate feathered military devices. Imperial tribute demands therefore not only stimulated specialized manufacturing in conquered regions, but they also encouraged and sustained interpolity interaction in those outlying areas, most likely through long-standing market and trading relations.

Indeed, a further dimension of the economic strategy involved the promotion of commerce. In the first place, this encompassed state-sponsored long-distance trading enterprises. Professional merchants (*pochteca*) from the Basin of Mexico engaged in private commerce on behalf of themselves or their relatives; for these exchanges they traveled extensively both within and beyond imperial boundaries (chapter 16). In addition, however, some specially designated pochteca ventures carried political, even diplomatic, overtones. Certain privileged pochteca, entrusted with the goods of the Mexica ruler, traveled beyond the empire to international trade centers, exchanging the ruler's goods with those from rulers in these trade centers (chapter 17). These exchanges provided rulers with desirable and valuable lowland luxuries, while at the same time establishing diplomatic ties with rulers of these energetic economic centers.

Additionally, one economic strategy involved in Aztec imperial policies was directed at marketplaces. In the Basin of Mexico, market taxes were assessed, providing some revenue to rulers (Berdan 1985). However, more significant meddling could take place: in some cases the imperial rulers dictated the presence and content of specific markets (Berdan 1985), thereby controlling the availability and flow of specific goods.

THE POLITICAL STRATEGY

The political strategy fostered goals of administrative integration and control. While the economic strategy was directed at controlling economic resources, the political strategy was aimed at controlling political competitors. If external territorial expansion were to be successful, it was imperative that the imperial powers solidify political control in their core zone.

With the landscape divided into numerous competing city-states, local rulers (tlatoque) competed with one another by forging alliances and engaging in open warfare (chapter 9). This was an unstable business, but nonetheless led to the possibility that strong political contenders to the empire could emerge. The imperial rulers were faced with the problem of diffusing local tlatoani power and of making "formerly autonomous states more dependent on the imperial center" (Hodge 1996:19). In the Basin of Mexico, imperial rulers solidified and stabilized their control by directly interfering with some local political offices and positions. They abolished some offices, as at Xaltocan and Coatepec, where the Texcocan ruler Nezahualcoyotl replaced local tlatoque with Texcocan calpixque. This was a political downgrade, since calpixque (tribute collectors) were of a decidedly lower social and political status than tlatoque. In other cases, imperial rulers created new administrative positions, as with the relatively frequent practice by the Mexica of adding new tlatoque to conquered Basin of Mexico city-states; these new rulers were, not surprisingly, relatives of the Mexica ruler (Hodge 1996:34–37). Also in the Basin of Mexico, the imperial rulers instituted separate but parallel hierarchies for tribute collection and political administration (Hicks 1984). This had the consequence of divorcing vertical flows of resources from the local rulerships, thus weakening constituent city-state political potency.

Some top-level decisions contained a somewhat more positive approach. As the empire expanded beyond the Basin of Mexico, conquered city-states within that core zone joined the Triple Alliance forces in distant conquests, gaining renown, prestige, lands, sacrificial offerings, tribute, and booty. Sharing in the spoils of war, the nobles of these polities became more firmly integrated with imperial goals and direction. Brumfiel (1998) explores the manner in which the Mexica state incorporated these regional elites into the imperial enterprise.

The political strategy is most noticeable in the Basin of Mexico core zone. Beyond, in the regions of the outer provinces, the empire engaged in little meddling, for local rulers were typically allowed to remain in positions of control following Aztec conquest. There are a few cases to the contrary. When Cuetlaxtlan was initially conquered, a Mexica governor was installed there (Durán 1967:2:182–183). A subsequent rebellion and reconquest resulted in the installation of a new governor and, surprisingly, new local leaders (the local populace apparently having risen up against its traditional rulers) (Berdan et al. 1996:286). Oztoma, near the Aztec-Tarascan border, was so severely defeated that colonists from central Mexico were selected and mobilized to repopulate the area, man the fort, and guard that insecure and dangerous frontier (chapter 14). In some other cases, the Aztec powers installed governors, military garrisons, or forts; these actions were most common in unstable, rebellious, or borderland areas.

THE FRONTIER STRATEGY

The frontier strategy focused on goals of security and containment along hostile imperial borderlands. From its inception in 1428, the Triple Alliance took an aggressive military stance, rapidly extending its domain farther and farther from the Basin of Mexico core. In this process, new frontiers were continually created, and the imperial powers needed to devise strategies for solidifying those frontiers, holding off military adversaries, and staging further conquests.

The frontier strategy consisted of both direct and indirect elements. The direct elements involved establishing military fortresses, dispatching and stationing garrisons of warriors, and sending colonists to strengthen frontier regions. At the time of Cortés's arrival, documented military installations were situated especially along the volatile borderlands with the Tlaxcalans to the east and

the Tarascans to the west. Almost constant warfare with the Tlaxcalans and their neighboring allies, and the frustrating inability of the Aztecs to vanquish these powerful kingdoms, most likely provided the incentives to fortify bordering imperial provinces. Provinces obstructing the Tlaxcalans' access to the Gulf coast and its rich resources were especially well fortified (see Berdan et al. 1996: figure 6.1). This did not, however, prevent the Tlaxcalans from causing considerable mischief in these eastern provinces (chapter 12).

The western spread of the Aztec empire was halted along the territories of the powerful Tarascans (chapter 14). It was here, in 1478 or 1479, that the Aztec forces suffered a disastrous and humiliating defeat at the hands of a superior force of Tarascans. Following that setback, the Aztecs refrained from testing that border again, instead being content with holding the border in a kind of equilibrium. This was achieved through the indirect elements of the frontier strategy, the establishment of a series of client states, or strategic provinces, along the border.

The forging of relatively reciprocal, mutually beneficial relations with client city-states provided the Triple Alliance with an efficient buffer zone against stubborn enemies. In the course of empire building, the Aztecs developed differential relations with their subjects: those in tributary provinces were conquered outright and paid specified tributes; those in strategic provinces rarely suffered outright conquest, sent "gifts" to the imperial rulers, and received "gifts" in return. These city-states owed their allegiance to the Triple Alliance (or some segment of it), but found themselves in special circumstances: they were situated along important trade routes or, especially, they were located along volatile military borderlands. Their further obligations therefore entailed the maintenance and accessibility of trade routes or the stability of hostile borders. As with fortresses and garrisons, strategic provinces were emphasized along the Tlaxcalan and Tarascan borders, and also to the north and south where the empire had reached its furthest extent and was facing future enemies. The volatile dynamics of the Aztec-Tarascan border are explored at greater length in Pollard and Smith, chapter 14.

THE ELITE STRATEGY

The elite strategy emphasizes the links among elites throughout the imperial domain. Elites from neighboring and distant city-states established economic, social, and political networks through reciprocal exchanges of luxury goods, marriage alliances, and shared use of common symbols and restricted cultural codes (such as writing and palace architecture).

The relationships between imperial rulers and local elite were somewhat precarious. As mentioned above, some local rulers, when conquered, were replaced with others chosen by the conqueror; the elite structure was maintained, with the loyalties of the office occupants more firmly assured. Arranged marriages between powerful elites also solidified these vertical political relations by establishing social obligations and consolidating resource control (Carrasco 1984). An added dimension of elite interaction involved exchanges of luxury goods. Such exchanges occurred frequently at state events (Brumfiel 1987b; Smith 1986), but may also have been an aspect of the recorded exchanges carried out on behalf of the Mexica ruler with rulers of the international trading center at Xicalanco (Sahagún 1950–1982, book 9).

Imperial conquerors dealt directly with the conquered local rulers and elite, not with the commoners. Local rulers and their elite contingent were approached by tribute collectors, invited to high-level state events, and were considered responsible for activities in their own realms. The event of imperial conquest increased the frequency and intensity of vertical elite interactions, necessitating successful communication. This is reflected in several innovations in long-distance interactions among elites. First, people in provincial regions adopted the Nahuatl language, and many nobles were multilingual in Nahuatl and other languages. Second, the new language-independent forms of Postclassic writing and iconography facilitated communication between widely separated nobles. The spread of specific forms of manuscript painting dedicated to historical accounts is the best-documented example of this process (chapter 27). Third, new forms of stylistic interaction involving painted ceramics, manuscripts, and mural paintings also helped bind spatially separated elite into a common interacting social class (chapters 10, 22, 24, and 31).

THE AZTEC EMPIRE IN THE MESOAMERICAN WORLD SYSTEM

The Late Postclassic Mesoamerican world system was, of course, considerably larger than the Aztec empire. The empire did, however, control extensive territories and command ample respect from those beyond its control. Its rapid growth and significant presence in Mesoamerica at the time of Spanish contact can illuminate two particularly interesting issues: the impact of the empire on other exchange circuits, and the nature of imperial interaction with the rest of Mesoamerica.

THE IMPACT OF THE EMPIRE
ON THE OTHER THREE EXCHANGE CIRCUITS
The Aztec imperial strategies discussed above resulted in economic, military, and political consequences beyond Aztec boundaries. These patterned differently with each of the three other exchange circuits. With west Mexico,

controlled primarily by the Tarascan empire, the consequences were predominately military: the presence of Aztec forces at the Tarascan borderlands required the Tarascans to respond in kind. They likewise fortified the long frontier border and needed to be on the alert for possible Aztec incursions. However, this precarious military situation did not deter economic exchanges: turquoise, copper, obsidian, and perhaps other goods moved from west to east into conquered Aztec provinces, a prime example of world-system exchanges that freely crossed even hostile political borders (chapter 14).

Aztec relations with the Mayan exchange circuit appear to have been primarily economic and diplomatic. Aztec merchants frequented at least one international trade center in the zone (chapter 17). Their commercial activities there undoubtedly stimulated the movements of goods produced throughout the Mayan zone (such as cacao and salt) to that trade center at least. Since some of these trading expeditions carried diplomatic overtones, we can also assume some political ties between the imperial powers and the fringes of this exchange circuit. Relations between the empire and the third exchange circuit, the southern Pacific coastal plain, appear to have been focused on the conquered province of Xoconochco and its international trade center (chapter 35). The tribute from this province was rich in cacao, tropical feathers, greenstones, jaguar pelts, and other fine items (Berdan and Anawalt 1992). This was a tributary province, and conquest of the region suggests that the imperial rulers expected reliable and regular payments of these goods through tribute, rather than relying on the less predictable vagaries of commercial exchange.

THE NATURE AND EXTENT OF IMPERIAL
INTERACTION WITH THE REST OF MESOAMERICA
As the empire expanded, new city-states continually found themselves at the borders of Aztec hegemony. This required these city-states to consider strategies themselves, such as military resistance or diplomatic discussions. The latter included possibilities of elite marriage alliances. In cases where a city-state sat close to a competing core, such as Tlaxcala, the city-state's options included alliance with the polities of that core. Economically, imperial tribute demands at times required conquered groups to go beyond imperial boundaries to fulfill their tribute obligations (chapter 12); this sustained trade and market relations between conquered and nonconquered regions, and maintained or stimulated production of those goods in extra-empire areas.

In general, the Aztec empire played a significant role within its domain in directing economic production and distribution to its expanding core. Increasing consumption needs of core elite also stimulated the commercial intensity (and perhaps the very number) of international trade centers and affluent production zones, whether within or beyond the bounds of empire. Similarly, resource-extraction zones must have felt increased demand (for instance, incessant warfare required large quantities of obsidian). As the empire expanded, it played an increasingly vital role in the dynamics of the Mesoamerican world system in the Late Postclassic period. One way to appreciate that role is to examine the nature of borders in the Aztec empire, the subject of the next chapter.

12

Borders in the Eastern Aztec Empire

Frances F. Berdan

Discussions of precapitalist world systems have been typically formulated around concepts of "center-periphery," "core-periphery," or "core-semiperiphery-periphery" (Abu-Lughod 1989; Chase-Dunn and Hall 1997; Rowlands et al. 1987). In this book we have modified and refined these units of analysis to consider exchange circuits, style zones, cores, affluent production zones, resource-extraction zones, international trade centers, unspecialized peripheral zones, and contact peripheries. These distinctions suggest that such units can be identified and spatially bounded. In this chapter I argue for the value of considering boundary complexities; especially significant is the likelihood that the same entity may be bounded differently for different purposes. For instance, regarding the Roman frontier, Elton (1996:4) observes that in "the region that was once Yugoslavia, political, social, ethnic, religious, linguistic, economic and military boundaries all overlapped." This notion of overlapping boundaries is a useful point of departure.

If, indeed, our spatial units consist of a multitude of dimensions (political, economic, social, and symbolic), then it is not surprising that each dimension may bound its entity in a distinct and meaningful fashion. Likewise, at the same time borders divide entities from one another, they also provide tantalizing corridors for interaction. So there is a multiplicity of interactions both within an entity (however defined) and across its borders with other entities (e.g., through trade, tribute, warfare, alliances, intermarriage, political administration, symbol sharing, or elite bonding).

Borders and boundaries encompass defined territories for specific reasons. When areas are mapped, boundaries are normally based on a set of culturally tied assumptions, imparting to the bounded areas a seemingly concrete reality and definition perhaps not shared by the people themselves. Robert Barlow (1949), for instance,

drew his well-known map of the extent of the Aztec empire to fully encompass all areas, whether those lands were documented as controlled by the empire or not. This was a top-down and geographically tidy approach, yet perhaps a bit dreamy if this vast territorial domination were indeed under the control of the Aztec military forces. A more recent bottom-up approach (Berdan et al. 1996) begins with the fundamental building block of central Mexican sociopolitical organization, the altepetl (roughly, city-state), resulting in smaller, discontinuous areas delineated by somewhat less tidy borders. Unfortunately, neither approach tells the full tale. The boundaries we draw are based on reasonably well-documented political arrangements and, as far as they go, are sound territorial delineations. However, they tell us little about how the borders themselves impinged on the lives of the people actually residing within those domains, or what those borders actually meant at the time.

SOME CHARACTERISTICS OF AZTEC-PERIOD BORDERS

What, then, are some of the salient characteristics of Aztec-period borders and borderlands? First, I suggest that these borders were *multidimensional*. Boundary lines varied over space depending on the type of activity—whether political, economic, military, social, or religious—and the level of activity (e.g., location of persons in a social hierarchy, or types of merchants). Thus the territory encompassed by a city-state as a hereditary political unit may not be coterminous with that city-state's marketing web, tributary obligations, military influence, or elite social networks (see Gibson 1971; Hicks 1984).

Second, and related to the first, is variation in the *intensity of borders* and borderlands depending on, again, different organizational dimensions and/or levels of activity. For some purposes, a border may be all but impermeable and sealed; for others, quite permeable and elastic. Long-distance professional merchants, for instance, trod over some borders only under severe duress, while more locally based traders crossed the same borders with impunity (Berdan 1988). Borders were therefore differentially sensitive to particular types of persons and their specific activities or goals.

Third, Aztec-period borders and borderlands exhibited a marked *instability*, perhaps related to their multidimensionality, that created an ongoing territorial tension. There was a fairly constant movement and reshuffling of people and groups around the landscape in Aztec-period Mexico. There also was an expected meander of domination and subordination (whether military or economic, or both) among different groups. Added to these was a pattern of on-again, off-again alliances and conflicts. Shifting and variably defined borders may be anticipated in such a dynamic, even volatile, context.

THE EASTERN EMPIRE

The eastern segment of the empire, while not overwhelmingly well documented, nonetheless exhibits considerable variation in geography and political history, certainly sufficient to make a discussion of borderlands interesting.

GEOGRAPHY

My definition of the eastern Aztec empire is somewhat arbitrary. For purposes of this study, this region stretches from the northernmost Aztec province, Oxitipan in Huaxteca country, to the southern edge of the province of Tochtepec, from whence Valley of Mexico merchants dared trek beyond imperial protection to profitable trading entrepôts. The region encompasses the highland valleys of Puebla-Tlaxcala and Tepeacac, then dips into semitropical mountainous zones, descending along the broad coastal plain to the Gulf of Mexico (figure 11.1) This eastern portion of the Aztec empire therefore encompassed three major geographic features: a high-altitude plateau, a semitropical mountain-and-valley landscape, and a lush, low-lying coastal plain.

In the delineation of the region's Aztec imperial provinces, it was not unusual for individual provinces to exhibit environmental diversity within their bounds, allowing, for example, wood products to be found at the higher elevations and cotton at the lower. With such provincial and regional diversity, it is likely that economic movements of goods involving marketplace exchange, long-distance trading, and tribute payments were complex and intertwined. Similarly, polities in and beyond this area competed openly for the region's resources, yielding an involved history of warfare, conquests, and unsteady alliances.

POLITICAL HISTORY

A wide diversity of peoples, notably Nahua, Huaxtec, Totonac, Otomí, and Tepehua, occupied the eastern region and had long traditions of specialized economic production, lively regional trade and trading centers, hierarchical social arrangements, and dynastic political systems. They were, in a word, complex. Under these conditions it may be anticipated that the spatial definitions of these peoples' many and varied activities would be likewise complex.

Much of the eastern empire, from highland plateau to Gulf coastal lowlands, was incorporated into the Aztec imperial domain during the mid-fifteenth to early sixteenth centuries. The political picture that emerged just before the Spanish conquest was the result of near-constant warfare, conquests, rebellions, and unstable alliances throughout the region. In this volatile situation, political, military, and economic borders relentlessly shifted about. The imperial conquest picture in the east is complicated by the reportedly significant role played by the Texcocan rulers Nezahualcoyotl and Nezahualpilli in these conquest events. Claims to tribute and other obligations by Tenochtitlan and Texcoco are similarly complicated. For instance, Xicotepec and Quauhchinanco in the northeast were reportedly subdued by Nezahualcoyotl, but later on Ahuitzotl became militarily involved to help quell rebellions in the region (Stresser-Péan 1995). It is not entirely clear to whom these city-states owed their economic obligations by the time of the Spanish conquest.

There were important consequences to these conquests: (1) they opened commercial avenues from the plateau to the coast for access to valuable lowland luxuries; (2) they allowed the conquerors access to locally available resources through tribute and the offering of "gifts"; (3) they extended the imperial territorial domain, shortening the "foreign" travel distance of highland merchants to valued external trading entrepôts; and (4) they bounded enemy Tlaxcala (and to a lesser extent, Metztitlan) with conquered or client subjects.

It is of special significance that this region contained important polities, especially Tlaxcala and Metztitlan, which successfully resisted Aztec conquest. The former also occasionally fomented rebellions among Aztec subjects in the eastern realm. The existence of persistent hostilities between these powerful polities and the Triple Alliance had an important impact on the nature of relationships throughout the eastern portion of the empire.

As elsewhere in Late Postclassic Mesoamerica, city-states (altepetl) served as the primary units of legitimized political and territorial organization both before and after Aztec conquest. Boundaries between these fundamental political units served to geographically delineate a city-state's hereditary dynastic tradition, claim to lands, and sometimes ethnicity. It is these boundaries that were so often described and also sometimes mapped in the colonial sixteenth century (see especially Gerhard 1993b). These bounded domains encompassed the lands and peoples from which a hereditary rulership could demand allegiance and economic support.

Although altepetl boundaries are the easiest to define on the ground, people did not bound their lives by altepetl alone: with it they combined commercial exchange networks, labor and tribute obligations, and aristocratic stratification with a hegemonic imperial overlay. These complex relations led to variously bounded domains as well as dynamic corridors of interaction (to borrow a handy term from John Pohl [1994b]; chapter 11). Geographically abstract relations, such as vertical tributary obligations, traditional internecine warfare, marketing interactions, and elite alliances created such corridors.

BORDERS AND BORDERLANDS IN THE EASTERN AZTEC REALM

How, then, do the posited borderland characteristics of permeability, instability, and multidimensionality measure up in this eastern segment of the Aztec empire? In particular, do these characteristics vary in regular ways according to extent of state or non-state involvement in border-relevant activities, distance from the core or other significant zones (such as international trading centers or affluent production zones), presence of competing cores, or length of time under imperial rule?

DEGREE OF PERMEABILITY

Aztec borders exhibited differing degrees of permeability, and this appears to be related at least in part to the nature and intensity of political relations between polities. In the economic realm, it appears that the larger and more politically charged the trading operations, the more intense and impermeable the political boundaries. For instance, only select Basin of Mexico professional long-distance merchants (pochteca) were actually given license to traffic beyond the defined imperial bounds. At least on the occasions that they trekked to Xicalanco on the Gulf coast, they were protectively escorted to this foreign destination (see Berdan 1988). The trade of these professional merchants, as well as that of their cohorts who were confined to trade within imperial bounds, was high in value, low in bulk, directed to wealthy noble consumers, and often state-sanctioned. Pochteca traveling in foreign domains did so under diplomatic protection or at their own considerable risk.

Many pochteca traded only within imperial bounds; apparently they did not have the blessing of the imperial powers to join diplomatic and economic ventures beyond the bounds of empire. Yet it appears that these merchants were given some opportunities to obtain extra-empire

luxuries without leaving the empire's confines. This was achieved through the institution of borderland markets such as that at Tepeacac (Berdan 1985). This market opportunity was attractive to professional merchants who would otherwise invite assassination by entering hostile lands; they could remain safely (relatively) within the bounds of imperial control while still trading for fancy exotic luxuries. This was a border cleft (or gateway community, à la Kenneth Hirth), allowing the goods in while constraining the movements of the imperial merchants. Obviously regional traveling merchants or some privileged pochteca were necessarily involved in transporting high-value goods across imperial boundaries to such markets. Yet those same borders were relatively impermeable to certain classes of professional merchants.

Merchants other than pochteca, operating on a regional or local-level scale and trafficking in smaller-value goods such as cotton or foodstuffs, probably crossed imperial and city-state borders with relative freedom. Trading in known markets undoubtedly conformed to long-standing patterns, established well before the institution of particular political boundaries, especially imperial ones. So, in the east, Acazacatlan was noted as a cotton-trading center, yet was too high itself to grow cotton. Acazacatlan merchants themselves focused on carrying cotton broadly throughout the region and repeatedly across city-state borders (García Payón 1965:41). Products from restricted ecologies—such as cotton, cacao, fish, wood, and salt (some being produced in affluent production zones or resource-extraction zones)—were carried far and wide by regional merchants. These merchants crossed city-state boundaries and passed in and out of the defined imperial domain (Berdan 1988:646–647). For instance, at a fringe of the eastern empire, the people of Teotitlan del Camino wove *huipiles* (women's tunics) and sold them to merchants who carried them as far as Xoconochco. There they exchanged the huipiles for cacao, needed by those of Teotitlan. And the cotton used in manufacturing huipiles was not grown locally, but obtained from distant coastal lands.

Political borders seem to have been crossed by these traders with some impunity. It should be emphasized that markets frequently served as venues for obtaining goods not directly produced in one's own political domain. In some cases it was imperative that markets beyond one's political boundaries be visited in order to satisfy specific imperial tribute demands (chapter 11). In the eastern empire, while most tribute goods were indeed produced within the designated provincial territories, a few were not. Most notably, people of the provinces of Atotonilco el Grande, Tlapacoyan, and Tlatlauhquitepec would have had to import precious feathers for the manufacture of warrior costumes and shields demanded in imperial tribute (see Berdan and Anawalt 1992:3: fols. 30r, 50r,

51r). This would have necessitated some sort of mercantile relations with city-states closer to the Gulf coast, although the sources are silent on the actual movements of these prized commodities. Nonetheless, not only were the borders permeable for commercial purposes, but were even required to be open for imperial economic purposes.

Imperial borders in this eastern hinterland also exhibited a marked degree of permeability with regard to political and military activity. A notable example involves little Ahuatlan province, completely surrounded by Tepeacac province. It can be expected that warfare was a common theme in economic and political relations, as both of these provinces lay along or close to the lands of Tlaxcala and its allies. With respect to the permeability of borders, warriors from towns in Ahuatlan province warred with Tlaxcala, Huexotzinco, Cholula, and Totimehuacan to the north, by necessity traipsing over a considerable span of Tepeacac lands (see Berdan et al. 1996: figure A4.18).

In the realm of political machinations, it appears that these distant imperial borders were likewise open to diplomats from enemies of the empire. On more than one occasion the Tlaxcalans attempted to foment rebellions among the people of coastal Cuetlaxtlan and perhaps the nearby provinces of Cempoallan, Misantla, and Xalapa (Berdan et al. 1996:286–288). The installation of numerous fortifications in these coastal areas was undoubtedly in part an imperial response to these enticements offered by the nearby competing core of Tlaxcala. Imperial borders appear to have been ineffective in keeping enemy diplomats out of Aztec-conquered lands.

INSTABILITY

Perhaps the best examples of border instability involve military actions. The Late Postclassic period in central Mexico was a volatile time, and the eastern portion of the Aztec empire was no exception. From at least the 1100s waves of peoples moved into areas of eastern Mexico, replacing or absorbing extant populations. Thus, for instance, many established Totonac settlements were replaced or pushed from areas of the Sierra Madre Oriental eastward toward the Gulf coast, largely by various militaristic Chichimec groups (García Martínez 1987). The territoriality of city-states was a fluctuating reality. The Aztec imperial administration typically did little to interfere with the internal politics of its conquered realms, but where it did establish officials and/or garrisons, their presence suggests unstable borderland conditions.

It appears that imperial borders had relatively little imperial meaning and were somewhat unstable in this distant corner of the empire. Consider that a town in Ahuatlan province warred with two towns in Tepeacac province, even though both realms were under the same imperial net. Similarly, a community in Tetela province warred incessantly with one in Tlapacoyan province (Berdan et al. 1996: 284, 289), and towns within and on the fringes of the southern province of Tochtepec warred continually with one another (Berdan et al. 1996:285–286).

It is also worth considering that this region was incorporated into the empire for only a short while, with little time to solidify borderlands. It was, it seems, still in the process of formation, with some very recently conquered city-states tagged onto existing provinces: Motecuhzoma II attached his conquests of Papantla to Tochpan, Tepexic to Tepeacac, Mictlan Quauhtla to Cuetlaxtlan, and Atzacan to Quauhtochco (Berdan et al. 1996:284–292). It was, still, a region under dynamic imperial development at the time of the Spanish conquest, and imperial boundaries were neither firm nor effective against very real and very close enemy incursions.

MULTIDIMENSIONALITY

Along with relative impermeability and instability, eastern empire borderlands exhibited aspects of multidimensionality; that is, areas were bounded differently for different purposes. Take, for instance, the complex matter of tribute. Tribute obligations were adjuncts of vertical political relations. While an individual (of all but the top social status) had such obligations within an altepetl, individuals also owed labor and goods to nobles and rulers of other domains. Such relations can be discerned in the eastern corner of the empire. For instance, two major northeastern centers, Cuauhchinanco and Xicotepec, owed rotational palace service to the Texcocan ruler and therefore had direct tribute obligations to that imperial center. Both of these city-states also housed imperial (perhaps Acolhua) tribute collectors, and Cuauhchinanco was additionally required to supply provisions and warriors for Aztec (Mexica? Acolhua? Triple Alliance?) campaigns (Berdan et al. 1996:290; Stresser-Péan 1995). One section of the Cuauhchinanco borderlands appears a bit vague, since some small towns were also claimed by neighboring Atotonilco el Grande (see Berdan et al. 1996: figures A4.23, A4.24). However, this may actually be due less to "vagueness" or to "documentary disagreements" than to the presence of dual obligations to two strong city-states (see Berdan et al. 1996: 346–347).

Many trade and market domains transcended political boundaries. Markets at Tochpan and Tzicoac attracted merchants from far beyond their provincial boundaries, and Huexotla, farther to the north, may have served as an international trading center. Even bulky pottery moved about across political borders, although apparently in small quantities. Ceramics found at Cempoallan include a few imports from the central highlands (notably the Puebla-Mixteca areas), and those uncovered at Quauhtochco and Cuetlaxtlan show predominant imports from Cholula, Tlaxcala, and Coixtlahuacan (Brüggemann 1990:146; Medellín Zeñil 1952). We may speculate that Cuetlaxtlan's on-again, off-again political relations with Tlaxcala may have been augmented with economic ties as well. Farther south, Tochtepec was a well-known trading center where professional merchants from Basin of Mexico cities (and probably elsewhere) assembled prior to venturing beyond areas of imperial control. Getting to Tochtepec, as to Tochpan, Tzicoac, and Huexotla, required successfully crossing several city-state, provincial, and imperial boundaries. These situations created commercial networks that had no necessary correspondence with political or tribute-paying boundaries, and indeed flowed across these boundaries.

Elite corridors also, by necessity, transcended political boundaries. Through political negotiations, military alliances, and marriage arrangements, elites associated with one another in a functional way. Mention has been made of the rather tattered negotiations and agreements made between Tlaxcalan and Cuetlaxtlan elites. Along a different line, it appears that a lingua franca, Nahuatl, was developing in the region, as noble officials in many of the major centers (e.g., Tochpan, Papantla, Tulancinco, and the principal towns of Tepeacac province) are recorded as speaking that language, often bilingually in conjunction with the local language.

SUMMARY

In this small corner of the Aztec imperial realm, the available data suggest that borders were defined along multiple dimensions, that they fluctuated in permeability according to the intensity of political involvement, and that they exhibited considerable fluidity in this militarily volatile environment. It may be posited that these borderland characteristics can be found, with some variation, throughout this (or any) imperial realm. Particularly significant factors in delineating and characterizing borders would include (1) the level and type of political interest in defining or maintaining a border; (2) distance from the core region of the empire; (3) the presence of actively competing cores; (4) relationships with specialized locales such as affluent production zones, resource-extraction zones, or international trading centers; (5) proximity to contact peripheries; and (6) length of time under imperial rule. An assessment of borderland dynamics in diverse regions throughout the Aztec empire yields useful insights into the interplay between imperial and local-level forces in the context of aggressive empire building. In a broader sense, borders and borderlands play critical roles in world systems, in that they can either impede or facilitate interaction among the units of the larger system. In that vein, consideration now turns to the Tarascan empire (chapter 13), followed by a focus on the hostile Tarascan/Aztec imperial border (chapter 14).

13

The Tarascan Empire

Helen Perlstein Pollard

In 1522, the Tarascan king ruled over a domain of more than 75,000 km² in the west-central highlands of Mexico, including the modern state of Michoacán. The Tarascan empire, at that time the second largest in Mesoamerica, was ethnically dominated by a population the Spaniards called Tarascan and who spoke the language of Michoacán, also called Tarascan or P'urepecha. This polity may have been the most strongly centralized state in Postclassic Mesoamerica, and its size and degree of centralization stand in contrast to the small polities prevalent in most areas. Nevertheless, the expansion and operation of the Tarascan empire were strongly influenced by the commercial dynamics of the Postclassic world system, and Tarascan imperialism in turn had major impacts on other polities in the world system.

Based on sixteenth-century documents, Borah and Cook estimate the population of the Tarascan empire at 1.3 million, and Beltrán, using similar documents, estimates the 1524 population at 750,000 (1994:119). Beltrán further breaks down the 1524 population estimate into the Bajío (352,316), the Sierra (248,648), and the Lowlands (140,071), emphasizing the high concentration of population in central and northern Michoacán (1994: 120). Regional archaeological surveys in the Zacapu, Pátzcuaro, Cuitzeo, and Sayula basins suggest that population density reached its highest level during the Late Postclassic. More than 90 communities, containing 60,000-105,000 people, were located in the Lake Pátzcuaro basin, the empire's geopolitical core (see chapter 29). Tribute records indicate the Cuitzeo Basin was densely populated. Indeed, the largest concentration of tributaries recorded in the empire were located in north-central Michoacán from the Zacapu Basin east to the Cuitzeo Basin (Beltrán 1982). Moreover, the data also suggest that the largest and most populous settlements within any single region, whether ceremonial centers or cities, also date to the Late Postclassic.

THE LEGENDARY AND HISTORIC CREATION OF THE TARASCAN TERRITORY

The historical sequence of conquest and consolidation of the kingdom over this vast region is primarily known to us from the *Relación de Michoacán*. Supplementing and confirming the material are several documents written within the Tarascan region as part of the early Spanish colonial administration, including the Relaciones Geográficas of 1579–1580, the Caravajal Visitación of 1523–1524, the Ortega Visita of 1528, the Suma de Visitas de Pueblos of 1547–1550, and early *encomienda* grants of 1523–1525 (Warren 1985). Documentary sources recording Aztec conquests along the eastern Tarascan border provide additional information (Hassig 1988). Finally, archaeological research within the Tarascan territory and along the frontiers amplifies the documentary record.

In the legendary history of the Tarascans, the great culture hero Taríacuri established himself as lord of Pátzcuaro in the Middle Postclassic period, and his two nephews, Hiripan and Tangáxoan, as lords of Ihuatzio and Tzintzuntzan, respectively. Between A.D. 1250 and 1350 this elite lineage under Taríacuri, the *uacúsecha*, effectively dominated political interaction within the Pátzcuaro Basin.

By 1350 Taríacuri, with his lineage in control of the largest and richest of Pátzcuaro Basin territory (Pátzcuaro, Ihuatzio, Tzintzuntzan), and his allies in Urichu, Erongarícuaro, and Pechátaro began to lead his followers on a series of military campaigns within and outside the Pátzcuaro Basin. Beginning with the southwest corner,

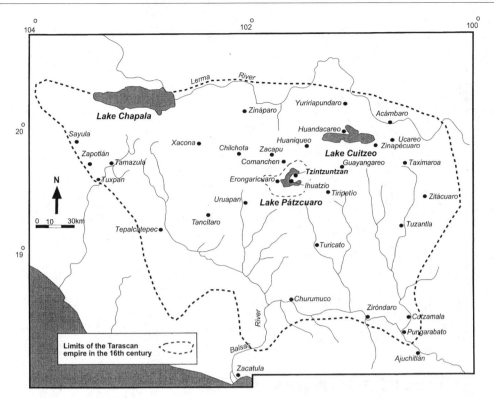

Figure 13.1 Map of the extent of the Tarascan empire. (After Pollard 1993: map 1.2.)

the conquests moved to encircle the basin. At this point Taríacuri died, and his nephew Hiripan of Ihuatzio continued the process of expansion out to the Lake Cuitzeo basin. These territories were the most densely settled at contact and greatly enriched the uacúsecha elite who led these campaigns. However, it is quite clear that at this point the military expansion was little more than a series of raids for booty, made by a war leader, Taríacuri, and later Hiripan, on behalf of a state that was little more than an amalgam of distinct polities, with a series of "capitals," that were residences of the highest-ranking members of the ruling lineage. The booty of military conquest was still being divided among the participating lords, and the conquests themselves were patchy.

Sometime around A.D. 1440, under the leadership of first Hiripan and later Tangáxoan, the first steps were made to institutionalize the military conquests and produce a tributary state. This involved the creation of an administrative bureaucracy and the allocation of conquered territories to members of the nobility. Rather than individual lords leading raiding parties, a series of lineages were allocated bureaucratic positions. In the words of the Relación, the Islanders took part of the *tierra caliente*, and the Chichimecs took the "right hand" or the Tarascan Sierra (Relación de Michoacán 1980:198). Some communities previously "conquered" were retaken, and a series of administrative centers established from which future conquests were made.

In the following decades, the pattern of expansion employed for the conquest and incorporation of central Michoacán was used in the series of conquests that followed. The first target was the Tarascan Sierra, followed by the Balsas Basin. Subsequent conquests expanded the borders of Tarascan control in all directions, probably reaching their maximum extent around 1470. A number of regions that were conquered under the Tarascan king Tzitzipandáquare were subsequently lost through rebellion or Tarascan consolidation in the face of Aztec expansion. By the 1460s the Tarascans had taken the province of Zacatula (on the Pacific coast at the mouth of the Balsas), advanced their northeastern frontier into the Toluca Basin, established centers north of the Lerma River, and moved north of Lake Chapala in the west.

During the 1470s the Tarascans faced military pressure along their eastern border from the Aztecs, and along their western border with Colima. In 1476–1477 the Aztecs under Axayacatl retaliated for Tarascan conquests with a major campaign that captured a series of frontier centers, including Taximaroa, and moved into the Tarascan heartland as far as Charo. After retaking their centers, the Tarascans fortified their eastern border by constructing a series of major military centers and resettling some ethnic Tarascans and several communities of Matlatzinca and Otomí exiles fleeing Aztec rule. The archaeological data suggest that the northern border, north of the Lerma River, was abandoned at this time by

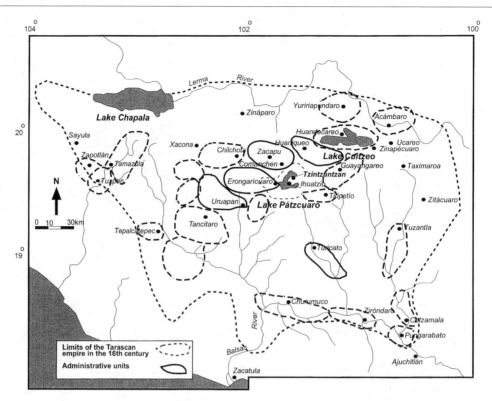

Figure 13.2 Map of the known administrative units of the Tarascan empire. (After Pollard 2000: figure 6.2.)

Tarascans. There are also indications that the Tarascans abandoned attempts to incorporate regions of Jalisco and Colima at this time, while consolidating their control in the Tamazula-Zapotlan and Coalcoman zones.

During the 1480s the Aztecs under Ahuitzotl—either directly or indirectly, through their Matlatzinca, Chontal, or Cuitlatec subjects—launched a series of attacks along the southern Tarascan border in the Balsas Basin. These attacks appear to have been stalemated during the 1480s and 1490s, but occupied much of Tarascan military strategy. In 1517–1518 a final major offensive against the northern Tarascan border was launched by the Aztecs under Motecuhzoma II and led by the great Tlaxcalan chief Tlahuicole. This campaign, which had reached Acámbaro in the north, was countered by the Tarascans in 1519 by two separate campaigns, one that marched from Zinapécuaro into the Toluca Valley, and the other from the central Balsas to the Aztec fortress of Oztuma. The preoccupation of both powers with the southern Balsas frontier may have provided the leverage for the local chief of Zacatula to remove that province from first Tarascan and later Aztec control.

POLITICAL STRUCTURE OF THE EMPIRE

The Tarascan state, in its sixteenth-century form, is renowned for its high degree of political centralization and relatively unchallenged control of its territory (Gorenstein and Pollard 1983; Pollard 1993). These

characteristics can be related to the emergence by the Late Postclassic (A.D. 1350–1525) of a social system with a fully Tarascan identity, produced by the conscious subordination and replacement of local ethnic-linguistic status as the basis for social or political power. Despite clear indications of earlier ethnic heterogeneity in central Michoacán in the Middle Postclassic period (Relación de Michoacán 1956), by the sixteenth century the Tarascan realm was self-identifying, and being identified by others as solely Tarascan (Relación de Michoacán 1956; Suma de Visitas 1905; Relaciones Geográficas 1985, 1987; Acuña 1987; Ochoa and Sánchez 1985; and Warren 1968, 1985, among others).

THE STRUCTURE OF AUTHORITY

The structure of the Tarascan administrative system has been the focus of study by numerous authors, including Beltrán (1982, 1994), Carrasco (1986), Castro-Leal (1986), García Alcaraz (1976), Gorenstein and Pollard (1983), López Austin (1976), Paredes (1976), and Pollard (1972, 1993). These studies are all based primarily on the documentary sources, especially the *Relación de Michoacán*, and what follows is a summary of this research.

The central administration of the state was located in the capital, Tzintzuntzan. There the Tarascan king (*irecha*) held his court, administered justice, and received emissaries from within and outside his territory. The court included members of the Tarascan nobility in a

Table 13.1
Titles and duties of officials in the Tarascan state bureaucracy

Title	Duties
Irecha	Head of the uacúsecha lineage; the king or *cazonci*
Angatacuri	Governor or prime minister
Captain	Chief military leader in warfare
Petámuti	Chief priest
Tribute minister	Steward in charge of the tribute collectors
Caracha-capacha	Governors of the four quarters of the state
Achaecha	Other members of the nobility acting as advisors
Quangariecha	Captains of the military units in wartime
Ocámbecha	Tribute collectors
Mayordomos	Heads of units that stored and distributed tribute, and produced crafts and services within the palace (at least 34 different units known)
Priests	Hierarchy of 10 levels below the chief priest; served in state temples
Angámecha	Leaders of towns and villages, referred to as caciques or señores

series of hierarchically organized offices (table 13.1). Below the court was a large bureaucracy composed of members of the nobility and commoners.

All positions appear to have been hereditary from father to son, with preference given to sons of senior wives. However, in most positions the Tarascan king had final approval of the officeholder. Local leaders were chosen by the king from among a number of possibilities; they could be replaced, and their decisions could be overruled by the king. In some instances the ties between the central dynasty and local leaders were reinforced by marriage to one of the king's daughters. These people are called *angámecha*, "los que tenian bezotes entre la barba y el labio" (those who had lip plugs between the beard and the lip) (Lagunas 1983:221). The removal of lip plugs was the symbolic act marking punishment by the king and removal from office (Relación de Michoacán 1956:201–202). This group included members of the hereditary nobility, *achaecha*, and apparently also included some commoners rewarded for military service. Their role as village leaders was the link between the Tarascan dynasty and the commoners, stressing the flow of authority from the central government and not from the local nobility.

This flow of authority from the center to the village was supported by the fundamental system of land and resource ownership. All land titles within the Tarascan domain were justified by having come from the king. This even included agricultural lands, fishing rights, mineral resources, and hunting territories within the Pátzcuaro Basin itself. Thus, for example, the people of Tiripitio had fishing rights in Lake Pátzcuaro by a grant from the king, despite their not being a basin community (Relación Geográfica 1985: Tiripitio; Ochoa and Sán-

chez 1985). Similar grants from the king are credited with laying out the lands and fishing rights of Xarácuaro, Zurumútaro, and Carapan (García Alcaraz 1976). The mechanisms for ensuring this distribution of resources is clear. In Carapan, we are told, if someone used fields not belonging to them, local judges would issue a death sentence, and the individual would be sent to Tzintzuntzan to be "offered to the gods."

Beltrán (1982) and Carrasco (1986) have studied the land-tenure system and isolated a series of categories including (1) patrimonial lands of the royal dynasty (uacúsecha), (2) fiscal lands of the state on which tributary goods were produced, (3) lands allotted to local lords, and (4) the lands of the commoners. To these categories I would add usufruct rights for hunting, fishing, and lumber, the control of state mines, and the control of long-distance merchants (Pollard 1982, 1987).

Labor to work the state lands was recruited from among the general commoners (*purépecha*), with additional lands worked by slaves. The slaves (*teruparacua-euaecha*) included war captives, criminals, those who sold themselves into slavery, and others bought in the market. In addition there were *acípecha* who appear to have been servants of the nobility (Carrasco 1986:80–81). Finally, each son of the ruling king was granted lands that were maintained by his mother's family, although how labor was actually recruited is unclear.

TERRITORIAL DIVISIONS WITHIN THE STATE
Administrative control was accomplished by the creation of a series of centers, each with a number of dependent communities. The administrative centers of these units reported directly to the palace in Tzintzuntzan. They in turn contained dependent villages and dispersed hamlets,

and in several instances were divided into subcenters. Beltrán (1982:118) suggests that these sub-cabeceras were the result of the splitting off of the noble lineages that ruled in the centers. Thus the administrative hierarchy contained up to five levels. Of the five units known in detail from the Caravajal Visitación, the number of subject communities varied from 12 to 44, and the number of *casas*, or households, reported varied from 244 to 863. At an average of six persons per household, the units reported varied from 1,464 to 5,178 persons. Despite the low density of population in regions farther from the Tarascan core, the units remained fairly similar in size, allowing one day's travel time between any community and its administrative center.

It is not clear whether there were any units above the level of these centers and below the capital. Documentary sources suggest, for example, that Tancítaro was a center for tribute collection for much of the southwestern territory. Furthermore, Xacona is described as one of the four centers for the administration of the Tarascan territory, the location of one of the four *caracha-capecha* (administrators). Analysis of the documentary sources suggests that the four-quarters division was either solely symbolic—as part of the cosmic design of the imperial enterprise—or that the four centers served as military massing centers in conjunction with a possible role as tribute-collection points. Thus, for example, we know that major military campaigns were organized from Xacona, Tacámbaro, and Zinapécuaro. The archaeological evidence from Huandacareo (Cuitzeo Basin) and Zirizícuaro (east of Uruapan)—single-period Tarascan administrative centers—suggests that where there were not already major population centers, Tarascans constructed public spaces to display state administration, justice, and ritual, and to bury local and imperial leaders.

The power of the central dynasty, however, was directly linked to headmen in each of the smaller administrative centers, and direct control of local decision making could reach even the village level. For example, we know of the sending of a judge by the king to settle disputes within the community of Tetlaman, near Tepelcatepec (Carrasco 1969:219). In the Sayula Basin, incorporated into the empire between A.D. 1440 and 1500, settlement during the Preclassic and Classic periods was dispersed in small communities and focused on the lakeshore exploitation of salt (Valdez and Liot 1994). During the Postclassic, settlement shifted to upland use of agricultural zones as communities clustered into what Sayula Project members term *señoríos*, or chiefdoms. Evidence of Tarascan occupation (or local leaders acting on behalf of the empire) is found at the largest sites associated with each local polity.

Within and along the frontiers of the Tarascan kingdom were a number of non-Tarascan ethnic enclaves composed of distinct communities that had been granted lands by the king within the Tarascan heartland, and also communities of non-Tarascans along the military borders. In the case of the Matlatzinca in the Charo-Undámeo zone, the communities were administered as a group and headed by Charo (Quezada Ramírez 1972:43; Warren 1977:247–250). As the location of the highest-ranked Matlatzinca nobility, the choice of Charo as administrative center implies little Tarascan "meddling" within Matlatzinca society, and a retention of Matlatzinca-defined status and authority. Along the military frontiers ethnic enclaves often provided their tribute in the form of specialized military service. Many of the frontier centers and fortified towns were multiethnic, including as many as four different ethnic groups in addition to small Tarascan communities sent to colonize the center. These communities were administered separately by ethnic group. Thus the Tarascan governor sent out to Acámbaro was in charge of only the Tarascan community (Celaya, in Ochoa and Sánchez 1985). Local lords of each ethnic group were selected, with the approval of the Tarascan king, to administer their own communities. When they fought in Tarascan military campaigns, they formed their own units, although serving under Tarascan leaders.

POLITICAL POWER, CLASS, AND ETHNICITY

As the state's territory enlarged, the economic and political success of the Protohistoric Tarascans required that the increasingly distinct communities be integrated to ensure the economic exploitation of populations and resources, and to protect the integrity of the frontier. This integration was designed to serve the best interests of the political core, the Lake Pátzcuaro basin. More particularly, it had to serve the interests of the sociopolitical elite living in the capital, Tzintzuntzan.

Within the heartland local leaders dealt directly with the central administration (Relación de Michoacán 1956; Gilberti 1975; Lagunas 1983; Caravajal Visitación, in Warren 1977). This region appears to have been under the direct control of the political capital. All local leaders were approved by the Tzintzuntzan elite and could be replaced, and their decisions could be overruled by the king. Their loyalty was assumed, and intervention in local affairs was considered unusual (Relación de Michoacán 1956:201–202). Such loyalty to the Tarascan royal dynasty was repeatedly demonstrated during the Early Colonial period (Warren 1977, 1985).

The second zone, that of active assimilation, presented quite different problems. It provided many resources basic to elite identification, including tropical fruit, cacao, cotton, copal, jaguar skins, tropical feathers, gold, silver, copper, and tin (Gorenstein and Pollard 1983; Pollard 1993). Absorbed into the expanding state only after 1440, this zone was increasingly basic to the maintenance of Tarascan elite society. If the kingdom was to successfully expand beyond it, the political loyalty of these tributaries had to be ensured. Revolts or insurrections, while unlikely in this region of low population density, nevertheless would have strained core Tarascan resources. By controlling access to local political offices, the core elite also controlled the local elite's access to power and prestige, now definable on Tarascan terms. All land titles within the Tarascan domain only had legitimacy because they were given to individuals and communities by the king. Among these were included agricultural lands, fishing rights, mineral rights, and hunting territories (Beltrán 1982; Carrasco 1986; Pollard 1993). By extending the Tarascan political ideology throughout this zone, non-Tarascan–based access to resources and social status became illegitimate and over time would have become irrelevant, fostering assimilation of local elites to Tarascan ethnicity.

Within the zone of ethnic segregation, along the military borders, loyalty to the Tarascan elite was assured in exchange for the security provided by the state military structure. Administrators were sent from the political core to articulate with the local population and ensure this loyalty. Nevertheless, the populations were regarded as subject allies, rather than subjects, and tribute included war captives and slaves (Acuña 1987). The inclusion of zones of segregation within the state was highly desirable; the risk to the state of losing their ultimate loyalty was balanced by the benefits of using these populations for military support, sacrificial victims, and economic brokers with neighboring societies. Carlos Herrejón Peredo (1978) has detailed the valuable role played by Matlatzinca and Otomí communities, both along the eastern border and at enclaves at Charo-Undámeo, in the Tarascan repulsion of the 1476–1477 Aztec military campaign. Such support brought harsh Aztec reprisals in the Toluca Valley itself, and resulted in additional refugees fleeing to Tarascan territory.

POLITICAL ECONOMY OF THE EMPIRE

Goods and services flowed through several institutional channels which fell into two basic classes: local and regional markets, and state-controlled agencies. The state-controlled agencies are believed to have included the tribute network, official long-distance merchants, state agricultural lands, state forest lands, state mines, and official gift exchange.

MARKET EXCHANGE
The primary sources about Tarascan economic networks say relatively little about markets and marketplaces, but we do know they existed and can locate specific centers (Relación de Michoacán 1956:223, 61, 92, 114, respectively). Gilberti recorded Tarascan terms for marketing (*mayapeni*), trade (*mayapecua*), merchant (*mayapeti*),

and marketplace (*mayepeto*) (1975 [1559]: 67, 403). Market activity included the renting of services, such as water carrying and maize grinding (Relación de Michoacán 1956:114); begging food; and the selling of slaves (Relación de Michoacán 1956:92, 178). There is no indication that the markets were state-controlled or regulated, despite an extensive description of the judicial system in the *Relación de Michoacán*. On only two occasions, the death of a Tarascan king and the appearance of Spaniards in the Tarascan capital (Relación de Michoacán 1956:246, 223), does the king forbid market activity. Both of these occasions are extraordinary, although they do indicate the ultimate subordination of marketing to centralized political control.

THE TRIBUTE SYSTEM
The most significant state agency involved in economic interchange was the vast, centralized, and hierarchically organized tribute network (see especially Relación de Michoacán 1956; Gorenstein and Pollard 1983; Pollard 1993). While it was fundamentally a political institution, the bulk of goods passing through various levels, from various regions of the state, ultimately found their way to the capital, Tzintzuntzan, where they were placed in central storehouses. To the extent that they were consumed within the basin—by the royal family, the political bureaucracy, the religious functionaries of the state temples, as gifts to foreign emissaries, and as emergency stores for the local population—they represent a significant portion of the local economy. In addition, these items were used to maintain the army, which during periods of war would have supported large numbers of men from central Michoacán.

The tribute system was under total control of the Tzintzuntzan-based royal family. Tribute was collected from regional tribute centers, each with its own known tributaries, on a fairly regular basis (e.g., every 80 days; see Warren 1968). Specialized bureaucrats were in charge of the collection, storage, and distribution of the tribute and are well described in the *Relación de Michoacán*. Tribute itself took the form of both goods and services. On the local level, tribute was used to support local state representatives, both administrative and religious, and only a portion was passed on to the regional collection center. From regional centers the amassed tribute was sent to Tzintzuntzan or to the military borders. The most common items appearing on tribute lists of goods that actually went to the capital include maize and cotton cloth and clothing. Other categories that regularly appear include slaves, sacrificial victims (from border zones), household services, metal objects, armaments, tropical fruit, cacao, cotton (raw), gourds, animal skins (jaguar, etc.), tropical bird feathers, gold, silver, and copper. Some goods that also appeared in the markets are occasionally mentioned in tribute contexts and include salt, beans, chile peppers, rabbits, turkeys, honey, maguey wine, local bird feathers, and ceramic vessels.

DIRECT STATE OWNERSHIP OF RESOURCES

In addition to the tribute network, there were state lands held in the Pátzcuaro Basin and elsewhere that were used to produce food directly consumed by the royal household, upper nobility, and the temple attendants (Relación de Michoacán 1956:173–180). Some of the land may have been planted as maguey plantations, reflected in illustrations in the *Relación de Michoacán* and the settlement of Aterio on the southern shore of the lake (Atero = "Place of Maguey Honey"). The value of this land is indicated by the capital punishment proscribed for "neglecting the king's fields" and "damaging the maguey" (Relación de Michoacán 1956:12).

The royal household also seems to have had exclusive rights to the products of certain local forests, including lumber, firewood, deer, and rabbit (Relación de Michoacán 1956:173–180). In a similar manner, waterfowl on the lake and, to a lesser extent, fish from the lake, are referred to as being provided to the royal household by royal duck hunters and royal fishermen (Relación de Michoacán 1956:173–180). These may have been, in fact, tribute items from lakeshore settlements, tribute made in the form of hunting service, or they may have reflected elite rights to certain general resources.

Indications exist that some of the copper mines were under the direct exploitation of the state. In a document from 1533, workers from the copper region of Turicato-La Huacana-Sinagua along the central Balsas River drainage indicated that delivery to Tzintzuntzan of copper occurred every 80 days or whenever the king asked for more (Warren 1968:47, 50). It suggests that the king sent workers to these mines to meet his needs. This seems to indicate a relationship greater than tribute (see Pollard 1993 for detailed discussion of the state's relationship to the mines). State gifts, from both foreign visitors and Tarascan leaders, that were brought into Tzintzuntzan include such items as tropical fruit, cotton and cotton cloth, and manufactured metal objects (Relación de Michoacán 1956:228, 238).

Artisans attached to the palace in Tzintzuntzan produced a wide range of goods for the royal household, including basketry, mats, pottery, featherwork, and metal objects of gold, silver, and copper (Relación de Michoacán 1956:173–180; Pollard 1972). Construction workers (numbered at 3,000) produced public buildings (Relación de Michoacán 1956:174–175). It is unclear whether these people were retained by the royal household or were paying their tribute in specialized activities and goods.

The last institutionalized mechanism by which goods flowed into the Pátzcuaro Basin was the state's long-distance merchants. These merchants were apparently retained by the royal household to provide specialized, rare goods obtainable only from the far reaches of the state or even outside it (Relación de Michoacán 1956: 178, 171–172). There is no indication whether these merchants sold any of their goods in the regional or Tzintzuntzan markets. One reference to merchants selling slaves (Relación de Michoacán 1956:184) may refer to these specialists or to local individuals who dealt strictly with local products.

RELATIONSHIPS BETWEEN THE STATE AND LOCAL, REGIONAL, AND INTERNATIONAL MARKETS

Commoners obtained goods through local markets or subsistence activities, while the elite obtained goods primarily through state-controlled agencies, especially state lands and usufructs. This means that settlements with immediate access to valued resources—such as prime agricultural land, marsh lands, and fishing zones—could exchange local surpluses for nonlocal items in the marketplace. Fish, for example, were dried to aid preservation and reduce bulk weight while maintaining full nutritional value; they were exported through regional markets. Other settlements specialized in the production of manufactured goods, including basketry, mats, ceramic vessels, and metal objects, especially in the core of the empire.

The role of regional marketing networks that integrated the empire as a whole, and which crossed the imperial borders, can be documented by the movement of goods whose sources within Michoacán are well known and whose distribution was primarily through markets; this largely limits evidence to obsidian (Darras 1998; Esparza López 1999; Healan 1997; Pollard et al. 1998; Pollard and Vogel 1994b) and salt (Williams 1999). Both commodities were distributed throughout the imperial territory, from the *mesa central* to the *tierra caliente* (e.g., Zináparo obsidian [Esparza López 1999]). Some foodstuffs moved through regional markets, and two zones are documented as food suppliers for the Pátzcuaro Basin: the Asajo zone to the northwest, covering the rich agricultural land of Comanja and Naranja, and the Curinguaro zone to the southeast, covering the lands of Tiripitio and Huiramba (Caravajal 1523, in Warren 1985; Relación de Michoacán 1956; Relación Geográfica of Tiripitio, see Pollard 1993).

However, the nobility, and possibly merchants, artisans, and other specialists, only minimally participated in such market exchange, obtaining similar products by outright ownership of production, such as through state mines, by state merchants, by tribute, and, in the case of war captives, by the exploits of the army. Imports for the elite came from all corners of the Tarascan state and beyond.

INTERNATIONAL EXCHANGE

From outside the state borders came turquoise and peyote from the northwest, marine shell from the Pacific, cacao from the Balsas Delta, rare obsidian and other stone from east-central Mexico and to the west in Jalisco, and serpentine, jade, amber, and pyrites from Oaxaca and farther south (chapter 29). There is no evidence that ceramics were imported from outside state borders. The small number of exotic sherds found usually are Aztec III Black-on-orange, found in contexts—the Tarascan king's palace and Tarascan frontier fortresses—associated with diplomatic missions between the Aztec and Tarascan states (Pollard 1993). The more distant the source of the item, the fewer the channels of acquisition and the rarer the use. The function of these imports was largely (but not exclusively) to maintain status differences between members of the elite and the rest of society as luxury goods (see chapter 18).

At present, only two types of commodities can be documented as having been exported to the rest of Mesoamerica: foodstuffs and manufactured metal objects, especially those of bronze and bronze alloys. The familiarity of the Aztec nobility with the fish, featherwork, and wood products of Michoacán (Sahagún 1950–1982, book 10:41) might be due to these products also moving across the eastern military frontier, but there is no independent evidence of such exchange. Sahagún (1950–1982, book 10:66–67) indicates that maize and chile from Michoacán were sold in the large Aztec market at Tlatelolco. Given the need for these products in central Michoacán, and the distances involved in their transport, the most likely place or origin for such exports is the frontier region of Michoacán, especially the eastern portion of the Lake Cuitzeo basin. This region, in the northeast of the Tarascan domain, was both productive enough to export basic commodities and close to the Aztec-controlled upper reaches of the Lerma River.

Metals found outside the Tarascan empire include large numbers of copper- and bronze-alloyed objects of Tarascan design and production (Hosler 1994). Many metal objects were mined and produced within the Tarascan empire and then exported throughout Mesoamerica, including Morelos, Oaxaca, Soconusco, Veracruz, and Belize (chapter 21). Some of the objects were made from ores coming from the Tarascan western frontier (or beyond) in Jalisco. It is not clear whether these objects were both mined and fabricated in Jalisco, or whether ores and/or ingots were imported (by trade or tribute) and then fabricated into objects within the core (chapter 29). They were probably exported by Tarascan long-distance merchants, but we know only what the merchants obtained from outside the empire, not what was exchanged in return (Relación de Michoacán 1956). As Hosler and Macfarlane (1996) point out, the evidence from Soco-

nusco suggests one avenue of export for distribution to southern Mesoamerica: canoe traffic from the port of Zacatula at the mouth of the Balsas. The fortress of Taximaroa is documented to have been a primary port of exchange between the Tarascan and Aztec merchants (Pollard 1993).

Finally, Tarascan merchants have often been seen as controlling the flow of turquoise from the American Southwest into central Mexico (Weigand and Weigand 1996:125) due to their position of control between Lake Chapala and Acámbaro along the Lerma River. While they certainly acquired turquoise for use within the empire, there is no direct evidence that they controlled the turquoise trade to central Mexico.

IMPERIAL IDEOLOGY AND IMPERIAL ELITES

The creation of the Tarascan state was accompanied by the establishment of a new ideology. The roots of this ideology came from the different cultural traditions that characterized Postclassic Michoacán populations, and the differing ways in which they related to the emerging elite (see Pollard 1993). Among the many deities known, it is Cuerauáperi, Curicaueri and Xarátanga who are mentioned most often, to whom the greatest number of temples seem to have been constructed, and who were linked most directly to the Tarascan state. The earth was conceived of as the body of the great creator goddess Cuerauáperi, who represented the forces that controlled fertility, including rain, birth, and death. She was the mother of all the gods and was actively venerated throughout the Tarascan territory (Relación de Michoacán 1980:15–17). The sun was embodied in Curicaueri, the great burning god and the god of fire. As the original patron god of the Tarascan royal dynasty and their Chichimec heritage, he was a warrior and the god of the hunt. The moon goddess, Xarátanga, was the daughter of the earth creator and wife of the sun, and was associated with childbirth and fertility. Patron deities of various communities were reinterpreted within the dual system of the four quarters (Curicaueri's four brothers) and the five directions, uniting all the solar deities in a manner that made the Lake Pátzcuaro basin the cosmic center.

In a similar manner, Tarascan art combined the common Mesoamerican heritage of Postclassic Mexico with features that were either limited to west Mexico or unique to Tarascan civilization. A specialized pyramid form, the *yácata*, consisting of a keyhole shape, was constructed at major religious centers associated with the Tarascan sun god, Curicaueri. Temples and elite residences included carved wooden lintels, portals, and posts, as well as painted posts and walls. Indeed, Tarascan culture used wood as the primary building material, unlike the peoples to the east and south, who relied upon wattle-and-daub, adobe bricks, and stone. Wood was also used for furniture, house posts, canoes, weapons, ceremonial drums, and figurines. Stone sculptures include chacmool (reclining warriors associated with human sacrifice) and animal sculptures of basalt. Much of Tarascan art was created with perishable materials that have rarely survived, such as woodwork, featherwork, and textiles; however, the most abundant medium for the expression of Tarascan beliefs and styles was fired clay. Certain ceramic forms were limited to the elite, were used for ritual offerings, or were part of major religious and political ceremonies. These were highly decorated, finely finished, and primarily nonrepresentational in style. Tarascan metalwork was different in style and form from that of contemporary central and southern Mexico, reflecting both the long west Mexican metallurgical tradition and specific Tarascan design canons (Hosler 1994). Only in gold design does the Tarascan metalwork reveal ties to central and southern Mexico.

The degree to which the Tarascans participated in Postclassic international style and symbol sets (chapter 24) is unclear. The Tarascan language has words for "scribe" (*carari*) and "to write, paint" (*carani*; Gilberti 1975), although the only known codices or lienzos from the empire's territory date to the Colonial period. Roskamp lists 19 pictographic documents, including the *Relación de Michoacán*, with its 44 illustrations (1999:

75). Several of the documents record land claims within the empire for Nahua communities, such as the Lienzo de Jucutacato; others pertain to ethnic Tarascan populations (e.g., the Títulos de Carapan); and all are in the Aztec codex style. Thus, in both belief and art, Tarascans and the Tarascan state shared basic Mesoamerican Postclassic technology and ideology while emphasizing a unique suite of forms and styles.

The picture that emerges is thus a mixed one for the Late Postclassic period. Raw materials and some finished goods were imported from beyond state borders in increasing quantities during the Postclassic, but basic elite identity was signaled with goods manufactured in central Michoacán (see chapter 29). On the other hand, during the Late Postclassic one of the most technologically complex and highly valued commodities, bronze and bronze-alloy objects, was produced within Michoacán and widely traded throughout Mesoamerica. Given the economic and political mechanisms by which this occurred within the imperial structure, the exchanges of manufactured metal goods for raw materials and objects necessary for elite status served to accelerate the processes of social, political, and economic centralization that made local and regional elites more dependent on state patronage and conversely made the royal dynasty more dependent on their participation in wider Mesoamerican exchange systems.

14

The Aztec/Tarascan Border

Helen Perlstein Pollard

Michael E. Smith

During the final century of the Late Postclassic period the Aztec and Tarascan empires were engaged in frequent hostile military actions along their common frontiers, even as they increased their volume of economic exchange. These seemingly contradictory processes illustrate the importance of world-system dynamics in Postclassic highland Mexico and provide one of the most dramatic examples of commercial exchange that crossed hostile political borders. The continual threat of invasions over the decades resulted in the construction of a series of parallel fortified citadels running from the Lerma River in the north to the Balsas River in the south, creating the only true territorial military border in Prehispanic Mesoamerica (Gorenstein 1985; Hassig 1988; Hernández Rivero 1994a, 1994b; Pollard 1993). Relatively little archaeological research has been done in the frontier zone (Contreras Ramírez 1985; Gorenstein 1985; Hernández Rivero 1994b, 1996, 1998; Silverstein 1999, 2000, 2001), and most of our understanding of the border comes from the Aztec and Tarascan documentary records (Beaumont 1932; Hassig 1988; Herrejón Peredo 1978; Pollard 1993; Relación de Michoacán 1956, 1980; Sahagún 1950–1982; Warren 1985).

HISTORY OF THE MILITARY CONFLICT

The Aztec/Tarascan military conflict was motivated by both economic and strategic factors. The southern part of the frontier zone in northern Guerrero was particularly rich in minerals and other resources. A desire to control sources of metals (copper, gold, and silver) was one motivation for Tarascan imperial expansion (Pollard 1987), and this area had numerous copper deposits (Hendrichs P. 1944–1945:1:202–206; Jiménez Moreno 1948). Tarascans received tribute from this region in copper, silver, and gold ingots (Pollard 1987). The Aztec

town of Alahuiztlan was one of the leading producers of salt in the western Aztec empire, and one function of the fortress of Oztoma was to protect the salt source from the Tarascans (Berdan et al. 1996:142), who attacked this fortress repeatedly. Thus both empires were interested in obtaining the rich mineral resources of northwestern Guerrero. Strategic forces came into play as the two expanding empires came up against each other and fought to a standstill.

In the 1440s the Aztecs, under Motecuhzoma Ilhuicamina, conquered areas south and southwest of the Toluca Basin as far as the modern Mexico-Guerrero border. Meanwhile the eastern expansion of the Tarascan empire under Tzitzipandáquare led to inconclusive campaigns into the Matlatzinca territory in the Toluca Valley between 1455 and 1462. In the 1470s the Aztecs took Tarascan-held areas of the Toluca Valley and defended them from subsequent Tarascan attempts to conquer the region. In 1479–1480 the Mexica king Axayacatl led an Aztec army of 32,000 soldiers into ethnic Tarascan territory for the first time. The Aztecs took the great fortress at Taximaroa (figure 14.1) and marched deep into Tarascan territory, coming to within 50 km of Tzintzuntzan, where they were defeated by a combined Tarascan-Matlatzinca force of some 50,000 soldiers. The decimated Aztec army was pursued back to the Toluca Valley, losing all of their conquests west of the frontier at Taximaroa. Twenty thousand Aztecs are said to have died at this battle, and Aztec armies never again penetrated the eastern border of the Tarascan empire. Continued hostility along their borders led the Tarascans to establish a series of fortifications at strategic points from the Lerma to the Balsas basins. Ethnic Tarascans were settled at some, and all were directly administered from the Tarascan capital. The Aztecs responded with fortifications built and manned by local populations, and in the case of

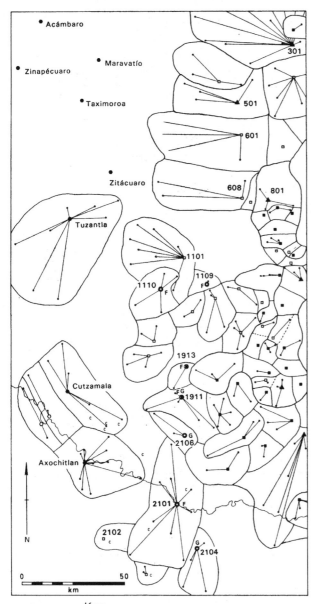

Key:

▲   Tributary Province Capital

■   City-State Capital, in Codex Mendoza

□   City-State Capital, Other Imperial State

●   Tarascan Border State

○   Other Tarascan State

⊗ F Aztec Fortress

⊗ G Aztec Garrison

•   Subject Town

c   Copper Source

Figure 14.1 Major military sites along the Aztec/Tarascan border

rebellious tributaries the settlements were repopulated with settlers from cities in the Basin of Mexico.

In 1515 the Aztecs attempted another military campaign along the central and northern portion of this militarized border. They attacked from the Toluca Valley, with the great Tlaxcalan general Tlahuicole in command. The Aztecs failed to take any sites but fought battles along the line, including Taximaroa, Maravatío, Acámbaro, Ucareo, and Zinapécuaro (figure 14.1). The Tarascans handed the Aztecs a major defeat between Maravatío and Zitácuaro; La Rea insisted that even in 1639 the bones from the battles were still visible (Beaumont 1932). Along the southern stretch of the border Tarascan armies repeatedly attacked the Aztec fortress of Oztoma but without taking the site. (These wars are discussed in greater detail in Herrejón Peredo 1978.)

The political tension between these empires is clearly seen in the way Tarascans reacted to Aztec requests for help against the Spaniards during 1519 and 1520. At least two embassies were ignored, and the Aztec ambassadors killed and sacrificed. In all cases the ambassadors traveled to the Tarascan frontier settlement of Taximaroa, where they were detained until a messenger was sent to Tzintzuntzan and permission was received from the king allowing safe passage, under escort, to the capital. A Tarascan party did go to Tenochtitlan in 1520 at Motecuhzoma II's request. The king, Zuangua, was suspicious that either the Aztecs would use a Tarascan alliance to defeat the Spaniards and then turn on them, or that Moctezuma would simply sell the Tarascan soldiers to the Spaniards as sacrificial victims. In the end they refused to help.

The most active sections of the border controlled access to the Lerma and Balsas river systems, with the Tarascans blocking Aztec penetration of either. This effectively prevented further Aztec penetration to the west and northwest along major trade routes. Over time, Aztec actions were both defensive, preventing Tarascan movement into the Toluca Valley, and offensive, finding alternative means of reaching the trade center at Zacatula. Hassig (1988) sees this as a policy of encirclement by the Aztecs. If that is so, it was clearly only a partial success, as only one of the Tarascan borders was effectively closed to further expansion by the Aztec actions. Other parts of the Tarascan border remained stable due to the inability of the Tarascan government to field armies for further expansion against increasingly distant populations to the north, west, and south.

ORGANIZATION OF THE BORDER ZONE

The Tarascan frontier with the Aztecs was a closed border. Although messengers could travel between Tzintzuntzan and Tenochtitlan in four days (Gorenstein 1985), movement was strongly restricted. Aztec messengers had to present themselves at the official ports of entry and await permission to pass into the Tarascan domain, under escort. Safety was clearly the enforcing principle, and continuing hostilities along the border bred suspicion that spies might precede raids or major campaigns. The movement of Tarascans within Aztec territory was probably also difficult, as their language was not spoken within the Aztec domain, and thus speakers would be quite noticeable. On both sides, one solution was to use Otomí or Matlatzinca messengers and spies, but this meant that communication between the elite of these states was indirect and intermittent.

Local populations in the border zone were neither Tarascan nor Aztec in ethnicity, and they typically paid their tribute to one of the empires in the form of military service. Although the border towns on both sides were administered indirectly, there was a greater state presence in the Tarascan border communities than in the Aztec towns. On the Tarascan side, border communities were administered directly by the central government, with their native leaders in charge locally (chapter 13). Tarascan populations were sometimes sent to build up the border settlement, as at Acámbaro (Gorenstein 1985), but in these cases the Tarascan governor only ruled the ethnic Tarascans, leaving local control in local hands. A chemical sourcing of obsidian artifacts from five of the Tarascan border sites (Acámbaro, Zirizícuaro, Taximaroa, Zitácuaro, and Tuzantla) identified 33 of 37 as Ucareo obsidian, including all 14 sourced artifacts from Tuzantla. While this may simply be due to market exchange in the eastern portion of the empire, the evidence that the state was probably controlling access to Ucareo prismatic blades (see chapters 13 and 28) suggests that the state may have provisioned the border communities.

Administration of most of the border communities on the Aztec side was through indirectly controlled client states (called "strategic provinces" in Berdan et al. 1996; see chapter 11). These Matlatzinca and Otomí city-states were not incorporated into the Aztec empire's system of tributary provinces as described in documents like the Codex Mendoza (Berdan and Anawalt 1992). Their payments differed from those of tributary provinces in three ways: military service was emphasized; the term "tribute" is avoided in favor of the term "gifts" to the Mexica king; and periods of payment were not regular (Berdan et al. 1996:147). With the possible exception of Temazcaltepec,[1] none of the capitals of these polities have been subjected to systematic archaeological fieldwork. Preliminary observations by Smith in 1997 at one such site, Cerro de las Minas (probably ancient Tlatlaya), revealed the presence of obsidian from the Pachuca source area, and redware ceramics from the Basin of Mexico or the Toluca Valley, indicating trade with the Aztec core area.

Documentary sources state that most of the Aztec client states along the border fought wars against the Tarascans, and that this military service was their major obligation to the Aztec empire. The sources mention a number of locally built fortresses and strongholds that were used in wars and skirmishes against the Tarascans, and archaeological surveys have located many such

Figure 14.2 Photograph of a local fortress, the Trincheras de Pedro Ascencio site on the Aztec side of the imperial border. (Photograph by Michael E. Smith, 1997.)

fortresses not mentioned in the (rather limited) documentary record (Hernández Rivero 1994a, 1994b). Figure 14.2 shows one such site, Trincheras de Pedro Ascencio, as it appeared in 1997. This is a small, protected mountaintop site with steep walls on all sides and a clear view of the various hilltops and passes into Tarascan territory to the west. It was located between the Aztec border towns of Amatepec and Tlatlaya.

TRADE ACROSS THE BORDER

Documentary sources note that Tarascan long-distance merchants, working directly on behalf of the royal dynasty, traveled to the state's borders to exchange goods with similar merchants. The fortress of Taximaroa is documented to have been a primary port of exchange for the Tarascan and Aztecs merchants (Gorenstein 1985; Pollard 1993), and one of the sourced artifacts from here is of Pachuca obsidian. Unfortunately, Aztec documentary sources have virtually nothing to say about trade across the Tarascan border. It appears that the ideology of conflict dominated Aztec official thinking on the Tarascans, to the point of ignoring an active cross-border exchange. Obsidian from central Mexican sources is present at Tzintzuntzan (Pollard and Vogel 1994a), and obsidian from Tarascan sources is present at Aztec sites in Morelos (see chapter 32). Various copper and bronze objects from Morelos are virtually identical to west Mexican bronze items (chapter 21). Hosler's initial lead isotope studies pointed to a Tarascan origin for some of these Morelos artifacts (Hosler and Macfarlane 1996), but more recent analyses (chapter 21) suggest that the metal in at least some of these artifacts may have come from Guerrero or Oaxaca rather than Michoacán. The trade connection between Morelos and the Tarascan zone probably went through one or more of the Aztec border towns, such as Temazcaltepec, Texupilco, and Tlatlaya. Sherds from Valle de Bravo (probably ancient

Temazcaltepec; see note 1) occur in small quantities at a number of sites in Morelos (Smith 2001c).

The *Relación de Michoacán* (1956, 1980) provides a record of the kinds of goods Tarascan merchants obtained from outside the empire, but it is silent on those exchanged in return. Finely crafted metal objects are likely commodities to have been used in these exchanges. Silverstein (1999, 2000) reports a broken ceramic vessel of Tarascan elite polychrome ware recovered at the Aztec fortress of Oztuma, probably a result of either diplomatic gift exchange or cross-border commercial trade.

Although the fortified Aztec/Tarascan border restricted political engagement between these two imperial powers, it did not stop an active trade in obsidian, metal, ceramics, and probably many other goods. Tarascan sources mention this trade, but the official histories of the Aztecs do not. Whether this is due to ignorance on the part of the Mexica historians, or to their deliberate omission of the subject for ideological reasons, it is likely that much of the cross-border exchange was in the hands of local and regional merchants not controlled by either empire. This black-market trade between enemy empires is a strong indication of the ability of commercial exchange to cross borders and integrate hostile polities into the wider processes of the Postclassic world system.

Part 3

Economic Networks

15

The Economy of Postclassic Mesoamerica

Frances F. Berdan

World systems are most commonly described in terms of economic relations. It is no surprise, therefore, that this book contains a substantial section devoted to exploring the role of the economy within the overall framework of regional and long-distance interactions. The purpose of this small chapter is to place significant economic processes (chapter 1) and economic units (chapter 3) within the broader framework of the Postclassic Mesoamerican world system. This overview also sets the scene for the following chapters on key institutions (chapters 17 and 22) and key commodities (chapters 18–21).

ECONOMIC PROCESSES IN POSTCLASSIC MESOAMERICA

Of the seven processes outlined by Smith and Berdan in chapter 1, three especially pertain to the economy. Each of these is considered in depth in the chapters of this section.

AN INCREASED VOLUME OF LONG-DISTANCE EXCHANGE

One important dimension of world systems is their economic integration over long distances and across political borders. Frequently this means travel over long distances by professional merchants who engage in economic transactions and politically tinged exchanges in centers far from their homelands. But this need not necessarily be the case, as much trading in Postclassic Mesoamerica was of a relay or down-the-line nature, allowing peoples and polities in broad areas access to a wide range of goods. As the Postclassic period progressed, increasing numbers of goods were imported across political borders. In the chapters that follow, this is especially reflected in an increase in production and distribution of obsidian (chapter 20) and metal objects (chapter 21). In addition, professional merchants were on the upswing (chapter

17). The use of money expanded during the Postclassic, indicating the need or desire to facilitate these increased volumes of exchange (chapter 21). Production increased, feeding into an expanding exchange system and necessitating an efficient and effective economic infrastructure. For some commodities, these production activities became more concentrated (chapter 16). As some specialized commodities became particularly well known for their high quality (or perhaps low price), they were transported over longer and longer distances. These goods found their way into (and then out of) international trade centers, regional markets, and the hands of professional merchants (chapter 17). If these highly desired commodities were to be exchanged across broad geographic regions, it was essential that borders be at least somewhat permeable, and political conditions at least somewhat accommodating (chapter 12). These production and exchange enhancements required an effective system of transport, and by Late Postclassic times there was apparently an abundance of overland burden bearers and canoe paddlers (admittedly of very low or slave status; see chapter 16).

AN INCREASE IN DIVERSITY OF TRADE GOODS

During Postclassic times, utilitarian goods were produced for local use, for tribute payments, for local or regional trade, or for long-distance exchange. Luxury goods were produced in noble households for noble use, but also manufactured in other settings for tribute payments and for trade at all levels, and for consumption by persons of noble and commoner status. As commercial and consumer options increased, so did the diversity of goods produced for trade. Commodities represent a vast range of types and styles: there were not only cotton capes, but capes of a multitude of colors and designs, perhaps embellished with some stylish rabbit fur or feathers. Similarly, metal and stone objects as well as ceramics increased in form, stylistic variety, and range of quality (chapters 20 and 21). There also seemed to be few hindrances to transporting commodities over long distances, even heavy and bulky materials such as salt, obsidian, cloth, metal objects, decorated ceramics, and cacao (see chapters 19, 20, and 21).

COMMERCIALIZATION OF THE ECONOMY

There are several indicators of an increased commercialization of the economy during the Postclassic. Markets flourished at all levels: small utilitarian markets; regional markets with a broader range of utilitarian goods and some luxury commodities; specialized markets focusing on known, quality products; borderland markets along particularly tense political boundaries providing access to distant and often exotic goods; international trade centers with their markets featuring goods from great distances; and the enormous and bustling cosmopolitan marketplace of Tlatelolco, where virtually everything in the realm could be found for sale (Berdan 1985). In general, buying and selling were featured activities in Postclassic Mesoamerican life, and everyone had access to a nearby marketplace or could venture farther abroad for a wider range of commercial offerings. A corollary of this extensive availability was the widespread access to luxuries by commoners as well as nobles (chapter 18).

A second indicator of increased commercialization is the widespread use of specific objects as standardized media of exchange (one important function of money). While several different objects are mentioned in the sources as "money," these are limited: cacao beans, white cotton capes, T-shaped bronze or copper axes, copper bells, feather quills filled with gold dust, salt, red shells, and precious stones. The first four items are mentioned most commonly by the sources and appear to have been accepted in exchanges over broad regions; this suggests a degree of standardization and economic agreement across diverse reaches of the world system. Hosler (chapter 21) particularly highlights the expanding use of metal objects as media of exchange, as well as serving storage-of-wealth and/or standard-of-value functions.

A third aspect of Mesoamerican commercialization is the increase in merchant activity. A suitable and sometimes extraordinary living could be gained from a career in trading. Aztec sources suggest that some professional merchants (pochteca) took considerable care to downplay their commercial successes and accumulated wealth (Sahagún 1950–1982, book 9). It is also here that we find an intersection between commercialized and political aspects of the economy. While many pochteca continued to gain economically, they also enjoyed privileged positions and roles within the political realm: some served as judges in the Tlatelolco marketplace, and some were entrusted with the ruler's goods for trade with foreign rulers in international trade centers. This heightened status of merchants in Postclassic society in central Mexico is paralleled by the already noble status of merchants in other parts of Mesoamerica (chapters 16, 22).

These aspects of Postclassic commercialization are explored at greater length in the next chapter.

KEY ECONOMIC UNITS IN POSTCLASSIC MESOAMERICA

In chapter 3 we outlined several spatial units that were key to the dynamics of the Postclassic Mesoamerican world's economy: international trade centers, markets, affluent production zones, and resource-extraction zones. In chapters 16–22 we examine these units in depth and consider their roles in this vigorous world system.

INTERNATIONAL TRADE CENTERS

International trade centers were key economic junctures in the Postclassic Mesoamerican world system. Not to be confused with the Polanyi/Chapman conception of ports of trade (Chapman 1957), these trade centers provided relatively safe and profitable venues for commercial activity at all levels, but were especially attractive to merchants traveling over long distances. Part of their attractiveness derived from the intensity of activity: high volumes of a wide range of goods passed through these centers. The expansion of international trade centers and their activities during the Postclassic is highly suggestive of increased economic interactions on a broad scale in Mesoamerica (chapter 17).

The importance of any specific center waxed and waned with the political and military fortunes of polities within the world system. Thus, for example, while we consider that Cohuaxtlahuacan qualified as an international trade center prior to its conquest by the Aztec empire, it subsequently lost that significance. Nonetheless, it appears that a center like Cholula, which combined economic and religious functions (as a pilgrimage site), weathered these political fluctuations quite well.

MARKETS

Markets were the lifeblood of the economic exchange system in Postclassic Mesoamerica. They ranged from small local affairs to the bustling cosmopolitan marketplace of Tlatelolco in the Late Postclassic (see above). Some markets on boundaries between core areas and between subsystems served interregional exchange functions and are of special interest in terms of world-system integration. At these locales, all levels of marketing (local, regional, and long-distance) took place, allowing goods to funnel vertically along the social and settlement scales as well as horizontally across regions.

AFFLUENT PRODUCTION ZONES

Affluent production zones were areas with dense populations, and whose economic activities were intimately linked to international exchange networks. Many of these areas were especially productive agricultural zones, while others produced more-specialized goods such as fine salt (chapter 19) and cacao (chapter 35). Recognition of these zones highlights the important notion that intense economic activity and commercialization were not monopolized by cores but were dispersed throughout the world system (chapter 16).

RESOURCE-EXTRACTION ZONES

Resource-extraction zones were located in politically peripheral areas where nonagricultural raw materials were obtained. We focus on zones that produced raw materials for the manufacture of key commodities in the Mesoamerican world system (chapter 18). The particular illustrative cases included in this section focus on salt (chapter 19), obsidian (chapter 20), and metal (chapter 21). Other extraction zones of special interest in this world system include concentrations of marine resources, chert, and greenstone. While extraction of all of these materials was by necessity localized, the raw materials or manufactured objects were desired and distributed broadly throughout the world system.

An interesting aspect of the Postclassic Mesoamerican economy is the apparent lack of direct political control of certain key resource-extraction zones. This is the case with mines in western Mexico (chapter 21), obsidian throughout Mesoamerica (chapter 20), and high-quality salt in northern Yucatán (chapter 19). While local poli-ties may have exercised some control over production arrangements, larger polities do not seem to have made major efforts to gain control over these resource areas. In the case of obsidian, Braswell (chapter 20) suggests that extraction and distribution were more the result of demand than political control, citing the politically peripheral location of obsidian sources, the uneven directional pattern of distribution from the sources, and a lack of obvious central places controlling the extraction locales. Generalizations, however, are still elusive since the archaeological evidence suggests a range of mechanisms—from local markets to regional markets to local elites—impacting the extraction and distribution of this important commodity (chapter 20).

CONCLUSION

As the Postclassic era progressed, economic expansion was accompanied by increased competition among the elite. This was manifested, at least in part, by an increase in reciprocity and gift-giving activities designed to solidify alliances and enhance political position (chapter 22). The pattern was widespread throughout the world system and added a further dimension to the system's economic integration. The competitive elite gift-exchange system not only provided a mechanism for establishing political linkages, but also stimulated the production and exchange of increasing quantities of luxury goods. The economic dimensions of this world system were intricately linked with political and social networks, as well as symbolic and informational realms (discussed in detail in part 4).

16

An International Economy

Frances F. Berdan, Marilyn A. Masson, Janine Gasco, and Michael E. Smith

The economy of Middle and Late Postclassic Meso-america was truly an international one. No single polity was self-sufficient (chapter 4), and no local or regional economic system was cut off from long-distance exchange networks. The expansion of commercial exchange throughout Mesoamerica—coupled with the intensification of intercommunication through symbols, styles, and codices—helped forge Mesoamerica into a single integrated economy. The tentacles of this international economy reached far into every Postclassic society, affecting not only political dynamics but also class structure, farming, religion, and numerous other institutions and processes that affected people's lives. This situation—an international economy that crossed political borders and affected myriad aspects of life for the bulk of the population—is the hallmark of ancient world systems. In this chapter we describe the contours of that economy.

LAND AND LABOR

The bases for wealth and power in ancient Mesoamerica lay in land and labor. In this essentially agrarian economy, control over land and its yields not only embellished one's lifestyle, but also signaled political power. As noted in chapter 1, land and labor were more directly under the control of nobles and kings than were the institutions and processes of exchange.

INTENSIVE AGRICULTURE
The Middle and Late Postclassic periods were a time of unprecedented agricultural intensification in many parts of Mesoamerica. In central Mexico, a record-level population surge led to the transformation of the entire landscape as hills, plains, and swamps were all turned into productive plots for growing maize and other crops. By

1519 virtually every non-mountainous area saw the construction of some combination of irrigation canals, raised fields, terraces, and house gardens, as well as fields for rainfall agriculture (Donkin 1979; Doolittle 1990; Evans 1990; López 1991). Recent simulations of population and carrying capacity in the Basin of Mexico suggest that agricultural intensification did not keep up with population growth, at least in the Basin of Mexico piedmont zone (Whitmore and Williams 1998). The pattern of Postclassic agricultural intensification was repeated in other areas, including Guerrero (Armillas 1949), Oaxaca (Winter 1985; Woodbury and Neely 1972), and the Tarascan realm (Fisher et al. 1999; Street-Perrott et al. 1989; see also Rojas Rabiela 1985).

Agricultural features such as terraces, irrigation systems, and raised fields required considerable labor investment. The application of comparative and theoretical models to archaeological and ethnohistorical data suggests that terrace agriculture was most likely organized on the household level, whereas irrigation fields were more likely subject to some form of state or elite supervision (see Smith 1996a:59–79). The case for chinampas is less clear; there is less comparative data, and the archaeological remains have yet to be analyzed in much detail. Chinampas may have been built and farmed under direct state control or as privately held estates owned by the nobility, or they may have been under the control of local communities (Brumfiel 1991; Parsons 1991; Smith 1996a:78–79).

LAND TENURE
In highland central and west Mexico, territoriality generally was directly associated with dynastic rulership. In central Mexico, some agricultural lands were designated for special purposes: *tlatocatlalli* were lands supporting the ruler, *teopantlalli* supported temples, and *milchimalli*

supported the army. In addition, *tecpantlalli* were lands belonging to the palaces of high-ranking nobles, *pillalli* were the patrimonial lands of the nobility, and *calpulalli* were lands pertaining to commoners residing in calpolli (Harvey 1984:84). Much of the land, and the labor required to make it productive, appears to have been controlled by persons occupying elevated political positions, by religious institutions, or by more communally oriented residential groups. The precise nature of communal control is unclear, however. This pattern from central Mexico compares fairly closely with that of the Tarascans of west Mexico, where lands in the core region were held by the state "to produce food directly consumed by the royal household, upper nobility, and temple attendants" (Pollard 1993:118).

This pattern contrasts significantly with the apparent pattern among the Maya. In Yucatán, land and labor were controlled through lineages, some of them merchant lineages (chapter 6). Similarly, highland Guatemalan K'iche'an land and labor were defined through "great houses," which combined lineality, residence, and territoriality (chapter 5). Among the Tzotzil and Tzeltal of highland Chiapas (Calnek 1988:17–18), much of the land may have been administered by the community as a whole, with communal lands subdivided into lineage holdings which were further subdivided into individual parcels, or *calaghibal*. Higher-ranking towns—city-states, or cabeceras—claimed the rights to certain commodities (e.g., salt, cacao, and perhaps cotton) produced in subject towns as well as tribute in subsistence goods. In addition, high-ranking nobles apparently held private lands that were worked by individuals attached to the land. Finally, the nobility may have also controlled other lands (called "office-lands" by Calnek) where crops such as maize and beans were grown for consumption by noble households; labor on these lands may have been a special form of tribute.

In Oaxaca the Mixtec land-tenure system placed land under the jurisdiction of aristocrats heading local, kin-based kingdoms (Spores 1967). A similar system is suggested for Zapotec kingdoms in the Valley of Oaxaca, where early colonial caciques controlled large territories that they presumably had also held in the Late Postclassic period (Appel 1982b:85–96; Oudijk 2000). The estates of local lords included agricultural lands worked by landless tenants, and other resources such as salt deposits and stone quarries. It is not clear if other lands were held, individually or communally, by non-nobles.

Warfare and conquest were persistent themes throughout Postclassic Mesoamerica. It was a customary and expected pattern for some of a conquered community's lands to be yielded to its conqueror, the dominating ruler then rewarding his valiant supporters with grants of these same lands (P. Carrasco 1999:37–39, 59, 145). Conquered communities typically were also required to make tribute payments to their new masters. The complex and fluctuating history of warfare resulted, for any city-state, in a mosaic of control over land, tributes, and labor drafts: some control resided with the local ruler, some with a conquering ruler, some with an earlier conqueror, some with esteemed noble warriors—all of whom doubtless also held lands in other city-states (P. Carrasco 1999; Gibson 1971).

CRAFT PRODUCTION

Beyond basic subsistence needs, Postclassic Mesoamerican peoples enhanced and embellished raw materials to produce a wide variety of utilitarian and luxury objects. These production processes entailed considerable knowledge, training, and labor organization.

SPECIALIZATION AND THE ORGANIZATION OF PRODUCTION
The commercialized international economy of Late Postclassic Mesoamerica was based in part on a high level of specialized craft production. Here we break the concept of specialization into several separate dimensions in order to explore the variation in Postclassic production processes. Our scheme follows that of Costin (1991).

Intensity of Production
Although one of the first questions often asked about craft production and specialization concerns the intensity of the labor input—was it full-time or part-time?—this is one of the most difficult dimensions to document with archaeological and historical data. Nevertheless, a number of patterns have been suggested for Postclassic production intensity. In an influential paper, Brumfiel (1987b) suggested that in Aztec central Mexico artisans producing luxury goods—featherwork, jewelry, sculpture— were urban-based full-time specialists attached to elite patrons, whereas many producers of utilitarian goods— pottery, basketry, stone tools—were rural part-time producers who worked independently and marketed their own goods. In ethnographic and historical accounts of many peasant societies, part-time rural craft production is taken up to compensate for declining land access or declining yields (Cook 1982; Kellenbenz 1974; Thirsk 1961), and this is a likely context for the development of rural craft production in many parts of Postclassic Mesoamerica. Although documentary sources in central Mexico and Yucatán list numerous specialists (Brumfiel 1998; Clark and Houston 1998; Rojas 1986), it is often not clear whether individuals practiced their specialties full-time or part-time.

Scale of Production
In Postclassic Mesoamerica the scale of production ranged from the household to the workshop. Many important commodities were produced at the household

level rather than at the workshop or industrial scales. The lowest level of production, termed "household production" by Peacock (1982), involves production at home for domestic consumption within the household. Although low levels of household production probably existed for a variety of utilitarian goods, this kind of production for use has fewer external economic connections and implications than do the larger-scale and more complex patterns of production for exchange.

Household production for exchange, termed "household industry" in Peacock's scheme, was widely practiced. Redundancy in production activities among Postclassic domestic zones within individual communities is a common observable pattern (Masson 2000a). Production of commodities such as textiles and ceramics was probably done at home on a part-time basis, with a small surplus destined for external exchange (chapters 32 and 34). Chert and chalcedony stone tool production in Belize, for example, was a home-based, part-time craft activity (Michaels 1987, 1994; Michaels and Shafer 1994). Other types of local production were carried out in marketplaces on demand. For instance, Feldman (1978:11) suggests that retail merchants in the highland Maya area produced and sold goods such as obsidian blades on this basis. Petty producers in Aztec markets performed similar activities (Anderson et al. 1976), and the presence of crucibles for smelting copper on the Maya trading canoe encountered by Columbus (chapter 1) suggests a similar pattern.

An example of variable specialization at the household level can be seen at the small Mayan island settlement of Laguna de On, where all domestic areas that were extensively tested yielded possible evidence of ceramic production in the form of features that might have been potting hearths (Masson 2000a). All domestic areas had spindle whorls. One area had greater proportions of lithic debris than other domestic zones, and another area had greater proportions of marine shell debris. No exclusive distributions of production or consumption debris were noted in areas tested at this settlement (chapter 34). These data suggest that household production was variable within this community. It is difficult to gauge the volume of production or the amount of surplus generated by each household, but the amount of debris is not great and suggests that cottage industries supported other activities of household maintenance at this small rural location. Similar patterns of low-level domestic craft production are reported at Aztec-period sites in Morelos (chapter 32).

A larger scale of production existed for several urban craft industries in central Mexico. The city-state center of Otumba had numerous areas with high concentrations of the remains of production of obsidian blades, bifaces, jewelry, figurines and other ceramic objects, and textiles of maguey fibers (Charlton et al. 1991; Nichols 1994;

Otis Charlton 1993). The localization of the artifact concentrations suggests either intensive household production or else workshops for these products. Many of the full-time luxury artisans working in Tenochtitlan were probably organized on a workshop level as well. Even so, the Codex Mendoza (Berdan and Anawalt 1992:3: f. 70r) suggests that luxury-craft skills were handed down within family units.

Some industries, such as obsidian extraction and salt production, were highly specialized, and their production approached an industrial scale (chapters 19, 20). These industries are archaeologically conspicuous because of the large quantities of debris and specialized facilities associated with production. An argument has been made that utilitarian ceramics in the Mayan area were mass-produced during the Postclassic period, since their form attributes are highly standardized (Rathje 1975; Sabloff and Rathje 1975b). These authors suggest that the standardization of ceramic form and the configuration of footed bowls were conducive to the transport of these artifacts in exchange around the Yucatán Peninsula. However, subsequent analysis of ceramic pastes has revealed that ceramics were made locally by most communities (Rice 1980), probably at the household level (Masson 2000a), and mass-production facilities for ceramic manufacture have yet to be located at any site. Increased standardization of paste attributes in areas such as the Petén may signify the monopolization of production by fewer specialized producers (Rice 1980). Many utilitarian and ritual ceramic forms bear close similarities at Postclassic Maya sites across the peninsula after A.D. 1150. This pattern is probably due to intensified economic interaction between the northern and southern lowlands after this time.

Concentration of Production

This dimension of specialization concerns the physical location of production facilities. Brumfiel's (1987b) model of Aztec rural utilitarian crafts and urban luxury crafts, mentioned above, is relevant here. It is clear that throughout Postclassic Mesoamerica many crafts were produced in both rural and urban settings. There was considerable variation among Postclassic cities in the scale or concentration of craft industries. For example, consider Otumba, Huexotla, and Yautepec, all Aztec city-state towns of equivalent size and political status. Otumba was a major industrial center (Charlton et al. 1991), Huexotla had few craft industries beyond the ubiquitous textile production (Brumfiel 1980, 1987a), and Yautepec had a level of production intermediate between the two (chapter 32). Yautepec, in turn, had considerably more craft activity than rural sites in Morelos such as Cuexcomate and Capilco.

The concentrated production of particular goods in certain residential districts has been documented in the archaeological record and from ethnohistorical accounts for a variety of crafts: the preparation of maguey cloth (Nichols 1994; Otis Charlton 1994), the working of obsidian objects (Otis Charlton 1993:160; Charlton 1994: 239), the fabrication of shell ornaments (chapter 34), and the fashioning of fine feathered items and manufacturing of precious stone and metal ornaments (Sahagún 1950–1982, book 9). The craft industries at Otumba varied in spatial location and concentration. For instance, obsidian core-blade and basalt workshops were scattered about the area, while lapidary, figurine, and maguey fiber workshops tended to be concentrated, perhaps into individual calpolli (Nichols 1994:182–183). With the exception of the centralized obsidian core-blade workshops, industries were located in residential areas, suggesting household-based production concentrated in specific community sections. Given their locations, these specialists were most likely independent operators rather than attached to elite patrons, and much of their production probably circulated through the region's lively marketplaces (Nichols 1994:184–186; Otis Charlton 1994). One exception may have been the lapidary specialists, who might have produced luxury objects for elite patrons (Otis Charlton 1994:198).

The Production Process
This dimension of specialization, not dealt with by Costin (1991), concerns issues such as the segmentation of tasks, level of standardization, and the volume of output. In complex economies like that of Postclassic Mesoamerica, the production of certain goods was frequently not limited to a single location. In many instances, a raw material was developed, altered, improved, and embellished in successive stages by different specialists on its way to becoming a finished and highly desired commodity. Consider, for example, the production of cotton clothing, a crucial commodity in the Postclassic world system. The evidence for cotton fiber and cloth production suggests a complex set of spatially separated sequences carried out across diverse regions.

While many inland valley areas of highland Mesoamerica qualified as cotton-growing areas (e.g., in present-day Morelos state), cotton was most widely grown along the coastal strips and long river valleys stretching inland from the Gulf and the Pacific. Cotton spinning and weaving, however, extended broadly across diverse ecological regions, from highland to lowland locales (with spindle whorls for cotton spinning being found widely across all inhabited elevations). Raw cotton was moved to spinners and weavers by the farmers and by long-distance merchants of the *oztomeca* variety (Berdan 1987b, 1988). The context for exchange was most likely the many marketplaces in both the highlands and lowlands. Indeed, in Aztec times an especially lively

marketplace for cotton was at Acazacatlan, a highland community in the eastern Sierra.

Cotton cloth was often creatively and painstakingly embellished. Adornments included spun rabbit fur, spun feathers, and dyed threads for embroidery. Spun rabbit fur and the spun feathers of "ordinary birds" such as ducks and turkeys were sold in the Late Postclassic period at the grand Tlatelolco marketplace and may have been purchased there by the weaver herself. These embellishments also may have been added by the purchaser (or producer) of a plain cotton cloth who might then personalize the item or create a designated piece of tribute cloth or an item for further sale. This entire process is not fully understood, but it does appear that, at a specific level, the rabbit fur merchant also specialized in dying those furs (Sahagún 1950–1982, book 10:77), that dyes were produced and sold independently of spun threads (10:77), and that the marketplace seller of spun turkey and duck feathers also spun those feathers (10: 92). So the creation of these embellishments involved specialists beyond the cotton spinners and weavers themselves.

Similar complexities in production processes can be seen for other commodities, particularly those destined for elite consumers, such as fine feathered adornments and valuable stone or metal jewelry. Each step and exchange of hands, of course, increased item's value (and cost).

Social Context of Production
Variation according to social status can be seen throughout Mesoamerica in the social context of various types of production. For instance, the distribution of spindle whorls at the highland Maya site of Canajaste suggests that spinning may have been an elite activity (Blake 1985:320), whereas at most Mesoamerican sites, virtually every domestic unit was engaged in spinning and probably weaving (Fauman-Fichman 1999; Masson 2000a, 2002). Ethnohistoric documentation stresses that every woman in Mesoamerica was expected to spin and weave (Berdan 1987a); some elite households may show a greater abundance of that activity due to polygynous practices.

In highland Mesoamerica some specialized production appears to have come under the control of specific groups, although "monopoly" is too strong a word to use. This is particularly the case in the production of luxury wares, which tended to be concentrated in urban contexts and performed by full-time specialists, sometimes under the sponsorship of elite patrons (Brumfiel 1987b). It is not surprising that producers of precious stone ornaments, shining metal jewelry, and fine featherwork would become concentrated and controlled: the raw materials were expensive, the training undoubtedly intensive, and the standards of elite consumers high.

PRODUCTION AND COMMODITIES
Production processes can also be analyzed in terms of the types of commodities produced.

Local Utilitarian Production
The local production of utilitarian commodities is represented in the manufacture of items such as everyday textiles, ceramics, stone tools (of chert, chalcedony, and other local raw material), fishing implements, animal or plant products, and grinding stones. This type of production occurred at the household level in most communities, with variation according to locally available resources. It also tended to rely on generalized knowledge and skills, and while there was some specialization, this was not extensive. (Perhaps the greatest amount of specialization was found in ceramic production, which required a significant outlay of equipment such as kilns.) The variations in resource availability led to intercommunity exchange in areas such as central Mexico, Oaxaca, and northern Belize (Berdan et al. 1996; McAnany 1991). Many commodities were circulated first through local market exchange before entering the long-distance (including maritime) trade network for more distant destinations.

Luxury Goods
By at least the Late Postclassic in the Basin of Mexico, luxury goods were produced in both workshops and households, and those households were incorporated into broader residential organizations (see chapter 18 for further discussion of luxury commodities). These urban residential "guilds" regulated membership, controlled quality in production, provided training, and involved their members in specific religious activities (Sahagún 1950–1982, book 9). They included, most notably, the featherworkers, fine lapidaries, and metalworkers (of gold and silver). In Oaxaca, where such artisanship attained a remarkable level of sophistication, luxury artisans were members of the nobility (chapter 22). In northern Belize, there are very few categories of locally produced luxuries represented in the archaeological record. Indeed, luxuries in the Maya area were often imported (Kepecs et al. 1994). Shell jewelry and carved bone are possible luxury goods produced in the eastern Maya lowlands at sites like Laguna de On (Masson 1999a, 2000a, 2002), and Colha (Dreiss 1994), and shell ornaments were imported into zones such as the Maya highlands in completed form (Blake 1985:332).

Production for Long-Distance Exchange
Production geared toward long-distance exchange can be seen where relatively unique or superior resources were concentrated and were in demand at distant destinations as well as locally. Salt, obsidian, and cloth were utilitarian items that fell into this category for both central

Mexican and Mayan areas. Other products such as cacao, honey, wax, dyes, and animal products also were produced for intra-lowland and international exchange in the Mayan area (Blom 1932; Piña Chán 1978), and commodities such as cochineal, copal, and paper moved in a similar fashion in central Mexico (Berdan 1988). Variation existed in the scale of salt and other commodity production at different localities (chapter 19). For the most part, salt, obsidian, and cloth were probably produced for export in greater quantities than other commodities due to a high continuous demand for these items. Granitic or basalt metates from highland Maya areas are another category of utilitarian item that was exchanged to the lowlands and to coastal ports, although in lesser quantities than other long-distance commodities destined for daily use. Luxury goods also were manufactured for long-distance exchange, though in smaller quantities (see below).

COMMERCIAL EXCHANGE

The Postclassic commercial economy entailed systems of transport, markets, money, traders and merchants, and international trade centers. Together these yielded vigorous economic interrelationships linking diverse polities and regions throughout the Mesoamerican world.

TRANSPORT
The technology of transportation in ancient Mesoamerica was quite rudimentary. Water transport using dugout canoes (like the ones encountered by Columbus and other European explorers; see discussion below) was relatively efficient but was largely limited to coastal routes (Edwards 1978) since only a few navigable rivers followed trade routes (Lee and Navarrete 1978). Overland transport costs, however, were quite high. Although the concept of the wheel was known—as evidenced in wheeled toys (Diehl and Mandeville 1987)—it was not put to work for transport purposes because of the lack of appropriate draft animals and the difficulties of the mountainous terrain in many areas (Hassig 1985). Thus on overland routes all goods had to be carried on people's backs.

These transport cost factors had several implications for the increased exchange in the Late Postclassic economy. First, specialized groups of burden-bearers assumed important roles in commercial transport. Overland carriers, called *tlameme* in Nahuatl, became prominent in Aztec trade (Hassig 1985), and Maya merchants used slaves as canoe paddlers. Second, most long-distance trade goods were high-value luxury items and special nonluxuries with high levels of demand and relatively low bulk, such as obsidian and high-grade salt.

Energetic reconstructions show the inefficiency of transporting bulky goods such as grain, ceramics, or ground stone over large distances, leading Drennan (1984a, 1984b) to postulate that long-distance ceramic exchange was never very extensive in ancient Mesoamerica. Smith (1990) responded that this is an empirical issue, and that in Postclassic central Mexico large quantities of decorated ceramics were exchanged over long distances (see also Smith 2001a; Smith, Neff, and Fauman-Fichman 1999). The fact that interregional ceramic exchange was so widespread, and that imported ceramic vessels were present in virtually all Middle and Late Postclassic commoner households (chapter 32), are indications of the high level of commercialized exchange in the Postclassic economy.

MARKET SYSTEMS AND MONEY

Marketplaces were a prominent feature of the Postclassic Mesoamerican landscape. Unfortunately, marketplaces leave little in the way of archaeological remains, and their presence and importance are largely gleaned from Late Postclassic documentary sources that portray the situation as it existed immediately prior to the arrival of the Spaniards. At that time, marketplaces were found throughout Mesoamerica but were especially common in regions that encouraged specialized production of a variety of products and hence required a venue for exchange of considerable quantities of utilitarian and luxury goods. Other regions were less diversified, yet the localization of important resources led to specialization of production in these areas as well.

Marketplaces varied in scale, function, and range. The largest and most diversified market in Mesoamerica in the Late Postclassic was at Tlatelolco, sister-city of the Mexica capital of Tenochtitlan. This metropolitan market may have served 20,000–25,000 people daily and 40,000–50,000 on every fifth day (Anonymous Conqueror 1971:392). Institutionally, this market contained judges and supervisors to assure order (possibly high-ranking members of the professional merchant "guilds") and other officials to collect taxes on vendors. This was a multipurpose market serving the luxury needs of the most discriminating noble as well as the everyday needs of virtually anyone. Vendors ranged from well-traveled, professional high-status merchants who offered precious feathers and valuable stones, to regional merchants carrying bulky cotton and cacao from lowland sources, to local vendors who traded small lots of goods such as chiles, pottery, and firewood.

While the Tlatelolco market was an economic attraction, it was not the only trading venue. Specialized markets developed reputations for the availability and quality of certain products: dogs at Acolman; ceramics, cloth, and fine gourds at Texcoco; slaves at Azcapotzalco and Itzocan; and turkeys at Otumba and Tepepulco (Berdan 1985:346–349). Durán (1971:278) states that these specialized sites were established through adminis-trative policy. However, those policies evidently did not dictate monopolies as all of the products listed above were common in markets throughout Mesoamerica.

Other markets enjoyed brisk activity and the attendance of local, regional, and long-distance merchants. Some of these, located along the fringes of major polities, can be considered borderland phenomena and exhibited some ambiguous characteristics of international trade centers. These included large markets at Cholula and Tepeacac along the Tlaxcalan/Aztec border in the early sixteenth century, at Coaixtlahuacan in Oaxaca in the mid-fifteenth century (Berdan 1985:354–355), and at Xicalanco on the Gulf coast (chapter 17). In the Mixteca Alta, and perhaps in the Valley of Oaxaca as well, borderland markets enabled populations of adjacent polities to exchange goods without having to cross each other's territory, and they may have also been linked to periodic religious celebrations and pilgrimages (Pohl et al. 1997).

Some markets are particularly interesting for how they integrated economic exchange with religion and politics. Cholula, for instance, was an important commercial and pilgrimage center that was also subject to some political manipulation when its market, like that of nearby Tepeacac, was required to stock jewels, precious stones, and fine featherwork (Durán 1971:278). While Cholula also drew travelers with religious goals, both it and Tepeacac also must have been havens for long-distance merchants dealing in high-value merchandise. These two markets were subject to political dictates that stimulated transregional trade and strongly encouraged professional merchants to cross politically defined borders.

Fairs were annual markets that integrated religious, commercial, and social activities (on fairs in general, see Allix 1922; Abu-Lughod 1989:51–75). Well known to the early explorers from Europe, fairs were mentioned from various parts of Mesoamerica. Freidel's (1981b: 378–381) pilgrimage–market fair model, featuring regularly scheduled calendrical festivities organized by community leaders, describes these important occasions for trade and exchange. Religious pilgrimage was closely linked to mercantile activity at the site of Cozumel (Freidel and Sabloff 1984). Feldman (1985:14, 56) also proposed that fairs were held on ritual occasions to promote trade between central Mexican traders and private traders from the Guatemalan highlands. References to markets in Tabasco associated with huge fairs and religious sanctuaries for pilgrimage are noted by Lee (1978:56; see also Blom 1932:545–546). Other market towns at the time of Spanish contact were of great commercial import but did not combine sacred and secular attributes. Freidel (1981b:381) refers to towns such as Chauaca and Conil as purely market towns where the primary activity was trade. Some markets observed in the Guatemalan highlands as early as the 1540s were held on a daily basis, and political officials presided to resolve disputes (Feldman 1978:12). Kepecs (chapter 33) reviews documentary evidence for markets and commercialization in Late Postclassic Yucatán.

The documentation of market exchange in the archaeological record is not easy. Marketplaces are quite elusive at archaeological sites, and in their effort to distinguish market exchange from other, more politically controlled forms of exchange, archaeologists have recently turned their attention to the effects of different exchange systems on household inventories. Hirth (1998) and Smith (1999) have argued that marketplace exchange results in the distribution of high-value goods to many households, irrespective of social class. In contrast, elite gift exchange and other politically controlled exchange systems distribute luxury goods exclusively to elites. In applications of this approach, Smith (chapter 32) and Masson (chapter 34) find such nonexclusive distributions of imported luxury goods (i.e., at both commoner and elite residential contexts) at sites in Morelos and northern Belize.

Market exchanges were facilitated by the use of various types of money as media of exchange. The most commonly mentioned money form was cacao beans, which served as widely distributed "small change." Although cacao was grown in various lowland areas (Bergmann 1969), Soconusco was the leading producer in Postclassic times (chapter 35). The use of cacao as money is known from central Mexico (Rojas 1998) to Yucatán (Piña Chán 1978) and as far south as Nicaragua, where Oviedo y Valdés described cacao beans as follows: "They guard them and hold them in the same price and esteem as the Christians hold gold or coin; because these almonds are regarded as such by them, as they can buy all things with them" (Oviedo y Valdés 1853:1:316, in Tozzer 1941:95 n. 417).

Exchanges of more highly valued goods were facilitated by the broadly accepted *quachtli*, or large white cotton capes (Rojas 1998). Another significant money form was the T-shaped bronze or copper "money-axe," which may have served not only as a medium of exchange, but also as a standard of value and a storage of wealth, albeit in a more restricted geographic arena (chapter 21). For Yucatán, Landa and other sources mention the use of various items as money: copper bells, T-shaped copper axes, red shells (perhaps *Spondylus* sp.), precious stones, and cacao (Piña Chán 1978:43). In highland western Guatemala, salt was noted as a form of money alongside cacao, textiles, and copper axes (Feldman 1985:21–23). The presence of these various forms of money in the Mesoamerican world system is another indicator of the high level of commercialization of the Postclassic economy. In addition, the development of money forms suggests some standardization in exchange processes across the world system.

MERCHANTS

Starting with their very first contacts with Mesoamerican peoples, the European explorers were impressed with native merchants, who ranged widely and carried a diversity of commodities along coastal routes. The canoe encountered by Columbus (chapter 1), with 25 people and a large supply of trade goods, was sufficiently noteworthy to be recorded in several written accounts (see Edwards 1978:199–204; Sauer 1966:128–129). Two decades later Cortés encountered a trade canoe loaded down with salt and maize that had just left from a "canoe port" along the north coast of Honduras (Edwards 1978:204).

Merchants from Xicalanco, an international trade center (chapter 17) along the Gulf coast, complained to Cortés that their trade with the east coast of Yucatán had been disrupted by Spanish activities. These coastal merchants had a broad knowledge of distant peoples and places; the first notice the Spaniards had of the Pueblo peoples of New Mexico came from a merchant's report to Nuño de Guzmán on the Gulf coast near Pánuco (Sauer 1966:129). The goods carried in the dugout canoes were all key commodities in the Postclassic world system: cacao, copper axe-money, copper/bronze bells, obsidian tools and weapons, decorated textiles, and salt (chapter 18).

Early descriptions from diverse areas of Mesoamerica suggest the existence of two types of professional merchants in many areas: high-status merchants who traded in luxury goods and were either members of the nobility or belonged to guilds that restricted membership; and regional merchants of lower status who often specialized in fewer commodities traded within individual regions. In addition, many market vendors were part-time, petty traders who sold goods produced by themselves or by their families; these individuals can be considered a third type of merchant. These three types are documented most fully in sources from the Basin of Mexico, but evidence from other areas suggests that similar patterns held in most of Mesoamerica.

Petty Vendors

At the smallest scale were local individuals marketing small quantities of their own surplus production, including relatively inexpensive commodities such as foodstuffs, herbs, pottery, baskets, and firewood. In these cases, household producers engaged in marketing as part of their overall economic strategies and typically did not travel far to attend a market. Early descriptions of the Tlatelolco market suggest that most of the sellers were petty vendors of this type, and Sahagún (1950–1982, book 9) provides the names and descriptions of many types of petty vendors. In highland Guatemala, petty vendors (termed "retailers" by Feldman [1985]) known as *ajaqabali* in Kaqchikel were also "the most common of all merchants" (Feldman 1985:21). These included artisans (such as obsidian workers) who made their products to order in the marketplace. Petty vendors are suggested for Tarascan markets in the *Relación de Michoacán* (Pollard 1993:113).

Regional Merchants

Beyond these many individuals were full-time regional traders who carried more-valuable goods across regions, traveling from market to market in an effort to gain a profit (Berdan 1988). The presence of a large number of these merchants (called *tlanecuilo* in Nahuatl) is indicative of the high degree of commercialization in the Mesoamerican world system. These merchants were instrumental in moving large quantities of "bulk luxuries" such as cotton, cacao, and salt over considerable distances and rough terrain, making these commodities broadly available beyond their more restricted production zones (chapter 33).

In his description of highland Guatemala, Feldman (1985:20–21) calls these merchants "petty traders." Compared to the high-status merchants, regional merchants made shorter trips and often dealt in a single commodity such as salt. The cotton vendors and fishmongers in Yucatán mentioned by Landa (Tozzer 1941:53 n. 294) were probably regional merchants, as were the itinerant peddlers described by Roys (1943:51–52) who carried their own packs (chapter 33). Pollard (1993:171–172) notes that neither Aztec pochteca nor Tarascan state merchants—both high-status merchants—crossed the Tarascan/Aztec border, and thus the cross-border exchange discussed in chapter 14 was probably in the hands of regional merchants—perhaps Otomí or Matlatzinca peoples—from the border area.

High-Status Merchants

This category of merchant received the most attention by early writers. In Aztec central Mexico, the high-status merchant category is represented by the pochteca, professional merchants who resided in specific calpolli in several Basin of Mexico cities. Membership in the pochteca organization was strictly limited. These merchants were not only successful entrepreneurs, but also very well connected politically. The Tlatelolco merchants, for instance, carried merchandise on expeditions on their own behalf as well as for the Mexica ruler, who, it appears, used these individuals as diplomatic envoys to extra-empire trade centers (Sahagún 1950–1982, book 9). In addition, these merchants were politically active in serving as spies (*oztomeca*) for the Mexica ruler and in overseeing the largest marketplace in the realm, Tlatelolco (Berdan 1978). The pochtecas' status was somewhat ambiguous in Aztec society: they were of commoner birth, but they provided essential goods and significant services to the state and to nobles, and many of them were accumulating enviable wealth by the time of the Spanish arrival. Less is known about Tarascan high-status merchants, but available information suggests even closer links to the state; indeed, Pollard (1993:119) calls these traders "state long-distance merchants."

In other parts of Mesoamerica high-status merchants were members of the elite. Many polities in Yucatán, for example, were ruled by merchants. We know of a Cocom lord who avoided the massacre at Mayapán because he was away on a trading expedition to Honduras (Roys 1962:33). Piña Chán (1978:44) quotes Herrera y Tordesillas as follows: "In this land of Acalan, they used to make the wealthiest merchant the lord, and thus it was Apoxpalon who had great trade…[and] agents in many towns where fairs were held." Two Maya terms for merchant are often mentioned, but it is not clear what these meant, nor how they correspond to our categories here: '*pplom*' meant "professional merchant," and '*ah pplom yoc*' meant "traveling merchant" (chapter 33).

In highland Guatemala, too, merchants were nobles. Chiapaneca lords, for example, went on long trading expeditions. The number of such high-status merchants in this area was quite low, suggesting restricted membership (Feldman 1985:20–21). In the small polities of the Mixtec and Zapotec areas of Oaxaca, merchants and luxury craftsmen were junior members of the nobility. The merchants undertook long expeditions to distant regions where they traded in luxury goods and the primary materials used in the manufacture of jewelry and other fine objects used for display, gifting, and bridewealth (chapter 22). The head merchant encountered by Columbus (chapter 1) was probably a high-status merchant, judging by the diversity of commodities carried, the size of the expedition (25 persons, including slave paddlers), and the haughty behavior of the head merchant when he first encountered the Europeans (Edwards 1978).

The cases reviewed above show two patterns for high-status merchants. In areas where small polities remained the sole political form, high-status merchants were members of the local nobility. In the Aztec and Tarascan empires, however, independent groups of high-status merchants came into existence. These merchants—the Aztec pochteca and Tarascan state merchants—served dual roles as agents of the state and as independent entrepreneurs. Several authors have suggested that in Aztec society the pochteca formed an emerging middle class between the nobility and the commoners (Sanders 1992; Hicks 1999).

INTERNATIONAL TRADE

Long-distance trade augmented and enhanced the availability of localized resources and manufactured goods among the many polities of the Mesoamerican world system. High-status merchants were the primary agents of this trade. While they traded in marketplaces throughout Mesoamerica, these entrepreneurs focused their energies at strategically located international trade centers that provided especially inviting and attractive venues for their commercial activities (chapter 17). At these locales, far-ranging merchants established and maintained contacts that transcended their own homelands, thus fostering an international flavor to the economy.

In the Maya area, such long-distance trading activity is known primarily through two sources of information: historical documents and the identification of exotic materials such as obsidian, greenstone (and other minerals), and metals at sites where they are not locally available. Ethnohistoric documents describe the circumpeninsular ties of northern Maya merchants (Scholes and Roys 1948:3; Sabloff and Rathje 1975b) and the travels of Aztec pochteca from highland bases to lowland trade centers (Sahagún 1950–1982, book 9). One example is the Cocom lord mentioned above who escaped assassination during the overthrow of Mayapán because he was away on a trading expedition to the Bay of Honduras. Trade centers were located around the peninsula during the Postclassic (chapter 17), and merchants who frequented these centers played an important role in distributing commodities produced in various territories of the Yucatán Peninsula as well as those obtained from more-distant locations.

The ports of Xicalanco and Potonchan were critical gateways between the Maya polities and those of the Gulf Coast, the isthmus, and highland Mexico (chapter 17). Merchant mercenaries from Tabasco were interested in the economy of the Maya peninsula, and their repeated interference with the regimes of Mayapán in northern Yucatán (Barrera and Morley 1949: table 6) attests to their desire to maintain political links that would promote international trade. While Mayapán exerted considerable power in the territories of northwestern Yucatán that surrounded it, its political control was weaker in territories of the northeast, the east coast, and the southern lowlands (Pollock 1962:11; Roys 1962). The site was influential in nonpolitical respects in these territories through promoting trade, forming political alliances, and disseminating religious doctrine that local elites adopted to promote their own prestige. Merchants in these eastern/southern territories probably negotiated their own trading relationships with Xicalanco (chapter 5).

Luxury items were major foci of long-distance interregional exchange. Cacao from Tabasco and Honduras was imported into northern Yucatán in substantial quantities for use as currency (Tozzer 1941:37; Scholes and Roys 1948:3; Bergmann 1969). Other luxuries imported into the Maya area were obsidian, gold, bronze, turquoise, dyed rabbit fur, and slaves (chapter 21). Luxury items traded from Xicalanco into the Aztec realm included tanned feline skins, carved tortoise shell, and precious stones such as amber and jade (Scholes and Roys 1948:29). While the international trade centers (chapter 17) served as lively exchange venues for luxury goods, they also were the scene of less prestigious exchanges. Aztec pochteca, for instance, carried trade goods attractive and appropriate to commoners as well as nobles from the Basin of Mexico to lowland Xicalanco (Sahagún 1950–1982, book 9).

In the Late Postclassic, merchants from the Basin of Mexico (and associated with Aztec imperial expansion) were particularly active. While most of these pochteca confined their entrepreneurial efforts to the imperial territory, others were granted special privileges to trade beyond the imperial boundaries in lucrative international trade centers such as Xicalanco. From the perspective of the Basin of Mexico, these merchants were especially active in acquiring high-value, low-bulk luxury objects and raw materials for consumption by the Aztec elite. These prestigious materials included tropical feathers, jaguar pelts, fine objects made of precious stones and metals, and cacao (see Berdan 1987b, 1992b). While these same products and goods were paid in tribute to the Aztecs by some of their richly endowed conquered provinces, this tribute was clearly not sufficient to meet the expanding standard of living of a burgeoning nobility.

POLITICALLY CONTROLLED EXCHANGE

Not all exchange in the Postclassic world system was open and commercialized. Ancient Mesoamerican forms of politically controlled exchange such as tribute and elite gift exchange continued to function in Postclassic times. One interesting feature of these exchange mechanisms in the Postclassic period was their close connection to commercialized exchange and the other institutions of the world system.

TRIBUTE

Tribute—a one-way, vertical transfer of goods and services—was the primary mechanism for financing expensive state enterprises and lavish standards of living for the elite. It also required an established hierarchy of officials to collect, record, and distribute this incessant flow of goods. Frequent and sustained military conflict in Postclassic times often resulted in the dominance of one city-state over others. One goal of such conquest was the exaction of tribute from subjugated peoples, and these demands accentuated the vertical movements of goods and services already entrenched in the hierarchical order of individual city-states themselves. In the best-documented example, at the time of Spanish contact the Aztec empire demanded regularly scheduled tribute payments from 38 conquered provinces and maintained "client" relations with 17 others (Berdan et al. 1996).

Such imperial tribute demands had important economic consequences. First, they stimulated an increase in local production in order to satisfy these additional requirements. Foodstuffs, textiles, raw materials, and specialized manufactures produced in the provinces were all transferred to the urbanized Basin of Mexico through tribute channels. This tribute had serious effects on donor areas. After Aztec conquest of the Cuauhnahuac area of Morelos, for example, the region experienced increased agricultural and textile production along with a decreased standard of living (chapter 32). Smith warns us, however, to also consider the possibility that other, more-localized economic processes may have contributed to the changes (Smith and Heath-Smith 1994).

A second significant consequence of imperial tribute imposition was the stimulation of long-distance exchange. Many tribute goods—particularly the elaborate feathered warriors' costumes—were manufactured from products that did not occur naturally in the tributary regions, and as a result provincial rulers or others had to engage in commercial exchange to obtain the products or raw materials demanded by the Aztec empire. Thus imperial tribute directly stimulated exchange in provincial areas; indeed this was part of a deliberate economic strategy on the part of the Aztec rulers (Berdan et al. 1996: 124, 135).

It should be kept in mind that, under Aztec hegemony, conquered nobles were obligated to give service and/or goods to a more powerful ruler, and conquered commoners paid in service and goods to not only their own rulership, but to the imperial powers as well. The quantities of goods and the extent of service moving vertically were considerable, but it is difficult to determine if the burdens were onerous. In one reconstruction of tribute levels from early Colonial documents, Smith (1994b) concluded that although imperial tribute in Morelos was modest at the household level (given the area's high population), the intermediate levels of tribute—to city-states and local nobles—were almost certainly quite a bit higher. Aztec imperial tribute quantities and collection procedures varied greatly by province, as documented in the Codex Mendoza (Berdan and Anawalt 1992). Variation in tribute among, or "gift giving" requirements for, Aztec client states ("strategic provinces") is summarized in chapter 6.

The Tarascan imperial administration appears somewhat more uniform and regular than that found in the Aztec empire. At the most basic level, tributes collected at the local level were partially allocated to the support of locally based state officials. The remaining amounts were passed on to regional centers, from where they were delivered to Tzintzuntzan or to military installations on the borderlands (chapter 13).

The centrally administered tribute systems of the Aztec and Tarascan empires contrast markedly with tribute in the smaller states of Oaxaca and the Maya region. None of the Late Postclassic Mixtec, Zapotec, or Maya polities held territories as large as those of the Aztecs or Tarascans, so tribute collection operated on a much smaller scale. Among the Mixtecs and Zapotecs the rulers of cacicazgos, or city-states, exacted tribute in goods and services from their subject populations; tribute was then redistributed to other members of the nobility, to religious and craft specialists, to servants and tenant farmers, and on ceremonial occasions to the population at large (Appel 1982a:139–141; Spores 1967, 1984; Oudijk 2000).

In Yucatán, tributes for the Middle-to-Late Postclassic Mayan polity of Mayapán included foodstuffs and clothing for the palace, military obligations, and other forms of service (Roys 1962:50). In the Guatemalan and Chiapas highlands, it is generally assumed that small Maya polities, as well as the expansionistic K'iche' polity, exacted tribute from subject communities. Several highland Guatemala polities controlled territories in the neighboring Pacific coastal lowlands, where they sent administrators to ensure the flow of tribute to the highland centers; tribute consisted of both goods and services (Orellana 1995:40–41). For highland Chiapas, there is little direct evidence regarding Postclassic tribute practices, but a sixteenth-century Tzeltal dictionary includes native words for "tribute payer," presumably referring to a Precolumbian social category (Calnek 1988:34).

GIFT EXCHANGE

Not all meaningful economic exchanges took place through markets or tribute channels. Elites frequently engaged in reciprocity and gift giving to solidify political relations and social standing. Throughout the Mesoamerican world system, the elevated status of elites was overtly exhibited, and one's achievements and social position were signaled with ostentatious displays of grandeur. Although no actual accounting exists, considerable quantities of luxuries must have passed hands as elite marriages were arranged, political alliances cemented, and a ruler's underlings rewarded for loyal service. Many of these transactions took place at restricted elite feasting events; Pohl (1994a, 1998a, 1999) has described these for the polities of the Mixteca-Puebla region (chapters 10, 22, 31); Smith (1986) and Brumfiel (1987b) review the evidence for feasting at Aztec imperial elite gatherings.

Some of this gift giving was relatively symmetrical, some asymmetrical. Gift giving among rulers of city-states appears to have been normative. Durán (1994:170, 340) describes two occasions in which rulers of enemy city-states were invited to Tenochtitlan by the Mexica ruler. The host impressed his recalcitrant visitors with lavish presents, including exquisitely worked clothing, sandals, featherwork, jewelry of gold and fine stones, and jaguar pelts. These gifts provided economic and display dimensions to the definition of social and political ties.

In asymmetrical contexts, cotton clothing was most commonly bestowed on underlings by rulers in a manner suggesting a personal payment for services. For instance, at differing events, the Mexica ruler bestowed clothing on priests for their role in religious ceremonies (e.g., Durán 1994:173, 306, 307) and on valiant warriors for their successful efforts on the battlefield (Sahagún 1950–1982, book 8). Other rulers presented Mexica emissaries with precious clothing, flowers, and tobacco (Durán 1994:333). Alonso de Zorita describes some of these events: "The lesser lords made gifts to the supreme ruler at certain festivals held every year; they did this in acknowledgement of their subjugation and vassalage.... When a festival had ended, the supreme ruler gave to the lesser lords, his vassals, and to the lords of neighboring towns who attended these festivals, rich cloaks and other presents, according to the quality of each lord. Thus these lords departed content and well rewarded for what they had brought" (Zorita 1963:188–189).

In imperial settings such as that described by Zorita, gift giving has a clear "display" dimension, but in areas where city-states were of a more equal standing, symmetrical reciprocity had the consequence of economically cementing meaningful social and political relationships (chapter 22). In either case, there were economic consequences beyond the more overt political aspects. In the first place, city-state rulers required sustained supplies of sumptuous luxuries for distribution, entailing the availability of precious raw materials and the "employment" of skilled artisans to fashion those materials into exquisite objects worth giving. For reliability, this may suggest a patron relationship. Second, highly valued luxuries changed hands across city-states and regions without the intervention of merchants, markets, or international trade centers. Despite the high degree of commercialization of the economy, other mechanisms for distributing goods operated in the Mesoamerican world system.

INTEGRATION OF THE ECONOMY

The Postclassic Mesoamerican economy was multidimensional. Economic units and processes were integrated and interwoven through political decisions and institutions, through commercialization and entrepreneurship, and through international relations and exchanges.

POLITICAL INVOLVEMENT IN THE ECONOMY

The degree of political control over the Postclassic Mesoamerican economy varied both by region and by economic sector. In some polities, particularly the Tarascan empire (chapters 13, 29) and the small states of the Mixteca-Puebla region (chapters 10, 22), many aspects of production and exchange were heavily influenced by political processes and institutions. In other areas, notably Aztec central Mexico and the Yucatán Peninsula, much of the economy was more open and commercialized. The greatest distinction in political control, however, was between economic sectors. In most Mesoamerican polities, land and labor were strongly controlled by nobles and the state, whereas most exchange processes (apart from tribute and gift exchange) were relatively autonomous of political control.

Throughout Postclassic Mesoamerica the basic economic factors of land and labor were predominately controlled by political leaders, whether they were city-state rulers and nobles (central and west Mexico), heads of lineages (the Maya area), or kin-based lords of kingdoms (Oaxaca). These elite with political power commanded rights to agricultural yields, personal services, and tribute in-kind from workers attached to those lands. These arrangements became more hierarchically complex following conquest, with suzerainty over conquered lands and labor claimed by conquest states or imperial powers.

Political control over craft production, while intense in a few cases, does not appear to have been pervasive. Extractive industries were situated largely on the fringes of political dominion and not directly administered by large polities, although Tarascan political control over copper mines in west Mexico may represent an exception. More direct political involvement can be seen in centralized urban contexts, particularly in the manufacture of luxury objects. Since the primary consumers of these products were members of the elite, some luxury artisans were directly attached to palaces (particularly in the Mixteca-Puebla polities described by Pohl in chapter 22), while others were concentrated in residential districts that controlled membership, production, and quality in exclusive, guildlike settings. Similar political control can be seen with the organization of professional merchants. In the Basin of Mexico, some of these pochteca traveled with state goods, acted as spies, and served as marketplace judges. In the Mayan exchange sphere, merchant lineages combined entrepreneurial interests with political power.

Although city-state rulers in many areas exercised rights to taxation in their marketplaces (Hicks 1986), most evidence suggests that the market systems and long-distance exchange systems were autonomous commercial institutions that flourished partly because they were outside of direct political manipulation (Blanton 1996). In some areas, as in Tlaxcala, political control may have been more intense; there the market was said to belong to the ruler of Ocotelulco (Blanton 1996:51). Nevertheless, the dominant characteristics of marketplace exchange in Postclassic Mesoamerica were its pervasiveness, independence, fluidity, and high degree of commercialization.

COMMERCIALIZATION AND ENTREPRENEURSHIP

As seen above, polities exercised some measure of proprietorship and control over commercial institutions. These same polities, however, stimulated commercial ventures and entrepreneurship. The stature of Mayan merchant lineages, for example, was based on success in trading ventures; Aztec imperial tribute demands often required a conquered populace to trade for goods in local or more distant markets; and professional merchants sponsored by city-states also traded aggressively in their own merchandise.

A further indication of increased commercialization involves the accumulation of wealth based on nonpolitical criteria. In central Mexico, there was considerable variation in property levels among commoners (Harvey 1984), suggesting that some were acquiring wealth through supplementary specialized production and/or commercial undertakings. Similarly, professional merchants differed in affluence, some achieving an abundance of riches (Sahagún 1950–1982, book 9). Commercialization had developed so extensively in the Postclassic that many merchants trading over regional and long distances could engage in trading on a prosperous full-time basis (Berdan 1988). Both markets and international trade centers were targets for the entrepreneurial ambitions of these traders. An essential contribution of the international trade centers to the world system was their role in stimulating exchanges across political borders and integrating merchants from distinct and distant polities.

The importance of commercialized marketplace exchange is also revealed at the level of the consumer. Households at even the smallest rural settlements in highland Mexico and lowland Belize had access to a wide variety of imported goods, including luxury goods also used by local elites (chapters 32, 34; see discussion above of Hirth's model). Markets and their impacts were felt strongly not only in highly urbanized contexts, but at all levels of society.

AN INTEGRATED INTERNATIONAL ECONOMY

The general processes identified here for the Postclassic economy—namely, an expansion of economic activity with a variety of complex institutional and processual contexts—took place across all of Mesoamerica and began well before the expansion of the Aztec empire. While the most detailed and voluminous evidence for markets, professional merchants, craft specialization, and tribute comes from Aztec records, we can adequately document all of these institutions for other areas of Mesoamerica and conclude that markets and commercial enterprises, in general, increased dramatically during the course of the Postclassic period.

Production efforts and exchange activities provided an interconnected web of spatial and hierarchical links. Both production and exchange enterprises transcended individual city-state polities in Late Postclassic Mesoamerica. In some cases, production of a single commodity required the hands of different specialists in separate city-states, or even regions, to reach its finished form, creating bonds of economic expectations. In addition, the uneven geographical distribution of resources encouraged specialization in production, with desirable products and commodities available in specific and known locales. These circumstances stimulated exchange specialists, and the movements of goods through polities and across regions often entailed the services of petty, regional, or long-distance merchants who carried not only merchandise but also information, ideas, and sometimes political clout.

Material goods and obligatory services also moved vertically through the hierarchical social and political structures of Postclassic Mesoamerica. Some production activities in workshop contexts may have been attached to rulers or other noble patrons; this patron-client relationship also pertained to some professional merchants who carried their rulers' goods for trade in distant areas. These production and mercantile activities were geared toward supplying elite consumers with prestige goods, and in some cases required the world system's most spatially far-flung relationships (chapter 17).

Tribute imposition, the most overt of the vertical economic links, served to channel surplus production vertically within and beyond individual city-states. In doing so, it also required, in some cases, the intensification of existing horizontal marketing ties, as well as the spread of local styles and designs in production. This can be seen in the payments of decorated textiles to Aztec emperors in the Late Postclassic: the designs do not derive from the Aztec repertoire, but from their provincial places of origin (Berdan and Anawalt 1992). In these economic movements, then, influence was from the bottom up as well as from the top down.

These economic relationships did not take place in isolation, but were tightly woven into the complex social, economic, and religious institutions of the Mesoamerican world system. Production was household-based, kin-based, or guild-based; it was "independent" or "attached"; it was completed by one individual/group, or by more than one; and it was directed toward universal, specialized, or elite consumers. Exchange took place in a variety of marketplace settings, at international trade centers, or through tribute, and was engaged in by a mosaic of merchants and traders with small-scale goals or heightened ambitions. Economic activities therefore not only linked the Mesoamerican world system along territorial dimensions, but also, given their high degree of commercialization, permeated the many dimensions and levels of Mesoamerican life. A particularly commercialized facet of the Postclassic economy was found at international trade centers, the subject of the next chapter by Gasco and Berdan.

17

International Trade Centers

Janine Gasco

Frances F. Berdan

The primary focal points for the extensive long-distance exchange described in chapter 16 were the numerous international trade centers, our notion of which contrasts markedly with the earlier influential notion of ports of trade as proposed by Anne Chapman (1957). Whereas Chapman saw these trade enclaves as politically neutral venues of exchange serving primarily political purposes, we view them as highly commercialized centers serving primarily economic purposes. In addition, we recognize considerable variation in the manner in which these entrepôts were situated, organized, and related to their constituent polities. We therefore identify considerably more trade centers than did Chapman.

The bulk of information regarding long-distance trade centers comes from documents written in the early Colonial period. Because many of these accounts describe the immediate preconquest period, they provide a snapshot view of the situation during the Late Postclassic. Much of the documentation emphasizes the influence of the expanding Aztec state on market systems, the movement of goods through tribute paid to the Triple Alliance, and the role of the pochteca in long-distance trade (see Berdan et al., chapter 16). In fact, many of the documents that we rely on heavily were written from an Aztec perspective. As a result, we have a good understanding of long-distance trade as it was conducted by the pochteca, but a much poorer understanding of trade conducted by other professional merchants. And we know more about the location and organization of long-distance trade centers on the eve of the Spanish invasion than we do for the earlier years of the Postclassic period.

Unfortunately, with the exception of Cozumel (Freidel and Sabloff 1984; Sabloff and Rathje 1975b), Naco (Henderson et al. 1979; Wonderly 1985), El Tigre (Ochoa and Vargas 1987; Vargas Pacheco 1994), and Wild Cane Cay (McKillop 1996), we have very little archaeological data from places believed to be trade centers that would enable us to observe their origins and development, and how their organization changed through time in response to the changing political and economic climate (see Andrews 1990a for a summary). The emphasis in the documentary record on the last decades of the Postclassic period, and the near absence of archaeological data mean that this chapter focuses mainly on long-distance trade centers as they existed in approximately 1520.

PORTS OF TRADE

More than 40 years ago the concept of a "port of trade" was introduced as a particular kind of economic institution in nonindustrial states that served as a principal mechanism for long-distance exchange between archaic states (Arnold 1957; Chapman 1957; Polanyi 1963; Revere 1957), and the term is still occasionally used today (see McKillop 1996, 2001). In that conception, ports of trade were a special kind of trade center found at ecological or cultural boundaries, or situated in buffer zones. Typically located in politically neutral locations, ports of trade made it possible for long-distance trade to be conducted safely between merchants from competing or even hostile polities.

Anne Chapman, in her application of the port of trade model to Late Postclassic Mesoamerica (1957), argued that the existence of ports of trade accounted for the volume and intensity of long-distance exchange across political boundaries. Briefly, Chapman focused on three factors that characterized ports of trade. First, Postclassic Mesoamerican ports of trade were located in neutral areas or buffer zones that were politically autonomous and could thus provide safe haven for enclaves of professional merchants. Second, trade was limited to luxury goods and their raw materials, making ports of trade structurally different and geographically separate from local markets. Third, traders who conducted their business at ports of trade did not act as individuals, but as members of a distinct social group whose activities were administered by professional organizations and authorized by the state. Chapman specifically identified as ports of trade the Xicalanco area along the Gulf of Mexico, the Acalan region, the northeastern portion of the Yucatán Peninsula, including Cozumel Island, the area around Chetumal Bay, the area around the Gulf of Honduras, and the Xoconochco region.

Chapman's discussion of ports of trade and the nature of long-distance exchange had a serious impact on conceptualizations of commerce and trade in Late Postclassic Mesoamerica. Subsequent research, however, has identified a number of problems with the port-of-trade model as it applies to Mesoamerica (e.g., Berdan 1978; Freidel and Sabloff 1984; McKillop 1996; Voorhies 1989b; see chapter 1 for criticisms of the port-of-trade model as applied in the ancient Old World). In contrast to Chapman's formulation, we now know that there was more variability in the organization of long-distance trade in Postclassic Mesoamerica than can be accommodated within a strict port-of-trade model. Many locations where long-distance trade was conducted do not conform to the specific conditions for ports of trade set out by Chapman and others as characteristic. Some of the more problematic issues include (1) the extent to which neutrality was required, (2) the nature of state involvement in the affairs of merchants, (3) whether or not there were strict divisions between local markets and locations where long-distance exchange was conducted, (4) the extent to which utilitarian goods as well as luxury goods were traded, and (5) the identity and organization of the long-distance merchants.[1]

In this chapter we explore the organization of long-distance trade centers frequented by merchants from across Mesoamerica. Given our differences with the port-of-trade model, we prefer to call these places "international trade centers." The use of this more neutral term allows us to consider a number of places that were not identified by Chapman, and to investigate the variable characteristics of these centers without assuming a priori how they were organized.

INTERNATIONAL TRADE CENTERS

The centers where merchants from diverse regions gathered to conduct long-distance exchange had several or all of the following characteristics: (1) they were the setting for trade between merchants from many different and distant areas, (2) they had a high volume of trade, and (3) they exhibited a great diversity of trade goods. Under this broad definition we include a variety of centers that at-

tracted merchants from across Mesoamerica. A general discussion of how these centers were organized is followed by a brief discussion of places that may have served as international trade centers.

Traditional port-of-trade models, including Chapman's, stressed that trade ports were located in neutral places or buffer zones. In Postclassic Mesoamerica, the issue of neutrality is complex, and trade centers were sometimes found within the territories of powerful states. Nevertheless, there must have been efforts to guarantee the safety of foreign merchants, or trade centers would not have been able to attract merchants from diverse, sometimes mutually unfriendly polities. Sabloff and Rathje have argued that successful centers must be flexible and pragmatic, and they must create culturally nonspecific features that maximize political and military neutrality (1975b:9–10). For example, a center might place an emphasis on religious elements embodied in shrines that appeal to pilgrims. Pilgrimage centers not only attract a constant stream of devotees, but they also create an atmosphere conducive to peaceful interaction—precisely the atmosphere that is desirable at an international trade center. We have evidence that some (e.g., Cozumel and Cholula), but by no means all, of the trade centers in Middle and Late Postclassic Mesoamerica were also important pilgrimage centers. A link between shrine locations and merchant activity may have actually begun during the Epiclassic period (Ringle et al. 1998), but at several centers we have no record of the existence of shrines. There were, however, other methods for ensuring merchant safety at trade centers. For instance, Aztec pochteca were escorted through open lands between the limits of Aztec hegemony and the trade center of Xicalanco on the Gulf coast, a service provided by the rulers of Xicalanco (Sahagún 1950–1982, book 9).

In the last decades of the Late Postclassic period, the Aztec state had conquered or established close ties with several previously independent commercial centers: Xicalanco, Xoconochco, Zinacantan, Huexotla, Coaixtlahuaca, Tochpan, Tochtepec, and Tehuantepec, among others. While it is sometimes held that the Aztecs prohibited trade by foreign merchants within Aztec-held territory (Hassig 1985:122), at least some of these centers apparently continued to serve as trade centers for merchants from outside the Aztec empire. Inasmuch as city-state rulers were strongly interested in assuring reliable quantities of exotic status-linked goods, they exercised some involvement in the activities of long-distance merchants. For instance, the Mexica ruler at Tenochtitlan apparently maintained diplomatic relations with the ruler of the trade center of Xicalanco through state-level economic exchanges conducted by pochteca at Xicalanco (Sahagún 1950–1982, book 9). In Tochtepec and Huexotla, traveling merchants from distant regions appear to have established permanent residential enclaves, indicating they must have been politically comfortable enough to do so (Sahagún 1950–1982, book 9; Berdan et al. 1996:293). The constant threat of Aztec military reprisals on persons who harmed Basin of Mexico pochteca is further evidence of political protection (Durán 1994).

One problematic feature of Chapman's port-of-trade model is that these so-called ports were said to be distinct from local markets, not only in location but also in their organization, and that only luxury goods were traded. In Postclassic Mesoamerica, there were certainly important distinctions between centers with local markets and what we are calling international trade centers, yet there appears to have been a considerable overlap in the kinds of goods being traded. At least some luxury goods could be acquired in local markets, and a very wide range of merchandise—ranging from common materials used in daily life to costly and exotic goods and raw materials—was available at larger trade centers. It is clear that at some of these centers access was not limited exclusively to professional merchants (McKillop 1996; Berdan 1978).

The day-to-day activities at international trade centers cannot be easily reduced to a single model. They apparently ranged from the large daily markets that catered to both local consumers and long-distance traders (e.g., Tlatelolco), to periodic markets held at certain intervals—often five days or twenty days (e.g., Tochpan). Some centers specialized in only certain products, but if these products were important enough, they would have attracted long-distance merchants (Hassig 1985:111; see Berdan et al., chapter 16). In other cases, long-distance exchange may have been carried out at fairs held to coincide with important days in the ritual calendar (Feldman 1978, 1985). Fairs are mentioned briefly in several early Colonial chronicles as occurring at Cholula, Xicalanco, Nito, and in the Guatemalan highlands (Freidel and Sabloff 1984:186–187).

Finally, there is the issue of the merchants themselves: their organization, their relationship with specific polities, and their economic and political activities. Both types of long-distance merchant—high-status merchants and regional merchants—frequented the international trade centers (Berdan et al., chapter 16).

Archaeologically, the layout of international trade centers varied. Many were on coasts, and some were in large cities (table 17.1; figure 3.5). In Yucatán and at Naco one feature appears to be single-unit structures that may have served as warehouses. Usually situated on low, agglutinated platforms, warehouses typically were not located right on the coast but at the inland population centers, presumably where they could be more easily guarded (Freidel and Sabloff 1984:190). One compelling example is Cozumel, where large substructures sat on massive agglutinated platforms. These were located inland, dispersed about the island, associated with relatively small communities, and do not exhibit structural

Table 17.1
International trade centers

	Center	Location	Scale
1	Tetellan	Inland	Town
2	Tlatelolco	Inland	City
3	Huexotla	Inland	Town
4	Cholula	Inland	City
5	Coaixtlahuaca	Inland	Town
6	Tochpan	Coastal	Town
7	Tochtepec	Inland	Town
8	Chontalpa	Coastal	Region
9	Xicalanco	Coastal	Region
10	Potonchan	Coastal	Town
11	Itzamkanac	Coastal	Town
12	Cozumel	Coastal	Region
13	Chetumal	Coastal	Town
14	Nito	Coastal	Town
15	Naco	Coastal	Town
16	Zinacantan	Inland	Town
17	Huatulco	Coastal	Town
18	Xoconochco	Coastal	Region
19	Zacatula	Coastal	Town

Note: Numbers are keyed to figure 3.5.

or artifactual features common to houses or shrines (Freidel and Sabloff 1984:136–137, 190). López de Gómara described a similar arrangement in the San Juan de Ulua region of Veracruz, including the observation that large superstructures were nucleated in their small community settings, an arrangement that resembles reports from the Bay of Honduras and northern Quintana Roo (see Freidel and Sabloff 1984:190–191). Overall, Freidel and Sabloff suggest "this particular form of nucleation, agglutinated or massive low platforms in combination with dispersed smaller platforms, is distinct from the general trend toward compact, fortified settlements in the years just preceding the Spanish Conquest" (1984:191). These settlement patterns would be highly conducive to filling the needs of thriving international trade centers.

A SAMPLING OF INTERNATIONAL TRADE CENTERS IN POSTCLASSIC MESOAMERICA

The following is a list and brief discussion of significant places that were involved in international trade. Most citations are to the secondary literature, and readers are referred to those sources for more in-depth discussions of primary sources and evidence. This list is meant to be more illustrative than definitive; future research may reveal other centers that should be added to the list, or may result in some centers being removed. It should also be kept in mind that some of the sites listed represent strings of settlements that served as trade centers, encompassing several distinct settlements. This is especially the case in coastal areas, such as the Yucatán Peninsula and the Pacific coast. The locations of the towns we have chosen as illustrative of international trade centers are shown in figure 3.5; see also table 17.1.

TARASCAN/AZTEC FRONTIER

We know of only a single center along this important frontier, although there may have been others.

Tetellan

This center was located on the Río Balsas along the volatile Tarascan/Aztec frontier. A high volume of trade suggests that this city-state (or larger area) served as an international trade center, as trade was conducted with towns subject to the Aztec empire, with Tarascan towns, and with towns on the Pacific coast. Lowland products such as cacao and cotton as well as local mineral deposits (copper and gold) and jade may have attracted long-distance merchants (Berdan et al. 1996:275–276). While Tetellan exhibited considerable Aztec political and military presence (following its client-like incorporation into the Aztec empire in the late fifteenth century), this does not seem to have deterred its energetic commercial proclivities. Some of the exchange across the Tarascan/Aztec border documented archaeologically (chapter 14) was probably channeled through Tetellan or else through trade centers farther north.

CENTRAL MEXICO

Tlatelolco

Tlatelolco, the major market for Tenochtitlan, was probably the largest market in Mesoamerica during the Late Postclassic. Clearly under Aztec domination and overseen by the pochteca, this market was not in a politically neutral location. Early Spanish descriptions express awe at the size, the diversity of goods offered, and the high degree of organization and order in the Tlatelolco market. This market was certainly a place where long-distance exchange was carried out. Goods from far-distant places—both utilitarian and exotic—were sold at Tlatelolco, and it was a gathering place for all kinds of buyers and sellers, from peasants to nobles, and from part-time petty craftspersons to full-time pochteca and other merchants (Berdan 1987b, 1988; Isaac 1986; Smith 1996a).

Huexotla

Located to the northeast of Tenochtitlan in a client state, or "strategic province" (Berdan et al. 1996:149), Huexotla lies in an ecological transition zone between low-

lands and highlands, and also occupies a political border zone. It was an important commercial center, and salt from as far away as Campeche was a featured commodity. Pochteca and other foreign merchants, perhaps Cholulans and Tepehuans, may have had permanent residences in the vicinity (chapter 12).

Cholula

An important commercial and religious center long before Postclassic times, Cholula was the site of a major shrine to Quetzalcoatl and the destination for pilgrims from all over Mesoamerica. A major market was held in the city, and merchants from Cholula traveled to many distant areas (McCafferty 1996a, 1996b; Durán 1994:349). There may have been some political entanglement in this market: Durán (1971:278) states that "it was ordered that the merchandise must consist of jewels, precious stones, and fine featherwork." The market at nearby Tepeacac, exhibiting a wide range of luxury wares, probably served international merchants as well.

MIXTECA ALTA

Coaixtlahuaca

In the Late Postclassic, this Mixtec city-state was home to a splendid market frequented by merchants from Tenochtitlan, Texcoco, Chalco, Xochimilco, Coyoacan, Tlacopan, Azcapotzalco, Toltitlan, and "other regions" (Durán 1994:182–183). These merchants brought to the market and traded such expensive and desirable commodities as gold, feathers, cacao, finely worked gourds, clothing, cochineal, and dyed rabbit fur (Durán 1994: 182). In the mid-fifteenth century, in a breach of international trade etiquette, the ruler of Coaixtlahuaca ordered Basin of Mexico merchants killed and their merchandise confiscated (Durán 1994:183). This indiscretion led to Aztec conquest, although this new political domination did not seem to inhibit international trade in Coaixtlahuaca. Exotic goods continued to be available there on a reliable basis, as Coaixtlahuaca and its conquered neighbors paid luxurious tribute to their Aztec overlords up to the time of the Spanish conquest (Berdan and Anawalt 1992:3: 431). Regionally, this city-state appears to have been one of "the lesser centers in terms of traditional hereditary rulership, strategic location, agricultural potential, and size" (Berdan et al. 1996:282). This political peripherality may have contributed to its growth as an international trade center.

GULF COAST

Tochpan

Tochpan, along with neighboring Tzicoac, was an important market center on the northern Gulf coast.

Conquered by the Aztecs in the mid-fifteenth century, Tochpan held an important market every 20 days that attracted Basin of Mexico pochteca as well as other merchants from distant places such as Tulancinco (Berdan et al. 1996:291–292). The region itself was economically rich in tropical resources. Tochpan's location on the coast and Tzicoac's siting along a major river, as well as the location of both of these centers at the political edge of the Aztec empire, may have contributed to their attractiveness as trade centers.

Tochtepec

In the Late Postclassic, Tochtepec sat at the fringe of Aztec hegemony and served as a trade center and assembly point for Basin of Mexico pochteca in their international entrepreneurial enterprises (Sahagún 1950–1982, book 9). Pochteca apparently established residences in Tochtepec, gathered there in considerable numbers, and conducted rituals appropriate to their guilds. The city-state was situated along a major coast-inland route and served as the most prominent political and military center of Aztec administration of the rich Tochtepec province. The considerable Aztec bureaucratic presence may have served, at least in part, to protect the economic interests of the pochteca. However, the extent of involvement in Tochtepec of merchants from other Mesoamerican areas remains unclear.

Chontalpa

This entire region—home to the Chontal Maya (sometimes called the Putun), notable long-distance merchants—was a focus of merchant activity (Izquierdo 1997; Scholes and Roys 1968; Thompson 1970). This entire area was described by Chapman as a port of trade, and she identified several specific locations: Coatzalcoalco, Cimatan, the Chontal coast, Potonchan, and Xicalanco (the latter two are discussed separately below). The region's neutrality may have been increasingly compromised with Aztec encroachment into most of these communities.

Xicalanco

An important long-distance trade center, Xicalanco by 1520 had close ties to the Aztecs and had resident Aztec merchants. Aztec soldiers may have been stationed there to ensure the safety of the pochteca (Izquierdo 1997: 131–143). Details of interactions among the Mexica ruler, the pochteca, and the Xicalanco ruler are recorded by Sahagún (1950–1982, book 9). The designation "Xicalanco" may refer to more than one actual center around the Laguna de Términos (see Ochoa and Vargas 1989; Vargas Pacheco 1994; Matheny 1970; Berlin 1960). This reference to Xicalanco as a region rather than a single port resembles our interpretation of Xoconochco (chapter 35).

Potonchan

An important commercial center, Potonchan was located near the mouth of the Río Grijalva (Izquierdo 1997:171–185). While this was a predominately Chontal community, numerous other towns in the region had considerable Nahuatl-speaking populations (Scholes and Roys 1968:24, 27). The presence of an intrusive Nahua element may indicate central Mexican commercial interest in this region, which is documented ethnohistorically. Merchants from Potonchan were active in Yucatán: pilgrims (perhaps with combined economic intents) visited the shrine of Ix Chel on Cozumel, and Potonchan merchants maintained factors (trading representatives) on the Río Ulua in northern Honduras (Scholes and Roys 1968:33–34, 317). Potonchan itself attracted Acalan merchants (Scholes and Roys 1968:58).

Itzamkanac

Capital of the Acalan province, Itzamkanac was home to long-distance merchants who actively traded around the Yucatán Peninsula and into Honduras. Acalan merchants reportedly occupied an entire ward at the trade center of Nito (Wonderly 1985). These energetic merchants traveled overland and by sea, trading cacao, cotton cloth, dyes, body paint, pitch pine (for torches), pine resin (for incense), and red shell beads (Scholes and Roys 1968:58). These may not have all been local exports, as they apparently also trafficked in salt, a nonlocal product, and local cacao production appears to have been insufficient for export (Scholes and Roys 1968:58–59). While Acalan merchants ranged far and wide, there is some question as to whether Itzamkanac itself (perhaps the archaeological site of El Tigre; see Ochoa and Vargas 1989; Vargas Pacheco 1994; Andrews 1943:49) was an important trade center, attracting merchants to its center (Izquierdo 1997:76–78).

NORTHEASTERN YUCATÁN/CENTRAL CARIBBEAN COAST

As with the Gulf and Pacific coasts, it appears that various lively commercial centers emerged along the northeastern Yucatán/central Caribbean coast during the Postclassic. These are reviewed by Andrews (1990a), but we single out Cozumel and Chetumal as strong and interesting examples. Other centers such as Isla Cerritos and Wild Cane Cay are also recognized as commercial centers linking the coastal trade corridors with major inland centers (Chichén Itzá and inland Belize, respectively; see McKillop 1996).

Cozumel

Cozumel is a rare example of an important trade center with both documentary and archaeological evidence (Freidel and Sabloff 1984; Sabloff and Rathje 1975b). Archaeological research has shown conclusively that the island was heavily involved in long-distance trade

(Freidel and Sabloff 1984). This trade was an integral part of the local economy, which saw production of products such as honey and wax stimulated due to the development of the island as an important trade center. Part of the allure of Cozumel for traders was the shrine of Ix Chel, which had become an important pilgrimage center by Postclassic times.

Chetumal

On the southeast coast of Yucatán, Chetumal enjoyed favorable port facilities and is described in Spanish reports as a center of lively commerce (Scholes and Roys 1968:124, 164, 317, 320). Like some of the other Mayan and Chontal trade centers, it was a center for cacao production (Scholes and Roys 1968:320). Chetumal's commercial tentacles extended beyond its local area; its merchants maintained entrepreneurial connections at least in the Ulua region of Honduras. These interests were strong enough to prompt a Chetumal military expedition against the Spaniards when they threatened the Ulua region (Scholes and Roys 1968:317).

GULF OF HONDURAS

Nito

Nito was an important commercial center near the mouth of the Río Dulce (but not yet identified definitively on the ground). It is reported that merchants of Acalan (see Itzamkanac above) occupied an entire ward of this community where they had their warehouses (Scholes and Roys 1968:4, 111).

Naco

Located in the Naco Valley of northwestern Honduras, Naco was reputed to be the region's major commercial center (Scholes and Roys 1968:320). Excavations at this site have suggested that the growth of trade may have been linked to the arrival of an intrusive population around 1250, possibly people from the Chontalpa region (Wonderly 1985:258 ff.). Other reports mention the presence of Maya nobles from Chontalpa, Chetumal, and elsewhere who maintained a presence in this region to keep an eye on their commercial interests (Scholes and Roys 1968:130; Wonderly 1985).

HIGHLAND CHIAPAS

Zinacantan

This Tzotzil town is mentioned in Sahagún (1950–1982, book 9:21) as a place where the "disguised merchants" (one variety of pochteca) visited, dressed like natives so they would not be recognized and would be able to trade without endangering themselves. Eventually, however, Zinacantan was reportedly conquered by the Aztecs (Berdan and Anawalt 1992:3:15v). These conquered people apparently did not pay tribute, but instead provided the Aztecs with some other service—perhaps protection for movement into and out of Xoconochco (Köhler 1978). Early Colonial records mention an Aztec garrison at Zinacantan (Remesal 1932:1:378). The importance of long-distance trade at Zinacantan is suggested not only by Sahagún's report, but also by an early Colonial account that notes that almost all of the people of Zinacantan were merchants (de la Torre 1545, in Ximénez 1999:362). Regional products that may have attracted foreign merchants included amber, numerous varieties of exotic feathers, and salt.

PACIFIC COAST/ISTHMUS REGION

It is likely that considerable long-distance trade was going on all along the Pacific coast. Although it is possible that many of the numerous Postclassic Pacific port towns served as international trade centers, there is only sufficient evidence to single out three of these: Zacatula, Huatulco, and Soconusco. Other ports have tantalizing clues, but insufficient information to include them in our list of centers at this time.

Zacatula

A port at the mouth of the Río Balsas, Zacatula was fought over by the Aztec and Tarascan empires (Relación de Zacatula 1945; Brand 1980) and was in an area rich in high-quality salt and cacao orchards. According to a document from 1525, "The Indians of the Zacatula coast say that often they heard their fathers and grandfathers relate that from time to time Indians from certain islands toward the south, which they point to, would come to this coast in large canoes, and they brought there exquisite things which they would trade for local products" (West 1961:133). The document goes on to say that these foreign Indians would sometimes stay for months in Zacatula waiting for the sea to become sufficiently calm to return home. The two likely origins for these merchants (based on other clues in the document) are the Cueva peoples of Pacific Panama and the Manteño peoples of coastal Ecuador (West 1961:133–134). Regardless of their specific origin, visits by such foreign merchants suggest that Zacatula may have served as an international trade center (see also Edwards 1978:204).

Huatulco

Huatulco may have been an important port for canoe traffic along the Pacific coast coming from Central America and Xoconochco. Early Colonial reports note that canoes traveled between Huatulco and Guatemala taking textiles from Teotitlan del Camino to Xoconochco and Xuchitepequez to trade for cacao (Paso y Troncoso 1905: 4:215).

Xoconochco

Another of Chapman's original ports of trade, Xoco-nochco was a tributary province of the Aztecs after the 1480s, so it could not have been neutral after that time (Berdan 1978; Voorhies 1989b). Its identification as a port of trade by Chapman was based on reports in Sahagún of pochteca trading there, but there is no other documentary evidence to suggest which other merchants might have also been active in the area. Nor is there any documentary evidence to suggest whether the long-distance trade mentioned in Sahagún took place in a particular town (perhaps the town of Xoconochco) or in the region more generally. An archaeological project currently underway at the site of Xoconochco promises to provide new information about activities at that site (chapter 35). However, if these sources refer to the entire region, there may be one or more coastal sites that were the actual sites of trade, perhaps resembling the Chontalpa and Xicalanco situations described above. The inner-coastal waterway that extends from Guatemala to Oaxaca would have been ideal for canoe traffic moving goods along this otherwise treacherous coastline. One location that is an ideal candidate for a coastal trade center is Paredón, a site located on a large lagoon just south of Tonalá, Chiapas. Archaeological collections from the site include a range of goods—including metal (chapter 21), other precious minerals and stones, and polychrome ceramics—suggesting that long-distance trade was an important activity.

INTERNATIONAL TRADE CENTERS IN THE POSTCLASSIC MESOAMERICAN WORLD

Archaeological and ethnohistoric evidence indicates the presence of numerous international trade centers during Postclassic (especially Late Postclassic) times in Meso-america. While each was unique, these centers shared several characteristics (see figure 3.5).

STRATEGIC LOCATION
BETWEEN ENVIRONMENTAL ZONES OR POLITIES

Many international trade centers were conveniently or strategically located at ecological or political disjunctions. Most were situated along coastlines separating (and joining) sea and inland settlements; these include those along the Gulf, Yucatán, and Pacific coasts. Another trade center, Huexotla, lay in a transition zone between highlands and lowlands. In the absence of attractive trade centers close to borderlands, political animosities could prohibit mutually beneficial trade between outwardly hostile (or inwardly seething) polities. Examples of such trade centers would be Cholula and Tepeacac along the tense Aztec/Tlaxcalan border, Tetellan on the forbidding Aztec-Tarascan fron-tier, and Coaixtlahuaca prior to its conquest by the Aztecs.

LOCATION ALONG TRADE ROUTES

Most international trade centers were situated along travel and transport corridors, facilitating commerce on a grand scale. Coastal centers enjoyed favorable ports for canoe traffic, and many of these sites (such as Tochpan, Chetumal, Wild Cane Cay, and those in Honduras) were also located near or along rivers that served as important coast-to-inland arteries. Trade centers such as Zinacantan, Cholula, and Huexotla were conveniently situated along well-traveled terrestrial routes, and Tlatelolco sat on an island that served as the focus for bustling highland lake traffic. As noted in Chapter 3, many international trade centers were located near the edges of exchange circuits (see figure 3.5).

OCCURRENCE IN CLUSTERS OR STRINGS

International trade centers often appear in commercial strings or clusters, which may explain to some extent our frequent difficulty in identifying specific sites as discrete commercial communities. Thus, it is reasonable to talk about a string of trade centers along the Pacific coast, a series of commercial sites (such as Chauaca, Cachi, Conil, and Ecab; see Scholes and Roys 1968:320) along the northeast coast of Yucatán, the "provinces" of Xicalanco and Xoconochco instead of single locales, and a cluster of sites on the Bay of Honduras, with Nito and Naco prominent. In other examples, it is difficult to include Tochpan as an international trade center without including nearby Tzicoac; the same is true with Cholula and Tepeacac. This string or cluster effect suggests that the scale of commercial activity was extremely large, and that some areas had become widely reputed as trading venues and could attract large numbers of merchants on a rather continuous basis. It also suggests that traveling merchants had several trading options once they arrived in an area, certainly another indicator of a strongly commercialized economy.

PREVALENCE OF SUSTAINED
AND CONTINUOUS COMMERCIAL ACTIVITY

International trade centers were locales of sustained commercial activity, not sporadic or in-and-out trading. There is considerable evidence for merchants maintaining connections and facilities in distant trade centers, indicating long-term and rather high-investment entrepreneurial goals. These were well-entrenched developments.

INTEGRATION WITH LOCAL
AND REGIONAL EXCHANGE SYSTEMS

International trade centers not only provided practical facilities and profitable interactions for long-distance merchants, but also were hotbeds for more-local and regional economic exchange activities. The interests of the long-distance merchants emphasized high-value, low-bulk luxuries, while regional merchants contributed to the bustle of commerce by profitably trafficking in bulk luxuries such as cacao, salt, and cotton. Smaller-scale trading activities moved primarily utilitarian goods within a more restricted geographic range. It is useful to view this commerce not as separate and distinct events, as the port-of-trade model suggests, but as dynamic, interlinked exchange networks (chapter 16).

INTEGRATION INTO REGIONAL POLITICAL AND RELIGIOUS SYSTEMS

International trade centers were not isolated or divorced from other aspects of Mesoamerican life. They varied considerably in terms of their political neutrality, ranging from Tlatelolco at the heart of Aztec imperial administration to the fairly marginal Coaixtlahuaca in the Mixteca Alta, and Tetellan on the Aztec-Tarascan frontier. Many were incorporated into the Aztec empire as conquered city-states (such as Tochpan and Xoconochco). All of the centers had political rulers and bureaucratic administrations with their own interests at heart. Some, especially Cholula and Cozumel, were also prominent pilgrimage sites that attracted travelers for religious as well as economic purposes.

THE IMPACT OF INTERNATIONAL TRADE CENTERS

International trade centers were pivotal contributors to the Postclassic Mesoamerican world system. They served not only as facilitators of exchange over long distances, but also as stimulants. The prospect of economic profit was an important motivation, and the development of cosmopolitan trade venues at accessible locales, where merchants from broad areas of Mesoamerica carrying a wide array of exotic and expensive goods could interact, encouraged traders to brave long treks and dangerous journeys. By the Late Postclassic, professional long-distance merchants had entrenched themselves in numerous well-established trade centers; this was not sporadic trading but institutionalized international commerce. The usefulness of such centers was also extended to alleviating trade along volatile political borders, where city-states such as Cholula and Tetellan facilitated the movements of high-value goods across otherwise closed borders. It is to be expected, then, that the actual locations of international trade centers would change over time in response to the world system's other political and economic dynamics. These centers served as venues for wide-ranging exchanges of key commodities in the Mesoamerican world system. These key commodities are the subject of the next chapter by Smith, and of the three subsequent chapters by Kepecs (salt), Braswell (obsidian), and Hosler (metals).

18

Key Commodities

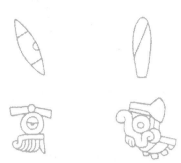

Michael E. Smith

Commodities are the building blocks of any commercialized economy, and they were the focus of the institutions and trade centers discussed in chapters 16 and 17. A commodity is "any thing intended for exchange" (Appadurai 1986:9). The anthropological analysis of commodities usually begins by contrasting them with gifts. In the framework of Chris A. Gregory (1982), the commodity/gift relationship can be summarized by the following dichotomies: alienable/inalienable; socially independent/socially dependent; value based on quantity/value based on quality; value marked by price/value marked by rank (see also Hart 1982). Later analyses go beyond the commodity/gift dichotomy by interpreting commodities within the framework of consumption, thereby adding greater social complexity to the concept (e.g., Appadurai 1986; Thomas 1991; Miller 1995). These newer approaches provide a social framework for the analysis of Postclassic exchange systems in Mesoamerica.

Appadurai (1986) points out that the functions and social significance of objects typically change during their life histories, and the status of "commodity" can be viewed as a phase in the life of an object. For example, a piece of fine gold jewelry may have begun life as a commodity sold by its maker to a noble. Later its commodity phase ended, and it became a gift when the noble presented it to another noble at a feast. If the recipient (or anyone else) were later to sell the jewelry, it would again become a commodity. Archaeological and ethnohistorical analyses can rarely approach the level of detail needed to follow the different phases in the life of an object, however, and in this book we are concerned with goods that served as commodities during some interval of their existence.

In less highly commercialized economies, most goods circulate through noncommercial channels such as gift exchange, trade partnerships, tribute payments, and patron-client interactions. This does not mean that commodities (goods produced for exchange) are absent from uncommercialized economies. Thomas (1991), for example, shows that even among the tribal-level, precapitalist societies of the southwestern Pacific that are known for their reliance on gift exchange, some goods served as commodities during parts of their existence. In commercialized economies, however, many or most goods are commodities at some stage of their life and circulate though market systems or similar institutions. This was particularly true of Postclassic Mesoamerica, where the number and variety of commodities were quite impressive.

William Roseberry (1989) argues that a fruitful approach to the anthropological analysis of the modern world system is to focus on key commodities. By following the production, distribution, and consumption of individual commodities, ethnographers can link their micro-scale research to the macro-scale processes of the modern world system. This approach is also useful for the archaeological and historical study of past world systems, where the linking of micro and macro scales is a crucial task. A further reason for the importance of commodities in the analysis of Postclassic Mesoamerica lies in the nature of the available data. Tracing the production and exchange of goods is one of the strengths of archaeology, and the ethnohistoric record also contains numerous lists of commodities that were available in marketplaces, carried by merchants, and paid in tribute.

CHARACTERIZATION OF COMMODITIES

The ethnohistoric record for Postclassic Mesoamerica contains information on several hundred goods that were exchanged and can thus be called commodities (e.g.,

Table 18.1
Key commodities in Postclassic Mesoamerica

	Mentioned for Maritime Trade
Cacao (as money and beverage)	x
Copper axe-money	x
Copper/bronze bells	x
Feathers and feather ornaments	
Gold jewelry	
Greenstone jewelry	
Obsidian and obsidian tools	x
Painted manuscripts	
Plain and decorated textiles	x
Polychrome pottery	?a
Raw cotton	
Salt	x
Slaves	x[b]
Turquoise jewelry	

Notes: Commodities marked as "mentioned in maritime trade" are those included in early written descriptions of maritime traders (Edwards 1978:205–207).

[a] Polychrome ceramics are not specifically mentioned, but one description includes utensils "marvelously made out of clay" (Edwards 1978:201).

[b] Slaves are not mentioned as commodities in these sources, but several sources do note that the paddlers were slaves (Edwards 1978).

Berdan and Anawalt 1992; Brand 1943; Feldman 1985; Landa 1941; Roys 1972; Sahagún 1950–1982; Scholes and Roys 1968). Many of these are also documented archaeologically, but this information has not been synthesized or summarized. The authors of this book drew up a list of about 50 commodities that were highly significant in Postclassic times; these are referred to here as "important commodities." From this list, we then highlighted 18 of these as "key commodities" whose production and exchange were particularly important for the functioning of the Postclassic world system. These are listed in table 18.1, which shows that many of these were included in early Spanish descriptions of maritime traders (Edwards 1978:205–207). Edwards also includes maize in his list, but that probably represented food for the merchants and their crew rather than a commodity for exchange. Four of the entries in table 18.1 are composite categories that are further broken down in the discussion and tables below (e.g., feathers and feather ornaments are considered separately below).

Important and key commodities had patterns of production, exchange, and/or consumption that had widespread influence within Postclassic society and economy. For example, commodities whose production required specialized technology or highly trained artisans were often more important than those easily obtained or produced. Commodities exchanged in large volumes or those exchanged over great distances were obviously important to the overall economy. And commodities with a high information content and whose use was restricted to elites had important social roles. These and other factors went into our categorization of important and key commodities. In this section I discuss the ways in which such commodities differed from others not included in our lists. An important point is that the key commodities in Postclassic Mesoamerica do not fit a single profile. Some were important because they were necessities with widespread demand, and others were important because they were luxuries involved in elite political dynamics.

FUNCTIONAL CLASSIFICATION

One of the most natural and useful ways to classify commodities or other goods is in terms of their uses or functions within society. Table 18.2 is our list of important commodities arranged by functional category. Key commodities are marked with an X. As the table shows, key commodities are found within every functional class. Table 18.2 also lists two other methods of characterization of commodities: their use-class and economic value. These alternative classifications are in fact more useful for our analysis than is the functional classification of commodities.

ECONOMIC VALUE

The economic value of commodities in archaeological and historical settings is usually very difficult to establish. The commercial economies of Postclassic Mesoamerica used several forms of money, and thus people probably measured the value of goods by their prices. Although some price equivalents have survived in documents (e.g., Anderson et al. 1976; Rojas 1998), there is not sufficient information to adequately assess the value of most commodities. There are two very different approaches to measuring or determining economic value: the labor approach and the scarcity approach. Leaving aside theoretical debates about the nature of value in various types of economies, it is likely that both the amount of labor involved in obtaining and/or producing a commodity and the relative scarcity of the good played roles in determining its value in precapitalist commercialized economies. I have argued that for archaeologists, labor input provides a more useful way to measure value of ancient goods than does scarcity (Smith 1987b:321), and this approach has been applied to Mesoamerican data by Abrams (1994), Feinman (1985), and others.

In order to approach the question of the labor value of Postclassic commodities, I have applied a rough measure to the commodities listed in table 18.2. This measure consists of the sum of the number of attributes present for six categories of labor investment.

Table 18.2
Important commodities listed by functional category

| | | Use-class | Value | Production/Exchange Attributes | | | | | |
				1	2	3	4	5	6
Food									
x	salt	1	4	x	x		x		x
x	fine salt	5	4	x	x		x		x
x	cacao	5	2	x					x
	fruits	1	0						
	grain	1	0						
	honey	2	0						
Domestic Tools and Materials									
x	obsidian tools	1	4	x	x			x	x
	ceramic vessels	1	1				x		
	ground-stone tools	1	1	x					
	chert tools	2	0						
Industrial Tools									
	copper/bronze needles	3	6	x	x	x	x	x	x
	bronze axes and awls	3	6	x	x	x	x	x	x
x	obsidian tools	2	4	x	x			x	x
	bark beaters	4	1	x					
	spinning tools	2	0						
	bone needles	4	0						
Raw Materials									
x	obsidian	4	3	x	x				x
x	raw cotton	2	2	x					x
x	feathers	4	2	x					x
	volcanic ash	3	2	x	x				
	paints and pigments	4	1						x
Clothing									
x	decorated clothing	5	4	x			x	x	x
	plain clothing	2	3	x			x		x
Serving Ware									
x	codex-style pottery	5	3				x	x	x
x	polychrome pottery	2	2				x		x
	other pottery	2	1				x		
	fine stone vessels	5	1	x					
	gourd bowls	2	0						
Jewelry/Display Items									
	copper/bronze jewelry	5	6	x	x	x	x	x	x
x	gold jewelry	5	6	x	x	x	x	x	x
x	greenstone jewelry	5	5	x	x		x	x	x
x	turquoise jewelry	5	5	x	x		x	x	x
x	obsidian jewelry	5	5	x	x		x	x	x

Table 18.2 continued
Important commodities listed by functional category

		Use-class	Value	Production/Exchange Attributes:					
				1	2	3	4	5	6
Jewelry/Display Items continued									
x	feather ornaments	5	4	x			x	x	x
	silver jewelry	5	6	x	x	x	x	x	x
	rock crystal jewelry	5	4	x			x	x	x
	shell jewelry	5	3	x				x	x
	amber jewelry	5	2					x	x
Money									
x	textiles	2	3	x			x		x
x	cacao	2	2	x					x
x	copper axe-money	3	6	x	x	x	x	x	x
Ritual									
x	copper/bronze bells	5	6	x	x	x	x	x	x
x	bloodletting knives	5	4	x	x			x	x
	rubber	5	4	x		x	x		x
	figurines	2	2				x		x
	drugs	5	2	x					x
	bark paper	5	2				x		x
	tobacco	2	2	x					x
	censers	2	1				x		
	copal	2	2	x					x
	stingray spines	2	1	x					
	flowers	2	0						
Special									
x	painted manuscripts	5	3				x	x	x
x	slaves	3	1						x

KEY:

	x	Key commodity
Use-Class:	1	Necessity
	2	Widely used goods
	3	Regionally limited
	4	Goods with specialized utilitarian uses
	5	Luxuries
Value:		This is the total number of attributes present.
Prod./Exch. Attributes:	1	Raw material limited to certain major environmental zones
	2	Raw material limited to a small number of locations
	3	Complex technology required
	4	Lengthy and/or complex production process
	5	Highly skilled craftworkers required
	6	High value in relation to weight

1. *Raw materials limited to certain major environmental zones.* This category is marked as present for goods whose raw materials were distributed differentially with respect to large environmental zones such as highlands versus lowlands, or coast versus inland. It contributes to economic value because such commodities, or their material constituents, were not available in many regions and had to be obtained through exchange. Thus cotton textiles were more valuable in the highlands since cotton can only be grown in lowland settings, whereas maize was

Table 18.3
Important commodities listed by use-class

	Functional Class	Value			Functional Class	Value
1. Necessities				**4. Goods with Specialized Utilitarian Uses**		
x salt	food	4		x obsidian	raw materials	3
x obsidian tools	domestic tools	4		x feathers	raw materials	2
ceramic vessels	domestic tools	1		x slaves	special	1
ground-stone tools	domestic tools	1		bark beaters	industrial tools	1
fruits	food	0		paints and pigments	raw materials	1
grain	food	0		bone needles	industrial tools	0
2. Widely Used Goods				**5. Luxuries**		
x copper axe-money	money	6		x copper/bronze bells	ritual	6
x obsidian tools	industrial tools	4		x gold jewelry	jewelry/display	6
x textiles	money	3		x greenstone jewelry	jewelry/display	5
x raw cotton	raw materials	2		x turquoise jewelry	jewelry/display	5
x polychrome pottery	serving ware	2		x feather ornaments	jewelry/display	4
x cacao	money	2		x decorated clothing	clothing	4
plain clothing	clothing	3		x fine salt	food	4
figurines	ritual	2		x codex-style pottery	serving ware	3
copal	ritual	2		x painted manuscripts	special	3
tobacco	ritual	2		x cacao	food	2
other pottery	serving ware	1		copper/bronze jewelry	jewelry/display	6
censers	ritual	1		silver jewelry	jewelry/display	6
honey	food	0		obsidian jewelry	jewelry/display	5
chert tools	domestic tools	0		rock crystal jewelry	jewelry/display	4
spinning tools	industrial tools	0		bloodletting knives	ritual	4
gourd bowls	serving ware	0		rubber	ritual	4
flowers	ritual	0		shell jewelry	jewelry/display	3
				amber jewelry	jewelry/display	2
3. Regionally Limited Goods				drugs	ritual	2
copper/bronze needles	industrial tools	6		bark paper	ritual	2
bronze axes and awls	industrial tools	6		fine stone vessels	serving ware	1
volcanic ash	raw materials	2				

Note: Key commodities are marked with an *x*. For an explanation of each commodity's value, please see chapter discussion.

less valuable since it can be grown in most environmental zones of Mesoamerica.

2. *Raw materials limited to a small number of locations.* This category marks goods whose raw materials were found only in a few discrete locations, regardless of how they occurred with respect to major environmental zones. Obsidian was found only in several discrete locations, as opposed to pottery clay, which was widely available in most areas.

3. *Complex technology required.* Most technological processes in ancient Mesoamerica were not highly com-

plex in terms of their use of special tools and facilities, and highly technical or specialized knowledge. Some important commodities produced through metallurgy and rubber processing are characterized as requiring complex technology, giving these products higher economic value.

4. *Lengthy and/or complex production process.* This category includes commodities whose production process required many separate and distinct steps. For example, the manufacture of ceramic vessels required mining clay and temper, mixing the clay, forming the vessels, drying and finishing them, and firing the vessels. The manufacture

of obsidian blades, although dependent on several steps, was a shorter process requiring fewer distinct tools and activities than ceramic production. Many Postclassic luxuries, such as featherwork, turquoise mosaics, and painted manuscripts, required lengthy and complex processes of production with many diverse activities.

5. *Highly skilled craftworkers required.* Commodities that required highly skilled producers had a higher value than those more easily produced. The production of tools and other items from obsidian and bronze required highly skilled workers, as did the weaving of highly decorated textiles and the painting of manuscripts or highly decorated ceramics.

6. *High value in relation to weight.* This category is a simple assessment of whether a commodity was easily transported for exchange, with the assumption that other things being equal, goods that were less bulky and less heavy were more valuable as exchange items.

The value measure in table 18.2 is the sum of the scores of each commodity for these six categories. This is a very rough measure, and no claims are made that the value scores reflect the actual economic values (or prices) of these commodities in Postclassic Mesoamerica. Nevertheless, these scores do correlate with our impressions commodity values, and they provide some insight into the nature of Postclassic commodities and the reasons that some were more important for the world system than others. Many, but not all, of the key commodities have high scores on the economic value scale. Another indication of the high value of some of these key commodities is their inclusion in early written descriptions of goods carried by maritime traders, including the Columbus description that opens chapter 1 (Edwards 1978:205–207; see table 18.1).

LUXURIES AND SOCIAL CONTEXT

The third approach to the classification of commodities involves the social context of their use. I have used a five-category classification of use-class into necessities, widely used goods, regionally limited goods, goods with specialized utilitarian uses, and luxuries (table 18.3). Because of the social and economic importance of luxury goods, it is worthwhile to discuss this concept in some detail. Douglas and Isherwood (1979:97) start with the definitions of luxuries and necessities used in classical economics: necessities are goods bought in the same quantities regardless of changes in prices or incomes, and luxuries are goods on which individuals will quickly cut down in response to a drop in income. They go on to suggest more-anthropologically useful definitions: necessities are items used in low-esteem, high-frequency events, whereas luxuries are goods used in low-frequency events that are highly esteemed (Douglas and Isherwood 1979:116).

Appadurai (1986) provides a more complete discussion of luxuries that is worth quoting in full:

I propose that we regard luxury goods not so much in contrast to necessities (a contrast filled with problems), but as goods whose principal use is *rhetorical* and *social*, goods that are simply *incarnated signs*. The necessity to which *they* respond is fundamentally political. Better still, since most luxury goods are used (though in special ways at a special cost), it might make more sense to regard luxury as a special "register" of consumption (by analogy to the linguistic model) than to regard them as a special class of thing. The signs of this register, in relation to commodities, are some or all of the following attributes: (1) restriction, either by price or by law, to elites; (2) complexity of acquisition, which may or may not be a function of real "scarcity"; (3) semiotic virtuosity, that is, the capacity to signal fairly complex social messages (as do pepper in cuisine, silk in dress, jewels in adornment, and relics in worship); (4) specialized knowledge as a prerequisite for their "appropriate" consumption, that is, regulation by fashion; and (5) a high degree of linkage of their consumption to body, person, and personality. (Appadurai 1986:38; emphases in original)

The five categories of goods, based on their social context, are as follows.

1. *Necessities.* Commodities classified as necessities are those that were required by most or all households for their normal functioning. These include food and certain basic domestic tools found in most Postclassic households. Two key commodities are considered necessities based on their importance in domestic consumption and their prominence in long-distance exchanges: salt and obsidian tools used in normal domestic tasks.

2. *Widely used goods.* This category includes goods that were in widespread use but less *essential* for basic survival than were necessities. This distinction is of course subjective, and some examples are open to argument. For instance, were items such as figurines and censers—used in household ritual—necessities or not? I have included them under widely used goods, but they could fit with either group. Key commodities in this category include industrial tools of obsidian (i.e., obsidian tools used to manufacture other products), textiles used as money and tribute goods, raw cotton, polychrome pottery, and cacao in its use as money.

3. *Regionally limited goods.* These are commodities that were widely used within some regions of Postclassic Mesoamerica, but rarely used in others. Bronze needles and awls, for example, were abundant in the Tarascan zone (where they were produced) and in Morelos (chapter 32), but rare in most parts of Mesoamerica; similarly, volcanic ash for pottery temper was a common product

in Yucatán but was not used widely in other areas. Although these goods were of great importance within their zones of use (see chapters 21 and 32 on bronze tools in Morelos), their limited occurrence or lowered importance in other areas prevents them from being considered key commodities.

4. *Goods with specialized utilitarian uses.* This category includes raw materials used in specific important craft industries, and slaves; the latter are included since they often contributed to the production of textiles and other products. The key commodities within this category are slaves and unworked (or only partially worked) obsidian and feathers.

5. *Luxuries.* These are goods that fit Appadurai's (1986) discussion quoted above. Although most have high values, it is the social and political contexts of their use that distinguish luxuries from other kinds of goods. These commodities had a high information content, and many of them required specialized knowledge for their appropriate consumption. Luxuries comprise the largest number of key commodities. Most of these were costly objects of personal adornment typically associated with elites: fancy decorated clothing and jewelry of gold, turquoise, and other precious materials. Key commodities among the luxury goods also included objects with high information content (painted manuscripts and the fanciest polychrome ceramics) and high-value imported foodstuffs (particularly fine salt and cacao).

In the commercialized Postclassic economy, only a few luxuries were restricted by law to elites. Commoners could purchase bronze bells, jade beads, or fancy feather ornaments if they could afford them, just as no one prohibited them from consuming cacao or fine salt. But since elites could better afford to purchase luxury goods in the markets, they tended to have many more of these goods than did commoners. This situation (Smith 1999) distinguishes commercialized economies like that of Postclassic Mesoamerica from the uncommercialized economies of tribes, chiefdoms, and centralized redistributive states. The widespread consumption of luxuries in Postclassic Mesoamerica highlights the very different systemic roles of luxury goods in commercialized economies from their roles in the prestige-goods systems that characterized these other types of societies. In prestige-goods systems, the production and exchange of valuable luxuries are controlled by elites, who are the only ones permitted to consume such goods. It is often suggested that the control of these goods is an important component of elite power in such systems (e.g., Clark and Blake 1994; Earle 1997; Friedman and Rowlands 1977; Frankenstein and Rowlands 1978; Schortman and Urban 1996). We prefer to use the term "luxury goods" in place of "prestige goods" to emphasize their role as commercial commodities and to distin-

guish the Postclassic world system from the prestige-goods systems mentioned above.

Susan Kepecs (2000; chapter 33) has suggested the phrase "bulk luxuries" for a subset of Postclassic luxuries that were traded in particularly large quantities; these included cacao, fine salt, and decorated clothing and textiles. Brumfiel (1987a, 1987b) describes the social and political dynamics of elite gifts of luxury commodities—particularly items of dress and personal adornment—among the Aztecs.

POSTCLASSIC COMMODITIES

This section provides brief discussions of the important commodities listed in tables 18.2 and 18.3, organized by the five categories of social context discussed above. Those commodities singled out (somewhat subjectively) as key commodities are indicated with an asterisk.

NECESSITIES

Salt
As a basic physiological necessity, salt was an important trade good throughout Mesoamerica. We have separated the finest white sea salt as another commodity, a luxury. Kepecs discusses salt in chapter 19.

Obsidian Tools
The widespread exchange of obsidian tools in Postclassic Mesoamerica qualifies them as key commodities. As domestic tools these were necessities, and as industrial tools used in the production of other goods, obsidian implements fall under the category of widely used goods. Braswell discusses obsidian in chapter 20.

Other Important Commodities
During most time periods in Mesoamerica, ceramic vessels were exchanged locally and regionally, with only limited long-distance trade (Drennan 1984b). In the Postclassic period, however, several varieties of central Mexican ceramics were widely traded over great distances (Smith 1990; Smith et al. 1999). The most elaborately decorated of these are singled out as luxury goods and discussed below.

WIDELY USED GOODS

Copper Axe-Money
These distinctive T-shaped copper/bronze "axes" are classified as a key commodity because of their widespread use as currency in most parts of Mesoamerica (chapter 21). They were very thin sheets of copper or bronze, and a number of archaeological finds indicate that many individual items were typically bound into standardized packets.

Obsidian Tools
See discussion above and in chapter 20 by Braswell.

Textiles and Raw Cotton
The high labor investment in spinning and weaving cotton textiles, coupled with their low weight, made them ideal commodities for a commercialized economy. They were exchanged through markets as a commodity and a form of currency, and through political channels as the predominant type of tribute at all levels (Anawalt 1981b; Berdan 1987a; Hicks 1994a). The distribution of spindle whorls for spinning cotton thread expanded throughout all of Mesoamerica in Postclassic times, and the use of small bowls for controlling the spindle was a technological innovation related to increasing demand for textiles (García Cook and Merino Carrión 1974; Smith and Hirth 1988; Stark et al. 1998). A trade in raw cotton is documented both in ethnohistoric sources and in the presence of spindle whorls for cotton in areas like the Basin of Mexico where cotton does not grow. Cotton textiles are discussed at greater length in chapter 16.

Polychrome Pottery
Ceramic vessels painted with geometric designs and simple symbols were widespread in Postclassic Mesoamerica (Nicholson and Quiñones Keber 1994a; Noguera 1975), and many of these were quite widely traded (chapters 26, 32). Elaborate codex-style polychrome pottery is listed separately below as a luxury good.

Cacao as Currency
Cacao was a key commodity because of its double use as money and food (Coe and Coe 1996; Bergmann 1969; Gasco 1996b; Rojas 1998). As a form of currency cacao is included here as a widely used good; cacao as a drink is discussed below under luxuries.

REGIONALLY LIMITED GOODS
Although no regionally limited goods are classified as key commodities for the whole Postclassic world system, their production and exchange were very important within certain areas. Bronze needles, awls, and axes, for example, were common in Morelos domestic contexts (chapter 32), and provide some of the best evidence for trade across the Aztec/Tarascan border (chapter 14).

GOODS WITH SPECIALIZED UTILITARIAN USES

Obsidian
Unworked, or more commonly, partially worked obsidian was certainly a key commodity that was exchanged extensively within local regions (chapter 20).

Feathers
Ethnohistoric sources reveal a heavy trade in tropical feathers. In many Aztec highland provinces, people had to trade with lowland areas for these feathers in order to meet their tribute obligations (Berdan and Anawalt 1992), and Aztec featherworkers must have obtained many of their materials through the markets as well as through tribute (Berdan 1987b).

Slaves
Because slaves were bought and sold, they can be considered a special form of commodity. Although most were used as household servants, many slaves made important economic contributions through craft production, particularly textile production by female slaves (Shadow and Rodríguez V. 1995).

Other Important Commodities
Bark beaters and paints such as hematite, limonite, and graphite were important commodities because of their use in the production of codices. Other pigments such as cochineal and purpura were exchanged for use as textile dyes (Dahlgren 1990a; Turok et al. 1988; Turok 1996).

LUXURIES

Bronze Bells
Small bells made of various kinds of copper alloys were the most extensively traded metal objects in Postclassic Mesoamerica; these are discussed by Hosler in chapter 21.

Gold Jewelry
Ornaments made of gold were among the most highly valuable and most intricate objects in Postclassic Mesoamerica (Bray 1989; Saville 1920), but their production and exchange are not yet well understood (chapters 21, 22).

Greenstone Jewelry
Beads, pendants, and other objects of jewelry and display carved from jadeite and other jadelike stones were important luxury goods in Mesoamerica in all time periods, and the Postclassic is no exception (Graham et al. 1998; Lange 1993; Thouvenot 1982).

Turquoise Jewelry
The importation of turquoise from the American Southwest was an important innovation in Postclassic Mesoamerica (Weigand et al. 1977; Harbottle and Weigand 1992; Weigand and Harbottle 1993), and this stone was quickly put to use in a large variety of mosaics, jewelry, and other fine objects (Carmichael 1970; Saville 1922). Turquoise jewelry was particularly important in the

Mixteca-Puebla area (chapter 22). Most reconstructions suggest that turquoise from the Southwest was traded through west Mexico, entering central Mexico through the Tarascan realm and entering the Mixteca-Puebla region through Tututepec in Oaxaca (Harbottle and Weigand 1992). This trade was the primary economic connection between Mesoamerica and the Southwest in Postclassic times (chapter 3).

*Feather Ornaments

Elaborate feathered ornaments (such as headdresses, fans, and capes) and warrior costumes and shields required complex production procedures with exotic materials. Their high value contributed to their uses as elite status markers and as signals of warriors' achievements (Berdan 1987b; Berdan and Anawalt 1992).

Decorated Clothing

This category denotes fancy decorated textiles, including both clothing and other items. These commodities were more important in the world system than plain clothing because of their higher value (and low weight), and because of their social roles in signaling status and other social characteristics (Anawalt 1981b; Berdan 1987a; Hicks 1994a).

*Fine Salt

The fine white salt of northern Yucatán was particularly highly valued by elites in many parts of Mesoamerica, and it was thus more extensively traded than was salt from other sources (chapter 19).

*Codex-Style Pottery

This category consists of the elaborate polychromes of the Mixteca-Puebla style, which were widely exchanged and highly prized, and which contained a high information content (chapters 22, 24, and 26).

*Painted Manuscripts

Painted manuscripts or codices were luxuries of only moderate economic value (table 18.2); their main significance was in the ideological realm, where they were a major part of Postclassic information networks (chapters 24, 27).

*Cacao as a Drink

Cacao in beverage form was a luxury good because of its high value and because of its social importance in elite feasts and rituals (Coe and Coe 1996).

DISCUSSIONS OF SELECTED KEY COMMODITIES

The descriptions given above are by necessity quite brief, and the reader is referred to the works cited for more information. Out of this list of key Postclassic commodities, three are singled out for in-depth treatment in the chapters that follow: salt (chapter 19), obsidian (chapter 20), and metals (chapter 21).

19

Salt Sources and Production

Susan Kepecs

Salt is a perfect commodity: production and distribution are easy to control since sources are localized, yet demand is broad (Adshead 1992:3). Salt is important for health, cuisine, and the preservation of perishables. The production and exchange of salt surplus is documented cross-culturally (e.g., Adshead 1992; Andrews 1983, 1998; Kepecs 1997, 1999; Kepecs et al. 1994; Mendizábal 1946; Multhauf 1978; Parsons 1994). Mesoamerica is no exception. In this chapter I examine salt in its role as a key commodity in the Postclassic Mesoamerican world system and describe the basic patterns of its consumption, production, and exchange.

SALT CONSUMPTION IN POSTCLASSIC MESOAMERICA

Salt satisfied both physiological requirements and culinary preferences. The amount of salt that human bodies require is highly variable, but 8 to 10 grams is typical for workers in tropical regions. Modern industrial statistics place salt consumption at that level throughout Mexico today (Andrews 1983:9). Further, the staples of modern Mexican cuisine—maize, chile, and salt—mirror the native sixteenth-century diet described in Spanish documents (see Gibson 1964:338; Mendizábal 1946:323–325).

Maize and salt went hand in hand at annual Aztec sacrifices to Huixtocihuatl, goddess of salt. According to Sahagún (1950–1982, book 2: chap. 7), singing, dancing, and drinking accompanied the sacrifice of a woman impersonating this deity and wearing "maize-ear insignias" (Cervantes de Salazar, cited in Mendizábal 1946:326). There is no published record of a parallel ritual in the Maya repertory, but salt was tied to sacred power; in the colonial-era Yucatec Books of Chilam Balam the governors of splendid coastal saltworks called themselves "priests of the white seashore" (see Edmon-

son 1982:70–72, nn. 1552, 1553; Kepecs 1999:95; Roys 1957:108).

Salt (sometimes in conjunction with chile) was taboo for participants in certain religious activities or military, trade, or exchange missions (Mendizábal 1946:327; Landa, in Tozzer 1941:107, 152, 158; Andrews 1983: 12). Today salt is used in syncretic life-cycle rituals rooted in the Prehispanic past (Andrews 1983:11–12; also personal observation).

Sahagún (1950–1982, book 10:585–594) listed 13 medicinal uses for salt. Mixed with warm water and certain crustaceans, it made earache drops; to cure cuts and swellings, it was blended with honey; and a cough-syrup recipe called for salt, herbs, and chile. The Maya used salt to stiffen the quilted cotton armor worn by warriors, and also to preserve fish (Landa, in Tozzer 1941:35, 190). And everywhere, wars were waged for salt. The Tlaxcalans, lacking local sources, were forced to raid salinas in enemy Aztec territory, which often cost them their lives or at least their liberty (Díaz del Castillo 1984:137, 146). Yucatán's richest salina—Emal, on the northeast coast—was fortified (Kepecs 1999; see also Roys 1957:107).

A localized resource, salt was clearly a valuable commodity in Postclassic Mesoamerica. Despite the limits of technology and transport in the ancient New World, salt was produced for both regional and macroregional exchange.

SALT PRODUCTION

Mesoamerican salt production was shaped by great diversity among geological conditions and salt-making techniques (see Andrews 1983; Ewald 1985:33). In a general sense, Mesoamerican salt sources can be broken down into three types: saline inland lakes or soil banks (playa lakes or salt playas), highland springs, and the

Table 19.1
Sodium chloride content of different types of salt

Product	Origin	Percentage of Sodium Chloride (range)
Tequisquites	Salt playas	4.6–37.5
Pure salts	Coastal estuaries	88.4–99.0

Data from Lefond 1969:131–135.

shallow edges of coastal estuaries. From these three contexts two basic kinds of salt were produced: earth-toned tequisquites—impure mixtures of sodium chloride, sodium carbonate, sodium sulfate, and clay—and "pure" white sodium chloride (Lefond 1969:133–134; see also Andrews 1983; Charlton 1969b; MacKinnon and Kepecs 1989; Mendizábal 1946; Paso y Troncoso 1905:1:176; Sahagún 1975:572). The difference between coastal salt and tequisquite is summarized in table 19.1 (Lefond 1969:131–135, charts 67 and 69).

The methods used to extract salt have changed to varying degrees, but the roots of these practices are reflected clearly in the ethnohistoric and archaeological records (e.g., Andrews 1983; Apenes 1944; Charlton 1969b; Dillon 1977; Eaton 1978; Ewald 1985:33; Kepecs 1999; MacKinnon and Kepecs 1989; McKillop 1995a; Mock 1994a; Parsons 1994; see also Kepecs, chapter 33). Mesoamerican salt making is an eclectic panorama of ingenious and often laborious methods adapted to specific circumstances. Yet these diverse techniques rest on three basic principles: boiling salt from brine (*sal cocida*); leaching brine through salt-laden earths to get tequisquite; and solar evaporation. These processes often are combined, but salt boiled from springs generally is purer than that leached from playa lakes, while the cleanest salt is produced through solar evaporation.

The complexity of Mesoamerican salt production defies simple description, but to provide some background I illustrate several fairly well documented examples. Andrews (1983), Mendizábal (1946), and Smith and Berdan (1996b: appendix 4) provide broader views of Prehispanic salt industries. The locations of key salt sources (including some not mentioned in the text) are provided in figure 19.1.

MAJOR PRODUCTION AREAS

Lake Texcoco
Salt industries were operating in dozens of towns around this great playa lake, according to sixteenth-century Spanish surveys (Gibson 1964:338, 562 n. 33; also see Mendizábal 1946[1]; Parsons 1994). Traditional salt-making methods (linked to ethnohistoric and archaeological descriptions) involve filtering water through blends of saline soils and then boiling down the juice to produce various kinds of tequisquite and salt (Apenes

1944; Parsons 1994). This laborious process requires a complicated inventory of filters, firing pits, and boiling pots. Archaeological remains of this practice include mounds of leached earth (*tlateles*) and associated sherds of Texcoco Fabric-marked boiling vessels (Charlton 1969b). At Zacatenco, evaporation tanks and hearths have been found associated with Aztec residential structures (Sánchez Vázquez 1984). Some salt also crystallizes naturally from lakeshore mud in the dry season (Apenes 1944; Parsons 1994:280). Among the various salts produced at Texcoco some—such as a black tequisquite (Parsons 1994:263)—may have had ritual or medicinal value. Whiter salt, tasty and scarce, probably was more valuable than most tequisquites (Kepecs 1999; Kepecs et al. 1994; MacKinnon and Kepecs 1989).

Tonatiuhco
A highland salt spring in the town of this name was known for its pure white salt. Two thousand loaves of this salt were paid to the Aztecs in tribute on an annual or semiannual basis (Barlow 1949:4; Berdan et al. 1996:269). Remains of very old saltworks at this site (Ewald 1985:42) include fossilized canals through which brine was channeled downslope into shallow evaporating ponds built to speed solar evaporation. Leach/boil methods may have supplemented this process, as they did at the end of the nineteenth century. An observer from this era (cited in Ewald 1985:42) noted that a dried salty crust was raked up from the ponds, and new saline water was poured through it to leach a high brine concentrate, which was then boiled to make high-quality salt. Among several other salt springs near Tonatiuhco, the best-known were Ixtapan de la Sal and San Miguel Ixtapan, in the polity of Texupilco. Small amounts of salt were produced at each of these sources. Solar evaporation was employed at the former (Mendizábal 1946:279), while more-complicated evaporation/boiling processes evidently were used at the latter (Ewald 1985:43; García Payón 1933).

Alahuiztlan
Alahuiztlan, in Tepequacuilco (an Aztec tributary in the Guerrero highlands), had the best source in the western Aztec realm (Berdan et al. 1996:274). Here several brine "wells" (springs?) yielded about 2,000 fanegas (ca. 230 metric tons) of salt per year (Paso y Troncoso 6:104). In the dry season, shallow resin-coated ceramic trays were filled with saline waters and allowed to dry out; this evaporation process, repeated daily, rendered trays full of salt in about a week (Mendizábal 1946:278; PNE VI: 103-104).

Acatlan and Piaxtla (Piaztlan)
At Acatlan and Piaxtla in the Mixteca Baja salt water from highland springs was left to evaporate in plaster-lined basins (Mendizábal 1946:289).

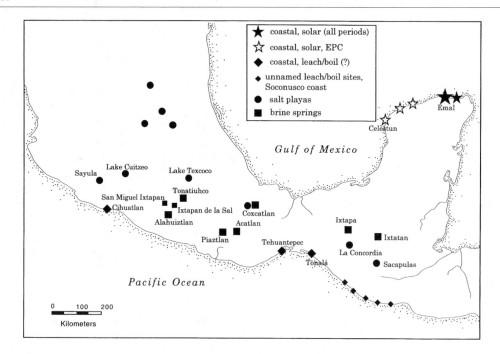

Figure 19.1 Key salt sources in Postclassic Mesoamerica

Coxcatlan

Coxcatlan, in southern Puebla, had two playa lakes (Lefond 1969:132, map 37) and some salt springs (Motolinía 1941, book 3: chapter 9). Tequisquite was leached from the former, while the latter provided good white salt that was crystallized through solar evaporation (Sisson 1973).

Lake Cuitzeo Basin, Michoacán

This basin was home to a pair of sites, Araró and Chucándiro, where tequisquite was leached from the earth. Eduardo Williams (1999) reports Spanish descriptions of the leaching process, complemented by archaeological mounds of leached soils with sherds at several sites around Lake Cuitzeo. Williams reports additional leached-earth features at archaeological sites in Colima's Sayula Lake basin.

Along the West Mexican coast in Michoacán and Guerrero

This area has several saline estuaries. Sixteenth-century reports mentioned in Williams (1999) describe white salt evaporating naturally in this zone. This estuarine salt was used in Spanish-era silver mining, but little is understood about Prehispanic production.

Sacapulas

Sacapulas (Andrews 1983:89–91) has a series of small salt playas on the eroded shores of Río Negro in the K'iche' highlands of Guatemala. Saltmakers here sprinkled hot spring water over the saline banks repeatedly over the course of three sunny days. This continuous

evaporation process turned the dark playa soils highly saline. The prepared soils were carried upstream to cooking huts for boiling. Here brine was filtered through the earthy mixture to make the final concentrate, which then was boiled over a fire in ceramic ollas. The black salts of Sacapulas reputedly had medicinal properties (particularly for treating glaucoma; see Andrews 1983:12).

Ixtapa

At Ixtapa (Andrews 1983:57–59), a salt spring in Chiapas, brine simply was boiled (today in iron cauldrons—in earlier times in ceramic pots) until the salt congealed; this salt was known for its medicinal qualities.

Tehuantepec, Tonalá, and the Xoconochco Coast

Spanish-era descriptions of salt production along this coast are lacking, but techniques probably were much like those used on Guatemala's Pacific coast, where sal cocida methods were reported (Mendizábal 1946:285). Some tequisquite may have been leached from estuary soils as well; this process was used early in the Prehispanic sequence of the Chiapas coast, where mounds of leached earth date to the Formative period (Andrews 1983:66). Modern traditional salt production along the Guerrero coast is described by Good (1995), who suggests a long historical depth for this industry.

Emal

Emal, on Yucatán's north coast (chapter 33), was the largest salt-making operation in Prehispanic Mesoamerica. Highly saline estuary waters evaporated naturally on the mudflats lining the Río Lagartos estuary, where this site is located. To speed evaporation, stone walls were built to divide the extensive flats into smaller units. A great deal of labor was needed during the dry season, but no boiling or filtration equipment was necessary to produce diamondlike white salt crystals.

PRODUCTIVITY AND EXCHANGE: SALT IN THE POSTCLASSIC WORLD SYSTEM

The parameters of the salt trade depended on demand, production potential, and availability of labor. In terms of output, the most limited of the three general source types were highland springs. The best springs yielded at most a few hundred metric tons annually (see Andrews 1983:115; Ewald 1985:41–42). In most documented cases such quantities were sufficient for regional-scale exchange. At a consumption rate of 8 gm/day, 1 metric ton would serve about 342 people per year; thus the 230 tons of salt produced annually at Alahuiztlan would meet the needs of about 78,600 consumers. Alahuiztlan salt was traded to several towns in a 50–100 km range,[2] spread across two western Aztec provinces: Tepequacuilco, where this source is located, and adjacent Tetellan. Spring salts from Acatlan and Piaxtla in the Mixteca (Berdan et al. 1996:284), and from San Mateo in the Guatemalan highlands (Andrews 1983:87), were marketed at similar distances.

Salt playas are more variable in terms of potential, yet despite considerable investments in labor and infrastructure, the product (except for certain specialty salts) is inferior. Further, tequisquite requires relatively complex production processes (economic value attribute #4, chapter 18 by Smith) and some technical skills (attribute #5), but lacks high value in relation to weight (#6). The combination of labor intensity and poor quality relegates tequisquite to the use-class of necessity, exchanged at the local and regional scales (chapter 18). At Sacapulas (a relatively small source) production probably never exceeded 70 tons, enough for local consumption with limited exchange (of black medicinal salt?) within a 100 km range (Andrews 1983:89–93). Saltworks around Lake Texcoco produced immense quantities of tequisquite (and various specialty salts)—enough for some regional trade beyond the densely populated Basin of Mexico. Spanish reports indicate that several towns in nearby Huaxtepec (Berdan et al. 1996:273) received Texcoco tequisquite—a claim supported with archaeological evidence, since Smith reports Texcoco Fabric-marked sherds at all excavated Late Postclassic sites in modern Morelos (chapter 32). Playa lakes (Sayula and Cuitzeo) supplied the Tarascan empire, but additional salt had to be imported—some of it from the Pacific coast (Helen Pollard, personal communication, 1999).

The potential yields of coastal salt making also were variable. High rainfall along the Veracruz and Central

American Atlantic seaboards was good for cacao, but detrimental to salt production (Andrews 1983:50; Ewald 1985:188). Thus there are only a few unreliable sources on the Veracruz coast. There is archaeological evidence that leach/boil procedures were used to extract tequisquite on the Belize coast during the southern Maya lowlands Classic period (McKillop1995a; MacKinnon and Kepecs 1989; Mock 1994a), but this source probably was supplemented by pure salt from Yucatán (MacKinnon and Kepecs 1989).

Freshwater rivers empty into coastal estuaries along the Oaxaca (Tehuantepec) and Chiapas (Xoconochco) coasts, diluting their salinity (Andrews 1983:67; Ewald 1985:157). Leaching and boiling were required to extract salt products. Nevertheless these salinas provisioned several Oaxacan provinces, including Miahuatlan, Teozapotlan, and Coyolapan. The distances involved in this exchange were relatively long—up to 200 km, as the crow flies.

Thus salt from the south Pacific coast was distributed over a considerable area.[3] Yet the best salt (in terms of both quality and quantity) is solar-evaporated on the banks of shallow coastal estuaries under dry, windy conditions. Modern Mexico has two such regions—the Baja peninsula, north of Mesoamerica (Ewald 1985:174–175; Lefond 1969:135, chart 69)—and Yucatán's north coast. Throughout history no Mesoamerican salt source has out-produced the rich salinas of Yucatán (chapter 33). The coastal strip is semi-arid and windy, and during the dry season salt crystallizes naturally along the mudflats lining its shallow estuaries. The richest salina by far is the one called Emal, in Chikinchel (chapter 33). The area around this site was highly populated throughout the Prehispanic period, so labor for large-scale production was readily available (Kepecs 1999). More salt could be harvested here in a dry-season day than at Alahuiztlan in a year. In Postclassic times, salt from this source supplied the peninsula through regional markets, and canoe loads were exchanged at international trading centers on the Gulfs of Campeche and Honduras (chapters 17, 33). With the growth of Maya sea trade, the Classic-period leach/boil operations on the Belize coast ceased (Andrews 1998; MacKinnon et al. 1989).

Landa (in Tozzer 1941:189) characterized Yucatán's solar salt as "the best salt which I have ever seen in my life, since it is very white when ground, and those who know about it say it is so good that half a *clemin* (1/12th of a *fanega*) of it goes further than a whole one from anywhere else." In contrast, common salt in the Aztec core was tequisquite, which the Spaniards thought was "noxious" (Gibson 1964:338; Sahagún 1975:572). Thus it is no surprise to find evidence that Yucatán's briny diamonds were available in important Aztec markets, including Coyaxtlahuaca and Huexotla (see chapter 33). In sum, salt products were a regional necessity everywhere in Mesoamerica, yet the gemlike white salt of Yucatán also was a bulk luxury, traded far beyond the regional level. In this context the Mayas' briny diamonds are best described as a world-system good that spread from international trading centers to regional markets in foreign territories, where it augmented regional supplies as a product of superior quality (see Blanton 1999). Similarly, obsidian was distributed throughout the Postclassic Mesoamerican world as a key commodity; its patterns are discussed by Braswell in the next chapter.

20

Obsidian Exchange Spheres

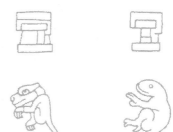

Geoffrey E. Braswell

Obsidian, a volcanic glass used for manufacturing chipped-stone tools, was the most widely circulated non-perishable good in Mesoamerica. Three factors make it particularly suitable for studying the exchange networks of the Postclassic world. First, because it was principally a utilitarian rather than a prestige item, it is found in a wide variety of contexts at both elite and humble sites. Second, the number of volcanic sources from which artifact-quality obsidian can be extracted is limited; most obsidian used in Mesoamerica came from 29 sources in west and central Mexico, and 12 sources in Central America (figure 20.1). Third, because of their unique geological histories, each source is chemically distinct, and many can be distinguished according to optical criteria or density measurements. It is possible, therefore, to ascertain the geological origin of an artifact and to reconstruct the exchange routes along which obsidian from different sources was traded.

The principal goal of this chapter is to present all published and many unpublished source assignments for obsidian artifacts recovered from Mesoamerican sites dating to the Epiclassic/Terminal Classic, Early Postclassic, and Late Postclassic periods.[1] The data are organized according to broad spatial patterns that I term "obsidian exchange spheres." Sites within a given sphere received obsidian from the same source or suite of sources. Obsidian exchange spheres are not intended to mirror political, ethnic, or linguistic boundaries, although their borders occasionally coincide. Most are much larger than any single Mesoamerican polity, so their existence implies international trade.

In order to examine this international trade, I extend the field of inquiry beyond the borders of Mesoamerica proper (chapter 3). Thus, source-assignment data are provided for sites stretching from the Loma San Gabriel region of southern Durango to Chorotegan communities

in northwestern Costa Rica, a linear distance of more than 2,300 km. The inclusion of Gran Nicoya in this survey is justified because many of the Sapoá/Ometepe–period inhabitants of that culture area came from Mesoamerica, made and produced ceramics traded to central Mexico, and used obsidian obtained from sources as distant as northern Hidalgo.

Although the focus of this volume is the Postclassic period, for two reasons I have opted to begin with the Epiclassic/Terminal Classic. First, the decline of Teotihuacan and polities in the Maya lowlands triggered important changes in the structure and organization of prehistoric exchange. The obsidian exchange spheres that coalesced in the Epiclassic/Terminal Classic period continued throughout the Postclassic period. Second, recent research in the northern Maya lowlands has forced a reevaluation of traditional chronology. Just as Tula is the quintessential Early Postclassic city of central Mexico, Chichén Itzá has long been considered the archetype of Early Postclassic Maya civilization. Nonetheless, it has become clear that Chichén Itzá was founded around A.D. 800 and was abandoned about A.D. 1050 (e.g., Braswell 1998a; Cobos 1998; Ringle et al. 1998; Schele and Mathews 1998).[2] In other words, the occupation of Chichén Itzá spans the two centuries of the Terminal Classic period. Since relations between Chichén Itzá and contemporary cities such as Xochicalco, El Tajín, and Tula are relevant to the development of the Postclassic Mesoamerican world, it is appropriate to include the Epiclassic/Terminal Classic in this discussion.

EPICLASSIC/TERMINAL CLASSIC OBSIDIAN EXCHANGE SPHERES (A.D. 650/800–1000/1050)

The period beginning about A.D. 650 in central Mexico and a century or so later in southeastern Mesoamerica

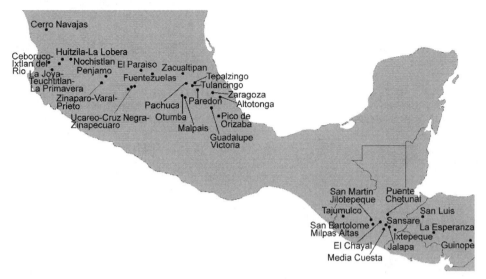

Figure 20.1 Principal obsidian sources of Mesoamerica

saw the disintegration of both interregional and long-distance Classic-period exchange networks. Although the extent and nature of the role played by Teotihuacan in the extraction, production, and exchange of obsidian are a matter of debate (e.g., Clark 1986; Santley 1983, 1989; Spence 1984), the demographic decline of that city represented the loss of the single largest source of demand for obsidian in northwestern Mesoamerica. Similarly, the collapse of Maya polities during the ninth and early tenth centuries minimally entailed a drastic revision in the nature and scale of exchange between the southern highlands and lowlands.

The disintegration of important regional states and the emergence of new power centers during the Classic to Postclassic transition required the formation of new exchange networks. I have identified 11 regional and interregional obsidian exchange spheres that characterize Mesoamerica during this transition (table 20.1 and figure 20.2).

NORTHWEST MEXICAN SPHERE

Although geographically and politically peripheral to Mesoamerica, northwest Mexico was the mythical home of several central Mexican groups, an important source of a wide variety of semiprecious stones and minerals, and possibly the place of origin of the patio-gallery, the tzompantli, the chacmool, Coyotlatelco ceramics, and the cult of Tezcatlipoca (Weaver 1993:187). For this reason, economic connections with regions to the southeast are of particular interest.

Northwest Mexico is home to a great number of obsidian sources, and this is reflected in the obsidian procurement patterns of sites in the region. Source areas that have been identified on the ground include Huitzila–La Lobera (located along the Jalisco and Zacatecas borders), Nochistlan (Zacatecas), Cerro Navajas (also called Llano

Grande, Durango), Ceboruco–Ixtlan del Río (Nayarit), and the La Joya–Teuchtitlan–La Primavera source area (sometimes called the Tequila and La Primavera source areas) of Jalisco (figure 20.1). Many more sources, whose geographic locations are not yet known, have been identified through chemical assay. Darling (1998) has identified nine chemical groups (called Unknown-A through -I), and Trombold et al. (1993) may have identified a tenth (called Group Z). Furthermore, many artifacts have chemical compositions that appear unique; that is, at present they cannot be attributed to either a known geological source or an identified chemical group. An assay of 25 artifacts from La Quemada, for example, revealed three known sources (Nochistlan, La Lobera, and Huitzila), two unidentified chemical groups, and nine unique pieces that could not be grouped statistically with each other or other artifacts (Trombold et al.1993). Darling (1998: table 5.3), in an analysis of five more artifacts from La Quemada, has additionally identified obsidian from Pachuca, Hidalgo, and Zináparo, Michoacán. Therefore, these 30 artifacts may have come from as many as 16 distinct sources.

Our understanding of the chronology of sites in northwest Mexico, such as La Quemada and Alta Vista, is changing. It once was thought that these two sites dated to the Early Postclassic period (e.g., Armillas 1969), but it now seems more likely that they span the Classic and Epiclassic periods (e.g., Kelley 1990; Nelson 1990; Trombold 1990). Other sites and regions in northwest Mexico, such as Las Ventanas in the Juchipila Valley, have long occupations beginning in the Formative and lasting until the Colonial period. Sites in the Bolaños Valley often are assigned to only two broad temporal periods: before A.D. 700 and after A.D. 700.

Given the wide variety of sources, poor chronologies, and the preponderance of artifacts that cannot be

Table 20.1

Obsidian procurement patterns for Epiclassic (A.D. 650–1000) northwestern Mesoamerica, Terminal Classic (A.D. 800–1050) southeastern Mesoamerica, and Late Bagaces period (A.D. 600–950) Gran Nicoya

REGION/SITE	N	MEXICAN SOURCES[1]										CENTRAL AMERICAN SOURCES[2]				UNKNOWN SOURCE	References
		ALT	GDV	OTU	PAC	PAR	PDO	UCA	ZAC	ZAR	OTHER	CHY	IXT	SMJ	OTHER SOURCE		
NORTHWESTERN MESOAMERICA																	
Atzcapotzalco[3]	604			30	11	✓		60	✓		✓						García Chávez et al. 1990
Cantona	58									100							
Cerro d. l. Minas[4]	21		14	19	24			33		10							Elam et al. 1992
Cerro Portezuelo[5]	2				100												Sidrys 1977b
Cholula[6]	89	15	8		18		3	2		54							Hester et al. 1972
Cuajilote	6	33								67							
El Pital[6]	3									67						33	Jack et al. 1972
El Tajín[6]	7							14		86							
Jalieza	50		4	2	24	2		4		62							Elam 1993
Lambityeco	3							33		67							Elam 1993
Lower R. Verde[7]	16		6	13	6		13	44		19							Joyce et al. 1995
Matacapan	2504				10												Santley et al. 1984
Mixtequilla Zone[8]	4379		✓	✓	9	✓	25		✓	66							Heller & Stark 1998
Monte Albán	6				17					83							Elam 1993
Southern Isthmus[9]		48			✓		✓			50+					✓		Zeitlin 1982
Tula[10]																	
Corral	—				<10			>90									Healan 1993
Terminal Corral	—				~30			~70									Healan 1993
Mixed	33	4	6	6	9			73									Hester et al. 1973

Table 20.I continued

Obsidian procurement patterns for Epiclassic (A.D. 650–1000) northwestern Mesoamerica, Terminal Classic (A.D. 800–1050) southeastern Mesoamerica, and Late Bagaces period (A.D. 600–950) Gran Nicoya

REGION/SITE	N	MEXICAN SOURCES[1]										CENTRAL AMERICAN SOURCES[2]				UNKNOWN SOURCE	References
		ALT	GDV	OTU	PAC	PAR	PDO	UCA	ZAC	ZAR	OTHER	CHY	IXT	SMJ	OTHER		
Urichu[11]	33				6			24	6		64						Pollard (this volume)
Xochicalco	116			4	3	1		85	5							2	Hirth 1989
SOUTHEASTERN MESOAMERICA																	
Acapetahua[12]	83				1		5					30		60	4		Clark et al. 1989
Aventura	19											100					Neivens et al. 1983
Becan	49	4								14		71	10				Nelson et al. 1983
Central Peten Lakes	20											65	20	5		10	Rice et al. 1985
Chicanna	37							3		3		73	22				Rovner 1989
Chichén Itzá	4[13]			25	50			25									Nelson et al. 1977
	2[13]							100									Moholy-Nagy and Ladd 1992
Cobá	2745			1	21	8	4	32	1	7		10	12	4			Braswell 1998c
	4											100					Nelson et al. 1983
Colha	307				1		<1	<1				96	1	2			Dreiss 1988
	3											100					Dreiss et al. 1993
	199[14]											48	51	1			
Copán[15]	551				4			<1				1	94	1	<1		Aoyama 1999
	518				11			2		3		3	83	<1			Braswell and Manahan 2001
Cozumel	6				33			17				17	33				Nelson et al. 1983

Table 20.1 continued

Obsidian procurement patterns for Epiclassic (A.D. 650–1000) northwestern Mesoamerica, Terminal Classic (A.D. 800–1050) southeastern Mesoamerica, and Late Bagaces period (A.D. 600–950) Gran Nicoya

REGION/SITE	N	MEXICAN SOURCES[1]										CENTRAL AMERICAN SOURCES[2]				UNKNOWN SOURCE	References
		ALT	GDV	OTU	PAC	PAR	PDO	UCA	ZAC	ZAR	OTHER	CHY	IXT	SMJ	OTHER		
Dzibilchaltun	22											91	5	5			Nelson 1997
Ek Balam[16]	198				2						1	97					Braswell 1998c
Huanacastal[12]	120						3					27		23	48		Clark et al. 1989
Isla Cerritos[17]	38				37		3	45				11	5				Cobos 1998
Izapa[12]	41				5							32		54	10		Clark et al. 1989
Kaminaljuyu	73											97		3			
Labna	123			2	6			6			3	80	3	1			
Lag. Cayo Francesa	12							17				50	33				McKillop 1995b
Las Lomas[12]	327									<1		26	3	70	1	<1	Clark et al. 1989
Las Morenas[12]	105				8		14	3				14	4	36	19	2	Clark et al. 1989
Mango Creek	3											100					McKinnon et al.1989
Nohmul	20											20	80				Hammond et al. 1984
Oxkintok[18]	362			1	44	1		19	<1	<1	8	20	4	2			Neivens et al. 1983
Patchchacan	6											83	17				
Placencia	7											100					McKinnon et al.1989
Quelepa	383											<1	99	<1			Braswell et al. 1994
Rancho Alegre[12]	35											17	6	74	3		Clark et al. 1989
Rio Arriba[12]	72							6			3	40	6	44		1	Clark et al. 1989
San Gervasio	12											33	67				
San Juan[19]	79				14			2				74	8			2	Guderjan et al.1989

Table 20.1 continued

Obsidian procurement patterns for Epiclassic (A.D. 650–1000) northwestern Mesoamerica, Terminal Classic (A.D. 800–1050) southeastern Mesoamerica, and Late Bagaces period (A.D. 600–950) Gran Nicoya

REGION/SITE	N	MEXICAN SOURCES[1]										CENTRAL AMERICAN SOURCES[2]				UNKNOWN SOURCE	References
		ALT	GDV	OTU	PAC	PAR	PDO	UCA	ZAC	ZAR	OTHER	CHY	IXT	SMJ	OTHER SOURCE		
Santa Rita Corozal	3											100					Neivens et al. 1983
Seibal	22										5	50	14	32			Nelson et al. 1978
Tenampua[20]	2														100		Braswell et al. 1995
Tikal	5				20							40	40				Moholy-Nagy and Nelson 1990
Tikal-Yaxha transect[21]	2												100				Ford et al. 1997
Tipu[22]	45											56	29			16	Baxter 1984
Topoxte	12											75	17	8			Braswell 2000b
Uxmal	10								10			90					Nelson et al. 1983
Wild Cane Caye[23]	442			<1	5	<1	2	13	<1		5	48	24	1			McKillop 1996
Xelha[24]	4									25		75			7		
Xkipche[25]	108			1	2			3	1	1		88	4				
Xunantunich[26]	290							<1		2		81	14	4			J. Braswell 1998
Yaxha	5											40		60			
Yaxuna	33			6	6			39	6			42					Braswell 1998c
Zacualpa[27]	5													100			
GRAN NICOYA																	
Ayala[28]	3													33	67		Salgado 1996
	338								<1					12	88		Braswell 1997

Table 20.I continued

Obsidian procurement patterns for Epiclassic (A.D. 650–1000) northwestern Mesoamerica, Terminal Classic (A.D. 800–1050) southeastern Mesoamerica, and Late Bagaces period (A.D. 600–950) Gran Nicoya

REGION/SITE	N	MEXICAN SOURCES[1]										CENTRAL AMERICAN SOURCES[2]				UNKNOWN SOURCE	References
		ALT	GDV	OTU	PAC	PAR	PDO	UCA	ZAC	ZAR	OTHER	CHY	IXT	SMJ	OTHER SOURCE		
Cacaulí I[29]	11											9				91	Braswell 1997
Güiligüisca[30]	46												15			85	Braswell 1997
La Cruz	8															100	
Playas Verdes[28]	34											3	6			91	

Note: Values shown under each source are expressed as percents; ✓ indicates present but no quantitative data available; if no reference is cited, data first appear here.

1 ALT=Altotonga, Veracruz; GDV=Guadalupe Victoria, Puebla; OTU=Otumba, México; PAC=Pachuca, Hidalgo; PAR=Paredón, Hidalgo; PDO=Pico de Orizaba, Veracruz; UCA=Ucareo-Zinapécuaro-Cruz Negra, Michoacán; ZAC=Zacualtipan, Hidalgo; ZAR=Zaragoza, Puebla.

2 CHY=El Chayal, Guatemala; IXT=Ixtepeque, Guatemala; SMJ=San Martín Jilotepeque, Guatemala.

3 Nine "gray" pieces analyzed by NAA, values shown for OTU and UCA are extrapolated from those results.

4 Oaxaca, Mixteca Baja region, Ñuiñe phase (A.D. 300–800).

5 Three additional pieces (two UCA, one OTU) are either Epiclassic or Early Postclassic in date.

6 Chronological placement insecure, perhaps Classic.

7 Coastal Oaxaca, Yuta Tiyoo Phase (A.D. 550–900).

8 Sources with ✓ identified chemically in zone. All appear in trace quantities except GDV, which drops considerably after the Preclassic period.

9 Other Mexican sources not specified.

10 Corral Phase = A.D. 700–800; Terminal Corral Phase = A.D. 800–900/950. Mixed Epiclassic and Early Postclassic samples chosen to represent full visual variation (i.e., not a random collection).

11 Michoacán, Lupe-La Joya Phase (A.D. 600–900). Other Mexican is Zináparo-Varal-Preito, Michoacán, source complex.

12 Chiapas, dated to A.D. 600–1000. Other Central American source (if present) is Tajumulco, Guatemala.

13 Material of uncertain temporal assignment from Sacred Cenote.

14 Late to Terminal Classic period.

15 Ejar-phase contexts (A.D. 950–1050), includes significant quantities of recycled earlier material as well as pieces from fill. Other Central American source is La Esperanza, Honduras.

16 Samples come from Late and Terminal Classic contexts.

17 Material dates to Chacpel/Jotuta and Early Joruta phase (A.D. 750–1050).

18 Other Mexican source consists of pieces that should be assigned to either Ucareo or Zaragoza.

19 Includes small quantities from other periods; unknown source most closely matches Tequila-La Primavera complex, Jalisco. Resourced by McKillop (1995).

20 Other Central American source is La Esperanza, Honduras.

21 Late to Terminal Classic contexts.

22 Some of source unknown material probably is from SMJ.

23 Late to Terminal Classic contexts; other Central American source is "Puente Chetunal," Guatemala.

24 Chemuyil phase (A.D. 600–900/1000). Other Mexican source is Ucareo or Zaragoza.

25 Includes some earlier material. Other Mexican source is Huitzila, Zacatecas.

26 Late Classic material.

27 Pokom phase.

28 Granada, Nicaragua. Other Central American source is Güinope, Honduras.

29 Madriz, Nicaragua. Other Central American source is Güinope, Honduras.

30 Carazo, Nicaragua. Other Central American source is Güinope, Honduras.

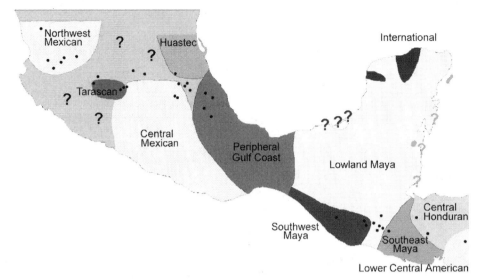

Figure 20.2 Obsidian exchange spheres of the Epiclassic (A.D. 650–1000) and Terminal Classic (A.D. 800–1050) periods

assigned yet to any known volcanic formation, I have not listed any sites in the northwest Mexican sphere in table 20.1. Instead, I discuss procurement data here in an abbreviated form. The interested reader is referred to Darling 1998 and Trombold et al. 1993, from which all the relevant data have been gleaned.

Darling (1998) suggests that two distinct obsidian procurement systems were used in the northwest Mexican sphere. First, most material was procured at local sources and used for ad hoc flake production and biface manufacture. Second, prismatic blades were imported in finished form from the Teuchitlan region of Jalisco, as well as from other areas in the Mesoamerican core. Sites where prismatic blades have been recovered tend to be large regional centers where ceremonial architecture, presumably inspired by Mesoamerica, also has been found. In this respect, the northwest Mexican sphere resembles the lower Central American sphere (see below), located at the opposite extreme of the Mesoamerican world. Prismatic blade importation began in the eighth century and apparently continued until the Spanish conquest.

Darling (1998) analyzed 167 artifacts from sites in northwest Mexico; only 16 are prismatic blade fragments. Eight prismatic blades recovered from sites in the Tlaltenango Valley region of Zacatecas were attributed to the La Joya–Teuchitlan–La Primavera source area. Thus, the inhabitants of the Tlaltenango Valley imported their prismatic blades from the Teuchitlan region of Jalisco. In contrast, most of the non-blade obsidian came from the closer Huitzila-La Lobera source area and Unknown-A, which probably is part of the Huitzila system (Darling 1998:329, table C.1). Two more prismatic blades analyzed by Darling (1998: table C.2) were recovered from sites in the Bolaños Valley of Jalisco and Zacatecas. These were attributed to the Huitzila–La

Lobera source area and Unknown-C. Most of the obsidian used to make flakes in this region came either from Huitzila–La Lobera or Unknown-B, -C, or -I. One prismatic blade from the Chapalanga Valley of Zacatecas came from the La Joya–Teuchitlan–La Primavera source area, but a second could not be assigned to any group (Darling 1998: table C.3). In contrast, most of the flakes and flake cores in the Chapalanga Valley came from Unknown-D, -H, or -J. As mentioned above, a single blade fragment from La Quemada came from the Pachuca source. Flakes and chunks from La Quemada and elsewhere in the Malpaso Valley of Zacatecas that were analyzed by Darling (1998: table C.5) came from the Nochistlan, Zináparo-Varal-Prieto, and Huitzila–La Lobera source areas, as well as from Unknown-C and Unknown-E. Finally, three prismatic blades found at sites in the Chalchihuites region of Durango came from the Pachuca and La Joya–Teuchitlan–La Primavera source areas, as well as from an unidentified source. In contrast, most of the ad hoc flakes and cores were attributed to the Cerro de Navajas source area of Unknown-B, -D, and -F (Darling 1998: table C.6). Thus, of the 16 blades from sites in the northwest Mexican sphere analyzed by Darling, 10 came from sources in the Teuchitlan region of Jalisco, and 2 from Pachuca, Hidalgo: both regions are generally considered part of Mesoamerica. One more comes from the Huitzila–La Lobera source area, just north of the Teuchitlan core. As Darling argues, this pattern strongly suggests that prismatic blades found in the northwest Mexican sphere were manufactured in the Teuchitlan region or elsewhere in Mesoamerica and were not made locally.

Obsidian from only two source areas in the northwest Mexican obsidian sphere—La Joya–Teuchitlan–La Primavera and Huitzila–La Lobera—has been found elsewhere. A recent study documents the use of La Joya–Teuchitlan–La Primavera obsidian in the Río Marques region of Michoacán (Esparza López 1999). Two more artifacts have been found very far afield at Maya sites dating to the Terminal Classic period. The first, from the minor Puuc center of Xkipché, has been assigned to the Huitzila-2 subsource (table C6.1). The second, from San Juan, Ambergris Caye, most closely resembles material from La Joya–Teuchitlan–La Primavera, but was not assigned unambiguously to that source complex. The presence of these exotic artifacts in the Maya region suggests contact, however indirect, with the Teuchitlan region. Connections between the Teuchitlan region and central Mexico have been demonstrated for the Classic period (e.g., Weigand 1985, 1990). During the period A.D. 700–900, however, the prosperity of the region declined, so it is not surprising that obsidian from these sources has not been found at Postclassic sites outside of west Mexico.

TARASCAN ZONE

Source provenance data for Epiclassic obsidian artifacts in the Tarascan obsidian exchange sphere are limited to just one site, Urichu, located near the western shore of Lake Pátzcuaro (chapter 29). Most obsidian at Urichu is found in the form of utilized flakes from the Zináparo-Varal-Prieto source complex located northwest of the Zacapu Basin. Smaller quantities of obsidian, including prismatic blades, are sourced to the Ucareo-Zinapécuaro–Cruz Negra (henceforth, Ucareo) source complex, as well as to Pachuca and Zacualtipan, Hidalgo. Although the Epiclassic sample is small, it is notable that no obsidian from sources in Querétaro or Guanajuato are present in the collection. Economic ties with distant trade partners to the east were more important than connections to closer sites north of the Tarascan region.

Ceramics from the Ucareo source area that date to the Epiclassic period show no close similarities to pottery from either the Tarascan region or Tula. It is likely, then, that extraction and production at this source were locally controlled (Hernández and Healan 1999). Thus, although a significant quantity of obsidian reached the Pátzcuaro region from Ucareo, the source was outside the boundaries of Tarascan economic and political control during the Epiclassic period.

HUASTEC SPHERE

No data have been published on obsidian procurement patterns in the Huastec region. Nonetheless, several researchers have observed that Huastec pottery can be found at Zacualtipan, the northernmost source in Hidalgo (Cobean 1991; Dan M. Healan, personal communication, 1999). Furthermore, Zacualtipan obsidian, with its characteristic dark black color and low surface luster, has been identified visually at several Huastec sites

(Cobean 1991), including the Late Postclassic center of Tamohí (table 20.3). Since Zacualtipan is the only source that appears to be represented in the Huastec region, and only small quantities ever were traded beyond this zone, I tentatively propose that a Huastec obsidian sphere existed in the Epiclassic and Postclassic periods.

Trace amounts of Zacualtipan obsidian have been noted at Azcapotzalco (García Chávez et al. 1990), Urichu (Pollard, this volume), and Xochicalco (Hirth 1989), and in the Mixtequilla (Heller and Stark 1998) and Maya regions (e.g., Braswell 1998c; Nelson et al. 1983). In fact, a small prismatic blade reused as a bipolar core was found at the Ayala site in Pacific Nicaragua, more than 1,600 km from the Zacualtipan source (Braswell 1997).

CENTRAL MEXICAN SPHERE

Epiclassic obsidian procurement patterns in central Mexico reflect a strong dependence on the Ucareo, Michoacán, source. Important regional centers such as Tula (Healan 1993), Xochicalco (Hirth 1989), and Azcapotzalco (García Chávez et al. 1990) received most of their obsidian in the form of cores imported from Ucareo. In fact, obsidian from this source was one of the most widely and intensely traded commodities of Epiclassic Mesoamerica.

Much smaller quantities of obsidian from Pachuca and Otumba also were distributed in Epiclassic central Mexico. Material from the second source, though, was not widely traded beyond the Basin of Mexico and was subject to a remarkably steep drop-off. Azcapotzalco, the nearest important site for which there are published data, received just 30 percent of its obsidian from Otumba during the Epiclassic period (García Chávez et al. 1990).

The fact that only a small quantity of Pachuca obsidian reached Tula during the Epiclassic period suggests that this important source was not yet controlled by the Toltecs (Healan 1993). In fact, given the rather limited distribution of Pachuca obsidian in central Mexico during the Epiclassic period, it seems unlikely that any major polity controlled its extraction or distribution.

PERIPHERAL GULF COAST SPHERE

Epiclassic sites along the Gulf coast and on the Isthmus of Tehuantepec received most of their obsidian from the Zaragoza, Puebla, source. This appears to have been the only extensively exploited Mexican source under the direct control of an important Epiclassic polity. Classic and Epiclassic Cantona, perhaps the most densely populated city in ancient Mesoamerica, is only 8 km south of Zaragoza (García Cook and Merino Carrión 1998; Ferriz 1985).

In addition to Cantona, which received nearly all of its obsidian from the Zaragoza source, Epiclassic samples from Cholula (Hester et al. 1972), El Tajín (Jack et al.

1972), the Mixtequilla region (Heller and Stark 1998), El Pital, and Cuajilote are dominated by obsidian from Zaragoza. It is likely that the majority of Epiclassic Matacapan obsidian also will prove to be attributable to Zaragoza.

Smaller quantities of obsidian from three additional sources within the boundary of this exchange sphere also were exploited in the Epiclassic period, although much less extensively. These sources are Altotonga, Guadalupe Victoria, and Pico de Orizaba.

Figure 20.2 depicts the boundary between the peripheral Gulf coast and central Mexican spheres as passing west of the Valley of Oaxaca and reaching the Pacific coast west of the Isthmus of Tehuantepec. Although we have relatively few data from central and coastal Oaxaca, sites in the western half of the state, including the Mixteca Baja and lower Río Verde regions, received most of their obsidian from Ucareo and the other sources exploited by the central Mexican exchange sphere (Elam 1993; Elam et al. 1992; Joyce et al. 1995). In contrast, sites in the Valley of Oaxaca and on the southern isthmus participated in the peripheral Gulf coast exchange sphere. As distance from the sources increased, however, the boundary between the two spheres became more tenuous.

LOWLAND MAYA SPHERE

During the Late Classic period, the vast majority of obsidian entering the central and northern Maya lowlands came from a single source: El Chayal, Guatemala. This pattern became attenuated during the Terminal Classic period, particularly in the northern lowlands and along the Caribbean littoral.

The declining importance of the El Chayal source may be attributed to two events. First, Kaminaljuyú, the largest Late Classic site in the central Maya highlands, was abandoned sometime in the ninth century. It is often assumed that elites residing at the site oversaw the extraction, production, and export of prismatic blade cores from El Chayal (e.g., Michels 1979), although I know of no evidence from the quarry region that supports this conclusion. Second, the political collapse and abandonment of the Petén during the ninth and early tenth centuries disrupted the overland trade networks that carried El Chayal obsidian into the lowlands. The decline of the lowland Maya obsidian exchange sphere may have been more rapid than suggested by data in table 20.1. Many of the obsidian artifacts found in Terminal Classic contexts at sites such as Topoxté and Calakmul appear to have been reused or scavenged from cores discarded in earlier periods (Braswell 2000b; Braswell et al. n.d.).

Obsidian was an uncommon good at Late Classic sites in the northern Maya lowlands. The overland trade network that supplied obsidian to Cobá, Dzibilchaltún, and sites in the Puuc region during the eighth century was insufficiently organized to bring significant quantities of prepared cores north of the Petén. Fall-off in the concentration of Classic-period obsidian in the central Maya lowlands is rather abrupt. Although more than a million obsidian artifacts were excavated by the Tikal project (Moholy-Nagy 1997), only 515 were recovered during three years of extensive excavations at Calakmul, just 100 km north of Tikal (Braswell et al. n.d.). In fact, jade is more common at Calakmul than obsidian (Braswell et al. 1998).

INTERNATIONAL SPHERE

Beginning about A.D. 800, obsidian began entering the northern lowlands via important ports on the west and north coasts of Yucatán. The first exotic obsidian to reach the northern lowlands in quantity probably came from Zaragoza. Obsidian from that source constitutes 17 percent of the Late Classic sample from Comalcalco, a site in the northwest periphery of the Maya region (Lewenstein and Glascock 1997). Importantly, no material from Ucareo is present in the collection. Late Classic Comalcalco, then, participated in the lowland Maya obsidian exchange sphere but also obtained significant quantities of obsidian through the peripheral Gulf coast exchange network.

An important Terminal Classic port of entry for Mexican obsidian was Isla Cerritos, associated with Chichén Itzá (Andrews et al. 1989). Terminal Classic collections from both Isla Cerritos and Chichén Itzá are dominated by obsidian from distant sources in Mexico, particularly Ucareo and Pachuca, the principal sources exploited by sites in the central Mexican exchange sphere. But the sources found in both collections are quite varied: prepared cores were imported from Zacualtipan in the Huastec sphere, Zaragoza and Pico de Orizaba in the peripheral Gulf coast sphere, and Paredón, a source of high-quality obsidian that was not widely exploited in Epiclassic highland Mexico. In addition to the seven Mexican sources, exhausted cores from all three major Guatemalan sources have been found at Chichén Itzá. Because of the wide variety of sources represented in collections from Chichén Itzá and related sites, they collectively form what I call the international exchange sphere.

Mexican obsidian also is found in the Puuc zone at sites with significant ninth-to-eleventh-century occupations; that is, sites with substantial mosaic-style Puuc architecture. These include Uxmal, Oxkintok, Labná, and Kabah. There is a general decline in quantity of exotic obsidian as the distance from the west coast increases and site size decreases. Although it is possible that Mexican obsidian was received in trade from Chichén Itzá, some probably entered the Puuc region through a port on the coast. Punta Canbalam, a site now under water, is one candidate. Green obsidian from the Pachuca source is found commonly on the beach near the site (Dahlin et al. 1998).

Obsidian from Ucareo and Pachuca is present at many Terminal Classic Maya sites. Blue-black obsidian from Ucareo and green Pachuca blades with ground platforms are two of the clearest diagnostics of ninth- to eleventh-century occupations at sites throughout the Maya area. For example, more than 13 percent of the obsidian artifacts recovered from Ejar-phase contexts at Copán come from these sources (Braswell and Manahan 2001; see also Aoyama 1999). Still, outside of the international obsidian exchange sphere, the proportion of Mexican material in obsidian collections is generally quite low and decreases as the distance from the Gulf coast and Caribbean shoreline increases.

Within the northern Maya lowlands, there are sharp territorial divisions between sites that received significant quantities of obsidian from Mexican sources and those that did not. Chichén Itzá and Uxmal apparently participated in the same international obsidian trade network, but sites like Cobá and Ek Balam did not.[3]

SOUTHWEST MAYA SPHERE

Sites in the Maya highlands and Pacific lowlands west of Kaminaljuyú participated in an obsidian exchange sphere that began to form as early as the Archaic period (Clark et al. 1989). Although the proportions of the three sources (San Martín Jilotepeque, Tajumulco, and El Chayal) that provided most of the obsidian consumed in this sphere shifted over time, suggesting that several distinct distribution mechanisms operated on the local level (e.g., Clark and Salcedo Romero 1989; Clark et al. 1989), regional procurement strategies were relatively stable until the Late Postclassic.

During the Early Classic period, most of the obsidian consumed in this zone came from the San Martín Jilotepeque source. In the Late and Terminal Classic (A.D. 600–1000), greater quantities of El Chayal obsidian were traded in the sphere, particularly in Chiapas. It seems likely that material from this source entered the western half of the obsidian exchange sphere via a trade route along the Pacific coast. I have observed significant quantities of both San Martín Jilotepeque and El Chayal obsidian at coastal centers such as El Baúl, but have found much less El Chayal obsidian at contemporary sites in the Kaqchikel and K'iche' highlands.

Although no Mexican obsidian is known from Late and Terminal Classic sites in the eastern half of the southwest Maya exchange sphere, a few pieces have been identified at sites in Xoconochco. In particular, Clark et al. (1989) have noted the presence of artifacts from the Pico de Orizaba, Zaragoza, Pachuca, and Ucareo sources at

six of seven sites dating to this period. Thus, it seems that small quantities of obsidian were entering the western edge of the zone from both the peripheral Gulf coast and central Mexican exchange spheres.

SOUTHEAST MAYA SPHERE

During the Classic period, Maya, Lenca, and other peoples in southeastern Guatemala, much of western Honduras, and all of El Salvador, relied almost exclusively on Ixtepeque obsidian. This high-quality source provided most of the raw material for making chipped-stone artifacts in this zone; at sites such as Copán, Tazumal, and El Cerén, chert artifacts are less common than obsidian blades from Ixtepeque.

Reliance on Ixtepeque obsidian is notable in parts of western Honduras and eastern El Salvador because La Esperanza, Honduras, is the closest source to sites in these regions (figure 20.1). Furthermore, although La Esperanza material lacks the shiny luster and translucence of Ixtepeque obsidian, material from the Honduran source is well suited for prismatic blade and biface manufacture. Differences in the quality of raw material do not explain the sharply delimited boundaries of the southeast Maya and central Honduran exchange spheres. The ceramic complexes of Quelepa and Tenampua also are quite dissimilar, supporting the hypothesis that little trade took place between eastern El Salvador and central Honduras.

During the Terminal Classic period, the southeast Maya obsidian exchange sphere began to expand, particularly along the Caribbean coast. Ixtepeque was the principal source of obsidian used at Terminal Classic Wild Cane Caye in southern Belize (McKillop 1996), Colha and Nohmul in northern Belize (Dreiss et al. 1993; Hammond et al. 1984), and San Gervasio on Cozumel Island. Significant quantities of Ixtepeque obsidian traveled inland from these coastal ports following major courses such as the Moho, Belize, Mopan, and New rivers, penetrating as far as Xunantunich (J. Braswell 1998), Tipu (Baxter 1984), Topoxté (Braswell 2000b), and Tikal (Ford et al. 1997; Moholy-Nagy and Nelson 1990).

CENTRAL HONDURAN SPHERE

Classic, Terminal Classic, and Postclassic sites in central and northern Honduras received nearly all their obsidian from the La Esperanza source, with smaller quantities coming from Ixtepeque and two low-quality Honduran sources: Güinope and San Luis. In central Honduras, where Lenca and other peoples built mound architecture and ball courts, and produced Uluá polychrome ceramics, obsidian from La Esperanza was used primarily for the prismatic blade industry. There is little evidence for blade production in northeast Honduras, where inhabitants seem to have produced casual flake tools and to have used imported blades.

Table 20.2

Obsidian procurement patterns for Early Postclassic (A.D. 1000/1050–1250/1300) Mesoamerica and Sapoa/Ometepe-period (A.D. 950–1550) Gran Nicoya

REGION/SITE	N	MEXICAN SOURCES[1]								CENTRAL AMERICAN SOURCES[2]				UNKNOWN SOURCE	Reference
		OTU	PAC	PAR	PDO	UCA	ZAC	ZAR	OTHER	CHY	IXT	SMJ	OTHER		
NORTHWESTERN MESOAMERICA															
Cerro Portezuelo[3]	4		75			25									Sidrys 1977b
Jalieza	20	10	10		10			70							Elam 1993
Mixtequilla Zone[4]	1859	✓	2	✓	87		✓	11							Heller & Stark 1998
Rancho Dolores[5]	4								100						Winter 1989
Southern Isthmus[6]	—	~7	~30		~52		✓		✓	✓				✓	Zeitlin 1982
Teopanzolco[7]	107	6	93	1										2	Smith et al. 1984
Tepozteco[7]	85	21	58			21									Smith et al. 1984
Tetla[7]	45	11	82	5										2	Smith et al. 1984
Tula	—		~85	✓		~15									Healan 1993
Urichu[8]	24		8			8	4		79						Pollard (this volume)
Xaracuaro[8]	10					40			60						Pollard (this volume)
Xochicalco[7]	237		49			51									Smith et al. 1984
Yautepec[9]	984	3	93	2		<1			2						Smith et al. 1996
SOUTHEASTERN MESOAMERICA															
Central Petén Lakes	26									19	58	15		8	Rice et al. 1985
Chuisac[10]	1214									9	1	90			Braswell 1996
Cihuatan	20									35	60	5			Fowler et al. 1987
Colha	10										100				Hester and Shafer 1983
False Caye	3		67							33					McKinnon et al. 1989
Frenchman's Caye	2		50							50					McKinnon et al. 1989
Isla Cerritos[11]	18	7	39	7		7		14		34					Cobos 1998

Table 20.2 continued

Obsidian procurement patterns for Early Postclassic (A.D. 1000/1050–1250/1300) Mesoamerica and Sapoa/Ometepe-period (A.D. 950–1550) Gran Nicoya

REGION/SITE	N	MEXICAN SOURCES[1]								CENTRAL AMERICAN SOURCES[2]				UNKNOWN	Reference
		OTU	PAC	PAR	PDO	UCA	ZAC	ZAR	OTHER	CHY	IXT	SMJ	OTHER	SOURCE	
Izapa[12]	147	1	3			4			1	27	1	50	13		Clark et al. 1989
Las Morenas[12]	4						25					75			Clark et al. 1989
Las Vegas[13]	52		2								23		73	2	Braswell et al. 1995
Moho Caye, Toledo	1										100				Hammond 1976
Pulltrowser Swamp[14]	3									67	33				Dreiss 1988
Río Claro[13]	3												100		Healy et al. 1996
San Gervasio	31			3		3					90	3			
Sula Valley[13]	1												100		Pope 1987
Wild Cane Caye[15]	75					1				8	84	1	6		McKillop 1996
Xelha	17											100			
Zacualpa	4										100				
GRAN NICOYA															
Ayala[16]	127									1	24		76		Braswell 1997
Bahia de Salinas[17]	1												100		Sheets et al. 1990
Caldera[18]	9									11	44		44		
La Pachona[19]	2											50	50		
Los Jocotes[18]	1									100					
Nindiri[18]	9										33		67		Sheets et al. 1990
Rio Sapóa[20]	1												100		Sheets et al. 1990
San Cristobal[21]	3										33		67		Healy et al. 1996
Santa Isabel "A"[22]	2										100				Healy et al. 1996
Tepetate[16]	35									3	66		31		
Vidor[23]	2										50	50			Sheets et al. 1990

Values shown under each source are expressed as percents; ✔ indicates present but no quantitative data available; if no reference is cited, data first appear here.

[1] OTU=Otumba, México; PAC=Pachuca, Hidalgo; PAR=Paredón, Hidalgo; PDO=Pico de Orizaba, Veracruz; UCA=Ucareo-Zinapécuaro-Cruz Negra, Michoacán; ZAC=Zacualtipan, Hidalgo; ZAR=Zaragoza, Puebla.

[2] CHY=El Chayal, Guatemala; IXT=Ixtepeque, Guatemala; SMJ=San Martín Jilotepeque, Guatemala.

Table 20.2 continued

Obsidian procurement patterns for Early Postclassic (A.D. 1000/1050–1250/1300) Mesoamerica and Sapoa/Ometepe-period (A.D. 950–1550) Gran Nicoya

3 Three additional pieces (two UCA, one OTU) are either Epiclassic or Early Postclassic in date.
4 Sources with ✔ identified chemically in zone. All appear in trace quantities except Guadelupe Victoria, which drops considerably after the Preclassic period.
5 Oaxaca; other Mexican source is Guadelupe Victoria, Puebla.
6 Oaxaca; other Mexican and Central American sources not specified.
7 Morelos; only 8 "gray" artifacts sourced; values extrapolated from this sample.
8 Michoacán; other Mexican source is Zináparo-Varal-Prieto.
9 Other Mexican sources are El Paraiso (1%), Tulancingo (<1%), and Fuentezuelas (<1%).
10 San Martín Jilotepeque, Guatemala.
11 Late Jotuta phase (A.D. 1050–1200); assay results extrapolated for unanalyzed "gray" obsidian.
12 Chiapas; other Central American source is Tajumulco, Guatemala.
13 Honduras; other Central American source is La Esperanza, Honduras.
14 Undifferentiated Postclassic.
15 Undifferentiated Postclassic. Other Central American sources are "Puente Chetunal," Guatemala (4%), and La Esperanza, Honduras (1%).
16 Granada, Nicaragua. Other is Güinope, Honduras.
17 Costa Rica; other Central American source is "Nica-2."
18 Masaya, Nicaragua. Other Central American source is Güinope, Honduras.
19 Chontales, Nicaragua. Other Central American source is Güinope, Honduras.
20 Costa Rica; other Central American source is Güinope, Honduras.
21 Managua, Nicaragua. Other Central American sources are La Esperanza (33%) and Güinope (33%), Honduras.
22 Rivas, Nicaragua.
23 Costa Rica.

LOWER CENTRAL AMERICAN SPHERE

Until quite recently, little was known about obsidian trade and production in lower Central America (Sheets et al. 1990). The Late Bagaces period (A.D. 600–850/950) is of particular interest. In Late Bagaces times and in the following Sapoá/Ometepe period, at least three waves of immigrants from Mesoamerica arrived in Pacific Nicaragua. The first group to arrive, the Chorotega, originally came from the region around Cholula, settled for a time in Xoconochco, and moved into Pacific Nicaragua about A.D. 800 (Healy 1980). The Nicarao, a Nahua group that also resided for a time in Xoconochco, arrived in the Rivas region around A.D. 1200. Finally, the Subtiaba, originally from the Tlapanec region of Guerrero, also came to Pacific Nicaragua at the end of the Mesoamerican Early Postclassic period (Fowler 1989:33–35).

The Late Bagaces–period inhabitants of Pacific Nicaragua produced neither prismatic blades nor bifaces. Like inhabitants of Caribbean Honduras and other parts of lower Central America, they made crude ad hoc flake and chopper tools out of chert, chalcedony, and obsidian. Most obsidian artifacts dating to this period are casual and bipolar flakes or cores from the Güinope, Honduras, source. Obsidian from Güinope was imported as small nodules and pebbles and worked locally. Drop-off in the quantity and size of Late Bagaces–period obsidian artifacts is monotonic, suggesting that nodules were exchanged in a down-the-line network.

Small quantities of prismatic blades made of Guatemalan obsidian also were traded through this loosely organized exchange network. The majority of these are made of Ixtepeque obsidian and are morphologically similar to prismatic blades found at Quelepa, Honduras (Braswell 1997). Since Delirio Red-on-white ceramics produced at Quelepa have been found at several sites in Nicaragua, it seems likely that the blades entered lower Central America from this community in the southeastern periphery of Mesoamerica. As noted, a single prismatic blade from the Zacualtipan source has been found at a site in Pacific Nicaragua. The lack of prismatic blade technology and the presence of blades imported from Mesoamerica is an important parallel with the northwest Mexican sphere.

EARLY POSTCLASSIC OBSIDIAN EXCHANGE SPHERES (A.D. 1000/1050–1250/1300)

During the two and a half centuries of the Early Postclassic period (A.D. 1000/1050–1250/1300), regional and interregional obsidian procurement strategies transformed as new centers of political power emerged in Mesoamerica. In the northwest, significant changes in the sources exploited by exchange spheres occurred (table 20.2), although the borders of these spheres shifted very little (figure 20.3). In southeastern Mesoamerica, changes

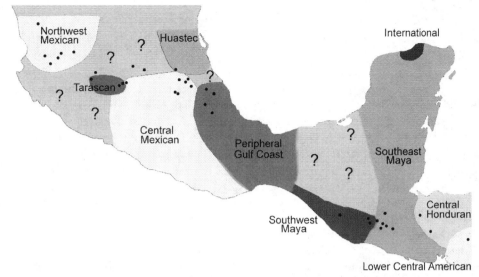

Figure 20.3 Obsidian exchange spheres of the Early Postclassic period (A.D. 1000/1050–1250/1300)

TARASCAN SPHERE

in the location of principal trade routes seem to have played a larger role. Few changes can be seen in several exchange spheres. For this reason, only regions exhibiting new Early Postclassic patterns are discussed.

TARASCAN SPHERE

Obsidian procurement data for the Early Postclassic period come from only two sites in the Tarascan region: Urichu and Xarácuaro. As in the Epiclassic period, material from the Zináparo-Varal-Prieto source complex comprises most of the sample, with lesser amounts coming from Pachuca and the Ucareo source area.

Pollard (chapter 29) divides the centuries I have assigned to the Early Postclassic into two ceramic phases: Early Urichu (A.D. 900–1000/1100) and Late Urichu (A.D. 1000/1100–1300). The Early Urichu sample, corresponding to the Epiclassic–Early Postclassic transition, contains no artifacts from Ucareo, the only portion of the Ucareo-Zinapécuaro–Cruz Negra source complex where high-quality obsidian is found. This phase is contemporary with the Terminal Corral and Early Tollan phases at Tula, when Ucareo obsidian constituted 60–80 percent of the material consumed at the site (Healan 1993:454; Ringle et al. 1998:222). It may be that the lack of Ucareo obsidian in the Tarascan region during the tenth and eleventh centuries was somehow related to heavy exploitation by the central Mexican exchange sphere. Although this hypothesis is quite plausible, only 14 artifacts dating to the Early Urichu phase were assayed. Thus, the lack of Ucareo material in the sample may be a reflection of its small size. Furthermore, some obsidian from the central Mexican exchange system did enter the Tarascan region during the Early Urichu phase. Two obsidian blades in the analyzed sample come from the Pachuca source, located east of Tula.

Ten pieces dating to the Late Urichu phase also were sourced. Two of these, one from each site, are assigned to the Ucareo portion of the greater Ucareo-Zinapécuaro–Cruz Negra source complex. If there was a barrier to trade across the Tarascan–central Mexican frontier during the tenth or eleventh centuries, it disappeared in the second half of the Early Postclassic period.

CENTRAL MEXICAN SPHERE

Two regional capitals emerged in central Mexico during the Early Postclassic period: Tula and Cholula.[4] The economic and political growth of these cities had important ramifications for the sources of obsidian that circulated in both the central Mexican and peripheral Gulf coast exchange spheres. At the beginning of the Early Postclassic, extraction and production at the Pachuca source increased dramatically. The vast majority of obsidian consumed at Tollan-phase Tula came from this source (Healan 1993). Diehl (1981:290) and Spence and Parsons (1972:29) have proposed that the Pachuca source came under the direct political control of Tula at this time. Although this remains a possibility, it may be that the growing demand for obsidian at Tula precipitated an increase in production at the source. Recent surveys around the mines themselves demonstrate a Toltec presence at Pachuca, but the vast majority of recovered ceramics date to the Late Postclassic period (Cruz Antillón 1994; Pastrana 1990, 1998).

Early Postclassic occupants of sites in Morelos (including Teopanzalco, Tepozteco, Tetla, and Yautepec) also received most of their obsidian from the Pachuca source (Smith et al. 1984; Smith et al. 1996). The sole exception is Xochicalco, where more than half of the Early Postclassic sample comes from Ucareo. But given the strong Epiclassic occupation of the site, this may be a result of stratigraphic mixing. Alternatively, Postclassic inhabitants of Xochicalco may have scavenged obsidian blades from Epiclassic contexts.

PERIPHERAL GULF COAST SPHERE

A similar shift of the principal exploited source occurred in the peripheral Gulf coast exchange sphere during the Early Postclassic period. In this case, the shift was away from Zaragoza, the primary source of the Epiclassic, to a reliance on the Pico de Orizaba source. This change was due in part to the decline of the city of Cantona. A second cause may have been the development of new mining technologies. During earlier periods, only the superficial layers of the obsidian flows at Pico de Orizaba were exploited. These layers yield small, irregular slabs of raw material that are not well suited for the prismatic blade industry (Daneels and Pastrana 1988:108). In the Postclassic period, however, shaft-mining techniques introduced from central Mexico allowed access to high-quality obsidian (Anick Daneels, personal communication, 1996).

A third cause for the shift to Pico de Orizaba obsidian may have been the rise of Cholula, the south pole of Early Postclassic central Mexico. Pico de Orizaba and Zaragoza, the two sources of high-quality obsidian closest to Cholula, are about 110 km away. When production at Zaragoza declined as a result of the abandonment of Cantona, increasing demand at Cholula probably served to intensify production at Pico de Orizaba. Unfortunately, no Postclassic obsidian artifacts from Cholula have been attributed to geological sources, so this remains a conjecture.

Who was mining obsidian at Pico de Orizaba? The source does not seem to have been under the direct control of any large site during the Early Postclassic period. Daneels (1997:249) hypothesizes that the Cotaxtla region, immediately east of Pico de Orizaba, was settled in the Early Postclassic by Nahua immigrants from Tlaxcala. Postclassic ceramics from the Cotaxtla zone include characteristic Mixteca-Puebla wares, as well as other types known from the altiplano (Daneels 1997:244–245). The presence of these ceramics near Pico de Orizaba supports the hypothesis that Postclassic exploitation of the source can be linked to Cholula.

Data from the Mixtequilla region provide some of the strongest evidence for a shift to Pico de Orizaba obsidian before the end of the Early Postclassic period (Heller and Stark 1998). Here, in contexts dating to A.D. 1200–1350 (and perhaps earlier), fully 87 percent of all obsidian artifacts are assigned to the Pico de Orizaba source. Data from the Valley of Oaxaca (Elam 1993; Winter 1989) and the southern isthmus (Zeitlin 1982) also demonstrate continued participation in the peripheral Gulf coast exchange sphere.

SOUTHWEST MAYA SPHERE

Few Early Postclassic sites in the southwest Maya exchange sphere have received significant investigation, despite the fact that Tohil Plumbate, one of the most widely traded ceramic wares in Mesoamerica, originated in the western half of this zone.

In the Xoconochco region, sites like Izapa and Las Morenas continued to receive most of their obsidian from San Martín Jilotepeque, El Chayal, and Tajumulco. At Izapa, significant quantities of obsidian from Ucareo, Pachuca, and Otumba also are represented in the collection. This suggests economic relations with sites in the central Mexican, but not the peripheral Gulf coast, exchange sphere. Perhaps, then, most Plumbate entered northwestern Mesoamerica before A.D. 1200 through Pacific and overland, rather than Gulf coast, trade routes.

SOUTHEAST MAYA SPHERE

The most notable change in obsidian procurement strategies in the Maya region during the Early Postclassic period was the expansion of the southeast Maya exchange sphere. Sotuta-Hocaba contexts at Chichén Itzá, dating to about A.D. 1050, contain the greatest proportions of Ixtepeque obsidian found at the site. At Isla Cerritos, however, no Ixtepeque obsidian has been found in Early Postclassic contexts, but the sample size (N = 18) is small. Still, it seems likely that this site continued to participate in the international exchange sphere after its inland capital was abandoned. Other coastal sites such as Xelha, San Gervasio, Wild Cane Caye (McKillop 1996), and Moho Caye (Hammond 1976) received most of their obsidian from Ixtepeque. What little data we have for inland sites in the Maya lowlands also support an Early Postclassic expansion of the southeast Maya exchange sphere (e.g., Braswell 2000b; Rice et al. 1985).

Who extracted obsidian from Volcán de Ixtepeque during the Postclassic? The nearest important Classic and Postclassic polities were centered at Copán, Chalchuapa, and Cihuatan, respectively 72, 81, and 75 km from the source. Copán was abandoned shortly after A.D. 820 and was briefly and lightly reoccupied about A.D. 950. Inhabitants of that site could not have supervised production at Ixtepeque during the Early Postclassic period, particularly after about A.D. 1050/1100, when Copán was again abandoned. Both Tazumal (in the Chalchuapa zone) and Cihuatan were extensively occupied during the Postclassic period, but no Pipil ceramics have been found near the source. Thus, extraction and production at Ixtepeque were likely managed by local inhabitants of the southeastern Guatemalan highlands.

LOWER CENTRAL AMERICAN SPHERE

The last six centuries of prehistoric Nicaragua are divided into two periods: Sapoá and Ometepe. In practice,

Table 20.3

Obsidian procurement patterns for Late Postclassic (A.D. 1250/1300–1520) Mesoamerica

| REGION/SITE | N | MEXICAN SOURCES[1] | | | | | | | | | | CENTRAL AMERICAN SOURCES[2] | | | | UNKNOWN | Reference |
		OTU	PAC	PAR	PDO	TUL	UCA	ZAC	ZAR	ZNP	OTHER	CHY	IXT	SMJ	OTHER	SOURCE	
NORTHWESTERN MESOAMERICA																	
Acámbaro[3]	8						75									25	Pollard &Vogel 1994
Apatzingan[4]	17		41				6			53							Hester et al. 1973
Cerro Portezuelo	3	33	67														Sidrys 1977b
Coatlan Viejo	—		98														Mason 1980
Copuju[5]	5						20			80							Pollard (this volume)
El Ciruelo A[6]	2613		97	<1			2										Smith et al. 1984
Milpillas[7]	39						10			79	10						Darras 1998
Mixtequilla Zone[8]	409	✓	33	✓	45			✓	22								Heller & Stark 1998
Olintepec[9]	65	68	32														Smith et al. 1984
Otumba[10]																	
Batch 1	—	97	3														Glascock et al. 1999
Batch 2	—	10	90														Glascock et al. 1999
Batch 3	—	39	61														Glascock et al. 1999
Batch 4	—	99	1														Glascock et al. 1999
Batch 5	—	25	75														Glascock et al. 1999
Batch 6	—	67	33														Glascock et al. 1999
Batch 7	—	16	75	2		4					1					4	Glascock et al. 1999
Pareo[6]	10						50			50							Pollard (this volume)
Quiahuitzlan[11]	56		2		21				71		2					4	Jack et al. 1972
Southern Isthmus[12]	—	10	45		45												Zeitlin 1982
Tamazulapan[13]	—		~50														Byland 1980
Tamohi[14]	5							100									
Taximaroa[3]	7	14					86										Pollard &Vogel 1994
Teotihuacan[15]	3672	19	81														Spence 1985

Table 20.3 continued

Obsidian procurement patterns for Late Postclassic (A.D. 1250/1300–1520) Mesoamerica

REGION/SITE	N	MEXICAN SOURCES[1]										CENTRAL AMERICAN SOURCES[2]				UNKNOWN	Reference
		OTU	PAC	PAR	PDO	TUL	UCA	ZAC	ZAR	ZNP	OTHER	CHY	IXT	SMJ	OTHER	SOURCE	
Tepeapulco[16]																	
Batch 1	—		35	63		2											Glascock et al. 1999
Batch 2	—	<1	94	5							1						Glascock et al. 1999
Batch 3	—		56	44													Glascock et al. 1999
Batch 4	—	<1	90	9							1						Glascock et al. 1999
Tuzantla[3]	14						100										Pollard & Vogel 1994
Tzintzuntzan[17]	3						67									33	Hester et al. 1973
Urichu[5]	381		8				44		1	40	4					6	Pollard (this volume)
[unclear][5]	48		6				82			6						4	Pollard (this volume)
Uruapan[18]	77		6				3			42	29					21	Esparza López 1999
Villa Morelos[19]	100	1	1				96		2								Hester et al. 1973
Xaracuaro[5]	19						16		2	79	5						Pollard (this volume)
Xochicalco[6]	292	4	82				11									4	Smith et al. 1984
Yautepec[20]	4596	1	93	3		1	1		<1		1					<1	Smith et al. 1996
Zempoala	39		22		44				33								Jack et al. 1972
Zirizicuaro[3]	6						83			17							Pollard & Vogel 1994
Zitacuaro[3]	2						100										Pollard & Vogel 1994
SOUTHEASTERN MESOAMERICA																	
Acapetahua[21]	176		18		27			1	1			13	2	30	7	1	Clark et al. 1989
Aldea Chimuch[22]	12											50		50			McKinnon et al. 1989
ALO:018[22]	2													100			
ALO:050[22]	2											50		50			
Cary Caye, Toledo	1											100					
Caserio El Hato[22]	4											25		25	50		
Casa Roja[22]	3											33		67			
Caye Coco	1466						<1					30	68	1			Mazeau 2000
Cerritos Tecpan[23]	5													100			

Table 20.3 continued

Obsidian procurement patterns for Late Postclassic (A.D. 1250/1300–1520) Mesoamerica

REGION/SITE	N	MEXICAN SOURCES[1]										CENTRAL AMERICAN SOURCES[2]				UNKNOWN SOURCE	Reference
		OTU	PAC	PAR	PDO	TUL	UCA	ZAC	ZAR	ZNP	OTHER	CHY	IXT	SMJ	OTHER		
Cerros	3											33	67				Nelson 1985
Chan Chen	7											29	71				Neivens et al. 1983
Chitaqtzaq[22]	1140											51	2	46	1		Neivens et al. 1983
Chiche[24]	2													100			
Chutixtiox[24]	4													100			
Corozal Beach	7												100				Neivens et al. 1983
El Aguacate[21]	155		39		18							9	27	4	3		Clark et al. 1989
El Rincon 3[23]	12													100			Braswell 1996
Finca Argelia[22]	3											100					
Finca El Pilar[22]	52											69		31			
Finca Magnolia[23]	27													100			Braswell 1996
Funk Caye, Toledo	1											100					McKinnon et al. 1989
Iximche[23]	16											19		75	6		Braswell 1996
La Cuchilla[23]	1													100			
Laguna de On[25]	658											27	67	3		3	Mazeau 2000
La Palma[21]	121		32		12							32	17	5	1		Clark et al. 1989
Las Brujas[26]	140		29		26						1	21	6	17			Maguire 2001
Las Carretas 1[23]	61													100			Braswell 1996
Las Gradas[21]	17		24		47							6		12	12		Maguire 2001
Las Morenas[21]	297		10		40				<1			13	10	24	1		Clark et al. 1989
Las Piedritas[21]	224		26		46							9	8	11			Maguire 2001
La Union 2[23]	34													100			Braswell 1996
Mayapan[27]	1241		<1	<1	<1				<1			1	98	<1		<1	
Media Cuesta[28]	72											8	46	3	43		
"Mixco" Viejo[23]	59											39		61			
Ocelocalco[21]	28		57									29		4	11		Clark et al. 1989
Patchchacan	9											55	33			11	Neivens et al. 1983

Table 20.3 continued

Obsidian procurement patterns for Late Postclassic (A.D. 1250/1300–1520) Mesoamerica

REGION/SITE	N	MEXICAN SOURCES[1]										CENTRAL AMERICAN SOURCES[2]				UNKNOWN	Reference
		OTU	PAC	PAR	PDO	TUL	UCA	ZAC	ZAR	ZNP	OTHER	CHY	IXT	SMJ	OTHER	SOURCE	
Pericon 2[23]	3													100			Braswell 1996
Pueblo Viejo[23]	167											3		97			Braswell 1996
Pblo. Viejo Tecpan[23]	13											38		62			
Q'umarkaj[24]	4											50	50				
San Gervasio	37						3						97				Neivens et al. 1983
Santa Rita Corozal	11		18		9							27	45				Neivens et al. 1983
Sarteneja	39		8										92				
Talpetate 4[23]	4													100			Braswell 1996
Tipu[29]	171		1									11	79	5		4	Baxter 1984
Topoxte	47											38	45	17			Braswell 2000b
Xelha	29											10	90				
Xesuj 1[23]	3													100			Braswell 1996
Xesuj 2[23]	4													100			Braswell 1996
Xesuj 3[23]	3													100			Braswell 1996
Xoconochco Bajo[21]	39	5			21							15	5	36	18		Maguire 2001
Xoconochco Viejo[21]	47	36			6							19	4	23	11		Maguire 2001

Note: Values shown under each source are expressed as percents; ✔ indicates present but no quantitative data available; if no reference is cited, data first appear here.
[1] OTU=Otumba, México; PAC=Pachuca, Hidalgo; PAR=Paredón, Hidalgo; PDO=Pico de Orizaba, Veracruz; TUL=Tulancingo, Hidalgo; UCA=Ucareo-Zinapécuaro-Cruz Negra, Michoacán; ZAC=Zacualtipan, Hidalgo; ZAR=Zaragoza, Puebla; ZNP=Zináparo-Varal-Prieto, Michoacán.
[2] CHY=El Chayal, Guatemala; IXT=Ixtepeque, Guatemala; SMJ=San Martín Jilotepeque, Guatemala.
[3] Frontier sites of the Tarascan empire; see chapter 11 for details.
[4] Michoacán. Pieces originally assigned to Guadalupe Victoria are probably from ZNP.
[5] Michoacán; other Mexican source (if indicated) is Pénjamo, Guanajuato.
[6] Morelos; results of assayed "gray" obsidian extrapolated for entire collection.
[7] Zacapú Basin, Michoacán. Other Mexican source is Pénjamo, Guanajuato. Sample analyzed by NAA. Additionally, 2,709 artifacts were visually sorted into black (87%, assumed to be from Zináparo-Varal-Prieto) and green obsidian (13%, assumed to be Pachuca). Given the easy confusion between PAC and Pénjamo obsidian and UCA and ZNP material, it is likely that the black and green visual categories include some UCA and Pénjamo.
[8] Sources with ✔ identified chemically in zone. All appear in trace quantities except Guadelupe Victoria, which drops considerably after the Preclassic period.
[9] Morelos, only two (of 44) gray artifacts sourced; context mixed with Epiclassic lithics.

Table 20.3 continued

Obsidian procurement patterns for Late Postclassic (A.D. 1250/1300–1520) Mesoamerica

10 Batch 1 (25 assayed "gray" artifacts) comes from a core-blade workshop; Batch 2 (22 "gray" artifacts) is from excavations in an elite residence; Batch 3 (25 "gray" samples) is from the surface of a rural site near Otumba; Batch 4 (25 "gray" artifacts) from a biface workshop; Batch 5 (25 "gray") is from surface contexts around three houses; Batch 6 (20 "gray") is from the surface of a single house; and Batch 7 (50 "gray" artifacts is from a lapidary workshop. In all cases, assay results extrapolated for entire collection. Other Mexican source is Tepalzingo, Hidalgo; unknown source is probably located near Pachuca.

11 Other Mexican source is Altotonga, Veracruz.

12 Oaxaca.

13 Mixteca Alta, Oaxaca. From area identified as prismatic blade workshop.

14 San Luis Potosí, also known as Tamuin.

15 From Aztec-period workshops; bifaces, some of which are Classic in date, are excluded. All "gray" obsidian assumed to be from OTU.

16 Batches 1 and 3 consist of random samples from prismatic blade workshop; 29 "gray" artifacts from Batch 1, and 25 from Batch 3 were assayed, and results extrapolated for the entire collections. Batches 2 and 4 consist of all "gray" obsidian from several surface collections; 29 gray artifacts from Batch 2, and 25 from Batch 4 were assayed, and results extrapolated for entire collection. Other Mexican sources are Malpaís, Hidalgo (Batch 2 and .4% of Batch 4) and El Paraiso, Querétaro (.4% of Batch 4).

17 Pieces assigned to PAC are high-quality green obsidian that appear to have been incorrectly assigned to the Jalisco sources; pieces assigned to ZAR originally sourced only to "Puebla."

18 Upper Río Marques region, Michoacán. Other Mexican sources include Tequila-La Primavera, Jalisco (27%) and Pénjamo, Guanajuato (1%). Only flakes were sourced, skewing data away from Ucareo, the primary source used for blades. Sourced artifacts are of uncertain chronological placement.

19 Michoacán; site is probably Postclassic in date; two samples originally assigned to Altotonga, Veracruz, and ZAR probably come from ZNP.

20 Atlan-Santiago phases (A.D. 1300 to Early Colonial period); results of assay of "gray" artifacts extrapolated to entire collection. Other Mexican sources are El Paraiso (.8%) and Fuentezuelas (.4%), Querétaro.

21 Chiapas; other Central American source is Tajumulco, Guatemala.

22 Sacatepequez, Guatemala; other Guatemalan source is San Bartolomé Milpas Altas.

23 Chimaltenango, Guatemala; other Guatemalan source is San Bartolomé Milpas Altas.

24 Quiche, Guatemala.

25 Belize; probably contains some earlier materials.

26 Chiapas; other Central American source is Guatemalan, but particular source unclear.

27 All pieces from Str. 163.

28 Santa Rosa, Guatemala; other Guatemalan source is Media Cuesta (Laguna de Ayarza), probable Xinca site.

29 Unknown source may be SMJ.

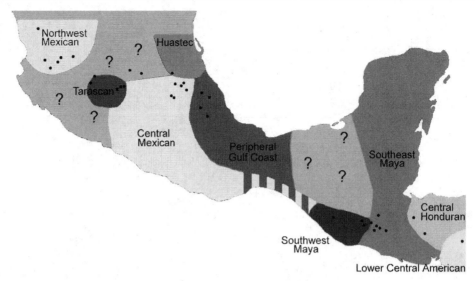

Figure 20.4 Obsidian exchange spheres of the Late Postclassic period (A.D. 1250/1300–1520)

it has proven difficult to distinguish two distinct and sequential occupations corresponding to these periods. At least some of the proposed differences in the Sapoá and Ometepe ceramic complexes reflect regional variation rather than temporal distinctions. For this reason, both periods are discussed together.

During Sapoá/Ometepe times, the proportion of Ixtepeque material in obsidian assemblages grew to more than double that of the earlier Late Bagaces period. This is related to a more than tenfold increase in the quantity of blades. Prismatic blade manufacture, although uncommon in Pacific Nicaragua, is demonstrated for two sites in the departments of Masaya and Rivas. Thus, while all Bagaces blades were imported as finished artifacts, at least some Sapoá/Ometepe blades were locally produced.[5] Moreover, the spatial pattern of obsidian in the department of Granada reveals a significant change in distribution. During the Bagaces period, obsidian artifacts were used at only the highest-ranked sites in the settlement hierarchy. In contrast, obsidian flakes and blades in Sapoá/Ometepe times were used by consumers at more modest villages and hamlets (Salgado González 1996).

LATE POSTCLASSIC OBSIDIAN EXCHANGE SPHERES (A.D. 1250/1300–1520)

The Late Postclassic was a period of remarkable integration. Although many Early Postclassic obsidian procurement and exchange spheres continued to operate, particularly near the sources, there were fewer barriers to trade in many regions (table 20.3 and figure 20.4). In particular, the division between the peripheral Gulf coast, central Mexican, and southwest Maya exchange spheres became less tangible.

TARASCAN SPHERE

The Late Postclassic period saw a major territorial expansion of the Tarascan empire. Ceramics dating to this period from the Ucareo region are related to types from the Tarascan heartland (Hernández and Healan 1999). It seems likely, then, that this source complex came under direct territorial control of the Tarascan empire during the final centuries of Mesoamerican prehistory. The Pénjamo, Guanajuato, source also was incorporated into the Tarascan empire during the Late Postclassic period.

Obsidian procurement data for the center of the Tarascan region come from five sites, including the imperial capital of Tzintzuntzan. Although each site received most of its obsidian from the Ucareo or Zinápuro source complexes, the relative quantities of material from each source differ among and within sites.

In particular, fully 76 percent of the obsidian at Tzintzuntzan came from the Ucareo source (and another 6 percent from the Zinapécuaro portion of the system). Residents of two locations at Urichu also received most of their obsidian from Ucareo, but those living in a third section of the site did not. Inhabitants of Xarácuaro, Copujo, and Pareo had only limited access to obsidian from Ucareo.[6] In general, the quantity of Ucareo obsidian in each collection is inversely proportional to the amount of material from the Varal portion of the Zinápuro source complex. Possible explanations for this pattern are discussed below.

Collections from peripheral regions of the empire also have been studied (e.g., Darras 1998; Esparza López 1999; Hester et al. 1973). Pollard (chapter 29) summarizes data from the Zacapu Basin (Darras 1998) and from a survey along the upper Río Marques, near Uruapán, Michoacán (Esparza López 1999). In both regions, obsidian from the Zinápuro source complex is predominant, although a surprising amount of material from Pén-jamo, Guanajuato, was identified in the Zacapu Basin. In the Río Marques region, 27 percent of the analyzed ob-sidian came from the La Joya-Teuchitlan–La Primavera source area in Jalisco. It seems as though consumers from the Río Marques region supplemented obsidian procured from sources within the empire with material from out-side of the Tarascan zone. Thus, the northwestern politi-cal frontier of the empire was not a sharp economic boundary (chapter 13). Collections from Villa Morelos and Apatzingan, located southeast and southwest of the Pátzcuaro Basin, were assayed more than 25 years ago by Hester et al. (1973). These collections are not well dated, but probably should be assigned to the Postclassic period. Nearly all obsidian from Villa Morelos comes from the Ucareo complex. Most material from Apatzin-gan was assigned originally to the Guadalupe Victoria, Puebla, source, but these assignments are implausible. X-ray fluorescence data for strontium, zirconium, and rubidium concentrations do not allow Zináparo-Varal-Prieto obsidian to be distinguished from material from several sources in Puebla (Michael Glascock, personal communication, 1999). Since the Zináparo complex is much closer to Apatzingan than to Guadalupe Victoria, I assume that the assignments reported by Hester et al. (1973: table 1) are inaccurate. A similar inaccuracy seems to exist in the identification of "Puebla" source obsidian at Tzintzuntzan (see table 29.4). Table 20.3 corrects the apparent errors in these data.

Data also are available for five Late Postclassic sites (Acámbaro, Taximaroa, Tuzantla, Zirizicuaro, and Zi-tacuaro) located near the Tarascan-Aztec frontier. Nearly 90 percent of the artifacts from these sites are attributed to the Ucareo source complex (Pollard and Vogel 1994). This proportion is even greater than that found at the capital of Tzintzuntzan. The abundance of Ucareo obsid-ian and lack of Zináparo-complex material may be re-lated to distance; these sites are closer to Ucareo than to the latter source area.

CENTRAL MEXICAN SPHERE
Late Postclassic source attribution data are available for eight cities and smaller centers in central Mexico. These are El Ciruelo A, Olintepec, Xochicalco (Smith et al. 1984), Otumba, Tepeapulco (Glascock et al. 1999), Yautepec (Smith et al. 1996), Coatlan Viejo (Mason 1980), and Teotihuacan (Spence 1985). For the last two sites, only the relative proportions of Pachuca and "gray" (i.e., not green) obsidian are reported. In the case of Teotihuacan, we probably are safe in assuming that nearly all gray obsidian comes from the Otumba source. Material from Otumba and Tepeapulco has been ana-lyzed in batches corresponding to a variety of residential and workshop contexts (Glascock et al. 1999). These col-

lections provide an important glimpse into procurement and production strategies at the sub-site level of analysis. The implications of these data are discussed below in an-other section.

Most central Mexican collections, not surprisingly, are dominated by prismatic blades from the Pachuca, Hidalgo, source. As mentioned, evidence for intensive shaft mining at this source dates to the Aztec period (Cruz Antillón 1994; Pastrana 1990, 1998), and there is little doubt that extraction and core preparation of obsidian were orchestrated by inhabitants of Pachuca, an administered center within the Acolhua state.

After Pachuca, Otumba is the second most common source for obsidian at sites in the Late Postclassic central Mexican exchange sphere. Obsidian from the Paredón source also was exploited, but its distribution largely was limited to the Tepeapulco region. Trace amounts from other sources within the northeast corner of the exchange sphere also are found, as are a few artifacts made of ob-sidian from El Paraíso and Fuentezuelas, Querétaro—two peripheral sources that were beyond the frontier of the Aztec empire. Finally, a few artifacts from Xochicalco have been sourced to Ucareo (Smith et al. 1984), but I suspect that these pieces either come from temporally mixed contexts or represent scavenged blades produced in earlier periods.

Within the Aztec empire, evidence for the importation of obsidian from sources in the peripheral Gulf coast sphere is limited to two prismatic blades from Zaragoza found at Yautepec. In fact, more obsidian from this source has been found at Tzintzuntzan and Villa Morelos in the Tarascan empire. The Aztecs, then, did not import obsidian from their eastern rivals.

Beyond the Aztec political frontier, however, the boundary between the central Mexican and peripheral Gulf coast obsidian exchange spheres is less evident. In the southern Isthmus of Tehuantepec, 45 percent of the Late Postclassic obsidian came from Pico de Orizaba, and 55 percent came from sources within the central Mexican sphere (Zeitlin 1982). At Tamazulapan, in the Mixteca Alta, about half the obsidian found in a pris-matic blade workshop came from Pachuca (Byland 1980). Given the relative proportions of Pachuca and Otumba obsidian in the central Mexican heartland, it is probable that most of the gray obsidian at Tamazulapan comes from other sources, some in the peripheral Gulf coast sphere.

PERIPHERAL GULF COAST SPHERE
The principal source for obsidian traded within the peripheral Gulf coast exchange sphere during the Late Postclassic period was Pico de Orizaba, but significant quantities of obsidian from Zaragoza and some Altotonga material also were exchanged. There are

indications that the Totonacs eventually came to consume most of the obsidian extracted from the Zaragoza source. Although relatively small quantities of Zaragoza obsidian are found in Late Postclassic contexts in the Mixtequilla zone (Heller and Stark 1998), most of the obsidian artifacts from Quiahuiztlan come from Zaragoza, as do a third of those in the assayed collection from Cempoalla (Jack et al. 1972).

Despite the prevalence of obsidian from Pico de Orizaba and Zaragoza in Late Postclassic collections from sites along the Gulf coast, significant amounts of green obsidian from Pachuca entered the exchange sphere. Thus, the boundary between the central Mexican and the peripheral Gulf coast spheres was more permeable than in earlier periods. In the Mixtequilla region, for example, a third of all Late Postclassic obsidian artifacts are attributed to Pachuca. Although the data are limited, it appears that the relative amount of Pachuca obsidian circulating in the peripheral Gulf coast sphere was greatest at the southern extremes of the exchange zone.

SOUTHWEST MAYA SPHERE

During the Late Postclassic period, the southwest Maya obsidian procurement sphere contracted, and the boundary between it and the two Mexican spheres to the west became diffuse. At the 10 Late Postclassic sites in Xoconochco for which we have data, 26–72 percent of the obsidian artifacts come from Mexican sources, predominantly Pico de Orizaba and Pachuca (Clark et al. 1989). The proportions of these two sources at each site differ. At Acapetahua, Las Morenas, Las Gradas, Las Piedritas, and Xoconochco Bajo, there is more obsidian from Pico de Orizaba. But at El Aguacate, Las Brujas, La Palma, Ocelocalco, and Xoconochco Viejo, Pachuca is the most common source.

Obsidian from four Guatemalan sources—El Chayal, San Martín Jilotepeque, Ixtepeque, and Tajumulco—also are found at these 10 sites. An interesting pattern emerges when we compare the quantities of obsidian from these sources to the Mexican obsidian present in the same collections. In general, sites that received most of their obsidian from Pachuca also acquired the bulk of their Guatemalan material from El Chayal and Ixtepeque. In contrast, sites with greater amounts of Pico de Orizaba obsidian tended to get most of their Guatemalan material from San Martín Jilotepeque.[7] Thus, at least two distinct local procurement networks operated within Xoconochco during the Late Postclassic period. I suspect that these two networks are temporally distinct, representing an early facet of the Late Postclassic (with more Pico de Orizaba and San Martín Jilotepeque obsidian) and a late facet of the Late Postclassic (with greater quantities of Pachuca, El Chayal, and Ixtepeque obsidian). Recent excavations and the careful analysis of stratigraphy lend credence to this hypothesis (Susan

Maguire, personal communication, 2001). It seems likely that the increase in the use of Pachuca obsidian was due to the Aztec arrival in Xoconochco at the end of the fifteenth century. The Aztec incursion, which has been difficult to detect in the ceramics of Xoconochco, may be discernable through analysis of obsidian exchange patterns.

Mexican obsidian is extremely rare in the Late Postclassic central highlands of Guatemala, and Pachuca is the only source that has been noted. With the exception of Saq Ulew (Woodbury and Trik 1953:229–231), the westernmost excavated Postclassic center, I know of no exotic obsidian at any major highland site.

Obsidian procurement patterns at Media Cuesta, a small site in the eastern highlands of Guatemala, are worth discussing for three reasons. First, the site is on the boundary between the southeast and southwest Maya exchange spheres, a fact reflected in the presence of obsidian from all three major Guatemalan sources in its Late Postclassic assemblage (table 20.3). Second, the site is only a few hundred meters from a small obsidian source known as Laguna de Ayarza or Media Cuesta (Braswell and Glascock 1998: figure 5). Despite the proximity of the outcrops, more than half of the obsidian used at the site was imported from more-distant sources. Media Cuesta obsidian is of sufficient quality for biface and casual flake production, but is not well suited for making blades. Third, two interesting polychrome paintings in the Postclassic international style are found above the lake 1 km west of the site. Finally, there is good reason to think that Media Cuesta was a Xinca, rather than Maya, site. Several indigenous place names in the region are derived from Xinca, and the few remaining Xinca speakers live in the same department. Thus, the stability of the boundary between the southwest and southeast Maya exchange spheres in this part of Guatemala might have been related to the presence of remnant Xinca populations.

SOUTHEAST MAYA SPHERE

Source provenance data are available for 14 Late Postclassic sites in the southeast Maya exchange sphere. In all but two collections (from Funk Caye and Pachchacan, Belize), the predominant source is Ixtepeque. Because these two sites are represented by a total of 10 artifacts, they do not seem to constitute significant exceptions.

Despite the paucity of data on Late Postclassic procurement patterns in the Maya lowlands, several facts are worthy of note. First, with the possible exception of Tikal, the density of obsidian artifacts at Mayapán is greater than that of any other lowland Maya site. The 1,241 artifacts for which source assignments are presented in table 20.3 come from only one building: a low range structure near the Castillo. Recent excavations in several buildings throughout Mayapán suggest that

Structure 163 is not anomalous (Peraza Lope et al. 1996). The quantity of obsidian at Mayapán and its general paucity elsewhere in the Late Postclassic Maya lowlands suggest that circum-peninsular trade was tightly regulated by this polity.

Second, obsidian from El Chayal, San Martín Jilotepeque, and several Mexican sources also reached the Maya lowlands during the Late Postclassic period. Most Mexican obsidian can be sourced either to Pico de Orizaba or the Pachuca source, but trace quantities from Paredón, Ucareo, and perhaps Zaragoza also have been noted. As in the Epiclassic period, obsidian from both the central Mexican and peripheral Gulf coast exchange spheres entered the Maya lowlands.

Third, in the southern lowlands, the quantity of obsidian seems to be greatest at sites near the coast or on major rivers. Again, this supports a model of circum-peninsular, rather than overland, trade routes.

DISCUSSION

Many aspects of the procurement data presented here are relevant to the emergence of transnational economies in ancient Mesoamerica. In this final section, I discuss several issues germane to Postclassic economies that these data elucidate.

LOCATION OF SOURCES
ON ECONOMIC AND POLITICAL FRONTIERS
Figures 20.2 to 20.4 suggest that most sources were peripheral, rather than central, to the exchange spheres in which artifacts ascribed to those sources circulated. In particular, the directed rather than radial pattern of distribution is striking. That is to say, instead of exhibiting a pattern of concentric decrement as distance from source increases, obsidian from a particular source is often absent from sites to one side of that source.

With the exceptions of Cantona and Zaragoza, and perhaps Tula and Pachuca, there are few indications that source areas were directly controlled by major polities during the Epiclassic and Early Postclassic periods. Epiclassic ceramics from the Ucareo source complex are local and show no particular affinities with pottery from Tula or sites in the Pátzcuaro Basin. Early Postclassic sites near Pico de Orizaba are small, and there is no nearby central place. In the Maya region, there is no evidence suggesting that Copán, Chalchuapa, or Cihuatan controlled Ixtepeque, despite the fact that this was the source of the most widely distributed obsidian in Postclassic southeastern Mesoamerica. Nor is there compelling evidence that Kaminaljuyú ever exerted direct control over the El Chayal source. Few important centers were located around the San Martín Jilotepeque source during the Classic and Early Postclassic periods, and during the Late Postclassic both Iximche' and Saqik'ajol Nimakaqapek

("Mixco" Viejo) were positioned equidistant from the source (Braswell 1996).

The peripheral or interstitial locations of obsidian sources, the directional pattern of distribution, and the lack of clear controlling central places all suggest that obsidian extraction and circulation were governed more by demand than by central planning. Rather than interpreting these patterns as indicating colonialist exploitation of hinterland resources, it may be that local populations residing near obsidian quarries manipulated their economic relations with more-powerful and populace regions to maintain political autonomy. One such strategy is tribute (when viewed from the perspective of the center) or gift giving (when viewed from the position of the periphery). If centers received enough obsidian from regions beyond their political control, it may not have been worth the military effort to incorporate small frontier communities with access to important resources.

INCREASED PRODUCTION AND EXCHANGE
There is strong evidence that extraction and production levels increased at most obsidian sources during the Postclassic period. At the Choatalum quarry of the San Martín Jilotepeque, Guatemala, source, topsoil was stripped away to afford easy access to obsidian-bearing deposits (Braswell 1996:239–242). During the last 500 years before the conquest, approximately 3000 m³ of lithic debitage—weighing nearly 3,000,000 kg—accumulated on the quarry floor (Braswell 1996:648). In central Mexico, evidence for increased production levels is even greater. New technologies, such as shaft and pit mining, were introduced during the Postclassic period (e.g., Charlton 1969a; Cobean 1991; Cruz Antillón and Pastrana 1994; Holmes 1900; Pastrana 1990, 1998; Stocker and Cobean 1984). Although it can be quite difficult to date quarry and mine features, most of the ceramic materials recovered from the major source areas of Pachuca and Otumba date to the Aztec period (e.g., López Aguilar and Nieto Calleja 1989; López Aguilar et al. 1989). Thus, it seems likely that extraction levels at those sources reached their peak during the Late Postclassic.

Recent research at the Ucareo, Michoacán, source has demonstrated the practice of large-scale "trench quarrying," but the chronology of such quarries is not yet clear (Healan 1997:90–92). Nonetheless, occupation of the Ucareo Valley was insubstantial until the end of the Late Classic period, so it is likely that trench quarries date to the Epiclassic or Postclassic periods (Healan 1997:93–98). There also is evidence for increased production at the Zináparo, Michoacán, source area during the Late Postclassic (Darras 1998).

Archaeological reports typically do not contain enough information to calculate consumption levels of obsidian artifacts. The problem is compounded by different recovery techniques. For example, some archae-ologists working in the Maya region do not sift exca-vated soils for small artifacts, so fragments of obsidian blades and flakes often are under-represented in collec-tions. Still, there is some evidence that the intensity of ob-sidian exchange and consumption increased during the Postclassic period. Carlos Peraza Lope has directed three field seasons of consolidation-oriented excavations at Mayapán. Bárbara Escamilla Ojeda, a student working on the project, currently is analyzing some 14,000 obsid-ian artifacts recovered from the site. This quantity, al-though small for a site in central Mexico or highland Guatemala, is much more than the total number of ob-sidian artifacts that have been reported for *all* other sites in the northern lowlands. Most of this material comes from Ixtepeque, the most distant obsidian source in the Maya region. Ixtepeque obsidian also became important in the K'iche'an highlands of Guatemala during the Post-classic period, suggesting the formation of new trade ties with the southeast Maya sphere. Finally, the presence of Mexican-source obsidian in significant quantities at Post-classic sites in Xoconochco, where little exotic material was present during earlier periods, is further evidence for an increase in long-distance obsidian exchange.

Population levels increased dramatically in many re-gions of Mesoamerica during the Late Postclassic period. Thus, one source of the increase in demand for obsidian was greater population. Another source seems to have been the proliferation and increased wealth of affluent production zones far from core areas. Residents of Xo-conochco, for example, may have imported more exotic obsidian during the Postclassic period because they were exporting more cacao. Similarly, inhabitants of the Balsas-Tepalcatepec drainage (including the upper Río Marques sites discussed by Pollard in chapter 29) may have been able to import more Zináparo obsidian be-cause they were mining for metal ores. Thus, as the de-mand for goods from affluent production zones increased in the core, wealth and the demand for core goods in-creased in affluent production zones. In some cases, inter-locking central-place systems developed, and commodities from different affluent production zones were exchanged without direct administration by the core.

ELITE CONTROL VERSUS MARKET EXCHANGE

Were intrasite and intraregional variations in procure-ment strategies the result of elite control or market ex-change? At the beginning of this chapter, I stated that obsidian was a primarily utilitarian rather than prestige good. Given the central role ascribed to preciosities in many discussions of the application of world-systems theory to preindustrial economies, it is important to examine the social value of obsidian in ancient Meso-america.

Obsidian may have served as a precious commodity in two contexts. First, in regions of Mesoamerica where ac-cess to material or skilled artisans was unusually low, im-ported obsidian could have been manipulated as a scarce quantity. The Pacific coast of Oaxaca and Guerrero, the Maya lowlands, and lower Central America all are re-gions where scarcity might have caused obsidian to be-come a preciosity. It is only in this third region, however, that there is clear evidence for differential access to mate-rial during the periods that concern us.

Salgado González (1996) describes the Late Bagaces settlement hierarchy of Granada, Nicaragua, as consist-ing of only two levels: nucleated and dispersed villages. The distribution of obsidian and imported ceramics (such as Delirio Red-on-white, Uluá polychromes, and Gallo Polychrome: Jaguar variety) was limited to nucleated vil-lages, which Salgado González argues were the centers of incipient complex polities. She suggests that the emerging elite of Granada monopolized the exchange of items re-ceived through long-distance trade, which helped stimu-late political elaboration.

In regions where access to obsidian was more com-mon, material from a distant source may have become a precious good because of its rarity and distinctive charac-teristics. Obsidian from the Pachuca source, for example, could have been a preciosity in the Maya region because of its green color. During the Terminal Classic period, however, there is little reason to suspect that access to Pachuca obsidian was limited to elites. Studies conducted in the southern Maya lowlands have not revealed a strong correlation between access to Pachuca obsidian and status (Stiver et al. 1994; Kindon and Connell 1999). Recent research has revealed significant quantities of both Pachuca and Ucareo obsidian throughout all Ejar-phase contexts at Copán. There is no evidence that the elite living in the epicenter of Chichén Itzá had greater access to exotic Mexican obsidian than did people living in more-humble and peripheral residential groups. Dur-ing the time periods in question, within- and between-site analyses in the Maya region do not suggest that access to exotic obsidian from distant sources varied with eco-nomic status. One possibility, then, is that exotic obsid-ian was not a prestige item. If access to all obsidian was related only to need, and not restricted by controlling elites, then this pattern also is consistent with Hirth's (1998) model of marketplace exchange. Elsewhere (Bras-well 2000a), I have argued that data from the northern lowlands are consistent with the emergence of partially and fully commercialized market economies during the Terminal Classic period.

Some evidence for differential access to exotic materi-als, and hence for redistributive and uncommercialized economies, can be seen in the Tarascan region, where most imported green obsidian is found in elite burials. Furthermore, the proportion of exotic obsidian in a collection, the number of remote sources represented, and the distance to those exotic sources all are greater for Tzintzuntzan than for the other Late Postclassic sites in the Pátzcuaro Basin. Residents of the imperial capital therefore had more access to obsidian brought to the region by long-distance traders than did the occupants of the outlying centers. This may be due in part to the higher status of the residents of Tzintzuntzan and the limited redistribution of obsidian by elites. But it also may reflect the role of the capital as a node of long-distance exchange, and the inefficiency of the local market system. Most likely, the procurement strategies of the Tarascan core were complex, consisting of both market exchange and the privileged provisioning of high-status individuals residing in the capital (chapter 29).

The distribution of Ucareo obsidian within the Late Postclassic Pátzcuaro Basin seems to suggest elite control of the exchange of material from that source. The pattern is complicated by the fact that most prismatic blades consumed in the Tarascan empire were made of Ucareo obsidian, but material from the Zináparo source area was used commonly to make ad hoc flake tools. Thus it is not clear if the Tarascan dynasty controlled the exchange of Ucareo obsidian or access to prismatic blade technology. Ucareo is more distant than the Zináparo source complex, a factor that would have been incorporated into its cost in the marketplace. Why trade for costly imported obsidian when cheaper material suitable for the dominant lithic industries is plentiful?

Recent data from Late Postclassic Tepeapulco (Glascock et al. 1999) appear to suggest the practice of marketplace exchange. Two collections from a variety of rural sites near Tepeapulco suggest an even distribution of obsidian from different sources, with Pachuca supplying 94 percent and 90 percent of the material in each sample (table 20.3: Batches 2 and 4). Collections from two prismatic blade workshops exhibit procurement patterns different from those of rural residential contexts, and also are distinct from each other (table 20.3: Batches 1 and 3). One workshop received 63 percent of its material from the Paredón source, and the other acquired 56 percent of its obsidian from Pachuca. Thus, although the prismatic blade workshops each had different procurement patterns, perhaps representing distinct dyadic relations with individuals who had access to the quarries, marketplace exchange appears to have homogenized the acquisition patterns of prismatic blade consumers. But why do households in Tepeapulco have radically different consumption patterns than the two sampled workshops?

The most complex local procurement pattern has been observed at sites around the city-state of Otumba (Glascock et al. 1999). Prismatic blade and biface workshops in that area exhibit similar procurement strategies: nearly all obsidian consumed in two workshops comes from the Otumba source (table 20.3: Batches 1 and 4). But collections from three residential zones display distinct procurement strategies. Nearly all the obsidian consumed at an elite household comes from the Pachuca source (table 20.3: Batch 2), a pattern similar to most sites in the Aztec empire. In contrast, a collection from three rural households reveals a somewhat greater reliance on Otumba obsidian (table 20.3: Batch 3), and a sample from a single house is dominated by obsidian from the Otumba source (table 20.3: Batch 6).

According to Hirth's (1998) models, this pattern is most consistent with elite control and redistribution, with Pachuca as the more-valuable obsidian. It does not suggest direct procurement from local workshops, because almost all obsidian from both the prismatic blade and biface workshop comes from the Otumba source. Thus, either the sampled workshops are anomalous, or distribution and consumption patterns are more complex than can be explained by Hirth's three models.

Most sites in the Aztec empire exhibit the same basic procurement strategy: 90–98 percent of all obsidian comes from Pachuca. This remarkably consistent pattern suggests the existence of a very large regional market system. It is likely that the source was controlled directly by the administered center of Pachuca, and indirectly by the Acolhua state, so we may assume that the proposed regional exchange system was heavily influenced by the economic concerns of Texcoco. Residents of the two sampled regions of Tepeapulco received almost all their obsidian from Pachuca, even though local workshops procured much of their raw material from Paredón. Thus, the hypothesized regional market system was sufficiently pervasive to overwhelm local production systems at Tepeapulco: a case of Winn Dixie versus the local roadside produce cart.

At Otumba, it seems that elites participated fully in the regional market system. In contrast, the occupants of rural households and non-elite portions of the city-state received the bulk of their obsidian tools from local producers exploiting the Otumba source. Hence, the local economy of Otumba was not as dominated by the regional market system as was that of Tepeapulco. The fact that local producers at both of these smaller city-states exploited distinct sources suggests that their two economies were not well articulated, at least as far as obsidian exchange is concerned (Glascock et al. 1999). In contrast, the distribution of Aztec-period ceramics is much more homogeneous, implying that the exchange of pottery was more strongly governed by the regional market system than was the obsidian trade.

Local variation in Epiclassic/Terminal Classic and Postclassic obsidian procurement patterns can be interpreted in a number of different ways. In Late Bagaces (analogous to the Terminal Classic) period Nicaragua, obsidian was a prestige good limited to and manipulated by local elites. This may be an example, therefore, of macroregional interaction stimulating local economic and political development. The Late Postclassic Tarascan case suggests a mixed system: Ucareo obsidian or core-blade technology was the domain of the elite, but material from the Zináparo source complex circulated in a regional market system. At Epiclassic Xochicalco, according to Hirth (1998), obsidian consumption patterns indicate the existence of a single market. Finally, the Late Postclassic city-states of the Aztec empire appear to have participated in both local market systems and a powerful regional market.

IDEOLOGY AND INTERNATIONAL INTEGRATION

The Postclassic Mesoamerican world not only was articulated by economic interdependence, but also was integrated by shared ideological principles (chapter 22). The two, in fact, are rarely separable. Regional cults or world religions that mandate pilgrimages may stimulate the growth of enormous international exchange networks; it is no accident that the hajj and global trade routes coincide. I close this chapter by observing that the two periods of greatest pan-Mesoamerican economic integration, as reflected in obsidian exchange spheres, seem to coincide with the spread of world religions in Mesoamerica.

The first period of economic integration that can be discerned from obsidian procurement data was the Epiclassic/Terminal Classic. At that time, Maya sites participating in the international exchange sphere received much of their obsidian from a wide variety of sources in highland Mexico. Ringle et al. (1998) have linked the broad distribution of the material traits collectively referred to as "Toltec" to the expansion of a cult centered on Quetzalcoatl/Kukulkan. They propose that sites exhibiting these characteristics formed a network of pilgrimage shrines spreading from Xochicalco, Teotenango, Cholula, Tula, and El Tajín in northwestern Meso-

america, to Uxmal and Chichén Itzá in the northern Maya lowlands. An important aspect of their argument is that the cult of Quetzalcoatl/Kukulkan dates to the Epiclassic, rather than Early Postclassic period. The establishment of these pilgrimage centers corresponds to the period of economic integration reflected in the international obsidian exchange sphere. Since sites from both the central Mexican and peripheral Gulf coast exchange spheres were major centers in this pilgrimage network, it is not surprising that the Mexican sources represented at sites in the international exchange sphere reflect connections with both regions of northwestern Mesoamerica.

The second period of economic integration corresponds with the Late Postclassic and the expansion of the Postclassic international style and the Late Postclassic international symbol set. These were brought into southeastern Mesoamerica and lower Central America along established Pacific and Gulf coast trade routes. The Pacific expansion can be linked to movements of Mesoamerican peoples, particularly the Pipil, Nicarao, and ultimately, the Aztecs. The appearance of round structures, twin pyramids, tzompantlis (skull racks), and the cult of Xipe Totec in Central America are tied to this migration.

Although there is very little evidence for the trade of Mexican obsidian in the Guatemalan highlands during the Late Postclassic period, ceramics and murals of the Postclassic international style, elite cremation, and numerous architectural features from northwestern Mesoamerica appear at sites like Iximche' and Q'umarkaj. The Nahuaization of K'iche'an culture, it appears, is related to the expansion of economic ties with both the Gulf coast and central Mexico (chapter 36). Ethnohistorians and archaeologists alike have struggled to discover the source and origin of these traits. Obsidian procurement data suggest that they are related, in part, to Late Postclassic economic integration along the Pacific coast.

21

Metal
Production

Dorothy Hosler

This discussion of Mesoamerican metallurgy begins in west Mexico just after or during the collapse of Teotihuacan. It is not surprising that metallurgy developed initially in west Mexico, where metallic ore deposits were plentiful, and small and dispersed polities flourished (chapter 8). The social fluidity characterizing these polities encouraged interactions between them and with people from South America who first introduced metal technology to Mexico (Hosler 1988b). These long-distance interactions were probably less likely in the more hierarchically organized areas of Oaxaca and the Basin of Mexico (Hosler 1994). Oaxaca and the Basin of Mexico also lack key metallic ore deposits. Both factors mitigated against the early emergence of metallurgy in either region. The ritually oriented copper-based metallurgy that developed in west Mexico provided Postclassic societies with a new medium for religious expression, for status display, and later, for exchange.

Major transformations occurred in Mesoamerican metallurgy after about A.D. 1300. Metallurgy appeared in Oaxaca, where an elaborate and unstudied copper-gold casting technology flourished (chapters 16 and 22). At the same time, peoples in Oaxaca, Gulf of Tehuantepec, eastern Guerrero, and eastern Morelos communities began to use a kind of common Euro-like metal currency: the axe-money—an ideal medium of exchange in these smaller commercialized economies (Hosler et al. 1990; Hosler 1994).

By contrast, the polities and states that coalesced in west Mexico's metalworking zone produced ever more elaborate ritual and elite paraphernalia but using new materials, specifically bronze and other copper-based alloys. Some west Mexican bronze items—bells, tweezers, and small hand tools—did make their way into market systems, ending up in Morelos, Belize, and elsewhere (Hosler and Macfarlane 1996). But so far, at least in the

west, no evidence suggests metal items were produced for commerce on any significant scale.

Here I am concerned with Mesoamerican metal production arrangements. The key questions are whether these changed through time, and whether the social function or use of metal changed through time in keeping with the increasing commercialization and interregional interaction that characterized Postclassic societies.

The data to address these questions vary regionally, temporally, and by material. A very large corpus of information exists from the west (and some, but less, from Morelos, Oaxaca, Chiapas, Belize, and Tamaulipas). These data derive from dated copper and copper alloy (bronze and copper-silver alloy) artifacts. We have investigated metal processing, production, and use from comprehensive laboratory studies of artifact chemistry, fabrication methods, and relations among alloy properties, design, and functionality. Artifact distributions, native and European texts, and geological data provide additional lines of evidence.

These sources furnish a reasonably clear picture of metal production technologies, their changes through time, their South American origins, and the arenas of cultural activity in which metal items played the most prominent role (Hosler 1986, 1988a, 1988b, 1994; Hosler et al. 1990). They also have provided most of the information concerning production arrangements (Hosler 1986, 1994), because until very recently (Hosler 2000, in press), no archaeological data existed from mining sites, smelting sites, or from sites where metal objects were fashioned. Provenience studies, now in their earliest stages (Hosler and Macfarlane 1996; Hosler 1999; López et al. 1999; Hosler n.d.), have clarified the picture somewhat because they locate ore sources and hence allow inferences concerning production and exchange patterns.

Here I deal with copper, bronze and other copper

159

Figure 21.1 Smelting ore in stone or pottery crucible. (Sahagún 1950–1982, book 11: plate 796.)

alloys (copper-silver, sometimes copper-gold), and occasionally silver and gold. Significant facets of Mesoamerican metal production (of gold and silver artifacts) lie beyond the scope of this chapter, and I comment only briefly on them. There is almost no contextual or analytical data for these objects; the information is mostly documentary, and even as such has never been assembled systematically.

TERMS AND DEFINITIONS

The term *metallurgy* encompasses various activities including extraction, processing, and fabrication of metal objects. The term is usually reserved for processing that requires smelting metal from an ore. Common Mesoamerican copper ores include malachite, azurite (copper oxides), and chalcopyrite and bornite (copper sulfides). Smelting involves winning (extracting) the metal from the ore by heating it to a liquid in an enclosure such as a furnace or crucible (figure 21.1). Often, when the ore is low-grade, metalworkers first crush the ore, select the most mineralized portions, and then smelt them. Sulfide ores are more difficult to smelt than the oxides, which are easily reduced by carbon monoxide generated in the furnace by burning fuel. Sulfur must first be removed by roasting the ore; the oxides that remain are then smelted to metal. Liquid metal can also be produced by co-smelting sulfide and oxide ores, which reduces the sulfide ores Lechtman and Klein 1999). Mesoamerican smiths smelted copper, silver, arsenic, and tin from their respective ores (Hosler 1986, 1994). During smelting, the liquid metal (copper, silver, or tin, for example) solidifies:

sometimes in small droplets or prills, sometimes in larger ingots. To produce alloys (mixtures of two or more metals) metalworkers either co-smelted the two ores (copper ores and tin ores in the case of tin-bronze), or smelted each ore separately and then reheated the tin and copper metal, melting the two together. These bronze and other alloys provide a material with mechanical properties superior to copper, exhibiting increased strength, hardness, or resistance to brittle fracture, for example.

To fashion objects from metal, Mesoamerican smiths sometimes cast the liquid metal into flat blanks which they subsequently cut into strips and hammered into items such as needles and punches. Axes and wedges were cast in open molds and subsequently cold-worked to shape them and to increase their hardness. Metalworkers also cast items such as bells and ornaments using the technically ingenious lost-wax method, in which the object is first modeled in wax, then enclosed in a clay and charcoal mold. The wax is melted out from this mold. The liquid metal is then poured into the mold and takes the shape of the original wax model.

THE EPICLASSIC AND EARLY POSTCLASSIC PERIODS (A.D. 600–1200)

THE WEST MEXICAN METALWORKING ZONE
The west Mexican metalworking zone (figure 21.2), defined from the data described earlier, is where Mesoamerica's earliest, and some of its most innovative, metallurgical developments took place. This region includes western Guerrero, Michoacán, the southern portion of the state of Mexico, and Jalisco, Colima, Nayarit, and southern Sinaloa. Nearly all Mesoamerican metal artifacts dating to this period have been recovered within the metalworking zone. This particular area that offered the unique combination of human and natural resources required for metal production. Here, large hierarchically organized agricultural settlements existed in fairly close proximity to a rich and varied array of ore minerals and native metals. The Mexican copper belt runs through portions of this area (Michoacán and Guerrero) and consists of a series of massive sulfide deposits and innumerable smaller copper outcrops. Other key ore minerals are also common in the metalworking zone; for example, native silver, argentite (the most abundant silver ore), silver sulfosalts, and arsenopyrite, the most abundant arsenic ore in Mexico. Small cassiterite deposits, the oxide ore of tin, occur sporadically along the northern boundary of this zone (Hosler 1994), and they also appear in the state of Mexico (Hosler 1986, 1994). Large copper deposits also occur in northern Mexico, but that area was sparsely inhabited, and principally by mobile desert foraging groups during the time period considered here. By contrast, large towns flourished in many areas of the metalworking zone. In the middle Balsas *tierra*

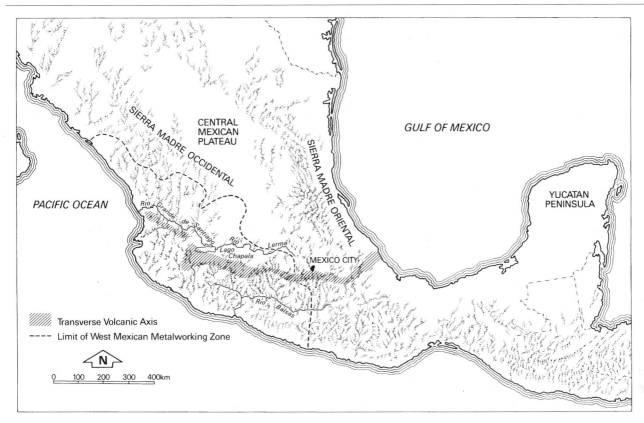

Figure 21.2 The west Mexican metalworking zone (from Hosler 1994:fig. 1.1.)

caliente region of Guerrero and Michoacán, for example, these settlements are distinguished by extensive public and ceremonial architecture, including large pyramids and ball courts (Hosler n.d.). Large settlements also developed during the same period in Colima, Nayarit, highland Michoacán, and Jalisco.

The earliest evidence for metallurgy in the west Mexican metalworking zone consists of artifact assemblages recovered at riverine or coastal sites: in Nayarit at Amapa; along the lower Balsas River between Michoacán and Guerrero; and at Tomatlan in Jalisco (figure 21.3). These date to between A.D. 600 and 900. Metal artifacts dating to a slightly later period (A.D. 800–900) occur at inland sites, for example in Jalisco's Lake Chapala basin. We assume that production activities likewise gradually moved inland. From the outset, metalworkers were particularly interested in the acoustical properties of metal, casting hundreds of small copper bells using the complex lost-wax method. They also hammered out various small implements and ornaments from cast copper blanks; for example, needles, tweezers, awls, and rings. Nearly all Epiclassic- and Early Postclassic–period artifacts were made from copper (Hosler 1988a, 1994), although archaeologists also occasionally have reported gold and silver items. Nonetheless, diagnostic trace elements in the artifact metal reveal that west Mexican smiths already had mastered fairly complex production (smelting) regimes. Tin, for example, sometimes appears

in concentrations between 0.10 and 0.40 weight percent in copper artifacts. Chalcopyrite, a copper sulfide ore, contains tin at these levels in disseminated form and is the only copper ore that does. When tin appears in copper artifacts in these trace concentrations, it signals the use of chalcopyrite and hence mastery of sulfide smelting regimes.

Production Arrangements

People living in a number of different areas within this large zone processed metal and manufactured metal objects. We have only vague ideas about their cultural affiliations, and these come usually from pottery. Unfortunately, securely anchored pottery chronologies are scarce for this region and for this time period. No direct evidence exists for mining at this time, yet we do have some, admittedly slim, evidence that metal was processed at some of these sites. At Amapa, Nayarit, archaeologists recovered several hundred copper artifacts and several pieces of metallic material which subsequent analyses showed to be slag (Root, in Meighan 1976). Meighan (1976) also recovered items he labeled as "slugs" of metal, which he thinks may have been ingots or blanks, cast for future use. These finds suggest that the metal for at least some Amapa artifacts was smelted there and, by inference, that some of the objects were made at Amapa. Archaeologists also report slaglike materials adhering to a potsherd at Peñitas, Nayarit (Carriveau 1976). They

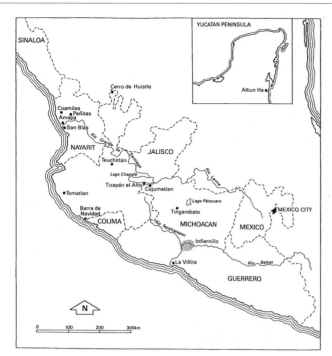

Figure 21.3 Map showing sites dating to before a.d. 1100 where evidence of metal production and metal artifacts were recovered (from Hosler 1994:fig. 3.1.)

argue that the potsherds were used to skim the slag from the molten metal. Only a few artifacts were excavated at Peñitas, but many more come from looters' collections. On the lower Balsas River at La Villita, Cabrera C. (1986) has identified amorphous metal adhering to stone crucible fragments. Cabrera C. excavated numerous copper artifacts at La Villita. His evidence suggests that metal was either melted or smelted at La Villita and that some of the objects he recovered were fashioned at the site. Metalworkers' tools have been identified at Tomatlan, Jalisco, by Joseph Mountjoy, who excavated several hundred copper artifacts there (Mountjoy and Torres 1985). Mountjoy and Torres think that metal was worked at Tomatlan. At Tizapan el Alto, Jalisco, Meighan and Foote (1968) excavated a number of copper artifacts and also "slugs" of metal that may represent ingots.

Apart from these archaeological data, the laboratory analytical evidence also supports the likelihood that people in many different areas of the metalworking zone were processing copper. The same object classes (for example, bell type 1a; Hosler 1994, figure 3.5) conforming to the same design criteria appear in many metalworking zone areas, but made from very different parent materials: sometimes from very pure copper oxide ores, at other times from copper sulfide ores (Hosler 1986). Even artifacts belonging to the same design type (for example, type 1a bells) and recovered at the same site can vary significantly in the presence and concentration of trace elements. This suggests that metalworkers were exploiting

many different ore deposits and were using different smelting techniques, which in turn argues for many, rather than a few, producing groups. These artifact types (type 1a bells), while similar in overall design (ratio of length to diameter), vary in key design parameters such as wall thickness (Hosler 1986, 1994) and the shape of the suspension ring. These attributes are unrelated to functionality—neither one affects acoustical properties—but the differences do suggest that the people who cast them were adhering to slightly different stylistic canons. Occasionally we find objects that are absolutely identical in design parameters and chemical composition (presence and concentration of elements). In these cases the evidence strongly indicates that these artifacts were fashioned from the same batch of metal and probably by the same metalworker(s).

Thus for the Epiclassic and Early Postclassic periods, the archaeological and laboratory evidence indicates that a number of metal-producing groups were working within a large region and that they fashioned the same object classes using similar fabrication techniques. At the same time, no evidence exists for standardization or recipes either in artifact design parameters or in metal composition. Standard processes and recipes appear where guilds or individuals attached to particular groups oversaw or controlled production: specifically, if metal was extracted at one or only a few mines, if metal was processed using standardized smelting methods, or if artifacts were manufactured to meet specific design specifications.

Technical Choices and Use: Sound and Cosmology
During the Epiclassic and Early Postclassic, smiths used metal primarily for ritual and status objects. Bells comprise some 60 percent of all items made from metal. Metalworkers also fashioned tools, but in far fewer numbers than bells. These people were particularly interested in the pitch of bells, casting bells that varied in those design parameters (internal volume and width of resonator opening) crucial to pitch. Data from burials show that different-sized bells (i.e., bells whose pitches varied) were worn together on the wrists or ankles, attached to waistbands, and sewn onto clothing. Metallic bell sounds were highly significant in Mesoamerican cosmology: they reproduced the sounds of thunder and rain, they engendered agricultural and human fertility, and the sounds they produced protected the individuals who wore the bells (Hosler 1994). I have argued elsewhere (1994) that this metallurgy's focus on sacred and supernatural spheres may respond to the particular circumstances surrounding its introduction from Andean South America; this exotic foreign material may have been especially attractive to chiefs and other elites in consolidating power and attracting followers.

South American Antecedents

I have documented the relation between the metalworking technology that developed in west Mexico and that in South America (Hosler 1986, 1988b, 1994). Briefly, the copper objects that appear at these early metalworking sites represent a complex of metallurgical techniques introduced through maritime trade to coastal west Mexico from Andean South America. The timing of these events roughly coincides with the collapse of Teotihuacan and may respond to the ensuing reconfiguration of west Mexican exchange patterns (Hosler 1994). The techniques that characterize west Mexican metallurgy derive from two external metallurgical traditions. One is from the central Andes, where people were working metal by 1000 B.C.; the other is from Colombia, where a technically complex lost-wax casting technology took shape by around 400 B.C. These two very different approaches to handling metal predated metallurgy in west Mexico by hundreds of years. In general, the evidence indicates that west Mexican societies incorporated knowledge rather than artifacts from South American traders. Data recently generated from lead isotope studies of Mexican copper ores and artifacts (Hosler and Macfarlane 1996) and of Andean South American copper ores and artifacts (Lechtman, personal communication, 2000) substantiate these inferences. The lead isotope ratios of Mexican and Andean ores differ sufficiently that it is usually possible to distinguish Mesoamerican from South American artifacts on the basis of lead isotope signatures. Thus far the lead isotope signatures for Mesoamerican and South American artifacts generally match the lead isotopic signatures of copper ores from those same two regions. Thus no evidence supports the idea that Mesoamerican people imported South American artifacts on any significant scale.

Observations

These data indicate that a number of independent metalworking groups were scattered across a broad and physically precipitous geographical area. These groups shared highly specialized metallurgical knowledge even though they differed in cultural affiliations and probably in ethnicity and language. They drew upon a common body of information concerning appropriate smelting regimes and fabrication methods, and they shared precepts concerning the significance of metallic sound, specifically bell sounds. Smelting and casting require substantial technical expertise. The fact that this metallurgical knowledge was so widely shared and crossed ethnic (and political) lines argues for face-to-face interaction throughout this large area, which is in keeping with other evidence for extensive trade and communication in Epiclassic/Early Postclassic Mesoamerica (chapters 3 and 24). The particularly rapid dissemination of highly specialized technical

know-how may reflect the fact that metallurgy was introduced from outside and as a kind of technological packet. Yet the early and profound interest in metallic sound that emerged in this metalworking zone was unique to Mesoamerica. South American smiths also cast bells (in Colombia) or hammered them (in Ecuador), but in neither case were bells a primary focus of those metallurgies (Hosler 1986, 1994).

EVIDENCE FROM OTHER AREAS OF MESOAMERICA

Archaeologists occasionally have recovered artifacts from outside of the metalworking zone dating to the period before about A.D. 800. Apart from a small cast figurine recently recovered at Teotihuacan and dated to A.D. 750 (Cabrera C., personal communication, 2000), nearly all of these come from the southeastern Maya area. One was recovered from Altun Ha, Belize; many others made from copper-gold alloys or from copper or gold metal have been dredged from the Cenote de Sacrificios in the Yucatán Peninsula. Some are lost-wax-cast copper-gold figurines, and all are difficult to date. Their design (stylistic) characteristics and composition make clear that these artifacts were imported from lower Central America (see Bray 1977 for what he calls "the Isthmian connection"). By A.D. 500, a complex lost-wax casting technology was flourishing in Colombia, Panama, and Costa Rica.

THE MIDDLE AND LATE POSTCLASSIC PERIODS (A.D. 1200/1300–1521)

The most significant developments after around A.D. 1200 to 1300 are: (1) the technical expertise of metalsmiths in the metalworking zone expanded in developing copper-tin and copper-arsenic bronze and copper-silver alloys which they elaborated and refined for ritual paraphernalia; (2) in Oaxaca, eastern Guerrero, coastal Chiapas, and the Gulf of Tehuantepec metalworkers began to produce and use axe-monies: thin, stackable, made of copper-arsenic alloys, and T-shaped; and (3) west Mexican metalworking zone artifacts appear at sites in Belize, Chiapas, Morelos, and Tamaulipas. Objects made in the west but found outside of it probably moved through market systems and middlemen; this occurs at about the same time that local people began to fashion metal objects in many of these same regions. By the time of the Spanish invasion, mining, processing, and manufacturing occurred in most Mesoamerican areas where ore minerals were found (highland Guatemala, San Luis Potosí, Honduras, Oaxaca), and metal was smelted and produced at innumerable settlements within the richly mineralized west Mexican metalworking zone. Production arrangements varied and represent a spectrum of structural possibilities. In some cases, mining, smelting, and production took place at a single site, particularly among smaller groups and polities in the metalworking zone. Sometimes ore was smelted, and the resulting ingots or blanks were exchanged. In areas where raw materials were scarce, itinerant metalworkers, probably traveling with their own tools and raw materials (Bray 1977), may have produced items on demand. Bray describes one such group traveling in canoes off the coast of Honduras. Sahagún may be referring to one of these itinerant smiths in his illustration of a needle seller who seems to be selling needle blanks and who is described as "the needle seller the copper caster who makes bells who melts copper… he makes bells, needles awls, punches" (Sahagún 1950–1982, book 10:87).

THE WEST MEXICAN METALWORKING ZONE

The evidence indicates in the metalworking zone smiths used bronze and copper-silver alloys to redesign the same elite and ritual artifacts they had previously made in copper. Their interest in metallic sound persisted, but they also became interested in metallic color, creating golden and silvery hues by using copper-tin, copper-arsenic, and copper-silver alloys. The superior mechanical properties of these alloys allowed them to cast large golden and silvery thin-walled bells; to shape large, elaborate, golden-looking tweezers through cold and hot work; and to cold-hammer into ritual paraphernalia large pieces of silvery-looking metal sheet from the copper-silver alloys. They also made bronze tools, but these appear in relatively small proportions (Hosler 1986, 1988a, 1994).

These new artifact designs—made using tin-bronze, arsenic-bronze, and copper-silver alloys—have been recovered in burials and household debris at sites throughout the metalworking zone (figure 21.4). At some settlements, the cultural affiliations of the people are clear; in Michoacán, artifacts appear at the Tarascan capital Tzintzuntzan (Cabrera C. 1988; Grinberg 1989; Hosler 1986; Rubín de la Borbolla 1944) and at the Tarascan centers of Huandacareo, Tres Cerritos (Macías G. 1989; Hosler 1994), Urichu (Hosler and Macfarlane 1996; Hosler 1999), and Huetamo (Hosler 1986). These bronze artifact types also appear at metalworking zone sites where ethnic affiliations are problematic. At Apatzingan, Michoacán, for example, Kelly (1947) recovered archaeological material she argues is unrelated to the Tarascan state, and this includes some of the metal artifact designs that characterize the period after A.D. 1200/1300. Cultural affiliations are similarly unclear at Milpillas, Michoacán (Hosler 1994), at lo Arado, Jalisco (Hosler n.d.), at El Chanal, Colima (Kelly 1980; Hosler 1986 and field notes), at San Miguel Ixtapan in the state of Mexico (Rubén Nieto, personal communication, 2000), and at Bernard in coastal Guerrero (Brush 1962), but copper-tin bronze artifacts are common at all of these sites. Moreover, hundreds of high-tin, tin-bronze artifacts

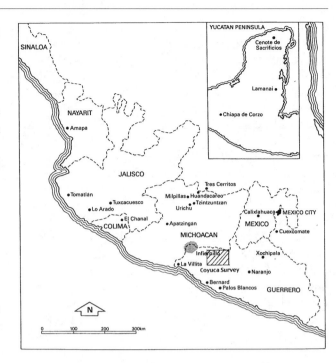

Figure 21.4 Map showing sites in west Mexican metalworking zone and adjacent areas where evidence for production and/or metal artifacts were recovered

(open rings) were recovered in the salvage operation in the Infiernillo region of the Río Balsas, and ethnic affiliations in these cases are likewise uncertain.

Production Arrangements

Archaeologists have reported evidence for metal production activities at various widely dispersed sites and regions in Colima, Jalisco, Michoacán, and Guerrero. The examples provided here are by no means exhaustive. Isabel Kelly (1949) identified slag in the Autlán area of Jalisco, and she also recovered copper ore as well as artifacts (already noted) at Apatzingán in Michoacán. Apatzingán lies in the Mexican copper belt and is very close to La Verde, one of Mexico's very large copper-belt mines. Metalworkers may have been smelting metal locally and fashioning objects at Apatzingán. Grinberg (1989) has identified slag at Churumuco and at the La Verde (Michoacán) mines, but the slag was not associated with archaeological material and thus may correspond to more-recent mining activities. These two mines have been subject to small-scale and commercial exploitation from the Spanish invasion into the twentieth century. Brush (1962) excavated slag at Bernard, Guerrero that, from his description, may be a by-product of tin smelting. This is especially significant because he also identified tin-bronze alloys at that site. Weitlaner (1948) identified slag at Naranjo, Guerrero. Two ingots were excavated at El Chanal, Colima, and we analyzed approximately 20 tin-bronze artifacts from that site (Hosler 1986, 1997).

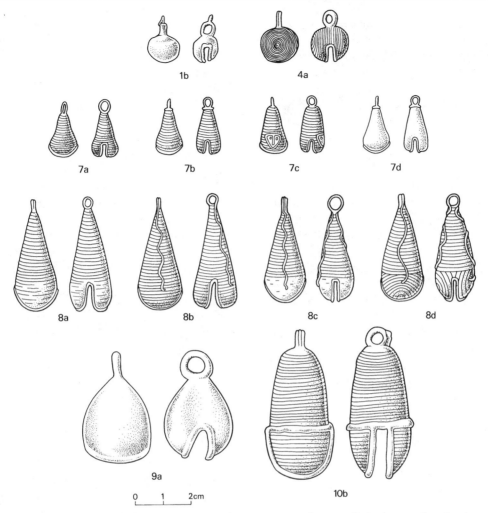

Figure 21.5 Bells made from copper-tin and copper-arsenic bronze alloys recovered at sites in the metalworking zone. Numbers refer to bell types discussed in Hosler 1994. (From Hosler 1994: figure 5.2.)

In my recent metallurgical site survey of the tierra caliente area of Guerrero and the adjacent Sierra Madre del Sur (figure 21.4; the cross-hatched rectangular area shows the area surveyed), I identified abundant evidence for preconquest mining, ore processing, and metal production. Eight of the 32 archaeological sites we located display evidence for some facet of metal production (e.g., ore, furnaces, processing tools, slag). Well-defined smelting areas appear at five of these sites, all containing large volumes of slag; four of the five also exhibit small, round, furnace-like structures as well as *morteros*—large flat rocks used for crushing ore. These smelting sites also display house mounds or other structures and Postclassic potsherds. In all but one case the smelting areas lie within 1 km or less of a copper mine.

These data suggest that metal processing and production took place throughout the metalworking zone. It is risky, except in very well documented cases, to associate these production areas with particular ethnic groups. For example, the multiethnic character of the Coyuca Survey area (the tierra caliente area that includes Coyuca, Pungarabato, Placeres de Oro, and mountain areas adjacent to them) was reported at the time of the Spanish conquest. None of the 32 sites I identified—just south of the Balsas River—shows unambiguous surface evidence (pottery or architecture) of Tarascan or Mexica presence. In fact, the largest and most impressive of the smelting sites lies outside of the area that scholars have ascribed to the Tarascan domain. The site is located at an altitude of 1,500 m in a remote area of the Sierra Madre del Sur, south of Placeres de Oro. It is unique in that it displays a large centralized production/smelting area and adjacent large habitation areas marked by long rectangular mounds, some of which are arranged around patios. Numerous potsherds were surface collected at this site, and several have been tentatively identified as exhibiting the Cuitlateca ceramic style (Cabrera C., personal communication, 2000). The quantity of copper artifacts reported from this general area (Coyuca, Pungarabato, Húetamo, Placeres de Oro) strongly suggests that people were manufacturing copper objects at least at some of these settlements. In other words, the probability is low that the sites just identified served exclusively to provide the processed raw materials (metal ingots, for example) as tribute to either the Mexica or Tarascan state.

Chemical analytical data also support the idea that metal processing and production were carried out in many regions of the metalworking zone. The hundreds of artifacts analyzed dating to this period show little evidence for standardization in alloy composition or design: the patterns are similar to those noted in the Epiclassic and early Postclassic period. Chemical compositions of artifacts of the same design type (e.g., wirework bells; see Hosler 1994 and figure 21.5) show that all are made from copper-tin or copper-arsenic bronze alloys. These designs require the properties of these bronze alloys. Nonetheless, these bells differ in the concentration of the alloying element and in the presence and concentration of trace elements. This indicates that metalworkers were not following technical recipes; that is, they did not adhere to strict norms for alloy compositions. Artifact chemical compositions suggest that the metal was smelted from quite different parent materials.

Perhaps most crucial to this argument are the results of my very recent lead isotope analyses of copper ores from the tierra caliente area and Sierra Madre del Sur in Guerrero (López et al. 1999; Hosler n.d.), which greatly expand the number of potential ore sources for artifacts we analyzed and published in *Science* (Hosler and Macfarlane 1996). At that time, the ore and artifact data pointed to several large Michoacán mines (Inguaran and Bastan) as major sources of copper ore for some 170 artifacts analyzed from sites in Jalisco, Michoacán, Morelos, Chiapas, Belize, and Tamaulipas. The Guerrero lead isotopic ratios (from 21 mines) overlap with those of Michoacán (Inguaran and Bastan mines) and occasionally with ore lead isotope ratios from Jalisco deposits. These data and data gained from other geochemical studies of Mexican ores now indicate convincingly that ore lead isotopic values alone will not allow us to distinguish copper deposits that are located along a north-south axis (between, for example, Jalisco, Michoacán, and Guerrero). But the data do confirm the evidence presented in the *Science* article that Mexico shows a west-east trend in lead isotopic ratios, making it possible to distinguish, for example, artifacts made from Jalisco ores from those made from ores from San Luis Potosí or Veracruz. This recent lead isotope evidence coupled with archaeological evidence for processing in the tierra caliente area indicates that many ore sources were exploited during the late Postclassic period.

Ethnohistoric sources from many Mesoamerican regions have provided insights concerning metal production prior to the invasion. The Relaciones Geográficas report copper and silver deposits in the province of Tenazmatlan, Jalisco (Acuña 1988:290), where, in the last several decades, many copper artifacts have been recovered by looters. The region is classified as a mining district by Mexico's Instituto Nacional de Geografía e Estadística (INEGI). The Relaciones Geográficas also describe a copper mine at Sinagua (Acuña 1987:254) in Michoacán. Sinagua is located in Michoacán's tierra caliente region and within about 25 km of the Inguaran, Churumuco, and Cocian mines, three of Mesoamerica's richest copper deposits. The historian Elinore Barrett (1981) argues that all three mines were subject to Sinagua prior to the invasion and were mined by local peoples. She cites Legajo 1204, a document written in 1533 and first published by J. Warren (1968) to support this contention, but she relies on other sources as well. Apart from identifying these mines, the Legajo reports that half of the metal was rendered as tribute to the Spanish Crown. It also describes copper smelting, but fails to do so in sufficient detail to facilitate useful reconstructions. In Guerrero, the Relaciones Geográficas from Tetela del Río (Hosler 1986; Paso y Troncoso 1905:36) mention two copper deposits and note that they had been mined prior to the invasion.

In summary, the archaeological, laboratory, and historical evidence cited here, together with evidence emerging from ongoing research, makes it clear that by Middle and Late Postclassic times, mining, smelting, and fabrication of copper, copper-tin and copper-arsenic bronze objects took place in many areas of the metalworking zone (Jalisco, Michoacán, Guerrero, Colima). This pattern is not surprising. The region is so richly mineralized, large and small copper sources are so common, and the area is so geographically precipitous that control of mining by any single group would have been nearly impossible.

If we have established that ores were smelted in many metalworking zone regions, what can we say about manufacturing? First, as discussed earlier, no evidence for standardization exists either in design or materials for metalworking zone artifacts. By "standardization in design" I mean that bells, tweezers, and rings conform to certain height and thickness specifications (for detailed reporting on this see Hosler 1986). The laboratory evidence shows no evidence of technical recipes in production such as those that obtained in ancient China, where, for example, during one period, bells of a given design always contained 20 percent tin and a lower but standard concentration of lead. (This is not to say that Mesoamerican metalworkers failed to manage the complex relations among alloy properties, design, and function: laboratory studies investigating precisely this issue show that they were highly skilled metallurgists.)

I also have shown that the same artifact classes are distributed throughout the metalworking zone (Hosler 1986, 1994), making it impossible to use metal artifact types as ethnic markers. For example, identical wirework

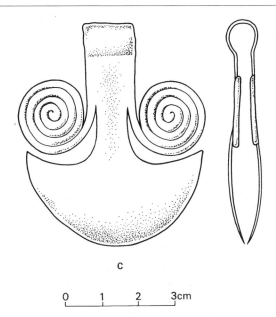

c

0 1 2 3cm

Figure 21.6 Tweezer design worn by Tarascan elites and priests. This particular design was restricted to Tarascan territories.

bells conforming to very similar design criteria appear in the Valley of Toluca, in Michoacán, at El Chanal in Colima, and in Guerrero. Whereas all are made from tin and arsenic bronze alloys, the presence and concentration of trace elements in the artifact metal differ, and as I noted in the case of Epiclassic and Early Postclassic bells, idiosyncratic design characteristics unrelated to functionality (dimensions and ratios of dimensions) differ. Their lead isotope ratios and hence metal sources also differ. Only one metal artifact type reliably marks ethnicity: the large spiral tin-bronze tweezers (figure 21.6) worn by Tarascan priests (as illustrated in the *Relación de Michoacán*) and recovered exclusively in Tarascan territory.

Technical Choices: Color, Sound, and Cosmology

The metalworking zone object designs that characterize the Middle and Late Postclassic periods appear at many sites throughout the area. Despite the range of new applications facilitated by the properties of bronze, metalworkers elected to continue producing sacred and status items rather than developing the tools and weapons, a development that did occur in other areas of the world. Their interest persisted in metallic sound, and they also began to produce objects in golden and silvery colors. They used high tin (golden-looking) and high arsenic (silvery-looking) bronzes for large, thin-walled bells cast with intricate, complex external zigzag design motifs (Hosler 1994). These alloys' strength allowed metalworkers to successfully cast larger bells, and these produced a range of new, lower pitches. Metalworkers also redesigned their tweezers, making them thinner and wider, cold- and hot-working the blade portion into delicate concave shapes. The spiral tweezer, a symbol of

Tarascan state power, displays complex, completely symmetrical spirals emerging from both sides of each blade (figure 21.6). Metalworkers also sometimes made tools from bronze; these were thinner and harder than their copper counterparts, containing tin or arsenic in concentrations up to about 5 percent by weight.

The most interesting aspect of these developments is that metalworking zone smiths elected to use these new materials to produce religious and status-bearing paraphernalia to strengthen, consolidate, and reify religious and social power, and to reinforce cosmological precepts. This ritual use of metal distinguishes this metalworking zone technology. Linguistic and other evidence suggests that metalworking zone peoples (some of whom lived in Mexica as well as in Tarascan and other territories) shared beliefs concerning the meaning of bell sounds and of golden and silvery metallic colors with the Mexica, and probably with the Huastec and other Mesoamerican groups as well. These sounds and colors helped define the Aztec paradise (Hosler 1994) described by Burkhart (1992) as a realm populated by deceased warriors and deified ancestors, and conceived as a shimmering, iridescent golden and silvery garden filled with the creative, generative sounds and songs of bells, birds, and human voices singing.

South American Connections

The development of the two bronze alloys and the widespread use of copper-silver alloys and of copper-arsenic axe-monies reflect continued contacts with South America (see Hosler 1988b, 1994). Nonetheless, as I have argued elsewhere, the Mesoamerican cultural interpretation of bronze as an elite and ritual material differed fundamentally from that of South America, where bronze was used primarily for utilitarian ends.

CURRENCY IN OAXACA

A second and striking change that occurred during this period is relevant to our discussion of increasing commercialization during the Postclassic. Sometime around A.D. 1200–1300, metalworkers in Guerrero and Oaxaca began producing an entirely new kind of metal object. These were axe-monies, a form of currency and a medium of exchange (figure 21.7). The concept and the design were South American. There, axe-monies appear in great numbers in coastal Ecuador and northern Peru, and hundreds of years before their appearance in Mesoamerica (Hosler 1986, 1988b; Hosler et al. 1990). Unlike the object types discussed previously, Mesoamerican axe-monies do meet the criteria for standardization in materials and design (Hosler 1986; Hosler et al. 1990). We do not know where they were produced, but they are abundant in collections in Guerrero and Oaxaca (Hosler 1986; Hosler et al. 1990), and they also sometimes appear in Chiapas (Hosler and Macfarlane 1996), in

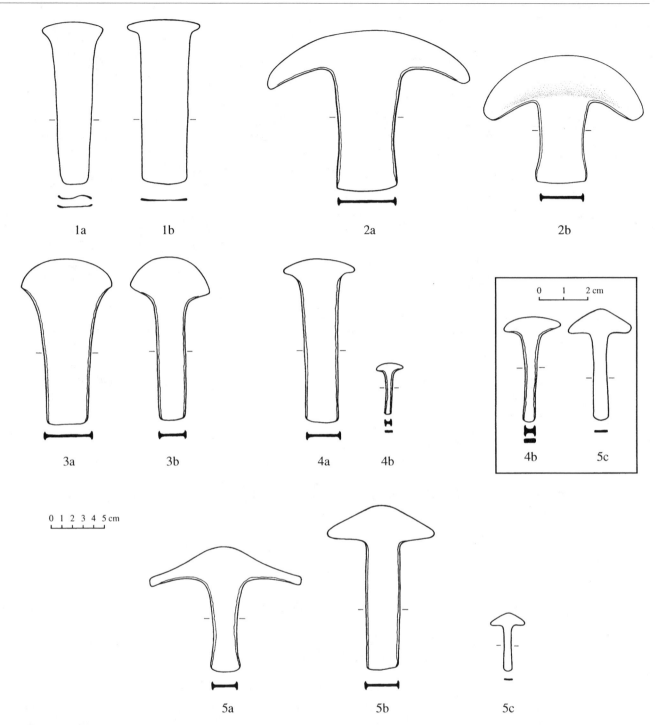

Figure 21.7 Axe-money types tend to appear in caches and are reported most frequently from Oaxaca, Guerrero, and Tehuantepec/northern Chiapas. Numbers refer to axe-money types discussed in Hosler et al. 1990. (From Hosler et al. 1990: figure 5.)

Morelos, and very occasionally in Michoacán, but never in significant numbers. With regard to numbers, axe-monies count as the second most abundant metal artifact class in museum collections (for example, in the National Museum of Anthropology storage facilities in Mexico City and also in the Regional Museum of Guadalajara) and probably comprise the second most abundant arti-

fact class in the entire Late Postclassic Mesoamerican metal corpus.

These thin, T-shaped axe-monies have been divided into various types (Hosler 1986; Hosler et al. 1990). Some are paper thin and have been found stacked in packets; others are heavier, mushroom shaped, and taper to a thin, fine blade. Microstructural studies of all vari-

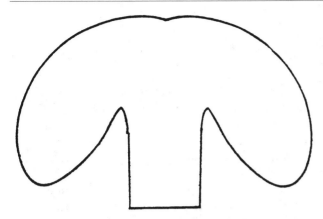

Figure 21.8 Drawing of type 2b axe-money in a sixteenth-century letter from López de Tenorio (Regidor de Antequera) to the Presidente del Consejo de Indias in Spain. López de Tenorio says in the letter that this is the kind of currency used in New Spain, and that four of these were worth five reales. (From Hosler et al. 1990: figure 31; after Medina 1912:563.)

eties show that the paper-thin type is mechanically un-suited for instrumental/tool-like applications. The mi-crostructural evidence is equivocal as to whether the oth-ers—whose heft and thickness might allow use—had utilitarian functions. Their design and mechanical prop-erty characteristics are such that they are capable of use. Francisco López Tenorio, the *regidor* de Antequera (the city of Oaxaca) illustrates this heavier type (figure 21.8) and explains its value in a 1548 letter to the president of the Consejo de Indias: "Esta es la forma de moneda que se usaba en la Nueva España...valían 4 de estas 5 reales y después siendo gastadas un poco no las querían recibir en precio alguno y venían por valer 10 por 1 real para tornarlas a refundir" [This is the kind of money used in New Spain...4 of these were worth 5 reales and after they became a bit worn no one wanted them at any price and when 10 were worth 1 real, they melted them] (Med-ina 1912). Other sources also refer to these items (*hachas* or *hachuelas*) as a medium of exchange. The Relación Geográfica from Tetiquiapa, Oaxaca, reports that "no tenían minas conocidas de donde sacar el oro ni otros metales que los hachas de cobre que solían tributar hera modeda que correria y se vendía en los tianguez y merca-dos que se hacian en todos los pueblos" [They did not have any known mines for gold or other metals...the copper axes they rendered as tribute were money and the axes were sold in the markets held in all the villages] (Troike n.d.).

Axe-monies have been encountered only rarely in ar-chaeological contexts, and they often appear in packets and caches. They are found almost exclusively in the region encompassing eastern Morelos, Guerrero, Oax-aca, and Chiapas. The most significant quantity recov-ered with reasonable archaeological associations comes from the site of Paredón, located in coastal Chiapas on the border with Oaxaca. There, archaeologists have surface-collected hundreds of the paper-thin variety, some of which were eroding out of mounds. Many others have been recovered from this site by looters (Barbara Voorhies, personal communication, 1995). The paper-thin axe-money type also appears in Guerrero. The thicker and heavier types are the most common in Oaxaca.

Axe-monies were probably manufactured in Oaxaca (and perhaps also in Guerrero, although for now the best evidence comes from Oaxaca). The incorporation of these South American items into the Mesoamerican repertoire after around A.D. 1200 and their subsequent local production mark a clear-cut shift in this region of Mesoamerica to a more formal commercialized economy.

METALWORKING IN OTHER AREAS

Maya Area

In 1977 Warwick Bray published a key article titled "Maya Metalwork and Its External Connections." He describes formal similarities between objects recovered in the Maya area and in Costa Rica and Panama, respec-tively, and cites evidence for metal production by itiner-ant smiths. He lists objects likely imported from Central America by Aztec merchants, and argues for local pro-duction in the Guatemalan highlands and in Belize. The question of production in Belize (at Lamanai) has now been thoroughly investigated (Hosler 1994). Chemical analytical evidence coupled with artifact design charac-teristics make it clear that some of these objects were made at Lamanai by remelting or recycling other arti-facts, whereas others (tin-bronze tweezers, for example) were moved through market systems to Lamanai from the metalworking zone, and still others, made from a very pure copper, were produced somewhere in the Maya region (similar bells have been dredged from the Cenote de Sacrificios at Chichén Itzá, for example), perhaps by Bray's itinerant smiths.

Oaxaca

The technically accomplished Oaxacan copper-gold cast-ing technology emerged after A.D. 1200. Similarities in this technology to the earlier copper-gold casting technol-ogy of lower Central America and Colombia indicate that the two are related. Unfortunately, Oaxacan metal-lurgy never has been systematically studied. Most arti-facts come from looted sites. Apart from the copper-gold cast alloy objects, copper (and bronze) bells and tools also have been recovered in Oaxaca, and these appear in significant numbers in museum collections. A few have been analyzed. Some artifacts seem to belong to a south-eastern Mesoamerican metallurgical tradition and resem-ble objects from Lamanai, the Cenote de Sacrificios, and other Maya sites. The chemistry and design characteristics of others resemble objects from Guerrero, Colima, and Michoacán, and they were probably imported from one or more of these areas (Hosler 1994, Hosler and Macfarlane 1996). We have no archaeological evidence for Oaxacan mining and processing, although the Relaciones Geográficas mention that copper was mined in Nexapa (Acuña 1984:357). The Relaciones also make frequent references to gold and silver.

Huastec Area

We also know that some tin-bronze items were produced by Huastec peoples (Hosler and Stresser-Péan 1992) in the late fifteenth or early sixteenth century. Archeologists have recovered bronze ingots (copper-arsenic-tin and copper-tin) and intermediate, partially smelted material in a Huastec burial at Vista Hermosa. This material was associated with a number of small copper bells and bell clappers. Several hundred copper and bronze objects also were recovered at Vista Hermosa and at Platanito, another Huastec site (Hosler and Stresser-Péan1992; Hosler 1994). Some bells apparently were cast locally, while other items were fashioned from metal from the west (Hosler and Stresser-Péan 1992; Hosler 1994; Hosler and Macfarlane 1996). Our most recent lead isotope studies of Guerrero ores indicate that this metal could have come from Guerrero, Michoacán, or Jalisco sources.

Morelos

At Capilco and Cuexcomate in Morelos (Smith 1992a, 1996a) we find copper and tin-bronze artifacts whose chemistry and design mark them as unambiguously west Mexican. These appear in assemblages alongside other metal objects whose design and chemistries (Hosler 1994) suggest they may have been made from recycled metal. Lead isotope studies of copper and bronze artifacts excavated by Michael Smith from Yautepec, an Aztec town in eastern Morelos, initially pointed to Michoacán and Jalisco copper sources, but recent research on Guerrero ores suggests that artifacts from all three sites could have been made from metal from copper deposits in Guerrero, which were within the Mexica domain.

DID PRODUCTION TECHNOLOGY AND USE OF METAL CHANGE THROUGH TIME?

Throughout the history of metallurgy in Mesoamerica, no single polity or group controlled metal production: mining, processing, manufacture, or distribution. The appearance of a standardized currency in Oaxaca does, however, reflect manufacturing specifications in that region for that artifact class. Overall, however, the pattern of localized or decentralized production did not change. Before A.D. 1200/1300 metallurgy was largely confined

to the mineral-rich metalworking zone, and we know little about the cultural affiliations of the producing groups. We know only slightly more about the cultural affiliations of metalworkers after A.D. 1200/1300. Smelting (and in some cases object manufacture) took place in Jalisco, near Autlan and lo Arado, in Colima in the El Chanal area, and in Michoacán in the vicinity of Apatzingan, and at Inguran and at other mines in the tierra caliente area. We know from the documents that in 1533 the Spanish Crown required tribute in copper from at least one Michoacán mine (Inguran), but we do not know who, if anyone, may have exploited the large and rich adjacent La Verde copper mine during that time or before the invasion. La Verde lies within 35 km of Inguaran. Archaeological evidence shows large-scale copper smelting in at least one large Sierra Madre del Sur site, and at various smaller sites in the tierra caliente of Guerrero. The recent lead isotope data now make clear that copper mining in the metalworking zone was not confined to four or five large mines. Rather, as our archaeological data are beginning to confirm, mining was carried out at hundreds of deposits.

Evidence from artifacts found outside the metalworking zone attests to varied production arrangements. People at Lamanai recycled metal by melting down artifacts and reworking them. Smelting and manufacture took place in the Huastec area. Evidence for metal recycling also appears in some artifacts excavated at Aztec towns in Morelos. We know that some artifacts found in Belize, Morelos, Chiapas, and Tamaulipas were made in the west and moved to these areas through market systems. The picture during this period reveals varied production regimes, because at such sites we find objects produced locally (for example, axe-monies in Oaxaca) in the same depositional context as tin-bronze wirework bells known from Guerrero or Michoacán whose lead-isotopic signatures also point to Guerrero, Michoacán, or Jalisco metal.

Changes did occur during the Postclassic in the primary role or social functions of metal items. After A.D. 1200/1300 metal production increased in the west Mexican metalworking zone and also took place outside of it. The primary emphasis in the west was on production of golden and silvery-looking ritual items, chiefly bells. In Oaxaca, by contrast, the evidence strongly argues for standardization of axe-money production. Unfortunately, we do not yet know where smiths were producing these items, but the best guess is along the Oaxaca/Guerrero border, based on axe-money distributions and the location of copper ores. The development of metal currency (axe-monies) stands out as the most significant event bearing on the question concerning economic integration during the Late Postclassic period. The appearance of metal currency signals a fundamental change in the use of metal in this region—Oaxaca, eastern Guerrero, northern Chiapas—where axe-monies circulated. The emergence of money economies in this particular area is another indication of the commercialization, commodification, and increased interaction that characterize most of Mesoamerica during the Postclassic.

One challenge in trying to understand the relations among Postclassic Mesoamerican polities is to develop a model that allows for the production of copper and copper alloys as a commodity—in fact, as money—that we observe in Oaxaca and the areas adjacent to it. The model also incorporates our metalworking zone evidence, where people continued to use copper and bronze (and gold and silver) primarily for production of ritual items.

The development of complex metallurgical techniques during the Postclassic adds a significant dimension to the growth and integration of the Mesoamerican polities during this period. It indicates long-range external connections between west Mexico and South America, and highlights linkages within Mesoamerica ranging from the Pacific coast to the Gulf coast, and extending as far southeast as Belize. Throughout Postclassic times these metal objects served sacred and status purposes, and their movements across polities may prove significant in linking elites in prestige-goods exchange. Along a different dimension, the development of standardized metal axe-monies—serving for exchange, storage of wealth, and/or standards of value—highlights the increasing commercialization of the Mesoamerican economy during the Postclassic period. The role that metal and other objects played in integrating elites in the Postclassic Mesoamerican world is explored in the next chapter by John Pohl.

22

Ritual Ideology and Commerce in the Southern Mexican Highlands

John M. D. Pohl

During the Postclassic period the Mesoamerican economy became inundated with new forms of elite wealth, most notably as a result of technological innovations for smelting precious metals introduced from South America, and the acquisition of turquoise from the American Southwest (Saville 1920; Harbottle and Weigand 1992). This emphasis on exotic material and technology reflects the profound increase in economic competition that attended the emergence of scores of newly empowered elite entrepreneurs, one that ultimately integrated large parts of North and Central America into what became the Postclassic Mesoamerican world system.

Archaeological evidence indicates that by A.D. 1200, emerging great houses throughout the central and southern highlands—the Mixteca-Puebla area—began to engage in fiercely competitive reciprocity systems to enhance their position in alliance networks. I examine these here for each of three regions: the Eastern Nahua region, and the Mixtec and Zapotec regions of Oaxaca.

THE EASTERN NAHUA

The *Historia Tolteca-Chichimeca* and the *Mapas de Cuauhtinchan* relate the legend of the Eastern Nahua peoples, led by the "sons" of Camaxtli-Mixcoatl who eventually settled in Tlaxcala and Puebla, including Quetzalcoatl, Mixtecatl, and Xelhua (Pohl 1994c). These fascinating paintings were commissioned by the colonial Indian leaders of a town in southern Puebla to document the foundation of their kingdom, its boundaries, and its relationships with neighboring states prior to their conquest by the Aztec Triple Alliance (Reyes García 1977; Yoneda 1991; Leibsohn 1994). There is something unusual about their composition, however. The Tolteca-Chichimeca migrants, dressed in deerskin cloaks and carrying bows and arrows, are shown hiking through the

Valley of Mexico, Tlaxcala, Puebla, and Oaxaca as if they were traveling on a seasonal hunting trip—an odd representation given the fact that the landscape over which they traveled was settled by thousands living in cities, surrounded by hundreds of square miles of cultivated land.

Elsewhere I have proposed that the Aztlan legend is metaphorical (Pohl 2001). The paintings reflect a traditional system of cognitive mapping in which legends associated with particular geographical features such as mountains, rivers, and so forth were recounted by tribal chiefs as directional locators in the course of seasonal hunting and foraging migrations. In the interest of emphasizing an outsider's divine right to rule, the stories were subsequently reconfigured to legitimize the establishment of Postclassic Tolteca-Chichimeca city-states, even though the political reality of the people employing the stories had little to do with the desert hunting strategies for which they were originally intended.[1]

The *Mapas de Cuauhtinchan* show us how the legend of Aztlan-Chicomoztoc functioned as a means of integrating peoples not only socially, but economically as well. There is a ritual quality about them, as if they prescribe annual religious pilgrimages as much as documenting any single historical event (Pohl 1994b:143–147; Leibsohn 1994; Boone 1991). Cuauhtinchan Map 2, for example, ascribes day signs calculated from the *tonalpohualli* (the sacred 260-day calendar) to the various place signs visited by the tribe traveling between Chicomoztoc and Cholula (figure 22.1a). The day signs make little sense as a chronology for events that took place over the course of more than a century, so what could they signify? The tonalpohualli was used to calculate the principal royal feasts and religious celebrations that bound communities together into systems of mutual support and obligation, much as the festivals of Christian saints

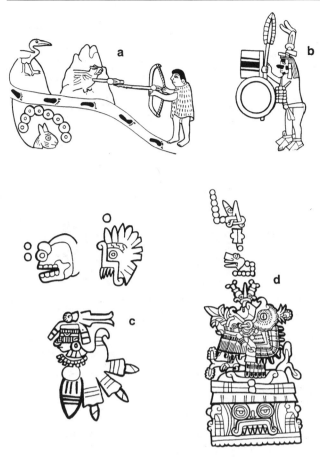

Figure 22.1 The role of myth and ritual in economic integration: (a) Cuauhtinchan Map 2 ascribes day signs calculated from the sacred tonalpohualli (260-day calendar) to the various place signs visited by the tribe traveling between Chicomoztoc, Aztlan, and Cholula; (b) Cuauhtinchan Map 1 portrays a leader of the Tolteca-Chichimeca migration wearing the ritual dress of Yacatecuhtli, the patron god of their merchants; (c) petroglyphs from the Acatlan Valley mark the feast days 1 Rain and 2 Death along with the sacred fetish of Camaxtli-Mixcoatl; (d) Codex Zouche-Nuttall depicts the deity-ancestor 8 Wind emerging from a tree growing from a cleft in Yucuñudahui, a major archaeological complex in the Nochixtlan Valley.

continue to do so throughout rural Mexico. The Spanish chroniclers tell us that these feasts were also the basis for an institutionalized system of periodic markets, the economic lifeblood of the Postclassic Mesoamerican world (Pohl 1998a; Pohl et al. 1997; see figure 22.1).[2]

Cuauhtinchan Map 1 portrays the leaders of the Tolteca-Chichimeca migration wearing the ritual dress of Yacatecuhtli, the patron god of their merchants (Sahagún 1950–1982, book 1:41–44; O'Mack 1991).[3] *Yacatecuhtli* is a Nahuatl term meaning "Vanguard Lord" in reference to his position as both a personage of royal blood and an extremely aggressive merchant entrepreneur (Sahagún 1950–1982, book 2:41; see figure 22.1b). The Florentine Codex depicts Yacatecuhtli wearing the *xiuhtlalpilli*, a blue, tie-dyed cloak worn only by para-

mount lords of royal blood in Late Postclassic times (Anawalt 1993:36). Yacatecuhtli was also an avatar of Quetzalcoatl (Garibay K. 1973:121). In this regard, it is significant that much of what characterized the Middle Postclassic world system was credited to the genius of the famous culture hero and his followers: "[I]n his life and in his time he [Quetzalcoatl] introduced great riches, jade, turquoise, gold, silver, redshell, whiteshell, quetzal plumes. And cotingas, roseate spoonbills, troupials, trogons, and herons. In addition, he introduced cacao of different colors and different colored cotton" (Bierhorst 1992:30).

While we view Tenochtitlan's Templo Mayor as a testament to the ideology of military dominance by a class of elites who made their war god Huitzilopochtli the primary focus of veneration (Brumfiel 1998), the cult of Quetzalcoatl at Cholula shows us an alternative path to power in Postclassic society through the competitive manipulation of temple and feast sponsorship by a ruling merchant elite. Quetzalcoatl-Yacatecuhtli was Cholula's merchant god and patron of the city's largest religious festival (Durán 1971:129, 139). The feast was held annually in the plaza before the main temple, which was said to have been even larger than Tenochtitlan's Templo Mayor. Cholulteca merchant-lords were known to invest as many as 20 years assembling enough capital to sponsor the feast, for which they were richly rewarded with royal titles, insignia, and positions of power as civic administrators.[4] Forty days prior to the celebration, a slave was purchased by the merchants and dressed to impersonate Quetzalcoatl. The slave sang and danced through the streets daily, collecting contributions for the feast from the homes of people throughout the city. Then, at the appointed time, he was sacrificed to the god he represented. The feast itself featured many days of dances, singing, dramas, and farces in and around a 10 m² central platform adorned with arbors of flowers. The general populace who attended the celebration contributed vast quantities of food. After dining on specially prepared dishes of bird and rabbit, the merchants danced in their finest ritual dress with actors pretending to be victims of disease and blindness, while at the same time solemn prayers were sung to Quetzalcoatl imploring him to protect the Cholulteca from disease.

Significantly, the Spanish chronicler Gabriel de Rojas described Cholula as the "Mecca" of the New World. Scholars studying the origins of major religious traditions such as Islam have identified a link between the spread of faith and the emergence of new alliance and economic systems. Eric Wolf (1951) proposed that Islam, in particular, was founded among a class of merchants who promoted it to override the divisiveness of kinship-based clans, while at the same time centralizing its cult at their major center of trade. Mecca thereby created an umbrella of some statelike political and economic structures, but still guaranteed political autonomy among its constituent kings, princes, and merchants.

Quetzalcoatl-Yacatuchtli's patronage of an interregional market system, as depicted in the Cuauhtinchan maps and Cholula histories, is a clear allusion to the establishment of trade networks being equated with the spread of religious ideology through Tolteca-Chichimeca confederacies. Ethnohistorical sources indicate that Cholula played a major role in trade with the tropical lowlands, known collectively as Anahuac, well into the Colonial period, using a route through the Tehuacan Valley. The Anales de Cuauhtitlan describe a continuation of the Tolteca-Chichimeca odyssey from northern Oaxaca east to Copilco, Topillan, Ayotlan, and Mazatlan. Copilco was a kingdom of mixed Nahua and Chontal peoples located on the Gulf coast between Veracruz and Tabasco. Topillan may have been the subject community now called Topilco. Ayotlan and Mazatlan, on the other hand, were located on the Pacific coastal Xoconochco (Scholes and Roys 1968:96–97; Gasco and Voorhies 1989).

Cuauhtinchan Map 1 confirms the account pictographically by portraying Nahua lords from Cholula seated in palaces along the Pacific coastal shoreline. According to Torquemada, Nahua peoples moved from Cholula to the Xoconochco region during the Early Postclassic and then subsequently founded kingdoms in coastal Guatemala, El Salvador, and Nicaragua, where they came to be known as the Pipil-Nicarao (Torquemada 1986:1:331–333; Orellana 1995:24; see also chapter 36). Close linguistic affiliations between the Nahua dialects of Veracruz, the Xoconochco region, and El Salvador appear to confirm Torquemada's account, but how large these migrations were and precisely when they occurred are still debated (Campbell 1976, 1985).[5] At the time of the conquest, both Cholula and the city-states of the Tehuacan Valley were trading heavily in textiles for cacao with the Xoconochco region and Guatemala, probably through Tochtepec and Zinacantan (Durán 1971:129; Acuña 1984:2:33; Feldman 1978; Köhler 1978). Tochtepec and other coastal Veracruz kingdoms were tributaries of Coaixtlahuaca prior to their conquest by the Mexica (Torquemada 1986:1:160; Bierhorst 1992:107; Dahlgren 1990b:74, 189). Zinacantan, a Tzotzil Maya city-state, remains virtually unknown archaeologically, but historical references suggest that it was the dominant Maya trading center in the Chiapas highlands (chapter 17).

Despite its diminished role in both the Late Aztec and Colonial Spanish worlds, the legacy of Cholula as a pilgrimage center was never lost. Every September 8, more than 350,000 people still journey to Cholula to celebrate the feast of the Virgin de los Remedios and to attend the richest indigenous market in central Mexico. Farmers travel by foot, mule, horse, truck, bus, and train from

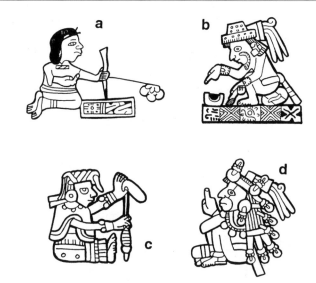

Figure 22.2 Images of noble women and men serving as court artisans: (a) An Aztec queen depicted as a painter in Codex Telleriano Remensis; (b) the Mixtec hero 9 Wind portrayed as a painter in Codex Vindobonensis; (c) a Mixtec queen weaving in Codex Vindobonensis; (d) the Mixtec hero 9 Wind named as a turquoise merchant-craftsman in Codex Vindobonensis.

Tlaxcala, Veracruz, Hidalgo, Morelos, Mexico, Guerrero, and Oaxaca along the same routes portrayed in the *Mapas de Cuauhtinchan* and the *Historia Tolteca-Chichimeca* (Olivera 1970). The market continues to inspire a vision of traditional Indian prosperity, featuring handwoven baskets from Tehuacan, painted pottery from Tlaxcala, and a bounty of fruits, vegetables, herbs, spices, and other specialized products as diverse as the mountains, deserts, and tropical coasts from which they are harvested.

THE MIXTECS AND ZAPOTECS

Oaxaca's mountainous environment—with its rugged topography, profound soil erosion, low annual temperatures, highly variable precipitation, and short growing seasons—severely inhibited regional exchange. While some kingdoms, notably Coaixtlahuaca, established themselves as international trade centers (chapter 17), exchange primarily took place during annual religious festivals held in outlying boundary areas, frequently on or near Classic-period ruins (Pohl et al. 1997). Abandoned by A.D. 1000, these ancient mountaintop shrines continued to be used as sources of mutual ancestral heritage by the otherwise divided royal houses of Postclassic kings and queens. For the Mixtecs these sites can be identified in the historical codices as wilderness locations where the founders of the principal dynasties miraculously first emerged from trees and stones. Timed to significant dates in the 260-day calendar, Mixtec lords and their retinue would gather to venerate the mummy bun-

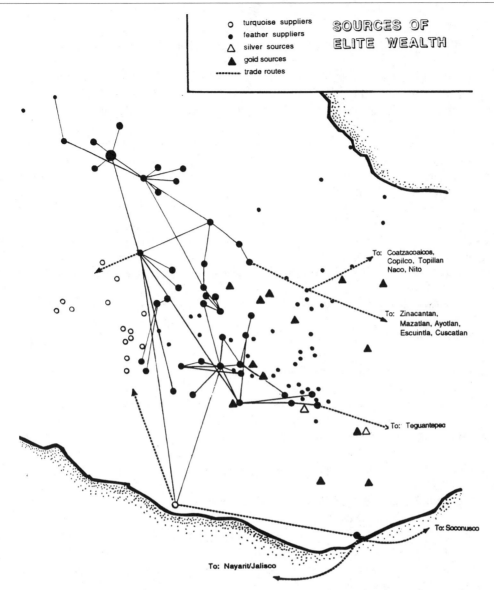

Figure 22.3 The distribution of primary elite commodities as depicted in the Codex Mendoza and other Colonial sources in relation to the Postclassic marriage networks (solid lines) that bound Eastern Nahua, Mixtec, Zapotec and other confederated peoples into systems of economic reciprocity. (Resource data are from Berdan 1992; Berdan and Anawalt 1992; and Relaciones Geográficas for the state of Oaxaca.)

dles of their deceased relatives, who were often grouped and buried in nearby caves, while their people danced, celebrated, and carried on trade through barter. Different Mixtec territorial units emphasized different sets of divine ancestors, so we would not expect to see the broad regional integration through ritual proposed for the fixed *veintana* festivals dedicated to the Aztec pantheon in Late Postclassic times.[6]

Both the Mixtec and Zapotec societies were traditionally divided into a hereditary nobility and a farming population. There is little evidence of any specialized class of merchants comparable to the pochteca (Spores 1984:72, 80–84). Rather, these positions were filled by a junior nobility (*toho* or *joana*) who acted as representatives of the rulers (*yya* or *coqui*) by mounting expeditions into foreign lands and transporting exotic goods back to the royal courts. There they were transformed into stunning works of art for prestige display, gifts, or bridewealth (Pohl 1994c:42–68; figure 22.2). Only a few examples of jewelry with the precious stones and metals that came to epitomize the luxury wealth of the Postclassic were known to exist until Caso's remarkable discovery of more than 140 gold and silver objects from Tomb 7 at Monte Albán in 1932 (Caso 1969). The ornaments consist of tiny brooches, bells, beads, and rings meticulously sculpted and cast in the form of eagles, quetzals, macaws, tortoise shells, and deities such as the patron god of artisans, 7 Flower-Xochipilli. The Mixtecs and Zapotecs appear to have monopolized gold extraction (Berdan 1992c:297). Placers were exploited throughout the Valley of Oaxaca, the Mixteca Alta, and the Chinantec region extending into Veracruz. Granular gold was measured in tubes for trade, but other standardized units of measure were created by smelting or hammering metals into such basic forms as bells or plates (figure 22.3).

Only turquoise surpassed gold in terms of value in the Postclassic elite economy, and hundreds of pieces of turquoise tesserae indicate that many works of mosaic art also had been placed in Monte Albán's Tomb 7. Turquoise procurement appears to have been dominated by the Mixtecs of the Costa and Baja regions lying between Acatlan and Tututepec (Berdan 1992c:301; Harbottle and Weigand 1992:82; Berdan and Anawalt 1992:2:90–94). Turquoise was mined and transformed into tesserae on Mesoamerica's northern frontier, where it was used as a currency in exchange for hides and parrot feathers (Harbottle and Weigand 1992; Pogue 1974: 97–98; Pohl 2001). The tesserae were then transported over tremendously long distances by Chichimec entrepreneurs into west Mexico, where the material was redistributed throughout Mesoamerica and transformed into astounding creations. Surviving examples include funerary masks, mirrors, shields, helmets, and sacrificial knives (Saville 1922). The amount of labor involved in assembling these masterpieces almost defies imagination. Given that turquoise sources were so far to the north, the Mixtecs must have imported it by dealing with west Mexican middlemen, possibly through the Río Balsas drainage by trail, but more likely by canoe along the Pacific coast.[7]

PALACE FEASTS AND GIFT EXCHANGE

We have seen that regional government became highly segmented and commercially oriented during the Early-to-Middle Postclassic throughout Tlaxcala, Puebla, and Oaxaca (chapter 10 and above). This was the time when architectural emphasis was placed on the development of great houses: networks of enclosed rooms and courts ideally suited not only to proliferation of an unequalled level of craft production, but also to the private feasting and drinking parties that were such an integral part of alliance formation (Pohl 1994a, 1998a). The value of wealth acquired from distant lands was amplified through artistic transformation. While the Aztecs maintained separate classes of artisans who transformed exotic raw materials into gifts and other valuable commodities (Sahagún 1950–1982, books 9, 10; Brumfiel 1987b; Soustelle 1961:59–70), there is considerable evidence that in earlier times the elite themselves served as the principal traders and craft producers. As the archetype of the Toltec lord, Quetzalcoatl was renowned as an expert craftsman: "And he was a great craftsman in all his works: his eating dishes, his drinking vessels, his

green-, herb-green, white-yellow, and red-painted pottery. And there was much more" (from Codex Chimalpopoca, Bierhorst 1992:30).

According to Codex Vindobonensis 48, the Mixtec culture hero 9 Wind "Quetzalcoatl" was conceived as not only a great prophet and warlord, but also an expert painter and jewelry craftsman (Furst 1978:102–105; Jansen 1982:143–145). Burgoa (1934a:210) wrote that the Mixtec codices were painted by the sons of nobles who had been taught this craft since infancy. There is evidence that ceramic wares were produced by women, who were probably trained in codex-style painting. The term *tacu,* or "painter," appears in several instances as the personal name of royal women in the Egerton and Muro codices (Smith 1973:67). Jewelry production was restricted to the elite. Burgoa (1934b:26:376–377) said that the commoners "did not use jewelry nor did they know of the art of mining, only the lords consumed the…gold and stones." Timed to the 260-day calendar recorded in codices, royal feasts were the primary means by which ranking lords bound their constituents into systems of mutual reciprocity and promoted their eligibility as potential alliance partners through lavish outlays of gifts crafted by court artisans.

Writing about the sixteenth-century Indian economy in general terms, the Spanish chronicler Alonso de Zorita described a reciprocal gift arrangement between the Mexican kings and their vassals: "The lesser lords made gifts to the supreme ruler at certain festivals held every year; they did this in acknowledgement of their subjugation and vassalage.… When a festival had ended, the supreme ruler gave to the lesser lords, his vassals, and to the lords of neighboring towns who attended these festivals, rich cloaks and other presents, according to the quality of each lord. Thus these lords departed content and well rewarded for what they had brought" (Zorita 1963:188–189).

Many Colonial sources tell us that precious stones, metals, and feathers—along with ornamental textiles called *mantas* (capes), specifically the *tilmatli*—were the most common form of gift given to Nahua lords by their followers (Anawalt 1981b:27). The Mixtec codices show us that a jacketlike garment called a *xicolli* was offered together with finely crafted gold, silver, jade, and turquoise jewels, and ornaments of quetzal and macaw feathers, to both reward loyal subjects for their services and to exchange with alliance partners for other goods and favors (Pohl 1994a). Perhaps the most famous gift portrayed in the Mixtec codices is the *yacaxihuitl* awarded to Lord 8 Deer by the Tolteca-Chichimeca priest Lord 4 Jaguar (Pohl 1994c:83–93). This turquoise jewel was inserted into the septum of the noses of Toltec princes who had been elected to the position of tecuhtli, the title of a landholding prince who served as a lineage head. The award was a significant achievement for Lord

Figure 22.4 The promotion of syndicates by royal intermarriage (schematic drawing)

8 Deer, who lacked the proper genealogical background to succeed to the throne of Tilantongo, and thereby sought alternative symbols of ritual power in his efforts to become the founder of Tilantongo's second dynasty. In return for this honor, 8 Deer apparently traded one form of political legitimacy for another by sending his son and daughter to the Toltecs for marriage into the royal house of San Miguel Tulancingo.

Among both Nahua and Mixtec peoples, marriages were the single most important occasions for gift exchanges. Muñoz Camargo (1984:198) describes a system of mutual exchange in which the relatives of both the Tlaxcalteca bride and groom exchanged gifts of cotton textiles, precious stones, gold, silver, cacao, and even slaves. The Mixtecs, in contrast, emphasized bride-price: "When a cacique wanted to marry he first took up the matter with the priests. He then sent his messengers to deal with the girl's parents and sent them presents of capes, jewelry, and feathers. These were given to the parents of the girl" (Spores 1965:984–985).

Herrera (1945:168) wrote that a Mixtec lord with many daughters thought himself a rich man for all the presents that were given for them in marriage. If the Early Colonial marriage of Doña Inés de Guzmán is in any way reflective of Precolumbian practices, then we may envision ceremonies with as many as 2,000 persons of royal blood in attendance contributing gifts of food and textiles to be measured in tonnage (Burgoa 1934b: 25:371).

Doubtless, bride-price was meant not only to emphasize the prestige of the givers and formalize the bond between two kin groups, but also to compensate a family for the loss of a valued royal woman's labor. Motolinía (1950:149) said that Nahua lords married many women because they valued their skills at weaving and practicing other crafts. Herrera (1945:167) wrote that the lesser wives or concubines of Mixtec noblemen were highly valued in that they "spent their time spinning to make the cacique and his lady their clothes." Considering that Nahua, Mixtec, and Zapotec kings had as many as twenty wives and just as many daughters, a single royal household could produce hundreds of textiles every year.

Many would be quick to see that the greater a royal house's ability to acquire exotic materials and to craft them into exquisite jewels, textiles, and featherwork, the better marriages it could negotiate. The better the marriages it could negotiate, the higher the rank a royal house could achieve within an emerging confederacy and, in turn, the better access it would have to more exotic materials, merchants, and craftspeople. In short, royal intermarriage promoted syndicates (figure 22.4), illustrating the close links between elite politics and world-system processes. The relationship between material acquisition, material craft, and exchange networks is the basis of what evolved into a Middle Postclassic world system. These elite connections provided an institutional context for the operation of significant information networks, the subject of the next section.

Part 4

Information Networks

23

Information Networks in Postclassic Mesoamerica

Michael E. Smith

During Postclassic times several distinctive styles and numerous symbols became prominent throughout Mesoamerica. Many of these elements have long been viewed as having an origin in, or at least a strong connection to, central Mexico. Indeed, the term *Mexicanization* is commonly used to describe the occurrence of such styles and symbols outside of central Mexico (e.g., Coe 1999: 187–188; Fox 1978:3; Miller 1982:65–74; Navarrete 1996; Thompson 1945:13; Sharer 1994:424–431; Sidrys 1983:404–406). Earlier scholars proposed a number of mechanisms to account for the spread of these elements from central Mexico to the distant corners of Mesoamerica, including mass migrations of peoples (Vaillant 1940:300; Ekholm 1942:128); travels by religious specialists carrying codices (Robertson 1970; von Winning 1977) or textiles (Lothrop 1966:189); the deliberate promotion of traits by the Aztecs in preparation for imperial conquest (Miller 1982:74; Navarrete 1976, 1996); and the diffusion of vague "waves of influence" (Nicholson 1960).

Today the term *Mexicanization* is used less frequently, and few scholars find the old explanations satisfactory (for discussion, see Smith and Heath-Smith 1980; Chase and Chase 1988; Nicholson and Quiñones Keber 1994b). Nevertheless, the presence of innumerable "central-Mexican-looking" elements throughout Postclassic Mesoamerica cannot be denied. Many of these traits and symbols were first identified in central Mexico, but that is not an argument in favor of a historical origin there. Some are more abundant in central Mexico simply because more codices have survived from the Aztec heartland than from other areas. The authors of this volume suggest that many of these elements were truly international in scope, meaning that they were widely distributed and did not necessarily originate in central Mexico.

The distribution and use of these styles and symbols were crucial components of the Postclassic Mesoamerican world system. As outlined in the chapters in part 1, our approach to world-systems analysis includes processes of information exchange alongside processes of economic exchange. The spread of styles and symbols was not just a by-product of economic exchanges: the peoples of Postclassic Mesoamerica—particularly elites—deliberately chose to use specific iconographic symbols and stylistic elements as crucial parts of their strategies of social and political interaction (e.g., Ringle et al. 1998). These pictorial elements communicated information, and as pointed out by Chase-Dunn and Hall (1997:52), information networks were important components of past world systems. We feel that our world-systems approach to styles and symbols provides a new and more convincing account of their occurrence and distribution than offered by past explanations. A historical review of the Mixteca-Puebla concept provides a background for our new concepts and units.

HISTORY OF THE MIXTECA-PUEBLA CONCEPT

George Vaillant (1938, 1940) coined the term "Mixteca-Puebla" to account for the pictorial styles of codices and ceramics of southern Puebla/northern Oaxaca (the Mixteca-Puebla region) and manifestations of that style in more-distant areas of Mesoamerica. He viewed Mixteca-Puebla alternatively as a culture and a "culture complex," and credited its spread from its Puebla/Oaxaca heartland to migrations and direct processes of diffusion. Perhaps because of Vaillant's broad and imprecise definition, other scholars soon began using the Mixteca-Puebla concept in a variety of ways (e.g., Ekholm 1942; Robertson 1959; Jiménez Moreno 1970).

In 1960, H. B. Nicholson (1960) reexamined the concept and tried to formalize and standardize its usage. He provided a clear definition of the Mixteca-Puebla style that emphasized its geometric precision, the standardization and conventionalization of symbols, and the use of color. Nicholson defined several "regional and temporal variants" of the Mixteca-Puebla style, including the Toltec, Aztec, and Mixtec. He accounted for the appearance of this style in distant areas of Mesoamerica through "waves of Mixteca-Puebla stylistic influence" that spread outward from the Mixteca-Puebla area (see also Meighan 1974). His ideas were developed further in several later papers (Nicholson 1982, 1996). Robertson (1959) defined and discussed the "Mixtec Pre-conquest manuscript style," which was quite similar to definitions of the Mixteca-Puebla style (e.g., Nicholson and Quiñones Keber 1994b).

Smith and Heath-Smith (1980) published a critique of Nicholson's model, arguing that he had lumped together three temporally and regionally distinct styles under the Mixteca-Puebla label. They pointed out that the earliest of these—which they labeled the "Postclassic Religious Style"—was widespread in coastal Mesoamerica, from Sinaloa in the north to Costa Rica in the south, during the Epiclassic and Early Postclassic periods. These occurrences predated the appearance of the Mixteca-Puebla style in its putative central Mexican heartland, and thus the "waves of influence" model cannot be appropriate. In a brief response to the Smith and Heath-Smith paper, Nicholson and Quiñones Keber (1994a) point out that those authors had confused style and iconography, an appropriate criticism (see discussion of these concepts in chapter 24). Here we refer to the standardized widespread Epiclassic/Early Postclassic symbols as the Early Postclassic international symbol set, a term that replaces the poorly named "Postclassic Religious Style."

Smith and Heath-Smith (1980) proposed calling the Middle and Late Postclassic manifestations of the Mixteca-Puebla style the "Mixtec Codex Style." They included the Mixteca and Borgia Group codices, the elaborate codex-style polychrome ceramics of Puebla and Oaxaca, and a series of Late Postclassic murals in central Mexico, Oaxaca, and Yucatán. It is now clear that there are really two distinct phenomena here: the Mixteca-Puebla style proper, and the more general international style (and symbols) of the mural paintings. Most scholars now use "Mixteca-Puebla style" to refer to the Middle and Late Postclassic codices, ceramics, and murals of the Mixteca-Puebla area (e.g., Nicholson and Quiñones Keber 1994b; Smith 2001b), a usage that we follow here. In our terminology, the Mixteca-Puebla style is a substyle of the more inclusive Postclassic international style (see below). Late Postclassic mural paintings from central Mexico to Yucatán share several key stylistic elements, a situation addressed by Robertson (1970), who grouped them as the "International Style of the Late Post-Classic." Smith and Heath-Smith (1980) also suggested a third

category—the "Mixteca-Puebla Regional Ceramic Style"—to describe local ceramic complexes in this area. Today this concept appears unnecessary: each region had its own history of changing ceramic complexes (corresponding to local ceramic phases), and these are different sorts of phenomena from the pictorial styles and symbols discussed above.

NEW UNITS AND CONCEPTS

With more information and new approaches to research on Postclassic Mesoamerica, we are now in a better position to identify the various chronological and spatial manifestations that were previously lumped together under the Mixteca-Puebla label, and to distinguish styles from iconographies in order to arrive at a better understanding of Postclassic Mesoamerican art and its social and cultural significance. Boone and Smith (chapter 24) discuss the issue of style versus iconography, a basic distinction for art historians that has become garbled when used by archaeologists, accounting for some of the confusion over the Mixteca-Puebla concept. They formally define the new concepts with illustrations, but it will be helpful to give a brief preview of them here.

The authors of this volume suggest the term *Postclassic international style* for a broad grouping of regional painting styles that exhibit similar use of form, line, color, spatial arrangement, and human figural conventions (chapter 24). We follow the lead of Donald Robertson (1970), who first proposed this concept for the Tulum and Santa Rita murals. At present, we can identify four regional styles within the general framework of the Postclassic international style (figure 23.1). We use the label *Mixteca-Puebla style* in its strict form as described above: to refer to the distinctive painting style found on codices, murals, and ceramics in the Mixteca-Puebla region of southern Puebla and Oaxaca (chapter 24; see also Nicholson and Quiñones Keber 1994a). The Aztec painting style is found primarily in pictorial codices, with some examples in mural paintings (chapter 27; see also Boone 1982a, 1990, 2000; Robertson 1959, 1963).

The *coastal Maya mural style* is our designation for the style of the mural paintings of Tulum, Santa Rita, Mayapán (newly discovered by Carlos Peraza), and other Postclassic coastal Maya sites (chapter 25; see also Miller 1982; Quirarte 1982; Robertson 1970). We suggest the name *southwest Maya style* for the mural paintings at Utatlan, Iximche', and other southwestern Maya sites. Only a few fragmentary examples have survived, and it is difficult to define this style with any precision (see discussion in chapter 24; see also Carmack and Larmer 1971; Guillemín 1965; Schele and Mathews 1998: figures 8.9, 8.10). It may be possible to define other regional polychrome painting styles within the Postclassic international style as more examples are brought to light. For

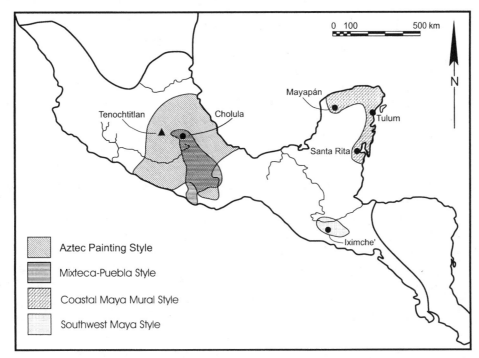

Figure 23.1 Map of regional style variants of the Late Postclassic international style. (Produced by Pamela Headrick, from base maps compiled by Timothy S. Hare.)

example, some west Mexican ceramics may qualify (chapter 24), and Postclassic murals and carved shells from the Huaxtec area might be considered another regional style (see Beyer 1934; Du Solier 1946).

Turning now from style to iconography, we propose the concept of an international symbol set to designate groups of related pictorial elements that are often found together in widely separated Postclassic representational contexts. As suggested above, the term *international* is important because it suggests the cosmopolitan nature of these elements and their lack of clear origin in, or strong association with, any particularly area. The Early Postclassic international symbol set includes iconographic elements from the Epiclassic and Early Postclassic periods originally labeled the Postclassic religious style by Smith and Heath-Smith (1980). These symbols—elements such as step-frets and serpents—were painted on polychrome ceramics along all of the coasts of Mesoamerica. Some or all of the symbols originated in Late Classic Maya iconography (Taube 2000:284). Their spread along coastal trade routes may have been associated with the spread of the feathered serpent cult throughout Mesoamerica at this time (Ringle et al. 1998).

These symbols of the Early Postclassic international symbol set preceded the development of the Postclassic international style and the related Late Postclassic international symbol set; in fact, they contributed strongly to the development of those later phenomena (Smith and Heath-Smith 1980; Day 1994). The elements of the Late Postclassic international symbol set were particularly widespread in Mesoamerica, and it is their distribution

that drew the attention of the early scholars who proposed the concept of Mexicanization. A closer look at this concept helps set the scene for the chapters that follow in this section.

BEYOND MEXICANIZATION

As noted above, the various early explanations for the spread of so-called central Mexican symbols and traits in Late Postclassic times all posited the origin of such traits in central Mexico, followed by their transmission to the distant reaches of Mesoamerica. In place of these notions, we suggest that many of the symbols, styles, and traits originated in other parts of Mesoamerica and then became incorporated into the active networks of commercial trade and information exchange that made up the Postclassic world system. Our approach to world-system dynamics suggests that the movement of ideas and symbols throughout the area is better viewed as a network with nodes than as a pattern of outward flow from a small number of centers (for similar models, see Ringle et al. 1998; Kepecs et al. 1994).

The advantages of our world-systems view over older, nuclear models of Mexicanization can be illustrated by a consideration of Carlos Navarrete's 1976 article "Algunas influencias mexicanas en el area Maya meridional durante el postclásico tardío" (Navarrete 1976; reprinted in 1996 with minor changes as "Elementos arqueológicos de mexicanización en las tierras altas mayas"). This paper is one of the most explicit and extensive treatments of the Mexicanization model. Navarrete lists more than

20 traits—organized into 12 categories of material objects—that he argues are central Mexican traits deliberately brought to the Guatemala highlands in preparation for Aztec conquest of the area. An examination of Navarrete's list, however, casts doubt on the central Mexican origin of many or most of the traits. Some are material objects that clearly originated in other parts of Mesoamerica (not central Mexico) such as copper/bronze items (from west Mexico; see chapter 21) and turquoise (from the Southwest; see chapter 18). Other items were imports from Aztec central Mexico (e.g., Aztec III Black-on-orange ceramics) whose presence outside of central Mexico resulted from commercial exchange that did not entail any necessary cultural or political affiliation with the Aztecs (Smith 1990). Still other items on Navarrete's list were general Postclassic traits widely distributed in Mesoamerica without any necessary priority or special affiliation with central Mexico. These include circular structures (Pollock 1936), mural paintings (Miller 1982; Pohl 1998a, 1999; Robertson 1970; Sisson and Lilly 1994a, 1994b), and human sacrifice (Massey and Steele 1997; Pijoan and Mansilla 1997; Ramírez and Acosta 1997; Welsh 1988), none of which had any temporal or cultural priority in central Mexico.

Even a trait like the double temple—often associated with the Aztecs because of the Templo Mayor—is suspect as an example of Mexicanization. There were many more double temples in the Maya area (Navarrete mentions 20; see also Smith 1955) than in Aztec central Mexico, where only five examples (Tenochtitlan, Tlatelolco, Tenayuca, Santa Cecelia, and Teopanzolco) are known (Pareyon Moreno 1972). Furthermore, the double temples in the two areas do not at all resemble one another in size, architectural style, or construction details. In short, most of Navarrete's traits were like the other international styles and symbols described above: they were distributed throughout Postclassic Mesoamerica along channels of commercial exchange and stylistic interaction. Local elites and others were in contact with people in distant regions, and they selected specific goods, symbols, and elements of style for their own reasons.

In the following chapter, Boone and Smith (chapter 24) discuss the concepts of style and iconography, and review the various international styles and symbols that characterized Middle and Late Postclassic Mesoamerica. That chapter is followed by three case studies that highlight the diversity of ways in which local elites deliberately selected and adopted specific elements or components of these styles and symbols for their own purposes. Masson (chapter 25) considers the well-known polychrome murals of the coastal Maya mural style at Tulum and Santa Rita, identifying the local and international elements in these paintings. She argues that coastal Maya elites adopted these symbols and styles in order to endow depictions of local rituals and scenes (with local mean-

ings) with an international flavor that contributed to their own political power and legitimacy (see also Chase and Chase 1988).

Pohl (chapter 26) looks at international styles and symbols on a smaller scale in his discussion of the social uses of polychrome ceramics in the Mixteca-Puebla region. Continuing the thread of his discussion of political alliances (chapter 10) and the linkages between religion and trade in this area (chapter 22), chapter 26 shows some of the ways in which the elaborate polychrome ceramics of the Mixteca-Puebla style contributed to regional political dynamics and interaction. The common occurrence of this style among the Eastern Nahua, Mixtec, and Zapotec peoples, albeit with distinctive local variations, shows how processes of interaction in the Postclassic world system served to dampen the importance of ethnicity as a force in regional political and social dynamics.

Boone (chapter 27) takes another important medium of the Postclassic international style—Aztec codices—and examines their role in forging a common religious and political ideology among widely dispersed local elites. This network of elite interaction, actively promoted by both the imperial rulers and local dynasts, was particularly strong within the expanding Aztec empire (Berdan et al. 1996), but it also crossed political borders and incorporated elites from all over Mesoamerica. The three media treated in chapters 25 through 27—murals, polychrome ceramics, and codices—provided the stylistic backbone for the networks of information exchange that helped create the distinctive nature of the Postclassic world system.

One point of disagreement among the authors of this book concerns the reasons why local elites chose to adopt international styles and symbols. Boone (chapter 27) emphasizes the political power of the Aztec empire and suggests that distant elites adopted these elements to ally themselves with the empire, presumably for the political and economic benefits that ensued. Masson (chapter 25) and Kepecs (chapter 33), on the other hand, argue that Maya elites chose to use central Mexican and other international symbols in order to consolidate their own political power and to manipulate commerce and production within their territories. Emulation of central Mexican styles is not a factor in their explanations for the coastal Maya murals. These two views can be seen as having different emphases rather than being opposing interpretations. Boone focuses more on the Aztec empire and on Tenochtitlan's relations within and beyond the empire, whereas Masson and Kepecs deal with the lowland Maya area, which had quite limited direct contacts with central Mexico. These scholars all agree that stylistic interaction and the exchange of information were two-way processes that easily crossed political borders in Postclassic Mesoamerica, and that old models of Mexicanization are not up to the task of accounting for the explosion of internationalization in the Postclassic world system.

CENTRAL MEXICAN TRAITS IN THE MAYA AREA

The network approach to information exchange in Late Postclassic Mesoamerica advocated in this book—which downplays central Mexico as the origin of traits—should not blind us to a number of cases where particular institutions or complexes of traits from central Mexico do appear in distant regions of Mesoamerica. For example, the Maya codices contain several passages that incorporate Aztec ritual concepts within the otherwise Maya religious content of the documents. There is a central Mexican–style almanac within the Madrid Codex, and several Aztec deity names are portrayed in the Dresden Codex (chapter 27; see also Whittaker 1986).

The sculpted skull platform provides an archaeological example of a Postclassic central Mexican feature found in southern Mesoamerica. Unlike the vague and unconvincing architectural similarities discussed by Navarrete (1996), the sculpted skull platform is a highly distinctive feature whose form and context in highland Guatemala duplicate examples in central Mexico. Klein (2000) first identified the sculpted skull platform as an architectural feature present in Aztec ritual codices (the codices Borbonicus and Tudela) and at archaeological sites (including Tula, Tenayuca, Tenochtitlan, and Cholula), and she differentiated these features from skull racks (tzompantlis), platforms used to display severed heads from sacrificial victims.

Sculpted skull platforms are low stone platforms, decorated with skulls and crossed bones in low relief, found attached to the fronts of large temple pyramids. Some have been classified previously as skull racks (e.g., Miller 1999), but the consistent iconography, low height, and spatial context of sculpted skull platforms suggest a distinctive significance and function. Stone effigy skull racks at Chichén Itzá and Tenochtitlan, on the other hand, are larger and have numerous repeating skull images without the crossed bones; these probably had different functions from the sculpted skull platforms. Klein (2000) shows that sculpted skull platforms have a symbolic association with the *tzitzimime* deities (celestial monsters) and with themes of health, fertility, and curing (see chapter 26 and Pohl 1998a). They were probably used in some kind of public curing ceremony or rites propitiating the tzitzimime.

The only known examples of a sculpted skull platform outside of central Mexico are two platforms at Iximche' described by Guillemín (1965, 1977).[1] The first, Structure 72, is attached to the front of Temple 2, a large pyramid in Plaza A. Excavation of the platform revealed polychrome paintings of skulls and crossed bones

(Guillemín 1965:16). A second likely example, Structure 104, is a low platform attached to the front of another large pyramid, Temple 4 in Plaza C. This platform has not been excavated, and it is not known whether it was decorated with paintings or sculptures. Deposits of decapitated skulls were excavated in front of both platforms (Whittington and Reed 1994). The very specific iconographic and contextual similarities between the Iximche' platforms and the central Mexican skull platforms discussed by Klein (2000) point strongly to a central Mexican origin for these highland Maya features.

Traditional accounts of Mexicanization would interpret the skull platforms at Iximche' as either an Aztec trait brought deliberately to the highland Maya city by Aztec agents (e.g., Navarrete 1976, 1996), or as a Toltec trait brought earlier by migrating Toltec warriors (e.g., Fox 1978:3, 1989). It is hard to imagine, however, why these central Mexican polities would want to impose a specific nonpolitical architectural form on the inhabitants of Iximche'. Braswell (chapter 6; see also Braswell 2001b), on the other hand, proposes a more likely explanation for this kind of Mexican feature at highland Maya sites. He suggests that Maya elites deliberately emulated specific central Mexican styles and symbols (e.g., the skull and crossed bones motif, and certain polychrome ceramic vessels) and adopted specific exotic luxury goods (e.g., gold jewelry) as part of their own system of status rivalry and social legitimation. Although we cannot yet identify the specific processes by which these concepts and goods reached Iximche' from central Mexico, it is clear that they were components of the information exchange networks that characterized Late Postclassic Mesoamerica.

These examples—Aztec deities and rituals in the Maya codices, and sculpted skull platforms at Iximche'—show that the adoption of Postclassic central Mexican concepts and elements in the Maya area went, in some cases, beyond the incorporation of individual symbols and styles into local artistic media to include the replication of entire complexes of traits. However, these examples are in the minority and provide no justification for claiming that the Mayas or other distant peoples became Mexicanized through their adoption of foreign ideas and traits. More likely, local elites deliberately chose to use or display such ideas and traits for their own purposes. It makes no more sense to claim that the use of such traits Mexicanized the Maya peoples than to claim that the use of Chinese porcelain in Europe and North America resulted in Sinicized local populations. Styles and symbols provide material evidence for the exchange of information in Postclassic Mesoamerica, and these networks of information exchange were crucial components of the Postclassic world system. The chapters that follow explore the nature of these processes of information exchange in Postclassic Mesoamerica.

24

Postclassic International Styles and Symbol Sets

Elizabeth H. Boone

Michael E. Smith

The similarities seen in art forms throughout much of Postclassic Mesoamerica have been attributed to the existence of a widespread artistic phenomenon that has been variously called the Mixteca-Puebla tradition or Mixteca-Puebla horizon style (Nicholson 1960, 1982; Paddock 1982), the Mixtec style (Robertson 1959:12–24; Ramsey 1975, 1982; Brockington 1982), the "International Style of the Late Post-Classic" (Robertson 1966, 1970), the codex style (critiqued by Quiñones Keber 1994), as well as the Postclassic religious style and the Mixtec codex style (Smith and Heath-Smith 1980). Most of these terms and characterizations embrace both the formal style of the relevant artworks and their iconography in attempting to explain how and why murals from eastern Quintana Roo, for example, look so similar to polychrome pottery from Cholula. Few scholars are fully content with these terms, however, which may explain the proliferation in nomenclature. One problem is that the term *style* has been differentially defined, and the so-called style's characteristics have been variously described as composing both formal (i.e., pertaining to form) style and iconography.

In this chapter we examine painting traditions from Postclassic Mesoamerica—distinguishing style and iconography—to examine the nature of the widespread "international" (Robertson 1970) styles and symbols that were so prominent at this time. We introduce several new concepts that help organize past research on this subject: the Postclassic international style, the Early Postclassic international symbol set, and the Late Postclassic international symbol set. The temporal and spatial distributions of these styles and symbols suggest some of the ways in which communication, ideology, and artistic production were integrated in the Postclassic Mesoamerican world system.

STYLE AND ICONOGRAPHY

Donald Robertson, as an art historian trained in the study of the formal styles of European art, was careful to limit his 1970 discussion of the Postclassic Maya murals at Tulum to the style in which the murals were painted (Robertson 1970). Being predisposed to separate style from iconography, he eschewed iconographic questions about the Tulum murals to focus solely on the manner in which forms were rendered and organized, noting that the murals are similar in formal style to central Mexican paintings but are iconographically Maya. This distinction between formal style and iconography is an important one, because the iconography and the style of a work may belong to different traditions, as is the case at Tulum.

Style, although a much debated and variously employed concept even within the realm of art history (e.g., Sauerländer 1983; Kubler 1979; Elkins 1996), is generally recognized to pertain to the manner in which forms are rendered and how they and larger compositions are structured. Ernst Gombrich (1968:352b) defined style as "any distinctive...way in which an act is performed"; Jules Prown (1980:197) characterized it as "a distinctive manner or mode" (as quoted in Elkins 1996:876). A more concrete definition is given in Meyer Shapiro's classic discussion of style written for *Anthropology Today*, where Shapiro (1959:289) defined style as referring to "three aspects of art: form elements or motives [motifs], form relationships, and qualities (including an all-over quality which we may call the 'expression')." Style thus refers to how forms are rendered, how they are organized and structured into coherent compositions, and such other expressive characteristics as the hardness or softness of line, the quality of light and color, and so on

(Shapiro 1959:289–290). Style is "the objective *vehicle* of the subject matter" (Shapiro 1959:304, emphasis added), rather than the units that compose the subject.[1]

The units that form the subject matter itself belong to the realm of iconography: representational forms, abstractions, icons, and symbols read by the viewer as animate and inanimate objects, places, actions, times, and concepts. When these units are structured into significant relationships with other units, and are thereby organized as an iconographic system, they convey specific meaning, a message disseminated by the artwork or artifact. Style is the vehicle that carries the message; the images and symbols are the components that make up that message.

Although a broadly defined art style can be marked by a preference for certain subjects and units of meaning, style and iconography usually should be analyzed separately. They provide different kinds of data. Iconography can yield the intended meanings of a work, whether these are expressed directly, indirectly, or metaphorically. Style qualifies these meanings and offers clues about the artists' training, and the cultural preferences and expectations of artist and audience. Both iconography and style can be used to document the movement of people, goods, and ideas.

THE POSTCLASSIC INTERNATIONAL STYLE

The Postclassic international style is distinct from earlier Classic styles (e.g., at Teotihuacan, Monte Albán, or among the Maya) and the Epiclassic and Postclassic Maya styles of the Chichén Itzá murals and the Maya codices. Its stiff lines and stocky proportions, for example, are somewhat reminiscent of Teotihuacan frescoes, but its figures are more naturalistic, less iconic, and therefore more easily read than those of Teotihuacan. Its lines and forms are quite distinct from the expressive contour lines or organic forms of Maya painting. H. B. Nicholson (1960, 1982) and Donald Robertson (1959:16–24), among others, have noted the style's characteristics, and the description below draws on their perceptions. Although Robertson's more-extensive discussion described the style of the Codex Zouche-Nuttall, which he used to define the preconquest style of Mexican manuscript painting, many of the attributes pertain to the international style as well.

The Postclassic international style is characterized by its rendering of form, the quality of line and color, its figural proportions and positions, and its employment of images in shallow space (figure 24.1). Forms are flat, precise, and almost geometric in their shape. As Robertson (1959:17) pointed out, "human forms...are not visually unified" but "can be divided into separable, component parts," such that "the figure is a totality created from the addition of the various appendages and the head to the

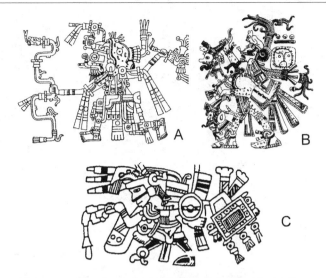

Figure 24.1 Human and deity figures as depicted in the Postclassic international style: (A) Codex Laud 2 (Anders and Jansen 1994:256); (B) Santa Rita mural, Mound 1, west wall (Gann 1900); (C) Tizatlan, painted Altar A, front (Marquina 1964:237.)

Figure 24.2 Example of the Aztec painting style: mural from Structure 1 at Malinalco. (García Payón 1946: opposite p. 20.)

torso." The forms are bordered by even, controlled, black outlines, which further flatten the forms and give a crisp edge. Robertson (1959:16) noted that "the treatment of line [which he called a 'frame line']...is one of its distinctive traits.... It is without purposeful variation of width or intensity, and its primary role is to enclose areas of color, to act as frames to flat color washes." This contrasts with the calligraphic or contour line preferred by the Classic and Postclassic Maya (e.g., Bonampak murals, Codex Dresden).

Colors are generally bright and fully intense, without any modeling or shading to suggest volume (figure 24.1). Proportions tend to be squat, with the most important elements (e.g., the heads of humans and animals) enlarged, and figures are usually posed in a way that exposes their

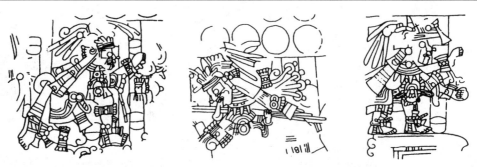

Figure 24.3 Example of the Southwest Maya style, a substyle of the Postclassic international style: mural paintings from different parts of Structure 2 at Iximche'. (Schele and Mathews 1998:303.)

Figure 24.4 Example of a possible west Mexican variant of the Postclassic international style: a ritual scene from a polychrome ceramic vase from Amapa, Nayarit. (From von Winning 1977:131.)

features in the fullest or most revealing way. For example, upper torsos may be presented frontally, whereas the hips, heads, and limbs are almost always in profile, as are feet and hands; plants are usually rendered with their roots exposed. Space tends to be ambiguous and shallow, and backgrounds are rare. Figures usually fill most of the two-dimensional space available to them, and often are rendered floating in space or tied to a ground line or register. Robertson (1970:80) called this feature "register space," and noted that many works contain more than one horizontal register filled with figures.

The most elaborate and extensive artworks painted in the Postclassic international style are the preconquest Mixtec and Borgia Group codices. The thousands of figures and pictorial symbols in these codices, and in the native-style Aztec pictorials, make up the greatest corpus of international-style images, which is the principal reason the style has been so closely linked to pictorial codices. Polychrome pottery from Oaxaca, Puebla, Tlaxcala, and the area in and around the Valley of Mexico comprises another large corpus, as do the relatively few extant murals in the same regions.

Although this international style appeared from the northern Gulf Coast to Guatemala, and from Guerrero to Quintana Roo, several regional substyles can be distinguished. A specifically Mixteca-Puebla substyle has been described by Robertson (1959:17–24). Like the international style, it is represented by the Mixtec and Borgia Group codices, especially the Zouche-Nuttall and Borgia

codices, and by the ceramics and murals from northwestern Oaxaca, Puebla, and Tlaxcala. This substyle has also been variously subdivided into Mixtec, Cholula, Borgia Group, Codex Borgia, and Codices Laud and Fejérváry-Mayer (Robertson 1959:17–24, 1963, 1966; Nicholson 1960, 1982; Nowotny 1961:13–16; Ramsey 1975, 1982; Smith and Heath-Smith 1980; Boone 1990, 2000; Sisson and Lilly 1994a, 1994b; Lind 1994). Examples are provided in figure 24.1 and in the illustrations in chapters 25 and 26.

A well-defined Aztec painting style is characterized by more naturalism in the rendering of form, by longer and leaner proportions, and by characteristic ways of rendering certain symbols (Boone 1982a; see figure 24.2). The Tulum and Santa Rita murals (figure 24.1B), also characterized by longer and leaner proportions, may represent another substyle (Quirarte 1975, 1982), and a southwest Maya substyle has been suggested for murals at the cities of Iximche' and Utatlan (Guillemín 1965; Carmack 1981; Carmack and Larmer 1971; see figure 24.3). Still other regional styles may emerge with more study. For example, Late Postclassic polychrome ceramics from Nayarit depict human or deity figures in a manner that exhibits most of the characteristics of the Postclassic international style (von Winning 1977; figure 24.4). Individual manuscripts, and indeed individual painters within the manuscripts, will have their own painting styles. Despite the detection of regional and codical variations, however, they all participate in the Postclassic in-

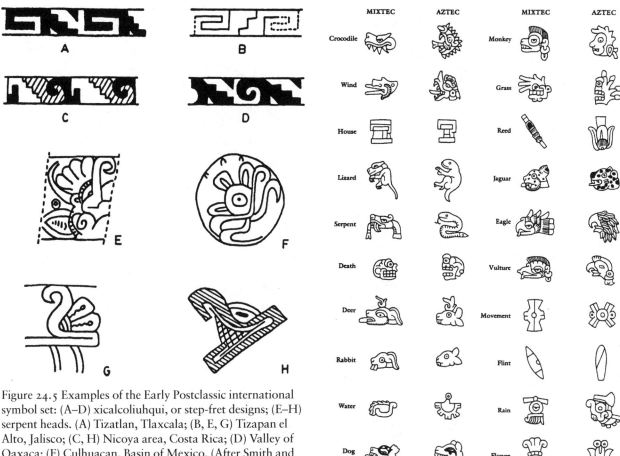

Figure 24.5 Examples of the Early Postclassic international symbol set: (A–D) xicalcoliuhqui, or step-fret designs; (E–H) serpent heads. (A) Tizatlan, Tlaxcala; (B, E, G) Tizapan el Alto, Jalisco; (C, H) Nicoya area, Costa Rica; (D) Valley of Oaxaca; (F) Culhuacan, Basin of Mexico. (After Smith and Heath-Smith 1980:23; see original source for citations.)

Figure 24.6 Mixtec and Aztec versions of the 20 day signs of the Late Postclassic international symbol set. (From Boone 2000:40.)

POSTCLASSIC INTERNATIONAL SYMBOL SETS

THE EARLY POSTCLASSIC INTERNATIONAL SYMBOL SET

During the Epiclassic and Early Postclassic periods, common iconographic elements were depicted on local painted ceramics throughout large parts of Mesoamerica (figure 24.5). These symbols, typically portrayed in horizontal bands around the exteriors of ceramic bowls, appeared first at sites in west Mexico and the Nicoya region of Costa Rica, only becoming popular in other areas (such as the Mixteca-Puebla region, the Basin of Mexico, the Gulf Coast) after the twelfth century, or the Middle Postclassic period (Smith and Heath-Smith 1980:18–31).

During Epiclassic and Early Postclassic times, the polychrome ceramics with symbols of the Early Postclassic international symbol set were associated with Fine Orange and Plumbate ceramics, the predominant pan-Mesoamerican trade wares of the period, and with distinctive pyriform vessels used in these and other ceramic types. The distributions and associations among these symbols and ceramic wares suggest a common participation in the extensive trade networks that spread throughout Mesoamerica in Epiclassic/Early Postclassic times. These networks emphasized coastal routes, and the peoples of highland areas such as central Mexico were only minor participants compared to lowland coastal and riverine peoples. Smith and Heath-Smith (1980) argued that the distribution of the Early Postclassic international symbol set (which they called the "Postclassic religious style") derived from these decentralized coastal networks of trade and communication, rather than spreading outward from a central Mexican heartland (as proposed by, among others, Nicholson [1960] and Meighan [1974]).

THE LATE POSTCLASSIC INTERNATIONAL SYMBOL SET

The Postclassic international style, a post-A.D. 1200 phenomenon, is almost always accompanied by a particular set of images and symbols that collectively can be called the Late Postclassic international symbol set. The painting style and image set evolved together from the same impetus in central or southern Mexico, and they are so

ternational style, which unites them as a common expressive phenomenon.

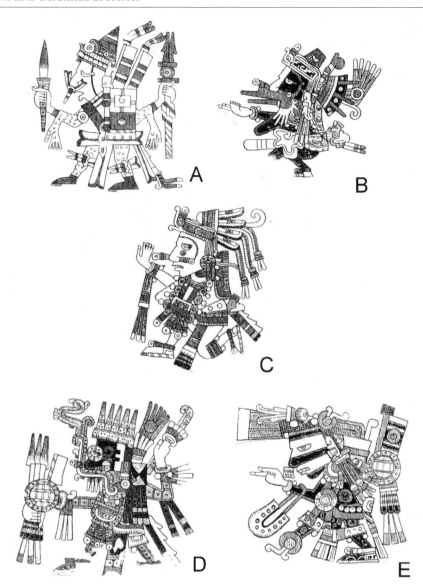

Figure 24.7 Central Mexican deities associated with the Late Postclassic international symbol set: (A) Xipe Totec (Codex Borgia 61; Seler 1963); (B) Quetzalcoatl-Ehecatl (Codex Borgia 9; Seler 1902–1903: figure 343); (C) Tonatiuh (Codex Borgia 66; Seler 1963); (D) Tlaloc (Codex Borgia 25; Seler 1963); (E) Tezcatlipoca (Borgia 57; Seler 1902–1903: figure 584).

interconnected that it is rare to find one without the other. The peoples of the Mixteca-Puebla region and central Mexico selected key symbols from the Early Postclassic international symbol set and other sources to create their own distinctive group of iconographic elements. This symbol set represents a Mexican versus a Maya perspective on the world, expressed in images that reflect Mexican customs and cosmology. The Late Postclassic international symbol set is characterized largely by imagery pertaining to the calendar and religious life, which is why several scholars have equated the international style with religious manuscripts (Robertson 1966; Brockington 1973:84; Smith and Heath-Smith 1980:29–31).

Nevertheless, the symbol set is also composed of more-secular and mundane imagery from Mexican pictography. Nicholson (1960:614, 1982:229) and Ramsey (1982) have listed many of the symbols in this set, and the listing below draws from their work.

Calendrical information in the symbol set reflects the Mexican calendar as it was represented especially in central and southern Mexico and used by the Aztecs, Mixtecs, Tlaxcalans, and their neighbors.[2] The 20 day signs (figure 24.6) are fairly naturalistic images of animals, plants, and objects (e.g., Jaguar, Reed, Flint), or they are symbols for concepts or phenomena (e.g., Movement, Wind). The day numbers are always expressed as a series

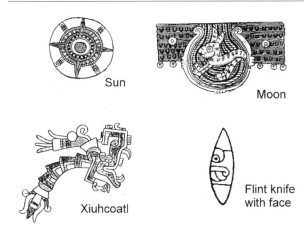

Figure 24.8 Some noncalendric elements of the Late Postclassic international symbol set: sun (Codex Borbonicus 16; Seler 1902–1903: figure 523); moon (Codex Borgia 71; Seler 1902–1903: figure 398); Xiuhcoatl, or fire serpent (Codex Zouche-Nuttall; Seler 1992:3:215); flint with fanged face (Codex Vienna 11a; Boone 2000: figure 4).

of linked or clustered disks rather than as bars and dots (although bars and dots can be used to express quantities). There is no use of place value within a vigesimal system, as one finds in the Maya Long Count or in Postclassic Maya codices such as the Dresden. It is the Mexican calendar that is being expressed.

The deities are Mexican also. Indeed a preponderance of the images belonging to the Late Postclassic international symbol set are those of the supernaturals seen in the central Mexican, Mixtec, and Borgia Group codices (figure 24.7). Present are the flayed god Xipe Totec (Our Lord, the Flayer), the culture hero and wind god Quetzalcoatl/Ehecatl (named 9 Wind in Mixtec codices), the sun

deity Tonatiuh (named 1 Death in Mixtec codices), Cihuacoatl (who may be 9 Grass for the Mixtec), and a good number of other deities. Each is represented with a generally consistent cluster of attributes. Accoutrements and costume elements of these gods include such things as flayed skins, wide collars of jade bordered by gold bells, as well as distinctive pectorals, headdresses, back devices, and arm and wrist bands. All of these individual elements take their place in the Late Postclassic international symbol set. Other elements, many associated with ritual action and religious concepts, are rayed sun disks, moon disks with U-shaped (pulque) vessels in them, Xiuhcoatls (fire serpents), flints with fanged faces, the symbol for gold, long-handled incense pans, and earth-monster mouths as openings into the earth, just to list a few spanning a broad range (figure 24.8).

Polychrome ceramics belong to this ritual world as well. Ceramic motifs that characterize the Late Postclassic international symbol set include rays, reeds, and bird heads that cut through or embellish concentric bands that ring vases, bowls, and plates. Other characteristic motifs are flints, night eyes or stars, disembodied hearts and hands, skulls and bones, step-frets, and tightly controlled scrolls, disks, and feathers. These motifs appear as separate images on the flat ground or borders of the vessel (figure 24.9; see chapter 25 for further discussion).

Outside the ritual sphere, the Late Postclassic international symbol set contains a number of mundane images and conventions as well. Women and men, for example, are distinguished by their clothing and hairstyles. Old age is represented by a toothless or snaggletoothed person with tousled hair. Stones, hill-signs, water, smoke, fire, earth, and sky-bands are all

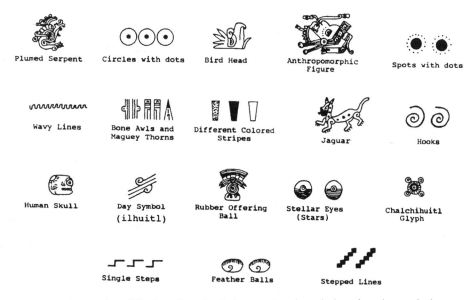

Figure 24.9 Examples of the Late Postclassic international symbol set found on polychrome ceramics from Cholula and Oaxaca. (From Lind 1994:94.)

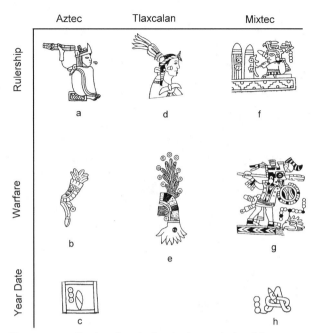

Figure 24.10 Regional variation in the symbols of the Late Postclassic international symbol set: (a) Aztec ruler Acamapichtli (Codex Mendoza 2v); (b) atl-tlachinolli, Aztec symbol for war (Teocalli de la Guerra Sagrada); (c) Aztec year 3 Flint (Codex Mendoza); (d) Tlaxcalan ruler (Lienzo de Tlaxcala 7); (e) atl-tlachinolli, the Tlaxcalan symbol for war (Tonalamatl Aubin 9); (f) Mixtec Lord 4 Wind ruling the Place of Flints (Codex Bodley 31c); (g) Mixtec Lord 13 Eagle going to war (Codex Bodley 28b); (h) Mixtec year 3 Flint (Codex Vienna). (Drawings of a–c, f–h by John Montgomery; d after Chavero 1900; e after Seler 1992:3:70.)

represented by well-established and widely shared pictorial conventions. The elements that compose the symbol set are the pictorial conventions on which the Mexican pictographic system is built. Many of these elements have been described and illustrated by Mary Elizabeth Smith (1973a:20–35), Joyce Marcus (1992a), and Elizabeth Boone (2000:31–61), among others.

Just as there are regional and more individual variations in the international style, there are regional, ethnic, and individual variations in the Late Postclassic international symbol set (figure 24.10). The central Mexicans, for example, used the turquoise diadem to signal a ruler's authority, and they often signaled war by combining the elements of water and fire (atl-tlachinolli). They placed their year signs in square cartouches. The Mixtecs used none of these conventions. Instead, Mixtec rule was expressed by the ruler sitting on his or her place sign; war was signaled by a chevron path (literally read as the path or road to the enemy); and years were signaled by the A-O year sign (Smith 1973a:20–35). The Tlaxcalans, for their part, identified their rulers by a royal headband of twisted cord (Nicholson 1967). Other regional and politically motivated variations can surely be teased out with further study.

STYLE AND SYMBOL IN THE POSTCLASSIC

The two aspects that define the widespread graphic phenomenon of Postclassic Mesoamerica are a Mexican painting style and a Mexican symbol set, which became international once they diffused more widely. The term *Mexican* is used here because this style and this symbol set were concentrated in central Mexico, Tlaxcala, Puebla, and Oaxaca, and they surely developed within this realm. Whether they actually originated in one part or the other is unknown, although we can say that the style and symbol set developed together and were carried outward together as complementary parts of the same ideological package (chapter 25). Despite the close association of the style with the symbol set, it is useful to recognize that the international style is a graphic and pictorial style of rendering and organizing form. The Late Postclassic international symbol set is a set of images and elements that carry meaning within a particular iconographic system. Usually the two moved together throughout Mesoamerica, but not always.

Because so many elements in the Late Postclassic international symbol set are calendrical and religious in nature, their widespread distribution may signal the existence of a pan-Mesoamerican religion. The religious unification of Mesoamerica was begun in Epiclassic and Early Postclassic times with the spread of the Early Postclassic international symbol set (Smith and Heath-Smith 1980) and the spread of the iconography and ritual paraphernalia of the feathered serpent cult (Ringle et al. 1998). Whether the expansion of the prominence and importance of international symbols and styles in Late Postclassic times simply expressed a preexisting religious unity, or whether that expansion was a major force in creating Mesoamerican religious unity, is difficult to judge.

The Postclassic international style and the Late Postclassic international symbol set were adopted in many areas of Mesoamerica long before the formation of the Aztec empire. For example, the Cholula polychrome ceramics and the codices and polychrome ceramics of the Mixteca region were all well established by the start of the Late Postclassic period (chapter 25), and the Tulum and Santa Rita murals were painted early in the Late Postclassic period, prior to the Aztec empire (Masson 2000a). Just as commercial exchange between the Basin of Mexico and exterior areas preceded processes of imperial expansion (chapter 31), so did the spread of Aztec styles in painting, sculpture, and architecture largely predate Aztec imperialism (Umberger and Klein 1993; Umberger 1996).

The expansion of the Aztec empire, however, contributed greatly to the further spread and adoption of these styles and symbols (chapter 27). They followed Aztec trade routes and were borne along with Aztec armies, ambassadors, and marriage alliances as the empire extended its domain over other, distant peoples. But since the adoption of the styles and symbols began well before imperial expansion, they are best viewed as markers of the networks of exchange and communication that comprised the Postclassic Mesoamerican world system.

And just as the Aztec empire was only one part of that wider world system, the imperial use and promotion of Postclassic international styles and symbols was only one facet of their importance in Late Postclassic Mesoamerica.

25

The Late Postclassic Symbol Set in the Maya Area

Marilyn A. Masson

The frescoes of Tulum and the murals of Santa Rita incorporate international symbols shared with art styles of highland Mexico (the Late Postclassic international symbol set), and the style of the paintings has features of the Postclassic international style. Yet the iconographic content of these murals derives from Maya culture (Robertson 1970). The actors portrayed in these mural programs are Mayas, and the objects they manipulate are local to the east coast of the Yucatán Peninsula (Chase and Chase 1988). The international aspects of the overall painting style—features such as the way the human body is depicted, icons, and the way space is filled—have been analyzed by Robertson (1970) and others (chapters 23, 24). Here I focus on the symbolism and iconography of these works—both international and local—and offer some new interpretations of their content. This case study illustrates some of the iconographic connections between distant areas in the Postclassic world system and shows how international symbols (and styles) were incorporated into local artistic programs.

The mural art of Santa Rita and Tulum most likely dates to the Late Postclassic period. While it might be possible to extract organic pigments from murals for the purpose of AMS dating, this has not been attempted. The most commonly discussed murals are those of Santa Rita Corozal (Gann 1900; Robertson 1970; Sidrys 1983; Chase and Chase 1988) and Tulum (Miller 1982; Love 1994: figure 2.2; Robles Castellanos and Andrews 1986), although murals are also present at Tancah, Xelha, Cobá, and other sites (Miller 1982). Several mural segments were reported from Mayapán (rendered in a composite drawing by Proskouriakoff 1962a: figure 3d), and new murals and frescoes have been discovered at this site (Peraza Lope 1998). Murals may have been more widely distributed throughout the Maya area (Robles Castellanos and Andrews 1986). Patches of poorly preserved

pigment are observed at sites on Cozumel Island (Freidel and Sabloff 1984), and structures in the monumental core of Mayapán, such as the Caracol (Structure Q-152), also have patches of painted murals. The primary basis for dating murals is style (Miller 1982, 1985). Miller believes the murals of Tulum were painted during the fifteenth century (Miller 1982:56–60), although Ball dates ceramics recovered from the associated buildings to the thirteenth to fifteenth centuries (Ball 1982:110–111). The murals of Santa Rita Structure 1 have similarly been attributed to the fifteenth century based on style (Gann 1900; Quirarte 1982; Robertson 1970). A single radiocarbon sample from a nearby midden yielded a date of A.D. 1425 (Sidrys 1983:126, 147).

INTERNATIONAL SYMBOLS AND STYLES IN LATE POSTCLASSIC MAYA MURALS

Murals of Tulum, Santa Rita, and Mayapán exhibit distinctive symbols that were part of the Late Postclassic international symbol set (Robertson 1970; Quirarte 1975, 1982; Smith and Heath-Smith 1980; Gann 1900; Peraza Lope 1998; see chapter 24). Figures 25.1 through 25.8 illustrate a number of symbols shared by highland Mexican and Mayan iconography of this period, including temple styles (figure 25.1), sun disks (figure 25.2), serpents (figure 25.3), star or rosette symbols (figure 25.4), step-terrace motifs (figures 25.5, 25.6), pottery vessel forms (figures 25.6, 25.7), and pottery vessel motifs (figure 25.8). Elements in these murals are very similar. Although some scholars attribute these symbols to direct foreign presence at Maya sites (Robertson 1970:88; Miller 1982:74), we believe that local elites in Yucatán and the eastern Mayan coast may have selected these international motifs for murals whose meaning and use were tied to local political and religious processes. The

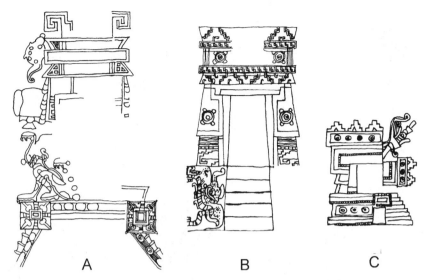

Figure 25.1 Temples in Maya and Mixtec art: (a) Santa Rita mural (Gann 1900: plate XXX); (B) composite hypothetical reconstruction of various architectural and iconographic elements at Mayapan (Proskouriakoff 1962: figure 3d); (C) Codex Nuttall (Nuttall 1975:77.)

incorporation of international motifs would also have emphasized the cosmopolitan ties of local leaders.

Late Postclassic international motifs show up in a variety of combinations and media at different sites. Proskouriakoff's (1962a:3d) illustration of motifs painted on temples at Mayapán in a composite reconstruction of a hypothetical temple (Structure Q-80) closely resembles temples shown in the Mixtec codices (figure 25.1B, C). Similar temples are observed in the Santa Rita mural (figure 25.1A) and among standing structures at Tulum (Lothrop 1924). Pollock (1962:14) describes the style of Mayapán structures as a mixture of Maya architecture with Aztec-inspired motifs. Recently discovered stucco facades on the side of Structure Q162 (The Castillo) at Mayapán (Peraza Lope 1998:53) bear a resemblance to figures found on the walls of Postclassic tombs at Zaachila, Oaxaca (Flannery 1983: figure 8.26). The stucco figures at Mayapán lack heads and instead have niches where the skulls of these individuals were placed (Peraza Lope 1998). Niches were also common in Oaxacan tombs from earlier times (Caso 1938: lam.1). Peraza suggests that the stucco individuals and their skulls were those of celebrated Mayapán warriors who may have been venerated at this monument (1998:52–53). These warriors also carry flags similar to those portrayed in highland codices. These individuals may be historically tied to the establishment of one of Mayapán's political regimes, which rose to power with the aid of Gulf Coast allies who provided military support (Roys 1962).

A sun cartouche motif common in highland codices is depicted at Mayapán and in murals of Santa Rita Structure 1 (figure 25.2A). At the southeastern corner of Struc-

ture Q162 at Mayapán, the back wall of a colonnaded structure (Q 161, "Sala de los Frescos") exhibits a series of sun symbols from which emerge descending supernaturals (Peraza Lope 1998:51, 53). Such disks are present earlier in the iconography of the Temple of the Jaguars at Chichén Itzá. Schele and Mathews (1998:225–239) interpret the figures in solar disks as founding ancestors. At Santa Rita, a serpent passes through this symbol (figure 25.3E), and in another wall segment (figure 25.2A), an ancestor or other supernatural is manifested from this symbol, which appears to be conjured from smoke or sound scrolls emerging from a censer or drum (Taube 1992). In all three Maya contexts, this symbol represents an important cartouche or portal through which supernatural beings emerge.

Other Late Postclassic international symbols in Maya

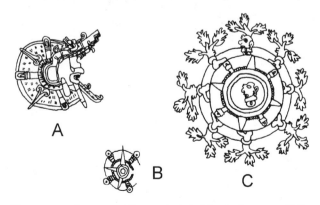

Figure 25.2 Sun cartouche symbols in Maya, Aztec, and Mixtec art: (A) Santa Rita mural (Gann 1900: plate XXIX); (B) Codex Telleriano-Remensis (Keber 1995:91); (C) Codex Nuttall (Nuttall 1975:76.)

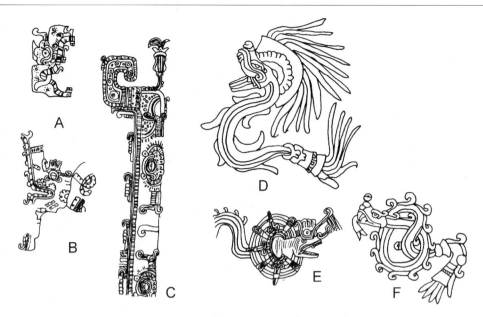

Figure 25.3 Serpents in Maya, Aztec, and Mixtec art: (A) Mayapan Structure Q-80, reconstructed side view (Proskouriakoff 1962: figure 3d); (B) Santa Rita mural (Gann 1900: plate XXX); (C) Tulum Structure 16 mural (Miller 1982: plate 37); (D) Codex Telleriano-Remensis (Keber 1995:39); (E) Santa Rita mural (Gann 1900: plate XXIX); (F) Codex Nuttall (Nuttall 1975: 75.)

murals include "Venus" or "star" eyes (figure 25.4). These eyes are in the celestial position at the top of mural programs (as in Structure 16 at Tulum, or in the Santa Rita mural), or they decorate entwined serpents that separate many of the Tulum scenes, such as those of Structure 5 (see figure 25.9) or Structure 16 (Miller 1982). The placement of "rosettes"—round, flowery medallions—along the celestial positions in the upper portion of Tulum Structure 16 (figure 25.4e) is also a convention shared with Aztec palaces (Evans 1991) and other structures (figures 25.1, 25.4). Rosette elements appeared earlier in the Classic-period highlands in the Teotihuacan

net murals, and star-eye motifs are present in the sky band of Tomb 105 of Monte Albán (Caso 1938: lam. 1). At Tulum, some of these rosette symbols contain the star-eye symbol, and others have essence scrolls emerging from them that Schele and Mathews (1998:229, 265) have interpreted as *itz*, a flowery, holy nectar. Star eyes are also shown in rosettes of painted mural fragments at

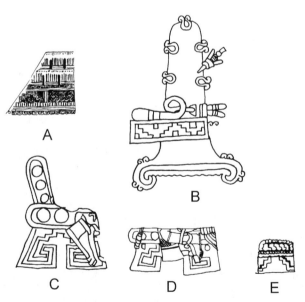

Figure 25.4 Star eye/rosette symbols in Mixtec, Aztec, and Maya art: (A) and (B) Codex Nuttall (Nuttall 1975:83, 75); (C) Codex Borbonicus (Códice Borbónico p. 18); (D) Telleriano-Remensis (Keber 1995:84); (E) Tulum Structure 16 (Miller 1982: plate 25); (F) Santa Rita mural (Gann 1900: plate XXIX.)

Figure 25.5 Step-terrace motif in Maya, Mixtec, and Aztec art: (A) Tulum Structure 5 (Miller 1982: plate 25); (b) Codex Nuttall (Nuttall 1975:75); (C) Codex Borbonicus (Códice Borbónico p. 4); (D) Codex Telleriano-Remensis (Keber 1995:51); (E) Tulum Structure 16 (Miller 1982: plate 37.)

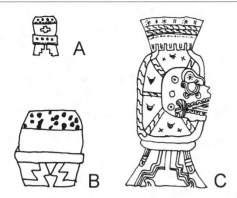

Figure 25.6 Step-terrace motif found on Mixtec, Aztec, and Maya pottery vessels: (A) Codex Nuttall (Nuttall 1975: 25); (B) Codex Borbonicus (Códice Borbónico p. 4); (C) Santa Rita mural (Gann 1900: plate XXXI.)

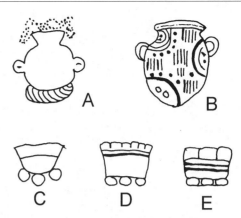

Figure 25.7 Similar pottery forms in Aztec and Maya art: (A) Codex Borbonicus (p. 5); (B) Tulum Structure 16 (Miller 1982: plate 37); (C, D) Codex Borbonicus (Códice Borbónico p. 4, 5); (E) Tancah (Miller 1982: plate 6.)

Mayapán (Proskouriakoff 1962a: figure 3d). By Postclassic times these elements were widely disseminated as part of the Late Postclassic international symbol set. Rosettes with star eyes also appear in the Aztec and Mixtec codices (figure 25.4). Rosettes are also a prominent form of decoration on non-effigy composite censers in the Maya area (Masson 2000a: figure 6.11). This decoration provides an important link within the Maya area between ritual facilities and portable ritual paraphernalia (Masson 2000a: figures 6.9–6.11).

Another international symbol in the Maya murals is the step-terrace motif (figures 25.5, 25.6), which can form the legs or flanges of ceramics or drums, or the legs of thrones. It is also found in cartouches alternating with woven mat symbols in Tulum Structures 5 and 16 (figure 25.5A). This motif is found in the roof bands of Mayapán paintings (figure 25.1B, Proskouriakoff 1962a: 3d) and in Mixtec examples (figure 25.1C). This symbol may represent several different things. The step-terrace motif is associated in the Maya area with the glyph Ik, which refers to wind and is associated with international feathered-serpent symbolism of the Epiclassic/Early Postclassic periods (Ringle et al. 1998: figure 19). It may also represent a general concept of place, especially when it has several tiers. Numerous place signs in the Mixtec Nuttall Codex are marked with step-terrace symbols (e.g., figure 25.5B). Thrones in the murals of Tulum Structure 16 and Codex Borbonicus have legs in this form (figure 25.5C, D, E), and its presence in celestial cartouches along with mat symbols at Tulum may imply its signification of place as well. Similarly, earlier art in Tomb 105 of Monte Albán has tiered mountain symbols beneath the ground line of a genealogical record (Caso 1938: lam. 1), and stone monuments from this site also frequently depict place signs in a step shape (Marcus 1983a: figure 4.15, 1983b: figures 5.7, 5.8). Step-terrace motifs are known in Maya art from the Early Classic period, when they were painted or engraved on basal-flanged bowls (Willey et al. 1965: figures 208, 211; Smith

1971: figure 41). This symbol was one that was internationally popular prior to the Postclassic period. It is notable that step-terrace motifs also occur on basal flanges of Late Postclassic Maya, Mixtec, and Aztec ceramic vessels (figure 25.6), and this technique may have been inspired by earlier traditions (Masson 2000a: 47). Other retrospective tendencies of Postclassic Maya pottery appear to recycle attributes of earlier pottery traditions (Willey et al. 1965).

Chevron bands and water bands are two other international symbols found in Tulum Structure 15 and Santa Rita that closely resemble those of the Mixtec codices (Sidrys 1983). Ceramic forms common to central Mexico and the Maya area are shown in Aztec codices (e.g., Codex Borbonicus 1974) and in murals of Tulum and Tancah (Miller 1982: plates 1, 37), including strap-handled ollas and tripod dishes (figure 25.7). Ladle censers with serpent handles are another example of ritual paraphernalia found in both the lowlands and highlands during the Late Postclassic period. In central Mexico these are depicted in many codices, including the Codex Borbonicus (1974) and the Codex Mendoza (Berdan and Anawalt 1992), and they have been recovered archaeologically at both temple and house sites (Smith 2002). In the Maya area ladle censers have been recovered archaeologically from the Epiclassic/Early Postclassic (Ringle et al. 1998) through the Late Postclassic periods (Smith 1971:95). Ceramic effigy censers of the Late Postclassic Maya area may have been a style that had spread from earlier Gulf Coast or Zapotec traditions (Sidrys 1983). At the site of Mayapán, these effigies include occasional depictions of Mexican deities (Thompson 1957). Outside of Mayapán, effigies depict primarily Maya gods or other local individuals.[1]

The convention of representing actors in Tulum Structures 5 and 16 may also be derived from traditions that originated in the highlands. The actors are separated by

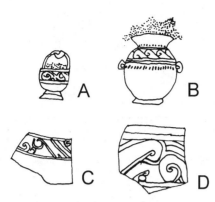

Figure 25.8   Similar decorative scroll motifs on Aztec and Maya pottery vessels: (A, B) Codex Borbonicus (Códice Borbónico p. 33); (C, D) sherds from Laguna de On, Belize.

serpent bands in these murals, in a style that is shared by contemporary Postclassic Maya codices (usually without serpents). The presentation of banded scenes is known earlier, from A.D. 600–900 in the Valley of Oaxaca inscribed on stone genealogical registers, which preceded Mixtec codices and may have been a prototype for them (Marcus 1983c:192). The convention of showing male/female pairs engaged in ritual offerings and relaying genealogical information is also shared by the Tulum murals and these earlier Zapotec funerary registers, as is the V-shaped frontal cape that distinguishes females from males in these programs (Masson 2000a:234–235). The Zapotec registers often feature conjured ancestors who emerge from the celestial realm to sanction marriages and other events in these scenes, and I have argued that the figures in the sky band (between the chevrons below the ceiling) in Tulum Structure 16 are also conjured, apotheosized ancestors, including perhaps the diving god (Masson 2000a: 229–234). These figures include a male seated on a throne and a female in the flying position who is grinding at a metate. In other Zapotec registers, senior ancestors are also shown in the lowest band (for example, the Noriega slab, Marcus 1983b: figure 7.5), and this may also be the case for Tulum Structure 16 (Mural 2), where the female shown in the lowest band has a face marked with age lines.

Although the origin of some of these Postclassic international symbols can be traced to locations outside the Maya area, their incorporation into late Maya art is most probably the result of centuries of exchange of goods and information. The distribution of these symbols may signal multiethnic participation in mutually intelligible ritual activities, much as Pohl (chapters 26, 31) argues for the Mixteca-Puebla region on a smaller scale. Miller (1982:75–76) suggests that the use of international symbols may have eased tensions at coastal ports such as Tulum and Santa Rita through religious integration. He further suggests that sacred ground in the form of shrine facilities may have provided a neutral zone for multieth-

nic economic interactions. Similar interpretations have been proposed for pilgrimage shrines at the trading communities on Cozumel Island (Freidel 1981a; Freidel and Sabloff 1984). During the Epiclassic/Early Postclassic periods, a similar network of shared religious participation accompanies an expanding world of international trade as reflected in the spread of feathered-serpent rituals and symbolism (Ringle et al. 1998). Cosmopolitan motifs are not limited to feathered-serpent iconography (Schele and Mathews 1998:197–257; Smith and Heath-Smith 1980; chapter 23).

LOCAL THEMES IN LATE POSTCLASSIC MAYA MURALS

The international aspects of Postclassic Maya art have received far more attention in the literature than the local themes that are portrayed. Nevertheless, the murals' content clearly derives from local Maya culture. Chase and Chase (1988:83–84) highlight the similarity of the characters of the Santa Rita murals to effigy censers from that site. The astronomical associations of Maya deities and these star symbols are the topic of a recent book by Milbrath (1999). Milbrath (1999) and Taube (1992) identify numerous Maya gods in the processions of the Tulum and Santa Rita murals that resemble those from the Maya codices, including God K, God M, God G, and others. Annual *tun*-ending Ahau dates (Long 1919) are associated with different characters in the Santa Rita murals, and 10 of these figures have Maya place-name glyphs (David Mora-Marin, personal communication, 1998). Only 5 of 25 characters in the bound procession of the north wall murals of Santa Rita Structure I have deity faces or masks, and thus the others may be historical individuals (Masson 2000a:245, table 6.7). A doorway in the north wall of Structure I is framed by a caiman mouth identified as Itzam Nab Cain by Taube (1992). This image is a Late Postclassic version of an old tradition of "monster mouth" doorways in Quintana Roo and Yucatán. A temple is shown in the mural segment to the east of the doorway. Marked by a shell, this temple may represent the coastal center of Santa Rita (Masson 2000a:247). A lord departs from the temple, carrying incense, and another lord enters, carrying an effigy. A feline figure is seated within it. The procession of lords on these murals may represent individuals of various political or territorial divisions within the Chetumal province who were bound together through rotating sponsorship of calendrical celebrations (Masson 2000a: 247). The individuals entering and leaving the temple may depict the rotation of offices. Rotating offices were a common mechanism for power-sharing in Late Postclassic Yucatán (Love 1994), and rotating geographical celebrations of calendrical festivities provided an important means of community and regional integration (Tozzer 1941:38; Chase 1985).

Figure 25.9 Tulum Structure 5 mural. (Redrawn by Becky Adelman from Miller 1982: plate 28.)

The mural themes of Tulum Structures 1, 5, and 16 also feature multiple ritual actors engaged in similar acts (Miller 1982: plates 15, 17, 25, 25, 28, 37). These temples all feature diving figures, as does Structure 25. These multiple temples may have commemorated the genealogies of important governing kin groups at this site, perhaps reflecting accession to office (Masson 2000a). The multiplicity of temples that reiterate common themes may reflect power-sharing institutions of the Postclassic period, perhaps even ruling councils known as *multepal* in Yucatán (Roys 1957). Though key actors are featured in these murals, the Tulum murals share with Santa Rita an emphasis on the depiction of groups without ostentatious glorification of specific individuals. While political and social inequalities certainly existed within Postclassic Maya polities through clearly defined, ranked offices (Roys 1957), elites at these communities chose not to represent such inequalities in the art of these temples. The iconography of the murals on all four buildings is closely related, involving males, females, and supernaturals engaged in ritual scenes demarcated by rosette-studded, interlocked serpents. Pedestal vessels containing tamales are featured in all three structures, as are mat symbols, which are either on the serpents or in the sky bands.

Although these basic elements unite the murals in all three structures, Structures 5 and 16 exhibit variation in their iconographic content that suggests different historical individuals are represented. They are engaged in similar rituals. The murals of Structure 1 are reported in fragmented form (Miller 1982: plates 15, 17, 19, 24), and their meaning is more difficult to fathom. Structure 5 features two sets of male/female pairs within entwined serpent bands (figure 25.9). The step-terrace and mat-marked sky band frames the scene, and two God K heads emerge from it at either end (Taube 1992). The heads of

the entwined serpents at the bottom right and left (south and north) corners of the scene differ from one another. The serpent on the right has a foliage-studded upturned snout that resembles the appendage shown on the heads of the God K figures emerging from the sky band. This God K serpent is also featured in the headdress of each male figure in the above scene. The serpent on the left exhibits a Chac snout. This same serpent is featured in the headdress of the female in the left pair of individuals in the scene, and she is seated on a sky throne that has Chac serpent legs The male in this left pair wears this same Chac mask. Both the left and right males have this Chac mask at the back of their headdresses, and they wear the God K figure in the front above their foreheads.

The dual representation of God K and Chac appears important in this scene. The male/female pair on the right each wear nose plugs, though the significance of this ornament is not known. In each pair, the seated female extends a staff or bundle to the male. The staff/bundle is marked with a sky (*kan*) glyph, a mat symbol, tamales, and a serpent head. Another set of entwined Chac serpents is shown below the ground line of this scene. A central swimming or flying figure appears encased in a shell and perhaps represents God N. The presence of star-eye markings beneath the celestial band and on both sets of entwined serpents suggests that the events shown on this mural were calendrically or astronomically timed. Perhaps the exchange of staffs represents accession of the males in this scene to political or religious office. It is noteworthy that two such scenes are shown. Jones (1999) documents the duality of rulership among the Petén Itzá, in which both a king and a high priest governed each polity. The same staffs or bundles exchanged in this scene are also prominent in the murals of Structure 16.

The murals of Structure 16 (murals 1, 2, 4, 5, and 6)

show seven male individuals holding this same staff (Miller 1982: plates 37, 40). Mural 2 is the most extensive published program of this group, and its content is more complicated than the murals of Structure 5. The scene emerges from the maw of a giant serpent mouth that frames the base and sides of the mural (figure 25.3C; Masson 2000a:234). A water band is present at the base of this serpent mouth, and it is lined by serpent teeth. The same serpent-toothed water band is present at the base of all other mural segments shown from this building, and another serpent mouth shown to the right of the doorway probably encases a similar scene. Four large open-mouthed serpents also adorn the back wall of the inner temple of Structure Q-80 at Mayapán. Each serpent interfaces with a different sky band. This mural may refer to one of the mythical founding events of the city, involving "four lineages from heaven" (Tozzer 1941:34). The reading order of the Structure 16 Tulum mural is unclear, but may be bottom to top as in some Zapotec registers (Marcus 1983c: figure 7.5). An old woman and a serpent-masked male face each other across a jar containing tamales in the scene at the bottom. The male holds one of the serpent/tamale staffs or bundles. In the second scene from the bottom, a four-legged supernatural and a small human or god are shown on the left, facing a similar tamale-filled jar. The four-legged figure holds a bundle marked with a snake, though it differs from other taller staffs in the scene. A woman on the right holds a small Chac effigy over a tamale vessel.

In the third scene from the top, a male on the left, wearing a God K serpent in his headdress, holds out tamales toward two approaching males on the right. The first male carries the serpent staff/bundle, and he is followed by a male with a Chac mask who wears Chac and God K effigies in his headdress (Taube 1992). The male on the left of this scene may be receiving this staff, and he may be the scene's central actor, perhaps acceding to ritual or political office (Masson 2000a:236). Another male and female are located between the rosette star and *itz*-marked chevron bands that mark the top celestial segment of this mural. The male (on the left) is seated on a throne and holds a serpent staff/bundle and faces a tamale-filled jar. He wears a Chac serpent in his headdress and a God K mask. Twin serpents open their mouths in the center of this section, and tamales emerge from them. A female flies to the right of these serpents, while grinding on a metate. She gestures toward a Chac figure.

KEY THEMES

A few key themes emerge from all of this detail. The repetition of Chac and God K imagery—along with tamale offerings, serpents, star signs, and serpent staffs or bundles—is common in both Structure 5 and 16 at Tulum.

Love documents the accession of Postclassic lords into a rotating *katun* office associated with a God K title in the Paris Codex (Love 1994:18–25), and rotation into a similar office may be represented on these Tulum murals. Chac rituals are also depicted on a mural at the nearby site of Tancah (Miller 1982: plate 1). Ancient versions of modern Cha-Chaac ceremonies may also be indicated on these murals. More-complex astronomical interpretations of the symbolism explore additional meanings of these murals (Miller 1982; Milbrath 1999). Astronomical correlations have long been used in the Maya area to sanction historical events sponsored by political elites (Freidel et al. 1993; Schele and Freidel 1990).

The presence of entwined serpent imagery and mat symbols suggests that the actors in these murals may have been members of powerful local lineages (Miller 1974; Masson 2000a:234–238), and the presence of at least four such temples at Tulum implies that rulership at this site was shared among multiple factions. The identification of Maya deities such as Chac and God K, as well as ancient Maya conventions such as the use of entwined serpents and serpent maws, indicates that the elements of the Late Postclassic international symbol set were incorporated into local agendas by governing elites at Tulum. Other local agendas are represented in the murals of Mayapán and Santa Rita, which incorporated this symbolism for different occasions.

The importance of external connections to Postclassic Maya elites is illustrated in the prominence and abundance of international symbols in Maya murals, as well as the use of a variant of the Postclassic international style. Past explanations that rely on the imposition of Aztec soldiers or merchants to account for the presence of these elements at Maya sites (e.g., Miller 1982:74–75) are no longer tenable: it is clear that many of the international symbols and elements did not originate with the Aztecs. Instead, a variety of peoples and cultures were responsible for these styles and symbols, many of which became popular throughout Postclassic Mesoamerica long before the rise of the Aztec empire (chapter 23; Ringle et al. 1998). Artists in the Yucatán, Quintana Roo, and Belize zones did not simply adopt foreign styles and symbols wholesale. Rather, they selected key elements from a broad repertoire of international possibilities and used these in creating paintings that depicted local and regional themes for a local audience. Their incorporation of cosmopolitan symbols also probably sanctioned local authority within these communities and with visiting merchant elites from other ports around the peninsula. The Postclassic Maya murals provide one of the best examples of the blending of local and international elements in the Postclassic world system. In the following chapter, Pohl examines similar phenomena within the Mixteca-Puebla region of central Mexico.

26

Ritual and Iconographic Variability in Mixteca-Puebla Polychrome Pottery

John M. D. Pohl

Artifactual evidence of the intensive feasting networks that were maintained by Eastern Nahuas, Mixtecs, Zapotecs, and their confederates is revealed in the development and spread of complex technologies for producing polychrome ceramics, and the development of a pictographic communication system for ornamenting them. During the Middle Postclassic period, the Mixteca-Puebla representational art style was widely adopted throughout central and southern Mexico (Nicholson 1960, 1982, 1994; Nicholson and Quiñones Keber 1994; Robertson 1959; Smith and Heath-Smith 1980). As one component of the wider Postclassic international style, the Mixteca-Puebla style was composed of highly conventionalized symbols characterized by an almost geometric precision in delineation. Colors were vivid, and imagery shared many of the attributes of contemporary cartoons, the exaggerated emphasis on the head and hands, in particular, reminiscent in overall design of characters made famous by contemporary animation studios like the Walt Disney Company (Nicholson 1960, 1982; Byland and Pohl 1994a:8–10).

In full figurative form the Mixteca-Puebla style was employed primarily to convey historical or ritual narrative, but certain symbols could also be reduced to simple icons that symbolized either an idea or a spoken word. For example, the depiction of repetitive designs of such common motifs as birds, butterflies, and jewels probably invoke the spirits of dead ancestors.[1] By A.D. 1300, the Mixteca-Puebla style had supplanted earlier pictographic and phonetically based scripts employed by the Classic-period civilizations of La Mojarra, Teotihuacan, Cacaxtla, Xochicalco, Nuiñe, Monte Albán, and to some extent even the Maya. There is considerable evidence that the old writing systems were intentionally rejected and that the new system was adapted from figurative symbolism used to ornament elite artwork in precious

metals, stones, wood, ceramics, and textiles (Pohl 1994a). Therefore, far from representing any decline in literacy, the employment of this new cartoon-like horizon style became an ingenious response to the redistribution of power among Postclassic confederations of city-states and great houses whose leaders communicated in as many as 12 different languages (Pohl 1994b; figure 26.1).

Mixteca-Puebla ceramics were highly refined in both form and design (Ramsey 1975, 1982). Manufacturing techniques were labor intensive.[2] After a plate or vessel was coil-built from fine-grain clay and shaped with wooden instruments, it was allowed to dry to a leather-like consistency. Next, its surface was burnished with smooth stones to prepare it for treatment with a white or orange base slip. Designs were handpainted in narrow dark lines without the use of templates, adding an element of spontaneity to each work. Paints were created by adding pigments to slips and carefully applying the colors in and around the line work with various brush sizes. The surface was then smoothed and burnished a second time. Ultimately, each vessel underwent at least one firing, and possibly as many as three. The effort put into producing the most refined pieces shows in their radiant colors, intricate geometric designs, and delicate figurative imagery.

Stratigraphic excavations carried out since the 1950s confirm a Terminal Classic–Early Postclassic origin for polychrome at Cholula, where it appeared following the erosion of Teotihuacan's influence in the central Puebla region after A.D. 750 (Noguera 1954; Lind 1994; McCafferty 1994). Although varieties of painted or burnished paste ceramics date to as early as the Formative in central and western Mexico, during the Late Classic the Olmeca-Xicalanca peoples of the Gulf Coast were producing variants of Maya polychrome, indicating a more direct technological and stylistic influence from the culture

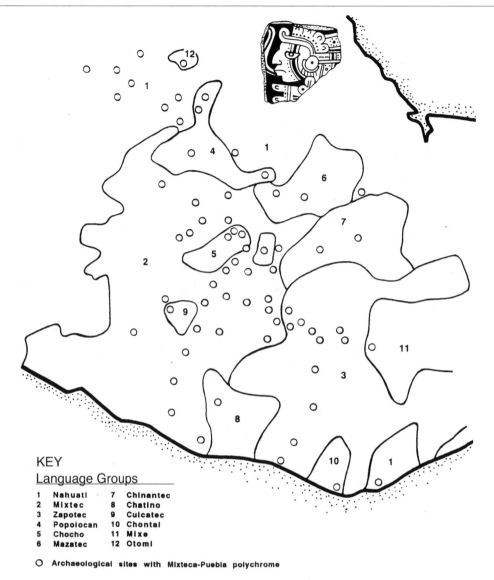

Figure 26.1 Map of sites with Mixteca-Puebla polychromes and their relationship to language groups

historically associated with Cholula prior to the Tolteca-Chichimeca intrusion (Lind 1994:98).

Michael Lind (1994) has documented stylistic changes in Cholula polychrome between A.D. 950 and 1350. The earliest varieties of Aquiahuac-phase plates, for example, were typically ornamented with lavish volute and floral designs. A figurative motif representing either a monkey or a personage possessing the attributes of Maya God M and the Aztec Ixtlilton appears during the subsequent Tecama phase.[3] It is only during the Martir phase, from A.D. 1350–1550, that iconography associated with the true Mixteca-Puebla style appears at Cholula—roughly the same time that polychrome was first introduced into Oaxaca (Neff et al. 1994). The fact that so many fourteenth-century court artisans in such a broad geographical area could paint the same set of icons with the same degree of precision in style is a testament to the

tremendous degree of elite integration that Nahua, Mixtec, and Zapotec royal houses achieved through their feast networks. Nevertheless, cultural differences in symbolic usage are also apparent.

Neutron-activation analysis allows archaeologists to identify the source of the clays employed by regional artisans and to map the geographical distribution of their finished pieces. Analysis of scores of polychrome sherds excavated from sites throughout the Mexican highlands has led Hector Neff, Ron Bishop, Edward Sisson, and their associates to identify a significant break in distribution between Oaxacan and Tlaxcalan-Pueblan polychrome (Neff et al. 1994:122). In other words, although there is a great deal of overlap in the exchange of ceramics between the Eastern Nahua kingdoms of Tlaxcala and Puebla, there is little or no comparable exchange between the Eastern Nahua and the Zapotecs and Mixtecs

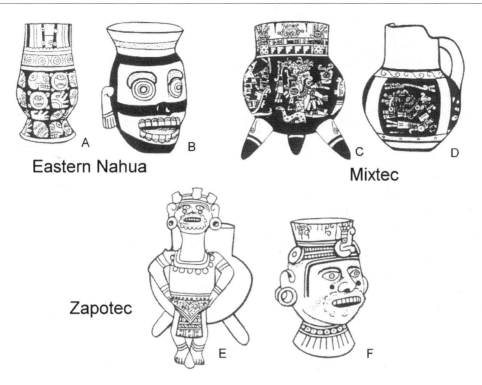

Figure 26.2 Polychrome drinking vessels used for cacao or pulque by Eastern Nahuas, Mixtecs, and Zapotecs: (A) Eastern Nahua goblet from Tlaxcala (Los Angeles County Museum of Natural History); (B) Eastern Nahua goblet from Cholula (Colección Televisa, Mexico City); (C) Mixtec tripod olla from Nochixtlan (Museo Nacional de Antropología e Historia, Mexico City); (D) Mixtec pitcher from Nochixtlan (Museo Nacional de Antropología e Historia, Mexico City); (E) Zapotec tripod olla from Miahuatlan (American Museum of Natural History, New York); (F) Zapotec goblet from Zaachila (Museo Nacional de Antropología e Historia, Mexico City.)

of Oaxaca. Michael Lind attributes such preferences in ceramic consumption to significant differences in the ritual contexts for royal feasts. He notes that the Eastern Nahua primarily served food and drink from goblets (figure 26.2A, B), vases, deep communal serving basins, and wide, flat plates, whereas the Mixtecs and Zapotecs employed pitchers and tripod ollas (figure 26.2, C–F) and platters (Lind 1994:87). Variance in these vessel forms is matched by different emphases in iconographic content as well. Lind quantified frequencies in the usage for more than 75 individual design motifs and found dramatic differences in symbolic usage. For example, Eastern Nahua artisans had a distinct preference for ornamenting pieces with precious jewels, butterflies, human skulls, crossed bones (figure 26.2A), extruded eyeballs or stars, sacrificial bloodletting instruments, and eagle or jaguar motifs. Mixtec-Zapotec artisans, in contrast, preferred plumed serpents, parrot heads, flowers, and shells. Lind interprets Eastern Nahua imagery as reflecting a bloodier, sacrificial nature related to Nahua ritualism. The figurative imagery of Mixtec-Zapotec art, on the other hand, provides clues about which gods, ancestors, or spirit forces were related to the various royal feasts.

THE EASTERN NAHUA

The ornamental bands of human skulls, hands, hearts, and shields that appear on vases were particularly diagnostic of the tzitzimime, the supernatural patrons of the court diviners who served as intermediaries with the souls of the dead (Lind 1994:92–97; Pohl 1998a). There are several outstanding examples of codex-style images of these spirit forces, as well as three-dimensional effigy goblets (figure 26.2). By some accounts the tzitzimime personified belief in an ideological relationship between death, disease, drought, and war as divine castigation, and appeasement through blood sacrifice (Taube 1993; Pohl 1998a; Boone 2000). The tzizimime were feared during climactic events, especially eclipses, because it was believed they would someday emerge as stars from their twilight world to attack the sun and bring an end to the present age of mankind. They were also associated with the chaos induced with drunkenness at banquets, and the murderous outcomes of arguments between factions over alliances, women, and land. Nevertheless, they exemplified an indigenous axiom that whatever causes disease or drought can also cure it. The tzitzimime could be benevolent when properly venerated, and midwives invoked their aid during childbirth and purification rituals. There was a profound fertility aspect to their cult, for they were said to travel as clouds to bring the first, life-giving rains of each year. This association clearly connects them to the worship of the royal dead, for the Eastern Nahuas believed that their kings and queens could be transformed into clouds (Mendieta 1971:97).

The supreme tzitzimitl was Mictlantecuhtli, ruler of the underworld (Anders and Jansen 1996:48). After death, Quetzalcoatl was transformed into a tzitzimitl, a personification of the morning star called Tlahuizcalpantecuhtli. Most importantly, the demons were primarily equated with a series of calendrical deities known as the *cihuateteo* and the *maquiltonaleque*. The cihuateteo were thought to be the souls of women who had died in childbirth (Sahagún 1950–1982, book 6:161). Invoked during the moveable feast days of 1 House, 1 Deer, 1 Monkey, 1 Eagle, and 1 Rain, they were patronesses of the five *trecenas* or divisions of the sacred calendar assigned to the west, or Cihuatlampa, a netherworld of women. The maquiltonaleque were consorts of the cihuateteo and presided over the feast days of 5 Lizard, 5 Rabbit, 5 Grass, 5 Vulture, and 5 Flower, the five trecenas of the south.[4] They were also the patrons of court diviners who employed the mantic divisions of the 260-day calendar portrayed in ritual manuscripts like Codex Borgia to foresee the future and to cure. Diviners invoked the maquiltonaleque as their own fingers, describing them as the "pearly headed" tzitzimime. Confirmation that their cult was pivotal to the more private ritual life of the royal palace is confirmed by a story of the first Franciscan friars sent to convert the lords of Tlaxcala. Upon entering the royal court of Tizatlan, they were shocked by the statue of a maquiltonal, which they described as being a frightening apparition of the dead (Torquemada 1986: 3:201).

THE MIXTECS

Mixtec artisans were best known for painting full-figure narrative scenes on polychrome ollas and pitchers, usually illustrating religious stories that are well documented in the Mixtec codices. An outstanding example in Mexico's National Museum of Anthropology and History was discovered in the ruins of a Postclassic palace near Nochixtlan around the turn of the twentieth century and illustrates people, places, and things that relate directly to Codex Zouche-Nuttall 15–21 (Byland and Pohl 1994a: 78). In the first scene on the olla we see an enthroned Mixtec god known as 10 Rain making a tobacco offering before a compound place sign composed of a double-peaked mountain marked with a flint knife from which grows a tree ornamented with a sacrificial paper bow. Beneath the mountain we see the bicephalic mouth of an earth monster representing a cave within which swims a

fish. In the second scene, the god 9 Wind is offering a decapitated human head before a temple over which rises an enormous serpent.

Ten Rain was a hero in the famous War of Heaven portrayed on Zouche-Nuttall 21, where he is also shown holding a decapitated head. On page 19 he is enthroned in much the same way as he appears on the Nochixtlan olla, within a large place sign that includes the bent mountain, the Hill of Flints, and the cave—actual sites in the southern Nochixtlan Valley. Nine Wind is recognizable by his protruding duck-bill mask. He is portrayed in Codex Vindobonensis 47–49 as a culture hero who was born from a flint, ascended to heaven to receive the sacred objects and ritual dress of the wind god, and finally descended to lift the earth from the sky at the site of Yucuñudahui. A pitcher that accompanied this olla also portrays personalities well-known from Mixtec legends. It is ornamented with the heads of Lady 9 Grass, Lord 1 Death, and other Mixtec gods as the patrons of the four directions (Seler 1990–1998:3:285–288).

Another pitcher—preserved in the Gilcrease Museum in Tulsa, Oklahoma—portrays a scene very similar to that of the Nochixtlan olla. A man dressed in a tight-fitting coyote suit is seated on a small throne and is making an offering of incense before a sacred tree in much the same way as 10 Rain. A famous Mixtec olla preserved in Oaxaca's regional museum may portray a series of creation-story heroes as well. The narrative consists of a group of seated men playing musical instruments. Two wear the masks of a monkey and a dog to identify them as priests. Others are wearing crowns and facial ornamentation related to a deity known as 7 Flower, patron of royal marriages, craft production, and gift giving (Pohl 1994a; see figure 26.2C).

THE ZAPOTECS

Archaeologist Roberto Gallegos Ruiz (1978) excavated an entire service of Zapotec polychrome feasting wares from Tombs 1 and 2 at Zaachila in 1962. The basic forms were comparable to those of the Mixtecs, being ornamented primarily with geometric designs and figurative images of crocodiles, serpents, parrot heads, flowers, and shells. Unique three-dimensional representations included a cup with a miniature hummingbird delicately perched on the rim, a pitcher with a spout formed as a deer head, and a uniquely formed vase representing the head of a deity wearing a crown ornamented with turquoise jewels and a butterfly (figure 26.2F). The painting of the face with the narrow red bands over the eyes and the white flower around the mouth identify this personage as Xochipilli, or Flower Prince, known to the Zapotecs as Bezelao, or 13 Flower (Pohl 1999; Ramsey 1982). A famous Zapotec tripod olla collected in Miahuatlan and now in the collections of the American

Museum of Natural History features a three-dimensional figure of Bezelao dancing with his hands on his hips (figure 26.2E). A tripod plate from Zaachila features a painting of Bezelao at the base of a bowl to which were added deer hoof supports. Piltzintecuhtli, an avatar of Xochipilli, was thought by the Nahuas to be able to transform himself into a deer (Serna 1987:423), and deer imagery is found in connection with many of the other Zaachila vessels, suggesting that the Zapotecs connected Bezelao to this animal in legend as well.[5]

SAME STYLE, DIFFERENT CULTS

Although the spread of the Mixteca-Puebla style throughout southern Mexico during the fourteenth century was clearly meant to facilitate elite communication between Tlaxcalan, Pueblan, and Oaxacan peoples, variations in vessel forms and iconography reveal that ceramic artisans were also motivated by differing world views. Significantly, the Spanish chronicler Diego Durán explained the differences between these peoples not in terms of language or race, but by comparing them to the principal religious traditions of his own time, saying:

> According to the native histories all these people (Eastern Nahuas) were of the same origin and that the only difference was that they belonged to different factions. However other nations such as the Mixtecs, Zapotecs, Huaxtecs and coastal peoples were to them as the Moors, Turks, or Jews are to us [Catholic Spaniards]. "Chichimec," a name of which the Aztec nation is so proud, is similar to our use of the word Castillian or Goth and the above named people did not use this title. Only those around the snow-capped volcanoes bore it and these people were the inhabitants of Tlaxcala, Huexotzinco, Cholula, and Tliliuhquitepec. All of them called themselves Chichimecs before they came to possess these lands. (Durán 1994:440)

The Eastern Nahua venerated supernatural beings known as the tzitzimime in their royal feasts. These spirit forces were frightening in their appearance, with fleshless human skulls and claws for hands and feet, imagery typically associated with death and the underworld, and yet they were clearly attributed progenerative powers as well. Codex Borgia pages 29–32 portray the creation of the world as a cosmic act initiated by a host of tzitzimime (Seler 1963). The climax of the event involves the supernatural birth of Quetzalcoatl and Tezcatlipoca from flints attached to the body of a decapitated giantess, either the tzitzimime Itzpapalotl or Citlalicue (Pohl 1998a:187–189).

For the Eastern Nahua, the ritual emphasis for palace feasts reflected in the ornamentation of their serving vessels did not appear to focus on the personality cults of lineal ancestors. In fact, few surviving written sources

list any ancestors of kingdoms beyond the great-grandparents, but it is easy to see why. When a Nahua king died, his body was dressed in both the clothing of the god who presided over the manner of his death and in that of the patron deity of the kingdom (López de Gómara 1987:438–440; Torquemada 1986:2:521). The body was then cremated, and the ashes were placed in urns that were buried either in the foundation of the principal temple or the palace. In this way the personality of the deceased was sublimated in favor of the identity of the god to whom he or she was dedicated, and then ultimately eliminated altogether. Consequently, the Eastern Nahua lacked religious cults like those of the Mixtecs, which were dedicated to the more than 25 generations of deified ancestors. What function would such accounts serve? The Tolteca-Chichimeca title of tecuhtli, or lineage head, was not inherited by divine right of descent but by being elected to participate in rituals of entitlement by the priests of Cholula. The *tetecuhtin* were never considered divine, and consequently the Tolteca-Chichimeca histories and king lists were not imbued with the sense of sacredness attributed to royal ancestors appearing in the Mixtec codices. On the contrary, there is little evidence to suggest that the Nahua invoked the souls of the dead as historical individuals at all, but rather as a collective of spirit archetypes. Like most Mesoamerican peoples, the Eastern Nahua perceived the soul to be a manifestation of the predetermined characteristics that were ascribed to the 260 days of the sacred calendar, the tonalpohualli; the term *tonal* can mean either "day" or "soul" in the Nahuatl language (López Austin 1988; Furst 1995; Monaghan 1998; Pohl 1998a).

The Mixtecs, on the other hand, were more interested in commemorating the rituals initiated by numerous culture heroes, priests, and oracles who first appeared on the earth and brought forth the first dynastic ancestors from trees. This is revealed not only in the representations of specific individuals on polychrome pottery and in pictorial manuscripts, but also by funerary customs. Mixtec kings and queens were endowed with a considerable degree of divinity: the term *yya* means both "high lord" and "god." At death, paramount kings and queens were transformed into religious objects of veneration by having their bodies mummified and placed in special reliquaries constructed in sacred caves in surrounding mountains; for example, the entire dynasty of the royal house of Tilantongo was preserved in a cave at Chalcatongo (Pohl 1994c:69–82). There the spirits of the dead were thought to pass into a royal paradise, but they could still communicate with their descendants through priestly intermediaries such as Lady 9 Grass who attended their mummy bundles and served as powerful oracles by consulting them on affairs of marriage and warfare among their descendants.

The maintenance of funerary cults focused on the

grouping of the remains of the royal dead in a central place was ingenious. The Mixtec yya's right to rule was largely based on direct descent from a deified ancestor and a preferred system of primogeniture. Social rank in general was therefore traced through one's familial relationship with a continuous royal lineage. The funerary cult, with its emphasis on historical individuals, supplied proof of the existence of these divine ancestors, became the focus of political unity, and ensured social stability among various members of otherwise factionalized royal kin groups. Colonial reports, court records, codices, and lienzos from the Mixteca Alta describe funerary cults dedicated to culture heroes and dynastic ancestors named in the Mixtec language. Although a few bear attributes that relate them to Nahua prototypes such as Tonatiuh, Cihuacoatl, and Xipe, most are characterized by unique combinations of ritual dress that distinguish them from the pantheon of Nahua gods portrayed in Codex Borgia, for example. Instead, they appear in the Mixtec codices as the heroes of legends clearly distinct from their Tolteca-Chichimeca counterparts.

We have seen that the narrative scenes appearing on the Nochixtlan olla are dedicated to the culture heroes Lord 10 Rain and Lord 9 Wind, who aided dynastic ancestors in establishing the first kingdoms. Three sixteenth-century Mixtec lords who were charged with idolatry in Yanhuitlan were accused of holding four feasts annually. These were dedicated to the gods Quiyo (Lady 10 Reed), Xiyo (Lady 11 Serpent), Sachi (Lord 7 Wind), and Sacuhu (Lord 7 Movement) (Jansen 1982: 283–286; Pohl 1996). Like 10 Rain and 9 Wind, all were leading participants in the War of Heaven and other foundation rituals depicted in Codices Vindobonensis and Zouche-Nuttall (Pohl 1994d:62, 1995:56–58).[6]

The Zapotecs had names for the spirit forces of rain, wind, clouds, and other natural phenomena, but these hardly constituted a pantheon comparable to that celebrated by the Eastern Nahua. Instead their worship focused on deified ancestors, each named for the day of his or her birth in the 260-day divinatory calendar. Names varied from community to community, suggesting that their cults were significant only to those who were directly related to them, and many bear the title of *coqui* (Lord) and *xonaxi* (Lady) (Marcus 1983f:348–349). Despite similarities to the Mixtecs in this regard, there are no surviving pre-Columbian historical annals and the few stories recorded by the Spaniards are too fragmentary to determine the exact nature of the relationships between Zapotec culture heroes and founding ancestors. The polychrome pottery that can definitely be attributed to Zapotec craftspeople lacks narrative scenes.

Although primogeniture appears to have been the preferred system of inheritance, it is not at all clear that the Zapotec royal title of coqui was necessarily dependent on proving direct descent from ancestors. The longest

Zapotec genealogy is found in the Lienzo de Guevea, which names eight generations for the royal house of Zaachila dating to between A.D. 1280 and 1563. However, Codex Zouche-Nuttall implies that this lineage only came to power when the founder Lord 5 Flower married a direct descendant of Lord 8 Deer of Tilantongo named Lady 4 Rabbit. Perhaps divine descent as a prerequisite of rulership was reintroduced by Mixtecs.[7]

In addition to the veneration of localized ancestor cults, the Zapotecs also believed in a "supreme universal god" called Bezelao, or Lord 13 Flower. He is mentioned in many of the Relaciones Geográficas for the Valley of Oaxaca and surrounding areas as far south as Coatlan. Like the Mixtecs, the Zapotecs mummified the remains of the dead and placed them in sacred shrines. The deceased of the highest-ranked dynasty, the royal house of Zaachila, were entombed at Mitla. Their spirits were thought to pass into a netherworld where they joined Bezelao in eternal paradise (Pohl 1999). Mitla's Palace of the Columns was the residence of a high priest called the Huijatao, or "great seer," a personage of considerable power who arbitrated disputes between the Zapotec kings and acted as a medium by claiming to be able to speak with the mummies of their ancestors. Some indication of the relationship between the cult of the ancestors and the cult of Bezelao is indicated by the account of the death and burial of Petela, Lord 5/9 Dog of Coatlan and Ocelotepec. When Petela died, he was mummified and worshipped as a god. An epidemic later swept through the region, and the Zapotecs invoked Petela to intercede with Bezelao on their behalf to cure them of the disease (Acuña 1984:1:89–90; Herrera 1945:4:172–173). Superseding even worship of the divine kings, it seems that the veneration of Bezelao unified the disparate cults of lineage segments among the Zapotecs. In this respect he was the equivalent to the Eastern Nahua's Tonacatecuhtli, the god above all gods who allocated the land and distributed it to the first royal ancestors for their kingdoms (Pohl 1999).[8]

CONCLUSIONS

The style, iconography, and distribution of the richly painted polychrome ceramics of central and southern Mexico—the Mixteca-Puebla region—provide a picture of social dynamics in one part of the Postclassic Mesoamerican world system. The great similarities in overall iconography and artistic execution of polychrome ceramics clearly helped promote shared social agendas and alliances in royal feasting networks that unified Eastern Nahua, Mixtec, and Zapotec royal houses as well as the other ethnic groups they dominated. At the same time stylistic preferences in vessel forms and the use of specific iconographic symbols clearly allowed for regional variations in ritual settings as well.

27

A Web of Understanding

Pictorial Codices and the
Shared Intellectual Culture of
Late Postclassic Mesoamerica

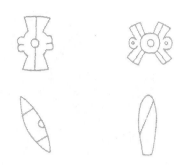

Elizabeth H. Boone

In the Late Postclassic, more so than in any other period of Mesoamerican history, elements of shared ideologies extended through the cultural life of Mesoamerica, particularly within the areas touched by the Aztec or Triple Alliance empire. Peoples on the very edges of the empire held many of the same beliefs and practiced many of the same customs as peoples in the core region of central Mexico. Although we cannot say that a single uniform ideology penetrated all aspects of religious, social, and political realms—for different regions kept also to their own local traditions—there is clear evidence of shared beliefs and patterns of action that bound distant peoples together regardless of the differences between them. The presence of these cultural elements corresponds generally to the economic and social network created by cross-Mesoamerican trade, tribute, and social interaction.

Shared ideologies and customs span a broad range of social activity. They include such things as painting styles (specifically manuscript painting), ways of conceptualizing and recording history, mythologies, the sources and iconography of royal power, and a calendrically based divination system. As might be expected, most of these shared elements pertain more to the elites, who were more socially interconnected and mobile, than to the commoners, who were more closely tied to local traditions. The realm of divination, however, extended to the laborers and farmers as well as the palace folk.

These ways of acting and thinking that bound Mesoamerica together in the Late Postclassic were carried in people's minds, but they were expressed in more permanent form in the pictorial codices. As bearers or containers of ideology for Mesoamerican people, the codices seem to have been the principal conduit for transmitting knowledge from one part of the Late Postclassic world system to another. Codices circulated throughout Mesoamerica within the valued baggage carried by long-distance merchants, leaders of moving armies, imperial governors, tribute collectors, ambassadors, as well as noble brides and grooms marrying into distant royal families. The codices followed the networks of trade, tribute, conquests, and social interaction that tied Mesoamerica together.

This movement of codices and of the ideological elements they contained was not the result solely of the imperial center (Tenochtitlan) imposing its art style, gods, calendars, and customs on the peoples around it, a push from the core into the periphery. Instead, the flow of ideas and styles was also the result of peoples in the provinces and on the edges of the empire choosing to embrace and emulate the customs of the center, a desire by the provincials to prove "We are Aztecs, too." After all, the Aztecs were eminently copyable, with their fine painting style, elaborate clothing and manners, and the powerful historical and mythic narratives that contributed so much to their success. Provincial lords probably also employed Aztec elements in order to accommodate the Aztecs visiting or living in their midst, which reflects a desire for accommodation that carried with it a reach toward cosmopolitanism.

Ideas moved the other direction as well, flowing from the provinces to the center. In some cases, the Aztecs consciously emulated the customs of their neighbors, as when the Aztec rulers strove to be more like the Oaxacan lords and adopted some of their royal regalia. The Aztecs were an intellectually ecumenical people who drew freely on the traditions of their predecessors and neighbors when fashioning their own customs and ideologies. In this way the Aztec pantheon became a collection of supernaturals gathered from many peoples. The House of the Diverse Gods in the ritual precinct of Tenochtitlan, where captured cult images of foreign gods were held and worshipped, stands as a

Figure 27.1 Example of the Aztec painting style from Veracruz, Lienzo Tochpan I, detail. (After Melgarejo Vivanco 1970: second plate.)

manifestation of this open and acquisitive spirit (Durán 1994:431).

In the Late Postclassic, then, ideas and styles flowed back and forth along many of the same routes as did trade goods and tribute. The following examples of shared elements suggest the depth of this phenomenon.

AZTEC PAINTING STYLES

In a 1996 article, "Manuscript Painting in Service of Imperial Ideology" in the book *Aztec Imperial Strategies* (Berdan et al. 1996), I argued that the Aztec painting style spread to the far reaches of the Triple Alliance empire and appeared especially in areas where the empire had vested interests. The Aztec painting style—characterized by a relative naturalism in rendering humans, animals, and objects; by taller and leaner human figures than are common in other Mexican (Mixtec and Borgia Group) styles; and by specific conventions—is perhaps best represented by the Codex Borbonicus (see figure 27.15 below) (see Boone 1982a for discussion of Aztec painting style). This style originated in the Valley of Mexico whence it was drawn to points on the outer edges of the empire. The style appears, for example, in the Lienzos de Tochpan from the northern province of Tochpan (figure 27.1), in the Codex Hueychiapan from the province of Xilotepec in Hidalgo, and the Codex Azoyu II from the province of Tlapa in Guerrero (figure 27.2). Since all these provinces were areas of special Triple Alliance interest and of significant Aztec occupation, it is natural that the Aztec painting style would be adopted there.

Figure 27.2 Example of the Aztec painting style from Guerrero, Codex Azoyu II, a tribute list from Tlapa. (Photo courtesy of the Stattsbibliothek Stiftung Preussischer Kulturbesitz, Berlin.)

In contrast, distinct regional painting styles prevailed in the Tlaxcalan realm (Tonalamatl Aubin; figure 27.16 below) and among the Mixtec and Zapotec polities of Oaxaca (see figure 27.4), both areas where Aztec control was lacking or less secure. The strong tradition of manuscript painting in the Mixteca seems especially to have kept the Aztec style at a distance. Where the Aztec and Mixtecs came together (along with Chocho and Cuicatec speakers) in the Coixtlahuaca Valley of northwestern Oaxaca, however, the lienzos and *tiras* (or strips) show a mingling of Aztec and Mixtec painting styles (Boone 2000:125–161).

ANNALS HISTORY

The annals history likewise spread within the core zone of the empire and to some distant provinces. In annals, the continuous count of the years is painted as a spine down or across the strip or page, and the events important to the altepetl (or community kingdom) are painted beside the year count, often attached to individual years

Figure 27.3 Codex Mexicanus (p. 71), an annals history. (After Codex Mexicanus 1952: plate 71.)

by lines (Boone 2000:197–237). Such are the Codex Mexicanus (figure 27.3), Codex Aubin, Fonds Mexicain nos. 40 and 85, Codex Moctezuma, Codex Saville, and the historical parts of the Codex Telleriano-Remensis and Codex Mendoza, all of which pertain wholly or largely to Tenochtitlan. Annals histories were also painted in the Texcocan realm (Tira de Tepechpan, Codex en Cruz), in Puebla (*Historia Tolteca-Chichimeca*), in the province of Xilotepec (Codex Hueychiapan and *Anales de Tula*), and from distant Tlapan (Codex Azoyu I); all but the *Historia Tolteca-Chichimeca* include Tenochtitlan's place sign or Tenochtitlan events in their accounts.

Since most of the extant pictorial annals embrace Tenochtitlan history into their stories, I argued in 1996 that the annals history was a historical genre developed or adopted by the Aztec-Mexica to tell the imperial story, to ground the imperium in the deep past, and to present its continuance as ongoing as long as the ribbon of time continued. This kind of history is especially suitable for the Aztec political system, in which rulers were chosen as much for their accomplishments as for their royal status, because it focuses not on the royal family but on events important to the community kingdom at large. In this way it stands in remarkable contrast to the event-oriented Mixtec genealogical history.

The genealogical history that characterizes the Mixtec screenfolds and tiras is distinct from other Mesoamerican histories because it focuses so insistently on the descent lines of the Mixtec rulers (Boone 2000:87–124). It includes the actions of the Mixtec rulers as they defended their territory from internal and external threats, and as they sought to expand their dominance over other polities, but it does so from the perspective of the royal families rather than the community kingdoms, and it concentrates on giving the genealogical history of these families, often in great detail (figure 27.4). These histories are appropriate for the Mixtec political system, where kingdoms were ruled according to primogeniture patterns of descent, and individuals took office because of who their parents (both father and mother) were (see chapter 10). The Mixtec codices lack long migration stories, which characterize Aztec histories, because their message is that the rulers had always been there, having emerged from the very lands they now occupied. The Mixtec stories are local stories, beginning when the ancient or supernatural ancestors emerged from the earth or from trees in the Mixteca (Mary Elizabeth Smith 1973a:82; Furst 1977).

Even though the Aztecs and Mixtecs stand apart in the events and structure of their histories, they still shared a number of mythological elements and rituals that reveal an ideological interaction within the Late Postclassic world system.

CAVE ORIGIN

One feature shared by many people in Mesoamerica is the notion that the first ancestors emerged from caves. The ideal of Chicomoztoc (as it is termed in Nahuatl), the place of Seven Caves, appears in Mixtec and Zapotec

Figure 27.4 Codex Zouche-Nuttall (p. 26), a genealogical history presenting the family of Lord 5 Crocodile. (After Anders, Jansen, and Pérez Jiménez 1992b.)

as well as Aztec sources, and it is expressed in at least one Tarascan-Nahua manuscript as well. Although the Mexica Aztecs believed that they themselves began their long migration when they left their ancestral homeland of Aztlan, the textual and pictorial histories of the Aztecs also include Chicomoztoc. In these accounts Chicomoztoc is either conflated with Aztlan, or it appears as a stop along the migratory journey, from where the Mexica and the other tribes emerge (Boone 2000:213–219, 239–240). In the Mexica realm, many sources—such as the Codex Mexicanus, the Codex Azcatitlan, Diego Durán's Historia (figure 27.5), and Domingo Chimalpahin's Historia and Relaciones—picture or speak of the peoples emerging from Chicomoztoc. From Cuauhtinchan in Puebla,

the *Historia Tolteca-Chichimeca* and Cuauhtinchan Map 2 feature the emergence of the people from Chicomoztoc before their migration to their homeland (Boone 2000: 173–176). Within Tarascan territory the Lienzo de Jucutacato (figure 27.6), whose creators claimed Toltec rather than Tarascan descent, likewise begins its migration story with the ancient people emerging en masse from a cave. Coixtlahuaca Valley documents that mingle Aztec and Mixtec elements and traditions often begin with a cave emergence, more specifically when the culture hero 9 Wind emerges from a seven-lobed cave (figure 27.7; Boone 2000:152–160).

Although the Mixtec origin stories lack long migrations and instead point out local origins, they do note that some of the ancient and supernatural ancestors emerged from the earth or, more specifically, from a place of Seven Caves (Boone 2000: 96-99). The Codex Zouche-

Figure 27.5 The beginning of the Aztec migration, with the Aztecs going forth from a cave. (From Diego Durán's *Historia de las Yndias* (fol. 4v). (After Durán 1967:2: plate 3.)

Figure 27.6 Cave emergence, the first scene of the Lienzo de Jucutacato. (After Mendizabal 1926.)

Figure 27.7 Chicomoztoc with the day dates (calendrical names) of 9 Wind and 1 Reed inside, Lienzo of Tlapiltepec. (Drawing courtesy of Nicholas Johnson.)

Figure 27.8 Lord 5 Flower emerging from a celestial Chicomoztoc, Codex Zouche-Nuttall (p. 14). (After Anders, Jansen, and Pérez Jiménez 1992b.)

Figure 27.9 Quetzalcoatl, Codex Magliabechiano (fol. 61r). (After Codex Magliabechiano 1970.)

Nuttall (1–2), for example, opens when 8 Wind "Flinted Eagle" emerges again and again from clefts in the earth, and later in the codex Lord 5 Flower emerges from a celestial Chicomoztoc, pictured as seven cavelike openings in the sky (figure 27.8). The Codex Selden also begins with the emergence of ancestors from clefts in the earth, although these crevices are not specifically seven-lobed caves. Additionally, Chicomoztoc is featured in the Colonial Zapotec "Genealogy of San Lucas Quiaviní" (Oudijk 1998b), which indicates that at least some Zapotecs shared the idea of cave origin. It is perhaps this ubiquity of cave origins in the ethnohistoric record of the Late Postclassic period that has led Mesoamericanists to view cave origins as a nearly universal feature of Mesoamerican culture.

QUETZALCOATL/9 WIND

Another featured shared by the Aztecs and Mixtecs, as well as by peoples in neighboring Morelos and Puebla, is the supernatural and culture hero known as Quetzalcoatl among the Aztecs, and Lord 9 Wind among the Mixtecs.

H. B. Nicholson devoted his 1957 doctoral dissertation to explaining the identity and multiple manifestations of Quetzalcoatl (published in 2001; see also Nicholson 1978, 2000; Ringle et al. 1998; and discussion in chapter 10). I will not attempt such a feat here, except to point out how remarkably parallel the Aztec and Mixtec manifestations are.

In the Aztec world, Quetzalcoatl contributed in a major way to the creation of the world (summarized in Nicholson 1971:399–401). He and Tezcatlipoca separated the sky from the earth. Quetzalcoatl descended into the underworld to retrieve the bones of the people from an earlier age, from which humans of the present age were created. Transformed into a black ant, Quetzalcoatl went into the mountain of sustenance and retrieved the grains of maize to feed humankind. He was the patron of the priesthood and of the *calmecac*, where knowledge was imparted (Nicholson 1971:428–430). As Ehecatl he was the wind god. As Tlahuizcalpantecuhtli, he was Venus, the morning star. Visually he appears with distinctive red, gold, and black face paint, a beard, and the black body paint of priests, wearing a conical jaguar-pelt headdress with four rounded-end panels that extend outward, and with an array of quetzal and other feathers in the back (figure 27.9). His earplugs are of white curved shell, and his pectoral is a sliced conch shell. Often he wears the red buccal mask of Ehecatl, from which wind is blown.

In the Mixtec world, 9 Wind figures early and often in the cosmogony told in the Codex Vienna (Nicholson 1978; Furst 1978:102–128; Boone 2000:92–96). Born from a great flint knife, 9 Wind's pictorial aspects include those that can read as metaphoric titles, such as Jaguar Singer, Manuscript Painter, He Who Has Song In His Heart, He Who Has the Earth Spirit (ñuhu) in His Heart,

Figure 27.10 Lord 9 Wind, Codex Vienna (p. 48). (After Anders, Jansen, and Pérez Jiménez 1992a.)

Figure 27.11 Lord 8 Deer getting his nose pierced, Codex Zouche-Nuttall (p. 52). (After Anders, Jansen, and Pérez Jiménez 1992b.)

Figure 27.12 Lord 8 Deer proudly wears his Mexican nose ornament, Codex Zouche-Nuttall (p. 53). (After Anders, Jansen, and Pérez Jiménez 1992b.)

He Who Has Royalty (?) (Xipe bundle) In His Heart (Monaghan 1990a:137–139). As pictured in the Codex Vienna (figure 27.10), Lord 9 Wind brings rule, in the form of accoutrements of office, down from the heavens to the Mixteca (Jansen 1982:1:89–90, 146–180; Furst 1990:129–130; Boone 2000:91–94); he carries the waters and heavens, seeming to separate them from the earth; he brings places into being; he makes an offering to an ancestral pair and thereby brings other supernaturals into being; he initiates the ritual that creates and consecrates temples and sweatbaths; and he participates in assigning the gods their personal names or attributes. Visually he is identical to the Aztec Quetzalcoatl, including the face paint, body paint, beard, conical jaguar-pelt hat, shell ear ornaments, and conch shell pectoral. In lienzos and tiras of the Coixtlahuaca Valley, such as the Selden Roll and Lienzo of Tlapiltepec, 9 Wind is associated with the date 1 Reed, which is his Aztec name; he comes down from the heavens and emerges through the Seven Caves to bring polity into being (see figure 27.7; Boone 2000:152–160).

As distinct as the Aztec and Mixtec are culturally, they share this same basic deity and identify him through the same iconographic elements. In the divinatory codices of the Borgia Group, Quetzalcoatl/9 Wind appears in the identical way.

ROYAL IDEOLOGY

Nahua and Mixtec rulers were clearly aware of each other's paths to rule. They seem also to have respected the way their counterparts gained power and how they used ritual and visual display to symbolize their political authority. We see this in evidence when Mixtec rulers turned to Aztec or Mexican rituals to help them gain political power back home, and also when Aztec rulers adopted Zapotec and Mixtec symbols of authority as their own.

THE NOSE-PIERCING CEREMONY

Two Mixtec rulers, Lord 8 Deer and Lord 4 Wind, both sought out a Mexican form of authority in order to rule the kingdoms to which they aspired. John Pohl, building especially on the work of Caso (1960:39, 61–62, 1966, 1977–1979:1:82, 2:172), has discussed this in several publications (Pohl 1994c: 83–93; Byland and Pohl

Figure 27.13 Zapotec Lord 3 Vulture with face paint and headdress of Xipe Totec, Codex Zouche-Nuttall (p. 61). (After Anders, Jansen, and Pérez Jiménez 1992b.)

Figure 27.14 Moctezuma Xocoyotzin in the costume of Xipe Totec, Codex Vaticanus A/Ríos (fol. 83v). (After Seler 1902–1923:2:596, figure 159.)

1994a:138–151). As the second son of a high priest, 8 Deer was not eligible to rule the prestigious polity of Tilantongo, although this was a goal. After embarking on a series of conquests, which brought him the rule of the powerful city of Tututepec, 8 Deer journeyed to a Place of Reeds where a Mexican ruler/supernatural/priest named 4 Jaguar conducted for 8 Deer the Mexican ceremony that conferred on him the title of tecuhtli, or lineage head. Since this ritual involved piercing 8 Deer's nose so that he could wear the distinctive turquoise nose ornament of Aztec rulers (the yacaxihuitl), 8 Deer proudly wore this nose ornament until his death (figures 27.11 and 27.12). Lord 8 Deer died at the hands of, or on the orders of, 4 Wind, a ruler who also then sought out the Mexican 4 Jaguar and had his own nose-piercing ceremony conducted. Thus, both 8 Deer and 4 Wind, the two most significant rulers whose stories are recorded in the extant Mixtec screenfolds, sought out the Mexican ceremony that conveyed political authority on potential lineage heads and rulers. Their nose-piercing ceremonies and their journeys to the Place of Reeds where the ritual was performed figure largely in the extant Mixtec screenfolds.

XIPE TOTEC REGALIA AND RITUAL

Emulations went the other way also, for it was not solely the Mixtecs who adopted Aztec ways when it suited their purpose. Mexica rulers recognized important Mixtec rituals and symbols and adopted them for their own. As William Barnes (1999) has shown, Moctezuma Ilhuicamina, Axayacatl, and Moctezuma Xocoyotzin adopted the costume and/or the cult of Xipe Totec (the Flayer God) from Oaxaca and used it to express their own power as Aztec rulers. As early as the Classic period, Xipe Totec was associated with the Zapotec royal line; Xipe braziers appear in elite Zapotec tombs, and later Zapotec rulers

consistently wore Xipe's distinctive face paint (Byland and Pohl 1994a:178–170), as the Mixtec codices are careful to note (figure 27.13). This Xipe cult also carried with it rituals whereby enemies were ceremonially executed both by arrow sacrifice and by hand-to-hand combat where the victim is tied to a great circular stone. Lord 8 Deer himself married into the ancient Zapotec line in order to increase his power and prestige, and when it came time to kill the two closest rivals to the Tilantongo throne, he adopted the Xipe-associated execution ceremonies.

When the Mexica advanced their conquest into Oaxaca, they took up the cult of Xipe Totec and installed it in Tenochtitlan (Barnes 1999). They also brought the rituals of arrow sacrifice and hand-to-hand combat (conducted during the second monthly feast of Tlacaxipehualiztli) to the imperial capital. More tellingly, however, the Mexica rulers clad themselves in the costume of Xipe Totec, using it as their principal war garb (figure 27.14). It is in the flayed skin and costume of Xipe that the Mexica rulers Axayacatl and Moctezuma Xocoyotzin appear in the Codex Cozcatzin (14v, 15r), Codex en Cruz (2b [F]), and Codex Vaticanus A/Ríos (83v), and carved in portrait on the side of the cliff at Chapultepec (Nicholson 1959). The Mexica rulers understood the importance of the ancient Zapotec royal cult and its god Xipe; they may have known about its adoption by Mixtec rulers, and they saw how it would work also to increase and symbolize their own power. Being politically and iconographically acquisitive, the Mexica rulers turned to ancient Oaxacan symbols of authority to increase their own power.

DIVINATORY IDEOLOGY

In the multilingual and multicultural system that was Late Postclassic Mesoamerica, one might expect to find considerable variation within religious and divinatory beliefs. This was the intellectual area that would have been most closely guarded by the temple priests, soothsayers/diviners, and daykeepers (calendar priests), and this was the realm that required the most training and the most esoteric knowledge to master. Thus one would expect that each people would guard and maintain its own system closely. One does find considerable variation, of course, but also a striking correspondence, especially in matters pertaining to divination. This correspondence does not merely obtain on a general level: it extends to the detail. Shared are such features as the division of the 260-day calendar into specific periods of time, the structure of the almanacs that pertain to these periods, the identity of the supernaturals and the elements associated with the different units of time, and the iconography and realms of these supernaturals. The correspondences are so many and so exact that it can be said that most of broader central Mexico (from the Gulf coast to Oaxaca) shared a single divinatory system.

The evidence for this Mesoamerican system appears primarily in the painted divinatory codices (the *tonalamatl*, literally "day books") of the Aztecs, Tlaxcalans, Mixtecs, and peoples of Puebla and Veracruz, as well as in a few textual accounts from the Colonial period that describe mantic themes, such as Sahagún's Book 4. Although these codices are painted in several different styles and come from different parts of Mesoamerica, their content is notably similar. The extant tonalamatl can be divided into two principal groups: the so-called "Aztec" divinatory codices and the manuscripts of the Borgia Group.

The Aztec divinatory codices include the Codex Borbonicus and Tonalamatl Aubin, (from the Valley of Mexico and Tlaxcala, respectively) that are painted in Precolumbian style on native paper, and the almanac sections of two cultural encyclopedias: the Codex Telleriano-Remensis (as well as its copy, the Vaticanus A/Ríos) and the Codex Tudela, which were both painted on European paper to explain the working of the Aztec tonalamatl to the Europeans.

The manuscripts of the Borgia Group have been grouped together partially because they were painted in the same general style, but primarily because they share much of the same content. The group is composed of five core members: the Codices Borgia (for which the group is named), Cospi, Fejérváry-Mayer, Laud, and Vaticanus B, to which can be added Aubin Manuscript No. 20 and the reverse side of the Codex Porfirio Díaz. All are hide documents, and all are screenfolds except Aubin 20, which is a single large panel; none have texts or glosses that explain the images. The provenience of these Borgia Group codices has been much debated ever since Eduard Seler grouped them together in 1887. Scholars have spoken of a "Borgia Group style" that is

Figure 27.15 Patron and elements governing the fifth trecena, Codex Borbonicus (p. 5). (After Seler 1904–1909:2: figure 221.)

distinct from the Aztec and Mixtec styles, but is still subsumed under Nicholson's (1960) all-encompassing Mixteca-Puebla horizon style or Robertson's (1970) international style of the Late Postclassic (chapter 23). It is clear, however, that the manuscripts fall into separate stylistic subgroupings and come from different places. Without presenting the detailed analyses here, it might suffice to note that the Borgia, Cospi, and Porfirio Díaz probably come from the corridor in Puebla that runs from Cholula and Huexotzingo to the Tehuacan Valley: the Cospi probably from near Cholula, the Borgia seemingly from the Tehuacan Valley, and the Porfirio Díaz more securely hailing from the Cuicatec area (Caso 1927; Nicholson 1960, 1966, 1994:113–114; Hunt 1978; Sisson 1983; Sisson and Lilly 1994b:37–44; Boone 1990; Uruñuela et al. 1994). The Fejérváry-Mayer and Laud are close stylistically to the Mixtec screenfolds, although costume elements and other features also link them to the Gulf Coast (Nicholson 1966; Anawalt 1981a). Aubin No. 20 is undoubtedly from the Mixteca, and the Vaticanus B is very probably a Mixtec document also (Nicholson 1966).

Thus the extant Postclassic Mexican divinatory codices (as opposed to the Maya ones) range from the Valley of Mexico, Tlaxcala, Puebla, Oaxaca, and possibly the Gulf Coast. They were painted by peoples who spoke Nahuatl, Mixtec, Cuicatec, and perhaps Chocho, and by peoples who were the bitter enemies of some of the others. Yet the contents of these manuscripts correspond closely with each other. Three examples provide a sense of the equivalence.

Figure 27.16 Patron and elements governing the fifth trecena, Tonalamatl Aubin (p. 5). (After Seler 1904–1909:2: figure 222.)

Figure 27.17 Patron and elements governing the fifth trecena, Codex Borgia (p. 65). (After Seler 1904–1909:3: plate 65.)

Figure 27.18 Patron and elements governing the fifth trecena, Codex Vaticanus B (p. 53). (After Seler 1904–1909:2: figure 219.)

TRECENA PATRONS: FIFTH TRECENA

One of the principal almanacs in the divinatory codices is the presentation of the 260-day tonalpohualli divided into 20 weeks of 13 days (or trecenas). In this almanac, the 13 day signs in each trecena are arranged in small compartments around the larger compartment that contains the trecena patrons as well as items that further qualify and characterize that period of time. The fifth trecena, beginning with the day 1 Reed, has Chalchihuitlicue ("Jade Her Skirt," goddess of groundwater) as its patron. The trecena is included in nearly identical fashion in the Codex Borbonicus (5), the Tonalamatl Aubin (5), the Codex Borgia (65), and the Codex Vaticanus B (53) (figures 27.15 to 27.18). In all, Chalchihuitlicue is pictured seated on a red throne spotted with disks symbolizing preciousness. Hanging from her neck is a long turquoise or jade collar with gold disks attached; she wears either a serpent headdress and white and red skirt and huipil (Borgia and Vaticanus B; figures 27.17, 26.18) or a blue, rubber-spattered headdress and blue-green shirt (Borbonicus; figure 27.15). The Vaticanus B and Borbonicus show her face painted red in an identical pattern. In all, water flows from her throne, carrying with it a small male, a small female, and a necklace of precious stones (Aubin, Borgia, Vaticanus B; figures 27.16, 27.17, 27.18). Other mantic elements in the panel include the symbol for war (either shield and spears or simply spears), a sacrificial platform, a box with a lid tied closed with cord, and a feather panache for a headdress. The contents of the Borgia and Vaticanus B representations are virtually identical, and the Aubin and Borbonicus are particularly close (sharing Toci's headdress of unspun cotton and an incense burner), but the Aubin shares more of the Borgia and

Vaticanus B elements than does the Borbonicus. Thus, there are differences in the four trecena panels, to be sure, but their similarities and shared elements are striking and indicate a unity of understanding about the forces governing this period of time.

THE FIVE CIHUATETEO

The five Cihuateteo (literally "goddesses," the souls of women who have died in childbirth) appear in the Borgia (47–48), Vaticanus B (77–79), and Aubin No. 20, where they are paired with the five *Macuilxochitls* (literally "Five Flower," usually associated with gaming, song, and dance, but also having solar associations). In the Borgia and Vaticanus B they accompany the trecenas commonly associated with the West (Cihuateteo) and the South (Macuilxochitls); in Aubin No. 20, each of the five pairs is associated with one of four cardinal directions and the center (the fifth). In all cases the Cihuateteo are linked to specific days (1 Deer, 1 Rain, 1 Monkey, 1 House, and 1 Eagle), and the Macuilxochitls are linked to other days (5 Lizard, 5 Buzzard, 5 Rabbit, 5 Flower, 5 Grass); additionally, they are paired the same way (1 Deer with

Figure 27.19 Marriage prognostication for day numbers totaling 18, Codex Laud 37, Codex Vaticanus B 35, Codex Borgia 58. (After Seler 1904–1909:2: figures 189, 190; vol. 3: plate 58.)

5 Lizard, 1 Rain with 5 Buzzard, 1 Monkey with 5 Rabbit, 1 House with 5 Flower, and 1 Eagle with 5 Grass).

Although Valley of Mexico sources do not specifically link the Cihuateteo and Macuilxochitls, both groups were important supernaturals in the Aztec realm. Sahagún's Florentine Codex pictures and describes

Macuilxochitl figures named 5 Flower, 5 Rabbit, and 5 Lizard, the latter being a standardbearer beside Huitzilopochtli's temple (Seler 1963:2:63–65). In the Valley of Mexico, the Cihuateteo were known to descend and cause harm to children on the days 1 Deer, 1 Rain, 1 Monkey, 1 House, and 1 Eagle (Sahagún 1959–1982, book 4:10, 41, 81, 93, 107), and sculpted images of the Cihuateteo found in Mexico City have one of these day names carved on the tops of their heads (see Nicholson and Quiñones Keber 1983:67–68). Thus, the Aztecs in the Valley of Mexico shared these specific minor supernaturals with the peoples in Puebla and Oaxaca.

MARRIAGE PROGNOSTICATIONS

A third example of shared ideology in the divinatory codices concerns the prognostications for marriage that appear in the Borgia, Laud, and Vaticanus B. The marriage almanac in these codices associates different images with the combined day numbers of the two individuals to be married, such that a man and woman whose birthdays are 12 Eagle and 6 Flower would have the prognostication of number 18, for example. In the three almanacs, the mantic scenes for number 18 feature a simply clad male and a bare-breasted female in association with a double-headed *coralillo* serpent and two vessels containing little jade elements that indicate the precious quality of the vessels' contents (figure 27.19). In the Laud and Vaticanus B, the coralillo is wrapped about the necks of the couple, whereas in the Borgia it is knotted around itself below. The Borgia couple also holds two small figures, perhaps a reference to twins, which would parallel the two precious vessels.

Another mantic scene, this one providing the fate for number 24, shows how a single basic message—infidelity on the part of the male—can be presented slightly differently (figure 27.20). In the Laud and Vaticanus B, the female holds a parrot or quetzal (potentially a symbol of preciousness) and faces the male, who holds a lizard; either he or the lizard is speaking. Since lizards could be associated with deceit, the implication is that the male is lying to his precious and presumably faithful wife; in the Vaticanus B the shield-and-spears symbol for war/conflict is painted at the top. The Borgia carries the same message but describes the deceit more graphically. On the left the wife has the quetzal tucked under her arm while she grasps her husband firmly by the hair. He twists awkwardly in space, moving away from his wife and toward the largely unclothed woman on the right, whose breast he grasps; he has clearly been caught in an adulterous affair. The coralillo tail that replaces his loincloth panel may refer to this infidelity, and the shield-and-spears motif painted above confirms the presence of conflict.

These various examples of parallel scenes and shared iconography in the divinatory codices reveal just how close the almanacs and prognosticatory messages were in

Figure 27.20 Marriage prognostication for day numbers totaling 24, Codex Laud 34, Codex Vaticanus B 33, Codex Borgia 59. (After Seler 1904–1909:1: figures 290a, b, c.)

the Valley of Mexico, Tlaxcala, Puebla, the Mixteca, and perhaps the Gulf Coast. The same almanacs appear in several of the codices, and their content is virtually the same throughout. Of the 27 almanacs in the Codex Borgia, all but two are also found in other codices. This sameness speaks of a single divinatory ideology that was widely shared throughout central Mexico.

THE MAYA CONNECTION

The Maya codices stand apart from the Mexican ones, belonging to another graphic and ideological world. Although the extant Maya codices are largely divinatory, their almanacs are structured differently than the Mexican ones, and they feature distinct texts, in the form of glyph blocks, that pair with images. Many Maya almanacs are topic specific, pertaining to such actions as

Figure 27.21 Xiuhtecuhtli in the Codex Dresden (p. 49). (After Taube and Bade 1991:14.)

beekeeping (cleaning hives, gathering honey, and so on), hunting, agriculture, and craft production (such as carving masks). The Maya codices also have astronomical tables that track celestial events forward and backward over long stretches of time; such tables are not a normal feature of Mexican codices. The Maya codices are in general so different from the Mexican ones that correspondences between them are noticeable. Such correspondences are few, but they show that the Maya were attuned to Mexican divinatory and religious traditions, and referenced or borrowed from them on occasion. Mexican features are apparent in the Codex Dresden, Codex Grolier, and Codex Madrid.

CODEX DRESDEN

It has long been noted that the Venus almanac in the Dresden (24, 46–50) pictures Mexican deities in two of its five compartments: the fire/year god Xiuhtecuhtli (figure 27.21) and the "blindfold" god Ixmiquilli (Thompson 1971:220, 1972:68–69). More recently, it has been pointed out that the hieroglyphic texts that accompany these illustrations and the previous one give phonetic soundings for Nahuatl deity names (Riese 1982; Whittaker 1986:57; Taube and Bade 1991). Thus the Dresden artists struggled to represent in Maya hieroglyphs the names Tlahuizcalpantecuhtli, Xiuhtecuhtli, and Cactonal (?). The Dresden artists did not change the structure of their Venus almanac, nor did they change its general iconography or meaning; rather, they inserted Nahuatl deities among their own.

CODEX GROLIER

Mexican elements are also present in the Venus almanac that composes the entire Grolier Codex (figure 27.22). The figures pertaining to the different phases of Venus are a blend of Maya and Mexican conventions and

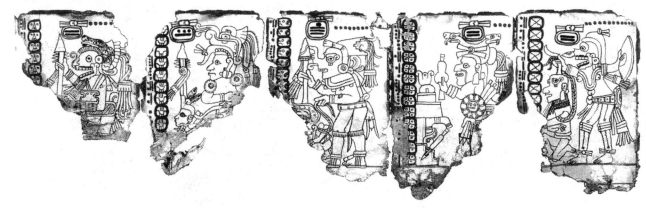

Figure 27.22 Codex Grolier (pp. 2–6). (After Coe 1973.)

elements (Coe 1973:151). Mexican elements that Coe identified as Toltec or Maya-Toltec traits include back shields and knee fringes, ruffled padding on one or both arms, Mexican atlatls and triangular dart points, and skulls with knives protruding from the nasal opening. Pointing out other Mexican resemblances, including the rendering of the double-headed serpent, Coe argued that the Grolier was particularly similar to the codices Fejérváry-Mayer and Laud.

In its use of numbers, the Grolier also varies from other Maya codices and looks toward Mexican usage, although the systems are garbled. Above each figure are a row of dots and a bar-and-dot number within a ring (looking exactly like a ring number typical of the Dresden). However, such a quantity of dots greater than four would not have been tolerated in the purely Maya system, for the traditional Maya would have used bars for quantities of five. These dots are to be read in the

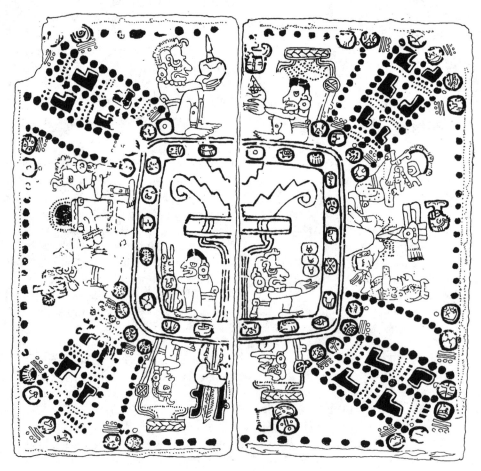

Figure 27.23 The 260-day cycle organized as a cross oriented to the four directions, Codex Madrid (pp. 75–76). (After Villacorta and Villacorta 1977:374–376.)

Figure 27.24 The 260-day cycle organized as a cross oriented to the four directions, Codex Fejérváry-Mayer (p. 1). (After 1971 edition.)

Grolier as representing 20 units each, and the "ring numbers" function as the extra quantities added to the multiples of 20. This combination of numbers gives the canonical duration of each phase of Venus; thus they function like the "spacers" that stand in for unpictured day signs in the Borgia Group codices but are absent from purely Maya almanacs. Thus, in painting style, deity iconography, and numeration, the Grolier Codex is an eclectic blend of Maya and Mexican features. Michael Coe (1973:151) hazarded a guess that it came from "some cosmopolitan trading center in the lowlands, most likely the great commercial port of Xicalango in Campeche."

CODEX MADRID

Although it contains fewer Mexican features than the stylistic hybrid that is the Grolier, the Madrid Codex has two Mexican-style almanacs of the kind found in the Borgia Group codices (V. Bricker n.d.). The best-known of the two is the "cosmogram" painted on pages 75–76, where the 260 days of the tzolkin/tonalpohualli are arranged in a Formeé Cross (often called a Maltese Cross) according to the four directions, each line of the cross composed of a 13-day trecena (figure 27.23). Gods and a sacrificial scene mark the four directions. This almanac, which represents such a departure from other Maya almanacs, is cognate with the famous first page of

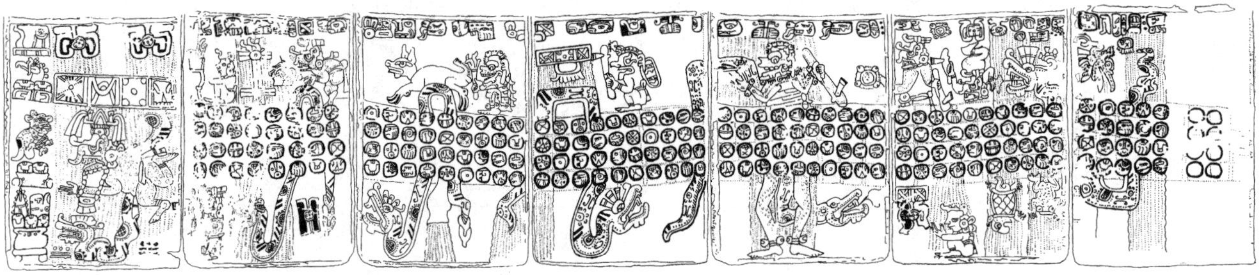

Figure 27.25 Serpent almanac in the Codex Madrid (pp. 112b–118b). (After Villacorta and Villacorta 1977:248–260.)

the Fejérváry-Mayer (figure 27.24), and it must be derived from a central Mexican source.

The so-called Serpent Almanac on Madrid 12b–18b also deviates from other Maya almanacs in its structure, calendrics, and iconography (figure 27.25). Following Bricker, Bryan Just (2000, n.d.) has recently shown how it is patterned after the "in-extenso" almanacs that open the codices Borgia, Cospi, and Vaticanus B, where the 260 days of the tonalpohualli are spread out in five long rows of 65 days each. Bricker et al. (1997:S28) note that the first Chac in this almanac wears the Mexican A-O sign in his headdresses, and Victoria Bricker (personal communication) notes that this Chac also has curled teeth in the Mexican style (cited in Just n.d.). The presence of these two almanacs in the Madrid does not make it a mixed codex like the Grolier, but it does indicate that the Madrid painter was aware of central Mexican divinatory almanacs and appreciated the mantic possibilities of their structure.

The Mexican elements in the Dresden, Madrid, and Grolier suggest that they were painted for three different audiences that had adjusted to or adopted Mexican ideology to varying degrees. The Nahuatl gods and their names in the Dresden are fully embraced within a Maya divinatory codex, and they are treated in the Maya manner. This suggests that the book's audience was Maya, but Maya who were familiar with Mexican gods and their realms, and may have appreciated the spice of added Mexican gods in their Venus almanac. The Madrid is also oriented to a Maya readership, but one that probably had firsthand familiarity with Mexican divinatory codices. The Madrid artist must have himself seen and handled codices of the Borgia Group type, and his audience was flexible enough to adopt foreign almanac forms to suit their own divinatory needs. The Grolier likely came from a mixed culture, where Maya and Mexican languages were spoken, and where Maya and Mexican ideological traditions were enmeshed. The awkward use of pseudo "ring numbers" and the dots representing quantities of 20—which is so at odds with both Maya and Mexican practice—suggests that the artist was working in a cultural frontier zone, far from the hearts of the two traditions, but where their edges

mixed. Coe may be right in guessing that its town of origin might be Xicalango on the southern Gulf coast, where Aztec pochteca often traded.

A WEB OF UNDERSTANDING

This chapter has examined a number of ideological elements that were differentially shared by peoples in various regions of Late Postclassic Mesoamerica. Most pertain to the ideological and artistic realms, and all are evidenced in pictorial codices from different areas. The range of these elements—the Aztec painting style, the annals history, cave origins, the culture hero 9 Wind/Quetzalcoatl, rituals and symbols pertaining to rulership, and details of the calendrically based divinatory system—suggests that a vast and diverse body of shared knowledge bound many Mesoamerican peoples together.

The peoples who shared these elements spoke different languages, worshipped different deities, had their own distinctive rituals, and lived and worked under different political systems. They thought of themselves as Mexica, Tlaxcala, Cempoalla, Mixteca, Cuicateca, Tlapaneca, and Maya (the Maya further distinguishing themselves ethnically and linguistically). Their differential choices to reject, accommodate, adjust, or adopt the ways of others were surely linked to the economic and social ties they had with those others, and also how powerful those others were.

The Triple Alliance empire, from its center in Tenochtitlan, dominated the ideological network of much of Postclassic Mesoamerica and shaped its character and extent. In building their own ideological and iconographic system, the Aztecs had looked within and outside their realm for goods, customs, and ideas, which they reshaped to fit their needs. Then, as Aztec representatives moved throughout the empire, they carried these ideas and customs with them. The peoples who came under direct political, tributary, and/or economic control of the Triple Alliance empire were forced officially to come to terms with Aztec systems and the Aztecs themselves. As exampled here, they chose to adopt a wide range of Aztec elements and ideas. Other peoples, such as the Maya, who remained outside the Triple Alliance empire but still participated in the Postclassic world system, embraced much fewer Mexican elements because they dealt with the Aztecs in different and more selective ways.

Embedded in the minds of travelers and recorded in their codices, ideology and customs spread across Mesoamerica. Human memories held perspectives and beliefs, and the specifics of ideology came painted in the books. Although some books were economic, others preserved the details of history, prescribed correct ritual, and revealed the mantic associations of time. The phrase "in tlilli in tlapalli" (the red, the black) was the metaphor for writing and the codices; it was also the metaphor for knowledge. In Mesoamerica, the books were the principal permanent containers of knowledge. These containers of knowledge had the additional benefit of easy portability, and the pictorial nature of the central Mexican codices (those spanning the Aztec to Mixtec realms) meant that they could be understood by anyone who shared knowledge of Mexican pictography, regardless of native language. As the painted books and their readers spread across and beyond the Triple Alliance empire, they carried customs and ideologies with them, creating a web of understanding in Postclassic Mesoamerica.

Part 5

Regional Case Studies

28

Themes in World-System Regions

Frances F. Berdan

The chapters in part 5 look at the Postclassic Meso-american world system from a different angle: whereas parts 1 through 4 delineate functional aspects of the world system, this section explores the roles of specific regions within the broader system. The purpose of including these case studies is to highlight regional and cultural variation within the world system, and to examine regional developments in the light of world-system processes.

MAJOR THEMES IN OUR REGIONAL SELECTION

Because the Postclassic world system included the entire area of Mesoamerica, all parts were in some sense important to the functioning of the world system. It is not feasible, however, to discuss every region, so we have guided our selection of the regional case studies that follow based on two factors. First, we have tried to include regions from most of our spatial categories—core zones, affluent production zones, and the like. Second, we have focused on regions that have the most complete archaeological and ethnohistorical evidence. There is no case study from an unspecialized peripheral zone, partly because these areas tend to be among the most poorly documented regions for the Postclassic period. Nevertheless, the chapters that follow do illustrate the overall processes of Postclassic Mesoamerica in many of the important regions.

While each region exhibits unique characteristics, and each author presents a particular perspective, the case studies collectively demonstrate some common concerns and patterns. Predominant among these are (1) relationships between cores and peripheries, (2) the interplay between internal and external processes, and (3) processes of change and forces for continuity during the Postclassic in Mesoamerica.

RELATIONSHIPS BETWEEN CORES AND PERIPHERIES
As emphasized in the first three chapters, the world-systems approach in this book does not conform comfortably to the traditional model of world-systems theory in terms of core/periphery relations. Not only do we find multiple competing cores, we also find that so-called peripheries were not so exploited as the standard model would predict. There is, of course, considerable variability in these patterns, as the following case studies demonstrate. Differences can be seen, for instance, between the more centrally controlled Tarascan empire (chapter 29) and the more internally competitive Basin of Mexico (chapter 30). In the former, the Tarascan core established and maintained controls over important resource-procurement zones and demonstrated a unified political economy (with muted commercialization), state religion, and ethnic identity. In the Basin of Mexico, the transformation from an affluent production zone to a core was signaled by increased commercialization and the strengthening of elite power already well established in a multitude of basin city-states.

While economic forces are notable in the formation and maintenance of cores, other factors also come into play. Pohl (chapter 31) emphasizes the role of elite inter-marriage in ensuring and expanding political interests, whether an area is defined as a core or an affluent production zone. A focus on two other affluent production zones reveals additional insights into core/periphery dynamics. Smith (chapter 32) argues that Aztec conquerors provided imperial support for subject rulerships in Morelos, in the sense that imperial conquest allowed local rulers to expand their own tribute base. In contrast to the traditional core/periphery model, this suggests that elites outside the core took some advantage of their conquered position (at the expense of their own commoners, of course). In northern Belize (chapter 34), emulation of core religious practices and symbolism suggests a similar pattern: the use of core power attributes in a strengthening of elite controlling outlying regions. Collectively, these case studies reveal dynamic, variable relations between cores and peripheries.

THE INTERPLAY BETWEEN
INTERNAL AND EXTERNAL PROCESSES

Related to core/periphery relations is the interplay between internal and external processes within the Postclassic Mesoamerican world system. While some of these relations involve cores and peripheries, it is important to emphasize that Mesoamerican polities were involved in intricate webs of interaction: affluent production zones interacted with affluent production zones; resource-procurement zones interacted with international trade centers; international trading centers interacted with affluent production zones, and so on—all without a required mediation of a core (although, of course, cores were actively involved in these webs).

Internal and external processes took many forms and had variable consequences. On a regional level, a clear distinction existed between wetland and inland communities in Soconusco in terms of hierarchical relations and wealth distribution that was significant within Soconusco but also responded to changes beyond the region (chapter 35). For the Tarascan realm, Pollard (chapter 29) suggests that the interplay between internal forces of state formation and increased interaction with other parts of Mesoamerica reinforced the centrality of the Tarascan state. The Basin of Mexico responded to different, more commercial forces and exhibited a receptivity for "things foreign" (chapter 30). Commercial forces extended to Morelos where, by the Late Postclassic, even humble households had access to far-ranging exotic goods (chapter 32). In addition, at Chikinchel in northern Yucatán, the effects of increased specialized salt production (for export) included a need to satisfy local requirements for essential domestic goods from outside sources (chapter 33). External forces influencing the Basin of Mexico included the ready adoption of foreign styles, and central Mexican influence on distant K'iche'an elites in the Guatemalan highlands resulted in culturally hybrid elites with exotic symbolic advantages over their own subjects, and an enhanced set of commonalities with their powerful central Mexican counterparts (chapter 36). Intermar-

riage was an abiding source of intercultural and interpolitical interaction, as emphasized by Pohl in chapter 31.

PROCESSES OF CHANGE AND FORCES FOR CONTINUITY

The regions of Mesoamerica were far from static during the Postclassic. Political fortunes waxed and waned, borders shifted, commercial relations flourished and faltered, and once-strategic centers became insignificant. Archaeologically, these dynamics are often best seen in the economic arena. In Late Postclassic-B Morelos, changes in the occurrence and distribution of imported goods suggest a decline in the standard of living accompanied by greater similarities between elites and commoners. Furthermore, some volatility in Morelos "trading partners" is evidenced in changes in the sources of imported ceramics and obsidian (chapter 32). Similar shifts in exchange networks are reported for Chikinchel (chapter 33) and Soconusco (chapter 35). Greater production stability, albeit with an overall increase in production and trade, can be seen in Postclassic northern Belize (chapter 34).

In some cases, affluent production zones were transformed into cores (chapters 29, 30). In other cases, resource-procurement zones gained or lost importance in the broader scheme; both salt from Chikinchel and cacao from Soconusco enjoyed the upswing (chapters 33, 35). Strategies of establishing and maintaining power were at times derived from beyond one's own region, and access to those strategies changed over time (chapters 31, 36).

OTHER REGIONAL ISSUES

The chapters in part 4 touch on a number of issues other than those already mentioned. These include (1) patterns of resource acquisition and distribution (chapters 29, 30, 32–35), (2) shifts in demography and settlement patterns (chapters 29, 32, 34, 35), (3) language and ethnicity (chapters 29, 30, 31, 36), and (4) sources of power (chapters 31, 36).

Although not every region of Mesoamerica can be represented here in a case study, those included offer an interesting comparative base in the context of the Postclassic Mesoamerican world system. They address a consistent set of topics and deal with different types of units within the world system. A discussion of the integration of these units and regions follows, in part 6.

29

Development of a Tarascan Core

The Lake Pátzcuaro Basin

Helen Perlstein Pollard

During the Postclassic period a major sociopolitical transformation occurred in central Michoacán resulting in the emergence of a new core region in central Mexico. This transformation involved the development of the first unified state to dominate the Lake Pátzcuaro basin, which was rapidly converted into the geopolitical center of an expanding conquest empire (chapter 13). Unlike other Postclassic Mexican cores, central Michoacán did not have a heritage of powerful city-states and empires. Instead, the region had been peripheral to the political economies of the Classic and Early Postclassic periods. By the early sixteenth century, however, the empire and the royal dynasty ruling from the Pátzcuaro Basin had become powerful forces in the Mesoamerican world. This transformation, and its impact on the Tarascan people, is known to us from the documentary record of the sixteenth century and, to a lesser extent, from the archaeological record.

This chapter focuses on the impact of this transformation on the communities of the Tarascan geopolitical core, the Lake Pátzcuaro basin. However, the region immediately encircling the basin, including the Zacapu Basin, was integral to its political economy and was part of the Tarascan ethnic heartland (Pollard 1993:100); it could thus be considered part of this west Mexican core. Therefore, data available from this larger region will be used to supplement that from Pátzcuaro. The region's basic chronology is derived from two recent projects in the Pátzcuaro and Zacapu basins; only that from the Pátzcuaro Basin currently distinguishes a Middle Postclassic, and it will be used here (see table 1.1).

Evidence from sediment cores, trenches, and wells studied in the Pátzcuaro, Zacapu, and Cuitzeo basins suggests that during the Late Urichu phase, lake levels were at their lowest since the Early Preclassic (2500 B.C.), and that during the Tariacuri phase they had returned to Classic-period high levels. These dates, based on the location of sites in the southwest portion of the Pátzcuaro Basin, the lowest (in elevation) of which date to the Early—Middle Postclassic, are toward the later end of the potential low lake level episode indicated in work based on sediment cores (A.D. 600–1100 [O'Hara et al. 1993]).

REGIONAL DEMOGRAPHY AND SETTLEMENT PATTERNS

Demographic and settlement trends within the Tarascan core can be documented from regional archaeological surveys in the Zacapu and Pátzcuaro basins. In the Zacapu Basin the Postclassic begins with an increase from 61 to 96 sites (Arnauld and Faugère-Kalfon 1998:16) and a shift from primarily lakeshore occupation to marked increases in sites located in the *malpaís* (the "badlands," a partially eroded lava flow) above Zacapu and the uplands toward the Lerma. In the Early Postclassic, the site of El Palacio was the first occupied and appears to have been the largest, with the most public architecture. In general, settlement appears to maximize three factors: access to agricultural land, defensive position, and continued development of the nearby obsidian mines of Zináparo. Sunken patios disappear from public architecture and are replaced by square rooms with columns and covered porticos reminiscent of La Quemada.

The Late Postclassic phase includes 83 sites—a drop in numbers that comes from the abandonment of sites immediately adjacent to the Zináparo obsidian mines. There is an increase in sites along the southern lakeshore associated with intensification of agriculture, and on the malpaís the density of settlement increases to urban levels: up to 20,000 people are estimated to have inhabited

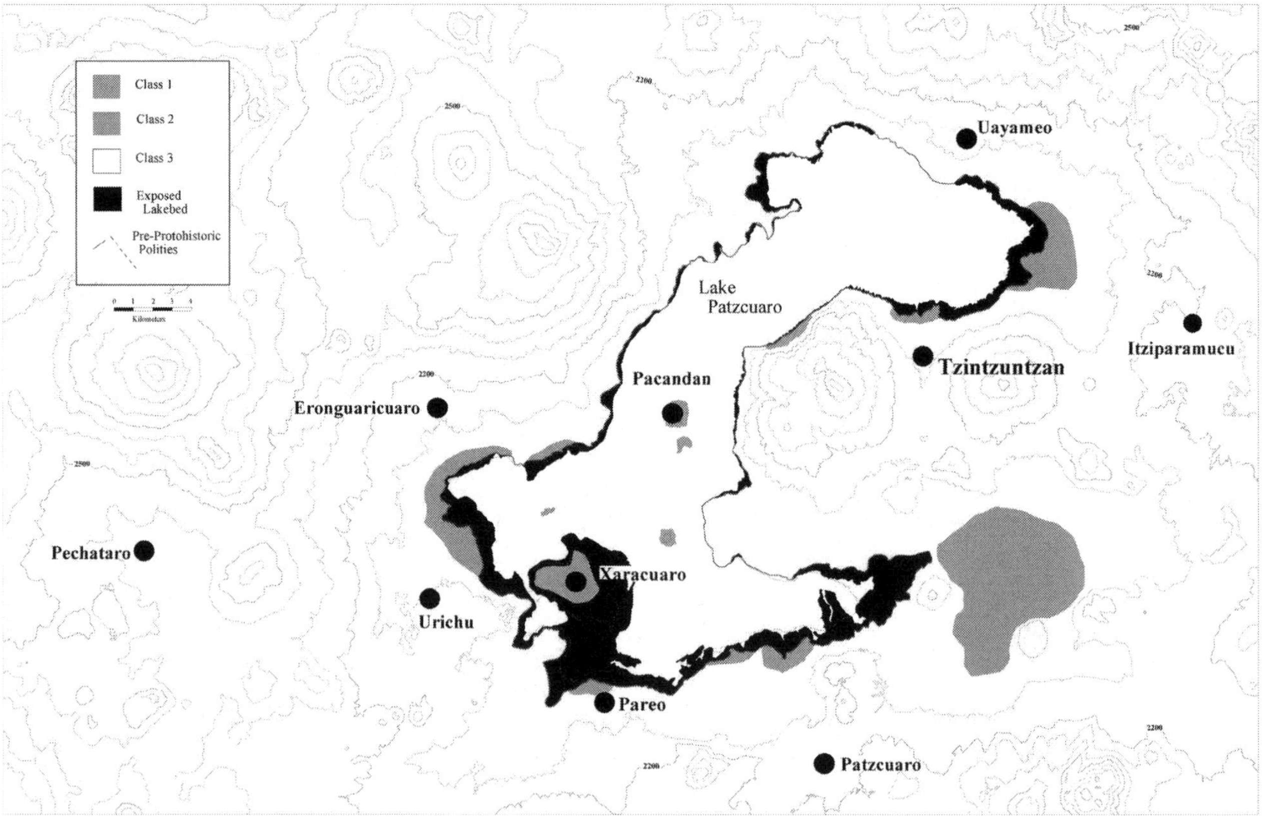

Figure 29.1 The Lake Pátzcuaro basin

the 13 sites covering 5 km² (Migeon 1998). The sites themselves include multiple barrios, each with public centers dominated by yácatas, with one plaza complex larger than the others. Michelet (1995) interprets this as reflecting relatively rapid movement of individual communities on to the malpaís, clustering together for defensive purposes, and shortly thereafter (A.D. 1250) each reorganizing under the control of a single authority.

The highest concentration of sixteenth-century documents pertains to the Pátzcuaro Basin (figure 29.1), as most were recorded in the Tarascan capital, Tzintzuntzan, located in the basin. Based on those documents and targeted survey, Gorenstein and Pollard (1983) identified 90 to 95 settlements dating to the Late Postclassic period. The total basin population is estimated to have been ca. 80,000 in 1522 (Gorenstein and Pollard 1983). Tzintzuntzan (901 ha) contained ca. 35,000 people (Pollard 1977), with secondary and tertiary administrative centers of 5,000–15,000 people located throughout the basin, including Erongarícuaro (250–300 ha), Ihuatzio (125 ha), Pátzcuaro (ca. 100 ha), and Urichu (>90 ha) (Pollard 1980, 1995). A number of communities were functionally differentiated, and settlements varied considerably in their area and population. There was general congruence between the location of elite families and administrative centers, but as table 29.1 indicates, this was not the case for other settlement functions. While the four largest settlements (Tzintzuntzan, Erongarícuaro, Pátzcuaro, and Ihuatzio) all had some specialized functions, there was no direct relationship between number of functions and population size. Indeed, only Tzintzuntzan was sufficiently differentiated to contain all community functions, making it a regional primate center on the basis of not only population size, but also on its overwhelming control of all other functional hierarchies.

Recent survey of 143 km² of the southwest portion of the basin provides the only diachronic information relevant to settlement and demography. As in other highland lake basins of Michoacán, settlement from Preclassic through Epiclassic times was generally lacustrine in orientation and widely scattered in small communities. Deeply buried evidence of canal irrigation associated with a Classic-period community, located above one of the marshes, documents more-intensive use of resources during a period of fluctuating lake levels (Fisher et al. 1999). Excavations at the site of Urichu (figure 29.2) revealed the presence of local elites during the Classic and Epiclassic periods (Pollard 1995). During the Early Postclassic, the number of sites increased, with almost a doubling of hectares occupied. In the Middle Postclassic, the number of sites increased again, and the area of occupation again doubled. A large proportion of the new sites were located on newly exposed islands and on fertile la-

Table 29.1
Central place functions of towns in the Lake Pátzcuaro basin

Town	Administrative Center	Resident Elite	Religious Center	Markets
Tzintzuntzan	X	X	X	X
Erongarícuaro	X	X		
Pechátaro	X	X		
Urichu	X	X		
Pareo	X	X		X
Pacandan-Xaracuaro	X	X	X	
Xaracuaro		X	X	
Itziparamucu	X	X		
Uayameo	X	X		
Pátzcuaro	X	X	X	
Ihuatzio		X	X	
Itzicuaro			X	
Ahterio			X	
Asajo				X

Sources: Data are from Pollard 1980; Gorenstein and Pollard 1983.

custrine soil exposed by the episode of lake regression. By the Late Postclassic these low-lying sites were flooded, and settlement shifted to the new lakeshore and to areas of high agricultural fertility back from the lakeshore. The number of sites and area occupied again doubled, including the maximum expansion of Urichu (>90 ha), Pareo (>45 ha), the entire exposed island of Xaracuaro, and densely occupied towns with public architecture at Tócuaro, Arócutin, Charahuén, and Ajuno (Axuni).

The data from all surveyed regions suggest that population density was highest during the Late Postclassic, and that the largest and most populous settlements within any single region, whether ceremonial centers or cities, also date to the Late Postclassic. Not all of this population growth was necessarily due to macroregional population increases. There is some evidence for population movement into the Pátzcuaro Basin from the Zacapu region, as well as a shift in population within the Zacapu Basin from the north to the south. Both suggest that the political and economic power of the state had a centripetal effect on settlement patterns, especially in the relocation of regional elites into the capital. The evidence from Huandacareo (Cuitzeo Basin) and Zirizícuaro (east of Uruapan)—single-period Tarascan administrative centers—suggests that where there were not already major population centers, Tarascans constructed public spaces to display state administration, justice, and ritual, and to bury local and imperial leaders.

LAND USE, RESOURCES, AND ECONOMIC EXCHANGE

Within the Pátzcuaro Basin intensive agriculture was practiced on lands that could be irrigated, and agricultural terraces were constructed on hillslopes between Tzintzuntzan and Ihuatzio. There is no evidence that chinampa agricultural plots were constructed along the lakeshore, and the relatively high lake levels during these centuries reduced the availability of exposed lacustrine soils along the lakeshore. Evidence of settlement location and soil erosion suggests this was a time of clearance of Class II and some Class III land back from the lakeshore (table 29.2). (Class I land is permanently or seasonally

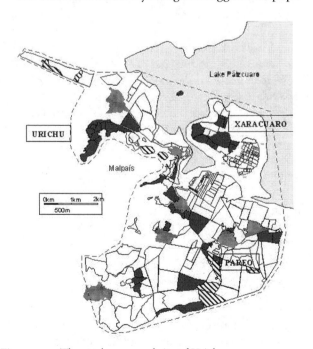

Figure 29.2 The study area and site of Urichu

Table 29.2
Late Postclassic agricultural potential of the Lake Pátzaro Basin

Land Class	Hectares	Productivity[a]	Fallow Cycle	Percentage of Total Land
Ia	321	2,200	1	0.4
Ib	212	2,000	1	0.2
II	11,922	1,000	1:2	13.0
III	29,600	450	1:4	32.0
Forest	36,045			39.0
Marsh	1,190			1.3
Open Water	13,600			15.0

Source: Data are from Gorenstein and Pollard 1983: appendixes 1–4; see original source for full discussion.
[a]Productivity is expressed in kg maize per hectare.

irrigated along the lakeshore; Class II land is the alluvial floor of the basin, farmed by rainfall agriculture; Class III land is on the lower slopes of the basin with relatively thin soils, also farmed by rainfall agriculture.)

Given the increasingly dense occupation during the Late Postclassic, which intensified during an episode of lake transgression when the water level rose and low-lying land was flooded, new economic mechanisms were required to support local populations. That is, by the Early Postclassic, lake levels had begun to fall, and they appear to have reached their lowest levels during the Middle Postclassic, opening up large tracts of fertile lacustrine soil. By A.D. 1300 lake levels began to rise again, forcing lakeshore communities and fields to be abandoned (O'Hara 1993; O'Hara et al. 1993; Fisher et al. 1999). By calculating the annual dietary needs of the estimated Lake Postclassic population, it is possible to determine indirectly the ability of the basin to support its population. To that end, I proposed a hypothetical Late Postclassic Tarascan diet based on foods consumed in the basin in the early sixteenth century, and weighted in significance according to ethnohistoric evidence and ethnographic diets (Pollard 1982; Pollard and Gorenstein 1980; Gorenstein and Pollard 1983).

With the estimated population of the Basin in 1522, and given the proposed diet, it was possible to determine the quantity of basic food resources needed to sustain the core Tarascans. For a population between 60,000 and 100,000 persons, the following foodstuffs would be consumed annually: 13,140,000–21,900,000 kg of maize/amaranth; 1,920,000–3,200,000 kg of beans; 1,560,000–2,600,000 kg of fish; and 624,000–1,040,000 kg of meat (primarily deer, rabbit, duck, and turkey). By determining the Late Postclassic land-use zones, including the open water, marsh, agricultural, and forest resources (see table 29.2), the maximum productivity of the basin for these products was calculated. When these figures—expressed either as kilograms produced per year or as numbers of people who could be supported—were compared to population needs, it became clear that the basin

would have been unable to produce sufficient maize/amaranth. The deficit was large, and between 25 percent and 55 percent of the maize consumed in the basin must have been imported. Beans were consumed in smaller quantities, and the basin was either able to produce a slight surplus of this item or, if the population was above 70,000, was importing up to 27 percent of its needs. The figures for meat are notably equivocal but suggest a deficit relationship of some unknown size. Of the basic resources consumed, only fish clearly produced a surplus, with up to 62 percent of the harvestable crop available for export (for more detail, see Gorenstein and Pollard 1983).

Other basic goods produced in the basin included wood products (especially firewood and lumber), basketry, mats, ceramics, and basalt tools. However, the basin naturally lacked salt, obsidian, chert, and lime—all products used by most households in the Late Postclassic period. It also lacked a wide range of elite goods. It is clear that the core of the Tarascan state in 1520 was not a viable autonomous economic unit. It existed, even thrived, only through the exchange of goods and services in regional and supraregional patterns. Goods and services were imported and exported through local and regional markets and various state institutions (chapter 13). Both the type and quantity of goods imported varied within the Pátzcuaro Basin by social class and community.

CHANGES IN PRODUCTION AND EXCHANGE

The most abundant information about Tarascan society after the state formed comes from historic and ethnohistoric records, but the best means of monitoring the impact of state formation on communities, and the emergence of a new core region, comes from the archaeological record. From this record it is possible to observe changes in the sources of raw materials and finished products used in communities of central Michoacán. Changes in production and economic exchange will be described by a focus on four artifact classes that provide

Table 29.3
Obsidian sources for sites in the Lake Pátzcuaro basin, by phase

Obsidian Source	Phase				
	Loma Alto	Lupe–La Joya	Early Urichu	Late Urichu	Tariacuri
Pénjamo-1					3
Zináparo-Varal	40	14	19	9	67
Cerro Prieto					1
Ucareo	8	1	4	1	315
Cruz Negra			1		1
Zinapécuaro			4		30
Pachuca-1	2	1	3		24
Zacualtipan		2	1		
Pizarrin					1
Puebla Sources					5
Unknown					22
Total pieces analyzed	50	18	32	10	469

Sources: Data are from Pollard and Vogel 1994; Pollard et al. 1998.

relevant information: (1) obsidian artifacts from the Pátzcuaro, Zacapu, and Uruapan-area drainages; (2) shell artifacts from the Pátzcuaro, Zacapu, and Cuitzeo basins; (3) metal artifacts from the Pátzcuaro and Sayula basins; and (4) ceramics from the Pátzcuaro Basin.

OBSIDIAN

Within the borders of the Tarascan empire were two extensive zones of obsidian: the Zinapécuaro-Ucareo zone in northeastern Michoacán, and the Zináparo zone in north-central Michoacán. Both were used by Prehispanic populations from the Preclassic to Colonial periods (chapter 20; see also Darras 1998; Healan 1997). Apart from the mines themselves, evidence of change in the consumption and exchange of obsidian within the Tarascan core comes from several sites within the Pátzcuaro Basin, and from comparisons with the Zacapu Basin to the northwest and the upper Marqués drainage (south of Uruapan) to the southwest.

Pátzcuaro Basin.

In 1987 almost 400 obsidian artifacts from the Late Postclassic Tarascan capital of Tzintzuntzan were analyzed by X-ray fluorescence (XRF). That analysis found that more than 94 percent of the gray-black obsidian artifacts came from the Zinapécuaro-Ucareo source zone, that the closer Zináparo source zone was used selectively for red and clear obsidians, and that small numbers of obsidians, primarily green prismatic blades, were imported from outside the borders of the Tarascan empire (Pollard and Vogel 1994a). Based on the intrasite distribution of obsidian artifacts and debitage at Tzintzuntzan and ethnohistoric data, it was suggested that obsidian from within

the empire was distributed through regional marketing systems, and that material from outside the imperial borders was acquired by long-distance merchants under the direct control of the royal dynasty.

In 1997, 198 obsidian artifacts from the excavation collections from the sites of Urichu and Xaracuaro, and surface survey collections from the sites of Urichu, Xaracuaro, and Pareo were analyzed by instrumental neutron activation (INA) at the University of Missouri nuclear reactor for the purpose of determining their sources (Pollard et al. 1998). This second analysis of artifacts from the Lake Pátzcuaro basin was designed to determine (1) whether the dominance of Ucareo obsidian observed at Tzintzuntzan during the Late Postclassic under the centralized state was also true at other basin centers under the state; (2) whether there was a shift in obsidian sources associated with the emergence of the state; (3) whether the specialized role of Zináparo-area obsidians found at Tzintzuntzan characterized other settlements; and (4) whether non-Michoacán obsidians are from similar quarries and in similar proportions outside the capital during the Late Postclassic and for periods before the emergence of the centralized state, when they were acquired by state-sponsored long-distance merchants.

This analysis (table 29.3) suggests four results. First, unlike the results from the Tzintzuntzan collection, in all phases the primary source of obsidian is Zináparo-Varal (50–90 percent). Second, in two of the three areas of the site of Urichu, during the Late Postclassic, Ucareo is the primary source of obsidian. Yet among the gray-black obsidian, Ucareo is not as dominant, and Zináparo-Varal is the second most important source. Third, the samples from the Epiclassic and Early and Middle Postclassic (Lupe—La Joya, Early and Late Urichu phases) contain very little Ucareo obsidian, although they do include Cruz Negra and Zinapécuaro obsidian from the same flow area during the Middle Postclassic. At Urichu the Ucareo obsidian comes only from elite residential deposits. This is the period when Ucareo obsidian is dominating other markets, including the urban center of Tula. Finally, there is a marked increase in prismatic blades (including prismatic blade cores) in the Late Postclassic following the emergence of the Tarascan state, but it is not universal, even for the elite centers sampled. The increase in the proportion of prismatic blades to flakes (the only measure that can be tracked with the sampled material) is noted at all excavated areas of Urichu, at Pareo, but not at the island polity of Xaracuaro (also sampled from excavated collections). In all phases except the Early Urichu, the majority of prismatic blades are from Ucareo, with the second most common source being Pachuca-1 (for more details see Pollard et al. 1998).

These data suggest that the pattern of obsidian procurement observed at the Tarascan capital, Tzintzuntzan, was not characteristic of the Lake Pátzcuaro basin as a whole, even during the Late Postclassic period. Ucareo obsidian, dominant at the capital, is a prominent source at only one of the three elite centers sampled, and is never prominent in periods before the emergence of the centralized state. This suggests that the differential distribution of Ucareo obsidian at the capital, and its significance at Urichu—associated in both cases with prismatic blade technology—may be due less to market exchange than to direct intervention by the state. Thus, in contrast to what has been written (Pollard 1993), there is good evidence to suspect that indeed the Tarascan central dynasty directly controlled either the Ucareo obsidian mines or the distribution of prismatic blades from the mines.

The pattern of distribution of the Zinaparo obsidians, including Cerro Varal and Cerro Zinaparo (and, in one case, Cerro Prieto) is also distinct from that of the capital. These obsidians are dominant for all phases prior to formation of the state, and dominant at Xaracuaro under the state. As the source area closest to the Lake Pátzcuaro basin, this pattern is the expected result of market exchange.

Finally, in all phases there are small quantities of obsidian from sources outside of Michoacán. All of the yellow-green obsidian was from Pachuca-1, primarily in the form of prismatic blades, with a dark green obsidian from Pénjamo-1. All, however, were from the Mesa Central of central and west Mexico, and were probably obtained through long-distance merchants. These nonlocal sources appear to have been fewer in number and closer in distance to the Pátzcuaro Basin than those represented at Tzintzuntzan. Thus, the emergence of state-sponsored long-distance merchants may have led to a larger number

of sources being represented, but the greater variety was distributed primarily in the capital.

Zacapu Basin

During the Late Preclassic—Early Classic (Loma Alta phase) 95 percent of the gray obsidian in the Zacapu Basin is believed to have come from the Zinaparo complex, and the only prismatic blades in this basin came from either Pachuca or Zinapécuaro-Ucareo (Darras, visual inspection, personal communication, 1998, and 1998:82). In the Late Classic and Epiclassic periods (Jarácuaro and Lupe phases) almost all prismatic blades disappear, including from the burials where they had been found earlier (and where they are still found in the Pátzcuaro Basin), and the gray obsidian continues coming from the Zinaparo complex. Darras believes that during the Early Postclassic a new technology was first used at the then-enlarged Zinaparo mining complex to produce percussion blades. Moreover, she believes that prismatic blades were only produced from Cerro Varal obsidian in the Middle—Late Postclassic, when most of the residential settlement in the mining complex zone had been abandoned (Darras 1998:83). Thus she associates the emergence of ground-platform prismatic blade technology in the Zacapu Basin with the emergence of the Tarascan state. Given the high levels of prismatic blade production at the Ucareo complex in the Cuitzeo Basin since the Preclassic, and the similar production of prismatic blades to the west in Jalisco during the Classic period, the absence of such technology from north-central Michoacán until the Middle Postclassic is unexplained. Indeed, the study of artifacts from Urichu includes two prismatic blade fragments excavated from Epiclassic and Early Postclassic deposits sourced to Cerro Varal.

The most detailed study, also by visual sourcing, comes from the analysis of 2,713 obsidian artifacts excavated from the Middle—Late Postclassic site of Milpillas (Darras 1998). Of the flakes (42 percent of the artifacts), 97.2 percent are of obsidian from the Zinaparo complex (either Cerro Varal or Cerro Zinaparo) and 2.8 percent are translucent green, probably from Pachuca. The bifacial artifacts (including projectile points) appear to be of the same range of obsidians, with the limited addition of Cerro Prieto (also from the Zinaparo complex). The prismatic blades and cores (48 percent of the artifacts) come primarily from Cerro Varal, but 24.2 percent are translucent green believed to come from Pachuca. The blades are primarily unretouched, and the cores are heavily reutilized. Darras does not believe that any prismatic blade production took place at Milpillas, but that limited flaking and production of bifacial tools did occur in households at the site. Of the 19 excavation units reported on, 2 (B6, an elite residence, and J21–26, a midden associated with a ball court) accounted for 51 percent of all the prismatic blades and 53 percent of the green prismatic blades. Of the 9 other houses excavated, green obsidian was found in 5, including 4 considered non-elite. It is not clear what the basis for this identification is, and the high proportion of green obsidian from the excavation units suggests to me that all units were in elite and ritual deposits, possibly reflecting the lower and upper segments of the nobility. On the other hand, Darras indicates that of 39 artifacts from Milpillas that were chemically sourced, 31 came from the Zináparo complex, 4 came from the Zinapécuaro-Ucareo complex, and 3 green-gray came from Pénjamo (personal communication, 1998). The unusually high proportion of green obsidian reported above thus may actually represent Pénjamo, and not Pachuca. This is a significant difference, since Pénjamo was located within the empire's territory, while Pachuca obsidian was imported by state long-distance merchants.

Upper Marqués (Southeast Uruapan)
The only other chemical sourcing of obsidian artifacts from communities within the Tarascan empire was done on artifacts from 10 sites located during a 1997 survey between Uruapan and Nueva Italia (Proyecto Carretara Uruapan–Nueva Italia, Salvamento-INAH) (Esparza López 1999). These sites are located in the upper reaches of tributaries of the Río Marqués, which flows south into the Balsas Basin. Under the Tarascan empire this was a region of active assimilation, with copper mines and tropical and subtropical crop production of value to the state (chapter 20). The sourcing study included only obsidian flakes from the 10 sites. The sample was small (29 artifacts studied by INA, and 48 by PIXE), and the chronological placement of the artifacts was not reported (table 29.4). As with the Pátzcuaro and Zacapu samples, the largest single source was the Zináparo-Varal complex (40–50 percent of known sources), and sources within the empire account for 50–63 percent of the sourced obsidian. The sourcing of only flakes probably means that Ucareo is under-represented. Unlike the Pátzcuaro and Zacapu samples, some of the gray-black obsidian was coming from the highland lake district of Jalisco (Magdalena-Teuchitlan), presumably through market exchange along the Tepalcatepec River routes (Esparza López 1999:193–204).

The site of Lagunillas has the largest quantity of obsidian from surface and excavated deposits (580 artifacts). Occupied during the Classic and Postclassic periods, the site has a large ceremonial precinct (Esparza López 1999:140). Of the gray-black flakes and blades from excavated deposits dating to before the Tarascan state (N = 179), 33 percent are blades. Of similar material dating to the Late Postclassic (N = 359), 52 percent are blades. This increase in blades relative to flakes following emergence of the Tarascan state appears similar

Table 29.4
Upper Marqués obsidian sources

Obsidian Source	PIXE	INAA
Zináparo-Varal	20	10
Cerro Prieto	0	2
Magdalena-Teuchitlan	16	5
Pachuca	1	4
Zinapécuaro-Ucareo	0	2
Pénjamo	0	1
Unknown	11	5
Total pieces analyzed	48	29

Source: Data are from Esparza López 1999.

to the pattern observed in the Pátzcuaro and Zacapu basins. Other sites, without ceremonial/elite zones, do not exhibit the increase in prismatic blades.

Summary
Obsidian procurement within the Tarascan core was a complex combination of market exchange, state control by provisioning elites and the capital, and state-sponsored long-distance merchants who exchanged with foreign merchants at the borders of their territory. Comparison to non-core zones suggests the core acquired relatively greater quantities of obsidian, and, in general, settlements that became administrative centers throughout the empire acquired marked increases in prismatic blades. Within the core, unlike the rest of the empire, these increases in prismatic blades and quantities of obsidian, although uneven, were not restricted to state or elite residences.

SHELL
In a synthesis of studies of shell artifacts from Michoacán, Suárez Díez (1997) found that during the Preclassic and Classic periods shell was imported from both the Caribbean and Pacific coasts, in addition to coming from freshwater deposits within the state. Although many of the studies used shell from older excavations that were poorly dated, the findings are consistent with results from the more recent projects in the Zacapu and Pátzcuaro Lake basins. In general, shell artifacts are rare and typically excavated from burials. The shell is far more likely to come from the Pacific Ocean. Excavations at Huandacareo (Cuitzeo Basin), Milpillas (Zacapu Basin), and Urichu (Pátzcuaro Basin)—all dating to the Middle–Late Postclassic—reveal shell only from local or Pacific coast origin (Suárez Díez 1997; Polaco, personal communication, 1997; Pollard and Cahue 1999). I know of no study of the materials excavated from the ceremonial platform at Tzintzuntzan, and the current sample of properly identified shell artifacts from all time periods is

Table 29.5
Analyzed sherds and compositional groups

Ceramic type	Main Group	Group 1	Group 2	Unassigned	Total
Yaguarto Cream	21	0	0	1	22
Querenda White	9	11	0	2	22
Tariacuri Brown	5	0	0	3	8
Sipiho Grey	4	4	0	0	8
Tarerio Cream	0	1	5	0	6
Tecolote Orange	1	2	0	1	4
Total sherds analyzed	40	18	5	7	70

Source: Data are from Pollard et al. 2001.

small. Nevertheless, the available data suggest that state expansion opened access to west coast merchants and ports, reducing the need to rely on Aztec merchants to acquire Caribbean shell.

METALLURGY
Metal objects of gold, silver, copper, and bronze alloys were produced within the territory of the empire and used for ritual, status, and utilitarian purposes (chapter 21; see also Hosler 1994; Pollard 1993; Warren 1968). The documentary record indicates that some of the mining, smelting, and production of objects was carried out by full-time craft specialists and tenants under the direct control of the state (Warren 1968). The production of ingots of smelted ore took place at smelting centers in the Balsas River drainage, and some portion of the crafting of objects took place in the Tarascan capital, possibly within the king's palace (Pollard 1993). Other metals or smelted ingots, particularly of gold and silver, were obtained through the state tribute system. Metal moving through the tribute system is recorded for the frontier zones of the southeast and the west. There is no direct evidence of independent production of metal goods that were sold in local or regional markets, although production for tribute suggests this was possible within these frontier zones. Within the Tarascan territory, metal objects are associated with ritual and elite deposits, although utilitarian objects such as needles and axes are more widely distributed. The looting of metal objects by the first Spaniards and subsequent generations has severely biased our samples from the core of the empire. Nevertheless, sourcing evidence from metal artifacts excavated from the sites of Atoyac (in the Sayula Basin) and Urichu (in the Pátzcuaro Basin), and dating to the Late Postclassic, support the interpretation that metal artifacts found in Michoacán were produced from ores mined in the Balsas Basin and adjacent Jalisco (Hosler and Macfarlane 1996). At both sites the metal objects are associated with elite administrators' residences, probably reflecting redistribution of state goods.

Most of the objects found both within and outside the Tarascan sphere have been dated to the Late Postclassic or after Tarascan imperial expansion. Copper artifacts are known from Early Postclassic occupations only in the Balsas (Infiernillo and La Villita) and Chapala basins (Tizapan el Alto and Cojumatlan) (Hosler 1994), probably reflecting routes of communication of this technology from the Pacific coast. Thus it is not possible to discuss changes in the production and distribution of metals during the Postclassic, at least based on the evidence from within Michoacán. Clearly the Tarascan empire emerged in a region that was already part of the west Mexican metallurgical tradition. Nevertheless, it appears that the emergence of a centralized state in the Pátzcuaro Basin and its subsequent expansion were associated with a marked increase in the scale of production and, possibly, a restriction of (some of) the control of the technology, raw materials, and products to core elites, especially the royal dynasty.

CERAMICS
Throughout the Postclassic period ceramic production is believed to have been local in scale and relatively unspecialized. A recent analysis of 70 sherds from the site of Urichu and 18 clay samples from the Pátzcuaro Basin by means of INA provides the only current data available concerning the scale of production and exchange of ceramics before and after formation of the Tarascan state. The sherds represent the six most common fine wares at Urichu, although only the two most common wares were sampled for all phases. The clay samples, collected by Amy Hirshman with advice from geologist Thomas Vogel (Michigan State University), were selected to give an indication of the chemical variability of sources within the Pátzcuaro Basin (Hirshman et al. 1999). The sherd and clay samples were prepared and analyzed using standard MURR procedures (Neff and Glascock 1999). The results of the analysis of the clay samples indicate that there is enough heterogeneity within the Pátzcuaro Basin to allow isolation of individual clay sources. For

the sherds, three compositional groups were recognized, and 7 sherds were unassigned (table 29.5). The compositional group to which 40 of the 70 sherds were assigned appears most similar in composition to clay samples from the southwest portion of the basin—that is, near the site of Urichu. The second compositional group, to which 18 sherds were assigned, is closest to clay samples from the southeastern portion of the basin. While none of the clay samples matches the third compositional group (5 sherds), the group is similar enough to samples from the southeastern basin that Neff and Glascock (1999) feel it likely that as-yet-unsampled deposits from this area will be found to have been the source for the clays.

All of the analyzed sherds appear to come from clays mined in the Pátzcuaro Basin; 63 percent of the assignable sherds came from clays near Urichu. Only one ware was assigned to the third group (Pottery Group 2); all the sherds come from a Late Postclassic deposit in front of a small yácata and associated with ceramic pipe fragments. The sherds are probably from vessels imported to Urichu for use in state ritual. The southeastern location of the clay source suggests that the pottery might have been produced in Ihuatzio, a settlement known to have contained other full-time craft specialists associated with state ritual.

The second compositional group included sherds from four wares, but only one ware is associated with this group during the Epiclassic, Early Postclassic, and Middle Postclassic periods (none is associated with this group in the Classic period). This is the ware associated with vessel form and decoration most Coyotlatelco-like in the Epiclassic and Early Postclassic periods. During the Late Postclassic, vessels of four different wares were produced from clays in the southeastern portion of the basin and imported into Urichu (12 of the 18 sherds in this group date to this period). Sherds assigned to the first compositional group date to all phases of occupation at Urichu. The fact that these were produced from clays mined locally indicates that ceramic production was a continuous part of the local economy at either Urichu or an adjacent settlement.

Clearly this study is too small and preliminary to support sweeping conclusions, but it suggests significant changes in the scale of exchange of decorated pottery following the emergence of the Tarascan state. All sherds tested from the Classic period were locally made; 67 percent of sherds tested from the Epiclassic and Early and Middle Postclassic were locally made, with the nonlocal pottery all of one ware; and 48 percent of Late Postclassic—assigned sherds were locally made, with nonlocal sherds representing five different wares. Ceramic exchange within the southern Pátzcuaro Basin would have been easily accomplished by canoe; the marketplace at Pareo along the south-central lakeshore is a logical location for such trade.

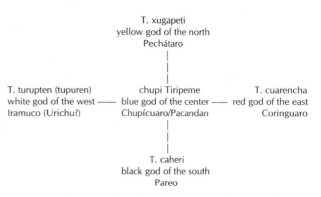

Curicaueri's brothers: the Tiripemencha

T. xugapeti
yellow god of the north
Pechátaro

T. turupten (tupuren)   chupi Tiripeme   T. cuarencha
white god of the west —— blue god of the center —— red god of the east
Iramuco (Urichu?)   Chupícuaro/Pacandan   Coringuaro

T. caheri
black god of the south
Pareo

Figure 29.3 Curicaueri and his brothers, the Tirpemencha

While production of polychrome vessels associated with state ritual and elite burials was not centralized in Tzintzuntzan, similar vessels found at imperial administrative centers outside central Michoacán are distinct enough from local ceramics, and rare enough, that they were probably imported from the Pátzcuaro Basin. Knowing whether such exported fine wares were produced at Tzintzuntzan, or at smaller centers like those represented in this preliminary study, will enable us to understand the degree to which state emergence altered ceramic production and distribution. However, until similar compositional analyses are done on other collections, this remains quite speculative.

IDEOLOGY OF THE TARASCAN CORE

The creation of the Tarascan state was accompanied by the establishment of a new ideology that made the Pátzcuaro Basin the center of cosmic power. The roots of this ideology came from the different cultural traditions that characterized Postclassic Michoacán populations. The patron gods of the newly dominant ethnic elite were elevated to celestial power, while the various regional deities and worldviews—themselves products of generations of change—were elevated, incorporated, or marginalized. The clearest evidence of this process involves the joining of the ethnic Chichimec or uacúsecha deity Curicaueri with the ethnic "islander" or P'urepecha goddess Xarátanga. In the prophetic language of a great epic, "Curicaueri will conquer this land, and you for your part will stand with one foot on the land and one on the water … and we shall become one people" (Relación de Michoacán (hereafter RM) 1980:40). Their joint worship at Ihuatzio and Tzintzuntzan was a direct product of this unification, reinventing them as husband (sun) and wife (moon).

Patron deities of various communities were reinterpreted within the dual system of the four quarters (Curicaueri's four brothers) and the five directions, uniting all

the solar deities in a manner that made the Lake Pátzcuaro basin the cosmic center (RM 1956:134–150; RM
1980:172–195; figure 29.3). For example, one of the
final conquests in the political unification of the Pátzcuaro Basin was the defeat of the island of Pacandan.
The island's patron deity became the god of sacrifice, exile, and the center direction. Four of these five locations
can be specifically located, and all are within or adjacent
to the basin, whose geographical center became the cosmic center of Curicaueri.

In the ritual of *Ecuata Conscuaro* ("the great gathering"), before the recounting of the official Tarascan
history in Tzintzuntzan, the chief priest would turn to
the east and invoke the goddess Cuerauáperi, turn to
the west and invoke the goddess Xarátanga, turn to
the north and invoke the solar god of Zacapu (Querenda-
Angapeti), turn to the south and invoke the gods of the
hot lands, and finally look up to the sky and invoke the
spirit of Curicaueri, the great sun (Pollard 1993:135).
This union of deities previously associated with distinct
ethnic/political groups can also be seen in the ritual centers constructed in the Tarascan core. A specialized
keyhole-shaped pyramid form, the yácata, was constructed at major religious centers associated with the
Tarascan sun god, Curicaueri. The greatest number (five)
were in Tzintzuntzan, but at Ihuatzio there were not only
three yácata, but also two rectangular pyramids associated with Xarátanga adjacent to a ball court. In the legendary history it was built on the orders of the goddess
Xarátanga, and it was here that the gods were to be fed
at midday ("Allí tengo de dar de comer a los dioses a
medio día" [RM 1980:174]). Stone chacmool sculptures
were placed in front of the yácatas at Tzintzuntzan and
Ihuatzio, the setting for major ceremonies celebrating the
state and cosmic order.

The centrality of the Pátzcuaro Basin in state ritual
and the union of the two major deities, not to mention
the value of metallurgy to the royal dynasty, were reflected in the location of the official state treasuries. The
chests of gold (Curicaueri, the sun deity) and silver (Xarátanga, the moon deity) were located at Tzintzuntzan (in
the king's palace) and on the islands of the lake, including
Apupato, Janitzio (Xanecho), Pacandan, the Urandeni,
and Utuyo (RM 1980:323–324).

Finally, the centrality of the Pátzcuaro Basin as a core
region was reflected in characteristic attitudes of urban
elites to the largely nonurban population. Ethnohistoric
documents refer to native speech as either "lengua de
Cintzuntza" (language of Tzintzuntza) (Lagunas 1983:
146) or p'urépecha (language of the people/commoners).
The dominant language of the Tarascan state is generally
referred to as Tarascan. While dialect divergence within
Tarascan is often believed to be relatively recent, Lagunas
made it clear in 1574 that he was basing his dictionary
and grammar on Tarascan as spoken in the Pátzcuaro

Basin. This version he viewed as the "courtly, cultured
and universal language of Michoacán, to be preferred to
the incongruous, barbarous and badly pronounced language that they use in some towns, inasmuch as the language of Michoacán is all one" (Lagunas 1983:343).

ETHNOGENESIS AND ELITE IDENTITY

Based on mortuary evidence from the site of Urichu, it
has been possible to propose that changes in the burial
practices of local elites document their transformation
from highly ranked local chiefs into a socially stratified
elite class associated with the emergence of the Tarascan
state (Pollard and Cahue 1999). Two distinctive mortuary patterns that represent the Classic—Epiclassic and
Late Postclassic periods are present. These patterns vary
in the age and sex composition of burial groups, the
preparation and treatment of the bodies, the mortuary
facilities, the types of burial goods, and the location of
the burials within settlements. This transformation involved a shift in elite identity from one associated primarily with imported finished goods from distant powerful
centers and control of prestige-goods networks, to an
identity primarily associated with locally produced, dis-
tinctively Tarascan goods and control of tributary, military, political, and ideological networks (for specific
evidence see Pollard and Cahue 1999).

Of significance here, Late Postclassic elite identity as
expressed at Urichu is specifically associated with finely
decorated pottery—both locally produced and imported
from other basin centers in distinctive Tarascan shapes
and designs—and metal ornaments and tools, also in distinctive Tarascan shapes and designs. Elite burial assemblages and ritual platform assemblages from Urichu are
indistinguishable from those excavated at the capital, Tzintzuntzan, and like those at Ihuatzio, they include both
rectangular pyramids and a yácata (Pollard 1995). This is
in spite of the distinctly different ethnic identity ascribed
to their elites before unification of the state in the legendary history. Thus, within the Tarascan core, the emergence of a new political economy was also associated
with a new state religion and a new regional ethnic
identity.

CENTRAL MICHOACÁN AS A CORE IN THE
MESOAMERICAN WORLD

During Middle and Late Postclassic times, central Michoacán saw two transformations: the emergence of the
Tarascan state, and the emergence of the center of that
state as a new core region in the Mesoamerican world.
Analytically distinguishing which of those processes produced the patterns discussed here is probably impossible.
Under conditions of hostile military borders (on the east
and west), the effects of increased commercialization of

interaction—which might have challenged the centrality of the state and the Pátzcuaro Basin—were muted (chapter 14). Thus both the internal process of state formation and the nature of increased interaction with Mesoamerica reinforced the rapid pace of cultural change that maintained the demographic, economic, and political centrality of the Pátzcuaro Basin. Internal and external processes also were active in the development of the Basin of Mexico as a core in the Late Postclassic. These dynamics are discussed by Berdan and Smith in the next chapter.

30

The Evolution of a Core Zone

The Basin of Mexico

Frances F. Berdan

Michael E. Smith

The Basin of Mexico, an important region since Classic times, offers us a well-documented view of world-system transformations through approximately 600 years of civilizational time. The focus of this chapter is on the internal and external forces stimulating change and continuity as the Basin of Mexico evolved from a rural backwater in Early Postclassic times to an affluent production zone in the Middle Postclassic period, to a core zone and seat of empire in Late Postclassic times. Although the broad outlines of this development paralleled the trajectory of the Tarascan core zone described in chapter 29, the resulting political economy of the Basin of Mexico was quite different from that of the Pátzcuaro Basin. In the Basin of Mexico, the formation of an empire did not wipe out the existing system of small polities as it had in the Tarascan core, and the continued vitality of the Aztec city-states contributed to the more extensive commercialization of the Basin of Mexico.

POSTCLASSIC DEVELOPMENTS IN THE BASIN OF MEXICO

The primary Postclassic trends described in chapter 1 were clearly present, if not magnified, in the developmental history of the Basin of Mexico. Beginning around A.D. 150, the gigantic city of Teotihuacan emerged in the northeastern area of the basin, completing the construction of its major structures by A.D. 200 and flourishing as a dominant influence in the basin and beyond for the next 400 years. After the city's collapse, perhaps as early as A.D. 600 (Cowgill 1996), the basin's population structure and settlement pattern became more diffuse, marking the start of a long-term trend toward smaller polities that culminated in the development of the altepetl, or Aztec city-states, after the twelfth century. The larger number of polities continued as the basin's basic territo-

rial building blocks throughout the Postclassic epoch, even in the context of Tula's Early Postclassic importance and Tenochtitlan's Late Postclassic dominance. Associated with these political arrangements was an increase in population size throughout the Postclassic period, although that population rearranged itself around the landscape differently with political and economic shifts during the Postclassic.

The economic trends noted for Postclassic Mesoamerica generally were vividly present in the Basin of Mexico. After the twelfth century, and perhaps before, marketplaces provided effective and efficient venues for exchange and were offered on a scheduled basis at communities throughout the basin. These marketplaces served as sites for the exchange of utilitarian and exotic goods, raw materials, and finished wares. Commercialization of the economy increased throughout the Postclassic, even in the face of Late Postclassic imperial developments and political involvement in the economy. Associated with this commercial posture was an increase in the diversity of trade goods available to marketplace purveyors and to professional merchants who operated in regional and long-distance contexts. This increasing diversity was to some extent linked to an increased volume of long-distance exchange and the enhanced economic and political importance of professional luxury merchants (pochteca) in several Basin of Mexico cities.

The Postclassic period also saw the development of new forms of writing and iconography. The pictorial manuscripts produced in the Basin of Mexico predominantly served historic, administrative, cartographic, economic, ritual, and calendric purposes (chapter 27). The pictorial histories are mostly local documents focused on individual altepetl rather than broader regional or cultural units (Boone 2000:244). Administrative, cartographic, and economic documents also tended to focus on specific altepetl, with the exception of the broader Late Postclassic tribute tallies that recorded income from provinces conquered by the Aztec empire (Berdan and Anawalt 1992). Writing and history worked in the service of individual city-states, which is consistent with the emphasis in the basin on these local-level politico-territorial units. Being formulated with few phonetic symbols and produced in a generally international style (see chapters 1 and 24), writings could be read and interpreted by persons speaking diverse languages, thus allowing for a potentially greater diffusion of information across linguistic and cultural groups.

The peoples of the Postclassic Basin of Mexico seem to have been strongly receptive to the adoption of foreign styles, relating to new patterns of stylistic interaction. Images of deities appeared with their original regional and cultural paraphernalia, such as the deity Xipe Totec from Oaxaca and/or Guerrero (chapter 27), or the Huaxtec-embellished deity Tlazolteotl (Nicholson 1971:420, 424). Offerings of Mezcala sculptures from Guerrero were deposited in caches at the Templo Mayor of Tenochtitlan at the end of the Postclassic period (González and Olmedo Vera 1990). Stylistic receptivity is even found in that most political of economic events, the imposition of tribute on conquered peoples: the Late Postclassic Aztec imperial tribute rolls clearly illustrate the payments of clothing tribute in local, often ethnically specific styles (Berdan and Anawalt 1992).

These related trends did not develop in a singular or uniform fashion in the Basin of Mexico, nor did they develop in isolation. The transformations that took place depended on internal as well as external forces at work in the more broadly defined Mesoamerican world system.

POLITICAL CHANGES

Small polities—with known boundaries, hereditary dynastic leadership, and sometimes notable economic specializations—were persistent and tenacious as the basic political building blocks in the Basin of Mexico during Postclassic times. However, their relationships were volatile as they vied for political and economic prominence. The power loci in the basin therefore shifted over time, reflecting this competitive situation. Aztec city-states are well documented for the Middle and Late Postclassic periods (chapter 9). Although most authors agree that the Epiclassic and Early Postclassic periods were also characterized by small polities (or, at least, polities much smaller than Teotihuacan), the applicability of the city-state model (chapter 4) to these periods is uncertain.

Teotihuacan was a massively dominant territorial state during the Classic period, apparently draining the basin's other polities of their population. As the capital of a modest central Mexican empire and a center of renown throughout Classic Mesoamerica (Smith and Montiel

2001), Teotihuacan transformed its valley heartland into a core zone for several centuries. Upon its demise, other areas of the Basin of Mexico were repopulated and, apparently, revitalized as some new centers appeared, perhaps settled by former inhabitants of Teotihuacan (Charlton and Nichols 1997b:193). With numerous relatively small, competing city-states, the region has been characterized as "Balkanized" (Hodge 1984:13): no one center dominated, and spatial buffer zones separated political entities from one another. Interestingly, a strikingly similar pattern is described for the Valley of Oaxaca after the collapse of Classic-period Monte Albán (Feinman 1999a:56).

The polities that thrived in the basin during the Epiclassic period (until ca. A.D. 900) were well defined and unequal in size. Even though Teotihuacan had suffered a severe depopulation, it entered the Epiclassic period as still the most densely populated settlement in the Basin of Mexico. Teotihuacan shared the northern part of the basin with two other settlement clusters (Charlton and Nichols 1997b:193). In the southern area of the basin, settlements appear to have been somewhat more continuous, and Charlton and Nichols (1997b) have posited a "confederacy" type of relationship for city-states in that region. Developments outside the basin may have impinged on these political arrangements: extra-basin settlements such as Xochicalco, Teotenango, and Cacaxtla took on a military/defensive posture (Diehl and Berlo 1989; Hirth 2000), and others began demonstrating unique styles suggesting the emergence of new ethnic groups or other major local changes.

During the Early Postclassic period (A.D. 900–1150), the basin's political arrangements were probably influenced by the large polity of Tula, north of the basin itself (Davies 1977; Diehl 1983; Healan 1989). Hodge (1984:13) suggests that Tula and Cholula, to the east, may have used the basin as a buffer zone in their competitive bids for power. Such external forces were certainly not a novelty to Basin of Mexico polities. Some authors suggest that Tula's influence can be seen in changes in settlements, which became skewed toward the northern part of the basin (Charlton and Nichols 1997b:196). Charlton and Nichols suggest that other changes—such as the emphasis on very small settlements, the repopulating of previously abandoned locales, and a slight decrease or evening of the population overall—also may have been due to Tula's influence. Smith and Montiel (2001), on the other hand, argue that Tula exerted very little political or economic influence over the Basin of Mexico in the Early Postclassic period. Davies (1980: 27–29) speculates that Tula's preeminence was shared by Culhuacan in the southern Basin of Mexico, and Otumba in the northern, in a sort of triple alliance; however, there is little evidence to support this claim.

The fall of Tula in the twelfth century coincided with a

new era of fundamental transformation in the Basin of Mexico. During this Middle Postclassic period (A.D. 1150–1350), the overall population increased dramatically. Rainfall increased (O'Hara and Metcalfe 1997; O'Hara et al. 1994), and significant migrations of Chichimecs from the north arrived in the basin, occupying available lands and merging with the resident basin peoples. As described by Smith in chapter 9, new dynasties with links to the ancient Toltec kings were established, and the pattern of Aztec city-state culture emerged. The growth of city-states was accompanied by processes of urbanization, particularly the growth of city-state capitals. Warfare appears to have been endemic but small-scale, and alliances were frequently established and just as frequently broken, but no one city-state mustered sufficient strength to gain control over others in the basin. Nonetheless, some city-states such as Azcapotzalco, Coatlinchan, Culhuacan, Tenayuca, and Xaltocan began to gain in population and importance during this time, each of them fleetingly acquiring conquered subjects, only to lose them in the basin's volatile military and political arenas (Davies 1980:134–156). Especially obvious are the increasing territorial ambitions and strains between the Acolhua polities on the eastern side of Lake Texcoco, and the Tepaneca ones to the west (Charlton and Nichols 1997b:199). It is important to keep in mind that similar processes were under way in nearby and adjacent areas, where city-states such as Cholula, Huexotzinco, Tollocan, and Cuauhnahuac were gaining in size and prominence to the east, west, and south of the basin (Smith 1996a).

The early portion of the Late Postclassic period (A.D. 1350–1520) saw the preeminent rise to power of two large competing political entities: the Acolhua city-states to the east of Lake Texcoco (centered at Texcoco), and the Tepanec ones to the west (focused on Azcapotzalco). Chalco, to the southeast, was a feisty contender throughout this period until its conquest by the Aztec Triple Alliance in 1465 (Berdan and Anawalt 1992:2:96). Hodge (1997) suggests the term "regional confederations" for these groups of allied city-states.

The basin's population continued to increase during Late Postclassic times, and urbanization intensified. At the culmination of this period, Tenochtitlan's population reached 150,000–200,000 inhabitants (Rojas 1986), the neighboring urban center of Texcoco housed as many as 25,000, while several others (Huexotla, Tepetlaoztoc, Chalco, Xochimilco, Chimalhuacan, and Amecameca) in the eastern and southern region of the basin supported 10,000–15,000 residents (Hodge 1997:219). Numerous other centers of around 5,000 inhabitants dotted the basin's landscape. This uneven increase in urbanization reflects unequal power relations between these numerous city-states, and the ability of some to effect conquests and institute imperial structures.

In 1430, an alliance of the Mexica of Tenochtitlan and the Acolhua of Texcoco overthrew the dominating yoke of the Azcapotzalco Tepanecas. This event set into motion the most impressive imperial endeavor in the basin's history. Along with the Tepanecas of Tlacopan, the Mexica and Acolhua formed a powerful Triple Alliance that initially subjugated city-states in the basin and then fulfilled their military ambitions across much of central and southern Mexico. In these conquests, they frequently enlisted the martial services of other basin city-states, thus integrating them into this complex system as subjects, participants, and recipients of rewards for valiant service. The growing dominance of Tenochtitlan created a hierarchy of political power that was only in its formative stages earlier in the history of the basin (Hodge 1997:224). This hierarchical structure suggests a strongly centralized system; in some cases (e.g., Cuauhtitlan and Chalco), hierarchical levels were reduced in subjugated basin city-states by the imperial rulers, thus curtailing the power of those city-states (Hodge 1997:220).

During the Aztec imperial period, the basin's numerous polities became more and more intertwined with polities external to the basin. Having emerged as a core zone in the Mesoamerican world system, the basin's powerful and expansionistic city-states confronted other powerful city-states, particularly those of the Valley of Puebla to the east (Tlaxcala, Cholula, and Huexotzinco) and those incorporated into the Tarascan empire to the west. Shifting alliances and serious warfare arrangements characterized these relationships as the Triple Alliance forces increasingly dominated other city-states throughout central and southern Mexico, as far south as the present-day border with Guatemala. Some of the most profound indicators of these world-system relations are found in the economic arena.

ECONOMIC CHANGES

During the Classic period, the flow and control of economic goods in the Basin of Mexico was the domain of Teotihuacan. With its own extraordinary population, and reduced population levels throughout the basin, economic production and distribution were geared toward supporting this massive urban center. Teotihuacan also served as a well-situated locale for trade between the basin and extra-basin regions. Flows of exotic goods from tropical zones were directed toward this center of elite activity, whether directed through hierarchical tribute channels or filtered through marketplaces to areas of high elite consumption demand.

With the fall of Teotihuacan and the fragmentation of the basin into a multitude of relatively small polities, it is likely that hierarchical movements of goods and services were contained within polities, with commoners supporting their own elite. Overall regional populations were low (Sanders et al. 1979), and the settlement patterns of the Early Postclassic period were the most ruralized of all time periods.

The inception of the Middle Postclassic period during the twelfth century A.D. matches the time when a five-century period of drought in central Mexico came to an end (O'Hara and Metcalfe 1997; O'Hara et al. 1994), and it is hard to avoid the conclusion that the increased rainfall contributed to the population surge that began at about that time. The arrival of the Aztlan migrants also contributed to the processes of demographic growth. The Middle and Late Postclassic periods witnessed a major surge of population in all parts of central Mexico for which data are available. Population across the Middle Postclassic to Late Postclassic transition in the Basin of Mexico grew at a rate of close to 1 percent (average annual increase), a very high figure for a preindustrial society (Sanders et al. 1979).

The result of this Postclassic population explosion is visible across central Mexico in the form of irrigation canals, raised fields, and terraces (Donkin 1979; Doolittle 1990; Evans 1990; López 1991). Every part of the landscape that could be cultivated was planted with maize and other crops to feed the growing population. Recent simulations of population and carrying capacity in the Basin of Mexico suggest that agricultural intensification did not keep up with population growth, at least in the Basin of Mexico piedmont zone (Whitmore and Williams 1998).

The growing populations that expanded across the landscape in Middle Postclassic times participated in active systems of market exchange (Blanton 1996; Minc et al. 1994). While regional marketplace integration (where buyers and sellers have commercial goals and move from market to market to seek out the greatest profit) is probably not an exact description of this highly fragmented and unstable political situation, marketplaces of a "solar" or rotating variety may more closely mirror the more highly localized, insular arrangements of polities. Minc et al. (1994:159) suggest that the boundaries of Middle Postclassic political entities (confederations more than individual city-states) placed a significant "constraint on exchange" of ceramics. Nonetheless, some ceramics (including Chalco-Cholula polychromes and Texcoco Fabric-marked salt vessels) did move more broadly, suggesting that these constraints were not absolute and that political boundaries were permeable to the flows of at least this type of economic ware. These authors argue for a "middle ground" between the regional and solar marketing models, one in which "exchange interactions, constrained by the major political divisions of the pre-imperial period, were organized through a series of sub-regional market systems that corresponded spatially to confederation territories of allied city-states" (Minc et al. 1994:164–165).

The marketing structure became more intensified, hierarchical, and commercialized during the Late Postclassic (chapter 16). At the time of Spanish contact, the economic draw of the great marketplace at Tlatelolco mirrored adjacent Tenochtitlan's political and military prominence. Vendors of all scales (from local producers to regional traders to haughty professional merchants) frequented this marketplace, and reportedly anything, from near or far, could be purchased there (Berdan 1985). This marketplace is the paramount example of the Postclassic economic trends described at the beginning of this chapter: an increased commercialization of the economy, an increased diversity of trade goods, and an increased volume of long-distance exchange. A plethora of additional marketplaces had developed during the Late Postclassic throughout Mesoamerica; the Basin of Mexico experienced a particular intensification of marketplace activity due to the political and military dominance of its city-states, its concentration of elite consumers, and its high degree of economic specialization. Some of that specialization may have been encouraged or stimulated by political decisions (chapter 16; see also Berdan 1985; Brumfiel 1980).

An increased volume of long-distance exchange is indicated by the success of professional merchants (pochteca). These long-distance traders had their headquarters in specific basin city-states and, with imperial support, brought precious sumptuary goods to the basin for use by that nobility (by trading state goods, or their own merchandise). By the time of Spanish contact, these merchants had, through entrepreneurial efforts, succeeded in accumulating extraordinary wealth and in gaining some political clout (for example, as judges in the Tlatelolco marketplace and as diplomatic emissaries of the ruler in international trading centers).

As a hegemonic empire, the imperial polities drew tribute and gifts from a large number of outlying conquered city-states (Berdan et al. 1996), thus underwriting an extraordinary standard of living for the elite and a more assured subsistence base for both commoner and elite. At this Late Postclassic time, then, the basin experienced a kind of "pax Azteca" allowing rather fluid movements of economic goods, although the defection of basin city-states to the Spanish conquistador Hernán Cortés suggests a certain lack of satisfaction with this arrangement.

THE TRANSFORMATION OF A CORE ZONE

When the political and economic changes outlined above are put together, they reveal the processes that transformed the Basin of Mexico from an affluent production zone into a core zone in Late Postclassic times. With the fall of Teotihuacan, the overall levels of population and economic activity in the Basin of Mexico declined.

Although Teotihuacan remained a major city in Epiclassic times, the most important central Mexican polities and cities at that time—Xochicalco, Cacaxtla, and Teotenango—were all outside of the basin. By the Early Postclassic period, Teotihuacan was largely abandoned, and the foci of political power and urbanization in central Mexico moved north to Tula and east to Cholula, leaving the Basin of Mexico as a rural backwater characterized by small, dispersed settlements and, presumably, weak polities.

The twelfth century marked the inception of major world-system processes in the Basin of Mexico. The demographic surge began at this time and continued steadily through the Spanish conquest. Intensive agricultural methods spread across the landscape along with new villages, towns, and cities. The basin quickly developed into an affluent production zone, and exchange with other parts of Mesoamerica became important to Aztec polities. Although small polities had been the norm since the Epiclassic period, the development of Aztec city-state culture was a key innovation. The new Aztec city-states had several features that contributed to processes of economic growth. Market systems flourished with only minimal political manipulation. Craft specialists, professional merchants, and the political elite formed symbiotic relationships that encouraged the twin processes of economic expansion and strengthening of elite power (Blanton 1996:83). The growing commercialization of the economy led to increased foreign trade, and by the fourteenth century, the polities of the basin had surpassed those of other areas in terms of population size, power, wealth, and urbanization. The Basin of Mexico had emerged as a core zone within the Postclassic world system.

The power and influence of Basin of Mexico polities only increased further in the Late Postclassic period. Confederations and mini-empires gave way to the Triple Alliance empire, which quickly came to exercise political and military dominance over extensive external areas and, therefore, to control and consume a steady supply of non-basin resources, both utilitarian and exotic. As noted in chapters 9 and 11, the expansion of the Aztec empire did not at all destroy the system of city-states at its base. In fact, the economic success of the empire was probably due in part to its adoption and promotion of economic practices and policies already successful at the city-state level, and to the continued vitality of Aztec city-states in the Basin of Mexico and surrounding areas. In the next chapter, Pohl discusses the dynamics of political relations in the eastern Nahua, Mixtec, and Zapotec areas in terms of networks of royal intermarriages.

31

Royal Marriage and Confederacy Building among the Eastern Nahuas, Mixtecs, and Zapotecs

John M. D. Pohl

Scholars tend to examine the Postclassic period either from the perspective of the Aztec empire centered in the Basin of Mexico or in terms of the regional ethnic divisions that continue to divide Indian peoples living throughout highland Mexico today. Nevertheless, the development and spread of the Mixteca-Puebla painting style together with innovations in both sculpture and architecture point to the florescence of elite social forms shared among the Eastern Nahuas, Mixtecs, and Zapotecs as well as with the peoples they dominated. These elite social forms both preceded Aztec conquest and transcended local differences in language and culture (chapter 22; see also Nicholson 1966; Umberger and Klein 1993).

James Lockhart (1992) proposed that the Eastern Nahua were distinct from the Aztecs settled around the Basin of Mexico in that they emphasized the authority of the tecuhtli as head of a teccalli, or lineage estate, over that of the calpolli and *tecpan*. The tecuhtli was in many ways the direct equivalent of the Mixtec yya or the Zapotec coqui, and emphasis on the role of an autonomous lord may very well have evolved in response to the pronounced interaction with the Oaxacan rulers with whom they were allied.[1]

Despite basic similarities in the size and distribution of Tlaxcalan, Pueblan, and Oaxacan political units, there were also significant differences in social complexity. Tlaxcala was divided into four pie-shaped quarters converging on a central point where government was dominated by the four highest-ranking kingdoms: Tepeticpac, Quiahuiztlan, Ocotelolco, and Tizatlan (figure 31.1; see Lockhart 1992:21–23). Located within two kilometers of each other, the rulers of these kingdoms, called tlatoque, formed a governing council. The council was led by the tlatoani of Tizatlan at the time of the conquest, but there

is evidence of a rotational power structure rooted in a fairly equal distribution of political, religious, and economic functions. The Tepeticpac tlatoani, for example, controlled the religious cult by preserving the ashes of the patron god himself, Camaxtli-Mixcoatl, while the principal market was supervised by the Ocotelolco king (Muñoz Camargo 1984; Lockhart 1992). Each of the four tlatoque governed their own territories through the tetecuhtin, who served as heads of noble estates in the interior of their jurisdictions. Comparable systems of organization have been documented for Huexotzinco, Cuauhtinchan, Tepeyacac, and Tecali (Carrasco et al. 1977; Chance 1996). Significantly less is known of Tehuacan, Coxcatlan, and Teotitlan, but initial surveys and excavations suggest that these kingdoms were also highly centralized city-states geographically, economically, and politically.

The limitations of a montane production strategy among the Mixtec, in contrast to the strategy of the Eastern Nahua, necessitated a much wider dispersal of population and inhibited the centralization of a highly complex elite administration (Spores 1967, 1984; Lind 2000). Consequently, I have characterized the Mixtec more as a system of great houses than of city-states per se (chapter 6). A typical Mixteca Alta kingdom, the *ñuu* or *yuhui tayu*, was dominated by a fortified palace, or *aniñe*, located on a prominent ridge in the center of a valley (Byland and Pohl 1994a; see Terraciano 1994 for discussion of Mixtec terminology). Each aniñe was generally separated from its neighbor by anywhere between 10 and 20 kilometers of rugged outlands. Dependencies, called *siña* or *siqui*, were governed by a secondary nobility called *toho* whose residences were located on *lomas* (ridges) that projected finger-like from the surrounding peaks onto the valley floor (figure 31.1).

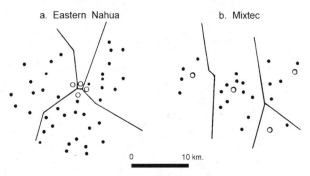

a. Eastern Nahua   b. Mixtec

0   10 km.

Figure 31.1 Idealized settlement patterns: (a) Eastern Nahua polity consisting of a capital center containing the highest-ranking royal houses, surrounded by a quadrupartite division of lands; (b) Mixtec polities with centers surrounded by subject settlements

Zapotec kingdoms called *gueche* were located throughout the Valley of Oaxaca and the Sierra Zapoteca. They generally emulated the organization of the Mixtec, with whom most were closely connected through trade and intermarriage (Appel 1982a; Oudijk 1998a, 1998b; Whitecotton 1977). For example, despite the lack of any major natural boundaries, Zapotec populations tended to be dispersed and removed from the paramount royal houses, or *gehui coqui*. Although certain communities such as Cuilapan and Mitla might be characterized as cities, these communities do not appear to have been centers of political control in and of themselves; they instead functioned as market and religious centers dominated by the rulers of the highest-ranked bloodline located at Zaachila, an elite administration center that served as a disembodied capital (Blanton et al. 1982; Appel 1982a).

Because of these differences in population density and the degree of concentrated political power, the region occupied by the Eastern Nahua possessed more of the attributes of a core zone in the Mesoamerican world system, while the areas dominated by the Mixtec and Zapotec might be better classified as affluent production zones. That said, however, it is wise to consider a few possible exceptions, such as Tututepec and Tehuantepec, city-states that eventually grew to dominate hundreds of square miles of coastal Oaxaca during the Late Postclassic, possibly in response to expansion of the Aztec empire into Oaxaca. The close social interaction between the dynasties of these regions, cutting across both ethnic lines and world-system functional zones, is one of the interesting features of this area in Postclassic times. One of the primary mechanisms of interpolity interaction was the royal marriage alliance.

ROYAL MARRIAGES

Royal marriages both perpetuated control over territory by the ruling families of individual kingdoms and linked these families into larger political constellations. (Spores

1974; Brumfiel 1983; Carrasco 1984). The Mixtecs preserved the most extensive genealogical records. In 1528, Yanhuitlan displayed a codex in a Spanish court that depicted a succession of 24 rulers who had governed the kingdom over the previous 500 years. Although the manuscript is now missing, its description in the court testimonial places Yanhuitlan's earliest ancestors at around A.D. 1028, a date coinciding with the outset of the Mixteca Alta's Postclassic era (Spores 1967, 1984:48; Smith 1998:55).

Surviving codices and lienzos indicate that other kingdoms—including Tilantongo, Jaltepec, Tlaxiaco, and Coaixtlahuaca—recorded genealogies nearly as old if not older than Yanhuitlan's (Caso 1949; Smith 1998). Codex Bodley Obverse portrays a genealogy of Tilantongo through 23 rulers from Lord 4 Crocodile, who lived around A.D. 950, to Lord 4 Deer, who was ruling in 1519 (Byland and Pohl 1994a). The account begins with a sequence of marriages between kingdoms that dominated the southern end of the Nochixtlan Valley at the end of the Classic period. The first genealogy ends with the death of the male heirs during the War of Heaven. In 990, Tilantongo created its first dynasty through marriage with a surviving female. However, when this dynasty also failed at the end of the eleventh century, the saga of 8 Deer is recounted to explain the institution of a second Tilantongo dynasty that continued relatively uninterrupted through the time of the conquest. Several different kingdoms are shown having intermarried with Tilantongo, including Teozacoalco, Tulancingo, Tlaxiaco, Chalcatongo, Jaltepec, and Yanhuitlan.

Some genealogies were structured to associate the families of two or three royal houses into extended alliance corridors (Pohl 1994c:111). Codex Zouche-Nuttall, for example, follows the Tilantongo genealogy through 8 Deer but then switches to recount first the dynasty of 8 Deer's son at Teozacoalco, and later a new dynasty at Zaachila through the marriage of the Teozacoalco Lady 4 Rabbit to the Zapotec Lord 5 Flower. Partners in these alliances subsequently supplied one another with heirs during times of successional crisis.[2] Eight Deer was not necessarily the preferred heroic ancestor, however. On Codex Bodley reverse the royal houses of Tlaxiaco and Achiutla are portrayed consistently intermarrying with each other from the thirteenth through the sixteenth centuries (Pohl 1996:84). In this case Tlaxiaco and Achiutla traced their heritage back to 8 Deer's son-in-law and assassin, Lord 4 Wind. The two royal houses later became so closely connected that by Colonial times they were considered to be a single cacicazgo (Spores 1967:223). There were apparently significant linkages between the kingdoms of Jaltepec, Yanhuitlan, and Cuilapan. A Colonial genealogy called the Yale document traces the ancestry of the cacique of Cuilapan back to Jaltepec's Lady 6 Monkey, 4 Wind's mother and 8 Deer's principal rival for control over the southern Nochixtlan Valley (White-cotton 1990:78–106). Codices Selden and Bodley reverse in turn allow us to extend the genealogy of both Tlaxiaco and Jaltepec back to the War of Heaven and the miraculous birth of the first ancestors from both the rivers of Apoala and a ceiba tree at Achiutla.

By 1500, virtually any ranking Mixtec and Zapotec lord or lady could connect themselves to all of the ancestors and places of creation depicted in the codices. So what led to decisions to associate oneself genealogically to any particular version of a saga? One factor may lie in a factional dispute that was being played out in the Valley of Oaxaca. In 1519, control of the valley was being contested by two distinct factions of Mixtecs that intermarried into the Zaachila dynasty (Byland and Pohl 1994a; Oudijk 1998a; Paddock 1983). The first were those of Teozacoalco, who allied themselves around A.D. 1280 through the union of Lady 4 Rabbit and Lord 5 Flower, while the second factions were those of Yanhuitlan, who intermarried around A.D. 1500. The first union led to the creation of the alliance corridor that linked Zaachila with Teozacoalco and Tilantongo for two centuries. The second was an extremely aggressive attempt by Yanhuitlan—possibly in league with Tlaxiaco—to expand its own corridor of influence south through the Nochixtlan and Etla valleys (Pohl 1994d:123).

The lands below Monte Albán once composed the northern portion of the kingdom of Zaachila until a Mixtec prince of Yanhuitlan married the daughter of the Zapotec king shortly before the conquest. The prince took up residence at what archaeologists refer to as Sa'ayucu (or Cuiban) and soon imported a large group of displaced Mixtec peasants from the Almoloyas area near Apoala to work the land. The two peoples lived together peacefully until they fell into dispute over the spoils of the Mixe war and divided the realm, thereafter remaining in a state of open hostility until the Spaniards entered the valley (Acuña 1984:2:157–158; Butterworth 1962:39; Burgoa 1934b:1:387, 392–393; Blanton et al. 1981:103–106; Kowalewski 1983; Paddock 1983; Whitecotton 1977:94–97).

Since we have no codex detailing Yanhuitlan's genealogy, it is difficult to say precisely why Cuilapan was advocating a connection to Lady 6 Monkey and Lord 11 Wind.[3] We know that Cuilapan claimed Apoala as an ancestral creation place, and that Apoala was tributary to Yanhuitlan at the time of the conquest (García 1981:327; Spores 1967:167–168). Codex Bodley reverse tells us that Lord 11 Wind's family was descended from Lord 1 Flower and Lady 13 Flower, who emerged from the rivers of Apoala. Lady 6 Monkey's grandfather, Lord 8 Wind, is depicted emerging from the rivers of Apoala in Codex Zouche-Nuttall 1.[4]

It appears from an examination of various codices, lienzos, and maps that Postclassic Oaxacan kings and

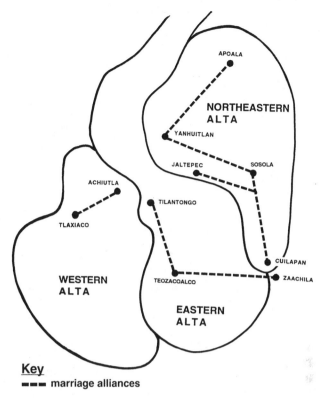

Figure 31.2 Dialect areas of the Mixteca Alta. (After Josserand n.d.)

queens structured their alliances symbolically along lines of descent from the factions born out of the 8 Deer saga. Evidence that these alliance corridors were so established that they could define territoriality is suggested by the distribution of the three dialect groups that continue to divide the Mixteca Alta today (Jiménez Moreno 1962; Josserand 1983). The Northeastern Alta dialect extends from Apoala through Yanhuitlan, Jaltepec, and Etla to Cuilapan. The Eastern Alta dialect extends from Coaixtlahuaca through Teposcolula and Tilantongo to Teozacoalco, whose eastern boundary is contiguous with Zapotec-speaking Zaachila. The Western Alta dialect extends from Ñumi through Achiutla and Tlaxiaco south to the Mixteca Costa (figure 31.2). As the Postclassic period progressed, political constructions became ever more intricate and widespread throughout Oaxaca as lesser-ranking kingdoms sought to increase their status by intermarrying with the highest-ranking royal lines. In the fifteenth century, Teozacoalco played a particularly significant role in this regard. According to Codex Muro, San Pedro Cantaros claimed that its dynasty was founded by a second son of the royal house of Teozacoalco (figure 31.3; see Smith 1973a).

Acatlan's ruling family claimed a Tolteca-Chichimeca heritage, but Codex Tulane suggests that a Teozacoalco prince initiated a system of hereditary rulership there as well (Smith and Parmenter 1991:38, 46).[5] Codex Edgerton indicates that Acatlan subsequently arranged several

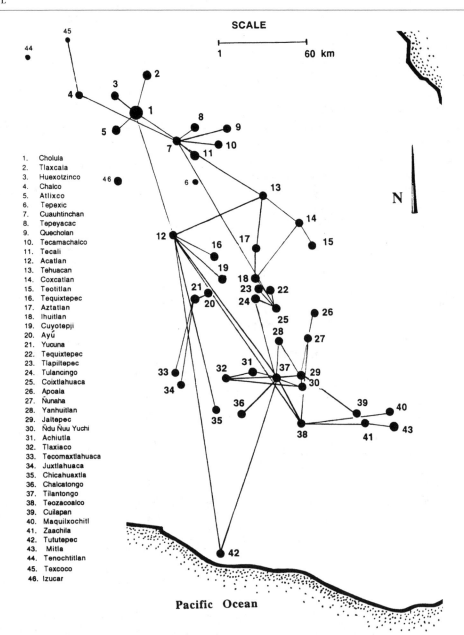

1. Cholula
2. Tlaxcala
3. Huexotzinco
4. Chalco
5. Atlixco
6. Tepexic
7. Cuauhtinchan
8. Tepeyacac
9. Quecholan
10. Tecamachalco
11. Tecali
12. Acatlan
13. Tehuacan
14. Coxcatlan
15. Teotitlan
16. Tequixtepec
17. Aztatlan
18. Ihuitlan
19. Cuyotepji
20. Ayú
21. Yucuna
22. Tequixtepec
23. Tlapiltepec
24. Tulancingo
25. Coixtlahuaca
26. Apoala
27. Ñunaha
28. Yanhuitlan
29. Jaltepec
30. Ñdu Ñuu Yuchi
31. Achiutla
32. Tlaxiaco
33. Tecomaxtlahuaca
34. Juxtlahuaca
35. Chicahuaxtla
36. Chalcatongo
37. Tilantongo
38. Teozacoalco
39. Cuilapan
40. Maquilxochitl
41. Zaachila
42. Tututepec
43. Mitla
44. Tenochtitlan
45. Texcoco
46. Izucar

Figure 31.3 Map showing marriage alliances that united paramount royal houses of Tlaxcala, Puebla, and Oaxaca during the Middle and Late Postclassic periods

marriages with a town called Place of the Jaguar, probably Cuyotepji in the Mixteca Baja (König 1979:54–55). This fascinating genealogy also portrays marriages with Tilantongo, Chicahuaxtla, Tequixtepec del Rey, and Cholula (Smith 1973a:150–151, 76–77; König 1979: 116–117). Marriages between Acatlan's Mixteca Baja neighbors to the south are shown in Codex Becker II and include Yucuna, Tecomaxtlahuaca, Ayú, as well as Tilantongo (figure 31.3; see M. E. Smith 1979).

Like Acatlan, Coaixtlahuaca advocated a connection to both Tolteca-Chichimeca migration heroes and Mixtec hereditary ancestors. On Codex Bodley 11–14 the children of 8 Deer's fourth wife intermarried with a twelfth-century dynasty at San Miguel Tulancingo, a kingdom

that may have dominated much of the Texupan and Coaixtlahuaca area prior to the establishment of Coaixtlahuaca itself (Smith 1973a:72–73). According to the Tlapiltepec and Seler II lienzos, Coaixtlahuaca subsequently instituted a system of dual rulership that continued through more than 20 generations. Descendants of Atonal the Elder (Lord 6 Water in the lienzos) founded the royal houses at Ihuitlan, Tequixtepec, Tulancingo, and Tlapiltepec (Caso 1961; König 1984; Parmenter 1982, 1993; Rincón Mautner 1994; van Doesburg and van Buren n.d.). The Lienzo de Ihuitlan relates that descendants of Ihuitlan's rulers in turn intermarried with Acatlan, Coxcatlan, and Tehuacan.

The Lienzo de Tlapiltepec portrays the journeys of

Mixtec-Chocho men and women into Puebla by connecting various place signs with either red or black lines (Parmenter 1982; Jansen and Gaxiola 1978; Johnson 1994, 1997; Pohl 1994b). In most cases the lines seem to identify intermarriages between Coaixtlahuaca, or one of its subjects, and various Tolteca-Chichimeca kingdoms, including Tecamachalco, Tecali, Tepeyacac, and Cuauhtinchan. The *Historia Tolteca-Chichimeca* states that shortly after Cuauhtinchan's founding, two Mixtec-Popolocan (Chocho) lords named Tecpatzin and 13 Rain went from Coaixtlahuaca to Cuauhtinchan, where they married two Tolteca-Chichimeca women. Nothing more is said of Tecpatzin, but he may have gone on to Tlaxcala. The last group of Tolteca-Chichimeca portrayed on Cuauhtinchan Map 2 traveled south past Coaixtlahuaca, turned north through Aztatla, continued past the Orizaba and Malinche volcanos, and finally descended into the Tlaxcala Valley to settle at Tepeticpac.[6]

Lord 13 Rain, on the other hand, established a barrio at Cuauhtinchan called Zacauilotlan (Kirchhoff et al. 1976:205–206; Johnson 1994:130–133). Thirteen Rain's son 1 Motion (or 8 Motion) later became ruler of Oxtotipan, and the Lienzo de Tlapiltepec suggests that 1 Motion's descendants either founded, or married into, royal lines at Tecamachalco, Tepeyacac, and Quecholac. Additional lines appearing in both the Cuauhtinchan maps and the Coaixtlahuaca lienzos indicate multiple marriages through time between these two regions (Johnson 1994:140–141). There are a few references to Mixtec populations settling even within the Basin of Mexico itself. The most famous is Ixtlilxochitl's account of the Tlailotlaque and Chimalpanecas, Mixtecs of "Toltec" heritage from either Cuauhtinchan, Acatlan, or Coaixtlahuaca who had gone first to Chalco and later Texcoco, where Quinatzin gave them lands to settle. They became renowned as artisans, painters, and diviners (figure 31.3; see Alva Ixtlilxochitl 1965:1:123–124, 2:69–70).

We know substantially more about marital alliances uniting Oaxaca with southern Puebla than we do about those uniting northern Puebla and Tlaxcala (Carrasco 1984). The few surviving genealogies for these kingdoms rarely extend beyond four or five generations.[7] Elsewhere I have proposed that the Tolteca-Chichimeca did not emphasize genealogies in their histories because a tecuhtli did not rule by divinely ordained hereditary descent, as did the Mixtec yya or the Zapotec coqui, but rather by being elected to his position (Pohl 1994a, 1994b; Pohl and Byland 1994; see chapter 25). The city-states of Chalco, Tlaxcala, Huexotzinco, Cholula, Atlixco, Cuauhtinchan, Tepeyacac, Tecali, and Tecamachalco maintained larger and more complex political institutions than those of their southern allies. The central administrations of Tlaxcala and Huexotzinco, for example, consisted of not one, but four autonomous royal houses aligned along adjoining hills (Anguiano and Chapa 1976;

Dyckerhoff and Prem 1976). Marriages were essential to maintain the allegiances within the landholding corporation composed of the teccalli and to define the territorial boundaries of a core city-state. We know that marriages between city-states must have been arranged regularly, but they were probably employed through lesser-ranking children both to confirm alliances and to secure tributary obligations following conflicts that periodically divided confederacy members.[8]

Cuauhtinchan became more diversified than either Huexotzinco or Tlaxcala. The original Cuauhtinchantlaca immigrants not only opened their lands up to Mixteca-Popolocan settlement, but incorporated Huexotzincan and Cholulan populations as well (Reyes García 1977:53–56, 62–64; Olivera 1976:186–187). The sites claimed by these peoples have been identified archaeologically between the present-day communities of Cuauhtinchan, Tepeyacac, Tecamachalco, Quecholac, and Tecali, reinforcing historical evidence that these communities were virtually a single political entity until they were divided by the empire of the Triple Alliance following Axayacatl's attack on Tepeyacac in 1466 (Reyes García 1977:145; Davila 1975; Olivera 1976:193). Connections to the north into the Basin of Mexico, east into Veracruz, and west into Morelos are more tenuous. There is little documentary evidence of any major extension of marriage networks into these regions aside from the establishment of the barrios of Mixtecs at Chalco and Texcoco discussed above, and Torquemada's account of the lord of Huexotzinco embracing Nezhualcoyotl as a "relative," perhaps in reference to a legend that Huexotzinco's first kings were related to Xolotl (Torquemada 1986:1:134; Alva Ixtlilxochitl 1965:1:110).

CONCLUSIONS: POLITICAL DYNAMICS IN A CENTRAL MEXICAN CORE ZONE

Cholula and the wider Eastern Nahua area was a core zone throughout the Postclassic sequence, but it was a very different kind of core zone than the Tarascan and Aztec cores discussed in the previous chapters. Populations were high, as in the Pátzcuaro Basin and the Basin of Mexico, but in this area empires did not emerge. The pre-Aztec confederacies in this zone (see chapter 10) may have signaled a move toward larger, more integrated political units, but if so, this development did not proceed very far. Instead, with Cholula serving more as a source of shared political ideology than of military dominance, political power remained in the hands of local city-state elites who used marriages as well as feasts involving the use of polychrome vessels and other serving wares to ensure their rule and promote their interests.

One of the interesting features of Postclassic political dynamics in this area was the close networks of intermarriage not just within the Nahuatl-speaking core zone, but between this area and the Mixtec and Zapotec affluent production zones (see also chapters 10 and 26). The multistranded, overlapping economic, political, social, and religious networks of this area provide a good example of the complexity and dynamic nature of interactions in the Postclassic Mesoamerican world system. Smith presents another prime example of these complexities and dynamics in his discussion of Morelos households in the next chapter.

32

Economic Change in Morelos Households

Michael E. Smith

How did the various large-scale processes of the Post-classic Mesoamerican world system affect people's lives? And how did the actions of individuals in turn influence world-system processes? In this chapter I examine the linkages between large-scale world-system dynamics and individual households in an affluent production zone of central Mexico. Morelos was an area of rich farmland whose grains and cotton—as well as bark paper, cotton textiles, and other products—were exported to the Basin of Mexico throughout the Middle and Late Postclassic periods. Most of the archaeological data presented here come from my excavations of Postclassic residential structures, both elite and commoner, at the sites of Yautepec in north-central Morelos, and Cuexcomate and Capilco in western Morelos. I also draw on a study of ceramics from Postclassic sites throughout the state of Morelos (Smith 2003).

EXCAVATIONS

I use the following designations for Postclassic time periods (see table 1.1): Middle Postclassic (A.D. 1100–1300; Temazcalli phase in western Morelos, and Pochtla phase at Yautepec); Late Postclassic-A (A.D. 1300–1430; Early Cuauhnahuac in western Morelos; Atlan phase at Yautepec); and Late Postclassic-B (A.D. 1430–1550; Late Cuauhnahuac and Molotla phases).

CUEXCOMATE AND CAPILCO

Located near Xochicalco on the huge alluvial fan known as the Buenavista Lomas, the sites of Cuexcomate and Capilco were first reported by Kenneth G. Hirth's Xochicalco Mapping Project (Hirth 2000) in 1978 (figure 32.1). In 1986, Cynthia Heath-Smith and I excavated a large number of houses and other structures at these rural sites (Smith 1992a; Smith and Heath-Smith 1994).

Because house foundation walls were visible on the surface, we were able to map most of the architecture and conduct energetic analyses of construction costs. We tested a large number of houses and excavated several structures completely. These houses had been abandoned gradually, probably as part of the Congregación de Indias policy of resettlement (Gerhard 1977, 1993b), and the inhabitants moved to the nearby village of Tetlama in the early or mid-sixteenth century; consequently, few artifacts were left on the house floors. Our excavation sampling emphasized midden deposits located with the help of soil phosphate tests. These middens furnished good samples of ceramics, obsidian, and other artifacts. A refined Postclassic chronology was developed for these sites (Smith and Doershuk 1991), resulting in a detailed picture of economic and social change in the Postclassic period. In addition to houses, we excavated several agricultural terraces and did reconstructions of regional population and carrying capacity in the vicinity of these sites.

Capilco was founded in the Middle Postclassic period as a tiny hamlet of a few commoner houses (the following reconstruction is based on Smith and Heath-Smith 1994). The founders may have come from the western edge of Xochicalco, where a small settlement had survived the eighth-century collapse of Xochicalco and continued in existence through the Spanish conquest. Regional population expanded greatly in the Late Postclassic-A period. Capilco grew in size, and Cuexcomate and numerous other settlements in the region were first settled. Agricultural terracing was initiated at this time in the form of hillside terraces and cross-channel terraces (check dams). An elite group built an impressive palace structure at Cuexcomate across a public plaza from a modest temple-pyramid. Imported goods from the Basin of Mexico increased in frequency, as did household production of cotton cloth and bark paper. Exotic imports—

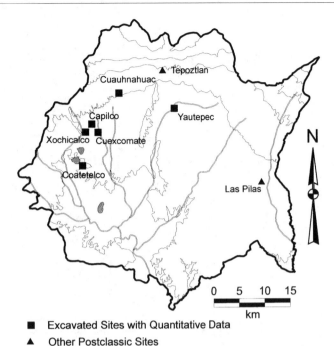

Figure 32.1 Map of Morelos sites mentioned in the chapter

ceramics, obsidian, jade, and bronze—were present in almost all residential middens, indicating that both commoners and elites had ready access to valuable goods. Elsewhere I have argued that this distribution pattern is indicative of the prevalence of marketplace exchange in provisioning these goods (Smith 1999). The overall impression at these sites is that the Late Postclassic-A period was a time of prosperity.

In the Late Postclassic-B period, population growth continued: Capilco became a village of 20 houses, and Cuexcomate a town of 150 houses. This growth was accompanied by terrace construction. The expansion of check-dam cultivation indicates that soil erosion was increasing upstream, and a reconstruction of agricultural productivity suggests that the population may have been approaching the carrying capacity. The elite compound at Cuexcomate was abandoned, and a much smaller and more modest elite compound was built in its place. Imported goods declined in frequency, but production of cotton cloth increased (as measured by frequencies of spindle whorls and spinning bowls). Artifactual wealth indices point to a decline in standard of living for both social classes, as well as a decrease in elite-commoner differences.

What caused the economic troubles in Late Postclassic-B times? Two likely processes are implicated. First, the demographic and agricultural processes suggest the presence of a regional agrarian crisis. The Buenavista Lomas, an upland area with little good alluvial land, was transformed from a pioneer situation of abundant land and limited labor to an overdeveloped situation of limited land and overabundant labor. This kind of agrarian

cycle has been documented for various parts of medieval and early modern Europe, with similar social consequences (Le Roy Ladurie 1972; Miller and Hatcher 1978). The second relevant process is the conquest of Morelos by the Aztec empire. Although imperial tribute was relatively modest compared to the population levels of Morelos (Smith 1994b), Aztec conquest had indirect effects that allowed local and regional elite to increase their own tribute demands under the empire. The net effect was probably a major increase in exploitation of the commoner class in provincial areas such as Morelos.

Neither of these overall processes—demographic increase and agricultural crisis, and imperial conquest—was unique to Morelos. Famines, malnutrition, and other crises became commonplace in the Basin of Mexico under the Aztec empire (chapter 30), whose imperial conquest affected large parts of Mesoamerica, both directly and indirectly (chapter 11). In order to investigate the effects of Aztec conquest in a broader zone of Morelos, we next undertook excavations at Yautepec.

YAUTEPEC

In 1992 we moved to Yautepec, an Aztec urban center in central Morelos, to excavate more houses. The goals of the project included the evaluation of the effects of conquest by the Aztec empire, along with the reconstruction of urban economic and social patterns. In Late Postclassic times, Yautepec was a powerful political capital whose king was lord over several smaller city-states in the Yautepec River valley (Gerhard 1970; Smith 1994b). Because the Aztec-period city lies under the modern town of the same name, it was much more difficult to sample this 200 hectare site with excavations. Through extensive test-pitting in open urban lots, we managed to excavate seven residences and a number of other midden deposits without associated architecture. The Postclassic deposits at Yautepec contained very dense middens, and we recovered more than a million sherds plus many thousands of obsidian artifacts.

We do not have much information about Yautepec's local agricultural context. Today it is in an area of major canal irrigation where sugarcane, maize, and other crops are grown. Documentary sources indicate that irrigation was widespread in Postclassic times (Maldonado Jiménez 1990; Smith 1994b), but we have yet to reconstruct the likely extent of Postclassic irrigation. Attempts to locate Postclassic canals through excavation were unsuccessful. Remnants of agricultural terraces are present near Yautepec, but these have not been excavated, and it is difficult or impossible to date these features, many of which are probably modern. Our full-coverage survey of the Yautepec Valley will provide far better regional context than we have in western Morelos, but the analysis of the survey data is not far enough along to describe here.

A Postclassic chronology parallel to that in western

Morelos was constructed for Yautepec (Hare and Smith 1996). As the results of quantitative and other analyses began to appear, there did not seem to be major changes concurrent with the Aztec conquest of Yautepec. In fact, the transition between the Middle and Late Postclassic periods seemed to mark greater economic changes, particularly in the realm of foreign trade, than the transition between the Late Postclassic-A and -B periods that signaled Aztec conquest.

My initial hypothesis to account for these changes at Yautepec was that the Mesoamerican world system expanded greatly in the Late Postclassic period, encompassing Yautepec at this time. In another work (Smith 2001c) I tried to distinguish the processes of the world system from those of Aztec imperialism. The timing of economic changes at Yautepec suggests that the economic processes of the Mesoamerican world system may have had greater impacts on local households in Yautepec than the conquest of this area by the Aztec empire. My interpretations of the Yautepec data are somewhat provisional, since analytical research on the artifacts is still in progress (Fauman-Fichman 1999; Norris n.d.; Olson 2001).[1]

PROCESSES OF CHANGE

The following discussion focuses on the Middle and Late Postclassic periods in Morelos. A major problem in interpreting Postclassic changes in Morelos is the absence of excavated Early Postclassic sites and the resulting lack of quantitative data for that period. My impression from survey results and from very limited excavations at Xochicalco (Smith 2003) is that the level of exchange was much lower in Early Postclassic times, and that the Middle and Late Postclassic periods witnessed tremendous increases in population, exchange, and economic activity in general.

DEMOGRAPHY AND AGRICULTURE
The Middle and Late Postclassic periods witnessed a major surge of population in all parts of central Mexico for which data are available. My demographic reconstruction for the area around Cuexcomate and Capilco indicates significant sustained population growth throughout the Postclassic sequence at the regional scale and at these sites (table 32.1). Every house occupied in the Middle Postclassic period continued to be occupied in later phases, and every house occupied in the Late Postclassic-A period was also occupied in Late Postclassic-B times. The only exception to this pattern of sustained growth is the Late Postclassic-A elite compound, Group 6 at Cuexcomate, which was abandoned in the Late Postclassic-B period.

The same pattern of sustained growth of households (none were abandoned during the sequence once they were occupied) is also found at Yautepec (Smith Heath-

Table 32.1
Population estimates for excavated rural sites

	Middle Postclassic	Late Postclassic-A	Late Postclassic-B
Capilco	30	70	120
Cuexcomate	—	240	800

Smith, and Montiel 1999), although our sample of excavated houses is neither as large nor representative as the samples at the rural sites. The Yautepec Valley Survey also found a pattern of major, sustained population growth at this time, but the demographic data have yet to be calibrated into population estimates. The inception of the Middle Postclassic period falls during the twelfth century A.D., which is when a five-century period of drought in central Mexico came to an end (Metcalfe et al. 1991; O'Hara et al. 1994).

I have applied Netting's (1993) model of smallholder intensive agriculture to terracing at Capilco and Cuexcomate (Smith and Price 1994). Population pressure led to the adoption of intensive farming methods at the household level, but probably did not lead to political centralization or other large-scale changes as argued by the population-pressure theorists of the 1970s and 1980s.

POLITICAL CHANGE
As described in chapter 9, the Middle Postclassic period was a time of city-state formation in Morelos and the Basin of Mexico. In the Late Postclassic-A period, several Morelos polities expanded at the expense of their neighbors, and by the Late Postclassic-B period, these more powerful polities—Cuauhnahuac, Yautepec, Huaxtepec, Totolapan, Yacapitztlan, and Ocuituco—controlled a total of about 60 subject city-states (Gerhard 1970; Smith 1994b). The larger conquest-states were in turn subject to the Aztec empire through the tributary provinces of Cuauhnahuac and Huaxtepec (Smith 1994b). The Cuauhnahuac province corresponded closely to the extent of the Cuauhnahuac conquest-state, whereas the Huaxtepec imperial province included several local polities. Sources are clear that this arrangement did not imply that the polity of Huaxtepec was dominant over the other polities, such as Yautepec or Yacapitztlan; the latter merely paid their imperial tribute through a calpixqui in Huaxtepec. There is some evidence that even after the Morelos polities were conquered by the Aztec empire and incorporated as imperial tributary provinces, they continued to expand their territories through conquest. For example, Cuauhnahuac was conquering new lands in northeastern Guerrero long after their own conquest by Tenochtitlan (Smith 1986). This suggests a pattern of imperial support for the subject kings and polities incorporated into the tributary provinces.

Table 32.2

Intensity of craft production at Morelos sites

	Cuexcomate/Capilco	Yautepec
Cotton textiles	Heavy	Moderate to Heavy
Chert tools	Low	Low
Smoothed items	Low to Moderate	Low to Moderate
Obsidian blades	—	Moderate to Heavy
Obsidian jewelry	—	Low
Ceramic figurines	—	Low to Moderate
Ceramic whorls	—	Low
Ceramic censers	—	Low
Bark paper	Moderate	Low
Bark beaters	Low	—
Painted items	Low to Moderate	Traces

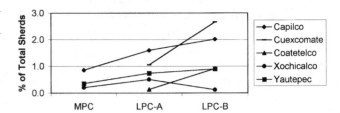

Figure 32.2 Frequencies of cotton-spinning artifacts at five Postclassic sites. (Data from Smith 2003.)

CRAFT PRODUCTION

Our excavations uncovered evidence for a variety of craft production activities in domestic contexts. There were few differences between Cuexcomate and Capilco in the presence and quantities of craft activities, but these rural sites present a contrast with Yautepec. Table 32.2 presents my subjective impressions of the intensity of craft production at these three sites. I have divided the crafts into three categories: those with equivalent expression in the two areas, those found exclusively at Yautepec, and those found predominantly at the rural sites.

Cotton Textiles

The production of cotton textiles was by far the dominant craft activity in Postclassic Morelos. Morelos was the only area of highland central Mexico with an appropriate climate to cultivate cotton, and a distinctive local tradition of small spindle whorls can be traced back to the Epiclassic period at Xochicalco (Smith and Hirth 1988). Ethnohistoric sources describe irrigated cotton cultivation, production of cotton mantas, and an active trade in mantas and raw cotton. Cotton spinning is indicated by ceramic spindle whorls and small tripod spinning bowls, artifacts that are ubiquitous and abundant in excavations of Postclassic houses. These items have been documented in quantitative studies of ceramics at a number of sites (Smith 2003), and the basic data are presented in figure 32.2. (More extensive and refined analyses of textile production in Morelos can be found in Fauman-Fichman 1999.) There is a pattern of increasing frequencies at all sites, with only a single exception (the Postclassic hamlet at Xochicalco from Late Postclassic-A to Late Postclassic-B times). Also notable are the higher frequencies at Cuexcomate and Capilco relative to Yautepec in all time periods.

Chert Tools

Chert is a minor part of chipped-stone inventories at Postclassic sites, and a small amount of tool production evidently took place at most sites (Norris n.d.; Sorensen 1988).

Smoothed Items

This category is based upon worked sherds and water-worn sherds, which are found consistently in low numbers at most sites. These may have been used to smooth ceramic vessels, or perhaps they were used in other craft activities.

Obsidian Blades

There is little evidence for obsidian blade production at Cuexcomate and Capilco sites (Norris, in process; Sorensen 1988). Inhabitants of these sites probably obtained obsidian from the nearby settlement of El Ciruelo, just north of Xochicalco, where a Postclassic obsidian blade production industry has been identified (Sorensen et al. 1989). Yautepec, in contrast, has abundant evidence for the production of obsidian blades, including debitage, small percussion blades and flakes, and exhausted and broken cores. This material is found in most of the excavations, but in higher concentrations in some locations. It is premature to talk of workshops or specialized production, however. Susan Norris (n.d.) is currently analyzing the obsidian from Yautepec, Cuexcomate and Capilco, focusing on the technological and social aspects of this industry.

Obsidian Jewelry

The Yautepec excavations uncovered a few pieces of obsidian broken in the process of making earspools and other jewelry; these were identified on the basis of Otis Charlton's (1993) reconstruction of the obsidian lapidary industry at Otumba. Although we cannot identify the place of origin of the finished earspools and labrets found at Yautepec, it is interesting that both forms of obsidian labret are present: the short, thick, polished cylindrical type manufactured from exhausted cores, and the long,

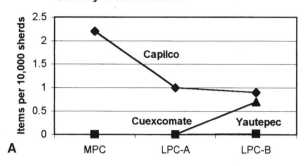

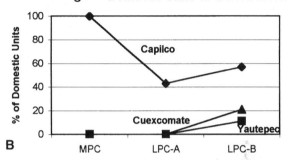

Figure 32.4 Quantities of bark beaters at three sites: (a) mean frequencies per 10,000 sherds; (b) percentage of domestic units with bark beaters.

Figure 32.3 Quantities of ceramic molds (for figures and spindle whorls) at Yautepec: (a) mean frequencies per 10,000 sherds; (b) percentage of domestic units with molds.

thin, cruder type made from blades (Brumfiel et al. 1994; Otis Charlton 1993).

Ceramic Objects
Small numbers of ceramic molds were recovered at Yau-tepec, but not at the rural sites. There are 22 molds for figurines, 5 for spindle whorls, and 2 for ladle-type censers with molded decoration. These molds provide evidence for the same sorts of ceramic production described at Otumba, but at a much lower level (Charlton et al. 1991). The figurine molds pertain to two categories of figurine: local styles found only at Yautepec, and figurines of the general Aztec style found in Morelos, the Basin of Mexico, and perhaps other areas (Olson et al. 1999). The molds for spindle whorls are for the small, cotton-spinning variety, and we also found a partially formed whorl. In addition, surface collections at another Postclassic site in the Yautepec Valley produced a mold for a larger maguey whorl. The two censer molds are for the standard Aztec ladle-type censer often classified as Texcoco molded.

Quantities of ceramic molds at Yautepec are portrayed in two ways in figure 32.3 (because of the difficulty in obtaining reliable quantitative interpretations for rare categories). The first graph shows the mean quantity of ceramic molds per 10,000 sherds in each phase, and the second shows the ubiquity of molds, or the frequency of domestic units yielding at least one mold. The two forms of quantification show the same pattern: a major reduc-

tion in molds between the Middle Postclassic and Late Postclassic-A periods.

Bark Paper
Bark paper was produced from the inner bark of the *amatl*, or wild fig tree. Fibers were stripped off, soaked, and then pounded into paper with the grooved stone implements known as bark beaters (von Hagen 1944; Wyllie 1994). Bark beaters are far more common at the rural sites, particularly at Capilco, than at Yautepec. Figure 32.4 shows the quantities of bark beaters through time. Morelos populations gave bark paper as tribute to the Aztec empire.

Bark Beaters
We found two types of evidence for the manufacture of bark beaters at Cuexcomate and Capilco. Bark-beater blanks are basalt preforms the same size and shape as beaters but without the characteristic grooves. Obsidian groovers consist of prismatic blades with heavily abraded edges that were probably used to cut the grooves.

Painted Items
This category pertains to paint or pigments recovered in excavations. Lumps of hematite (red), limonite (yellow), and graphite (black) are relatively common at Cuexcomate and Capilco, but much rarer in the Yautepec excavations. One patio group at Cuexcomate (Group 10)

Total Imported Ceramics by Site

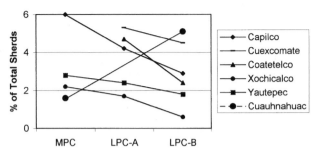

Figure 32.5 Trends in the quantities of imported ceramics

produced unusually high frequencies of both bark beaters and pigments in the Late Postclassic-B period, suggesting a possible specialization in the production of paper and painted manuscripts. This group was located near the Late Postclassic-B elite compound.

Discussion

There are clear differences in emphasis between the rural sites and Yautepec in terms of their craft production activities. All sites were heavily involved in cotton textile production, although the rural sites had greater quantities of production artifacts. The urban site had ceramic and obsidian industries lacking at the rural sites, which engaged in more craft activities relating to paper and perhaps manuscript production. Two quantitative trends in these data stand out. First, there was a steady increase in frequencies of cotton-spinning artifacts at all sites over all three periods. This was probably the result of both an increasing commercial use of cotton textiles and an increase in the economic exploitation of commoners by increasingly powerful elites (cotton textiles were the predominant item of tribute). Second, there is a large drop in frequencies of molds (at Yautepec) and bark beaters (at Capilco) after the Middle Postclassic period. One possible cause of this pattern could be a growing economic interdependence among settlements and regions in Late Postclassic-A times that might have reduced the need for specialized local products in some regions; however, this hypothesis is difficult to evaluate with our present sample of excavated sites.

EXCHANGE

Several lines of evidence indicate that market systems were important institutions in the regional economies of Late Postclassic Morelos. Documentary sources mention markets in Morelos communities of all sizes, from the largest cities to small villages (Smith 1994b); the high volume of imported goods at all sites points to active commercial exchange (Smith 2002), and the distribution of high-value imports among both elite and commoner houses is consistent with the operation of a market sys-

tem (Hirth 1998; Smith 1999). Ceramics are a particularly useful class of commodities for monitoring market exchange since they are generally not included in imperial tribute documents. Ceramic vessels were probably part of the tributary receipts of local lords, but it is unlikely that they were included in long-distance tribute payments (Berdan and Anawalt 1992; Rojas 1993). The overall trends in the quantities of imported ceramics are given in figure 32.5.

Exchange within Morelos

Distinctive regional ceramic types comprise the main category of evidence for exchange within Morelos, particularly the geometric polychromes of the Tlahuica Polychrome style found outside of their presumed locus of production. These trade sherds are a low-frequency but consistent component of most of the domestic inventories in Postclassic Morelos. I have suggested places of origin for many of the ceramic types of the Tlahuica Polychrome style based on distributional data (Smith 2003), and recent neutron-activation studies have confirmed these hypotheses for the tested types (Smith, Neff, and Fauman-Fichman 1999).

There was a steady decrease at most sites in the frequencies of imports from other parts of Morelos. A large part of this decline is probably due to the chronological situation of the Teopanzolco ceramic complex. The site of Teopanzolco has a large twin-stair pyramid dating to the Middle Postclassic period, and this was probably the Middle Postclassic capital of Cuauhnahuac. Ceramics at this site exhibit a tremendous variability in decoration within the Tlahuica Polychrome style (Smith 2003), and several of these types are the predominant Morelos trade wares (i.e., numerically most abundant at other sites). The Teopanzolco phase, when these types were made and used, dates to the Middle Postclassic period and the first half of the Late Postclassic-A period. At the same time, there was a trend toward greater regional uniformity of non-Teopanzolco Polychrome types, making it much more difficult to identify imported sherds without characterization data. Nevertheless, there is other evidence that suggests declining ceramic trade between Yautepec and western Morelos apart from these two factors. Imports of the Yautepec type B-7 at Cuexcomate and Capilco declined between Late Postclassic-A and -B times, perhaps suggesting hostilities between the expanding Cuauhnahuac and Yautepec polities. Another trend was a reduction in the number of regionally distinct ceramic complexes, and a corresponding increase in the areal extent of ceramic complexes. This was most notable in western Morelos, where two or three ceramic complexes in Middle Postclassic times were reduced to the single Late Cuauhnahuac complex in the Late Postclassic-B period (see chapter 16).

Exchange with the Basin of Mexico

Almost all sites in Morelos engaged in active exchange with the Basin of Mexico in all periods. The trend of basin ceramic imports at Morelos sites is one of initial increase (Middle Postclassic to Late Postclassic-A) followed by decline (Late Postclassic-A to -B). The most abundant imported type was the Texcoco Fabric-marked basins used to produce and transport salt from the basin's saline lakes (chapter 19). This is followed by various individual types of the Aztec Black-on-orange category. The basin origin of the latter types has been confirmed by neutron activation (Smith, Neff, and Fauman-Fichman 1999b). Most of the Aztec Black-on-orange at Yautepec (types Aztec II and III) is from the Tenochtitlan production area. In Late Postclassic-B times, the Aztec III/IV type appears, and tested sherds fall into the Texcoco production group. It is difficult to determine whether this signals a reorientation of Yautepec's ceramic exchange from Tenochtitlan to Texcoco, or the addition of Texcoco ceramics to existing imports from Tenochtitlan. Other imported types include Xochimilco Polychrome, an uncertain number of Chalco polychromes (see discussion below), and some figurines.

Very small quantities of Morelos sherds have been found at sites in the Basin of Mexico, including Xaltocan, Culhuacan, Tlahuac, Amecameca, and Tenochtitlan (these are reported in Smith 2003: table 16.8).

Obsidian Quantities and Sources

The data described here are highly provisional, pending completion of current research. Some preliminary data were presented in Smith and Heath-Smith 1994 and in Smith et al. 1996. The data in table 32.3 show lower quantities of obsidian at the village site, Capilco. Quantities at Yautepec drop by half in the Late Postclassic-B period, whereas Cuexcomate has even greater amounts in that period.

We collected an excellent sample for sourcing at Yautepec, consisting of pseudo-random samples of gray and green blades selected from each well-dated domestic unit, but the results of sourcing through x-ray fluorescence are not yet available. We did complete the sourcing of a preliminary sample of artifacts by NAA and XRF (Smith et al. 1996), and the basic chronological trends are that Basin of Mexico gray sources decline in frequency through time, whereas other central Mexican sources increase.

Exchange with More-Distant Areas

Three categories of artifacts were imported from areas other than Morelos or the Basin of Mexico: obsidian, ceramics, and rare valuable goods. The people of Yautepec made considerable use of obsidian sources from the northern frontier of the Aztec empire and in the Tarascan

Table 32.3
Frequency of obsidian by period

	Middle Postclassic	Late Postclassic-A	Late Postclassic-B
Capilco	1.5	2.0	2.1
Cuexcomate	—	3.5	4.2
Yautepec	3.4	3.6	1.8

Note: Frequencies expressed as number of items per 100 sherds.

area. The most common area of origin for ceramic imports, after the Basin of Mexico, is a large zone west and northwest of Morelos. This category includes ceramics from the Toluca Valley, the Valle de Bravo area on the Tarascan border, and parts of northeast Guerrero. As might be expected, these are more common in western Morelos than in Yautepec or eastern Morelos, but their frequencies do not show any clear trends through time. The neutron-activation research revealed some interesting patterns. Of the 10 complex polychrome sherds we classified as Chalco-Cholula polychromes, only one was sourced to Chalco, and none to Cholula (Smith, Neff, and Fauman-Fichman 1999). Most were assigned to the Huexotzinco and Ocotelulco source areas of the Puebla/Tlaxcala area (see discussion in Neff et al. 1994). Furthermore, a number of spindle whorls included in that analysis were assigned to a southern Puebla source in the Late Postclassic-A and Late Postclassic-B periods.

Valuable, low-frequency imported goods included bronze objects and exotic jewelry. These are both quite rare, and they are quantified (figures 32.6, 32.7) following the two methods described above for ceramic molds. Most of the bronze objects are sewing needles; there are also other tools (awls and an axe) and a few elite objects (bells and tweezers). Research by Hosler (chapter 21) shows that the bronze objects were imported from Michoacán and Jalisco. Exotic jewelry consists of beads and ornaments of greenstone, rock crystal, and shell imported from distant areas. The quantified data in figures 32.6 and 32.7 suggest that these exotic imports were more common at Capilco and Cuexcomate than at Yautepec, where both categories were absent in Middle Postclassic times.

STYLISTIC INTERACTION

There are several kinds of evidence for stylistic interaction with areas outside Morelos. Many ceramic traits are shared with Postclassic sites in the Basin of Mexico. Some of these are items of food preparation and serving suggestive of similar food habits (e.g., thin, flat comals and basic forms of cooking and storage jars), and others pertain to the realms of ritual (e.g., figurines and ladle-type censers). There are architectural similarities between

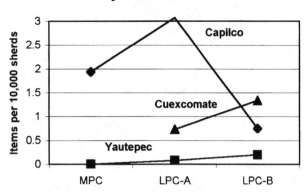

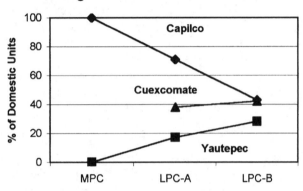

Figure 32.6 Quantities of bronze artifacts at three sites: (a) items per 10,000 sherds; (b) percentage of domestic units with bronze

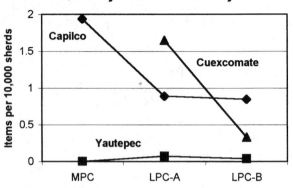

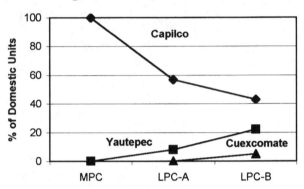

Figure 32.7 Quantities of exotic jewelry (greenstone, rock crystal, shell) at three sites

Postclassic palace plans in the two areas, suggesting some kind of common elite culture, or at least interaction. Early Colonial–period lienzos and codices from Morelos are very similar to those from the Basin of Mexico and pertain to the same artistic tradition (Boone 2000; Robertson 1959). The iconography and style of carved stones at several sites are identical to the Aztec style of the Basin of Mexico; these include the pulque reliefs at the temple of Tepozteco (Nicholson 1991; Seler 1990–98, v.4:266–280) and the Los Reyes rock carvings in the rural Yautepec Valley (Krickeberg 1969). No polychrome murals are known from Postclassic Morelos.

DISCUSSION

This section contains observations on how the data presented above relate to some of the wider processes of the Postclassic Mesoamerican world system.

POPULATION GROWTH

The Postclassic population surge in Morelos described above was a major force driving some of the changes observed archaeologically, including the spread of popula-

tions into marginal areas like the Buenavista Lomas, the intensification of agricultural practices, urbanization, and perhaps political expansion.

PROLIFERATION OF SMALL POLITIES

Postclassic Morelos was united ethnically and commercially, but fragmented politically. This situation, also found in many other parts of Postclassic Mesoamerica (see chapters in part 2), is typical of many ancient and historical city-state cultures around the world (Hansen 2000b). Several aspects of Hansen's model are relevant to the present discussion. First, political fragmentation in city-state cultures is not a barrier to trade. This certainly fits Morelos, where trade in ceramics, obsidian, cotton, and other goods was generally not restricted by political boundaries. Second, city-state cultures tend to develop in periods of economic prosperity, which also fits Postclassic Morelos in the Middle Postclassic and Late Postclassic-A periods.

The data presented above also demonstrate trade across imperial borders (chapter 14). Sherds from Valle de Bravo (one of the Aztec border towns) at Xochicalco and Coatetelco provide evidence of commercial links between Morelos polities and the border area. There is no reason to think that the Tarascan artifacts arrived via

Tenochtitlan or the Basin of Mexico; in fact it is more likely that trade across the imperial borders was accomplished outside of state controls through smuggling operations. The small polities of Postclassic Morelos were conducive to the operation of a vigorous market-based and multilevel exchange system.

INCREASED VOLUME OF EXCHANGE

The period of greatest expansion of exchange in Morelos—the Early-to-Middle Postclassic transition—is also the most poorly documented, due to the lack of excavations at Early Postclassic sites. Based on very limited Early Postclassic samples from Xochicalco (Smith 2003) and preliminary judgments from a survey of the Yautepec Valley (Hare et al. n.d.), it appears that there was only very limited trade between Morelos polities and outside areas (such as Tula) during Early Postclassic times. Beginning with the initial documented Middle Postclassic occupations at Yautepec, Capilco, and other sites, the peoples of Morelos engaged in active exchange with a large number of areas for a wide variety of goods. Patterns of imported ceramics and other materials changed in various ways during Postclassic times in response to both local factors and wider world-system processes.

GREATER DIVERSITY OF TRADE GOODS

The same difficulty noted above for the volume of exchange applies to the diversity of trade goods. My subjective impression is that there were fewer types of imports in Early Postclassic Morelos, but the lack of quantified data from excavated contexts prevents firm conclusions on this point.

COMMERCIALIZATION OF THE ECONOMY

One indication of the importance of commercialization in Postclassic Morelos is the degree to which major sectors of the economy were outside of elite control. There is little evidence from our excavations to suggest that elites exerted much control over those aspects of the economy described here (agriculture, crafts, and commercial exchange). Cross-culturally, terraced agriculture is almost always organized at the household level, without elite or state control (Netting 1968, 1993). The elites may have owned or controlled the land around Capilco and Cuexcomate, and "rented" it to farmers, as in the Morelos communities covered in early sixteenth-century census documents (Carrasco 1972; Cline 1993), but it is likely that labor and its products were under the control of the individual farming households. The situation with irrigation agriculture in the Yautepec Valley may have been different, but there is little empirical evidence on this.

Documentary sources mention cases in Morelos where commoner women went to elite households to spin and weave textiles for their local lord (see discussion in Smith 1994b or Fauman-Fichman 1999), suggesting some level of elite control over the textile industry. It was therefore surprising to find that elite houses did not have higher frequencies of spindle whorls or spinning bowls than found at commoner houses (at either Cuexcomate or Yautepec). Cotton mantas were the main tribute good at all levels, from tribute to a local lord to imperial tribute, and thus elites had some level of control over these goods. Nevertheless, the available evidence from Morelos and elsewhere indicates that women produced textiles in their homes without outside interference or control. Some of these textiles were destined for tribute payments, others were for household clothing needs, and others were undoubtedly exchanged in the market for other goods.

There does not seem to be any evidence for elite control over other craft industries. Craft indicators such as obsidian debitage and bark beaters are not found in greater quantities at elite residential compounds, nor do they appear to be more common at commoner houses adjacent to elite compounds. The only exception here is the possible paper-makers and manuscript painters of Group 10 at Cuexcomate, located near (but not adjacent to) the Late Postclassic-B elite compound.

The arguments outlined above for the importance of marketplace exchange in Postclassic Morelos also indicate the economy's high degree of commercialization. All kinds of goods—from cooking pots to exotic jade and obsidian jewelry—were traded through the markets, where they were purchased by both commoners and elites.

MORELOS HOUSEHOLDS IN THE POSTCLASSIC WORLD SYSTEM

The basic processes of change in the Postclassic world system affected life at both rural and urban settlements in Morelos. Postclassic commercial-exchange systems reached far into the central Mexican countryside, drawing inhabitants of small villages like Capilco into the world system as active participants. Even the poorest peasant households at the village of Capilco and the city of Yautepec had access to an abundance and a diversity of exotic imported goods. The economic prosperity of the Middle-to-Late Postclassic-A periods that resulted from the growth and transformation of the world system benefited Morelos households, and the economic contraction of the Late Postclassic-B period (caused by overpopulation and exploitation by the Aztec empire) worked to their detriment. But these rural and urban peoples were not just the recipients of large-scale changes from the imperial and metropolitan centers. The cotton grown by the men, and the textiles woven by the women of Morelos were important commodities whose production and exchange produced effects that were felt throughout the world system. An adequate understanding of the Postclassic world system requires a consideration the lives, actions, and conditions of individual people and households, and thus the excavation of houses and domestic contexts is a necessary part of ongoing research on the distinctive processes and conditions of Late Postclassic Mesoamerica. Our attention now turns to activities at Chikinchel, an affluent production zone on the northern Yucatán coast, described by Kepecs in the following chapter.

33

Chikinchel

Susan M. Kepecs

The contributors to this volume agree that major Postclassic trends include population growth, the proliferation of small polities, an increase in the volume of long-distance exchange, a greater diversity of trade goods, commercialization of the economy, and new patterns of stylistic interaction. In chapter 5 I review the issue of small polities in Chikinchel. Below I summarize documentary and archaeological evidence for the other categories on this list, and outline the Postclassic history of my study region as an affluent production zone in the context of the Mesoamerican world system.

THE WRITTEN RECORD

The written record contains little direct information on the economy of the Epiclassic or Early Postclassic periods. Two keys—the so-called Itzá migration legend in the Chilam Balam of Chumayel, and Spanish accounts of flourishing canoe routes—led Sir Eric Thompson (1970: 10–11) to describe the Itzá as seafaring merchants from southern Campeche who arrived by boat on Yucatán's east coast and established Chichén Itzá after "long wanderings" across the peninsula. Thompson did not trace their route, but recent site identifications trace it through Chikinchel (Kepecs 1999). After marrying local women on the east coast, the Campechanos traveled north and then west to Aké—a large Chikinchel site on the coastal tier where the Itzá were "born" (Kepecs 1997, 1999, 2000; also Edmonson 1986:82–91; Krochock 1998; Roys 1973:70–73). From Aké they traveled to Alaa, and then to Tixchel (a small Epiclassic/Early Postclassic center on Chikinchel's coast) where they offered prolonged discourse. From Tixchel the pilgrims turned south, passing through several towns in neighboring Cupul (see figure 5.2) on their search for the perfect spot for their new inland capital (Kepecs 1997, 1999).

Information is richer for the later end of the Late Postclassic through the "contact period." The 1517 de Cordoba expedition landed at Ecab, a trading port on the northeast coast that Díaz del Castillo (1984:29) flamboyantly nicknamed "El Gran Cairo." A decade later Montejo's invading army rode across the northeast plains. According to Oviedo (1853, book 32, chapter 3:229–231) the Spanish conquistadors established their base not far from Ecab and then marched north along the coast. Eventually they turned southwest toward Cachi, a thriving inland market town near the eastern edge of Chikinchel (as drawn on the Roys map, figure 5.2). The next stop was Sinsimato, where great groves of copal were cultivated for regional trade. Resuming a northward route they came to Chauaca, an impressive town on the coastal support tier with many prosperous merchants. The invaders passed through several other Chikinchel towns on their loop through the region (Kepecs 1997, 1999; cf. Roys 1957).

The Spaniards did not discover the north-coast saltworks on this first visit, but it soon became apparent that briny diamonds were the peninsula's most valuable commodity. Some salt was collected by families for household use (e.g., Landa, in Tozzer 1941:87; Chi, in Tozzer 1941: appendix C:230), but great quantities also were produced for exchange at large saltworks. Landa (in Tozzer 1941:189) described certain saltbeds as property of the Euan family, batabs of Caucel in the western territory called Chakan. And Chikinchel *encomendero* Juan de Urrutía (*Relaciones Histórico-geográficas de la Gobernación de Yucatán* [RHGY] 2:249) wrote that "particular pueblos had and possessed [salinas] like real estate, from which they sustained themselves and made profits, especially the pueblo of Chauaca." Some salt surely circulated regionally, but Spanish eyewitnesses described canoes heaped with salt on their way to international markets on the gulfs of Mexico and Honduras (Díaz del Castillo 1984:497; Landa, in Tozzer 1941:94). According to Landa, salt, and other Yucatán goods, were exchanged for cacao grown intensively on the humid plains surrounding these market regions.

Economic references in the Chilam Balams are veiled, but Emal—Mesoamerica's most productive salina—was important in the native scheme (Kepecs 1997, 1999). Emal's rulers were "the children of the Itzá." Three times during the first 150 years of Spanish rule the 20-year ritual *katun* cycle was seated there, with swearing-in ceremonies on the white seashore (Edmonson 1982:37, 43, 70–72, 141). The Tizimín (Edmonson 1982:35) chronicles chaos at Emal on edge of the sea during the katun surrounding the Spanish invasion. The rulers of the white sands were members of the Chan lineage (Edmonson 1982:35–36, 38).

Chikinchel's Chans had economic ties to relatives on both gulfs, where salt was sold in international markets. They spoke a distinct dialect—probably Chontal, from the Gulf Coast (Jones 1989:96; Miller 1986:203; Kepecs 1997, 1999). *Chan* was a common Chontal name in the sixteenth century. Chontal and Yucatec naming practices differed, but Scholes and Roys (1948:64–65) suggest that the similarity of many Chontal names to Yucatecan patronymics reflects "what one might expect if a number of people with Chontal names had at some time settled among the Yucatecan Maya and some of their names had become patronymics in their new homes."

Chikinchel's links to the east are similarly documented. The Chans spread across Tases, Ecab, Uaymil, and farther south (Okoshi 1995; Thompson 1977; see figure 5.2). Chikinchel means "west woods" (Roys 1957: 103), marking a territorial position in this lineage scheme. The Chans of Emal were closely allied with their kin in Uaymil, who also spoke a Gulf Coast dialect (Jones 1989:31, 96; Scholes and Roys 1948:321; Thompson 1970:45). Both groups were called "the guardians of the sands, the guardians of the seas" (Roys 1973:156; Edmonson 1986:212, 1982:35), and they collaborated in a violent rebellion against Spanish rule in the mid-seventeenth century (Edmonson 1982:141, 1986:213; Roys 1973:157). Theirs was an economic tzucub (chapter 5), and they resisted taxation together in the seventeenth century. On the eve of the sixteenth century, Uaymil's Chans specialized in large trade canoes (Oviedo 1853, book 2, chapter 6:25).[1] These craft must have carried salt (and other goods) around the peninsula to international trading ports on the gulfs of Mexico and Honduras (chapter 17).

COMMERCIALIZED ECONOMY

Although interpretations of the Late Postclassic Maya often have a substantivist bent (e.g., Chapman 1957; Clendinnen 1987; Farriss 1984), various chroniclers—Yucatán's first bishop, Diego de Landa, key among them—described the native economy in commercial terms (see Clark and Houston 1998; Kepecs 1999). There were numerous professions. Farmers, fishers, merchants, potters, carpenters, idol-makers, and *curanderos* were specialists, and "the greatest number were cultivators and men who apply themselves to harvesting maize and other grains, which they keep in fine underground places and granaries, so as to be able to sell their crops at the proper time" (Landa, in Tozzer 1941:94–96, 190). Cotton, an important crop, was "gathered in wonderful quantity and grows in all parts of the land" (Landa, in Tozzer 1941:200). Surplus maize was stored in "great silos" at Ek Balam (Garza et al. 1982; Garza 1983 [RHGY 2:138]).

Fishing was pursued "on a very large scale, by which they eat and sell fish to all the country. They are accustomed to salt the fish, to roast it and to dry it in the sun without salt, and they take into account which of these methods each kind of fish requires, and the roasted keeps for days, and is taken 20 or 30 leagues for sale" (Landa, in Tozzer 1941:190). Fishermen used boats, capturing a great variety of species with nets, hooks, and spears. The catch was prepared on the coast for inland sale. Commercial fishing and agriculture were both fueled with slave labor (Roys 1943:35; Tozzer 1941:190 n. 995).

There were various kinds of traders. Roys (1939:61), consulting Colonial Maya dictionaries, found professional merchants called *pplom*, and those who traveled were *ah pplom yoc*. Itinerant peddlers carried their own packs (Roys 1943:51–52), and cotton vendors and fishmongers sold merchandise in towns along inland routes (Tozzer 1941:64 n. 294). Wealthy operators owned slaves to haul cargo overland and to paddle the big trade canoes that circled the coast (Roys 1943:35).

According to Landa (in Tozzer 1941:96, 127–129), the Maya traded everything they produced in markets. The best-known and most elaborate references to exchange emporia concern international trading ports (like El Gran Cairo). Women produced and sold household goods (cloth and clothing, and birds for meat and feathers), probably in local or regional markets. Some women also were midwives and sorceresses.

The Maya used cacao-bean currency, gave credit, and sealed business contracts with public toasts (Landa, in Tozzer 1941:94, 96, also n. 425; RHGY 2:44). There is no clear information on Prehispanic prices, but Landa (in Tozzer 1941:98) describes cacao being counted out in lots for trading purposes. Gaspar Antonio Chi, in his own relación on native customs (in Tozzer 1941:231), reported that prices for provisions were fixed (although the worth of maize fluctuated according to availability), and that money (cacao and also certain beads and copper bells) was used to pay for these goods. He also mentions that costs rose with the advent of Spanish administration.

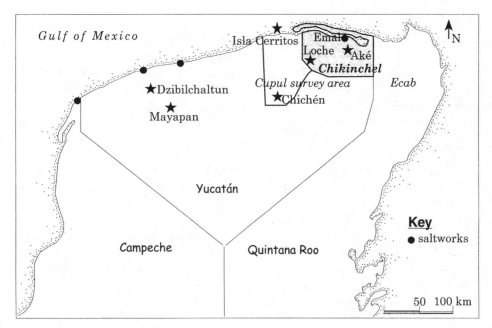

Figure 33.1 Chikinchel in Yucatán

Trade was sanctified. Ek Chuah, god of merchants and cacao, was feted in the native month of Muan, with sacrifices of dogs with chocolate-colored spots and offerings of incense. Other specialists, including sorcerers, beekeepers, and hunters, also had celestial patrons and performed special annual rituals (Landa, in Tozzer 1941: 153–164).

Some Spaniards reported that the natives were self-sufficient agriculturalists (RHGY 2:43, 92, 104, 158, 188, 247, 250, 277; Landa, in Tozzer 1941:87, 96–97). These comments, along with the agrarian "ethnographic present" and Yucatán's relatively unspectacular Late Postclassic architecture, led substantivists and traditional culture historians (e.g., Chapman 1957; Clendinnen 1987; Farriss 1984; Proskouriakoff 1955; Thompson 1966) to ignore the above-cited material (which they viewed, perhaps, as Spanish hyperbole). Yet domestic and specialized production coexisted. Regional and whole-site archaeological information from my surveys in Chikinchel supports a more formalist interpretation (Kepecs 1997, 1999).

CHIKINCHEL'S MATERIAL RECORD

The Chikinchel survey was my dissertation project (figure 33.1). I collected ceramic and architectural data on the centers of 79 sites in this zone, and surveyed three entire settlements—Emal, San Fernando Aké, and Loche—from their monumental cores to the settlements' edges, where "outfield" spaces begin. Two of these sites are particularly important in the following discussion: Emal, an elite settlement fronting Mesoamerica's most productive saltworks, and San Fernando

Aké—its inland support center 12 km south (Kepecs 1997, 1999).

My regional survey was designed to be roughly compatible with a similar project carried out by Tony Andrews, Tomás Gallareta, and Rach Cobos (1988) in the strip between Chichén and the coast in the northern portion of Cupul, adjacent to Chikinchel. We combined our data to get a broad regional view of diachronic regional settlement patterns (Kepecs and Gallareta Negrón 1995). Archaeological periods were dated through ceramics; the roughly compatible ceramic chronologies from our two surveys are reported elsewhere (Andrews et al. 1988; Andrews et al. 1989; Kepecs 1998, 1999; Robles Castellanos 1987).

To estimate the number of central places and the relative importance of smaller sites in our combined sample, we used simple criteria based on the size of a site's monumental core and, associated with this architecture, the quantity and variety of trade and common ceramics per archaeologically recognizable period. We plotted changing regional settlement patterns using simple geographers' models (summarized in Blanton et al. 1993; Kepecs 1999). The results of this analysis—Chichén's large regional state, followed by city-state culture in the Late Postclassic—are described in chapter 5. Here I discuss economic shifts that accompanied political change in Chikinchel.

THE LATE CLASSIC

Throughout the Classic period, Yucatán was on the far periphery of a prestige-goods network—an archaic world system—that spread along the sierra from Teotihuacan to Kaminaljuyú (Blanton et al. 1992; Kepecs 1999). As

Teotihuacan waned, technological developments in the peripheries began processes of world-systems change that had profound effects on local economies across the macroregion. Innovative new ceramics abundant only on the Campeche coast—Fine Gray wares and the ash-tempered Celestun group—were added to standard Classic-period assemblages at a limited number of Yucatán sites. These ceramics have somewhat different distributions, but Celestun is especially important as a marker of change. Celestun wares are reported in moderate amounts, but only at coastal saltworks and two centers on the inland support tier—Dzibilchaltun in the west, and San Fernando Aké (close to Emal) in Chikinchel (Ball 1978; Kepecs 1998, 1999; Simmons and Brem 1979; Sierra Sosa n.d.). Like the Itzá migration myth, Celestun ceramics mark the arrival of Gulf Coast entrepreneurs on the north coast—and their first steps toward establishing control over Chikinchel's rich salinas.

THE EPICLASSIC/EARLY POSTCLASSIC

In the following era new cores rose up in parts of the macroregion that were peripheral in Teotihuacan's world (Blanton et al. 1992; Kepecs 1999, 2000; Thompson 1970:4). Among these cores three stand out: Chichén, Tula, and El Tajín. Shared public symbols constituted a lingua franca for an "international superculture" (e.g., Freidel 1986:425; Kepecs et al. 1994; Kowalski 2000; Ringle et al. 1998) oriented toward the Gulf coast.

The written record for this period is poor, but archaeological patterns are relatively rich. The Itzá—ancestors of Chikinchel's Chontal-speaking Chans of the sixteenth century—reorganized the zone from Chichén to the coast to expedite control over the flow and production of goods for this new world system. Classic-period single-center polities were replaced with a new administrative hierarchy (see figure 5.1) with strings of secondary centers stretching from the core to the coast, at Isla Cerritos (the port) and Emal (the saltworks). An additional line of large towns crossed the coastal support tier (Kepecs 1999, 2000; Kepecs et al. 1994).

Political centralization is reflected in Sotuta slatewares, the common slipped ceramics of Chichén and all other settlements within its administrative domain. From petrographic analyses of hundreds of sherds (Bey and Kepecs 1999; Chung 1993; Kepecs 1998, 1999; Shepard 1951, also cited in Smith 1971, appendix D) we know that other regional variants of Epiclassic/Early Postclassic slate ceramics are somewhat variable, but Sotuta sherds are remarkably homogeneous. This pattern typifies what happens when production is politically controlled: reduced competition, coupled with the demands of high-intensity manufacture, leads to product standardization (Costin 1991; Feinman 1985:196–197; Feinman et al. 1984:299; Rice 1991:270).

Other hallmark Itzá artifacts include Silho Fine Orange and Dzibiac redwares,[2] and green Pachuca obsidian. These items, while less common than slateware ceramics, are recorded consistently in surface collections from the centers of key settlements in the Itzá domain, and also at coastal sites from Campeche to southern Belize (e.g., Andrews 1978; Andrews et al. 1988; Eaton and Ball 1978; Kepecs 1999; Kepecs et al. 1994; McKillop 1996). This distribution could reflect political ties (patron-client chains) or market exchange (Andrews 1990b; Kepecs et al. 1994).[3] Regardless, this complex of artifacts links secondary administrative sites to Chichén, and places the peninsula's sea lane squarely within the Itzá network.

New infrastructure was built to handle growing sea traffic. At Emal and Isla Cerritos stone foundation braces that probably were docks stretch into the water perpendicular to the shore (Andrews et al. 1988; Kepecs 1999, 2000). Since Isla Cerritos was all but abandoned after the Epiclassic/Early Postclassic, these features probably date to this period in both cases. And behind Emal's plazas on the white seashore, a premodern salt "factory" (see below) was built or expanded during this period of growth.

After several hundred years the Itzá polity folded, along with the other regional states of the period. This drastic decline must have been related to world-scale shifts, since Tula and El Tajín also faded.

THE MIDDLE THROUGH LATE POSTCLASSIC

World-systems restructuring went hand in hand with the development of new polities throughout Mesoamerica (see part 2). With Chichén's decline the Cupul territory (including Isla Cerritos) was practically abandoned (Andrews et al. 1989). The secondary sites on Chichén's route to Emal also faded, yet the rest of Chikinchel floresced (figure 33.2; see also Kepecs 1997, 1999). The total number of sites in the regional sample increased slightly, from 68 in the Epiclassic/Early Postclassic to 71 in the Late Postclassic. Emal continued to thrive, and occupations on the coastal tier grew. At San Fernando Aké 756 platforms had evidence of occupation during the Late Postclassic, up from 547 in the Epiclassic/Early Postclassic. New sites sprang up in the eastern zone, which the Itzá failed to incorporate. Especially important in this area was Chauaca (see above). Late Postclassic development continued east of Chikinchel: Conil and San Angel, sites in western Ecab, provided links between Chikinchel and late Prehispanic trading developments on the Caribbean seaboard (see Andrews 1993; Romero y Gurrola 1995; Taube and Gallareta Negrón 1988).

As noted in chapter 5, there was no overarching regional capital in this period. Instead, Chikinchel had nine first-order centers, each the capital of an independent city-state or batabil. Political decentralization was accompanied by economic competition. The salt industry expanded as entrepreneurship replaced political control.

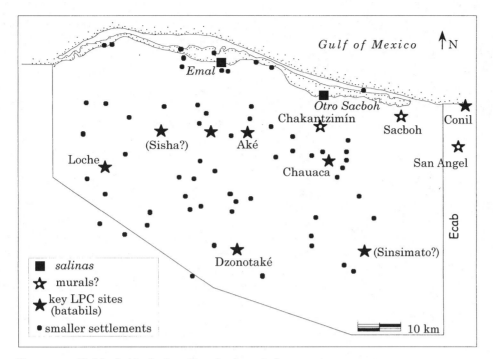

Figure 33.2 Chikinchel in the Late Postclassic period

Emal continued as the center of a large industry, but instead of a single factory-style facility, now there were two. The second—which has only minimal evidence of Itzá-era occupation—is 20 km east of Emal, at Otro Sacboh (see figure 33.2). Emal's inland base probably was San Fernando Aké, given proximity and a long history of symbiosis between these two sites (Kepecs 1999). In contrast, Otro Sacboh was within walking distance of three Late Postclassic centers: San Fernando Aké, Chakantzimín, and Chauaca. Thus control over this facility probably was hotly contested. (The written sources support this idea. According to Oviedo [book 32, chapter 3] Chauaca and Aké were not on friendly terms; during the course of Montejo's march across this territory the citizens of the former raided the latter with great delight. At that moment Otro Sacboh may have been controlled by Chauaca, known for its prosperous merchants. One of the keys to their success must have been salt.)

Ceramic paste also fits expectations for competitive production. In contrast to homogeneous ceramics made under political authority, stylistically related wares made by multiple groups of specialists within an interacting region should exhibit patterned diversity (Kepecs 1997, 1998, 1999; see also Costin 1991:35). Across the peninsula Epiclassic/Early Postclassic slatewares were replaced by Late Postclassic (Tases) redwares, which in the Chikinchel collections fall into five distinct paste varieties. This variation was noted by eye on thousands of sherds, in hand-lens observations on many, and through petrographic analysis of a few. Apparently these differences

are not related to function, since a range of forms occurs in each paste group. Traditional recipes and localized geological conditions are key factors in paste composition (Feinman et al. 1989), and small local differences abound in Yucatán's superficially homogeneous northeastern plains. Thus the five paste groups among Chikinchel's Late Postclassic redwares should reflect multiple production loci.

Analysis of my whole-site surface collections (from San Fernando Aké, Emal, and Loche) reveals that while each paste was most prevalent around its probable site of production, all five paste groups were present at each site (figure 33.3). This distribution is what I would expect if multiple pottery producers competed in regional markets. This exchange was not negligible; at each site ceramics in these distinct paste groups were broadly distributed (Kepecs 1997, 1998, 1999; see also Hirth 1998). Overall, non-elites had access to a greater variety of ceramics produced by specialists than ever before (Kepecs 1999). In addition to more choices in slipped serving wares, incensarios came into popular use. Censer fragments in the Chikinchel collections fall into the same paste varieties as the redwares, as do unslipped (Navula) pots. Matillas Fine Orange, while less broadly distributed, rounds out the ceramic inventory of this period.

CHIKINCHEL AND INTERPENETRATING ACCUMULATION

More ceramics were produced for regional exchange because interpenetrating accumulation (IPA) is systemic:

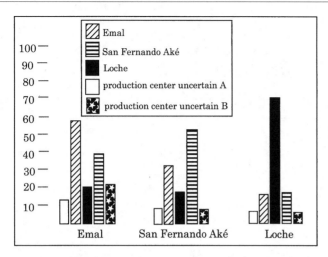

Figure 33.3 Percentage of Late Postclassic platforms with ceramics in each paste group

it engages people from multiple social strata, creating a complex political economy that shifts some labor (formerly invested in domestic production) to surplus production for exchange (see chapter 2). As more workers are tied up in production for long-distance trade, more surplus in essential domestic goods also is needed to meet local and regional demands.

THE SALTWORKS

Factories are single, large-scale production systems operated by a coordinated labor force (Costin 1991; Feinman 1999b; Muller 1997). The creation of factory-scale infrastructure requires resources and thus generally is the province of elites. Control over labor is placed directly in the hands of rulers—or entrepreneurs—by removing the means of production from the household context.

Emal is just such a facility. The plazas on the white seashore (figure 33.4) consist of a walled complex of ruined but relatively elaborate structures. The ceramic assemblage from this site, which spans the Classic through Spanish periods, includes impressive quantities of fine pottery, including Classic-period polychromes and Postclassic Fine Orange wares.

Blanquizal—salt-encrusted mudflats—spread out around the settlement. Eroded rough-cut stone divisions stretch across 25 ha of this crusty mud, possibly the remains of a once larger system. Though somewhat fragmentary, these features resemble modern solar evaporation systems in which large natural pools are divided into successively smaller units through which brine is channeled to speed evaporation. Today the white crust is thin, but when Emal was in use, canals probably were used to flood the ponds with highly saline waters from the shallow Río Lagartos estuary.

There is no evidence of non-elite settlement at Emal. Instead, labor must have come from the large sites on the inland support tier, including San Fernando Aké (figure 33.5). These sites have vast tracts of common house platforms and are within a day's walk range (9 to 12 km) from the saltworks. Regional and whole-site survey data show that while the size of individual sites shifted through time, substantial populations are represented within the tier zone during all archaeological periods (Kepecs 1999).

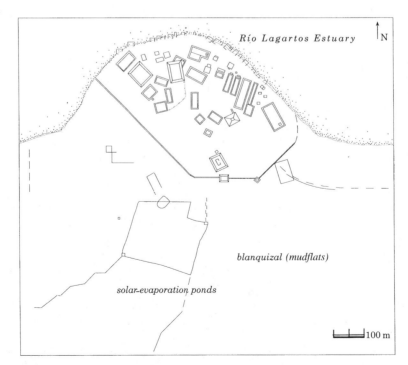

Figure 33.4 Emal site map

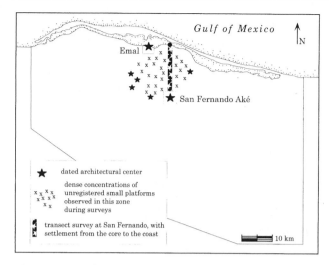

Figure 33.5 Settlement on the coastal tier, showing potential labor for Postclassic salt production

Except in cases of modern mechanization, salt harvesting is a dry-season activity. Crystallization processes begin in January, and the product is reaped from late April through May. When evaporation is accelerated with built infrastructure, some labor is required during the crystallizing phase, but the actual harvest involves the largest number of workers. During the rainy season a reduced workforce can handle maintenance (of both the facility and its stores of salt) and distribution.

We can get a heuristic notion of Prehispanic labor and production from historic-period reports (in Andrews 1983; Ewald 1985). In 1605 the Emal saltworks produced 50,000 fanegas (ca. 5,750 metric tons) of salt. I used an account from the mid-nineteenth century (still based on nonmechanized technology) to estimate how much labor this harvest might require. According to this document, five workers could produce 20 fanegas of salt in a one-day shift. A fanega is roughly a bushel and a half in size, and weighs roughly 115 kg (Andrews 1983:137–138). Thus 500 men divided into 100 groups could collect 2,000 fanegas per shift, or 60,000 fanegas in an intensive 30-day dry-season harvest. Even if 500 men worked half as hard in Prehispanic times they still could have produced 30,000 fanegas (close to 3,500 metric tons) in a season. The inland support sites near Emal easily could have provided this number of workers. San Fernando alone could have carried this burden in any of the Prehispanic periods, and the spread of unsurveyed platforms around other nearby sites must have contributed significantly to overall population during any specified epoch.

Although I may be overestimating, it seems reasonable on the basis of high regional population and the scale of the Emal facility to project that a great deal of salt was harvested on an annual basis in Prehispanic times. Some of this perishable mineral surely was traded regionally, but Yucatán's briny diamonds also were exchanged on the world scale.

THE EPICLASSIC/EARLY POSTCLASSIC: SALT FOR OBSIDIAN

One key item the Itzá received in return for salt was obsidian (Kepecs 1999, 2000; Kepecs et al. 1994; Simmons and Brem 1979). In the Epiclassic/Early Postclassic most volcanic material traveled south along the Gulf coast from central Mexican sources (Ucareo and Pachuca) and Pico de Orizaba in Veracruz (chapter 20; see also Andrews et al. 1988; Braswell, chapter 20, this volume; Healan 1993). Mexican obsidian also reached the Puuc region, but not until the later part of the Epiclassic/Early Postclassic, when Uxmal evidently was allied with Chichén (Dunning and Kowalski 1994; Kowalski and Dunning 1999; cf. chapter 20). Ek Balam and Cobá were out of this loop; small quantities of obsidian at these sites came mainly from Central America (chapter 20; see also Bey and Kepecs 1999).

Obsidian, like salt, was extracted in large-scale factory contexts. Both pit and shaft mines are reported at Pachuca, Ucareo, and Orizaba (Charlton and Spence 1982; López Aguilar et al. 1989; Pastrana 1992, 1998; Stocker and Cobean 1984). Pits measure as much as 40 m in diameter by 10 m deep, and some have tunnels branching laterally from their sides into deep obsidian deposits. Shafts can reach 12 m or more in depth, connecting to complex interior tunnel networks. To operate these facilities, infrastructure and coordinated labor were required. Without ventilation, miners cannot work more than 4 m deep; drainage or water collection must be managed; and materials have to be hauled out (Craddock 1995:73–74). Mining at Ucareo was heaviest in the Epiclassic/Early Postclassic (Healan 1991b, 1992, 1993, 2000). And Pastrana (1992:220, 1998:61–67) has identified a Toltec-era component of unknown extent at Pachuca. Although the most active mining at this source evidently occurred in the Late Postclassic, Healan (2000) cautions that the intensity of Aztec exploitation may have destroyed or engulfed much of the evidence from the preceding period.

Tula played a key role in long-distance obsidian trade. Blade fragments from central highlands sources are extremely common at the Toltec core. The degree of political control Tula held over sources of raw material remains unknown, but large quantities were received through tribute or trade (Healan 1993). Close ties between Tula and Chichén (and also El Tajín on the Veracruz coast) are underscored by a shared military motifs cult that probably facilitated interpenetrating accumulation in several ways. Warrior images inspired crusades (for god and booty), and the public threat of force probably helped keep workers in line (e.g., Hirth 1989; Kepecs 1999, 2000; Ringle et al. 1998).

In addition to obsidian, the Itzá imported volcanic ash

temper for Sotuta slate ceramics. Petrographic studies of hundreds of common slate sherds from the Puuc region, Chichén and its hinterland sites, and Ek Balam reveal close links between the use of ash temper and the obsidian trade pattern (Bey and Kepecs 1999; Chung 1993; Kepecs 1998, 1999;[4] Shepard 1951, 1964, 1974; Simmons and Brem 1979). Sherds from Ek Balam (where obsidian import was light) appear virtually ash-free. Less than half of the Puuc sherds were tempered with the microscopic shards. Yet all of the Sotuta examples contained ash—not surprising given Chichén's role as Yucatán's largest consumer in the international obsidian exchange sphere of the Epiclassic/Early Postclassic. I envision this glassy powder being used as packing for the fragile obsidian blades that arrived at Isla Cerritos docks in henequen bags.

Recently George Bey and I (Bey and Kepecs 1999) carried out a very heuristic calculation to estimate how much ash the Itzá had to import annually to produce the Sotuta slates. Based on ethnographic observations, medium-sized utilitarian pots—jars and ollas—are replaced about once a year (e.g., DeBoer 1985). Larger pots are stronger and last longer, while smaller serving vessels are curated carefully and break less often. Medium-sized pots generally weigh about 4 kg. The average amount of volcanic ash relative to paste in Sotuta slate sherds (determined through point counts in both Chung's [1993] study and my own) is about 17.5 percent—roughly 700 gm per 4 kg vessel. At an annual replacement rate of one jar and one olla, consumption of ash as temper amounted to 1,400 gm per household. We used generalized survey observations to get a very rough estimate of the number of households at each site with Sotuta ceramics in Chichén's domain, and totaled those figures to get 10,750 households.[5] We then multiplied this number by 1,400 gm to get 15 metric tons. We tried to be conservative, but even half this much ash imported on an annual basis would involve substantial trade in bulk goods over long distances.

Based on the hypothetical quantities of salt and volcanic ash that moved through the Epiclassic/Early Postclassic world system, we can begin to talk about the production and exchange of bulk goods in terms of metric tons, rather than a few exotics. White salt and ash temper were quasi-luxuries, since temper and salt—albeit inferior varieties—were regionally available. Yet shipping in bulk was revolutionary. The prestige-goods networks of the Classic period were an archaic kind of world system, but the large-scale, regular exchange of these bulk goods in the Epiclassic/Early Postclassic marks Mesoamerica's first step toward a premodern economy.

The Epiclassic/Early Postclassic world system came to an end with the roughly concurrent decline of Tula, El Tajín, and Chichén (e.g., Andrews et al. 1988; Healan et al. 1989; Brüggemann 1994a, 1994b; Kepecs et al.

1994). The causes of this decline are not entirely clear. Established elites may have been weakened by class struggles, as more laborers worked at least part of the time in factory settings. And a new generation of coastal traders evidently developed advanced boat-building technologies that provided a competitive edge in the restructuring world system (Kepecs 1999).[6]

THE LATE POSTCLASSIC: SALT FOR CACAO

The world system underwent a series of developments that culminated in the fifteenth century with the cores and affluent production zones (chapter 3) witnessed by Spanish chroniclers. Foreign goods received in return for salt changed with these world-systems shifts. In Late Postclassic Yucatán, most obsidian came not from central Mexico but from Ixtepeque, Guatemala (chapter 20; also Barrera Rubio 1985; Nelson 1989), and volcanic ash no longer was used as ceramic temper. Copper artifacts, earlier very rare except from Chichén's famous cenote, are reported in various excavated contexts (Freidel and Sabloff 1984; Lothrop 1952; Peraza Lope et al. 1998; Proskouriakoff 1962b; Root 1962). Yet there are few gray (Ixtepeque?) blade fragments and no copper bells whatsoever in the Chikinchel surface collections—perhaps in part because these items are more likely to be recovered in excavation, but also because in well-functioning mercantile systems traders do not hoard goods (Rathje and Sabloff 1975:13).

Nevertheless, Chikinchel was in the loop. During my surveys I collected small quantities of Cunduacan Fine Orange, a Terminal Postclassic ware from the Laguna de Términos region (Berlin 1960; Matheny 1970:93–102), at Emal, San Fernando Aké, and Chakantzimín (see figure 33.2). I also recorded fragments of black and blue plaster—probable evidence of Late Postclassic murals—from recently destroyed small Late Postclassic shrines at Chakantzimín, Sacboh, and Otro Sacboh. In Yucatán, codex-style murals—evidence of participation in the Late Postclassic international style and/or symbol system—once seemed limited to the east coast (Tancah, Tulum, Santa Rita). Yet a decade ago a new example was discovered at San Angel, in western Ecab (Taube and Gallareta Negrón 1988; Andrews 1993)—within day's walk range of the sites at which I found painted plaster in Chikinchel. Thus the material record complements documentary and linguistic links between Chikinchel, Laguna de Términos, and the east coast, and also marks trade routes described by Landa (in Tozzer 1941:94, also see n. 415; Scholes and Roys 1948:30, 244), who wrote that Yucatán's briny diamonds were exchanged (along with cotton cloth and slaves) for cacao and stone beads (the native currencies) at trading ports on the gulfs of Mexico and Honduras.

From these depots Chikinchel's salty gems were dispersed deeper into the complex trade maze of the Late

Postclassic. Some salt apparently reached Aztec markets, where one could buy clean, fat loaves of pure white salt "without disagreeable taste," but also poor-quality salts that were sandy or tasted harsh (Sahagún 1975:572). Aztec nobility had a marked preference for unadulterated white salt, demanding 2,000 loaves of this mineral in annual or semiannual tribute (Barlow 1949; Smith and Berdan 1996b:269) from the province of Ocuilan, where small quantities were produced from salt springs. Yet salt consumption in the Texcoco palace alone was reported to be 20 loaves daily (Ixtlilxochitl, in Berdan 1975:123), or 7,200 annually. The Ocuilan tribute (the only salt payment listed in the Matrícula/Mendoza) would have been insufficient to sustain this level of consumption throughout the year. At least about half of the white salt destined for royal use in Texcoco alone would have come from other sources; much more would have been needed for Tenochtitlan and Tlacopan (Kepecs 1999; MacKinnon and Kepecs 1989). Two additional references to Prehispanic Aztec salt tribute come from the Dominican friar Diego Durán, writing in the mid-sixteenth century (cited in Berdan 1996:127–128; table 33.6), who noted that "ocean salt" was a required donation from Coaixtlahuacan, in Oaxaca. Salt (variety unspecified) also was paid by Tepeacac, adjacent to the Basin of Mexico. Yet a great deal of salt probably was distributed through the market system.

Coaixtlahuacan was a key market town (Appel 1982a) where pochteca procured cacao, among other goods (Berdan 1988:643–644). Nearer coasts were not great salt producers (chapter 19), so most ocean salt (for tribute and trade) probably was purchased at Laguna de Términos entrepôts. Another important Aztec market was in the strategic province of Huexotla, north of the basin at the junction of busy trade routes linking the highlands with the Veracruz plain. Huexotla was a major center for cotton and salt—some of the latter "from Campeche" (Smith 1996b:149; Smith and Berdan 1996b:293). Yet there is little evidence that Campeche's saltbeds and those of neighboring northwest Yucatán were exploited in the Late Postclassic.[7] Thus the reference to "Campeche" salt sold at Huexotla probably indicates shipment from Laguna de Términos, rather than the mineral's original provenience. Much of the salt here and at Coaixtlahuacan probably came from Chikinchel.

Cacao, which was used to pay for salt, was produced (like salt and obsidian) in high-intensity, large-scale contexts. Great portions of the humid plains of the southern Gulf coast and the Pacific plain were dedicated to cultivating the sweet chocolate beans (e.g., Millon 1955; Orellana 1995; Pérez Romero 1988). Cacao is a delicate plant requiring specialized growing and harvesting techniques, and the fruits of labor invested in this industry were enjoyed across political boundaries.

Cacao received by Chikinchel salt merchants at inter-national entrepôts equaled pure purchasing power (Kepecs 1999). Cacao supported the intensification of domestic staples since it could purchase slaves whose labor was used in large-scale fishing and agriculture as well as for paddling canoes and hauling goods overland (Roys 1943:35; Tozzer 1941:190 n. 995). Chocolate cash also allowed traders to buy surpluses of salt, maize, fish, cotton, copal, ceramics, and other basic necessities. Thus profits accrued through international trade underwrote at least some regional economic activities. As more labor was tied up in specialization and transportation for both regional and macroregional exchange, markets developed in Chikinchel to supplement what once was produced at home.

CONCLUSIONS: THE MAYA, THE AZTECS, AND THE MEDIEVAL OLD WORLD

Currency was the *sin qua non* of international trade in the medieval Old World (Abu-Lughod 1989:15). No single subsystem prevailed (chapter 2); contacts were mediated through essentially hinterlandless trade emporia, and people and goods moved across the various parts of the world system via sea lanes, rivers, and overland routes. Some of these subsystems (Europe, the Islamic world of the Persian Gulf/Arabian Sea) were characterized by multiple city-states; in others (Mamluk Egypt, the Mongolian empire of central Asia, and especially China), cities were bound hierarchically in imperial domains (Abu-Lughod 1989:39 n. 9). The Aztec system somewhat resembled China's (Blanton 1985), while the Maya were more like medieval Europeans in a number of interesting ways (Kepecs 1999, 2000).

One of two critical factors leading (over the long term) to mercantilism or incipient capitalism in medieval Europe was a well-developed system of long-distance trade, which increased circulation, and thus profits (Braudel 1986:2:582–594; also Blanton 1985). The advantages of water shipping over land transport gave merchants in coastal zones a great advantage. Braudel (1986:2:472), describing the social mobility of European merchants, wrote that their edge over old-guard, landed nobility was strongest near the sea, where water transport facilitated the movement of goods. Thus Venice, long the center of a coastal trading port empire, emerged at the core of the Old World economy in the late fourteenth century (Braudel 1986:3:119–132). The Venetians built great ships to shuttle goods—and Crusaders—from Europe to the Middle East. These boats were the precursors of late-fifteenth-century *galere da mercato* that carried Spaniards to the New World. The Venetians were salt merchants, too, turning great profits from briny spice evaporated in solar holding tanks on the marshes of the Adriatic (Braudel 1986:3:123; Kraft and Aschenbrenner 1977:28–29).

Figure 33.6 Chontal diaspora in the Late Postclassic period

Growth in long-distance trade generated corresponding increases in surplus production for regional economies, removing labor from domestic contexts and rendering common populations at least partly dependent on exchange (e.g., Costin 1991:4). As exchange became regularized, market systems emerged to handle the flow of goods (see Plattner 1989:181). Yet here is the key: in Braudel's (1986:2:600) words, long-distance trade and market economies are necessary but not sufficient conditions of incipient capitalism. The crucial factor is the appearance of economic forces independent of the state (Braudel 1986:2:589; Blanton 1985). Strong states control accumulation and dampen competition; thus unfettered economies flourish in small, weak polities (such as the seigniorial regime of feudal Europe). Under weaker political conditions, merchants can reach the top of the economic ladder, from which they can control surplus production and distribution (Braudel 1986:2:594).

These conditions were not unique to Europe. Braudel (1986:2:589–594), drawing on the works of other historians, notes parallels between the European case and late feudal Japan. To these examples I add the northern Maya lowlands of the post-Itzá period. But Braudel emphasizes that mercantile classes do not simply emerge overnight. Change is slow. It can take generations for social mobility to occur between old patricians and new merchant classes (Braudel 1986:2:476), and conditions over the *longue durée* are not always parallel. Feudal Japanese emperors and Yucatán's Itzá presided over strong centralized polities that eventually broke apart, while western Europe's seigniorial regime survived nearly a thousand years (Braudel 1986:2:258–261). Nevertheless, in all three cases merchants eventually were able to overcome royal barriers to social mobility. To move up the ladder, Braudel observed (2:258–261, 382, also 2:600–601), merchants needed "a good start in life." This meant having the right social connections, and material inheritance built up through long processes of accumulation.

The children of the Itzá were born to such conditions. Chichén—built by Gulf Coast entrepreneurs who married into powerful Yucatán families (Krochock 1998)—marks Yucatán's participation in an innovative economic shift that began on the peripheries of Teotihuacan's world. Maritime developments were crucial in this change, but, as in Europe, sea technology improved (e.g., Edwards 1978; MacKinnon et al. 1989; Thompson 1951). The sons-of-Putun (with apologies to Tony Andrews and Fernando Robles [1985]), like the Venetians, prevailed in strategic coastal regions (figure 33.6), selling bulk quantities of salt and building large seagoing vessels. With the fall of Chichén, entrepreneurs broke free of political authority, holding the Itzás' fortunes in their hands. As in Europe, the best opportunities for profit were along the coast, hence the coastal orientation of Chikinchel's Late Postclassic settlement pattern (see figure 33.2).

In Chikinchel, as in Europe and Japan, this free-market political economy developed over the *longue durée*. I am not sure that modern industrial capitalism would have evolved on its own in the Maya lowlands if only the Spaniards had stayed home. Some of the economic institutions of thirteenth-century Italy—such as banking and the stock market—failed to develop in the ancient Americas. Nevertheless, the Maya and the Europeans had a great deal in common. Masson presents an additional perspective on affluent production zones in the Maya area in the next chapter.

34

Economic Patterns in Northern Belize

Marilyn A. Masson

Northern Belize, an area rich in natural resources, functioned as an affluent production zone in the Early and Late Postclassic periods. A perspective is offered here from the communities of Caye Coco and Laguna de On, located along the Freshwater Creek drainage that penetrates the interior of northern Belize southward from its mouth at Chetumal Bay of the Caribbean Sea (figure 34.1). Caye Coco is a political center on an island in Progresso Lagoon (figure 34.2). This center measures 400 by 600 m and has 17 mounded structures. Laguna de On Island is a smaller settlement on Honey Camp Lagoon (known previously as Laguna de On), one-quarter the size of Caye Coco and lacking mounded architecture (figure 34.3).

The archaeological record at these communities suggests that patterns of production and exchange established during the Early Postclassic period (eleventh–twelfth centuries, as defined in this volume) continued in an intensified form during the thirteenth through fifteenth centuries (Middle and Late Postclassic periods, as defined in this volume; referred to here as Late Postclassic). While production techniques such as ceramic firing become more standardized and technologically proficient over time (Masson and Mock n.d.), pottery throughout this sequence exhibits basic continuity in style and function (Graham 1987). From the eleventh to the sixteenth centuries, occupants of Caye Coco and Laguna de On engaged in the production of textiles, local stone tools, and shell tools. Fishing and turtle harvesting were common activities at these inland lagoons. The inhabitants also relied on imported commodities such as obsidian, greenstone celts and ornaments, and small quantities of exotic ground stone. These sites, like most of northern Belize, were directly linked to world-system exchange networks in the Early and Late Postclassic periods. These periods coincide with the reign of two centralized states in north-

ern Yucatán—Chichén Itzá and Mayapán—and there is little doubt that producers of northern Belize contributed significantly to the regional exchange systems connected to these centers.

EARLY POSTCLASSIC

The expansive economies of Chichén Itzá and Mayapán stimulated maritime trade around the Yucatán Peninsula, and the exchange networks of each period affected the development of inland communities such as Caye Coco and Laguna de On in distinct ways. The Terminal Classic period (A.D. 800–950) was a time of dramatic settlement shifts in the southern lowlands, as Petén-centric interior cities and upland sites were vacated in favor of riverine, aquatic localities that allowed agrarian self-sufficiency and access to burgeoning coastal trade (Culbert 1988, Masson and Mock n.d.). This was a time of settlement growth for key resource-rich localities in northern Belize. New opportunities were created for residents of northern Belize and probable migrants from the Petén zone. For example, new coastal settlements experimented with salt-making and marine resource extraction (Mock 1994a). Much of the Maya settlement at Progreso Lagoon was newly established during the Terminal Classic period.

In northern Belize, interaction with Chichén Itzá is reflected in the emulation of slateware technologies, incised decorative techniques, and ceramic forms (Mock 1994b; Masson and Mock n.d.; Masson n.d.a). Our AMS radiocarbon dates for these Terminal Classic materials coincide well with the new chronology for Chichén Itzá that places it in the Terminal Classic (Andrews et al. 2000). A break with northern traditions is indicated during the Early Postclassic—a narrow temporal episode ca. 950–1100—in which pottery specific to northern Belize is prevalent (Masson and Mock n.d.).

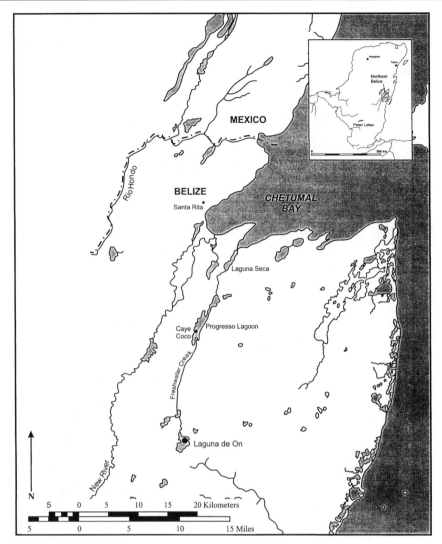

Figure 34.1 Map of northern Belize showing the location of Caye Coco and Laguna de On

This slipped pottery resembles the elaborate Buk-phase chalices from Lamanai that were more fully developed during the twelfth century (Graham 1987).

Direct contact with Chichén Itzá has not been reported from many sites, with the exception of Nohmul (Chase and Chase 1982) and Colha (Nash 1980; Hester 1982, 1985; Shafer 1979; Michaels 1987:178; Michaels and Shafer 1994). Trickle wares of Chichén Itzá's Sotuta complex are reported in low numbers this far south at sites like Becan (Ball 1977). Many other artifact assemblages from northern Belize exhibit a similar trend that appears to reflect exchange at a distance—a comfortable distance—from Chichén Itzá's hegemonic northern regime. However, the recent recovery of a Terminal Classic–period round temple suggests more than casual contact with Chichén Itzá may have occurred at Caye Coco (Masson and Digrius 2001). Chichén-related wares have been identified at Caye Coco, and this also implies

more direct contact with the north, as argued for Nohmul and Colha.

Many northeastern Belize Postclassic sites were growing during this time, capitalizing on burgeoning coastal trade systems inspired by Chichén Itzá's activities, but most communities were probably politically autonomous from the northern center (Masson and Mock n.d.). During the Terminal Classic and Early Postclassic, northern Belize was a resource-rich region in an optimal location for trading with northern and southeastern Maya lowland areas. Trade was facilitated by its lengthy coastline and the existence of three north-south waterways (Rio Hondo, New River, Freshwater Creek) and one east-west waterway (Belize River) connecting the coast to the interior. This coastal focus is reflected in the combination of southern and northern traits in the Terminal Classic ceramic styles of this period. Most closely related to the sites of Quintana Roo, northeast Belize

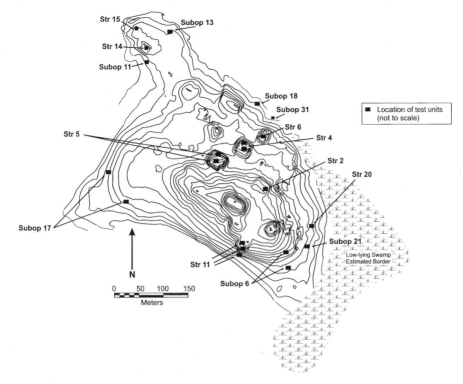

Figure 34.2 Map of Caye Coco showing the location of contexts mentioned in the text

sites join the sites of Ichpaatun (Sanders 1960), Tulum (Sanders 1960), Cozumel (Connor 1983; Peraza Lope 1993), and El Meco (Robles Castellanos 1986) in developing an east coast variant of Late Postclassic slipped and unslipped wares. These are referred to as "Payil Red" (Smith 1971) or "Tulum Red" (Sanders 1960) and Navula (or Tulum) Unslipped, ceramic types produced from the twelfth through fifteenth centuries (Masson and Mock n.d.).

THE LATE POSTCLASSIC

Polities in northern Belize interacted intensively with Mayapán during the Late Postclassic period (Masson 2000a). Local potters emulated modes of ceramic decoration characteristic of Mayapán and incorporated these new traits into Payil Red slip and paste technologies. This pattern is found at the sites of Lamanai (Graham 1987), Santa Rita (Chase 1982; Chase and Chase 1988), and Caye Coco (Masson and Mock n.d.), although Mayapán-like wares are classified as Rita Red at Santa Rita (Chase 1982). Local elites also emulated Mayapán's religious practices associated with the production and use of effigy censers (Sidrys 1983; Chase and Chase 1988; Chase 1986, 1988; Masson 2000a). These effigy censers were common throughout Yucatán, the east coast of Quintana Roo (Lothrop 1924), Belize (Sidrys 1983), and the Petén lakes (Bullard 1970; Rice 1987a) during the latter fourteenth and fifteenth centuries. Their distri-

bution suggests an extensive network of symbolic interaction among Postclassic elites at this time.

Religious interaction was closely tied to trading activities at sites on Cozumel Island and elsewhere at the time of Spanish arrival (Freidel and Sabloff 1984; Freidel 1983). Other items of ritual paraphernalia in northern Belize resembling forms at Mayapán include composite (non-effigy) censers (Barrett 1999; Mazeau 2000a) and plaster turtle sculpture offering vessels at Caye Coco (Barrett 2000; Masson 1999a) and Santa Rita (housed in the Department of Archaeology vault, Belmopan, Belize). Similar turtle sculptures at Mayapán are inscribed with Ahau dates (Proskouriakoff 1962a), suggesting they were used in calendrical period-ending celebrations. Mayapán also invoked an earlier tradition of stela erection (Proskouriakoff 1962b), and this practice was emulated at Tulum and Ichpaatun in the recycling of earlier monuments (Lothrop 1924) and in the dedication of blank stelae at the sites of Chan Chen and Sarteneja in Belize (Sidrys 1983). Strong political and economic alliances between Mayapán, eastern Quintana Roo sites, and those in the northern Belize/Chetumal Bay vicinity are indicated in Colonial accounts (Pollock 1962; Roys 1962; Freidel and Sabloff 1984).

INTERPENETRATING REGIONAL ECONOMIES DURING THE LATE POSTCLASSIC

Although polities in the eastern and southern portions of the peninsula were probably politically autonomous

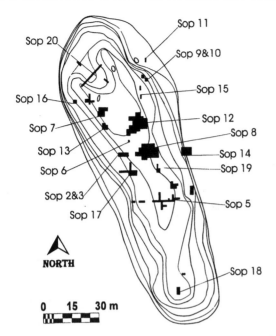

Figure 34.3 Map of Laguna de On showing the location of contexts mentioned in the text

from Mayapán (chapter 5), their economic prosperity was linked to their amplified participation in the circum-Yucatecan exchange network and to the interpenetrating nature of community economies throughout the peninsula (chapter 33). Piña Chán (1978) and Jones (1989) identify specific sets of commodities produced within different polities of the lowlands at the time of Spanish contact. It is clear from these accounts that resource heterogeneity was conducive to community and regional specialization, and encouraged trading interdependencies in bulk utilitarian goods during this period. While such resource diversity had existed during previous periods— when it encouraged the development of intercommunity exchange networks within subregions of the Maya lowlands (McAnany 1993, 1994)—most utilitarian products were made and obtained locally during the Classic period (Rice 1987b; Fedick 1991). In contrast, prestigious and more highly valued items were exchanged over longer distances (Hester and Shafer 1994). This pattern is illustrated by the shrinking geographic extent of utilitarian ceramic style zones during the Classic period, suggesting that economic exchange of everyday items became more localized from A.D. 250 through 900 (Masson n.d.b).

More-extensive exchange of bulk utilitarian items across the Maya lowlands accompanied the major amplification of a maritime trade network established by Chichén Itzá (chapter 32; see also Sabloff and Rathje 1975a, 1975b; Kepecs et al. 1994; Friedel and Sabloff 1984). The broad extent of more standardized ceramic (and other artifact) styles across the Maya lowlands during the Middle/Late Postclassic periods is one indication

of extensive economic integration (Sabloff and Rathje 1975a, 1975b; Rathje et al. 1978; Masson n.d.b). Although vessels themselves may not have been commonly exchanged beyond batabil or cuchcabal boundaries, broad similarities in the wares of such polities along the east coast of the peninsula reflect considerable communication and interaction (Masson n.d.b).

Archaeological evidence of interpenetrating accumulation is difficult to assess with the research carried out to date. Nevertheless, evidence for community economic specialization from ethnohistoric sources and archaeological data from Laguna de On and Caye Coco suggest the development of this sort of interpolity economic dependency. Canoe trade along the Caribbean coast (chapter 33) provides another line of evidence. The large quantities of obsidian debris found in domestic contexts at northern Belize Postclassic sites provide the best indication of these communities' reliance on a utilitarian resource obtained from outside the region (chapter 33; see also Rice 1987b; McKillop 1996). During the Terminal Classic/Early Postclassic, northern Belize obsidian came from a variety of sources, including several sources in the Guatemalan highlands and highland Mexico (Dreiss and Brown 1989). During the Late Postclassic, in contrast, most of the obsidian in northern Belize came from the Ixtepeque source in the Maya highlands (Dreiss and Brown 1989; Masson and Chaya 2000). This trend provides an example of interpenetrating accumulation between the Maya highlands and the lowlands.

Factory-style facilities analogous to those of Chikinchel (chapter 33) have not been identified in northern Belize. However, it is possible that small industries in perishable goods—such as honey, wax, cacao, or forest products—have not been detected from scant evidence that might be found from enigmatic features or processing tools. Functional analysis of lithic and ceramic assemblages may be helpful in identifying such industries. An example from Caye Coco illustrates the potential for inferring perishable industry locales. A small circular structure (1.5 m in diameter) was detected at Caye Coco from a posthole alignment in white limestone bedrock. In the dark earth midden overlying this miniature structure, at least nine small limestone disks (10 cm diameter) were recovered. Such disks were used to plug logs in which honey-producing bees were housed (González 1994, Cramp 1998), and the miniature structure at Caye Coco may have been a beekeeping facility. Similar circular stone structures associated with limestone disks may represent apiaries at Cozumel (Freidel and Sabloff 1984: 121–125). According to the Spaniard Alonso Luján, the Chetumal community specialized in honey production. He observed 1,000 to 2,000 hives made of logs plugged at each end with limestone mortar (Jones 1989:33). This scale of production surely exceeded community consumption, as only 2,000 houses were recorded at this center by the same observer (Jones 1989:32).

Another series of enigmatic features at the site of Laguna de On consists of a set of deep fire pits (1 m deep, 1 m in diameter) filled with broken, burned metate fragments, ash, and various domestic debris. These pits closely match ethnographic descriptions of ceramic-firing pits in the Maya highlands (Deal 1988; Masson 2000a). Fragments of pigment matching the color of red-slipped wares at this site were found in one of these pits. At both Laguna de On (Rosenswig and Stafford 1998) and Caye Coco (Barrett 2000; Roddick 2000), we found deep pit intrusions (2–3 m in diameter) into clay deposits that may represent quarries for clays for ceramic production.

During the Late Postclassic period in northern Belize, many of the production activities detected through artifact analysis reflect household-scale crafts, and some forms of production specialization are identified at the communities of Laguna de On and Caye Coco. Low numbers of spindle whorls are associated with various households at Laguna de On, and possible pottery-firing features were also distributed among several domestic zones at this site. Net weights are also broadly distributed among the site's domestic areas, suggesting that each household caught ample quantities of fish and turtle from the lagoon waters.

Lithic debris appears in greater quantity and quality in one domestic zone at Laguna de On, which suggests the presence of a resident flintknapper on the island (Masson 2000a). The volume of debris in this vicinity (Suboperation 13), however, does not approach the cottage workshop scale documented for the site of Colha, 10 km southeast of Laguna de On (Michaels 1987). There is little evidence to suggest that residents of Laguna de On produced stone tools for exchange beyond the community, although they probably exchanged chalcedony in raw material form. A chalcedony quarry (Locality 11) 5 km northeast of Laguna de On does exhibit large quantities of primary debris, suggesting that chalcedony cobbles were trimmed and extracted systematically from this vicinity (Oland 1998, 1999). Although a paucity of tool blanks and manufacturing failures suggests toolmakers were uncommon at Laguna de On, the site has much lithic debris. This debris reflects considerable processing of lithic raw materials, perhaps some of which were exchanged with nearby sites. Chalcedony from Locality 11 matches much of that found in domestic assemblages at the sites of Laguna de On and Caye Coco (Oland 1998, 1999; Oland et al. 2000), and it resembles the type that Colha artisans imported in raw form to furbish into finished tools. Laguna de On may have extracted chalcedony from this site for exchange with neighboring communities. The vicinity of Progresso Lagoon—where Caye Coco is located—has much coarser local lithic re-

sources. Caye Coco residents had a taste for finer materials such as Laguna de On chalcedony and Colha chert tools, which they probably obtained from these communities to the south (Oland 1999, 2000b).

As evidence for production beyond the household scale has not yet been identified in northern Belize, these data are inconclusive for comparing the economic structures of the Chetumal polity with those of Chikinchel (chapter 33). Inland sites such as Laguna de On and Caye Coco may have experienced less economic development than coastal sites such as Emal. The nature of some of the resources being extracted—such as copal, honey, wax, or dyes—may also have been more conducive to household production. Activities such as spinning and weaving were carried out on a larger scale in highland Mexico (chapter 32) and probably could have been performed on this level in Belize if the demand or organizational structures had been in place. Belize (referred to in Colonial accounts as Honduras) was one of the southern Maya regions where cacao was grown, and Mayapán lords actively maintained their vested interests in extracting cacao from southern orchards (Tozzer 1941:37; Scholes and Roys 1948:3). Cacao was also a major export from the Maya area to highland Mexico (chapter 16). The scale of cacao cultivation is difficult to gauge in northern Belize because the archaeological record lacks traces of this industry (McAnany et al. n.d.). Nevertheless, this product is one of the most likely to have been produced beyond the household scale because this resource was owned and controlled by powerful kin groups at certain times in Maya history (McAnany 1995:74–84). Contact-period Spanish accounts refer to substantial orchards at sites such as Chetumal (Jones 1989:33), and communities specialized in cacao production and paid cacao as tribute to the Crown (Jones 1989:32).

HIERARCHICAL DEVELOPMENT AFTER A.D. 1200

During the thirteenth century, a developmental upswing occurred at Laguna de On, Caye Coco, and other sites in northern Belize. This growth is indicated by the following evidence: a moderate increase in imports such as obsidian; greater investment in nonperishable domestic architecture at upper-status households; the construction of shrines, temples, meeting halls, and other religious architecture; the erection of stelae (plain or formerly painted but now eroded) and altars; the re-erection of inscribed monuments recovered from Classic-period sites; and an increase in censer rituals (Masson 2000a). Laguna de On Island was artificially extended by terraces at this time, and a shrine and ball court were built at the site. Large elite residences at Caye Coco, up to 4 m high and 20 m wide at the base, were constructed in single building episodes after about A.D. 1300. All of the site's 17

Table 34.1
Temporal comparisons of artifact frequencies of Caye Coco (percentage of total items)

Context	Ceramics	Lithic Tools	Lithic Flakes	Obsidian Blades	Spindle Whorls	Net Wghts.	Marine Shell	Ground Stone	Fauna	Total Items
Late Classic										
1 Subop 18 Level 5-7	42.8	7.8	30.0	1.4	0.0	10.5	0.4	0.1	6.9	3,036
Early Postclassic										
2 Subop 18 Level 3-4	62.6	0.3	5.7	2.8	0.1	5.0	0.3	0.0	23.3	11,725
3 Subop 31 Level 5-6	38.8	0.4	2.6	1.5	0.2	2.1	1.9	0.2	52.2	1,819
4 Subop 31 L3-4	42.9	0.2	2.5	0.9	0.0	0.6	2.3	0.6	50.1	527
5 Subop 13h early L4+	45.0	1.3	8.8	1.1	0.0	1.5	1.3	0.0	41.0	4,726
Mean	47.3	0.6	4.9	1.6	0.1	2.3	1.4	0.2	41.6	4,699
Late Postclassic										
6 Subop 31 L1-2	52.4	1.0	1.9	1.9	1.0	6.8	4.9	0.0	30.1	103
7 Subop 13h late L 1-3	69.0	0.9	4.9	2.3	0.1	2.2	1.0	0.1	19.6	8,945
8 Subop 18 Level 1-2	48.5	1.2	8.9	2.4	0.1	3.5	0.6	0.0	34.7	6,915
Mean	56.7	1.0	5.2	2.2	0.4	4.2	2.1	0.0	28.1	5,321

mounded structures exhibit modification at this time, and this flurry of construction activities reflects a surge in labor mobilization tied to the site's emergence as a local center. Most of the structures were elite residences, suggesting that monumental construction was undertaken primarily to symbolize the status of elite families. Six stone altars—circular limestone disks, ca. 60 cm in diameter and 40 cm high—are located around the site's surface and may be contemporary with the construction of this architecture (Barnhart 1998).

These trends suggest that local elites became active in promoting greater integration of northern Belize polities through ritual festivities, as ritual paraphernalia such as shrines, censers, caches, and altars are located adjacent to upper-status residential units and are lacking in lower-status domestic contexts at Laguna de On and Caye Coco. This trend has been observed for Santa Rita (Chase 1986; Chase and Chase 1988) and Lamanai as well (Pendergast 1981). The similarity in these rituals across the lowlands indicates that this surge in elite activity occurred across a broad area that extended from the northern Yucatán to the Petén lakes. Participation in this form of symbolic integration promoted mutual economic interaction and furthered the social ambitions of local elites (Freidel and Sabloff 1984). Regional settlement trends also reflect the amplified development of political hierarchy during the latter half of the Postclassic period.

During the thirteenth century, a settlement shift occurred in the vicinity of Chetumal Bay in northern Belize. Prior to this time (during the Early Postclassic) four large sites probably served as political centers: Aventura, Sarteneja, Santa Rita/Wilson's Beach, and Shipstern (Masson 2000a). At least 15 supporting settlements of

this period are currently known. In the Late Postclassic, five centers are known in the area: Santa Rita, Ichpaatun, Caye Coco, Sarteneja, and Bandera. At least 26 additional supporting settlements date to this period. Full-coverage survey is likely to reveal greater numbers of centers and supporting settlements. Of the five Late Postclassic centers, only Santa Rita and Sarteneja overlap with the Early Postclassic centers. The rise of Mayapán to power in northern Yucatán—coeval with this settlement shift—may have resulted in shifting alliances as new political opportunities opened for elites in northern Belize. The shift in location of political centers also correlates with the amplification of elite-sponsored monumental works and long-distance trading activities described above for the thirteenth to fifteenth centuries in northern Belize.

Although several centers have been identified for northern Belize during the Early and Late Postclassic periods, the criteria by which they are classified as centers is variable. Size is a primary criterion, although this can be measured through spatial extent, as at Santa Rita, or through monumental works, as at the circumscribed island center of Caye Coco. Rankings devised by Sidrys (1983: table 1) used a combination of such criteria. The signatures of power at these sites differ considerably (Masson 2000b). Santa Rita was an extensive settlement along a coastal bluff characterized by dispersed barrios and large, low elite residential platforms with rich caches and burials (Chase and Chase 1988; Chase 1992). The elite of Caye Coco built a series of square residential structures clustered in front of a communal rectangular public building. They also sponsored the production of circular stone markers and maintained rear altars in their

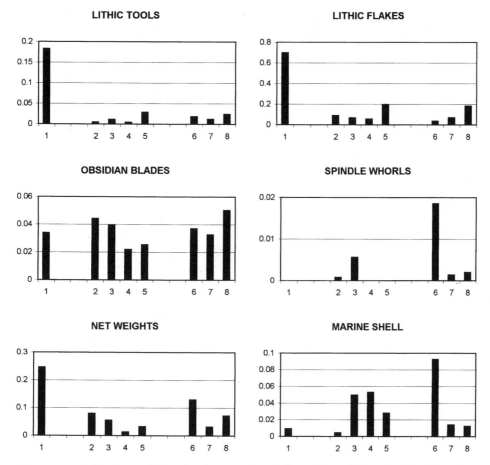

Figure 34.4 Artifact/ceramic sherd ratios over time in Caye Coco middens: (1) Late Classic; (2–5) Early Postclassic; (6–8) Late Postclassic. (See table 34.1 for key to proveniences.)

homes. Ichpaatun was a walled community with colonnaded halls like those at Mayapán and Tulum. The occupants of this site recycled stelae from earlier periods, as was the case at Tulum (Lothrop 1924; Escalona Ramos 1946). Less is known about the other large Early and Late Postclassic centers. Further south, the elite at Lamanai expressed power through the modification of a structure built in earlier times (Pendergast 1986). Also, elaborate funerary ceramics were used at this site (Pendergast 1981).

The presence of multiple elite residences at Santa Rita and Caye Coco is consistent with a model of assembly rule described for Mayapán (Masson 2000b), or multepal (Landa 1941; Roys 1957). Although individual leaders are known from fifteenth- and sixteenth-century Maya communities, power was negotiated at Mayapán through assemblies or councils composed of confederations of heads of powerful landholding kin groups (Landa 1941). Evidence for such power organization in the archaeological record is indirect. In chapter 25, I describe the depiction of multiple, equivalently ranked actors in the political and religious art of temples at Tulum and Santa Rita. This art corresponds to community settlement data at these sites and at Caye Coco, and it

also reflects the presence of a number of upper-status households of resident elites. Such elites may have rotated through ritual and political offices (chapter 25).

While social ranking within central communities is difficult to distinguish, it is likely that Postclassic centers were functionally differentiated on a regional level, and they were probably ranked in a regional hierarchy. Spanish documents state that the Chetumal territory (northern Belize/Chetumal Bay) was governed by a halach uinic who resided at the capital city of Chetumal (Roys 1957), which has been identified as the site of Santa Rita Corozal (Chase and Chase 1988). Other sites such as Caye Coco were probably subordinate communities led by batabil who collected tribute and represented other interests of the halach uinic at secondary centers (chapter 6; Roys 1957). Little is known of the exact relationships between these communities, which may have been at times compliant and at times competitive in their dealings with the capital center of Chetumal. Earlier seats of rulership may have been at other locations, and after the fall of Chetumal in the early fifteenth century, another center—Chanlacan—took its place (Jones 1989). Caye Coco is probably this site of Chanlacan (Masson and Rosenswig 1998b). Coastal sites such as Santa Rita,

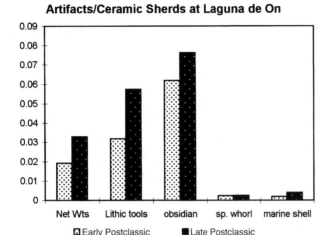

Artifacts/Ceramic Sherds at Laguna de On

☑ Early Postclassic   ■ Late Postclassic

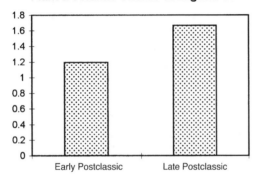

Flakes/Ceramic Sherds at Laguna de On

Figure 34.5 Artifact/ceramic sherd ratios over time at Laguna de On

Sarteneja, and Ichpaatun were probably engaged in a greater degree of trading activity with coastal merchants than were sites at inland locations. Inland sites like Caye Coco may have performed a greater role in extracting resources from the interior and moving them out to coastal trading centers along riverine networks (Masson 1999a). Four north-south running aquatic-focused settlement systems probably existed for northern Belize (Masson 1999a), including the Río Hondo, the New River, the Freshwater Creek drainage, and the coast and cayes (Andrews and Vail 1990; Vail 1988).

In addition to capital centers and subordinate centers, a third tier of settlement is represented in northern Belize by small settlements such as Laguna de On and Colha. These smaller sites, which lack Postclassic monumental architecture, were highly significant in the regional economy. The inhabitants of Colha manufactured chert and chalcedony stone tools that were widely distributed (Michaels 1987, 1994; Michaels and Shafer 1994), and it is located on perhaps the finest outcrop of chert in the Maya area. Laguna de On, located near fine chalcedony beds, may have extracted this raw material for exchange with other sites, including Colha. Textile production was

also an important industry at Laguna de On (Masson 2000a), which was located near the headwaters of the Freshwater Creek drainage that connected it to Caye Coco and the Caribbean Sea. Colha was further inland. Commodities such as stone tools, lithic raw materials, cotton textiles, and probably cacao and honey were moved through these communities northward and eastward to coastal trading centers.

ECONOMIC TRENDS OVER TIME AT CAYE COCO AND LAGUNA DE ON

The acceleration of trade in the latter half of the Postclassic period is reflected in the archaeological record of Caye Coco and Laguna de On, although the changes are not dramatic. The frequencies of artifact types in three domestic midden deposits at Caye Coco (table 34.1) illustrate these changes. In figure 34.4 these data are expressed as ratios of artifact type counts to counts of ceramic sherds by time period. Context no. 1, with Terminal Classic ceramics, yielded AMS radiocarbon dates with eighth- to tenth-century ranges (Masson 2000c). Early Postclassic radiocarbon samples date primarily to the late tenth and eleventh centuries A.D., and Late Postclassic contexts date from the twelfth through fifteenth centuries (Masson and Rosenswig n.d.).

Some interesting trends are observed at Caye Coco (figure 34.4). Local lithic tool use and the production and use of net weights appear proportionately more significant during the Terminal Classic than in Late Postclassic deposits. Obsidian blades were used in similar proportions throughout all time periods, though the drop-off in quantities of local stone tools in the Postclassic levels indicates that obsidian was relied upon to a far greater degree (relative to all chipped stone) in the Postclassic compared to the Terminal Classic. The increased significance of obsidian in Postclassic times may be due to its declining exchange value; the Classic/Postclassic transition marked a transformation of obsidian from a prestige good to a commonplace utilitarian item (Sidrys 1977a; Freidel 1985; Rice et al. 1985:602; Rice 1987b). Weaving and marine shell ornament production increased substantially in one context (Suboperation 31) during the Late Postclassic, but not in other areas. This context was adjacent to an elite residence.

The trends at Laguna de On (figure 34.5) differ from the Caye Coco middens. Proportions of net weights, lithic tools, flakes, and obsidian increased over time, while the quantities of spindle whorls and marine shell remained nearly constant. The most important pattern reflected in the data from these sites (figures 34.4, 34.5) is the similarity in assemblage composition throughout the Postclassic levels at each site, a pattern that reflects these communities' long-term stability.

Table 34.2
Artifact frequencies at Caye Coco domestic contexts (percentage of total items)

Context	Ceramics	Lithic Tools	Lithic Flakes	Obsidian Blades	Spindle Whorls	Net Wghts.	Marine Shell	Ground Stone	Fauna	Total Items
Mounded Architecture										
Structure 2	84.9	1.7	7.6	1.4		0.8	3.1	0.5		2,063
Structure 11	82.8	1.5	7.3	1.4	0.1	0.3	0.9		5.7	2,669
Structure 6	74.0	1.2	11.3	1.3	0.1	0.6	0.6	0.2	10.8	2,712
Structure 4	81.1	3.1	7.4	1.1		0.4	1.5	0.2	5.1	891
Structure 5	73.3	1.8	0.8	1.8	0.1	0.5	5.6	0.1	15.9	3,335
Structures 14, 15	69.4	3.3	26.0	0.7					0.6	883
Structure 20	53.6	0.0	40.6	2.9			1.4	1.4		69
Mean	74.2	1.8	14.4	1.5	0.1	0.5	2.2	0.5	7.6	1,803
Off-Mound Domestic Areas										
Subop 11	66.1	4.0	16.3	4.4		2.0	0.5		6.6	2,226
Subop 16	71.3	1.7	10.7	5.1		1.1		0.2	9.9	533
Subop 17	90.6	2.9	4.5	0.6		1.0	0.2	0.2		512
Subop 21	92.4	0.3	4.5	2.4		0.1	0.1	0.1		672
Subop 18 (Levs. 1-4)	57.5	0.6	6.9	2.6	0.1	4.5	0.3		27.5	18,621
Subop 31 L1-4	44.4	0.3	2.4	1.1	0.2	1.6	2.7		46.8	630
Subop 13h (Levs. 1-4)	60.7	1.0	6.2	1.9	0.1	2.0	1.1		27.0	13,671
Mean	69.0	1.5	7.3	2.6	0.1	1.7	0.8	0.2	23.6	5,266
Mean for all contexts	71.6	1.7	10.9	2.1	0.1	1.2	1.5	0.4	15.6	3,535

COMMUNITY INDUSTRIES

Several features hint at ceramic production activities at Caye Coco. Two deep, irregular pits into clay deposits (Mazeau 2000b; Barrett 2000) may represent clay quarrying activities. One large fire pit of Early Postclassic date—containing numerous large fragments of only two ceramic types (Roddick 2000)—may have been used to fire pottery. As mentioned above, Postclassic fire pits have also been found at Laguna de On, and these were associated with pigment fragments, stone slab linings, and large sherd concentrations, which suggests they were used for ceramic production (Masson 2000a). More research is needed to determine whether ceramic manufacture was performed at many communities or at a few specialized settlements.

Community-based specialization in craft production is reflected in the proportions of lithic debris at each site (Masson n.d.c, 2002). Lithic tools are present in similar proportions at each site (mean percentages of 1.4–1.7; tables 34.2, 34.3), but manufacturing debris is far more common at Laguna de On (mean percentages of 45.2–48.6) compared to Caye Coco (mean of 10.9 percent). As described previously, this trend implies a specialization in

lithic raw material processing at Laguna de On. Marine shell working is more common at Caye Coco, and this may correlate with a higher regional social position of elites at this political center (Masson 2002).

HOUSEHOLD VARIATION

The presence of multiple ruling elites of varying occupational specializations during the Late Postclassic is well documented in ethnohistory and archaeology, and these individuals provided leadership in matters of governance, economy, war, and ritual (Landa 1941; Roys 1957; Chase 1992; Masson 2000a). Elites controlled valuable resources such as cacao orchards (McAnany 1995), and they actively oversaw the exchange of such goods for commercial profit with distant consumers in the Yucatán network. Despite well-established elite tribute networks, however, marketplace exchange was well developed at the time of Spanish contact (Blanton et al. 1993; Freidel 1981b, 1986). It is likely that most members of society participated in open exchange, trading items produced at home for items produced at neighboring communities or more distant areas.

The degree of economic differentiation between

Table 34.3
Artifact frequencies at Laguna de On (percentage of total items)

Context	Ceramics	Lithic Tools	Lithic Flakes	Obsidian Blades	Spindle Whorls	Net Wghts.	Marine Shell	Ground Stone	Fauna	Total Items
Early Postclassic										
Subop 8	29.4	1.1	47.0	3.1	0.1	0.4	0.1	0.0	18.8	3,590
Subop 12	63.1	0.7	13.1	2.4	0.1	0.6	0.1	0.0	19.9	1,912
Subop 17	42.5	0.8	37.0	1.5	0.1	0.9	0.1	0.0	17.1	3,186
Subop 5	28.5	1.3	52.4	1.9	0.0	1.1	0.0	0.1	14.6	2,958
Subop 7	5.2	3.4	49.7	3.4	0.9	1.7	0.3	0.0	35.4	698
Subop 18	62.3	2.3	22.5	0.8	0.0	0.7	0.0	0.0	11.4	613
Subop 20	8.6	1.1	74.6	3.4	0.0	0.0	0.1	0.0	12.2	755
Subop 14	9.0	1.5	65.6	2.7	0.0	0.5	0.0	0.1	20.6	1,000
Mean	31.1	1.5	45.2	2.4	0.1	0.7	0.1	0.0	18.8	1,839
Late Postclassic										
Subop 8	26.6	0.7	37.0	2.2	0.0	0.7	0.2	0.0	32.5	10,002
Subop 12	40.4	0.8	30.5	2.2	0.2	1.7	0.0	0.0	24.2	3,296
Subop 17	13.9	0.8	69.9	1.8	0.1	1.0	0.0	0.0	12.5	4,604
Subop 5	40.0	0.8	28.9	1.7	0.0	1.0	0.0	0.0	27.6	4,219
Subop 16	5.6	0.9	81.1	0.9	0.0	0.0	0.0	0.0	11.5	1,334
Subop 7	27.6	2.6	48.3	5.1	0.3	0.9	0.0	0.1	15.1	1,012
Subop 13	12.0	1.1	70.5	1.7	0.0	0.6	0.0	0.0	14.1	1,362
Subop 18	22.2	2.0	37.5	1.6	0.0	0.0	0.0	0.0	36.7	248
Subop 20	32.6	3.9	48.4	2.1	0.0	0.4	0.7	0.0	11.9	285
Subop 14	34.1	0.7	34.1	1.9	0.0	0.8	0.0	0.2	28.3	1,059
Mean	25.5	1.4	48.6	2.1	0.1	0.7	0.1	0.0	21.4	2,742

Postclassic elites and commoners is difficult to determine. Comparisons of domestic architecture and ritual activity suggest that social status varied along a continuum at most communities (Chase 1992). Differential investment in domestic architecture suggests that elites possessed more resources than commoners. Nevertheless, luxurious funerary goods such as metal occur in both upper- and lower-status domestic zones, though not in even proportions (Chase 1986; Chase and Chase 1988; Pendergast 1981). Ritual paraphernalia is one means by which elites can be identified at Postclassic sites. This pattern is found at Santa Rita, where caches are found primarily in elite residential courtyards (Chase 1986), and at Caye Coco, where caches are found at rear altars of the site's largest elite residential structures (Barrett 1999, 2000; Masson 1999a). The manufacture of shell ornaments is also primarily associated with elites at Laguna de On (Masson 2000a, 2002) and Caye Coco.

Market economies facilitate a more even distribution of valuable commodities—including luxury goods— across categories of social status, as the marketplace in-

creases the accessibility of these goods to all potential consumers (Hirth 1998; Smith 1999). An examination of the domestic assemblages of elites and commoners provides a means for measuring the differences in production and exchange among members of different social classes within a community.

Frequencies of key artifact categories (expressed as ratios to counts of ceramic sherds) are shown in figure 34.6. The left series of bars in each graph represents elite residential mounds, and the series of bars on the right in each graph represents off-mound domestic middens and rubble floors, assumed to represent commoner contexts. Lithic tools, spindle whorls, obsidian blades, and flakes appear in variable proportions among both mound and off-mound contexts, and these items are not more abundant in either setting (figure 34.6). For each of these artifact categories, some domestic zones exhibit greater quantities of these materials, reflecting either normal household variability or else a degree of household specialization within the community. Examples include the greater ratio of spindle whorls for Suboperation 31, flakes

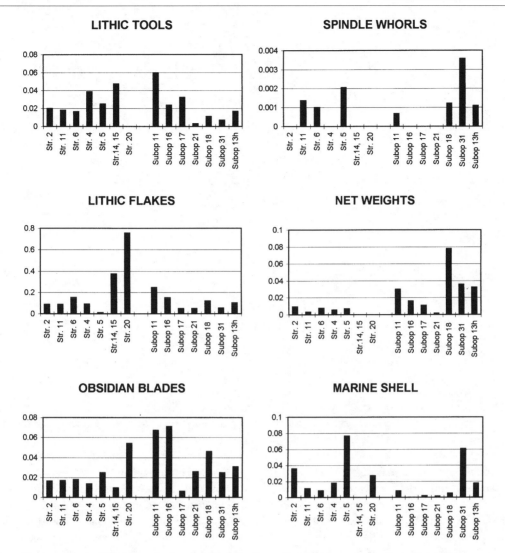

Figure 34.6 Artifact/ceramic sherd ratios in various domestic contexts at Caye Coco. Bars on the left are mounded contexts; bars on the right are off-mound contexts.

for Structure 20, and obsidian blades for Structure 20 and Suboperations 11 and 16.

Net weights appear in greater proportions in off-mound contexts, most of which are in shoreside locations (figure 34.6). Marine shell, mostly production debris, is more common in mound contexts (figure 34.6), with one off-mound exception, Suboperation 31, which is adjacent to a mounded elite residence (Structure 6). Shell ratios exceed .01 for four out of six mounded contexts, but only two out of seven off-mound contexts (table 34.2). This suggests that upper-status members of this site more commonly undertook the manufacture of shell ornaments. Other artifact categories do not indicate elite-specific activities at Caye Coco, and their distribution conforms to Hirth's (1998) expected distributions for open market exchange. Although shell is associated with status, it is significant that this item is not found exclusively in elite contexts (see chapter 32 for a similar pattern in Morelos households). Similar broad distributions

are observed for ornamental objects such as mica, worked bone, ceramic effigy faces, and small pieces of carved stone (table 34.4). With the exception of mica, all of these items were probably crafted locally at Caye Coco. These data suggest that differences in wealth and status were less strongly expressed in domestic artifact assemblages than they were in architecture and ritual features at this site.

Metal was probably the most highly valued luxury good in this region of the Postclassic Maya world. It was present in greater quantities at major centers such as Lamanai (Pendergast 1981) and Santa Rita (Chase and Chase 1988), where it is found primarily in elite contexts. This commodity was probably obtained by local elites through maritime trading partners (chapter 21), and it may have formed an integral part of elite gift exchange within or between communities.

Artifact/ceramic sherd ratios for Late Postclassic contexts at Laguna de On are displayed in figure 34.7.

Table 34.4
Valuable objects in Caye Coco contexts

	Mica	Worked Bone	Pigment	Ceramic Effigy	Greenstone	Carved Stone
Mounded Architecture						
Structure 2	1					
Structure 4			1	1		
Structure 5		1	2		1	2
Structure 6						
Sructure 11	1					
Structures 14, 15			2			
Off-Mound Domestic Areas						
Subop 11						
Subop 13 (Lev. 1–4)		6		1		1
Subop 16					2	
Subop 17			2			
Subop 18 (Level 1–4)			4	1	4	2
Subop 31 (Lev. 1–4)	2			2	1	1

Upper-status and ritual contexts include the four bars on the left of the graph, including Suboperation 20, a ball court. Patterns similar to those of Caye Coco are observed for ratios of lithic tools, flakes, and obsidian, which do not appear concentrated in either upper- or lower-status contexts. Similarly, net weights exhibit no clear pattern. Spindle whorls are almost exclusively recovered from upper-status or ritual contexts, with the exception of one domestic zone that has a higher ratio than the others (Suboperation 7). Marine shell is exclusively distributed in upper-status and ritual contexts. These data suggest that marine shell ornament manufacture was primarily an elite activity at this site, as observed for Caye Coco. Textile production may also have been an activity more commonly practiced by the upper-status members of the Laguna de On community.

DISCUSSION

The upper-status families at Laguna de On were not of equivalent regional rank to those of Caye Coco. The difference between upper-status residences and other residences at Laguna de On—as defined by architectural characteristics such as stone foundation alignments, plaster floors, and proximity to ritual features—is slight (Masson 1999b, 2000a). The lack of mounded residential architecture of Postclassic date at Laguna de On contrasts with the multiple residential mounds at Caye Coco. The architecture of Laguna de On's "upper-status" households is similar to the off-mound architecture at Caye Coco. Despite these differences in settlement scale, two important patterns emerge. First, within each com-

munity, ritual paraphernalia, marine shell debris, and rare ornaments of local or exotic material distinguish the domestic zones with the highest social rank. Second, other artifact classes show few differences in their proportions at upper- and lower-status contexts, suggesting that inhabitants of various domestic zones had many production and exchange activities in common and were able to obtain many of the same commodities useful in everyday life, including imported obsidian.

These data point to the operation of well-developed market networks in northern Belize. While obsidian represents the primary category of material not of local derivation, its distribution was likely paralleled by other perishable commodities such as salt, fur, or fibers that may have been imported into northern Belize from distant locations. The substantial quantities of obsidian at Laguna de On and Caye Coco reflect the degree to which "interpenetrating accumulation" (chapter 33) was manifested among northern Belize communities through their participation in broader mercantile exchange networks.

Few differences in everyday economic activities distinguished the elite from the non-elite occupants of Caye Coco and Laguna de On. Elites may have enjoyed more prestige and power, as suggested by their occupancy of mounded architecture and their manufacture of ornaments for displaying their status or for gift giving (as in Formative Soconusco; see Clark and Blake 1994). There is no evidence, however, that elites controlled bulk goods production or exchange. Elite activities were probably linked to the promotion and scheduling of market events and ritual occasions that provided regional integration (Masson 2000a), and this role would have been benefi-

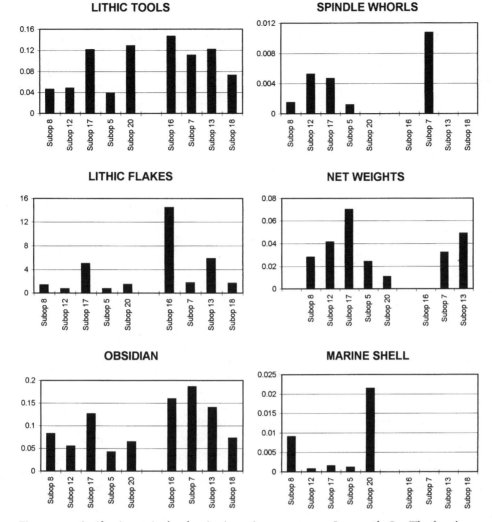

Figure 34.7 Artifact/ceramic sherd ratios in various contexts at Laguna de On. The four bars on the left include upper-status and ritual contexts (Suboperations 8–5), including a ball court (Suboperation 20); the remaining bars are lesser-status domestic zones.

cial to a society characterized by small-scale entrepreneurs who operated at the household level or beyond (chapters 32, 33).

The data from northern Belize, as currently represented, provide no archaeological indications of suprahousehold scale production of lithic, ceramic, or textile commodities for local and regional exchange, although such industries probably existed for perishable items. This region was known for its rich groves of cacao and its production of honey and wax (Piña Chán 1978), and the scale of production of these commodities was probably much grander than those reflected by preserved household artifacts. Such activities are difficult to iden-

tify in the archaeological record, and systematic efforts to detect these are sorely needed. Much continuity over time is observed in the artifact assemblages in Late Postclassic levels at Caye Coco and Laguna de On. This pattern suggests long-term stability—around four centuries—at these northern Belize Postclassic sites. Northern Belize participated in the Postclassic world system not as an exploited and underdeveloped periphery, but as an affluent production zone characterized by economic activity and dynamism. Another vital affluent production zone was the Soconusco area of the Pacific coast, an area discussed by Gasco in the next chapter.

35

Soconusco

Janine Gasco

The Soconusco region, one of the primary cacao-producing areas of Mesoamerica, is located along the Pacific coastal zone of Chiapas, Mexico (figure 35.1). A portion of southwestern Guatemala is within the traditional boundaries of Soconusco, but there has been little fieldwork in the Guatemalan portion of the region, and there is only brief mention of Postclassic sites in reports from this area (Coe 1961; Coe and Flannery 1967; Shook 1965).

The Soconusco region is hot and humid. There are, however, significant climatic differences as one moves from northwest to southeast (it gets wetter toward the southeast, with rainfall reaching 3–5 m annually in some areas) and from the coast inland to the piedmont of the Sierra Madre (it gets wetter toward the mountains). Apart from the climatic differences between northwest and southeast, the entire region can be divided into two environmental zones. Near the coast is a large estuary system made up of mangrove swamps, large lagoons, and navigable canals. Inland are a narrow flat coastal plain and the Sierra Madre foothills. Archaeological research in the Soconusco region has been limited to the estuary zone, the coastal plain, and foothills or piedmont zone. The Sierra Madre above the piedmont zone is almost completely unknown and quite inaccessible.

There is some debate about what really constitutes the Soconusco region. During the Colonial period the Province of Soconusco included the entire coastal region of what is today Chiapas and a small part of Guatemala (Gasco 1989b). But the few preconquest references to the region only mention towns in the southeastern half of what became the Colonial province (from Mapastepec to the southeast), and beginning late in the Colonial period and continuing until today there has been a similar division between the southeastern half of the region—the Soconusco district—and the northwestern half—the

Tonalá district, now sometimes called La Costa (Bassols Batalla et al. 1974; Lowe et al. 1982; Voorhies 1989a). I focus mainly on the southeastern portion of the greater Soconusco region, the area with the greatest population density and the area where cacao can be grown.

In contrast to many parts of Mesoamerica, much more is currently known about the Archaic and Early Formative periods in Soconusco than about later periods (e.g., Blake 1991; Blake et al. 1995; Clark 1991; Clark and Blake 1994; Ekholm 1969; Kennett and Voorhies 1996; Lesure 1997; Voorhies and Kennett 1995). Our vision of the Postclassic period has been shaped largely by the appearance of Soconusco towns in the Codex Mendoza and other Aztec documents (see Gasco and Voorhies 1989). Because little else was written about Postclassic Soconusco, scholars have relied heavily on the documents that describe the Aztec conquest of Soconusco and subsequent tribute lists (chapter 7). Yet this conquest occurred a scant 25 to 35 years before the fall of Tenochtitlan to the Spaniards. Clearly the Aztec conquest of Soconusco was an important event for people in the region, but we also need to consider what happened in Soconusco for the other 500 years or so of the Postclassic period.

The data I present here come primarily from work carried out by Barbara Voorhies and myself over the past 24 years in the Soconusco region. Voorhies directed the Proyecto Soconusco from 1978 to 1983. This project consisted principally of survey and excavations of sites within a 755 km² area in the vicinity of Escuintla (figure 35.2). During a subsequent field season in 1988, Voorhies directed a survey of the wetlands northwest of the original survey area and conducted a brief investigation of the site of Paredón (figure 35.2). The Proyecto Soconusco and the subsequent wetland survey never focused specifically on the Postclassic period, but a number of issues can be addressed with Voorhies's data from survey and

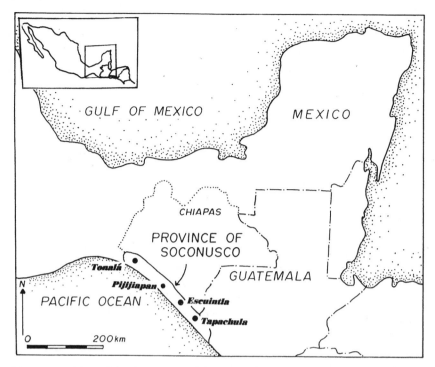

Figure 35.1 Map of the Soconusco region in southern Mexico

excavations at several sites that were occupied during the Postclassic. The Proyecto Soconusco data for the Postclassic period will be published soon in a monograph (Voorhies and Gasco 2002).

My own work initially focused exclusively on the Colonial period in Soconusco (Gasco 1989a, 1989b, 1992, 1993). My long-term goals, however, always have been to better understand the Postclassic period and to trace the changes from the Postclassic to Colonial periods. To do this, it became clear to me as we worked on the monograph mentioned above that it would be necessary to expand on what had already been done and de-

velop a project whose goals were specifically to investigate the Postclassic period. Consequently, in 1997 I began the Proyecto Soconusco Posclásico. During the first field season, test excavations were carried out at five Postclassic sites (Gasco 1998a, 1998b; figure 35.3). During the summer of 2000 the area in the vicinity of the Late Postclassic and Colonial town site of Soconusco was investigated (Gasco 2001).

Our previous efforts to interpret the Postclassic period had been hampered by the fact that virtually all of the sites investigated by Voorhies were multicomponent sites. Because the regional ceramic chronology had not been developed when Voorhies's excavations were carried out, it was not obvious at the time that most of the excavation units were dug into mixed fill. To sidestep this problem, in my 1997 excavations I purposefully selected sites that appeared to be single-component Postclassic sites. Analysis of the materials recovered during the 1997 and 2000 seasons is still in progress, but I include as much as I am able to in the following discussion.

CHRONOLOGICAL CONSIDERATIONS

We have not yet solved a number of problems related to the chronology or periodization of the Postclassic period in Soconusco. Apart from the post-1487 period of Aztec domination of some sort, we have no firm independent basis for subdividing the rest of the Postclassic period. Whereas it is highly desirable to distinguish this Aztec period or phase, it is not clear whether or not we will ever be able to identify such a short phase archaeologically.

Figure 35.2 Map of archaeological study areas in the Soconusco region

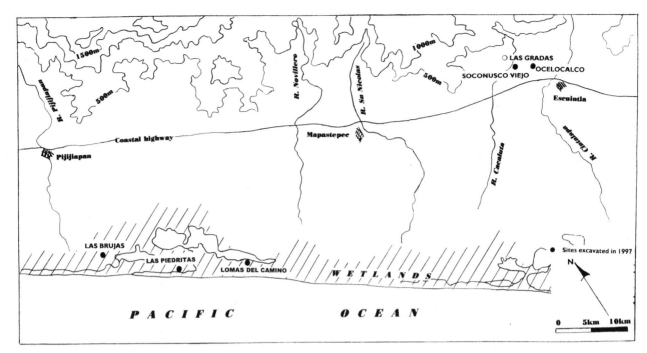

Figure 35.3 Map of archaeological sites excavated in 1997

Lowe et al. (1982:153–157) briefly discuss what they identify as the Early Postclassic (A.D. 900–1200) occupation at Izapa. The primary diagnostic pottery for the Early Postclassic at Izapa was Tohil Plumbate, and we now know there are some serious problems with the earlier Plumbate sequence (for example, a greater overlap between San Juan and Tohil Plumbate than previously thought). In the Proyecto Soconusco survey, very few sherds were identified as Tohil Plumbate, and because this was the primary criterion we used to identify Early Postclassic sites, we have identified only 4 sites with an

Early Postclassic occupation (out of 90 dated sites). This is almost certainly an underrepresentation, but we still have virtually no information about other ceramic types in use during the Early Postclassic period. In their work at Izapa, Lowe et al. noted that it is difficult to distinguish Late Classic utilitarian ceramics from those of the Early Postclassic (1982:157).

This problem of identifying Early Postclassic sites is not unique to Soconusco, and my sense is that many Late Classic ceramic types continued to be used in the Early Postclassic period in other areas as well. Within the

Table 35.1
Radiocarbon dates for Soconusco sites

Lab #	Site	Context	Range, A.D.	Intercept
110207	Las Piedritas	operation 2, level 5	1635–1700	A.D. 1670
110205	Las Piedritas	operation 2, level 7	1410–1650	A.D. 1455
110206	Las Piedritas	operation 4, level 3	1285–1470	A.D. 1410
110209	Las Brujas	operation 7, level 2	1705–1950	—
110208	Las Brujas	operation 7, level 4	1415–1655	A.D. 1490
110210	Las Brujas	operation 8, level 4	1450–1690	A.D. 1550
110204	Soconusco Viejo	operation 10, level 3	1535–1545 1635–1700 1720–1820 1855–1860 1920–1950	A.D. 1665

*Note: 2-sigma ranges listed. Calibration based on Pretoria Calibration Procedure; shell corrected using a correction of 225 +/– years for reservoir effect. Dates determined by Beta Analytic, Inc.

Table 35.2
Obsidian hydration dates for Soconusco sites

Site	Sample no.	Date, A.D.	Site	Sample no.	Date, A.D.
Las Brujas	282	741	Las Piedritas	84	810
	278[a]	1103		41	1067
	271	1206		37[a]	1114
	273	1209		95	1244
	327[a]	1226		59[a]	1264
	269[a]	1233		120[a]	1290
	291[a]	1259		223[a]	1307
	329	1273		86	1314
	402	1281		213	1323
	251[a]	1281		160	1343
	258	1314		9	1357
	244	1319		156	1358
	253	1349		191	1413
	229	1445		169[a]	1431
	290[a]	1453		175[a]	1490
	255	1462		78[a]	1508
	287	1474		64	1622
	356	1518			
	359[a]	1681	Soconusco Viejo	395[a]	1346
	332[a]	1785		383	1451
	301	1819		388	1465
				267	1507
Ocelocalco	207	1388		387	1534
				394	1566
				396	1672
				265	1727
				374[a]	1717[b]
				377[a]	1753[b]
				376	1791[b]

[a]Samples that yielded more than one date; the latest date is reported here.
[b]These samples come from the Colonial component of the site.

Proyecto Soconusco survey area, 66 sites were occupied during the Late Classic period (based on ceramics types); if some of the ceramic types identified as Late Classic continued to be used in the Early Postclassic, this would alter considerably our understanding of Early Postclassic settlement patterns.

Unfortunately, my 1997 excavations have not helped much in this regard. Of the almost 4,000 diagnostic sherds analyzed, only 12 are Plumbate of any kind (most sherds are too small to accurately identify them as San Juan or Tohil). I still plan to carry out additional attribute analyses or some other measure to seriate the ceramic

assemblage, but it now seems likely that the sites excavated in 1997 date exclusively to the Middle-to-Late Postclassic period. All 7 radiocarbon dates and a group of obsidian hydration dates (50 samples) indicate that occupations at the excavated sites began after A.D. 1100–1200 (tables 35.1, 35.2). I am hopeful that eventually ceramic seriation will allow me to identify two or more phases within the Late Postclassic, but this probably will not add anything to our understanding of Early Postclassic ceramics or the Early Postclassic period. In this chapter I use the term Late Postclassic for the period from A.D. 1100/1200 through the Spanish conquest.

POSTCLASSIC DEMOGRAPHY

Population estimates for the period immediately preceding the Spanish conquest range from 67,500 to 90,000 (Gasco 1989c; Gerhard 1993a). Population density was almost certainly higher in the southeastern half of what became the Colonial province of Soconusco. In fact, the northwestern zone was referred to as the Despoblado beginning early in the Colonial period, presumably reflecting both low population and the absence of towns; only 4 of the more than 40 towns in the sixteenth-century province of Soconusco were in the northwest. This pattern of greater population densities in the southeastern area continues to the present day.

Population estimates for earlier periods in the Prehispanic era are virtually nonexistent. Within the Proyecto Soconusco study area there are more than twice as many sites with Late Classic–period occupations as there are sites with Late Postclassic–period occupations. This might mean that the Late Classic population was larger than the Late Postclassic population, but it also may reflect a significant change in settlement patterns, an issue discussed more fully below.

ETHNOLINGUISTIC GROUPS IN POSTCLASSIC SOCONUSCO

Soconusco lies within a major natural corridor for the movement of peoples and goods between Mexico and Central America. Linguists have concluded that Mixe-Zoquean peoples have lived in the area since the Formative period, and that Tapachultec, a Mixean language, was the region's mother tongue in the sixteenth century (Campbell 1988; Ciudad Real 1976; Thomas 1974). Speakers of other languages, however, frequently passed through the area, sometimes staying. For the Epiclassic/Postclassic periods there is documentary evidence for the arrival of Nahuatl-speakers, Otomanguean-speakers (Chiapanec/Mangue), and Mam-Maya-speakers, all of whom apparently settled in the Soconusco region. Unfortunately, none of these immigrant populations have been identified in the archaeological record.

Torquemada, writing in 1615, referred to a population of Nahuatl-speakers who resided in the northwestern portion of Soconusco during the Epiclassic period (1969:1:331–333). Similarly the Codex Chimalpopoca (Bierhorst 1992:42) lists places where migrant Toltecs settled, including towns named Ayutla and Mazatan, where Toltecs reportedly settled around 1060.[1] Admittedly, these are place names that can be found in other regions, so we cannot be certain that this report refers to Soconusco towns, but the Soconusco towns that bear these names are linked in other documents, and they are close to each other geographically, making it likely that this reference does refer to the Ayutla and Mazatan in

Soconusco. Moreover, linguistic evidence for the Colonial period and twentieth century supports the presence of a Pipil-like Nahuatl language ("mexicana corrupta") in the Soconusco region that has been called in recent times "Waliwi" (Bruce and Robles Uribe 1969; Campbell 1988; Knab 1980). Waliwi may be derived from the Nahua populations mentioned by Torquemada and the Codex Chimalpopoca. Some of the original Nahuatl-speakers eventually migrated to Nicaragua to become the Pipil-Nicarao, while others may have stayed in the Soconusco (Campbell 1988; Fowler 1989). The impact of this Nahua migration into the Soconusco is unknown. There has been little archaeological research within the region on this time period, and there is so far no obvious evidence for an intrusive population, nor does archaeological evidence from subsequent time periods (also relatively scarce) allow us to identify the presence of a Nahua population that is distinct from the native Mixe population.

We know less about the Otomanguean immigrants to Soconusco. Torquemada (1969:1:331–333) mentions that Manguean speakers lived for a time in the Soconusco until they were driven out by invading Olmecas in the Epiclassic period (see further discussion below). According to this account, one group then moved into Nicaragua to become the historic Mangue, and a second group moved into the Grijalva Valley to become the historic Chiapanec (Campbell 1988:268–269; Navarrete 1966:5–7). There is no good evidence to suggest that any Manguean speakers remained in the Soconusco region. One Colonial document, however, notes the presence of Chiapanec or Mangue speakers in the Soconusco town of Huixtla in 1656 (Reyes 1961:178). We do not know if this was a remnant population of Manguean speakers whose ancestors had lived in the area in the Prehispanic period, or if these were people who had moved into Huixtla in the Colonial period, when there was a good deal of migration into the Soconusco region (Gasco 1989c).

Mam Maya (or possibly the recently identified Teco Maya, a close relative of Mam) is or was spoken in several Soconusco towns from late prehistoric times to the present (Campbell 1988; Schumann 1969). Mam incursions into Soconusco are thought to have occurred late in the Postclassic period, and Mam speakers continued to move into the region in the Colonial period. A single Colonial document presents information about the relationship between Postclassic Mam immigrants and local Soconusco communities.[2] In 1599 the Mam residents of the Soconusco communities of Cuilco, Tepeguis, Ilamapa, and Nejapa complained to the Audiencia of Guatemala that they were forced to work for the Indians of Huehuetan. According to testimony by both sides, this arrangement was based on an agreement between Mam immigrants, who had arrived in Soconusco sometime prior to the arrival of the Spaniards, and the residents of Huehuetan, who had given the immigrants land in return for an annual labor obligation. The descendants of these original immigrants, who now lived in the four towns listed above, argued that because they were all now vassals of the king of Spain, the original work obligation was no longer required. So at least in this one case, an immigrant population had been given land in return for an annual labor levy.

In addition to these immigrant populations, powerful neighboring or distant polities sometimes engaged in violent confrontation with the people of Soconusco through raiding or outright conquest, although with the exception of the Aztecs, there is little evidence that these intrusive groups had a lasting impact on the region's ethnolinguistic makeup. There are vague references to invading "Olmecas" (Olmeca/Xicalanca), who drove groups of Nahuatl-speakers and Otomanguean-speakers out of the Soconusco region sometime between A.D. 800 and 1040 (Campbell 1988:277–279; Fowler 1989:36; Navarrete 1966:5–7; Torquemada 19691:331–333). There is somewhat better evidence of K'iche' raids on the southeastern Soconusco towns of Ayutla, Mazatan, Tapachula, and Naguatan in the mid-fifteenth century (Recinos 1957: 79–81).

Finally, there is the well-documented conquest of several towns in the Soconusco region by the Triple Alliance during the reigns of Mexica rulers Ahuitzotl and Motecuhzoma Xocoyotzin (see chapter 7). Apart from the political and economic implications of this conquest, it also resulted in the spread of Nahuatl into the Soconusco region. In contrast to what we know about earlier invasions of Soconusco, we know that following the Aztec conquest at least a few Aztec officials began to reside in the province. Aztec documents report that two high-ranking Aztec officials, a tezcacoacatl and a tlillancalqui, were stationed in the town of Xoconochco (Berdan and Anawalt 1992:3:f. 18r; P. Carrasco 1999:394). The usual Aztec provincial strategy was a hands-off policy with regard to local political rule (Berdan et al. 1996; see chapter 11), although in some areas, like Soconusco, officials from the capital oversaw tribute collection and were charged with maintaining order. There are other reports of an Aztec military garrison in Soconusco (Diaz del Castillo 1950) that would have created a more significant Aztec presence in the Soconusco. Although there is some debate about the real meaning of the term "garrison" (Davies 1978; Smith 1996b:141–147), Soconusco and a handful of other towns were clearly identified as having some special military installation. P. Carrasco (1999: 386–400) concludes that these can best be thought of as military colonies where colonists from the Valley of Mexico served as part of their military obligation to the Triple Alliance. These settlements were supplied by tribute paid by local peoples.

Archaeologically we have not yet seen obvious evidence for an intrusive Nahuatl population at Late Postclassic sites in Soconusco. But so far only limited test pits have been excavated at Soconusco, the town that was designated as the capital of the Aztec province, where Aztec officials were stationed and where a garrison may have been located.

If there is little material evidence so far to indicate Aztec hegemony in the region in the last decades of the Postclassic period, linguistic evidence suggests that local political leaders had adopted Nahuatl, perhaps as a lingua franca, and that they had taken Nahuatl surnames. Several Early Colonial documents from Soconusco are written in Nahuatl, and in these documents local caciques and other principales use Nahuatl surnames or titles. A 1565 letter from the indigenous leaders of Huehuetan is written in a variety of Nahuatl that is identified as provincial, similar to the Nahuatl being used in the western fringes of the Aztec empire (Anderson et al. 1976:190–195). Curiously, there do not seem to be any colonial documents written in Tapachultec; all of the native-language documents from Colonial-period Soconusco (perhaps a dozen in all) are written in Nahuatl. This suggests to me that elites were fluent in Nahuatl and may have been accustomed to using it in all of their extra-provincial affairs, a practice that continued into the Colonial period. In fact, it is worth mentioning the possibility that former Aztec officials actually became the local leaders in the Colonial period.

SETTLEMENT PATTERNS

Late Postclassic settlement patterns have been difficult to identify in the Soconusco region because the physical characteristics of sites changed dramatically at some point between the Late Classic and the Late Postclassic periods. Across Mesoamerica there was a decline in the amount of monumental construction by the Late Postclassic period (Blanton et al. 1993). This included a shift away from the construction of house platforms to building houses at ground level. These trends have affected our ability to locate Late Postclassic sites in the Soconusco region. Dense vegetation prohibits good ground visibility, so sites without large mounds are virtually invisible. Almost all of the Late Postclassic sites we have found are associated with earlier sites (with the exception of a small number of sites in the wetlands). Much of the mound construction at these sites predates the Late Postclassic period, and the Late Postclassic occupation is often ephemeral, identified only by the presence of a few sherds. This situation has serious implications; if there are Late Postclassic sites that lack mounds and that are not associated with an earlier site, we have not found them. It seems unlikely, however, that we have missed any large Late Postclassic occupations.

Table 35.3
Postclassic site hierarchy, and intensity of occupation per period

Sites by Category	AR	EF	MF	LF	Pr	EC	MC	LC	EP	LP
Primary, Terra Firma										
Acapetahua/CAP-1				4	4	4	4	4		4
Secondary, Terra Firma										
Lomas Juana/CAP-35						3	3	3	1	4
Secondary, Estuary										
La Palma/CAP-2				4	4	4	4	4		4
Las Morenas/MAP-5				4	4	4	4	4	3	4
Coquito 2/CAP-22					4	4	4	4		4
La Concepción/CAP-24				4	4	4	4	4	1	3
Tertiary Terra Firma										
Doña María/CAP-67							4	4		3
Dos Amates/CAC-2				4	4	4	4	4		3
Filapa/CAP-13				3	3	3	3			4
Flor de Carmen/CAC-3					4	4	4	4		3
Las Lomas/COM-6				3	3	3	4	4		2
Loma Bonita/CAP-31					4	4	4	4		4
Loma Cacao/CAP-68						4	4	4		3
Loma de Piedra/CAP-11						4	4	4		4
Loma Eduardo/CAP-52								4		4
Lomas Lopez/CAP-56					4	4	4	4		3
Santa Elena I/CAP-71						3	3	3		4
Tepalcatenco/CAC-1		2	2	4	4	4	3	3		2
Tertiary, Estuary										
Apazotal/CAP-27				4	4	4				3
Castaño 2/CAP-17	1									2
Campito/CAP-15		3	3			4	4	4	1	3
Chantuto/CAP-3	4				3	3				2
Coquito 1/CAP-21						4	4	4		3
El Conchal/CAP-14				4	4	4	4	4		3
Herrado/CAP-5				4	4	4	4	4		3
Is. Tamarindas/CAP-33	1	3	3	2	2	2	2	2		2
La Ceiba/CAP-18	1	3	3	2	2	2	2			2
Zapotillo 2/CAP-39	1	3	3	2	2	2	2	2		2
Zoológico/CAP-23						3	3	3		4

Notes:
AR=Archaic; EF=Early Formative; MF=Middle Formative; LF=Late Formative; Pr=Proto-Classic; EC=Early Classic; MC=Middle Classic; LC=Late Classic; EP=Early Postclassic; LP=Late Postclassic. For intensity of occupation, 1=possible occupation; 2=minor occupation; 3=moderate occupation; 4=major occupation.

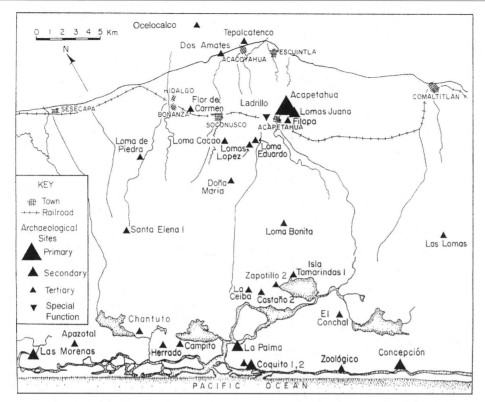

Figure 35.4 Map of Proyecto Soconusco study area showing archaeological sites dating to the Late Postclassic period and identifying their position in the regional site hierarchy

THE PROYECTO SOCONUSCO STUDY AREA

The data from the Proyecto Soconusco study area indicate a dramatic shift in settlement patterns sometime between the Late Classic and Late Postclassic periods. There is a decline in the total number of sites occupied (but this undoubtedly reflects our inability to identify small residential sites), a decline in the number of primary centers, and a shift toward a greater proportion of sites in the wetlands.

A total of 29 habitational sites (of 90 dated sites) within the Proyecto Soconusco study area have some evidence of a Late Postclassic occupation (see Voorhies and Gasco 2002). Sites in the study area were classified along two dimensions. One dimension is synchronic and places the sites within a three-tiered site hierarchy for the Late Postclassic period. Sites are classified as primary (tier 1), secondary (tier 2), or tertiary (tier 3) based on the following criteria: the apparent size of the Late Postclassic occupation; the estimated amount of construction; the quantity, quality, and diversity of ceramics; and ethnohistorical evidence. In addition, the location of sites either on terra firma or in the estuary is noted in table 35.3 (and see figure 35.4). The second dimension is diachronic and is a measure intended to estimate the relative intensity of occupation at each site for each time period. For this measure, Voorhies evaluated relative proportions of surface ceramics from each time period as well as the physical characteristics of each site. From these data, it was

possible to estimate whether a site had a major, moderate, or minor occupation during each time period (based on Voorhies 1989e).[3] Using these two schemes, it is possible to see simultaneously the occupational history of each site and how each of the 29 sites fit into a site hierarchy for the Late Postclassic period (table 35.3).[4]

In terms of the Late Postclassic site hierarchy, the site of Acapetahua, one of the Soconusco towns listed in the Codex Mendoza, is the area's only primary center; five sites are categorized as secondary centers (Lomas Juana, La Palma, Las Morenas, Coquito 2, and La Concepción); 23 sites are classified as tertiary (see table 35.3 and figure 35.4). All of the primary and secondary centers were in locations that had been occupied since at least the Classic period, and in most cases since the Late Preclassic (with the caveat that we have not identified an Early Postclassic occupation at three of the six sites). With only one exception, these primary or secondary centers had experienced a major occupation in the Late Classic period. The majority (57 percent) of sites that had a major occupation during the Late Classic period, however, had been abandoned by the Late Postclassic period. To become a primary or secondary center in the Late Postclassic period, it apparently was important for a site to have had a major occupation during the Late Classic period. Nevertheless, having a major occupation in the Late Classic period did not guarantee that a site would survive to the Late Postclassic: not only were many abandoned, but

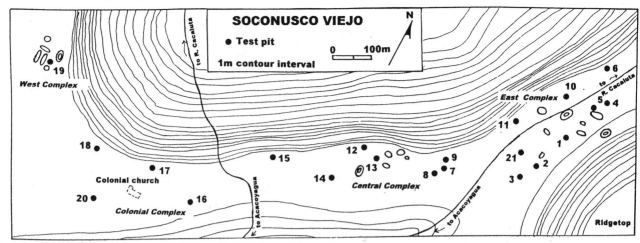

Figure 35.5 Map of Soconusco Viejo showing locations of test pits

others had only moderate or minor occupations in the Late Postclassic.

Another settlement shift involved the increased importance of estuary sites. Although the single primary site of Acapetahua is an inland site, four of the five secondary centers were in the estuary along the inner-coastal canals. The fifth secondary site, Lomas Juana, might be best thought of as a satellite community of Acapetahua. Of all 29 Late Postclassic sites in the Proyecto Soconusco study area, 15 are in the estuary zone. This is in sharp contrast to the pattern in the Late Classic period, when only 25 percent of the sites were in the wetland zone. The higher proportion of Late Postclassic sites in the wetland zone almost certainly reflects the increased importance of the canal system for trade and transport in the Late Postclassic period.

The missing Early Postclassic occupations remain troublesome. The large majority of identified Late Postclassic sites are on top of, or adjacent to, Late Classic centers, suggesting a certain degree of continuity, but missing an Early Postclassic component. As mentioned above, I suspect that many of the sites we have identified as Late Classic sites continued to be occupied into the Early Postclassic. If this is true, then the shift in settlement patterns noted above may have taken place between the Early Postclassic and the Late Postclassic periods. Obviously, determining more precisely when this shift occurred will be a critical component of future work on Postclassic sites in the Soconusco.

THE 1997 AND 2000
PROYECTO SOCONUSCO POSCLÁSICO DATA

During the course of planning the first phase of the Proyecto Soconusco Posclásico, I selected five sites that, based on surface ceramics, appeared to date exclusively to the Postclassic period in order to avoid our earlier problems with mixed deposits (figure 35.3). Test excavations carried out at these sites in 1997 confirmed that

they do indeed date exclusively to the Late Postclassic period (or the Middle-to-Late Postclassic). These sites, identified in earlier surveys, are near but not within the original Proyecto Soconusco study area. Two of the sites (Soconusco Viejo and Ocelocalco) are in the inland zone, and three (Las Piedritas, Las Brujas, and Lomas del Camino) are in the estuary zone.

The sites also were selected because they appeared to occupy different tiers of the settlement hierarchy established for the Proyecto Soconusco study area. Soconusco Viejo was by far the largest of the five sites in areal extent. It extends over 1.5 km across a long, narrow ridge, and the Postclassic site lies adjacent to the abandoned Colonial town site of Soconusco Viejo (Gasco 1990; figure 35.5). Like Acapetahua in the Proyecto Soconusco study area, this town appears in the Codex Mendoza. Furthermore, we knew that this town had been designated as the provincial capital by the Aztecs. The ethnohistorical data certainly suggested that this was a primary center (see chapter 7).

The estuary sites of Las Brujas and Las Piedritas are on islands that face large canals. These sites are much smaller in area than Soconusco (figure 35.6), so following the scheme devised for the Proyecto Soconusco material, these sites were tentatively classified as secondary sites. The other two sites, the inland site of Ocelocalco and the estuary site of Lomas del Camino, are very small, with little or no standing architecture. These sites were placed into the tertiary site category; presumably they were hamlets during the Postclassic period.

Based on the physical characteristics of these sites and on artifact distributions, we can now identify some rather striking differences between the site of Soconusco Viejo, on one hand, and the two island sites of Las Piedritas and Las Brujas on the other. I had long been interested in the site of Soconusco because it was named as the provincial capital when the region was conquered by the Aztecs in the 1480s. Curiously, despite its apparent

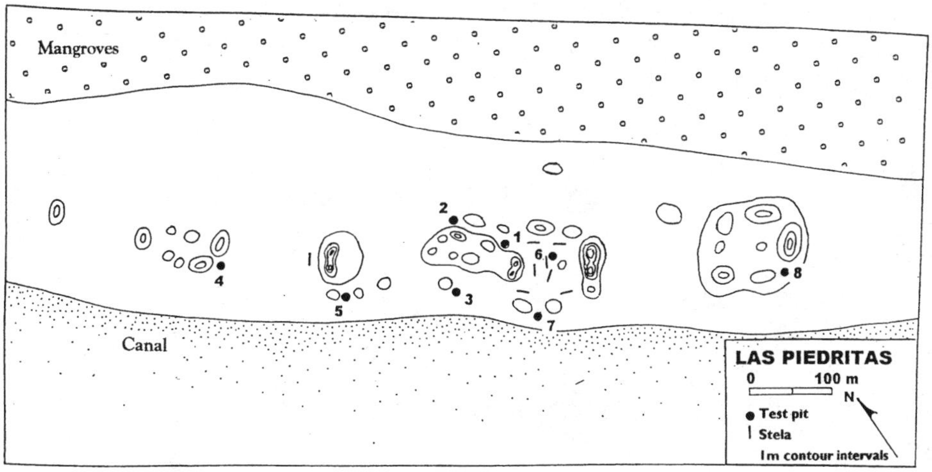

Figure 35.6 Map of Las Piedritas showing locations of excavation units

importance and its size, Soconusco Viejo is a quite unimpressive site in terms of architecture. There are only 15 small mounds, all less than 2 m high. Even in the portion of the site where artifact and mound densities are highest (the East and Central complexes), there are no large mounds. In fact, most of the site is flat and featureless, yet wherever we excavated we found household refuse, and in some units we uncovered foundation stones, suggesting that most of the houses were ground-level constructions. The situation at Soconusco Viejo became more complex in 1998 when we located a Late Postclassic site on a neighboring ridgetop. This second site, called Las Gradas by locals, has a commanding view of the entire coastal plain (figure 35.3). It has a few stone-faced mounds up to 2–3 m high, and the slopes of the ridge have been terraced. The site is littered with Late Postclassic sherds.

Soconusco Viejo and Las Gradas were the focus of further investigations during the summer of 2000. After survey and limited excavations at both sites and in the area between them, we now know that the two sites are separated by approximately 400 m of unoccupied terrain. The ceramic evidence, however, suggests that they were roughly contemporary. The relationship between these two sites is not yet well understood; one or the other may date exclusively to the period after the Aztec conquest of the region (and in this case it is possible that Las Gradas was the site of an Aztec garrison), Las Gradas may have served as some other special-function site (a ceremonial or shrine site, or the site of elite residences), or the two sites may have been occupied sequentially. Our ceramic chronology is not sufficiently refined to rule out this possibility. Because Soconusco Viejo is also the site of a Colonial occupation, it seems likely that this area was occupied at the time of the Spanish conquest. So far there is no evidence for any Colonial occupation at Las Gradas. Future research is currently being planned to resolve these issues.

Even with the uncertainties that still surround the Soconusco Viejo/Las Gradas sites, we can identify important differences between these inland sites and the estuary sites. In contrast to Soconusco Viejo/Las Gradas, the two island sites of Las Piedritas and Las Brujas have many more mounds (more than 30 each), some of which are 5 m high (figure 35.6). Another important difference between Soconusco and the two island sites is the presence of seven to nine plain stelae at the island sites, some still in situ. We assume that these were once painted. This stone is not available in the estuary and had to be brought in from inland area. At Soconusco Viejo only a single stela was located.

Both the amount of construction and the presence of stelae suggest that there was a greater investment of labor at the estuary sites. While we are still in the early stages of artifact analysis, there are some early indications of significant distinctions between estuary and inland sites for several classes of artifacts that will be discussed below in the section on imported commodities.

INLAND AND WETLAND SITES

One issue that warrants further discussion is the relationship between inland and littoral sites during the Late Postclassic period. Within the Proyecto Soconusco study area the proportion of sites in the wetland zone increased from 25 percent in the Late Classic period to around 50 percent in the Late Postclassic period. Presumably this reflects a greater role for wetland sites in the Late Postclassic because of increased use of the canal system for transport. The occupational history of the three wetland sites I excavated during the 1997 field season lends further support to this possibility. Las Piedritas, Lomas del Camino, and Las Brujas all appear to have had their initial occupation in the Middle-to-Late Postclassic period. In contrast to the Late Postclassic wetland sites within the Proyecto Soconusco study area, all of which had earlier occupations, in the area between the study area and

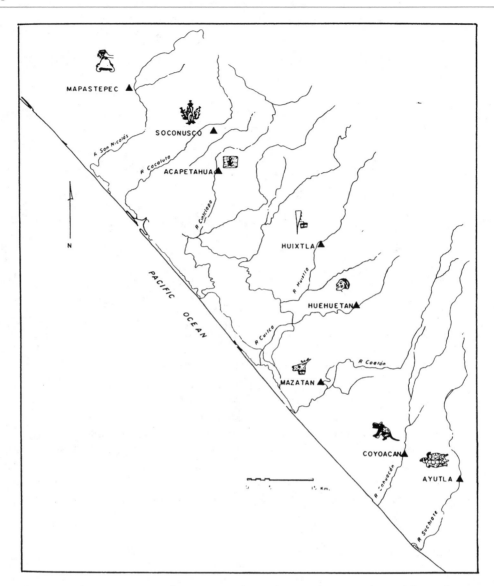

Figure 35.7 Soconusco towns that appear in the Codex Mendoza. (Berdan and Anawalt 1992:4: f.47r.)

the Isthmus of Tehuantepec entirely new communities were established in the Middle-to-Late Postclassic. Paredón, a major site on a large lagoon within the estuary system, closer to the Isthmus of Tehuantepec (figure 35.2), also seems to date exclusively to the Middle-to-Late Postclassic period. This suggests that canoe transport between southeastern Soconusco, where cacao was produced, and the isthmus may have become more extensive in the Middle-to-Late Postclassic period, prompting new communities to become established along the coast.

A second aspect of the relationships between inland and wetland sites has to do with their hierarchical relations. Data from the 1997 and 2000 excavations suggest that we may need to refine our notions about the settlement hierarchy. Site layout and labor investment in architecture and other features as well as the artifact distribution (particularly the distribution of luxury goods such as

metal and certain ceramic types) suggest a more complex relationship between inland and wetland sites.

Finally, there are questions regarding the absolute dates of occupation of the inland and littoral sites. Curiously, not a single littoral site appears in any town list in the Aztec and Early Colonial documents. Were important centers like Las Morenas, La Palma, Las Brujas, and Las Piedritas abandoned before the Spanish or even the Aztec invasion? Were the Aztecs and Spaniards simply unaware that there were communities in the estuary zone? Did the Aztecs purposefully discontinue the use of the coastal waterways in favor of overland transport, resulting in the abandonment of the wetland towns? For whatever reason, Aztec records such as the Codex Mendoza and later Colonial documents mention only inland towns (figure 35.7), even though the archaeological data suggest that the wetland communities were flourishing well into the

Table 35.4
Sources of obsidian at Postclassic Soconusco sites

	Guatemalan Sources	Pachuca	Orizaba	Other	Sample Size
Early Postclassic					
Las Morenas	75%			25%	4
Izapa	91%	3%		6%	147
Late Postclassic					
Las Morenas	47%	10%	40%	3%	297
La Palma	55%	32%	12%		121
Acapetahua	53%	18%	27%	2%	176
El Aguacate	43%	39%	18%		155
Ocelocalco	43%	57%			28
Las Piedritas	27%	26%	46%	1%	225
Las Brujas	44%	29%	26%	1%	140
Soconusco Viejo	55%	38%	7%		45
Las Gradas	33%	20%	47%		15

Sources: Las Piedritas, Las Brujas, Soconusco Viejo, and Las Gradas data from 1997 and 2000 excavations; all other data from Clark et al. 1989.

fourteenth and even fifteenth centuries. Something must have happened late in the Postclassic period to affect these towns.

AGRICULTURAL PRACTICES AND TROPICAL FOREST RESOURCES

The Soconusco, with its rich soils and heavy rainfall, was one of the most fertile regions of Postclassic Meso-america. Until just a few decades ago, the region was covered by tropical forest vegetation. Residents who are in their 50s and 60s vividly remember widespread use of forest resources, and wild game was a large part of their diet (Alvarez del Toro 1985). Most of the forest at lower elevations has been cut in recent years, and while in much of the Soconusco region subsistence farming has given way to agribusiness and cattle ranching, many people continue to grow a variety of crops for family consumption on small parcels of land. In most of the southeastern half of the region two corn crops can be planted without irrigation. A wide variety of vegetables and legumes are cultivated, and in some areas rice is an important crop. Tree crops also are highly valued.

Historically, the most important tree crop in So-conusco has been the cacao tree. The importance of cacao in Mesoamerica is widely recognized (e.g., Millon 1955; Bergmann 1969), and its role in the economy of Postclassic Soconusco has also been discussed previously (e.g., Gasco and Voorhies 1989). Important issues that have yet to be resolved include the extent to which cacao production in Soconusco increased in the Postclassic period, and how and when cacao became a medium of

exchange. I suspect that production did increase, and it also seems possible that cacao did not become a medium of exchange until the Postclassic period (Gasco 1996b). If these notions are correct, then it also seems likely that the organization of cacao production would have changed in Postclassic Soconusco, and this in turn would have brought about significant changes in the lives of cacao farmers. This issue will be addressed in future research.

IMPORTED COMMODITIES

The evidence from the Proyecto Soconusco and Proyecto Soconusco Posclásico sites suggest that consumption of certain imported commodities reached unprecedented levels in the Late Postclassic period. The 1997 and 2000 data also indicate significantly different consumption patterns for inland and wetland sites. I review here the data for obsidian, ceramics, and metal.

OBSIDIAN
Obsidian artifacts from several Postclassic sites in the So-conusco region have been analyzed by John Clark (Clark et al. 1989). In addition to these published data I include here an analysis (conducted by Susan Maguire and John Clark) of the 425 obsidian artifacts recovered during the 1997 and 2000 excavations at the sites of Las Brujas, Las Piedritas, Soconusco Viejo, and Las Gradas.

Table 35.4 identifies the sources for obsidian artifacts from two Early Postclassic and nine Late Postclassic sites in Soconusco. One particularly notable difference between the two Early Postclassic sites and the Late Post-classic sites is the much greater use of Guatemalan obsidians in the Early Postclassic (75 percent and 91 percent). By the Late Postclassic the percentage of Guatemalan obsidians had dropped at all sites to somewhere between 27 percent and 56 percent, and there was a clear shift to Pachuca and Pico de Orizaba obsidians, which together made up between 45 percent and 72 percent of the artifacts studied. Even during the period of strong Teotihuacan influence during the Early and Middle Classic period, Guatemalan obsidian sources accounted for between 78 percent and 100 percent of the obsidian at five sites; of 390 obsidian artifacts from the Early and Middle Classic periods, only 5 artifacts from a single site were from Pachuca obsidian. Similarly, artifacts from the Pico de Orizaba source were rare before the Late Postclassic period (Clark et al. 1989; see also chapter 19).

CERAMICS

We have not yet carried out sourcing studies on the Soconusco ceramics, but certain ceramic groupings exhibit strong influences from outside the immediate region (Voorhies and Gasco 2002). Some of these are almost certainly imported from elsewhere, whereas others may be locally produced imitations. As was the case with obsidian, the ceramics (or mental templates for the ceramics) came into the Soconusco region from either Guatemala to the south or Oaxaca, Veracruz, and central Mexico to the north.

Ceramic groups that seem to be most closely related to ceramic types reported from other areas include polychromes that resemble Chiapanec polychromes (Navarrete 1966), and bichromes and polychromes that are similar to those reported for the Guatemalan highlands (Wauchope 1970). There is also a very unique ceramic type among the Soconusco ceramics that has a fine gray paste and appears to be identical, in paste and form, to the Fine Gray wares from the Valley of Oaxaca. Among all the materials recovered so far—including ceramics from the Proyecto Soconusco and Proyecto Soconusco Posclásico sites—there is a conspicuous absence of ceramics that are similar to Aztec types and wares.

The analysis of ceramics from the sites excavated during the 1997 and 2000 seasons of the Proyecto Soconusco Posclásico reveals an interesting distinction between the estuary and inland sites. First, there are higher proportions of bichromes and polychromes at the estuary sites, and second, the Fine Gray wares occur almost exclusively at the estuary sites (227 of the 229 sherds in this ceramic grouping were found at estuary sites). Minimally, this suggests that residents of the estuary sites had greater access to "fancier" pottery. And if these pots were actually imported from outside the area, this means that estuary residents had greater access to imported products.

METAL

Several copper/bronze artifacts have been found at the sites of Acapetahua and Las Morenas within the Proyecto Soconusco study area and at the sites of Las Brujas and Las Piedritas; these include needles, bells, tweezers, a ring, and axe-monies (chapter 20). It is interesting to note that most of these artifacts were found at estuary sites. Particularly noteworthy is the fact that all of the 12 copper axes or axe-monies (Hosler et al. 1990) come from estuary sites (6 from Las Morenas, 4 from Las Piedritas, and 2 from Las Brujas).

CRAFT PRODUCTION

We have very little evidence regarding craft production for Postclassic Soconusco. From the presence of bead spindle whorls in Late Postclassic deposits (Voorhies 1989d; Voorhies and Gasco n.d.) it is clear that cotton threads were spun, and presumably cotton textiles also were produced. Textile impressions have been found on sherds that date to the Late Postclassic period. Because the ceramic types with textile impressions are exclusively plain utilitarian wares, and because spindle whorls are found, we assume that cotton textiles were produced locally. Unfortunately, we cannot even speculate about the extent of spinning and weaving during the Postclassic period. It is perhaps significant that textiles were not among the items the Soconusco towns paid in tribute to the Aztecs. Similarly, there is no mention of textile or cotton production in the hundreds of Colonial documents that I have worked with. It seems probable, therefore, that cotton production and textile production were not major economic activities in Postclassic (or Colonial) Soconusco. In my 1997 excavations seven bead spindle whorls were found at the site of Las Piedritas. None have been found at Soconusco Viejo. This absence may be significant; perhaps farmers at Soconusco were devoting most of their time to cacao cultivation to the exclusion of other activities. Also, the use of copper axe-monies as currency in this region (chapters 15, 20) may have reduced the need for cotton textiles as currency for long-distance exchange.

Other evidence for craft production includes a possible ceramic production area east of the site of Acapetahua. Although initially identified as two separate (but adjacent) sites, this area can be treated as a single archaeological phenomenon (Voorhies and Gasco 2002). Currently a number of open clay pits along the west bank of the Río Filapa are being mined for clay for brick and tile production. Voorhies noted that as the brickmakers were excavating the clay pits, they encountered dense concentrations of sherds. Controlled excavations subsequently were carried out near the clay pits, and the great majority of sherds (85–98 percent) came from a single ceramic type, Acapetahua Coarse. In other deposits at the site of Acapetahua the percentage of Acapetahua Coarse sherds ranged from 5–32 percent. Although there is no definitive evidence that this pottery was being produced in this location (that is, no kilns were found), a large number of "wasters" were identified. This, together with the exceptionally high percentage of Acapetahua Coarse sherds found, suggests that this may have been a production center for Acapetahua Coarse pottery. Acapetahua Coarse vessels are found at sites throughout the Proyecto Soconusco study area and at all the sites excavated in 1997 and 2000. Perhaps this utilitarian pottery was all being produced at the regional center of Acapetahua.

Finally, Clark's analysis of the Proyecto Soconusco obsidian and obsidian from other Soconusco sites (1989) provides the best information about obsidian tool production in the region. Clark concludes that during the Classic and Postclassic periods the major obsidian technology was the manufacture of pressure blades. What changed from Classic to Postclassic was the availability of obsidian at different stages of manufacture from different sources. In the Classic period, polyhedral cores—from which pressure blades were produced—were imported mainly from the Guatemalan sources of El Chayal and San Martín Jilotepeque. Obsidian from more-distant sources was imported in ready-made blades. In the Postclassic period polyhedral cores were imported from greater distances, primarily from the Pico de Orizaba source in Veracruz. Clark notes, however, that obsidian from the even more distant Pachuca source continued to be imported as blades. The obsidian analysis from the 1997 and 2000 excavations is still in progress, but if these data conform to the materials already analyzed by Clark, it appears as if obsidian production strategies did not change dramatically from Classic to Postclassic periods in the Soconusco.

ELITES

Soconusco elites presumably were involved in the exchange of esoteric information that linked them with other Mesoamerican elites. There are no known codices or mural paintings from the Soconusco region, however, and evidence for participation in elite networks comes from indirect evidence of exchange of elite goods such as certain ceramics, metal goods, and jewelry (lip and ear plugs of obsidian, amber, and gold). At present it is unclear precisely how Soconusco residents (presumably elites) came to acquire these goods. There is no evidence regarding marital alliances either between elite Soconusco families, or Soconusco families and outsiders. Similarly, there is simply no evidence regarding visitation with elites from elsewhere. One objective of future work, which will focus on excavation of residences, is to determine precisely who had access to certain luxury goods that in other parts of Mesoamerica were used extensively by elites.

STYLISTIC PATTERNS

We have noted a general stylistic similarity in the polychrome ceramics found at Soconusco sites and the polychromes that were popular across Mesoamerica during the Postclassic period (Voorhies and Gasco 2002). There are some vague similarities with Mixteca-Puebla ceramics and with ceramics from the Guatemalan highlands. Without sourcing studies, we do not yet know which of the vessels were imported and which were produced locally as imitations of popular styles.

In terms of architectural style, some Postclassic Soconusco sites (including Las Piedritas and Las Brujas) have double-temple pyramids, a style that was popular in central Mexico and highland Guatemala (Navarrete 1996; see chapter 36).

SOCONUSCO IN THE POSTCLASSIC MESOAMERICAN WORLD

From the data presented above, it is possible to arrive at certain conclusions about Soconusco's participation in the larger Mesoamerican world system. A key to understanding how and why Soconusco became more closely linked to other regions within Mesoamerica is cacao, the area's most important product. Although cacao had been cultivated in the Soconusco region since Formative times, production almost certainly increased in the Postclassic period. Presumably the significant increase in the amount of obsidian from central Mexico and Veracruz that began in the Late Postclassic (or Late Middle Postclassic) and the appearance of copper axe-monies at around the same time suggest that the cacao trade, too, may have increased markedly at around 1200. Ceramic styles—if not the pots themselves—also seem to have been introduced into the region at around the same time, and double-temple pyramids appear at sites that were first built at about the same time.

The growing importance of communities within the estuary zone, along an inner coastal canal that facilitated canoe traffic from Guatemala to Oaxaca, is also indicated by the archaeological data. Curiously, even though the archaeological record suggests that estuary sites were actively engaged in exchange well into the fifteenth century, these sites are virtually absent in documents that describe events of the last decades of the Late Postclassic period. This is precisely the time that the Aztecs conquered Soconusco and began exacting tribute; perhaps the Aztecs also interfered with earlier trade routes along the coast and began to dominate trade into and out of the region.

After the Aztec conquest the annual imperial tribute from the eight conquered Soconusco towns consisted of 200 cargas of cacao, 2 strings of greenstone beads, 2 blocks of amber, 4,000 bunches of colored bird feathers, 40 jaguar pelts, 800 gourds, 160 bird skins, and 2 amber lip plugs set in gold. Except for the gourds, all of these items were luxury goods (chapter 17); thus Soconusco towns were participating in a luxury-goods network through forced tribute payments of what were largely raw materials obtained from the local forest habitat or, in the case of the cacao, from local orchards. The gold and amber, and probably the greenstone, were obtained from elsewhere, however.

This situation only pertained to the final decades of the Postclassic period, so we need to also consider how Soconusco was connected to the rest of Mesoamerica before the 1480s. It is clear from the archaeological evidence that prior to the Aztec conquest, Soconusco participated in long-distance exchange networks. Aztec documents record the trading expeditions of the pochteca into the Soconusco region, and according to some sources, local attacks on pochteca prompted the Aztec conquest of the entire Soconusco region. I suspect that this may have just been a pretense, and that the real reason for the Aztec conquest of Soconusco has more to do with the region's valuable products.

Although Xoconochco was identified by Chapman (1957) as a "port-of-trade," the data presented here and in chapter 17 show that this is not an adequate characterization of the region. No single site immediately jumps out as a large trading port, although Paredón does seem to be larger than any of the other known sites. Perhaps it would be more accurate to view the entire region as one whose location and resources attracted traders. The bulk of trade almost certainly took place at sites within the estuary that served as stopping-off places for merchants traveling along the coast in canoes.

Soconusco's neighbors to the southeast in the western Guatemalan highlands were the K'iche'. We have already seen that the K'iche' carried out raids into the Soconusco region in the fifteenth century. In the following chapter Geoffrey Braswell explores K'iche'an origins.

36

K'iche'an Origins, Symbolic Emulation, and Ethnogenesis in the Maya Highlands

A.D. 1450–1524

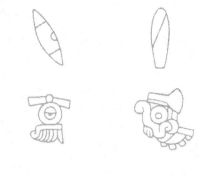

Geoffrey E. Braswell

No topic in K'iche'an archaeology and ethnohistory has been the subject of more speculation than the source and timing of central Mexican influence in the central and western highlands of Guatemala. Evidence for an important connection between the two regions is undeniable, and is manifest in indigenous historical accounts such as the *Popol Wuj* (Brasseur de Bourbourg 1861; Saravia E. and Guarchaj 1996) and the *Memorial de Tecpán Atitlán* (Arana Xahilá and Díaz Xebutá Queh 1573–1605),[1] in Postclassic architecture and mural painting, in portable artifacts, in burial practices, and even in the vocabulary and personal names used by K'iche'an peoples.

The foremost concern of archaeologists of K'iche'an culture has been chronology, specifically whether the period of the most-intense intercultural contact was the Early or Late Postclassic (e.g., Lothrop 1933, 1936; Thompson 1943, 1954; Wauchope 1949, 1970, 1975). The goal of this research was to determine if central Mexican cultural traits found in the Guatemalan highlands were more properly associated with a "Toltec" horizon or with the Aztec expansion into Xoconochco. Borhegyi (1965:39–41) saw as many as three waves of intense and intrusive interaction, each characterized by the migration of central Mexicans into the Guatemalan highlands. Each of his conjectured migrations involved groups that he called the Pipil: the Teotihuacan-Pipil of A.D. 400–500, the Pipil-Nicarao (also called the Tajínized-Teotihuacan-Pipil) of A.D. 700–900, and the Nonoalca-Pipil-Toltec-Chichimec of A.D. 1000–1200. Thus, in a complex way, the appearance of central Mexican traits in highland Guatemala also was linked with movements of the Nahua-speaking Pipil and Nicarao into Guatemala, El Salvador, and Nicaragua. More recently, a variation of Thompson's Putun hypothesis has been championed by ethnohistorians as accounting for a

Mexicanized Maya presence in the Guatemalan highlands (e.g., Carmack 1968, 1973, 1981; Fox 1978, 1980, 1991; Fox et al. 1992; Nicholson 1957; Recinos and Goetz 1953). Although these scholars are concerned with temporal issues, their research has focused on reconstructing a migration route for K'iche'an "lineage" founders from the Gulf coast lowlands. Thus, archaeological and ethnohistorical discourse has concentrated on demic diffusion. In contrast, few scholars have considered the economic, social, and political implications of the adoption of a central Mexican cultural veneer by K'iche'an elites (cf. Brown 1983, 1985; Navarrete 1976, 1996); that is, Postclassic interaction rarely has been discussed as an example of elite emulation.

In this chapter, I briefly review the archaeological, linguistic, and ethnohistorical evidence for contact between the highlands of Guatemala and Mexico during the Postclassic period, and conclude that evidence for the long-distance or interregional migration of K'iche'an elites is unconvincing. In contrast, a growing body of archaeological data suggests that K'iche'an peoples originated in the western highlands of Guatemala and entered the central highlands by the beginning of the Early Classic period. I then turn to the social context of central Mexican cultural traits in the K'iche'an realm, and note that it is limited to expressions of elite identity. Finally, I consider the economic and political implications of emulation and the creation of an elite ethnic identity within the framework of factional competition within a house society.

ARCHAEOLOGICAL EVIDENCE OF POSTCLASSIC CONTACTS WITH CENTRAL MEXICO

In two works, Navarrete (1976, 1996) provides an exhaustive list of Postclassic material traits from the highlands of Chiapas, Guatemala, and El Salvador that may have originated in central Mexico. These include architectural forms and features (such as I-shaped ball courts, twin temples on a single platform, round structures, and sacrificial blocks placed in front of temples), mural paintings (particularly those from Temple 2 of Iximche', in a style reminiscent of Mixteca-Puebla murals; see chapters 23 and 24), sculptural forms (such as two chacmools from El Salvador), ceramics (including Aztec pottery found in Chiapas and El Salvador, and Mixteca-Puebla ceramics from Chiapas and Guatemala), and various other items of material culture.

Several aspects of this list are noteworthy. First, although a few architectural traits and portable objects may date to earlier periods, virtually all the items in Navarrete's list are firmly dated to the Late Postclassic period, particularly after A.D. 1450. Second, most of the portable artifacts are limited in distribution to Chiapas and El Salvador, and hence may be attributable to the physical presence of Nahua speakers in those areas.[2] In fact, no Aztec pottery and only two Mixteca-Puebla style vessels (from Q'umarkaj and an unknown site) have been found in the K'iche'an highlands (Navarrete 1996:328). A second vessel, from Zacualpa, carries images of crossed bones with "star eyes" and a skull with a chert knife embedded in its nasal cavity (Lothrop 1936:33, figure 30). Nonetheless, it is classified as Chinautla Polychrome, an autochthonous ware of the central highlands of Guatemala. Apparently, highland Maya potters only rarely copied foreign motifs.

Third, most of the architectural features of probable central Mexican origin are found at paramount sites such as Saq Ulew, Iximche', and Saqik'ajol Nimakaqapek ("Mixco" Viejo). For the most part, these elements are associated with temple structures, but some range structures of the type known as nimja also have sloping balustrades surmounted by vertical blocks. Although certain architectural forms may be of central Mexican origin, it is uncertain how they were used by the highland Maya. Specifically, it is not known to which gods double pyramids were dedicated, and if round structures should be associated with Ehecatl, a wind deity and avatar of Quetzalcoatl. There is no clear evidence that the highland Maya participated in the pan-Mesoamerican cult of the feathered serpent, so this identification seems unlikely.[3]

Fourth, nearly all features of material culture that may have a central Mexican origin are associated with elite contexts, such as possible royal burials (e.g., feature E 27-A of Iximche' [Guillemín 1961]), and are found in the epicenters of regional "capitals." The ownership, display, and use of items of foreign origin were quite restricted, perhaps even by sumptuary laws. Despite the strong desire of K'iche'an elites to emulate Nahua culture, they apparently had little access to imported status goods.

LOAN WORDS FROM NAHUATL IN K'ICHE'AN LANGUAGES

Also providing evidence for contact between K'iche'an and Nahua peoples are the numerous loan words from Nahuatl found in Colonial documents and dictionaries from the Guatemalan highlands. Campbell (1977: 104–109) has compiled a list of 74 Nahuatl loan words, almost all of which are nouns, that appear in K'iche'an sources. As others have noted (e.g., Carmack 1965, 1968, 1981; Whorf 1943), many of these are related to warfare (e.g., *xkapupul*, 'cotton armor'), religion (e.g., *nawal*, 'spirit' or 'alter ego'), social and territorial organization (e.g., *kalpul*, a social unit), elite architecture (e.g., *tekpan*, 'palace'), and status goods (e.g., *xit*, 'greenstone').

It is tempting to suggest that the elite semantic domain that encompasses these loans mirrors the social context of their borrowing. In fact, such an interpretation is consistent with the argument I make below. But, as Campbell (1977:109) points out, many more loans describe common objects (e.g., *ikom*, 'jug'), domestic architecture (e.g., *xan*, 'adobe'), and especially animals (e.g., *tamasul*, 'toad'), plants (*witzitzil*, a type of tree), and food (e.g., *xunakät*, 'onion'). He suggests that an overemphasis on religious and military terms has caused scholars to miss the more intimate nature of contact between Nahuatl and K'iche'an speakers (Campbell 1977:109). It also may be that by privileging texts that focus on the origin myths and military exploits of elites, ethnohistorians have limited the *apparent* context of Nahuatl loans to an elite semantic realm. The *Popol Wuj* and *Memorial de Tecpán Atitlán*, after all, are texts written by, for, and about the K'iche'an elite.

When and from what region did Nahuatl loans enter the K'iche'an languages? Some probably were adopted during the Colonial period (e.g., *mes*, 'cat'), perhaps from the Tlaxcalans brought to Guatemala by the conquistadors. Others may have come from the Pipil who lived in El Salvador and southern Guatemala during the Postclassic period. But Campbell (1970, 1977:109) suggests that the principal source of loans was a dialect spoken in the Isthmian Gulf Coast.[4] He argues that, as in the Nahuatl of that region, loans in K'iche'an languages are typified by the change of *kwaw-* sequences to *ko-* (e.g., *kot*, the Kaqchikel word for 'eagle', is reduced from the Classical Nahuatl *quauhtli*) and *-iwi-* is changed to *-i-* (e.g., the Classical Nahuatl *chalchihuitl*, 'greenstone,' is reduced to *xit* in Kaqchikel).

This interpretation often is viewed as supporting the conjecture that K'iche'an forefathers, called "Toltec overlords" by Campbell (1977:109), came from the Gulf coast of Tabasco or Veracruz (e.g., Carmack 1981:44–52). But it also is consistent with other kinds of contact with speakers of Isthmian Nahuatl. In chapter 20 I suggest that during the first part of the Late Postclassic period, sites in Xoconochco received significant quantities of obsidian from the Gulf Coast exchange sphere. At the same time, considerable interaction with the K'iche'an highlands is demonstrated by the presence of Guatemalan obsidian in Xoconochco. It may be that the inhabitants of Xoconochco mediated economic and linguistic exchange between K'iche'an and Isthmian Nahuatl speakers during the first half of the Late Postclassic period.

There is considerable evidence from both Colonial sources (e.g., Torquemada 1969:1:331–333) and contemporary studies (e.g., Bruce S. and Robles Uribe 1969; Campbell 1988:277–281; Knab 1980; Navarrete 1975; Reyes García 1961; van Zantwijk 1963; Vivó 1942) that Nahua was spoken in southwestern Guatemala and southeastern Chiapas before the arrival of the Aztecs in Xoconochco. Several K'iche'an documents discuss Nahua peoples in Xoconochco, including the *Macatlecat* (Mazateca) and the *Ayutlecat* (Ayuteca), both identified as *Yaqui Vinaε*: "Nahua people" (Carmack and Mondloch 1983:162–163; Recinos and Goetz 1953:194). Other communities—such as Naguatecat, Tapaltecat, and Xicalapa—are called by Nahuatl names in the *Títulos de la Casa Ixquin-Nehaib Señora del Territorio de Otzoya* (Recinos 1957:79–81). Little is known about the dialect(s) spoken in these towns at the time of conquest, but studies of modern Chiapan Nahuatl provide some information about linguistic affinity. Although the dialectology of modern Chiapan Nahuatl, including Waliwi, is somewhat in doubt, Campbell (1988:280) presents a strong case that it is more closely allied to the Core Nahuatl dialects of Veracruz than to Central American Pipil. In particular, there is evidence of the reduction of *kwaw-* to *ko-* (see entry for "firewood" in Campbell 1988:287). I suggest, therefore, that the source of loans in highland Maya languages may have been pre-Aztec Chiapan Nahuatl, rather than a dialect spoken in the Gulf coast region. Consequently, there is no need to posit a migration from the Gulf coast to the Maya highlands in order to account for the presence of Nahuatl loan words in K'iche'an languages.[5]

MIGRATION MYTHS AND THE PROBLEM OF K'ICHE'AN ORIGINS

With the exception of linguists, most scholars have relied on native documents dating to the Colonial period as the principal source of information on the origins of K'iche'an peoples. There has been a tendency to accept the *Popol Wuj*, the *Memorial de Tecpán Atitlán*, and other documents as texts that, after analysis, yield western-style history. Several documents describe the creation of the mythical founders of K'iche'an civilization,

how these ancestors of the K'iche', Kaqchikel, and Chajoma' (also called the Aqajal Winäq or the Sacatepéquez) arrived at a place called Tulan, how they eventually departed, and how after a period of migration settled in their current territories in the western and central highlands of Guatemala. One of the longest and most detailed accounts, the *Memorial de Tecpán Atitlán*, also describes how the ancestors of the Kaqchikel made war against a people called the Nonoalca after leaving the mythical Tulan. The *Popol Wuj* and the *Título de Totonicapán* (Carmack and Mondloch 1983; Recinos and Goetz 1953) both name places in the Verapaz early in their accounts of K'iche' migrations. Thus, these native documents are regarded as presenting strong evidence that the appearance of Postclassic central Mexican cultural patterns was the result of a southerly migration of peoples from the Gulf coast lowlands to the northern and southern highlands of Guatemala.

Ethnohistorians frequently link descriptions of K'iche'an migrations to particular geographical features and archaeological sites, and attempt to trace the route followed by the founders of the elite houses during the Postclassic period. Carmack (1968, 1981), Fox (1980, 1991), and other scholars argue that the forefathers of the K'iche' elite were Ch'ontal-Nahua speakers from the hot lowlands of the Gulf Coast.[6] This interpretation is based on a rather literal and selective reading of certain K'iche'an texts, most notably the *Popol Wuj* and the *Título de Totonicapán*, which are notably vague about the place of K'iche' origin and the location of the mythical Tulan. Some scholars privilege these ambiguous documents over the more specific descriptions of migrations presented in the *Memorial de Tecpán Atitlán* and the *Título de Jilotepeque* (Crespo M. 1956). The first of these two texts describes a journey limited to the highlands and Pacific slopes of northern Central America, and notes that the ancestral founders of the Kaqchikel elite passed through a town called Teozacuanco before fighting the Nonoalca.[7] Teozacuanco, Nonoalco, and Tula all are toponyms from El Salvador, suggesting that the Xajil faction of the Kaqchikel may be describing an expedition into the lands of the Pipil. Thus the Nonoalco of the *Popol Wuj* may not have been located in the lowlands of Veracruz or Tabasco, and we need not turn to a variant of the Putun hypothesis to explain K'iche'an origins. The *Título de Jilotepeque*, the principal document of the Kaqchikel-speaking Chajoma', is even more specific, noting that their place of origin was just north of the Río Motagua in the area of Joyabaj and Zacualpa, two municipios in the department of Quiché.

The problem of K'iche'an migrations has been compounded by the frequent misconception that Tulan was a place of origin. The *Popol Wuj*, the *Memorial de Tecpán Atitlán*, and the *Testamonio de los Xpantzay* (Recinos

1957) all describe how mythical ancestors *arrived* at Tulan and were given images of their gods; that is, Tulan was a place of gathering and legitimization, but not a homeland. Many Mesoamerican peoples claim some ancestry or stay at the fabled Tulan/Tollan/Tula, and assert that they are not native to the places they occupied during the Colonial period. By asserting that their progenitors and the ancestors of their neighbors were at Tulan, the authors of K'iche'an documents contextualize themselves at the center of the Mesoamerican world.[8] A seventeenth-century Kaqchikel legal document, the *Testamonio de los Xpantzay*, illustrates this principle taken a step further. In this work, the Xpantzay claim that they are descendents of Adam, Abraham, Isaac, and Jacob, and that they helped build the Tower of Babel. After dispersing from that place, they assembled at Tulan, only to move to the central highlands of Guatemala. Thus, the Xpantzay contextualize and legitimate themselves before both Spanish and Maya audiences.[9]

Which origin story should we use to reconstruct migration routes? The modest and specific migration myth of the Chajoma' recounted in *Título Jilotepeque*, the detailed account of the Kaqchikel Xajil faction described in the *Memorial de Tecpán Atitlán*, or the vague claims laid out in the *Popol Wuj*? Or, for that matter, why not try to reconstruct a migration route from ancient Babylon to Tulan, a journey that the Xpantzay and the authors of the *Título de Totonicapán* claim to have made with other K'iche'an peoples? In the end, the origin and migration stories of the Maya of the Guatemalan highlands are not objective sources of western-style history. These portions of the documents relate much about how Maya people viewed their past. They also show us how certain Kaqchikel and K'iche' factions intended others to perceive their histories. But the documents are not accurate Postclassic road maps (chapter 22).

Linguistic studies provide a very different perspective on the origins of K'iche'an civilization. Most Mayan linguists argue that the homeland of Common Mayan (also called Proto-Mayan) was somewhere in the highlands of western Guatemala or Chiapas, Mexico: the portion of the Maya area that today shows the greatest linguistic diversity, and hence the region that has been occupied by Mayan speakers for the longest time (e.g., Kaufman 1976). Although there is considerable evidence that K'iche'an languages contain loan words from the Ch'olan subgroup of languages, they do not appear to come from Ch'ontal. Instead, the period of borrowing was considerably earlier than the Postclassic period. In particular, it seems most likely that linguistic borrowing was from Southern Classic Mayan, the Classic-period ancestor of Ch'olti' and Ch'orti' (Houston et al. 1998). Thus, if the progenitors of the leading great houses of the K'iche', Kaqchikel, Chajoma', and Tz'utujil did speak

Ch'ontal, their descendants completely abandoned the ancestral language.

Lexicostatistical evidence, however controversial, suggests that Greater K'iche'an began to diverge before the current era, and that K'iche'an languages began to separate about A.D. 900–1000 (Kaufman 1976; McQuown 1964).[10] Thus, linguistic studies suggest that the K'iche'an languages evolved in the Maya highlands not far from where K'iche', Kaqchikel, and Tz'utujil are spoken today. Furthermore, if the territorial expansion of K'iche'an languages represents actual population movements, migrations began long before the Postclassic period.

New archaeological data support the model that Greater K'iche'an peoples came from the western highlands of Guatemala and entered the central highlands at the beginning of the Early Classic period. Popenoe de Hatch (1997), analyzing material from the San Jorge section of Kaminaljuyú, describes a punctuated and dramatic break in the ceramic sequence between the Protoclassic Santa Clara phase and the Early Classic Aurora phase. She interprets this sudden and near total ceramic replacement as a case of site-unit intrusion (Popenoe de Hatch 1998). Dramatic changes in settlement patterns, the cessation of the erection of carved monuments, the apparent disappearance of hieroglyphic writing, and the advent of a new stone-tool technology at Kaminaljuyú during the Early Classic period all are consistent with Popenoe de Hatch's conclusion (Braswell 1998b; Braswell and Amador 1999:908–909). For these reasons, it is likely that at about A.D. 200, a new group of settlers entered the Valley of Guatemala and either forced out or rapidly assimilated the previous inhabitants of the region. The same pattern, particularly the replacement of the Las Vacas ceramic tradition by the Solano tradition (Popenoe de Hatch 1998), can be seen throughout the Kaqchikel region (e.g., Braswell 1996; García García 1992; Gárnica Vanegas 1997; Robinson 1990). Since the oldest known examples of Solano-tradition pottery are found in the department of Quiché, Popenoe de Hatch (1997, 1998) has posited that the Classic-period inhabitants of the central highlands came from the northwest.

Were the Classic-period inhabitants of Kaminaljuyú and the central highlands the ancestors of later K'iche'an peoples? The abandonment of Kaminaljuyú at the end of the Late Classic period makes it difficult to establish a direct link between that site and the Postclassic inhabitants of the central highlands. Recent excavations at Chuisac, however, provide important data (Braswell 1996). Located in the mountains of San Martín Jilotepeque between the Late Postclassic capitals of the Chajoma' and Kaqchikel, Chuisac was settled in the Early Classic period by people who made and used Solano ceramics related to those found at contemporary Kaminaljuyú.

Significantly, Solano-tradition ceramics were found in Early Postclassic middens that also contained imported Tohil Plumbate and locally produced micaceous wares and dichromes related to Chinautla Polychrome. Hence, the Early Postclassic inhabitants of Chuisac continued to make Solano ceramics, but also used new wares that became characteristic of the Late Postclassic period. The Classic-to-Postclassic transition at Chuisac is marked by gradual and continuous changes of form, surface treatment, and paste, and not by the sudden and total replacement of one ceramic tradition by another. Fox (1977) and Carmack (1979) have identified Chuisac as O'ch'al Kab'owil Siwan, a site founded by the ancestors of the Xpantzay. Some time in the fifteenth century, O'ch'al Kab'owil Siwan became the capital of the Chajoma'. Thus, a direct link between Late Postclassic K'iche'an groups and Classic Solano-using people has been established (Braswell 1996).

These archaeological and linguistic interpretations, of course, do not preclude the possibility that the Guatemalan highlands saw the arrival of a small, elite population segment during the Postclassic period, or that this segment somehow came to found several of the K'iche'an great houses. Nonetheless, the data suggesting that such a migration occurred—drawn primarily from a few K'iche'an texts—are both slim and contradictory. The presence of Nahuatl loan words in highland Maya languages may be attributed to an elite migration from the Gulf Coast, but is more parsimoniously explained by the fact that Chiapan Nahuatl speakers already were living in close proximity to the highland Maya. Moreover, there is rather a lot of negative evidence. Ch'ontal loan words are, at best, quite rare in K'iche'an languages. Material goods from or inspired by the Gulf Coast generally are absent from Postclassic elite assemblages. Finally, several important ethnohistorical sources describe other places, some quite nearby, as the place of origin of the elite great houses.

THE SOCIAL CONTEXT OF EMULATION AND ETHNOGENESIS

If we rule out migration as an explanation for the Nahuaization of K'iche'an culture during the Late Postclassic, we must conclude that a central Mexican cultural veneer was emulated by K'iche'an peoples. Although interregional interaction led to cultural borrowing in many areas and at many time periods in Mesoamerican prehistory, the degree to which K'iche'an peoples tried to emulated Nahua culture is striking. In two works, Thompson (1943, 1954) argues that in the Late Postclassic period, the Maya of the Guatemalan highlands recast "Mexican innovations" adopted in the Early Postclassic to conform to their own cultural norms. Navarrete (1996:348), in

contrast, does not believe this to be the case and asserts that the Late Postclassic process of Nahuaization was a "preamble for a violent intervention interrupted by the Spanish Conquest." Although I hesitate to predict what would have happened had Alvarado not conquered Guatemala, and prefer to consider local reasons for the adoption of central Mexican cultural traits, Navarrete's point is well taken. The Nahuaization of K'iche'an culture was transformative, to the extent that we may consider it an example of ethnogenesis.

Although many Nahuatl loan words in K'iche'an languages pertain to non-elite realms of discourse, the vast majority of central Mexican cultural traits adopted during the Late Postclassic are limited to the social and spatial contexts of the apical elite. These include gold artifacts from burials in Iximche' and Saq Ulew, mural paintings at Temple 2 of Iximche' and the palace at Q'umarkaj, imported and imitation Mexican pottery from Saq Ulew and Q'umarkaj, and cremation burials at all the Late Postclassic capitals. Other examples include titles and names of elite members of the most-powerful great houses (Braswell 2001a). Thus, the social context of symbolic emulation and ethnogenesis was the uppermost class of K'iche'an society.

Why did K'iche'an elite find it advantageous not only to emulate their Nahua neighbors, but also to create a new ethnic identity for themselves? The answer may lie in the factionalized and highly competitive fabric of K'iche'an society. The problem can be addressed from three perspectives: social differences within the great house, factionalization between the great houses, and competition between the various polities of the Maya highlands and Pacific lowlands.

K'iche'an social structure, although stratified, was conceptualized in terms of kinship. The metaphor of kinship acted to undermine the elaboration of class structure. Since K'iche'an origin myths do not propose a separate divine creation for the ruling class (Braswell 2001a, 2001b), alternative distinctions were needed to sustain class structure. Two ways that elites can justify their elevated status is through the monopolization of esoteric knowledge and the adoption of a foreign identity. The fixing of religious titles in certain lines and the creation of a new hybrid Nahua-K'iche'an ethnicity would have served to create social distance between classes and to justify the subordinate status of members of the *alk'ajol* class. The use of imported items, the practice of cremation, the erection of temples and palaces with Mixteca-Puebla–style murals and central Mexican architectural features, and the adoption of Nahuatl-derived names and titles all would have engendered and supported social distinction. In this sense, the genesis of a new elite ethnicity is not different in kind from symbolic emulation, but is novel in intensity. The adoption and display of a hybrid ethnicity also may have played a role in competition among families within great houses, and particularly in the factional conflict between great houses. If elevated status and Nahuatl-derived titles became associated with a hybrid ethnicity, it would not be surprising for great houses competing for those titles to display a Nahua-K'iche'an identity.

INTERACTION WITH THE AZTECS (A.D. 1501–1519) AND THE PROCESS OF ETHNOGENESIS

It is unfortunate that there are few descriptions of relations between the Aztecs and K'iche'an polities, and that those that do exist are maddeningly terse. The first *entrada* of the Aztecs into the Guatemalan highlands took place in A.D. 1501, during the reign of Ahuitzotl. If Fuentes y Guzmán (1932–1933:6:47–48) and his now-vanished, third-party Pipil text may be relied upon, pochteca sent by Ahuitzotl to the south coast of Guatemala visited Q'umarkaj and then were ordered out of the K'iche' kingdom. Perhaps their presence was viewed as imperiling K'iche' interests in the Pacific region.

The second phase of contact took place in A.D. 1510, after the conquest of Xoconochco. The *Memorial de Tecpán Atitlán* (p. 52) reports the arrival of messengers from *Modecçumatzin* (Motecuhzoma Xocoyotzin) on the day 1 Toj, but does not say why they came. The authors of the *Títulos de la Casa Ixquin-Nehaib, Señora del Territorio de Otzoya* (Recinos 1957:84) report that in the same year, K'iche' lords from Quetzaltenango and Momostenango began to pay tribute to Motecuhzoma. It is important to note, as Recinos (1957:84, footnote) does, that this is the only suggestion that the highland Maya ever paid tribute to the Aztecs. An illustration found in the same collection of documents has been interpreted as indicating that the K'iche' were further subordinated by the marriage of two daughters of Motecuhzoma to the lord of Q'umarkaj (Carmack 1973:371, 1981:142–143). This image and the accompanying caption, however, are more reasonably explained as a depiction of Cortés, Alvarado, and their two Mexica concubines (Ridder 1993). Given the lack of corroborating evidence and the appeasing stance that the authors present regarding the payment of Spanish tribute, tribute might not have been paid to the Aztecs. There is little evidence demonstrating that after A.D. 1510 there was a "more or less continuous presence of Mexica representatives in [Q'umarkaj]" (Carmack 1981:143), and we cannot be sure that relations with the Aztecs changed significantly during the last 14 years before the Spanish conquest.

K'iche'an polities and the alliances of great houses of which they were comprised competed with each other and with their Maya and Nahua neighbors for access to the cacao, cotton, fish, salt, and other resources of the Pacific piedmont and coast. The Aztec conquest of Xoconochco must have been viewed by K'iche'an elites as both a threat and an opportunity. On the one hand, K'iche'an elites may have been concerned that encroachment would limit their own access to coastal resources. On the other, the Aztec presence in Xoconochco presented an unrivaled opportunity for trade and the formation of alliances against traditional competitors, some of whom were Nahuatl-speakers. From either perspective, an increase in the pace and intensity of ethnogenesis would have been a pragmatic strategy for K'iche'an elites.

The arrival of the Aztecs greatly increased the movement of goods along the Guatemalan and Salvadoran coasts. Resources from this zone, as well as feathers, jade, obsidian, and other highland goods, became more valuable to K'iche'an elites because of the new proximity of potential trading partners. Moreover, the position of K'iche'an polities between the domains of the Pipil and Aztec Xoconochco gave additional strategic importance to the Pacific piedmont and coast. K'iche'an great houses that controlled lands in the south may have tried to tax or somehow monopolize transportation across their territory, as the Pipil did until conceding that right to the K'iche' and Kaqchikel late in the fifteenth century (Carmack 1981:140).

Cortés's (1961:218–219) fourth letter to the Crown describes a meeting with a delegation of Kaqchikel ambassadors, an encounter that is extraordinary because it took place near Pánuco, in northern Veracruz. These Kaqchikel ambassadors sought an alliance with the Spaniards against the K'iche'. It is reasonable to suspect that other *lolmay* or *lolmet*, as K'iche'an ambassadors were called, visited the Aztecs in Xoconochco for similar political reasons. K'iche'an lords probably viewed the Aztecs as powerful potential allies who could aid them in their own ambitions.

CONCLUSIONS

Evidence for the Nahuaization of K'iche'an culture is extensive and is found in language, social forms and practices, and material culture. The highland Maya engaged in significant, if sporadic, interaction with peoples from central Mexico since at least A.D. 800, when the Nahua migrations to Central America began. Most loan words from Nahuatl do not come from Central American Pipil, but we need look no farther than southeastern Chiapas for a suitable dialect from which the loans were derived. Nonetheless, it is clear that the borrowing of cultural traits reached its greatest intensity during the Late Postclassic, particularly during the 70 years immediately preceding the Spanish conquest. During this period, the transformation of elite culture was so profound that we must either consider the possibility of the arrival and incorporation of a new, ethnically distinct elite stratum into highland Maya society, or characterize the process of extreme emulation as ethnogenesis.

Several ethnohistorians (e.g., Carmack 1968, 1973, 1981; Fox 1978, 1980, 1991; Fox et al. 1992; Nicholson 1957; Recinos and Goetz 1953) have preferred the former explanation and have posited the migration of small groups of bellicose "Nonoalca-Pipil-Toltec-Chichimecs" (Borhegyi 1965) or "Epi-Toltec warlords" (Carmack 1981) from the Gulf coast to the Guatemalan highlands. In contrast, most linguists have argued that K'iche'an languages evolved in the highlands, although Campbell (1977:109) once attributed the presence of Nahuatl loan words to a migration of "Toltec overlords" from Tabasco or Veracruz. Migration and conquest, of course, are not the only mechanisms that account for linguistic borrowing, so should be considered only two of several possible scenarios.

Until recently, most archaeologists have been concerned more with the timing of the appearance of foreign traits and less with the mechanisms of their transmittal (e.g., Thompson 1943, 1954; Wauchope 1970, 1975). In more recent years, two archaeologists have challenged the notion of K'iche'an migrations. The first, Navarrete (1976, 1996), does so obliquely by interpreting the process of Nahuaization as a vanguard of Aztec conquest. Brown (1985) explains the appearance of the few foreign items found at K'iche'an sites as an indication of trade with merchants traveling through the southern piedmont, and believes that highland myths about Tulan ultimately may be tied to Teotihuacan. Archaeological research conducted in the past 15 years has cast new light on K'iche'an origins and suggests that the ancestors of the Postclassic Chajoma', Kaqchikel, K'iche, and Tz'utujil were living in the central highlands of Guatemala during the Classic period (Braswell 1996, 1998b; Popenoe

de Hatch 1997, 1998). These new data and their interpretation not only are consistent with the body of linguistic evidence, but also are congruent in a general way with important ethnohistorical documents that describe short-distance movements within the highlands of northern Central America. Although it is conceivable that small, elite groups did migrate from the Gulf coast to the Guatemalan highlands during the Postclassic period, there is no compelling evidence supporting this conjecture.

The process of Nahuaization that transformed the elite stratum of K'iche'an society during the Late Postclassic can be seen as a pragmatic adaptive strategy. The emergence of a stratified, class-based society during the Postclassic period necessitated the development of distinctions between commoners and elites belonging to the same great house. The creation of a new, elite identity through the appropriation and display of exotic symbol sets is consistent with the distancing of the ajawa' from the alk'ajola', as is the adoption of foreign names, titles, and ways of behavior. Moreover, competition between the great houses that made up K'iche'an society could have escalated cultural emulation and led to ethnogenesis. Finally, the adoption of a hybrid Nahua-K'iche'an ethnicity would have lessened the cultural distance between the highlanders and their powerful Aztec neighbors in Xoconochco. This may have been seen as a way to foster trade in prestige goods, to build alliances in a factionalized and militarized political climate, and even to forestall an eventual conquest.

ACKNOWLEDGMENTS

I thank Lyle R. Campbell for his generous help with certain key aspects of this chapter.

Part 6

Synthesis and Comparisons

37

Different Hemispheres, Different Worlds

Philip L. Kohl

Evgenij N. Chernykh

Archaeologists have attempted to apply the world-systems model to both Postclassic Mesoamerica and Bronze Age west Asia. This chapter briefly compares and contrasts the large-scale integration evident in these two areas. One major problem with this comparison is immediately apparent. The exercise implies that there is some developmental similarity between the two areas, a perspective classically espoused by Robert McC. Adams in his seminal comparative study, *The Evolution of Urban Society* (1966). There Adams skillfully combined archaeological, historical, and ethnohistorical data to compare the processes leading to increased social complexity, the emergence of social classes, and the appearance of nucleated urban centers on the alluvial plain of southern Mesopotamia with those so richly documented in the central Valley of Mexico in Postclassic times. Using a broad range of sources for both cases, Adams convincingly traced increasing social differentiation within these regions and then attempted to account for the similarities in the processes that resulted in both cases in the breakdown of older kin-based societies and in the emergence of sharply differentiated, class-stratified formations. But what happens to these comparisons when one expands 'the spatial horizons beyond the central Valley of Mexico and southern Mesopotamia to incorporate broader "worlds" of interaction, based on processes—as demonstrated here—that were also basic to the overall development of social complexity? Are developmentally comparable phenomena being analyzed, or are the patterns of interregional interaction or the structure of each "world system" fundamentally distinctive, and, if so, how then does one explain these differences? This chapter explores these issues.

Certainly, some basic similarities can be noted. Economic and ideological integration was achieved in both areas on a macroregional scale. Some bulk trade in surplus cereals and possibly dates and dried fish linked the southern alluvial plain of southern Mesopotamia with the rich dry-farming zone of northern Mesopotamia. This trade extended at least into northern Syria, and possibly occasionally included more sparsely populated cultures stretching to the southeast along the Persian/Arabian Gulf to the Oman Peninsula. There are also numerous references to the large-scale surplus production and exchange of woolen textiles, which were produced on the great temple and palace estates and which were differentially valued in terms of the quality of their manufacture. Both areas exhibit even more highly developed exchange networks in precious and semiprecious materials—with restricted natural distributions—and in luxury prestige goods that were differentially accumulated by the emergent noble classes. Some of these exotic goods were traded as finished commodities and were ideologically charged or meaningful for both producers and consumers. Thus, for example, soft stone vessels elaborately carved with specific geometric and naturalistic motifs relating to the supernatural world were produced on tiny nonurban sites in eastern Iran and "consumed" by the priests and rulers in Sumer and in the proto-Elamite center of Susa in southwestern Iran (Kohl 1978). As in Postclassic Mesoamerica, this trade in luxury goods was significant for distinguishing the emerging classes, particularly the elite, from one another. Just as it is impossible to conceive of a Sumerian *en* (or Egyptian pharaoh) without his ceremonial insignia and gold and lapis lazuli ornaments, neither can one imagine an Aztec tlatoani without his jade and feathers.

It can be argued that in both hemispheres this trade in exotic luxury goods was structurally more significant relative to the trade in bulk staples than is characteristic of the modern world system. To pursue this structural comparison further, the so-called "development of underdevelopment," which is supposedly a hallmark of the modern world system, was itself underdeveloped in both Postclassic Mesoamerica and Bronze Age west Asia. Few economic dependencies could be deliberately established and maintained for long periods, primarily because the linkages between more developed "cores" and less specialized "peripheries" (if this term even applies in the Mesoamerican case) were more fragile and easily severed. The fragility of such dependent relationships was causally related to the means of transportation and communication that linked disparate areas, and such means were qualitatively less developed in premodern times. Similarly, technologies were easily transferred and adopted by peoples with less complex social orders, and important innovations in the Old World, such as the domestication of the horse and quite possibly the adoption of wheeled vehicles, often first occurred in these less complex or "peripheral" areas.

Such points of similarity between developments in the hemispheres could be extended, but the contrasts are even more striking and revealing. First, Mesoamericanists seem to know the limits of their "world." Even if there is debate over whether or not to include (or, better, how to incorporate) the American Southwest or lower Central America in the broader Mesoamerican world—an inclusion which would roughly double the geographical extent of this system—there are real limits both to the south and north which nearly all specialists would agree fall outside this world (for an iconoclastic alternative view, see Kehoe 1998:150–171). In Bronze Age west Asia/Eurasia these boundaries are far less distinct, and the system continuously appears to expand over time. From Mesopotamia, important connections can be traced east across the Iranian plateau at least to the Indus Valley, southeast along the gulf and onto the Arabian Peninsula, north into Syria and Anatolia, particularly along the upper Euphrates and Tigris valleys, and west to the Levant. The Mesopotamian and Egyptian "worlds" overlap in the eastern Mediterranean region, and of course, early Egyptian civilization is also economically linked with the Sinai Peninsula and areas farther south in Nubia and in sub-Saharan Africa more generally. The vast Eurasian steppes that stretch from eastern Ukraine north of the Black Sea east across the Don, Volga, and Ural rivers and across Kazakhstan to Mongolia and the borders with China are themselves interconnected in systems of the production and exchange of materials, above all metals. With the development of more-mobile, pastorally based economies, technologies were shared and peoples moved freely across these steppes. By the end of the Middle Bronze period peoples began to regularly interact—peacefully or aggressively—with their more settled neighbors to the south. The problem of where to draw boundaries or to "close the system"—at any point in time—in the Old World Bronze Age is real and not mutually agreed upon by relevant specialists. This contrast with Postclassic Mesoamerica is striking and deserves further examination.

Mesoamerican cities—at least from the Classic period onward—were much larger than their Old World Bronze Age counterparts. The largest Sumerian city-states extend for a few hundred hectares at most. For example, the extraordinarily large Early Dynastic I city of Uruk extends only over ca. 400 ha (Adams and Nissen 1972: 18; Van de Mieroop 1999), and those of other early Bronze Age west Asian civilizations were smaller, rarely exceeding 100 ha in extent (e.g., the famous cities of the Indus Valley civilization, such as Mohenjo-daro and Harappa [Kenoyer 1998]). Curiously, the only nucleated settlements comparable in extent to the largest Sumerian centers are the so-called gigantic sites of the even earlier Late Chalcolithic Tripol'ye culture (ca. 4200–3500 B.C.)—such as Majdaneckoe (270 ha), Dobrovody (250 ha), and Tal'janki (400 ha)—found between the Bug and Dnepr rivers in Ukraine (Videjko 1995). But these fortified settlements show very little indication of craft specialization or internal social differentiation, and functionally seem to resemble overgrown villages more than cities.

Many of the major cities and city-states of Postclassic Mesoamerica discussed here were larger, and Tenochtitlan considerably so. They exhibit clear evidence for social differentiation and agricultural and craft specialization; some had populations significantly exceeding those of the earliest west Asian cities (e.g., 212,500 at Tenochtitlan [Smith et al. 1994]) compared with a maximum estimated population of 40,000 at Uruk). It is not until later in the Iron Age (first half of the first millennium B.C.) that some sites, such as the various capitals of the Neo-Assyrian empire, begin to approximate in size the major cities of Postclassic Mesoamerica, but none approached the overall scale of Tenochtitlan (ca. 1,350 ha). Thus, for example, the city of Nineveh, the famous final capital of the Neo-Assyrian empire, which was burned down at the end of the seventh century B.C., encompassed an area of ca. 750 ha with an estimated population of ca. 75,000 (Stronach 1994:103). Neo-Babylonian Babylon in the early sixth century B.C. was even larger (890 ha) and apparently more densely populated, with an estimated population of "well over 100,000" (Stronach, personal communication). Other major centers were smaller, comparable to the largest Bronze Age cities, and functioned as capitals sequentially; for example, Dur-Sharukin (Khorsabad) at 300 ha and Nimrud (Kalhu) at 360 ha (Eleanor Barbanes, personal communication, 2000).

It is really only during the subsequent Classical period that a few cites, such as imperial Rome, surpassed the Mesoamerican centers in spatial extent and, presumably, in their nucleated populations. These differences in scale had obvious overall demographic consequences. The population estimate for Aztec central Mexico is 4.5 million (Smith 1996a:60–64), and reasonable estimates for all of Mesoamerica at the time of European contact range as high as 15 million; Adams (1981:149), on the other hand, has estimated the total population of the southern Mesopotamian alluvium during the highly state-centralized Ur III period (or roughly the end of the third millennium B.C.) at closer to 500,000 than to 1,000,000.

Although such figures are approximate, they reveal a real difference between Bronze Age west Asia and Post-classic Mesoamerica—a contrast that also must reflect underlying differences in the aggregate output of each area's food production systems. The riverine civilizations of the Old World relied on different systems of irrigation agriculture to produce typically one winter-grown crop each year (two in the case of the Indus Valley). Such systems substantially modified the natural landscape and can be considered more intensive than those practiced over greater areas in the dry-farming zones that received sufficient natural precipitation in northern Mesopotamia and elsewhere, but they were not nearly as productive as the multi-crop chinampa and raised-field systems of Mesoamerica.

The intensity of a food production system is, to a certain extent, a relative concept, and, relatively speaking, Mesoamerican agricultural production was much more intensive than that practiced by the early Bronze Age civilizations of the Old World. More food per unit area was produced in Mesoamerica simply because the land was under more or less continuous cultivation. Clearly also, the exploitation in west Asia of large domesticated animals such as sheep, goats, cattle, and pigs for food, secondary products (such as wool and milk), and draft purposes also affected the fallow cycle and the overall intensity of the agricultural regime; some land was deliberately kept out of more-intensive cultivation to sustain these animals. The harnessing of animals—oxen at least by the second half of the fourth millennium B.C. (if not earlier), Bactrian camels by the latter half of the third, and horses probably by the end of the third/beginning of the second millennium—also changed the nature of the agricultural system, both in terms of preparing the arable land for cultivation and for transporting the harvest to storage and consuming areas. Not only was more land brought under cultivation with these developments, but the west Asian systems as a whole became less intensive in terms of the expenditure of human labor-power, and more extensive in terms of the total area brought under cultivation. Mesoamerica did not experience these interrelated innovations or improvements; instead the region's agricultural systems became ever more involuted (in Geertz's 1966 sense) and capable of producing more foods and sustaining more peoples on the same limited,

though constantly transformed and highly productive, landscape.

Stock raising for meat and pastoral products became a specialized component of the food-producing economy throughout west Asia, a development that culminated in the emergence of southwest Asian and Eurasian pastoral nomadism. These specialized herders, and eventually mounted nomads, often migrated annually over long distances with their livestock; they were far more mobile than the hunting and gathering Chichimecs of northern Mexico who moved into central Mesoamerica in times of political crisis and collapse, and adopted sooner or later the lifestyle of the area's earlier settled inhabitants. Unlike their Southwest and Eurasian counterparts, these Mesoamerican nomads only represented a real threat to the established order after they had transformed themselves into intensive agriculturalists and/or allied themselves with such groups. The more-settled literate societies in both hemispheres looked down on these less developed intruders with a mixture of fear and contempt, but—to use an earlier nineteenth-century terminology—a division or recurrent trope in west Asia was between civilization and barbarism, whereas in Mesoamerica it was more between civilization and savagery.

The availability of pack and harnessed animals pulling plows, sleds, and then wheeled vehicles not only enhanced the mobility of the Old World herding societies and facilitated their large-scale migrations into different areas and different ecological zones, such as the open steppes, but also transformed the nature of long-distance exchange and cross-cultural contact. That is, many of the illiterate "barbarian" societies surrounding the socially more complex, "civilized" centers of Bronze Age west Asia developed highly mobile, pastorally based economies that allowed them to move into areas and interact—often on a more or less equal footing—with their settled neighbors. Over time the continuous improvements in metal weapons and enhanced mobility often gave these nomads a military advantage over the more complex societies that were tied to the landscape through their irrigation systems. As a consequence, peoples from the highlands or surrounding steppes periodically invaded and conquered the settled areas. Migrations and conquests occurred both in Mesoamerica and west Asia, but differed qualitatively in their nature and significance.

The development of wheeled transport, of course, had far-reaching social and economic effects. Currently, the earliest pictographic representations of wheeled vehicles come from southern Mesopotamia, and the earliest remains of actual carts (Hayen 1989, 1991) come from northwestern Europe and date roughly to the same period—the second half of the fourth millennium B.C. (Häusler 1981, 1994; Bakker et al. 1999). If anything, current direct archaeological evidence suggests the diffusion of the technology of wheeled transport from

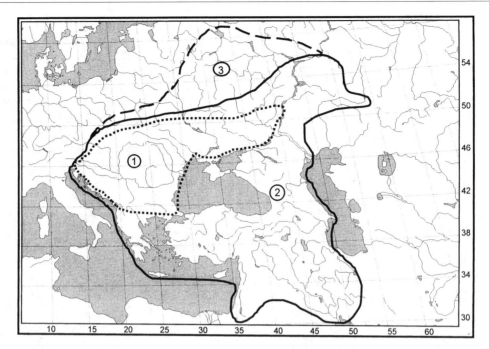

Figure 37.1 Map of metallurgical provinces in Bronze Age west Asia: (1) the Carpatho-Balkan province, Copper Age, fiftieth to thirty-eighth centuries B.C.E.; (2) the main area of the Circumpontic province, Early and Middle Bronze Ages, thirty-third to nineteenth centuries B.C.E.; (3) area of expansion of the Circumpontic province during the Middle Bronze Age, twenty-sixth to nineteenth centuries B.C.E.

northwestern Europe, with its forests of usable hard woods, to the more open steppes and alluvial plains to the southeast. This is the reverse of the traditional direction for presumed cases of diffusion, which moved from the Mesopotamian heartland of the urban revolution to the more peripheral, less differentiated societies farther north. Future discoveries may alter this reconstruction, but it is equally possible that archaeological evidence—even aided by reliable sequences of radiocarbon determinations—will be unable to resolve the question of the origin of wheeled vehicles, since, once invented, this technology diffused rapidly throughout much of Europe and west Asia/Eurasia. Similarly, the development of horseback riding quickly transformed interregional relations throughout much of Eurasia, though the origins of this process are less clear and more hotly debated; this too was a development that spread so rapidly it may prove impossible to ascertain precisely where and when horses were first ridden. What is indisputable is that in both cases such innovations were quickly adopted by societies at different levels of development, leading to the increased mobility and even migrations of some of these societies, and facilitating the exchange of materials over long distances.

In both hemispheres it was cheaper and easier to move goods over seas and rivers than overland. Though impossible to quantify, this may have been even more true in Mesoamerica than west Asia given the former's lack of

pack and transport animals. Deserts seemed to represent more-formidable barriers to interregional communication and exchange than mountain ranges in west Asia and Mesoamerica, though in the Old World, deserts too were ultimately bridged with the development of improved means of transportation and the use of animals, such as Bactrian camels, peculiarly adapted to these harsh, water-deficient inland "seas." Throughout pre-Columbian times, deserts continued to impede the movements of materials and peoples, particularly from the Mesoamerican world to the north. The availability of pack animals, wheeled vehicles, and riding in the Old World meant more goods could be carried overland over longer distances than in Mesoamerica. Interregional trade, even in relatively bulky items such as textiles and metals, was not principally confined to waterways or coastlines, a reality which makes it even more difficult to define the precise borders of the interconnected Bronze Age west Asian world system.

It is no accident that European prehistorians adopted the Three-Age system in the early nineteenth century to order their materials. Arguably, large-scale developments and processes in later Eurasian prehistory are most clearly discerned by documenting changes in metallurgical production and exchange. There are several reasons for this. As Childe perhaps overly emphasized, the birth of true metallurgy—the smelting of metal ores and the melting, alloying, and casting of metal objects—implied the emergence of full-time craft specialization: to pursue their craft, smiths had to be fed by societies capable of regularly producing food surpluses. Metallurgical developments were technologically cumulative, and conveniently for prehistorians, this progression was traceable. Each step in the sequence from native copper to arsenic-bronze, tin-bronze, and iron required technological advances, particularly those associated with the control and manipulation of fire (pyrotechnology) and the exploitation of different metal resources. These resources, the components of bronze more so than iron, are unevenly distributed spatially, and this reality distinguishes the value of metals for reconstructing prehistory on a broad scale from, say, ceramics, whose technological progression is also related to pyrotechnological advances and can be traced archaeologically. That is, in the Old World the exchange of metals was as, if not more, important than their production for transforming late prehistoric societies.

These technological changes did not proceed in a gradual, cumulative fashion, but rather were characterized by sudden punctuated changes, such as the sudden appearance of new metal types and the exploitation of new resources which distinguish Late Chalcolithic from Early Bronze remains, or what Chernykh (1992) has referred to as the collapse of the "Carpatho-Balkan Metallurgical Province" (or CBMP) at the beginning of the fourth millennium B.C. and the subsequent rise of the substantially more extensive "Circumpontic Metallurgical Province" in the second half of that millennium (figure 37.1).

The concept of a metallurgical province (Chernykh 1992:8–9), in turn, is a lumping category meant to order the archaeological record on the general typological uniformity of metal tools and weapons, and on the fundamental similarity in the technological production within it and/or the use of common ore sources. This archaeologically derived concept is particularly useful for tracing the interregional relations associated with the integration of the Eurasian steppes into the "civilized" agricultural world of west Asia. Thus, for example, the earlier Carpatho-Balkan metallurgical province (ca. 5000–3800 B.C.) has been reconstructed on the basis of the analysis of more than 8,000 metal artifacts, principally copper and gold; stretching from the Carpathian Mountains and the Balkan Peninsula in the southwest to the Middle Volga region in the northeast, this province encompassed ca. 1.2–1.3 million km². The subsequent Early and Middle Bronze circumpontic metallurgical province (ca. 3300–1900 B.C.)—which is based on the collection of more than 84,000 artifacts of gold (ca. 54,000 samples), silver (ca. 6,400 samples), and copper (ca. 24,000 samples), including the analysis of ca. 7,000 copper and arsenical and tin-bronze artifacts—stretched much farther

to the south and northeast, encompassing ca. 4.9–5.0 million km² during the Early Bronze period and ca. 5.6–5.8 million km² during Middle Bronze times. Mostly, semiprocessed metals and ingots, not finished goods, were exchanged throughout these vast Old World provinces; strikingly similar metal tools, weapons, and ornaments were produced locally by smiths sharing uniform metalworking technologies, resulting in largely balanced and relatively stable systems of exchange between pastoral and agricultural societies at different stages of development.

In Mesoamerica, metallurgy was introduced relatively late (ca. 650 A.D.) from South America, but as Hosler (chapter 21) and others have demonstrated (see also Hosler and Macfarlane 1996), by 1200 A.D. copper, arsenic-bronzes, tin-bronzes, and copper-silver alloys were being produced, and there was a well-developed trade in west Mexican ores and finished artifacts, such as bells and axe-monies, far to the south. In both hemispheres most of the earliest metals produced were ornamental, often ideologically charged exotica which then circulated in prestige-goods exchange networks that had significant transformative effects on the local elites acquiring them. Not only were the Bronze Age metallurgical provinces of west Asia/Eurasia spatially more extensive than those of Postclassic Mesoamerica, but also more functional items—tools and, above all, weapons—were increasingly produced and exchanged, adding a critically important new dimension to the significance of metal production and exchange in the Old World. An increase in militarism characterizes both Postclassic Mesoamerica and the Late Bronze Age of west Asia, but in the former case, warfare was promoted by the increased production of largely preexisting weaponry, such as obsidian-tipped swords, while in west Asia there was a transformation of metallurgical production and the appearance of new, and dangerously effective, cast-metal weapons such as daggers, swords, and spears. In many areas of the interconnected Bronze Age world of west Asia/Eurasia, metal tools such as sickles and metal-tipped plows became increasingly utilized in essential agricultural production. The bronze tools of Mesoamerica, such as awls and tweezers, were obviously less significant for the continued reproduction of their societies than these basic, continuously improved agricultural implements were for the societies of the west Asian Bronze Age. In other words, a very important change in the function of metals in the Old World is not paralleled in the New. In the former, prestige-goods exchanges of metal ornaments and ceremonial objects, however significant in their own right, were transformed into the trading of metal tools and weapons essential for the basic reproduction and defense of the societies acquiring them. It is also not an accident that the Three- (or even Two-) Age system was not adopted by New World archaeologists trying to order their materials.

Where, then, does this brief comparison/contrast leave us? For both hemispheres, it is impossible to understand developments in a single region without considering the interconnections—the exchanges of materials and the movements of peoples—between regions. It is far easier to define the interacting world or world system of Mesoamerica than it is to demarcate the boundaries of a west Asian/Eurasian world system. In Mesoamerica everything is much more concentrated and restricted: the numbers of people, the commodities produced and exchanged, and the amount of foodstuffs continuously cultivated and traded. In west Asia/Eurasia, interconnections can be traced over far greater areas, but it is much harder to quantify their scale or assess their regularity.

Many of the difficulties in reconstructing a west Asian Bronze Age world system are associated with the nature of the evidence. Archaeologists recover largely mute artifacts of varying quality and from uneven contexts, and the available historical records only occur sporadically and in limited regions of this interconnected Bronze Age world. These documents are ultimately less informative than the rich historic and ethnohistoric documents that Mesoamericanists so productively mine. It can be argued that it is precisely the quality of the Postclassic Mesoamerican data that allows for the convincing reconstruction of an integrated Postclassic Mesoamerican world such as presented in this book, while the more limited data available for the west Asian Bronze Age makes such an exercise more problematic and speculative. Such limitations admitted, the contrasts between the hemispheres adumbrated here seem to be more interesting and real than the similarities and certainly deserve more extended analyses. If apples are being compared and contrasted with oranges, the question remains why the fruits differ in the first place.

38

A Perspective on Late Postclassic Mesoamerica

Frances F. Berdan

Susan Kepecs

Michael E. Smith

The previous chapter points out striking differences between the New and Old Worlds (see also chapter 2). Nevertheless, Bronze Age west Asia, the medieval Old World, and Postclassic Mesoamerica all manifest key processes that fall under the rubric of world-systems theories. One of these processes is that world systems restructure through time, with periods of decline alternating with epochs of heightened integration (chapter 2). Given cumulative technological change, these systems tend to increase in terms of overall size and integration through time (Abu-Lughod 1989:366–368; Chase-Dunn and Hall 1991:16). The Late Postclassic Mesoamerican world system is no exception. Despite clear evidence of regional diversity, the archaeological and documentary records point toward greater levels of trade, communication, and stylistic similarity across the macroregion at this time than during any prior period.

Researchers long have focused on Mesoamerica as a broad culture area sharing traditions including art styles, language, and subsistence strategies (Kirchoff 1943; Trigger 1989:122–124; Guzmán and Martínez O. 1990; Blanton et al. 1993:2–3). In particular, Mesoamerican societies in the Late Postclassic period exhibited an enticing array of common traditions. Our modified world-systems approach offers an avenue for appreciating the extent, nature, dynamics, and significance of the interregional interactions that shaped those commonalities in Postclassic times.

Earlier theories of interaction—such as migrations, imperial conquests, and vague diffusionism (Vaillant 1940)—presented generalized processes that were only sporadically applicable to understanding particular cases of interaction, and then only incompletely. More-recent notions of the impact of trade (Feldman 1978; Parsons and Price 1971; Santley 1983; Shepard 1948; Tourtellot and Sabloff 1972) and of the dispersion of the Mixteca-

Puebla style (Meighan 1974; Nicholson 1960, 1982) only treat single dimensions of the interaction mosaic. Ideas emphasizing the spread of central Mexican traits to the Mayan lowlands (e.g., Navarrete 1996) contain an inherent highland-lowland bias and tend to emphasize an unrealistic one-way transfer of ideas and goods. In a somewhat different vein, Polanyi's substantivist approach found no room for noncapitalist commercial economies such as those that indeed characterized Postclassic Mesoamerica (chapters 2, 16, and 17). None of these approaches contain the breadth and flexibility of the world-system approach, particularly as conceived and modified in this book, and none of them provide satisfying accounts of the rich archaeological and documentary record for Postclassic Mesoamerica.

THE STRUCTURE OF THE POSTCLASSIC MESOAMERICAN WORLD SYSTEM

One advantage of viewing Postclassic Mesoamerica as a world system is that a broad and meaningful structure for interaction unfolds. It has been an established pattern in Mesoamerican research to divide up the Mesoamerican world according to definable linguistic or cultural groups, usually with some geographic designation (such as lowland Maya, Oaxaca, or the Gulf coast). This is useful from the standpoint of categorizing cultural diversity and variation.

If, however, the goal is to reveal broad networks of interaction at a large scale, a different set of structural units is needed. We have focused on individual city-state polities as the basic building blocks of social and political life. These fundamental units were defined by specific geographic boundaries, dynastic leaders, established traditions and mythologies, and often widely known reputations (for qualities such as certain levels of acceptable morality or fierceness in battle, as with the scandalous Huaxtec or the aggressive Mexica, respectively—to achievements such as the elegant poetry or the production of exquisite jewelry—as with the Texcocans and the Mixtec, respectively). These polities engaged in trade, joined alliances, became incorporated into empires, exchanged marriage partners, and shared in common symbols of communication.

Additionally, we find that some of these polities exhibited characteristics of other types of units particularly significant in the structure of this Mesoamerican world system. These are core zones, exchange circuits, international trade centers, affluent production zones, resource-extraction zones, and unspecialized peripheries.

The core zones that we have defined for Mesoamerica shifted about somewhat over the Postclassic period, and certain trends are discernable. Core zones for the Early Postclassic (Chichén Itzá, El Tajín, Tula, and Cholula) were all individual sites. The same holds for the Middle Postclassic core of Mayapán, but the Cholula core grew in size and is identified as the Tlaxcala/Cholula region. The four core zones we have defined for the Late Postclassic (Tlaxcala/Cholula, Basin of Mexico, Mixteca/Valley of Oaxaca region, and the Lake Pátzcuaro basin) all contained numerous city-state polities. These changes from single dominant polities to regional collections of polities may reflect, in part, the nature of the archaeological data and ethnohistoric documentation, but they were probably the consequence of the development of a greater number of more powerful polities within more closely defined geographic spaces. The common thread of these cores, whether individual city-states or groupings of them, was their ability to influence and even dominate city-states beyond their immediate vicinity. Their effects on distant polities ranged from imperial conquest, to control of trade, to stylistic emulation. We have no problem with seeing multiple cores within a single world system, particularly that of the highly competitive Mesoamerican scene.

The various Late Postclassic core zones were surrounded by large areas of intensive commercial exchange that we call exchange circuits. Trading activities were most intensive within these circuits, as were the various forms of stylistic interaction and visual communication that linked politically independent elites into larger social networks. Each exchange circuit—Aztec, west Mexican, Maya, and southern Pacific coastal plain—was a miniature world system of its own, comparable in functional terms to the localized but extensive subsystems identified by Abu-Lughod (1989) for the world system in the Old World from the eleventh through thirteenth centuries A.D.

International trade centers provided structural focus for broad-ranging economic exchange, particularly trade that took place beyond the four exchange circuits (see the maps in chapter 3). The profusion of such trade-based cities and towns in the Postclassic and, especially, Late Postclassic periods is indicative of the high degree of commercialization of Mesoamerica at that time. While Chapman (1957) saw these entrepôts as diplomatic meeting grounds, the data better fit a model of strategically situated centers that attracted traders from distant areas, enjoyed a high volume of trade, and exhibited a great diversity of trade goods. Political neutrality was not a requirement, although the safety of merchants and their wares was a consideration (chapter 17). The presence of a large number of these centers allowed merchants from the numerous, culturally varied, and sometimes mutually hostile city-states to still maintain a high volume of economic exchange, especially in the luxury goods so important to the elite.

Affluent production zones are singled out because of their production impact on the world system. These areas did not develop the powerful polities and large cities found in the core zones, but nonetheless they were scenes of large overall populations and hotbeds of vigorous economic activity. The considerable number of these, and their high levels of agricultural and/or craft production, contributed significantly to the energy of the world system. Many of these were also regions that thrived on production of high-value prestige raw materials; they included, for example, cacao from Soconusco, salt from northern Yucatán, and precious feathers from coastal Veracruz and highland Guatemala (chapters 3, 16). An extension of this localized production was extensive and predictable exchange networks, since materials such as these were in high demand by elites throughout the world system.

Resource-extraction zones also were areas of specialized production, but rather of materials in more generalized, utilitarian demand and use. These zones focused on the production of nonagricultural materials, particularly the extraction of stones, metals, and salt. Especially significant were the obsidian zones of central Mexico and highland Guatemala, the metal zones of west Mexico and northern Guerrero, and the northern Yucatán salt beds. Economic extraction activity obviously developed in these zones because of the natural presence of the desired raw materials. It is interesting that, as the Mesoamerican world system developed, these zones did not have sufficient attraction to develop as cores and, despite high demand for the materials, remained relatively small-scale operations.

Obviously these specialized units do not encompass the entirety of the Postclassic Mesoamerican world system. Many city-states fall into none of these categories, yet provided a context for local economic, social, political, and religious life. We prefer to not describe these as peripheral zones in the common parlance of world-systems theory, since that notion is usually accompanied by a sense of dominance by a core. We have, nonetheless, called these "unspecialized peripheries" to highlight their generalized contribution to the world system as a whole—as opposed to the more-specialized and focal functions of international trade centers, affluent production centers, and resource-extraction zones.

THE DYNAMICS OF THE POSTCLASSIC MESOAMERICAN WORLD SYSTEM

The dynamics of this system—with its profusion of city-state polities, powerful cores, and specialized foci for trade, production, and extraction—can be summarized under the seven processes outlined at the outset of this book in chapter 1.

POPULATION GROWTH

There are only a few highland areas for which we have good data on Postclassic demographic patterns. Postclassic population change cannot be studied for regions like Oaxaca which have few chronological subdivisions (chapter 1), and for many lowland areas (and the highland Maya region) there are simply insufficient data on phased Postclassic sites to reach firm conclusions (chapters 33–36). For those areas where demographic trends can be examined—such as the Basin of Mexico, Morelos, and the Lake Pátzcuaro basin—the picture is uniformly one of steady and dramatic population growth in the Middle and Late Postclassic periods. This "population explosion," in highland areas at least, was linked to widespread adoption of intensive methods of agriculture that transformed much of the rural landscape.

Although we have no desire to adopt the demographic determinism of the 1970s (e.g., Cohen 1977), it seems clear that these processes of population growth and agricultural intensification played important roles in generating the economic dynamics of the Postclassic world system. These processes helped turn many of the highland valleys and parts of Yucatán into affluent production zones, and the increased economic demand of larger regional populations contributed to the expansion of exchange throughout Mesoamerica.

PROLIFERATION OF SMALL POLITIES

On the eve of the Spanish invasion—and with the exception of the Tarascan empire (chapter 13)—the prevailing pattern of political organization was one of city-state culture. The small political units of Postclassic Mesoamerica were far from identical. As described in the individual chapters in part 2, Aztec central Mexico, Oaxaca, and Yucatán (the areas with the most complete documentation) all had distinctive types of interacting small polities. Nevertheless, the basic patterns of small size and limited political power were the same, and they had similar effects on processes of exchange.

The small size of Postclassic polities was tremendously advantageous in an increasingly commercialized world, since economic competition thrives in the absence of steep political hierarchy (e.g., C. Smith 1976, 1982; Chase-Dunn and Hall 1997:33–35). This does not mean that all exchange was unfettered; as noted in chapter 16, some merchants did carry out diplomatic exchanges with foreign rulers. Yet even in centralized, hierarchical polities (the Tarascan empire, the Aztec tributary domain, and probably Tlaxcala) independent trade was encouraged, at least to some degree. For example, while the Aztecs received volumes of exotics in tribute, amounts probably were insufficient to meet elite demands. By encouraging international commerce, Aztec rulers were assured provisions of additional supplies that could be purchased in markets (Blanton 1996:48; also see Berdan 1987b).

INCREASED VOLUME OF LONG-DISTANCE EXCHANGE

Although difficult to quantify with existing data, the archaeological record suggests much higher levels of long-distance exchange in the Late Postclassic period compared to earlier times. Imported goods such as ceramics, obsidian, and metal were more prevalent at sites in most areas. Increased trade in obsidian resulted in innovations such as deep shaft mines, and the expanded distribution of Texcoco Fabric-marked ceramics throughout the Aztec exchange circuit points to heavier exploitation and trade of salt from lakes in the Basin of Mexico.

A number of key ethnohistoric sources contain long lists of goods for sale in markets and through merchants (e.g., Berdan and Anawalt 1992; Brand 1943; Cortés 1961; Feldman 1985; Landa 1941; Roys 1972; Sahagún 1950–1982; Scholes and Roys 1968). These lists, as well as conquerors' and chroniclers' remarks on trade, provide additional evidence for the high level of long-distance exchange in Late Postclassic times. The use of currency highlighted in many ethnohistoric accounts (chapter 16) is further evidence that trade in Postclassic Mesoamerica was voluminous (Kepecs 2000).

GREATER DIVERSITY OF TRADE GOODS

The documentary lists of goods mentioned above are remarkable for the great diversity of commodities that they contain. The Spanish conquerors were amazed at the number and variety of goods in Aztec markets; of the Tlatelolco market, for example, the conqueror Hernando Cortés wrote, "Every kind of merchandise such as may be met with in every land is for sale there, whether of food and victuals, or ornaments of gold and silver, or lead, brass [*sic*; Cortés probably meant bronze], copper, tin, precious stones, bones, shells, snails and feathers" (Cortés 1961:87). He goes on to enumerate hundreds of different goods sold in the market. Although Tlatelolco was the largest market in Late Postclassic Mesoamerica, lists of goods from smaller markets contain most of the diversity found in this central marketplace.

COMMERCIALIZATION OF THE ECONOMY

The macroregional economy of Postclassic Mesoamerica relied on an increasingly intensified production of key commodities, including metals, cotton and cotton cloth, cacao, obsidian, and salt (chapter 18). Some of these industries—especially cacao, obsidian, and coastal salt—were large-scale, but in many cases specialized production was a part-time activity carried out within household contexts (Feinman 1999b). All production for exchange removed some labor from the domestic economy, making local and regional markets essential for the provision of some basic goods (as noted in chapters 2 and 33).

At the heart of the commercial economy was money. Braudel (1981:442) wrote that wherever commodity exchange developed, one of the more sought after or plentiful goods played the part of money. Money is a technique (Braudel 1981:477)—one that allows fixing of the value of an item according to predetermined prices set by outside parties. It replaces face-to-face barter, in which worth is calculated by the involved individuals' need or desire for the items being exchanged. Mesoamericans no doubt bartered in some cases, but Spanish documents repeatedly record the common use of several kinds of currency: axe-monies, shell beads, cotton mantles, and especially cacao (chapter 16). These were true currencies of the "primitive" kind, serving as standards of exchange.

Not all of the information on currency is documentary. In chapter 21, Hosler summarizes archaeological evidence for axe-monies that adds a substantial material component to ethnohistoric descriptions. Further, the locations of major cacao-producing regions coincided with some of the strategically located international trade areas, and increases in cacao production probably occurred in the Postclassic (chapter 35). This information broadens our picture of the link between cacao and exchange, and the ways in which this link increased hand in hand with increasing commercialism.

Local and regional markets in the Aztec domain are well represented in the written record (Berdan 1985; Feldman 1978). Documents for the Maya area also mention markets (chapter 33), but substantivist historians such as Farriss (1984) and Clendinnen (1986) claim these references describe only international trade emporia for diplomatic exchange (Chapman's discredited port-of-trade model). This approach perpetuates the notion that traditions are immutable, and that Prehispanic commoners were just like the self-sufficient peasant agriculturalists of the twentieth-century "ethnographic present," who had little need for market exchange (see Kepecs 1999; Feinman 1997).

Yet in Yucatán, as in the Aztec domain, the material record helps build a picture of local or regional markets. In chapter 33 Kepecs describes archaeological patterns reflecting the regional exchange of locally produced ceramics in Chikinchel (also see Kepecs 1997, 2000a). And in chapter 34, Masson reports the presence of non-local trade goods—especially obsidian—in excavations that cut across the social range of household contexts in northern Belize. A similar pattern is described by Smith (chapter 32) for Morelos, where even the most valuable imported commodities—greenstone and rock crystal jewelry, and various objects of bronze—are found in both commoner and elite contexts. These data support the arguments of Hirth (1998) and Smith (1999) that the lack of exclusively elite goods (and the presence of valuable imports in non-elite contexts) can be seen as evidence for the operation of commercial market systems.[1]

NEW FORMS OF WRITING AND ICONOGRAPHY

One of the innovative features of our world-systems approach is the role accorded to non-economic processes and institutions. Writing and iconography were crucial components of the system of interregional communication in Postclassic Mesoamerica. The Middle and Late Postclassic periods witnessed an expansion of pictorial texts with limited phonetic content that could be read by speakers of diverse languages. These "international" writing systems—particularly the Aztec and Mixtec scripts—reduced the separation between linguistic signs and iconography, and they were understandable by elites or their agents over much of Mesoamerica.

NEW PATTERNS OF STYLISTIC INTERACTION

Beyond the formalized Aztec and Mixtec scripts, Postclassic Mesoamerica witnessed a dramatic expansion of international symbols and styles (chapters 24 and 25). These elements and styles were adopted and exchanged rapidly among many far-flung parts of Mesoamerica. In contrast to prior accounts that try to find central Mexican origins for these traits, we believe that they are better seen as international in character, providing evidence for dynamic two-way interactions between distant elites. It was no accident that various forms of "international" writing and the various international symbols and styles developed in Postclassic times. The widespread adoption of these traits went hand in hand with the expansion of commerce, with each process reinforcing the other.

POSTCLASSIC MESOAMERICA AS A DYNAMIC WORLD SYSTEM

The chapters in this volume reveal Postclassic Mesoamerica as a setting for dynamic systems of economic exchange, stylistic communication, and political competition. The contrasts between the Postclassic period and earlier periods are dramatic. Economic activity was carried out at a much higher level, and for the first time, a strongly commercial economy developed in Mesoamerica. The ubiquity of small polities in all areas was a new phenomenon. Postclassic writing systems were innovative in their international character, and the spread of international symbols and styles was unprecedented.

It is difficult to make sense of these developments—in all their detail and at a variety of scales from the household to the community to the region and even greater—using the theoretical approaches that have long dominated Mesoamerican studies. Old, outdated models that explained everything by migrations and "diffusion" do contain kernels of truth, but they are inadequate as explanatory models today. Ecological approaches provide important parts of the picture, and traditional studies of "trade" furnish crucial empirical data. Theories of cultural evolution provide broad descriptive outlines of trends, but seem incapable of explaining the dynamism of Postclassic society. In short, none of these traditional approaches can account for the archaeological, ethnohistoric, and art historical data presented in this volume.

It was a combination of dissatisfaction with prior models and an abundance of new data that led to the production of this volume. The authors of the above chapters have collectively crafted our own modified world-systems approach (chapters 2, 3) to bring together the diverse data on Postclassic Mesoamerica. This theoretical approach seems most capable of integrating the various types of information (archaeological, documentary, and visual) from a large number of ethnically and culturally distinct regions into a coherent whole. Although many questions remain unanswered, we believe that we have made a significant step forward in demonstrating the nature of interrelations between diverse societies throughout the broad Mesoamerican culture area. The creativity and dynamism of Postclassic Mesoamerican societies were extraordinary, and we are now starting to glimpse the contours of this remarkable civilization in a comprehensive fashion.

Notes

CHAPTER 1

1. The merchants in this large dugout canoe said they were from a place called "Maia." Lothrop (1927) showed that the designation "Maya" was used in the early sixteenth century to refer to several different parts of the Caribbean, including northwest Yucatán and the north coast of Honduras, where Columbus encountered the merchants. Thus Edwards (1978: 199–204) views the merchants as local Hondurans, not Mayas from Yucatán (see also Sauer 1966:128–129). Blom (1932:534) points out, however, that the term the merchants used for cotton cloak—*zuyen*—was a Yucatec Maya term (*zuyem* in the Motul dictionary), and on that basis argues that these merchants were indeed Mayas from Yucatán (Edwards does not cite Blom nor refer to this evidence). Regardless of the merchants' origin, however, the important point is the diversity of origins of the many trade goods they carried.

2. In an important article summarizing ethnohistorical evidence for Postclassic Maya commercial institutions, Franz Blom (1932) anticipated Rathje and Sabloff's mercantile model. Blom's article had little influence on views of the Postclassic Maya, however, perhaps because scholars in the early and mid-twentieth century were not prepared to accept its implications for the Postclassic economy and society.

3. One reason that scholars can interpret the same data in such different ways is the lack of generally accepted methods for the identification and analysis of social and economic phenomena from archaeological data. The development of material-culture models for institutions and processes in complex societies is still quite underdeveloped. Recent contributions in this direction include Costin 1991; DeMarrais et al. 1996; Hirth 1998; Smith 1999; and Stark 1990. Particularly important for the theme of this volume is the ability to identify market exchange in the absence of written descriptions, and for this purpose several chapters rely on the models of Hirth (1998) and Smith (1999) (see chapters 16, 32, and 34).

4. Polanyi's substantivist economic anthropology still has a few adherents among scholars of ancient economic history. Rather than promote Polanyi's model, which is largely discredited today, they focus their energy instead on criticizing the works of Morris Silver (1983, 1985). Silver is a formalist economic historian who goes far beyond other scholars by attributing not just commercial exchange, but a whole range of capitalist institutions and practices to the ancient societies of the Near East. Just as scholars cited in the text criticized the distortions of Polanyi's antimarket interpretations of the historical data, others criticize Silver for parallel distortions from the opposite perspective (Renger 1995; Mayhew et al. 1985).

CHAPTER 2

1. Chase-Dunn and Hall extend the notion of core/periphery structures to relations among small, kin-based societies—a controversial notion that lies beyond the issues addressed in this book.

2. Chase-Dunn and Hall (1997:233–234) envision cycles of change in premodern world-systems in typically substantivist terms. Cycles of centralization and decentralization occurred within empires, and empires themselves rose and fell. Yet the balance of the world system as a whole did not shift toward a multistate pattern until the shift to "capitalist logic"—by which they mean the advent of price-setting markets and profit-driven competition. Although they recognize weak tendencies toward this direction earlier, as noted in the text they place the definitive shift at the end of the sixteenth century.

3. Chase-Dunn and Hall (1997:61) use several specific terms for nonsystemic and weakly systemic peripheries, but in general the authors in this book focus on well-integrated subsystems, so we do not make these distinctions.

CHAPTER 3

1. Many authors have pointed out religious symbols and traits in Southwestern cultures that appear to have a Mesoamerican origin (e.g., Hays-Gilpin and Hill 1999; Pohl 2001; Taube 2001). We do not see these similarities as sufficiently extensive or precise to warrant inclusion of the Southwest in our model of the Postclassic Mesoamerican world system.

CHAPTER 4

1. Because of its careful specification of criteria and its broad cross-cultural framework, Hansen's (2000b) model of city-state culture is more useful as an analytical construct than other recent comparative treatments of city-states, such as Trigger (1993) and Charlton and Nichols (1997a, 1997b). Marcus (1998) is critical of the city-state concept as a comparative category, a position criticized by Adams (2000) and Hansen (2000b).

CHAPTER 6

1. Elsewhere, I have argued that there is no ethnographic evidence that the highland Maya ever were organized into moieties (Braswell 2000b).

2. The notion of the house as a societal type relevant to Mesoamerica was first proposed by Gillespie (1995) in a critique of the lineage model as applied to the Classic Maya. More recent discussions (Gillespie and Joyce 1997; Joyce

1996, 1999, 2000a; Ringle and Bey 2001) have applied Lévi-Strauss's model to Formative Mesoamerica and the Postclassic northern Maya lowlands. Cultural anthropologists, in contrast, have been cautious in adopting the house as a societal type, seeing it as another example of Lévi-Strauss's classificatory, essentialist, and processual paradigm. Instead, they have emphasized the house as a fetish (e.g., Macdonald 1987) or as a "living being" (e.g., Carsten and Hugh-Jones 1995). For inspiring analyses of the house concept, see Gillespie 2000a, 2000b.

CHAPTER 7

1. Archivo General de Indias (Seville)–Contaduría 657, Primer tributo de Soconusco, 1530–31.

2. The site of Tepalcatenco, classified as a tertiary site, is adjacent to the modern town of Acacoyagua, presumably the "Yacacoyauacan" mentioned in the "Memorial de Tlacopan" (Paso y Troncoso 1939–42:14:121–122). It is possible that the main part of the site lies beneath the modern town, and that our classification of the site as tertiary is in error.

3. Acapetahua, however, became a sujeto within the partido of Soconusco.

4. A relationship of some sort between leaders of the towns of Soconusco and Huehuetan in the late sixteenth century is suggested on a fragment of a map published by Navarrete (1978:78) in which a line is drawn between individuals—presumably leaders—from the two towns.

5. Archivo General de Indias–Mexico 3102, "Informe de Fructos Gómez Casillas sobre la población…en las cinco provincias del obispado," 1611.

CHAPTER 10

1. Among the best of the general ethnohistorical studies of the composition of Postclassic great houses and city-states discussed here are: Appel 1980; Byland and Pohl 1994; Carrasco, Broda et al. 1976; Flannery and Marcus 1983; García Cook 1981; Lind 1999; Martínez 1984; and Reyes García 1977.

2. See Taggart 1983 for a discussion of the functional ideology behind variations on religious stories, myths, and legends that distinguish neighboring Nahua communities.

3. A Mitla painted lintel depicts Camaxtli-Mixcoatl's battle with Itzpapalotl. Pictographs and carved bones depicting both gods or emblems associated with their cult have been identified from Acatlan, Coixtlahuaca, and the Huautla areas (Pohl 1999; Pohl and Winter n.d.). The Nicarao worshiped a god called Mixcoatl (Fowler 1989:233, 242). A codex-style pictograph was carved on a boulder above Acatlan portraying both Camaxtli-Mixcoatl and Itzpapalotl (Seler 1998), and a Tula atlantid-style warrior column known from Tututepec probably represents Itzpapalotl as well (Piña Chán 1960:68).

4. In a provocative article, Ringle, Gallareta Negrón, and Bey (1998) propose that the Epiclassic was characterized by the spread of competing feathered serpent cults, with Tula and Chichén Itzá gaining dominance by the outset of the Postclas-sic. They discuss the significance of the fact that the Mixtecs do not buy into the Tollan myth directly but rather appear to introduce the Quetzalcoatl cult on their own terms by having their priests magically descend from ropes from the heavens with the first sacred bundles dedicated to 9 Wind. Monaghan (1995:272–275) has shown that a comparable process of miraculous appearance remains a key factor in the appropriation of Christian saints' cults together with their associated feasts and markets in the Mixteca even today. Miraculous appearance is the means by which a foreign cult is introduced as "home grown."

5. By the time of the conquest, Zaachila was fighting with Cuilapan for control of the central Valley of Oaxaca, while farther south, Miahuatlan, Ozolotepec, and Coatlan were fighting with one another. In the Mixteca Alta, Mitlantongo was fighting Tlaxiaco and Tututepec. Tututepec was also fighting Tamazola, Zacatepec, and Tehuantepec. Tejupa was fighting with the Chochos of the Coixtlahuaca area, and Tilantongo was fighting with Teposcolula (Spores 1965). Elsewhere I have proposed that many of these disputes, especially the war between Cuilapan and Zaachila, were associated with competing alliance corridors dominated by kings and queens who differentiated themselves by advocating descent from the various factions who participated in the War of Heaven and 8 Deer sagas played out in the Nochixtlan Valley (Pohl 1994b, 1998b).

CHAPTER 14

1. José Hernández has suggested that the rich Postclassic site in the town of Valle de Bravo, which has seen limited excavations (Hernández Rivero and Escobedo Ramírez 1997; Reinhold 1981), may have been the location of ancient Temazcaltepec (personal communication to Smith, 1998). Smith was unable to locate Prehispanic remains in a brief examination of modern Temazcaltepec in 1997, lending support to this hypothesis.

CHAPTER 17

1. It is hardly surprising that when we acknowledge the highly commercialized nature of the Postclassic economy, the port-of-trade model—with its state control of merchants and markets, and the disassociation between long-distance and local or regional exchange systems—looks inadequate. Mesoamericanists and other archaeologists are only now freeing themselves from the "anti-market mentality" (Blanton 1982) fostered by Karl Polanyi's substantivist economic anthropology, which was, and continues to be, very influential in archaeology (see discussion in chapters 1 and 2).

CHAPTER 19

1. Most of Mendizábal's information was taken from the Papeles de Nueva España (Paso y Troncoso 1905, 1939).

2. Measurements were taken from maps in Berdan et al. 1996 and the 1999 *National Geographic World Atlas*.

3. Saltworks in other areas also must have provided salt

for trade on this medium-range scale. Some salt was produced for export on the Cihuatlan (central Pacific) coast (Berdan et al. 1996:277), and some of this salt ultimately reached the Tarascan empire (Helen Pollard, personal communication, 1999); yet according to Ewald (1985:35, 162–163), Prehispanic operations on the central Pacific were small in scale and involved laborious leaching processes. Coxcatlan in southern Puebla is poorly documented (Smith 1996a:147), but probably was an important regional source of both spring salt and tequisquite. And finally, sparsely populated regions beyond the Mesoamerican heartland had good salt-making potential that went untapped during the Prehispanic era, including the Sinaloa coast and the playa lakes of Zacatecas and San Luis Potosí in interior northern Mexico (Ewald 1985; Lefond 1969).

CHAPTER 20

1. Throughout this volume, we advocate the definition of a distinct Middle Postclassic period. Unfortunately, the chronological tools needed to distinguish this period from Early and Late Postclassic occupations are insufficiently developed for many regions outside of the Tarascan and Aztec zones. Despite significant advances in each area, Postclassic Oaxaca and Sapoá/Ometepe-period Gran Nicoya remain particularly problematic. For this reason, I have chosen a simpler chronology for this chapter. In cases where a Middle Postclassic can be defined, I have incorporated the obsidian data into the Late Postclassic period.

2. Until quite recently, the ceramic chronology of Tula was tied to an absolute calendar by only a handful of chronometric dates. Cowgill (1996:327) suggests that the beginning of the Corral phase at Tula should be pushed back to before A.D. 650, and currently there are no chronometric dates for the site later than the eleventh century. According to the chronology adopted by most authors in this volume (table 1.1), the occupation of Tula spans the Epiclassic and only the first century (A.D. 950–1050) of the Early Postclassic period. Thus, as for Chichén Itzá, the traditional assessment of Tula as a quintessentially Early Postclassic city is open to question.

3. Elsewhere, I have argued that Terminal Classic obsidian procurement strategies at Uxmal can be divided into two periods. Before about A.D. 900, Uxmal had little access to Mexican-source obsidian, but significant quantities of the same sources represented at Chichén Itzá reached the Puuc capital during the period A.D. 900–1050 (Braswell 2000a). I interpret this pattern as indicating the incorporation of Uxmal into a pan-Mesoamerican competitive obsidian market during the second half of the Terminal Classic.

4. The chronological assignment of Tula's period of grandeur is now being reassessed. See note 2, this chapter.

5. During her 1999 field season, Karen Niemel recovered three exhausted polyhedral cores from N-Ri-17, a site in the department of Rivas, Nicaragua. To date, these are the only well-documented polyhedral cores of certain provenance recovered from an archaeological site in Nicaragua. As such,

they provide the strongest evidence for the local production of prismatic blades in Sapoá/Ometepe times. They remain to be sourced, but appear to come from Güinope, Honduras.

6. Four artifacts from this sample come from the Zinapécuaro portion of the source system, but only one is traced to Ucareo.

7. Las Piedritas is an exception to this generality.

CHAPTER 22

1. The ritual ideology of the Aztlan-Chicomoztoc migration saga originated with the subsistence behavior of foraging peoples living in northern Mexico and the American Southwest (Pohl 2001). Later, as demand for rare commodities unique to their home ranges (such as turquoise and peyote) began to increase throughout Mesoamerica, the Chichimecs became ever more adept at systematically procuring these commodities, transporting them along their annual hunting and migration routes, and then monopolizing their distribution into the Postclassic world system through west Mexico. Even though commodity specialization subsequently had the effect of fostering migratory behavior long after it had lost its functional appeal as a subsistence strategy, the ritual ideology remained intact as an essential element of a new exchange strategy between chiefdoms and ultimately legitimization for the expansion of conquest states.

2. Hassig (1985:67–84) proposed that the 260-day calendar evolved in Meosamerica as a device for creating periodicity for regional market systems. Among the Eastern Nahua, markets were held in conjunction with palace feasts. Market periodicity thereby fell under elite control over the divinatory calendar.

3. Yacatecuhtli also displays attributes associated with two avatars of Tezcatlipoca, Omeacatl and Tlacochcalco Yaotl (Seler 1990–1998: 2:238, 261, 266). Facial ornamentation consisting of squares of black painted at the nose, forehead, ears, and chin is virtually the same. O'Mack (1991) emphasizes the similarities in ritual behavior during festivals dedicated to Yacatecuhtli and Tezcatlipoca as well.

4. In this respect Cholula's elites appear to have been engaged in competitive systems of reciprocity and redistribution comparable to contemporary institutions such as *mayordomía* (see Monaghan 1990b).

5. There are a few legends of conquests by Camaxtli-Mixcoatl and his son Quetzalcoatl in both the Morelos and Veracruz regions (see Davies 1977:315–318 for discussion). By some accounts, Quetzalcoatl led his people to found Cempoalla, the great Totonac city-state in Veracruz, before journeying south to Tlapallan, where he died (Garibay K. 1973:38). Tlaxcala subsequently wielded political influence over Cempoalla until the middle of the fifteenth century (Durán 1994:175–176). Morelos, on the other hand, appears to have been connected more with the city-states around the Basin of Mexico than those of Tlaxcala, Puebla, or Oaxaca (see chapter 31). While we tend to equate the Tolteca-Chichimeca with the Nahua ethnically, in fact there is a

distinction. Technically, anyone can adopt Toltec cults and even Nahua language to assimilate them. This is particularly true of peoples in marginal areas claiming to be Toltecs.

6. Citing a collection of divinatory calendars from the Sierra Zapoteca showing that every valley maintained a distinct system of reckoning, Nancy Farris (personal communication) and Arthur Miller (personal communication) pointed out to me that the profound variability in environment and agricultural production that characterize Oaxaca would have made any broad regional exchange system based on feasts timed to the solar year pointless (Alcina Franch 1993). The problem is comparable to the Andean situation discussed by Murra (1975). While there is no mention of a veintana or fixed-feast system south of Teotitlan del Camino, a Nahua-Popolocan kingdom on the Oaxaca-Puebla border, some moveable feasts pictured in the Mixtec codices bear striking similarities to veintana ceremonies. Eight Deer's execution of his two half nephews, a Tlacaxipehualiztli-like ritual appearing in Zouche-Nuttall 81, is a good example, as is the Mixtec fire ceremony appearing on Zouche-Nuttall 17 that resembles Borbonicus 34 (Seler 1963; Taube 2000). To what extent Nahua veintana ceremonies might have affected, or been affected by, Mixtec and Zapotec ritualism remains to be determined.

7. Alvarado Tezozomoc (1980:609) confirms that turquoise was a highly valued commodity in Tututepec that was collected as tribute by the Aztecs. A list of the estate of Don Pedro de Alvarado shows that this sixteenth-century Tututepec cacique valued the stone above all other commodities, boasting a treasure of "tres sartas de piedras turquesas, dos sartas de turquesas más menudas, otras dos sartas de piedras turquesas; digo sartas grandes, tres sartas de piedras turquesas entreverados y engastadas en oro, otra seis sartas de turquesas solas, tres conejos entallados en tres piedras turquesas" [three strings of turquoise stones, two strings of smaller turquoise stones, another two strings of turquoise but of a larger kind, three strings of turquoise stones set with gold, another six strings of turquoises only, three rabbits carved in turquoise stone] (Berlin 1947:31). Tantalizing evidence of a coastal trade route between west Mexico and Tututepec is found in Alva Ixtlilxochitl 1965:2:27–28, which describes an odyssey of Tolteca-Chichimeca from Aztlan through Jalisco to Huatulco, Oaxaca. Huatulco served as Tututepec's port due to the inaccessibility of its own coastline (chapter 17). Burgoa (1934b:26:293) alludes to sea craft from South America landing at Huatulco, and Janine Gasco (personal communication) has documented regular canoe traffic in cacao from the Xoconochco region. It is certainly significant that a highly refined manifestation of polychrome ceramics in the Postclassic international style is associated with the Amapa area of west Mexico (chapter 24), an area of mixed ethnicity but dominated by a Nahuatl-speaking elite. The forms are unique to the area, and some stylistic elements reflect Central American influence, but the preference for depicting narrative scenes and certain iconographic details such as the Mixtec *ñuhu*, or earth lord, is indicative of Oaxacan contact (Smith and Heath-Smith 1980; von Winning 1976).

CHAPTER 23

1. There is an earlier representation of skulls and crossed bones on a Puuc-period stone platform at Uxmal (Pollock 1980), but its style and architectural context differ from the central Mexican and Iximche' examples.

CHAPTER 24

1. The large literature on style in archaeology is concerned primarily with artifact styles and their social significance. Although this literature does have some relevance to our discussion, there is not space to discuss it here (see, for example, Carr and Neitzel 1995; Conkey and Hastorf 1990; Hegmon 1992; Wobst 1999).

2. John Pohl (personal communication, 2000) points out that the 20 day signs only make sense in Nahuatl. When they appear in Oaxaca, used by a diversity of other language groups, the symbols remain the same but the words applied to them differ greatly. For example, the Mixtecs use the symbol for flower as the twentieth day sign in their codices, but the actual word is *huaco* ("macaw"). Similarly, the Zapotec term is *lao* or *loo*, meaning "face of a lord" (like *Ahau*). The implication is that the day names, and by extension the larger Late Postclassic international symbol set, were being generated and spread by Nahuatl-speaking peoples at least as early as A.D. 1300.

CHAPTER 25

1. In the second half of the Late Postclassic period, the Mexica adopted effigy censers specifically for offerings at the Templo Mayor of Tenochtitlan. Many of the finely made ceramic vessels in these offerings were censers and other forms with human or deity effigies (Bonifaz Nuño 1981; Matos Moctezuma 1989), a feature otherwise absent from the Aztec ceramic tradition (Smith, Wharton, and Olson n.d.). The adoption of this non-Aztec ceramic form for Templo Mayor offerings, whether borrowed from Maya or Zapotec censers, was one example of the incorporation of foreign styles and objects into the ritual offerings at the central imperial monument in Tenochtitlan (Broda 1987; Heyden 1987; López Luján 1994).

CHAPTER 26

1. Mendieta (1971:97) wrote that the souls of Tlaxcalan lords were transformed into clouds, birds of rich plumage, and precious stones. Furst (1995:23–32) has written extensively about the same concept in contemporary indigenous belief that includes references to butterflies and other creatures.

2. Mixteca-Puebla—style ceramics were produced using techniques first developed by the lowland Classic Maya in Mesoamerica (see Reents-Budet 1994:210–217 for discussion).

3. Several Tecama-style plates depict the profile head of a

being who is frequently painted entirely black and/or with paint around the mouth and eye that is diagnostic of both the Nahua Ixtlilton and the Maya God M (Spranz 1973:339; Taube 1992). Other details linking these two conceptions include clown-like attributes with distended lips, oddly shaped heads, and either phallic or pug-shaped noses (see Taube 1989 for discussion of clowns). A star symbolized as an eye appearing overhead also accompanies both gods. The face painting is frequently marked or labeled as ash in codices, and the two gods clearly share attributes with the "ash-mouths," a common name for the clowns of the Zuni, Hopi, and Rio Grande Pueblo peoples (Wright 1994).

4. In a previous article I related the cult of the cihuatateo and the maquiltonaleque to the veneration of the souls of the dead (Pohl 1998b). I do not believe that these creatures were the souls of all deceased persons who were destined to live in Mictlan, an underworld associated with the north. They appear to be more the patrons of palace diviners, curers, weather prophets, and midwives who were charged with mediating between the living and the dead. The tzitzimime equated with the cihuateteo as souls of those who died in childbirth were represented as fleshless women who occupied the second level of the heavens (Garibay K. 1973:69). The maquiltonaleque resided in the fifth (Garibay K. 1973:103). This, combined with the fact that these spirit beings were thought to reside in the west and south as well, suggests a belief in special afterlife places for female and male spiritual practitioners distinct from Mictlan, a tradition still maintained in Tlaxcala today.

5. Creation stories involving a patriarch who appears as an anthropomorphic deer are found throughout Oaxaca today (Bierhorst 1990:103).

6. The *Relación de Tilantongo*, on the other hand, refers to 10 moveable feasts that were held annually in that community.

7. For example, the Relación Geográfica of Chichicapa describes a Tlatoani Itzcuintli, or Lord Dog, who introduced the cult of Lord 7 Rabbit and Lady 3 Deer into his kingdom from the Mixtecs. On the other hand, Petela, or Lord 5/9 Dog, of Coatlan and Ocelotepec claimed direct lineal descent from "those who survived the general flood," which is to say ancestors who had lived since time immemorial. It is not known, however, if Petela is the same man as Tlatoani Itzcuintli (Acuña 1982:1:84, 89).

8. Tonacateuchtli was also known as 7 Flower. His cult was prevalent in the Tehuacan Valley, where he is widely depicted on *xantiles*, household incense burners, a major artifactual component in the region. Seven Flower, or Sahuaco to the Mixtecs, probably fulfilled much the same role as Tonacatecuhtli did for the Nahuas, and Bezelao for the Zapotecs (Pohl 1994a).

CHAPTER 31

1. The title of tecuhtli was then adopted by peoples who were either conquered by the Eastern Nahua or who perceived advantages in appropriating a Tolteca-Chichimeca identity; these included certain groups of Mixtec and Zapotec as well as the Popoloca, Chocho, Mazatec, Cuicatec, Trique, Chontal, and Chatino. The tendency was for less complex societies to assume Eastern Nahua titles. We have seen how 8 Deer had himself made a tecuhtli to facilitate his rise to power at Tilantongo, but still maintained Mixtec traditions of dynastic succession as well. It is significant that peoples who wished to seize lands to which they were not otherwise entitled claimed to be Tolteca-Chichimeca. This was especially true of the Mixtecs and Chochos of the Coaixtlahuaca area and the Mixtecs of Tututepec.

2. Elsewhere I have argued that Mixtec genealogies were used to symbolize alliance corridors in much the same way as the legendary migrations of the Tolteca-Chichimeca (Pohl 1994a, 1994b).

3. Yanhuitlan itself was a late invention. Its name means "New Town." In two ethnohistorical documents we can connect Yanhuitlan in Colonial documents to individuals appearing in Codex Bodley, but they are not associated with the present site but rather with two towns called Andua or Saandua (Place of Arrows) and Chindua (Place of the Spiderweb), both a few kilometers away. At the time of the conquest they had become Yanhuitlan's subjects.

4. The Cuilapan-Zaachila conflict appears to have been a continuation of an earlier dispute. The Genealogy of Maquilxochitl tells us that sometime in the first half of the fifteenth century, a Maquilxochitl lord helped Lord Quixicayo wage war against Huitzo and Mazaltepec, two kingdoms in the Etla Valley closely associated, if not actually intermarried, with Jaltepec (Byland and Pohl 1994a). Whitecotton (1990:18) proposes that Quixicayo was Lord 5 Reed Ocoñana of Teozacoalco. Oudijk (1998a:31–32), on the other hand, proposes that the name translates in Zapotec as Lord 6 Water of Zaachila. In either case the text sets a precedent for the conflict between the two rival Mixtec-Zapotec alliance groups at Cuilapan and Zaachila.

5. According to the *Relación de Acatlan*, they also worshipped two Mixtec gods named 7 Deer and 9 Eagle appearing in Codex Vindobonensis (Smith and Parmenter 1991:25). Place of the Jaguar may also represent either Cuquila, a subject of Tlaxiaco in the Mixteca Alta, or Tehuacan in southern Puebla (König 1979:54–55). Repetitive marriages with women from Mixteca Baja kingdoms like Acatlan and Tequixtepec del Rey are the basis for the Baja identification of Cuyotepji ascribed here. Smith identified a marriage between a Place of the Jaguar woman and a Chicahuaxtla lord (1973a:150–151). Jansen (1994:184, 187) suggests that there may be place signs represented for spouses from Guerrero and Morelos.

6. Lina Odena Güemes (1994:213) proposes that a Tecpatzin of Tlaxcala portrayed in the *Historia Tolteca-Chichimeca* is the same as a man she identifies as Ce Tecpatzin Tlailotlaque in Tlaxcala's XVI Relación Geográfica (Acuña 1984b:148, 163–164). If Odena Güemes is correct, then 13 Rain's partner might be the same man. On the other hand,

there appear to be differences in the spelling of the name between "Tecpatzin" and "Tetzpatzin" in the sources, perhaps indicating that these are different men. Alva Ixtlilxochitl (1965:1:123–124, 2:69–70) said that the Tlailotlaque were a group of Mixtecs of "Toltec lineage" who migrated to the Basin of Mexico from the Mixteca. A pictographic sign for these people appears in Codices Xolotl and Quinantzin as a road of footprints forming a loop to signify "those who returned."

7. Extensive genealogies for the rulers of Chalco and Tecamachalco appear in Chimalpahin and Lienzo Vischer 1. The former is a central Mexican anomaly for which we have no comparison. The latter appears to be a genealogical sequence of Tecamachalco's rulers, but this is an invention. Cross-referencing the marriage pairs in other documents reveals that they ruled at different communities at different times (Johnson 1994). In studying the profound antiquity of the royal line advocated for the kingdom of Texcoco by Ixtlilxochitl, Victor Zamudio-Taylor (personal communication) suggested to me that such anomalous Nahua genealogies might have been fabricated as a response to the requirements of Spanish courts adjudicating claims to *mayorasco* (primogeniture), for which a family had to submit proof of entailment. In fact the Archivo General de la Nación has a separate division for these cases.

8. Muñoz Camargo (1984 [1892]:115) wrote that the Huexotzincas, Tlaxcaltecas, and Cholultecas claimed to be relatives of one another.

CHAPTER 32

1. Fieldwork at Cuexcomate and Capilco was funded by the National Science Foundation and Loyola University of Chicago. Yautepec fieldwork was funded by the National Science Foundation, the H. John Heinz III Charitable Trust, and the University at Albany, SUNY. I thank the Consejo de Arqueología of the Instituto Nacional de Antropología e Historia for granting permits for the fieldwork, and the Centro INAH Morelos for many kinds of help over the years. Cynthia Heath-Smith and a number of students participated in the fieldwork and analyses of these projects.

CHAPTER 33

1. Spanish reports describe very large canoes holding up to 40 "indios" (Díaz del Castillo 1984:30–31; also see Edwards 1978; Thompson 1951, 1970:153).

2. In contrast to the slatewares, which are utilitarian in form, both Silho and Dzibiac ceramics are typified by thin, elegant vessels that often bear incised designs (see Brainerd 1958:56; Smith 1971:1:181).

3. At Cobá and Ek Balam, Silho wares and Pachuca obsidian are quite rare (Bey et al. 1998; Bey and Kepecs 1999; Robles Castellanos 1990; also Kepecs, chapter 19); in the Puuc region they are somewhat more common, though only late in its trajectory, when Uxmal was allied with Chichén (Dunning and Kowalski 1994; Kowalski and Dunning 1999; and see Kepecs and Masson, chapter 5; Kepecs, chapter 19).

4. My various petrographic studies were aided and abetted by Jim Stoltman, Jim Burton, and Sherman Banker.

5. There are 15 large secondary administrative sites in the Itzá system, and one of those—San Fernando Aké—has more than 750 house platforms with Sotuta ceramics. Based on this information, we hypothesized that each secondary site had roughly 500 houses in use at any given time in the Epiclassic/Early Postclassic. Ninety smaller sites reported in the Itzá polity range in estimated size from 10 to 250 platforms. We used a heuristic average number of platforms per small site per year: 25. Thus we calculated a total of 7,500 platforms for the large sites and 2,250 platforms for the smaller sites. Since Chichén is primate, we assigned it a size double that of the secondary centers: 1,000 platforms. This exercise gave us a housemound count of 10,750.

6. We cannot be sure that the Itzá were limited to three-man canoes (like those depicted in the famous Guerreros mural), but to date we have no evidence that the 40-passenger craft of the sixteenth century were in use in the Epiclassic/Early Postclassic.

7. Andrews (1996) notes a few documentary references to salt-making in this area and speculates that the lack of archaeological evidence for Late Postclassic occupation may reflect a pattern of migrant workers. Given the prominence, however, of Late Prehispanic murals and prestige ceramics at the eastern coastal sites, I suspect these documents refer to salt collection for local or regional use rather than for world-scale exchange.

CHAPTER 35

I would like to thank the Instituto Nacional de Antropología e Historia for providing permits for archaeological research in Chiapas. The H. John Heinz III Charitable Trust funded the 1997 fieldwork, and the Foundation for the Advancement of Mesoamerican Studies funded the 2000 fieldwork. An RSCAAP grant from California State University, Dominguez Hills, funded the obsidian hydration analysis.

1. Whether these migrants were actually from Tula or—if the term was being used in a more generic way—from elsewhere, I presume this population spoke a Nahuatl language.

2. Archivo General de Centroamerica (Guatemala City) A3.16-351-4485.

3. Voorhies used the terms *primary, secondary,* and *tertiary,* but since we also use these terms for site hierarchies, I am using *major, moderate,* and *minor* to describe intensity of occupation during any single period.

4. Note that a site can be classified as tertiary in the site hierarchy for the Late Postclassic, but at the same time have a major rating for intensity of occupation (e.g., Loma Bonita, Santa Elena I). This would mean that relative to other Late Postclassic communities ranked as secondary or primary, this community was relatively unimportant, but in terms of the site's occupational history, the Late Postclassic was the most important period of occupation. Similarly, a site can be classified as secondary, but the intensity of occupation can be

moderate (e.g., La Concepción). In this case, the site seems to have been a secondary center during the Late Postclassic, but in terms of its occupational history, it had a more intense occupation at earlier time periods.

CHAPTER 36

1. Also known as the *Annals of the Cakchiquels* (Brinton 1885; Recinos and Goetz 1953). All references are to page numbers in the original document, now at the University of Pennsylvania.

2. In this chapter, I use the term *Nahua* in a deliberately ambiguous way to refer to Central American Pipil, Pochutec, and all dialects of "Aztec" (Canger 1980:16).

3. The K'iche' patron god Tojil (a thunder god similar in many ways to the Classic Maya God K) is said in the *Popol Wuj* to be the same as the Yaqui (Nahua) god Quetzalcoatl, but Tohil is not a feathered serpent. The comparison seems to indicate nothing more than the centrality of both gods to their respective peoples. The *Memorial de Tecpán Atitlán* (p. 23) does mention *eucumatz* (quetzal snake) as the name of a group of people, and there was a K'iche' ruler by this name. Thus, the concept of the feathered serpent was known to K'iche'an peoples, but there are no unambiguous data supporting the existence of a cult dedicated to that divinity.

4. Campbell (1985:926–935) proposes that although Pipil may be more closely related to dialects spoken in the Isthmian Gulf Coast region than to others of so-called Core Nahua, it is distinct from those dialects and should be considered a separate language.

5. Lyle Campbell (personal communication, 2000) concurs that Chiapan Nahua is a logical source for loan words in K'iche'an languages. He also notes that at the time he focused on this question, he was most concerned with demonstrating that the vast majority of loans could not have come from Classical Nahuatl or Pipil, a conclusion that still is unassailable.

6. Because of their aristocratic and militaristic behavior, Carmack (1981:47–48) favors the phrase "Epi-Toltec warlords" to "Putun merchants" (Thompson 1970).

7. "*Teoçacvancu*" and "*ah nonovalcat, ah xulpiti*" in the *Memorial de Tecpán Atitlán* (p. 22). A close reading does not reveal that the battle occurred in a place called Nonoalco, only that the people were "of" that place. Thus, it may be that the *ah nonovalcat, ah xulpiti* were new to the area where they were fought by the Kaqchikel. It is striking that the people who are often translated as "Nonoalca" are given a double name, the second half of which seems to be derived from the Classical Nahuatl *xolopitli* (foolish person) (Frances Berdan, personal communication, 2000). It is conceivable, albeit

unlikely, that the Salvadoran national nickname *guanaco* (simpleton) is a translation of this Precolumbian ethnic name. Borhegyi (1965:41), for reasons that are linguistically implausible, equates the *ah xulpiti* with the Xiu of Mayapán and Uxmal.

8. All K'iche'an versions of this myth describe how their neighbors, in some cases including Nahua-speakers, gathered at Tulan. The myth of origin and migration, then, also serves to partition the Mesoamerican world, in the sense explored by Dumézil (1973). From this perspective, Tulan is analogous to Mount Ararat, from which Shem, Japhet, and Cham dispersed and populated the world. In a rather enlightening passage in the *Memorial de Tecpán Atitlán* (p. 18), the people arriving at Tulan are said to come from four *other* places called Tulan, associated with east, west, God (north?), and the underworld (south?). Hence, the partitioning of the world took place at the center (the fifth Tulan) and is described in ethnogeographic terms.

9. The authors of the *Popol Wuj*, a document written for a Maya audience, conflate Babel with Tulan, noting that the K'iche'an languages became differentiated while the ancestors were at the mythical city. The *Título de Totonicapán*, written for both Spanish and Maya readers, describes Tulan as being across the sea, near Babylon.

10. Given the contiguous pattern of the regions where Tz'utujil, K'iche', and Kaqchikel are spoken, and the regular contact between these groups that is documented in indigenous texts, we may ask if these languages have diverged at a slower rate, and hence if that divergence began before A.D. 900.

CHAPTER 38

1. The documentary and archaeological evidence for commodities, money, markets, and merchants in Postclassic Mesoamerica is crucial, since the available historical records say little about the kinds of commercial institutions and practices that were common in other early commercialized economies. Did Mesoamerican merchants use promissory notes? Did they form partnerships or joint-stock companies? Were there professional moneychangers? In comparison to other ancient commercial economies, from Assyria to Rome to the Islamic world (Abu-Lughod 1989:15–25; Chaudhuri 1991:435–440; Harris 1993; Subrahmanyam 1990), we know very little about the infrastructure of commercial exchange in Postclassic Mesoamerica. Yet even without detailed documentary descriptions of such practices and institutions, the record for commodities, money, merchants, and markets in Mesoamerica provides impressive evidence for the commercial nature of exchange in the Late Postclassic period.

References Cited

Abrams, Elliot M.
  1994 *How the Maya Built Their World: Energetics and Ancient Architecture*. University of Texas Press, Austin.
Abu-Lughod, Janet L.
  1989 *Before European Hegemony: The World System, A.D. 1250–1350*. Oxford University Press, New York.
Acuña, René
  1984a *Antequera*. Relaciones Geográficas del Siglo XVI, vols. 2–3. 2 vols. Universidad Nacional Autónoma de México, Mexico City.
  1984b *Tlaxcala*. Relaciones Geográficas del Siglo XVI. Universidad Nacional Autónoma de México, Mexico City.
  1985 *Tlaxcala*. Vol. 2. Relaciones Geográficas del Siglo XVI. Universidad Nacional Autónoma de México, Mexico City.
  1987 *Michoacán*. Relaciones Geográficas del Siglo XVI, vol. 9. Universidad Nacional Autónoma de México, Mexico City.
  1988 *Nueva Galicia*. Relaciones Geográficas del Siglo XVI, vol. 10. Universidad Nacional Autónoma de México, Mexico City.
Adams, Robert McC.
  1966 *The Evolution of Urban Society: Early Mesopotamia and Prehispanic Mexico*. Aldine, Chicago.
  1974 Anthropological Perspectives on Ancient Trade. *Current Anthropology* 15:239–259.
  1981 *Heartland of Cities: Surveys of Ancient Settlement and Land Use on the Central Floodplain of the Euphrates*. University of Chicago Press, Chicago.
  2000 Scale and Complexity in Archaic States: Review of *Archaic States*, edited by Gary M. Feinman and Joyce Marcus. *Latin American Antiquity* 11:187–193.
Adams, Robert McC., and Hans J. Nissen
  1972 *The Uruk Countryside: The Natural Setting of Urban Societies*. University of Chicago Press, Chicago.
Adshead, Samuel A. M.
  1992 *Salt and Civilization*. Macmillan Academic and Professional, London.
Aguilera, Miguel A.
  1999 Off-Mound Feature Investigations at Suboperations 13 and 22, Caye Coco, Belize. In *Belize Postclassic Project 1998: Investigations at Progresso Lagoon*, edited by Marilyn A. Masson and Robert M. Rosenswig, pp. 7–25. Occasional Publication, vol. 3. Institute for Mesoamerican Studies, Albany, NY.
Alcina Franch, José
  1993 *Calendario y religión entre los zapotecos*. Universidad Nacional Autónoma de México, Mexico City.
Alexander, Rani T.
  1999 Site Structure at Isla Cilvituk, Campeche, Mexico: Political Economy on the Frontier. Paper presented at the 1999 Annual Meeting of the Society for American Archaeology (Chicago).
  n.d. Frontier Settlement and Development Cycles in the Maya Lowlands: Postclassic Isla Cilvituk, Campeche, Mexico. Unpublished manuscript.
Allix, André
  1922 The Geography of Fairs, Illustrated by Some Old-World Examples. *The Geographical Review* 7:532–569.
Alva Ixtlilxochitl, Fernando de
  1965 *Obras históricas*. 2 vols. Editorial Nacional, Mexico City.
Alvarado Tezozomoc, Hernando de
  1944 *Crónica mexicana*. Leyenda, Mexico City.
  1980 *Crónica mexicana escrita en el año de 1598*. Porrúa, Mexico City.
Alvarez del Toro, Miguel
  1985 *Asi era Chiapas*. Universidad Autónoma de Chiapas, Tuxtla Gutierrez.
Anales de Cuauhtitlan
  1945 *Códice Chimalpopoca, anales de Cuauhtitlan y leyenda de los soles*. Translated by Primo Filicrono Velásquez. Imprenta Universitaria, Mexico City.
Anales de Tlatelolco
  1948 *Anales de Tlatelolco: Unos anales históricos de la nación mexicana, y códice de Tlatelolco*. Edited by Heinrich Berlin. Antiguo Librería Robredo, Mexico City.
Anawalt, Patricia R.
  1981a Costume Analysis and the Provenience of the Borgia Group Codices. *American Antiquity* 48:837–852.
  1981b *Indian Clothing Before Cortés: Mesoamerican Costumes from the Codices*. University of Oklahoma Press, Norman.
  1993 The Riddle of the Emperor's Cloak. *Archaeology* 46(3):30–36.
Anders, Ferdinand, and Maarten Jansen
  1996 *Religión, costumbres, e historia de los antiguos mexicanos: Libro explicativo del llamado códice Vaticano A*. Fondo de Cultura Económica, Mexico City.
Anders, Ferdinand, Maarten Jansen, and Gabina Aurora Pérez Jiménez
  1992a *Crónica mixteca: El rey 8 Venado, Garra de Jaguar, y la dinastía de Teozacualco-Zaachila: Libro explicativo del llamado Códice Zouche-Nuttall*. Fondo de Cultura Económica, Mexico City.
  1992b *Origen e historia de los reyes mixtecos:Libro explicativo del llamado Códice Vindobonensis*. Fondo de Cultura Económica, Mexico City.
Anderson, Arthur J. O., Frances F. Berdan, and James Lockhart (editors)
  1976 *Beyond the Codices: The Nahua View of Colonial Mexico*. University of California Press, Berkeley.
Andrews, Anthony P.
  1978 Puertos costeros del postclásico temprano en el norte de Yucatán. *Estudios de Cultura Maya* 11:75–93.
  1983 *Maya Salt Production and Trade*. University of Arizona Press, Tucson.
  1990a The Role of Trading Ports in Maya Civilization. In

Vision and Revision in Maya Studies, edited by Flora
S. Clancy and Peter D. Harrison, pp. 159–168. University of New Mexico Press, Albuquerque.

1990b The Fall of Chichen Itza: A Preliminary Hypothesis. *Latin American Antiquity* 1:258–267.

1993   Late Postclassic Lowland Maya Archaeology. *Journal of World Prehistory* 7:35–69.

1996   The Northern Maya Lowland Coasts: Settlement, Trade, and Political Organization. Paper presented at the 61st Annual Meeting of the Society for American Archaeology (New Orleans).

1998   El comercio maya prehispánico de la sal: Nuevos datos, nuevas perspectivas. In *La sal en México*, edited by J. C. Reyes G., pp. 3–28. Universidad de Colima, Colima.

Andrews, Anthony P., E. Wyllys Andrews IV, and
Fernando Robles Castellanos
2000   The Northern Maya Collapse and Its Aftermath. Paper presented at the 65th Annual Conference of the Society for American Archaeology (Philadelphia).

Andrews, Anthony P., Frank Asaro, Helen V. Michel, Fred H.
Stross, and Pura Cervera Rivero
1989   The Obsidian Trade at Isla Cerritos, Yucatán, Mexico. *Journal of Field Archaeology* 16:355–363.

Andrews, Anthony P., Tomás Gallareta Negrón, Fernando Robles
C., Rafael Cobos P., and Pura Cervera Rivero
1988   Isla Cerritos: An Itzá Trading Port on the North Coast of Yucatán, Mexico. *National Geographic Research* 4:196–207.

Andrews, Anthony P., and F. Robles Castellanos
1985   Chichen Itza and Coba: An Itza-Maya Standoff in Early Postclassic Yucatan. In *The Lowland Maya Postclassic*, edited by Arlen F. Chase and Prudence M. Rice, pp. 62–72. University of Texas Press, Austin.

Andrews, Anthony P., and Gabriela Vail
1990   Cronología de sitios prehispánicos costeros de la península de Yucatán y Belice. *Boletín de la Escuela de Ciencias Antropológicas de la Universidad de Yucatán* 18(104–105):37–66.

Andrews, E. Wyllys, IV
1943   The Archaeology of Southwestern Campeche. In *Contributions to American Anthropology and History*, no. 40, pp. 1–100. Publication, vol. 546. Carnegie Institution of Washington, Washington, D.C.

1968   Dzibilchaltun: A Northern Maya Metropolis. *Archaeology* 21:36–47.

Anguiano, Marina, and Matilde Chapa
1976   Estratificación social en Tlaxcala durante el siglo XVI. In *Estratificación social en la Mesoamérica prehispánica*, edited by Pedro Carrasco and Johanna Broda, pp. 118–156. Instituto Nacional de Antropología e Historia, Mexico City.

Anonymous Conqueror
1971   Relación de algunas cosas de la Nueva España y de la Gran Ciudad de Temestitan Mexico; escrita por un compañero de Hernán Cortés. In *Colección de Documentos para la Historia de México* 1:368–390, edited by Joaquín García Icazbalceta. Editorial Porrúa, Mexico City.

Aoyama, K.
1999   *Ancient Maya State, Urbanism, Exchange and Craft Specialization: Chipped Stone Evidence from the Copán Valley and La Entrada Region, Honduras / Estado, urbanismo, intercambio, y especialización artesanal entre los Mayas antiguos: Evidencia de lítica menor del Valle de Copán y la región de la Entrada, Honduras*. Univer-

sity of Pittsburgh Memoirs in Latin American Archaeology, vol. 12. University of Pittsburgh, Pittsburgh.

Apenes, Ola
1944   The Primitive Salt Production of Lake Texcoco. *Ethnos* 9:24–40.

Appadurai, Arjun
1986   Introduction: Commodities and the Politics of Value. In *The Social Life of Things: Commodities in Cultural Perspective*, edited by Arjun Appadurai, pp. 3–63. Cambridge University Press, New York.

Appel, Jill
1982a A Summary of the Ethnohistorical Information Relevant to the Interpretation of the Late Postclassic Settlement Pattern Data: The Central and Valle Grande Survey Zones. In *Monte Alban's Hinterland, Part I: The Prehispanic Settlement Patterns of the Central and Southern Parts of the Valley of Oaxaca*, edited by Richard E. Blanton, Stephen Kowalewski, Gary M. Feinman, and Jill Appel, pp. 139–146. Memoirs, vol. 15. University of Michigan, Museum of Anthropology, Ann Arbor.

1982b Political and Economic Organization in the Late Postclassic Valley of Oaxaca, Mexico: An Evolutionary Perspective. Ph.D. dissertation, Department of Anthropology, Purdue University.

Arana Xahilá, F. H., and F. Díaz Xebutá Queh
1573–
1605   *Annals of the Cakchiquels*. University of Pennsylvania Museum Library, Philadelphia.

Armillas, Pedro
1949   Notas sobre sistemas de cultivo en Mesoamérica: Cultivos de riego y de humedad en la cuenca del Río del Balsas. *Anales del Instituto Nacional de Antropología e Historia*, serie 6, 3:85–113.

1969   The Arid Frontier of Mexican Civilization. *Transactions of the New York Academy of Sciences*, Series II, 31:28–48.

Arnauld, Charlotte, and Brigitte Faugère-Kalfon
1998   Evolución de la ocupación humana en el centro-norte de Michoacán (proyecto Michoacán, CEMCA) y la emergencia del estado Tarasco. In *Génesis, culturas y espacios en Michoacán*, edited by Véronique Darras, pp. 13–34. Centre D'Études Mexicanes et Centroaméricanes, Mexico City.

Arnold, Rosemary
1957   A Port of Trade: Whydah on the Guinea Coast. In *Trade and Market in Early Empires*, edited by Karl Polanyi, Conrad M. Arensberg, and Harry W. Pearson, pp. 154–176. Free Press, Glencoe, IL.

Bakker, J. A., J. Kruk, A. E. Lanting, and S. Milisauskas
1999   The Earliest Evidence of Wheeled Vehicles in Europe and the Near East. *Antiquity* 73:778–790.

Ball, Joseph W.
1977   *The Archaeological Ceramics of Becan, Campeche, Mexico*. Publication, vol. 43. Middle American Research Institute, Tulane University, New Orleans.

1978   Archaeological Pottery of the Yucatán-Campeche Coast. In *Studies in the Archaeology of Coastal Yucatán and Campeche, Mexico*, pp. 69–146. Publication, vol. 46. Middle American Research Institute, Tulane University, New Orleans.

1982   Appendix I: The Tancah Ceramic Situation: Cultural and Historical Insights from an Alternative Material Class. In *On the Edge of the Sea: Mural Painting at Tancah-Tulum, Quintana Roo, Mexico*, edited by

Arthur Miller, pp. 105–111. Dumbarton Oaks, Washington, D.C.

Barlow, Robert H.
1949 *The Extent of the Empire of the Culhua Mexica*. Ibero-Americana, vol. 28. University of California Press, Berkeley.

Barnes, William
1999 Aztec "Zapotecizing": The Imperial Significance of Mexica Acculturation. Paper presented at the Annual Meeting of the College Art Association (Los Angeles).

Barnhart, Edwin
1998 The Map of Caye Coco. In *The Belize Postclassic Project 1997: Laguna de On, Progresso Lagoon, and Laguna Seca*, edited by Marilyn A. Masson and Robert M. Rosenswig, pp. 107–111. Occasional Publication, vol. 2. Institute for Mesoamerican Studies, Albany, NY.

Barrera Rubio, Alfredo
1985 Littoral Marine Economy at Tulum, Quintana Roo, Mexico. In *The Lowland Maya Postclassic*, edited by Arlen F. Chase and Prudence M. Rice, pp. 50–61. University of Texas Press, Austin.

Barrera Vásquez, Alfredo, and Sylvanus G. Morley
1949 The Maya Chronicles. In *Contributions to American Anthropology and History*, no. 48, pp. 1–85. Publication, vol. 585. Carnegie Institution of Washington, Washington, D.C.

Barrett, Elinore M.
1981 The King's Copper Mine: Inguarán in New Spain. *The Americas* 38(1):1–29.
1987 *The Mexican Colonial Copper Industry*. University of New Mexico Press, Albuquerque.

Barrett, Jason W.
1999 Investigating Architecture and Phases of Construction at Structure 4: Subop 5 and 15 Excavations, Caye Coco. In *Belize Postclassic Project 1998: Investigations at Progresso Lagoon*, edited by Marilyn A. Masson and Robert M. Rosenswig, pp. 103–124. Occasional Publication, vol. 3. Institute for Mesoamerican Studies, Albany, NY.
2000 Excavations at Structure 5: Postclassic Elite Architecture at Caye Coco. In *Belize Postclassic Project 1999: Continuing Investigations at Progresso Lagoon and Laguna Seca*, edited by Robert M. Rosenswig and Marilyn A. Masson, pp. 31–58. Occasional Publication, vol. 5. Institute for Mesoamerican Studies, Albany, NY.

Bartra, Roger
1975 *Marxismo y sociedades antiquas: El modo de producción asiático y el México prehispánico*. Editorial Grijalba, Mexico City.

Bassols Batalla, Angel
1974 Realidad y problemática de la costa. In *La costa de Chiapas: Un estudio económico regional*, pp. 11–93. Instituto de Investigaciones Económicas, Universidad Nacional Autónoma de México, Mexico City.

Baus Czitrom, Carolyn
1985 The Tecuexes: Ethnohistory and Archaeology. In *The Archaeology of West and Northwest Mesoamerica*, edited by Michael Foster and Phil Weigand, pp. 93–115. Westview Press, Boulder.

Baxter, Kevin H.
1984 Obsidian Source Analysis and the Economy of Tipu, Belize. Paper presented at the 24th Annual Conference of the Northeastern Anthropological Association (Hartford, CT).

Beaumont, Pablo
1932 *Crónica de Michoacán (1776–80)*. Archivo General de la Nación, Mexico City.

Bell, Betty
1971 Archaeology of Nayarit, Jalisco and Colima. In *Archaeology of Northern Mesoamerica*, part 2, edited by Gordon F. Ekholm and Ignacio Bernal, pp. 694–753. The Handbook of Middle American Indians, vol. 11. University of Texas Press, Austin.

Beltrán, Ulises
1982 Tarascan State and Society in Prehispanic Times: An Ethnohistorical Inquiry. Ph.D. dissertation, Department of History, University of Chicago.
1994 Estado y sociedad tarascos en la época prehispánica. In *El Michoacán antiguo*, edited by Brigitte Boehm de Lameiras, pp. 31–163. El Colegio de Michoacán and Gobierno del Estado de Michoacán, Morelia.

Berdan, Frances F.
1975 Trade, Tribute, and Market in the Aztec Empire. Ph.D. dissertation, Department of Anthropology, University of Texas.
1977 Distributive Mechanisms in the Aztec Economy. In *Peasant Livelihood: Studies in Economic Anthropology and Cultural Ecology*, edited by Rhoda Halperin and James Dow, pp. 91–101. St. Martin's Press, New York.
1978 Ports of Trade in Mesoamerica: A Reappraisal. In *Cultural Continuity in Mesoamerica*, edited by David Browman, pp. 179–198. Mouton, The Hague.
1985 Markets in the Economy of Aztec Mexico. In *Markets and Marketing*, edited by Stuart Plattner, pp. 339–367. University Press of America, Lanham, MD.
1987a Cotton in Aztec Mexico: Production, Distribution, and Uses. *Mexican Studies/Estudios Mexicanos* 3:235–262.
1987b The Economics of Aztec Luxury Trade and Tribute. In *The Aztec Templo Mayor*, edited by Elizabeth H. Boone, pp. 161–184. Dumbarton Oaks, Washington, D.C.
1988 Principles of Regional and Long-Distance Trade in the Aztec Empire. In *Smoke and Mist: Mesoamerican Studies in Memory of Thelma D. Sullivan*, edited by J. Kathryn Josserand and Karen Dakin, pp. 639–656. British Archaeological Reports, International Series, no. 402, Oxford.
1992a Glyphic Conventions of the Codex Mendoza. In *The Codex Mendoza*, edited by Frances F. Berdan and Patricia Rieff Anawalt, pp. 93–102, vol. 1. University of California Press, Berkeley.
1992b The Imperial Tribute Roll of the Codex Mendoza. In *The Codex Mendoza*, edited by Frances F. Berdan and Patricia Rieff Anawalt, pp. 55–79, vol. 1. University of California Press, Berkeley.
1992c Economic Dimension of Precious Metals, Stones, and Feathers: The Aztec State Society. *Estudios de Cultura Náhuatl* 22:291–323.
1996 The Tributary Provinces. In *Aztec Imperial Strategies*, by Frances F. Berdan, Richard E. Blanton, Elizabeth H. Boone, Mary G. Hodge, Michael E. Smith, and Emily Umberger, pp. 115–136. Dumbarton Oaks, Washington, D.C.

Berdan, Frances F., and Patricia R. Anawalt (editors)
1992 *The Codex Mendoza*. 4 vols. University of California Press, Berkeley.

Berdan, Frances F., Richard E. Blanton, Elizabeth H. Boone, Mary G. Hodge, Michael E. Smith, and Emily Umberger
1996 *Aztec Imperial Strategies*. Dumbarton Oaks, Washington, D.C.

Bergmann, Richard E.
1969   The Distribution of Cacao Cultivation in Pre-Columbian America. *Annals of the Association of American Geographers* 59:85–96.

Berlin, Heinrich
1947   *Fragmentos desconocidos del Códice de Yanhuitlan y otra investigaciones mixtecas.* Antigua Librería Robredo de José Porrúa e Hijos, Mexico City.
1960   Late Pottery Horizons of Tabasco, Mexico. In *Contributions to American Anthropology and History*, no. 59 pp. 95–154. Vol. 606. Carnegie Institution of Washington, Washington, D.C.

Bernal, Ignacio
1979   *A History of Mexican Archaeology: The Vanished Civilizations of Middle America.* Thames and Hudson, New York.

Berrocal L., G., and F. Querol S.
1991   Geological Description of the Cuale District Ore Deposits, Jalisco, Mexico. In *Economic Geology, Mexico*, edited by G. P. Salas, pp. 355–363. The Geology of North America. Geological Society of America, Boulder.

Bey, George J., III, T. M. Bond, W. M. Ringle, C. A. Hanson, C. W. Houck, and C. Peraza Lope
1998   The Ceramic Chronology of Ek Balam, Yucatan, Mexico. *Ancient Mesoamerica* 9:101–121.

Bey, George J., III, and Susan Kepecs
1999   The Yucatan States in Economic Context: A Petrographic Approach. Paper presented at the 98th Annual Conference of the American Anthropological Association (Chicago).

Beyer, Hermann
1934   Shell Ornament Sets from the Huaxteca, Mexico. In *Studies in Middle America*, edited by Maurice Ries, pp. 153–215. Publications, vol. 5. Tulane University, Middle American Research Institute, New Orleans.

Bierhorst, John
1985   *Cantares Mexicanos: Songs of the Aztecs.* Stanford University Press, Stanford.
1990   *The Mythology of Mexico and Central America.* William Morrow, New York.
1992   *History and Mythology of the Aztecs: The Codex Chimalpopoca.* University of Arizona Press, Tucson.

Binford, Lewis R.
1962   Archaeology as Anthropology. *American Antiquity* 28:217–225.
1968   Some Comments on Historical Versus Processual Archaeology. *Southwestern Journal of Archaeology* 24:267–275.
1983   *In Pursuit of the Past: Decoding the Archaeological Record.* Thames and Hudson, New York.

Bittmann Simons, Bente
1968   *Los mapas de Cuauhtinchan y la historia tolteca-chichimeca.* Serie investigaciones, vol. 15. Instituto Nacional de Antropología e Historia, Mexico City.

Blake, Michael
1985   Canajaste: An Evolving Postclassic Maya Site. Ph.D. dissertation, Department of Anthropology, University of Michigan.
1991   An Emerging Early Formative Chiefdom at Paso de la Amada, Chiapas, Mexico. In *The Formation of Complex Society Southeastern Mesoamerica*, edited by William L. Fowler, pp. 27–46. CRC Press, Boca Raton, FL.

Blake, Michael, John E. Clark, Barbara Voorhies, George

Michaels, Michael W. Love, Mary E. Pye, Arthur A. Demarest, and Barbara Arroyo
1995   Radiocarbon Chronology for the Late Archaic and Formative Periods on the Pacific Coast of Southeastern Mesoamerica. *Ancient Mesoamerica* 6:161–183.

Blanton, Richard E.
1982   Urban Beginnings: A View from Anthropological Archaeology. *Journal of Urban History* 8:427–446.
1983   Factors Underlying the Origin and Evolution of Market Systems. In *Economic Anthropology: Topics and Theories*, edited by Sutti Ortiz, pp. 51–66. University Press of America, Lanham, MD.
1985   A Comparison of Early Market Systems. In *Markets and Marketing*, edited by Stuart Plattner, pp. 399–426. University Press of America, Lanham, MD.
1996   The Basin of Mexico Market System and the Growth of Empire. In *Aztec Imperial Strategies*, by Frances F. Berdan, Richard E. Blanton, Elizabeth H. Boone, Mary G. Hodge, Michael E. Smith, and Emily Umberger, pp. 47–84. Dumbarton Oaks, Washington, D.C.
1998   Beyond Centralization: Steps Toward a Theory of Egalitarian Behavior in Archaic States. In *Archaic States*, edited by Gary M. Feinman and Joyce Marcus, pp. 135–172. School of American Research Press, Santa Fe, NM.
1999   Complexity and Long Range Interactions in Mesoamerica. Paper presented at the American Sociological Association Symposium "Before the Flood: Precolumbian World-Systems in the Americas," Chicago.

Blanton, Richard E., and Gary M. Feinman
1984   The Mesoamerican World System. *American Anthropologist* 86:673–682.

Blanton, Richard E., and Mary G. Hodge
1996   Appendix 2: Data on Market Activities and Production Specializations of Tlatoani Centers. In *Aztec Imperial Strategies*, edited by Frances F. Berdan, Richard E. Blanton, Elizabeth H. Boone, Mary G. Hodge, Michael E. Smith, and Emily Umberger, pp. 243–246. Dumbarton Oaks, Washington, D.C.

Blanton, Richard E., Stephen A. Kowalewski, and Gary M. Feinman
1992   The Mesoamerican World-System. *Review* 15:419–426.

Blanton, Richard E., Stephen Kowalewski, Gary M. Feinman, and Jill Appel
1982   *Monte Alban's Hinterland, Part I: The Prehispanic Settlement Patterns of the Central and Southern Parts of the Valley of Oaxaca.* Memoirs, vol. 15. University of Michigan, Museum of Anthropology, Ann Arbor.

Blanton, Richard E., Stephen A. Kowalewski, Gary M. Feinman, and Laura M. Finsten
1993   *Ancient Mesoamerica: A Comparison of Change in Three Regions.* 2nd ed. Cambridge University Press, New York.

Blom, Frans
1932   Commerce, Trade, and Monetary Units of the Maya. In *Middle American Papers*, edited by Maurice Ries, pp. 531–556. Publication, vol. 4. Middle American Research Institute, New Orleans.

Boehm de Lameiras, Brigitte
1986   *Formación del estado en el México prehispánico.* El Colegio de Michoacán, Zamora.

Bonifaz Nuño, Rubén, and Fernando Robles
1981   *El arte en el Templo Mayor: México-Tenochtitlan.* Instituto Nacional de Antropología e Historia, Mexico City.

Boone, Elizabeth H.

1982a Towards a More Precise Definition of the Aztec Painting Style. In *Pre-Columbian Art History: Selected Readings*, edited by Alana Cordy-Collins, pp. 153–168. 2nd ed. Peek Publications, Palo Alto.

1982b *The Art and Iconography of Late Post-Classic Central Mexico*. Dumbarton Oaks, Washington, D.C.

1990 The Painting Styles of the Manuscripts of the Borgia Group. In *Circumpacifica: Festschrift für Thomas S. Barthel*, edited by Bruno Illius and Matthias Laubscher, pp. 35–54, vol. 1. Peter Lang, Frankfurt.

1991 Migration Histories as Ritual Performance. In *To Change Place: Aztec Ceremonial Landscape*, edited by David Carrasco, pp. 121–151. University Press of Colorado, Niwot.

1994 Aztec Pictorial Histories: Records Without Words. In *Writing Without Words: Alternative Literacies in Mesoamerica and the Andes*, edited by Elizabeth Hill Boone and Walter D. Mignolo, pp. 50–76. Duke University Press, Durham.

1996 Manuscript Painting in Service of Imperial Ideology. In *Aztec Imperial Strategies*, by Frances F. Berdan, Richard E. Blanton, Elizabeth H. Boone, Mary G. Hodge, Michael E. Smith, and Emily Umberger, pp. 181–206. Dumbarton Oaks, Washington, D.C.

2000 *Stories in Red and Black: Pictorial Histories of the Aztec and Mixtec*. University of Texas Press, Austin.

Borhegyi, Stephan F.

1965 Archaeological Synthesis of the Guatemalan Highlands. In *Archaeology of Southern Mesoamerica, Part 1*, edited by Gordon R. Willey, pp. 3–58. Handbook of Middle American Indians, vol. 2. University of Texas Press, Austin.

1980 *The Pre-Columbian Ballgames: A Pan-Mesoamerican Tradition*. Contributions in Anthropology and History, vol. 1. Milwaukee Public Museum, Milwaukee.

Bourdieu, Pierre

1977 *Outline of a Theory of Practice*. Cambridge University Press, Cambridge.

Bradley, Ronna Jane

2000 Recent Advances in Chihuahuan Archaeology. In *Greater Mesoamerica: The Archaeology of West and Northwest Mexico*, edited by Michael S. Foster and Shirley Gorenstein, pp. 221–240. University of Utah Press, Salt Lake City.

Brainerd, George W.

1958 *The Archaeological Ceramics of Yucatan*. Anthropological Records, vol. 19. University of California, Berkeley.

Brand, Donald D.

1943 *An Historical Sketch of Geography and Anthropology in the Tarascan Region, Part 1*. New Mexico Anthropologist, vol. 6/7.

1971 An Ethnohistorical Synthesis of Western Mexico. In *Archaeology of Northern Mesoamerica*, part 2, edited by Gordon F. Ekholm and Ignacio Bernal, pp. 632–656. The Handbook of Middle American Indians, vol. 11. University of Texas Press, Austin.

1980 A Persistent Myth in the Ethnohistory of Western Mexico. *Tlalocan* 7:419–436.

Brasseur de Bourbourg, C. E.

1861 *Popol Vuh, Le livre sacré et les mythes de l'antiquité américaine, avec les livres héroïques et historiques des Quichés*. Collection de documentos dans les langues indigenes de l'Amérique ancienne, vol. 1. Arthus Bertrand, Paris.

Braswell, Geoffrey E.

1993 Ri Rusamäj Jilotepeke: Investigaciones en una antigua zona productora de obsidiana: Kanojki'l pa jun ojer xoral rub'anon chay. In *VI simposio de investigaciones archaeológicas en Guatemala, 1992*, edited by Juan Pedro Laporte, Hector Escobedo, and S. Villagrán de Brady, pp. 479–498. Museo Nacional de Arqueología y Etnología, Guatemala City.

1996 A Maya Obsidian Source: The Geoarchaeology, Settlement History, and Prehistoric Economy of San Martín Jilotepeque, Guatemala. Ph.D. dissertation, Department of Anthropology, Tulane University.

1997 El intercambio comercial entre los pueblos prehispánicos de Mesoamérica y la Gran Nicoya. *Revista de la Universidad del Valle de Guatemala* 6:17–29.

1998a Trade, Procurement, and Population: Obsidian and the Maya of the Northern Lowlands. Paper presented at the 97th Annual Meeting of the American Anthropological Association (Philadelphia).

1998b The Origins of K'iche'an Civilization: The Early Classic Period. Paper presented at the conference "Mayan Culture at the Millenium (Part 1)" (Buffalo).

1998c La arqueología de San Martín Jilotepeque, Guatemala. *Mesoamérica* 35:117–154.

1998d El Epiclásico, Clásico Terminal y Postclásico Temprano: Una visión cronología desde Teotihuacan, Chichén Itzá y el altiplano guatemalteco. In *XI simposio de investigaciones arqueológicas en Guatemala, 1997*, edited by Juan Pedro Laporte and Hector Escobedo, pp. 803–806, vol. 2. Museo Nacional de Arqueología y Etnología, Guatemala City.

2000a The Emergence of Market Economies in the Ancient Maya World: Obsidian Exchange in Terminal Classic Yucatán, Mexico. Paper presented at the 65th Annual Conference of the Society for American Archaeology (Philadelphia).

2000b Industrie lítica clase tallada: Obsidiana. In *El sitio maya de Topoxté: Investigaciones en una isla del lago Yaxhá, Petén, Guatemala*, edited by Wolfgang W. Wurster, pp. 208–221. Materialien zur Allgemeinen und Vergleichenden Archäologie, vol. 57. Verlag Philipp von Zabern, Mainz am Rhein.

2001a Postclassic Maya Courts of the Guatemalan Highlands: Archaeological and Ethnohistorical Approaches. In *Royal Courts of the Ancient Maya*, edited by Takeshi Inomata and Stephen D. Houston, pp. 308–331, vol. 2. Westview Press, Boulder.

2001b Ethnogenesis, Social Structure, and Survival: The Nahuaization of K'iche'an Culture, 1450–1550. In *Maya Survivalism*, edited by Ueli Hostettler and Matthew Restall, pp. 51–58. Acta Mesoamericana, vol. 12. Verlag Anton Saurwein, Markt Schwaben, Germany.

Braswell, Geoffrey E., and Fabio Estéban Amador Berdugo

1999 Intercambio y producción durante el Preclásico: La obsidiana de Kaminaljuyu-Miraflores II y Urías, Sacatepéquez. In *XII simposio de investigaciones arqueológicas en Guatemala, 1998*, edited by Juan Pedro Laporte and Hector Escobedo, pp. 905–910, vol. 2. Museo Nacional de Arqueología y Etnología, Guatemala City.

Braswell, Geoffrey E., E. Wyllys Andrews V, and Michael D. Glascock

1994 The Obsidian Artifacts of Quelepa, El Salvador. *Ancient Mesoamerica* 5:173–192.

Braswell, Geoffrey E., and Michael D. Glascock

1998 Interpreting Intrasource Variation in the Composition of

Obsidian: The Geoarchaeology of San Martín Jilotepeque, Guatemala. *Latin American Antiquity* 9:353–369.

Braswell, Geoffrey E., Joel D. Gunn, M. del R. Domínguez C., William J. Folan, Lorraine Fletcher, and Michael D. Glascock
n.d. Defining the Terminal Classic at Calakmul. In *The Terminal Classic in the Maya Lowlands: Collapse, Transition, and Transformation*, edited by Don S. Rice, Prudence M. Rice, and Arthur A. Demarest. Westview Press, Boulder.

Braswell, Geoffrey E., Joel D. Gunn, M. del R. Domínguez C., William J. Folan, and Michael D. Glascock
1998 Late and Terminal Classic Obsidian Procurement and Lithic Production at Calakmul, Campeche, Mexico. Paper presented at the 63rd Annual Meetings of the Society for American Archaeology (Seattle).

Braswell, Geoffrey E., Silvia Salgado González, and Michael D. Glascock
1995 La obsidiana guatemalteca en Centroamérica. In *VIII simposio de investigaciones arqueológicas en Guatemala, 1994*, edited by Juan Pedro Laporte and Hector Escobedo, pp. 121–131, vol. 1. Museo Nacional de Arqueología y Etnología, Guatemala.

Braswell, Geoffrey E., and T. Kam Manahan
2001 After the Fall: Obsidian Production and Exchange at Terminal Classic and Postclassic Copán. Paper presented at the 66th Annual Meeting of the Society for American Archaeology, New Orleans.

Braswell, Jennifer
1998 Archaeological Investigations at Group D, Xunantunich, Belize. Ph.D. dissertation, Department of Anthropology, Tulane University.

Braudel, Fernand
1980 *On History*. University of Chicago Press, Chicago.
1981 *The Structures of Everyday Life*. Translated by Sian Reynolds. Civilization and Capitalism, 15th–18th Century, vol. 1. Harper and Row, New York.
1982 *The Wheels of Commerce*. Translated by Sian Reynolds. Civilization and Capitalism, 15th–18th Century, vol. 2. Harper and Row, New York.
1984 *The Perspective of the World*. Translated by Sian Reynolds. Civilization and Capitalism, 15th–18th Century, vol. 3. Harper and Row, New York.
1986 *Civilization and Capitalism, 15th–18th Century*. Vol. 2, *The Wheels of Commerce*, and vol. 3, *The Perspective of the World*. Perennial Library Edition, Harper and Row, New York.

Bray, Warwick
1977 Maya Metalwork and Its External Connections. In *Social Process in Maya Prehistory*, edited by Norman Hammond, pp. 365–403. Academic Press, New York.
1989 Fine Metal Jewelry from Southern Mexico. In *Homenaje a José Luis Lorenzo*, edited by Lorena Mirambell, pp. 243–275. Colección Científica, vol. 188. Instituto Nacional de Antropología e Historia, Mexico City.

Bricker, Harvey M., Victoria R. Bricker, and Bettina Wulfing
1997 Determining the Historicity of Three Almanacs in the Madrid Codex. *Archaeoastronomy* 22:17–36.

Bricker, Victoria R.
n.d. Comparison of Maya Manuscripts with Borgia Group Codices, Class Notes from the 1999 Seminar "Mesoamerican Divinatory Manuscripts," Tulane University.

Bricker, Victoria R., and Gabrielle Vail (editors)
1997 *Papers on the Madrid Codex*. Publications, vol. 64. Middle American Research Institute, New Orleans.

Brinton, D. G.
1885 *The Annals of the Cakchiquels: The Original Text, With a Translation, Notes, and Introduction*, vol. 6. Library of Aboriginal American Literature, Philadelphia.

Brockington, Donald
1973 *Archaeological Investigations at Miahuatlan, Oaxaca*. Vanderbilt University Publications in Anthropology, no. 7.
1982 Spatial and Temporal Variations of the Mixtec-Style Ceramics in Southern Oaxaca. In *Aspects of the Mixteca-Puebla Style and Mixtec and Central Mexican Culture in Southern Mesoamerica*, edited by Jennifer S. H. Brown and E. Wyllys Andrews V, pp. 7–13. Occasional Paper, vol. 4. Middle American Research Institute, Tulane University, New Orleans.

Broda, Johanna
1987 The Provenience of the Offerings: Tribute and *Cosmovision*. In *The Aztec Templo Mayor*, edited by Elizabeth H. Boone, pp. 211–256. Dumbarton Oaks, Washington, D.C.

Brown, Kenneth L.
1983 Some Comments on Ethnohistory and Archaeology: Have We Attained (or Are We Even Approaching) a Truly Conjunctive Approach? *Reviews in Anthropology* 10(2):53–71.
1985 Postclassic Relationships between the Highland and Lowland Maya. In *The Lowland Maya Postclassic*, edited by Arlen F. Chase and Prudence M. Rice, pp. 270–281. University of Texas Press, Austin.

Bruce S., R., and C. Robles Uribe
1969 La lengua de Huehuetán (Waliwi). *Anales del Instituto Nacional de Antropología e Historia, Epoca 7* 1:115–122.

Brüggemann, Jürgen Kurt (editor)
1990 *Zempoala: El estudio de una ciudad prehispánica*. Serie Arqueología. Instituto Nacional de Antropología e Historia, Mexico City.
1994a Tajín en numeros. *Arqueología Mexicana* 1(5):57.
1994b La ciudad de Tajín. *Arqueología Mexicana* 1(5):26–30.

Brumfiel, Elizabeth M.
1980 Specialization, Market Exchange, and the Aztec State: A View From Huexotla. *Current Anthropology* 21:459–478.
1983 Aztec State Making: Ecology, Structure, and the Origin of the State. *American Anthropologist* 85:261–284.
1987a Consumption and Politics at Aztec Huexotla. *American Anthropologist* 89:676–686.
1987b Elite and Utilitarian Crafts in the Aztec State. In *Specialization, Exchange, and Complex Societies*, edited by Elizabeth M. Brumfiel and Timothy K. Earle, pp. 102–118. Cambridge University Press, New York.
1989 Factional Competition in Complex Society. In *Domination and Resistance*, edited by Daniel Miller, Michael Rowlands, and Christopher Tilley, pp. 127–139. Unwin Hyman, London.
1991 Agricultural Development and Class Stratification in the Southern Valley of Mexico. In *Land and Politics in the Valley of Mexico*, edited by Herbert R. Harvey, pp. 42–62. University of New Mexico Press, Albuquerque.
1996a The Quality of Tribute Cloth: The Place of Evidence in Archaeological Argument. *American Antiquity* 61:453–462.
1996b Figurines and the Aztec State: Testing the Effectiveness of Ideological Domination. In *Gender and Archaeology*,

edited by Rita P. Wright, pp. 143–166. University of Pennsylvania Press, Philadelphia.

1998 Huitzilopochtli's Conquest: Aztec Ideology in the Archaeological Record. *Cambridge Archaeological Journal* 8:3–14.

Brumfiel, Elizabeth M., and Timothy K. Earle

1987 Specialization, Exchange, and Complex Societies: An Introduction. In *Specialization, Exchange, and Complex Societies*, edited by Elizabeth M. Brumfiel and Timothy K. Earle, pp. 1–9. Cambridge University Press, New York.

Brumfiel, Elizabeth M., Tamara Salcedo, and David K. Schafer

1994 The Lip Plugs of Xaltocan: Function and Meaning in Aztec Archaeology. In *Economies and Polities in the Aztec Realm*, edited by Mary G. Hodge and Michael E. Smith, pp. 113–121. Institute for Mesoamerican Studies, Albany.

Brush, Charles F.

1962 Pre-Columbian Alloy Objects from Guerrero, Mexico. *Science* 138:1336–1337.

Bullard, William R., Jr.

1970 Topoxte: A Postclassic Maya Site in Peten, Guatemala. In *Monographs and Papers in Maya Archaeology*, edited by William R. Bullard, pp. 245–308. Papers, vol. 61. Peabody Museum, Harvard University, Cambridge.

Burgoa, Francisco de

1934a *Palestra historial*, vol. 24. Publicaciones del Archivo General de la Nación, Mexico City.

1934b *Geográfica descripción*, vols. 25–26. Publicaciones del Archivo General de la Nación, Mexico City.

Burkhart, Louise M.

1992 Flowery Heaven: The Aesthetic of Paradise in Nahuatl Devotional Literature. *Res* 21:89–109.

Butler, Mary

1959 Spanish Contact at Chipal. *Mitteilungen aus dem Museum für Völkerkunde und Vorgeschichte in Hamburg* 25:28–35.

Butterworth, Douglas

1962 Relaciones of Oaxaca of the Sixteenth and Eighteenth Centuries. Translated and edited by Douglas Butterworth. *Boletín de Estudios Oaxaqueños* 23:36–53.

Byland, Bruce E.

1980 Political and Economic Evolution in the Tamazulapan Valley, Mixteca Alta, Oaxaca, Mexico. Ph.D. dissertation, Department of Anthropology, Pennsylvania State University.

Byland, Bruce E., and John M. D. Pohl

1994a *In the Realm of 8 Deer: The Archaeology of the Mixtec Codices*. University of Oklahoma Press, Norman.

1994b Political Factions in the Transition from Classic to Postclassic in the Mixteca Alta. In *Factional Competition and Political Development in the New World*, edited by Elizabeth Brumfiel and John W. Fox, pp. 117–126. Cambridge University Press, Cambridge.

Cabrera C., Rubén

1976 Arqueología en el bajo Balsas, Guerrero y Michoacán: presa La Villita. M.A. thesis, Department of Anthropology, Escuela Nacional de Antropología e Historia.

1986 El desarrollo cultural prehispánico en la región del bajo río Balsas. In *Arqueología y etnohistoria del estado de Guerrero*, pp. 117–151. Instituto Nacional de Antropología e Historia y Gobierno del Estado de Guerrero, Mexico City.

1988 Nuevos resultados de Tzintzuntzan, Michoacán, en su décima temporada de excavaciones. In *Primera reunión sobre las sociedades prehispánicas en el centro occidente de México*, pp. 193–218. Instituto Nacional de Antropología e Historia, Mexico City.

Caley, Earle R., and Dudley T. Easby

1964 New Evidence of Tin Smelting and the Use of Metallic Tin in Preconquest Mexico. In *35th International Congress of Americanists*, pp. 507–517, vol. 1. Proceeding of the International Conference of Americanists, Mexico City.

Calnek, Edward E.

1988 *Highland Chiapas Before the Spanish Conquest*. Papers, vol. 55. New World Archaeological Foundation, Provo, UT.

Campbell, Lyle

1970 Nahua Loan Words in Quichean Languages. *Chicago Linguistic Society* 6:3–13.

1976 The Linguistic Prehistory of the Southern Mesoamerican Periphery. In *Las fronteras de mesoamérica (XIV Mesa Redonda)*, pp. 157–183, vol. 1. Sociedad Mexicana de Antropología, Mexico City.

1977 *Quichean Linguistic Prehistory*. University of California Press, Berkeley.

1985 *The Pipil Language of El Salvador*. Mouton, Berlin.

1988 *The Linguistics of Southeastern Chiapas, Mexico*. Papers, vol. 50. New World Archaeological Foundation, Provo, UT.

Canger, Una

1980 *Five Studies Inspired by Nahuatl Verbs in -oa*, vol. 19. Travaux du cercle linguistique de Copenhague, Copenhagen.

Carmack, Robert M.

1965 The Documentary Sources, Ecology, and Culture History of Pre-Hispanic Quiché-Maya of Highland Guatemala. Ph.D. dissertation, Department of Anthropology, UCLA.

1968 Toltec Influence on the Postclassic Culture History of Highland Guatemala. In *Archaeological Studies of Middle America*, pp. 42–92. Publication, vol. 26. Middle American Research Institute, Tulane University, New Orleans.

1973 *Quichean Civilization: The Ethnohistoric, Ethnographic, and Archaeological Sources*. University of California Press, Berkeley.

1977 Ethnohistory of the Central Quiché: The Community of Utatlán. In *Archaeology and Ethnohistory of the Central Quiche*, edited by Dwight T. Wallace and Robert M. Carmack, pp. 1–19. Publication, vol. 1. Institute for Mesoamerican Studies, Albany, NY.

1979 La verdadera identificación de Mixco Viejo. In *Historia social de los Quichés*, edited by Robert M. Carmcack, pp. 131–162. Editorial José de Pineda Ibarra, Ministerio de Educación, Guatemala City.

1981 *The Quiché Mayas of Utatlán: The Evolution of a Highland Guatemala Kingdom*. University of Oklahoma Press, Norman.

1996 Mesoamerica at Spanish Contact. In *The Legacy of Mesoamerica: History and Culture of a Native American Civilization*, edited by Robert M. Carmack, Janine Gasco, and Gary H. Gossen, pp. 80–121. Prentice-Hall, Englewood Cliffs, NJ.

Carmack, Robert M., and Lynn Larmer

1971 *Quichean Art: A Mixteca-Puebla Variant*. Miscellaneous Series, vol. 23. Museum of Anthropology, University of Northern Colorado, Greeley.

Carmack, Robert M., and J. L. Mondloch

1983   *El título de Totonicapán: Texto, traducción y comentario.* Universidad Nacional Autónoma de México, Mexico City.

Carmichael, Elizabeth

1970   *Turquoise Mosaics from Mexico.* British Museum, London.

Carr, Christopher, and Jill E. Neitzel (editors)

1995   *Style, Society, and Person: Archaeological and Ethnological Perspectives.* Plenum Press, New York.

Carrasco, David

1990   *Religions of Mesoamerica: Cosmovision and Ceremonial Centers.* Harper and Row, New York.

1991   *To Change Place: Aztec Ceremonial Landscapes.* University Press of Colorado, Boulder.

1999   *City of Sacrifice: The Aztec Empire and the Role of Violence in Civilization.* Beacon Press, Boston.

Carrasco, Pedro

1964   Los nombres de persona en la Guatemala antigua. *Estudios de Cultura Maya* 4:323–334.

1969   Nuevos datos sobre los Nonoalca de habla Mexicana en el reino Tarasco. *Estudios de Cultura Nahuatl* 8:215–221.

1972   La casa y hacienda de un señor Tlahuica. *Estudios de Cultura Náhuatl* 10:235–244.

1978   La economía de México prehispánica. In *Economía política e ideología en el México prehispánico*, edited by Pedro Carrasco and Johanna Broda, pp. 13–74. Nueva Imagen, Mexico City.

1981   Comment on Offner. *American Antiquity* 46:62–68.

1982   The Political Economy of the Aztec and Inca States. In *The Inca and Aztec States, 1400–1800: Anthropology and History*, edited by George Collier, Renato Rosaldo and John Wirth, pp. 23–40. Academic Press, New York.

1984   Royal Marriages in Ancient Mexico. In *Explorations in Ethnohistory: Indians of Central Mexico in the Sixteenth Century*, edited by Herbert R. Harvey and Hanns J. Prem, pp. 41–81. University of New Mexico Press, Albuquerque.

1986   Economía política en el reino tarasco. In *La sociedad indígena en el centro y occidente de México*, edited by Pedro Carrasco, pp. 63–102. El Colegio de Michoacán, Zamora.

1996a *Estructura político-territorial del imperio tenochca: La triple alianza de Tenochtitlan, Tetzcoco y Tlacopan.* Fondo de Cultura Económica y El Colegio de México, Mexico City.

1996b La Triple Alianza: Organización política y estructura territorial. In *Temas mesoamericanos*, edited by Sonia Lombardo and Enrique Nalda, pp. 167–210. Instituto Nacional de Antropología e Historia, Mexico City.

1999   *The Tenochca Empire of Ancient Mexico: The Triple Alliance of Tenochtitlan, Tetzcoco, and Tlacopan.* University of Oklahoma Press, Norman.

Carrasco, Pedro, and Johanna Broda (editors)

1976   *Estratificación social en la mesoamérica prehispánica.* Instituto Nacional de Antropología e Historia, Mexico City.

Carriveau, Gary W.

1976   Application of Thermoluminescence Dating Techniques to Prehistoric Metallurgy. In *Application of Science to the Examination of Works of Art*, edited by W. J. Young, pp. 58–67. Museum of Fine Arts, Boston.

Carsten, Janet and Stephen Hugh-Jones (editors)

1995   *About the House: Lévi-Strauss and Beyond.* Cambridge University Press, New York.

Caso, Alfonso

1927   Las ruinas de Tizatlán, Tlaxcala. *Revista Mexicana de Estudios Históricas* 1:139–172.

1938   *Exploraciones en Oaxaca, quinta y sexta temporadas, 1936–1937.* Publication, vol. 34. Instituto Panamericano de Geografía e Historia, Mexico City.

1949   El mapa de Teozacoalco. *Cuadernos Americanos* 7(5):145–181.

1958   *The Aztecs: People of the Sun.* University of Oklahoma Press, Norman.

1960   *Interpretation of the Codex Bodley 2858.* Sociedad Mexicana de Antropología, Mexico City.

1961   Los lienzos mixtecos de Ihuitlán y Antonio de León. In *Homenaje a Pablo Martínez del Rio en el XXV aniversario de la edición de "Los orígenes americanos,"* pp. 237–274. Instituto Nacional de Antropología e Historia, Mexico City.

1965   Lapidary Work, Goldwork, and Copperwork from Oaxaca. In *Archaeology of Southern Mesoamerica*, part 2, edited by Gordon R. Willey, pp. 896–930. Handbook of Middle American Indians, vol. 3. University of Texas Press, Austin.

1966   *Codex Colombino.* Sociedad Mexicana de Antropología, Mexico City.

1969   *El Tesoro de Monte Albán.* Memorias, vol. 3. Instituto Nacional de Antropología e Historia, Mexico City.

1977–
79   *Reyes y reinos de la mixteca.* 2 vols. Fondo de Cultura Económica, Mexico City.

Castillo Farreras, Victor M.

1974   Matrícula de Tributos, comentarios, paleografía, y versión. *Historia de México* 27–30:231–296. Salvat Editores de México, Mexico City.

Castillo Peña, Patricia

1995   *La expresión simbólica del Tajín.* Serie Arqueología, Colección Científica, vol. 306. Instituto Nacional de Antropología e Historia, Mexico City.

Castro Leal, Marcia

1986   *Tzintzuntzan, capital de los tarascos.* Gobierno del Estado de Michoacán, Morelia.

CDIU

1885–
1932   *Colección de documentas inéditos, relativos al descubrimiento, conquista, y organización de las antiguas posesiones españoles de ultramar.* 25 vols. Real Academia de la Historia, Madrid.

Chadwick, Robert

1971   Archaeological Synthesis of Michoacan and Adjacent Regions. In *Archaeology of Northern Mesoamerica*, part 2, edited by Gordon F. Ekholm and Ignacio Bernal, pp. 657–693. Handbook of Middle American Indians, vol. 11. University of Texas Press, Austin.

Chance, John K.

1996   The Caciques of Tecali: Class and Ethnic Identity in Late Colonial Mexico. *Hispanic American Historical Review* 76:475–502.

2000   The Noble House in Colonial Puebla, Mexico: Descent, Inheritance, and the Nahua Tradition. *American Anthropologist* 102:485–502.

Chapman, Anne C.

1957   Port of Trade Enclaves in the Aztec and Maya Civilizations. In *Trade and Market in the Early Empires*, edited by Karl Polanyi, Conrad M. Arensberg, and Harry W. Pearson, pp. 114–153. Free Press, Chicago.

Charlton, Thomas H.

1969a On the Identification of Obsidian Mines in Southern Hidalgo. *American Antiquity* 34:176–177.

1969b Texcoco Fabric-Marked Pottery, Tlateles, and Salt-Making. *American Antiquity* 34:73–76.

1994 Economic Heterogeneity and State Expansion: The Northeastern Basin of Mexico During the Late Post-classic Period. In *Economies and Polities in the Aztec Realm,* edited by Mary G. Hodge and Michael E. Smith, pp. 221–256. Institute for Mesoamerican Studies, Albany, NY.

Charlton, Thomas H., and Deborah L. Nichols

1997a The City-State Concept: Development and Applications. In *The Archaeology of City-States: Cross-Cultural Approaches*, edited by Deborah L. Nichols and Thomas H. Charlton, pp. 1–14. Smithsonian Institution Press, Washington, D.C.

1997b Diachronic Studies of City-States: Permutations on a Theme—Central Mexico from 1700 B.C. to A.D. 1600. In *The Archaeology of City-States: Cross-Cultural Approaches*, edited by Deborah L. Nichols and Thomas H. Charlton, pp. 169–208. Smithsonian Institution Press, Washington, D.C.

Charlton, Thomas H., Deborah L. Nichols, and Cynthia Otis Charlton

1991 Aztec Craft Production and Specialization: Archaeological Evidence from the City-State of Otumba, Mexico. *World Archaeology* 23:98–114.

Charlton, Thomas H., and Michael W. Spence

1982 Obsidian Exploitation and Civilization in the Basin of Mexico. In *Mining and Mining Techniques in Ancient Mesoamerica*, edited by Phil C. Weigand and Gretchen Gwynne, pp. 7–86, vol. 6. Anthropology, Stony Brook, NY.

Chase, Arlen F., and Prudence M. Rice (editors)

1985 *The Lowland Maya Postclassic*. University of Texas Press, Austin.

Chase, Diane Z.

1982 Spatial and Temporal Variability in Postclassic Northern Belize. Ph.D. dissertation, Department of Anthropology, University of Pennsylvania.

1985 Ganned But Not Forgotten: Late Postclassic Archaeology and Ritual at Santa Rita Corozal, Belize. In *The Lowland Maya Postclassic*, edited by Arlen F. Chase and Prudence M. Rice, pp. 104–125. University of Texas Press, Austin.

1986 Social and Political Organization in the Land of Cacao and Honey: Correlating the Archaeology and Ethnohistory of the Postclassic Lowland Maya. In *Late Lowland Maya Civilization: Classic to Postclassic*, edited by Jeremy A. Sabloff and E. Wyllys Andrews V, pp. 347–378. University of New Mexico Press, Albuquerque.

1988 Caches and Censerwares: Meaning from Maya Pottery. In *A Pot for All Reasons: Ceramic Ecology Revisited*, edited by Charles C. Kolb and Louana M. Lackey, pp. 81–104. Temple University, Laboratory of Anthropology, Philadelphia.

1992 Postclassic Maya Elites: Ethnohistory and Archaeology. In *Mesoamerican Elites: An Archaeological Assessment*, edited by Diane Z. Chase and Arlen F. Chase, pp. 118–134. University of Oklahoma Press, Norman.

Chase, Diane Z., and Arlen F. Chase

1982 Yucatec Influence in Terminal Classic Northern Belize. *American Antiquity* 47:596–614.

1988 *A Postclassic Perspective: Excavations at the Maya Site of Santa Rita Corozal, Belize.* Monograph, vol. 4. Precolumbian Art Research Institute, San Francisco.

Chase-Dunn, Christopher, and Thomas D. Hall

1991 Conceptualizing Core/Periphery Hierarchies for Comparative Study. In *Core/Periphery Relations in Precapitalist Worlds*, edited by Christopher Chase-Dunn and Thomas D. Hall, pp. 5–44. Westview Press, Boulder.

1997 *Rise and Demise: Comparing World-Systems.* Westview Press, Boulder.

Chaudhuri, K. N.

1991 Reflections on the Organizing Principle of Premodern Trade. In *The Political Economy of Merchant Empires*, edited by James D. Tracy, pp. 421–442. Cambridge University Press, New York.

Chernykh, Evgenij N.

1992 *Ancient Metallurgy in the USSR: The Early Metal Age.* Cambridge University Press, Cambridge.

Chung, H. J.

1993 *Análisis tipológico y petrográfico de la cerámica arqueológica de Chichén Itzá, Yucatán.* Licenciatura thesis, Escuela Nacional de Antropología e Historia, Mexico City.

Ciudad Real, Antonio de

1976 *Tratado curioso y docto de las grandezas de la Nueva España.* Serie de Historiadores y Cronistas de Indias, vol. 6. Edited by Josefina García Quintana and Victor M. Castillo Farreras. Instituto de Investigaciones Históricas, Universidad Nacional Autónoma de México, Mexico City.

Clark, James C. (editor)

1938 *Codex Mendoza: The Mexican Manuscript Known as the Collection of Mendoza Preserved in the Bodleian Library, Oxford.* 3 vols. Waterlow and Sons, London.

Clark, John E.

1986 From Mountains to Molehills: A Critical Review of Teotihuacan's Obsidian Industry. In *Economic Aspects of Prehispanic Highland Mexico*, edited by Barry L. Isaac, pp. 23–74. Research in Economic Anthropology, Supplement, vol. 2. JAI Press, Greenwich, CT.

1989 Obsidian Tool Manufacture. In *Ancient Trade and Tribute: Economies of the Soconusco Region of Mesoamerica*, edited by Barbara Voorhies, pp. 215–228. University of Utah Press, Salt Lake City.

1991 The Beginnings of Mesoamerica: Apologia for the Soconusco Early Formative. In *The Formation of Complex Society in Souteastern Mesoamerica*, edited by William L. Fowler, pp. 13–26. CRC Press, Boca Raton.

Clark, John E., and Michael Blake

1994 The Power of Prestige: Competitive Generosity and the Emergence of Rank Societies in Lowland Mesoamerica. In *Factional Competition and Political Development in the New World*, edited by Elizabeth M. Brumfiel and John W. Fox, pp. 17–30. Cambridge University Press, New York.

Clark, John E., and Stephen D. Houston

1998 Craft Specialization, Gender, and Personhood Among the Post-Conquest Maya of Yucatan, Mexico. In *Craft and Social Identity*, edited by Cathy Lynne Costin and Rita P. Wright, pp. 31–49. Archaeological Papers of the

American Anthropological Association, vol. 8. American Anthropological Association, Washington, D.C.

Clark, John E., Thomas A. Lee Jr., and Tamara Salcedo Romero
1989   The Distribution of Obsidian. In *Ancient Trade and Tribute: Economies of the Soconusco Region of Mesoamerica*, edited by Barbara Voorhies, pp. 268–284. University of Utah Press, Salt Lake City.

Clark, John E., Thomas A. Lee Jr., and Tamara Salcedo
1991   La distribución de la obsidiana. In *La economía del antiguo Soconusco, Chiapas*, edited by Barbara Voorhies, pp. 313–331. Translated by Raúl del Moral. Universidad Nacional Autónoma de México and Universidad Autónoma de Chiapas, Mexico City.

Clark, John E., and Tamara Salcedo Romero
1989   Ocós Obsidian Distribution in Chiapas, Mexico. In *New Frontiers in the Archaeology of the Pacific Coast of Southern Mesoamerica*, edited by Frederick J. Bové and Lynette Heller, pp. 15–24. Arizona State University Anthropological Research Papers, vol. 39. Arizona State University, Tempe.

Clendinnen, Inga
1987   *Ambivalent Conquests: Maya and Spaniard in Yucatán, 1517–1570*. Cambridge University Press, Cambridge.

Cline, S. L.
1986   *Colonial Culhuacan, 1580–1600: A Social History of an Aztec Town*. University of New Mexico Press, Albuquerque.
1993   *The Book of Tributes: Early Sixteenth-Century Nahuatl Censuses from Morelos*. U.C.L.A. Latin American Center, Los Angeles.

Cobb, Charles R., Jeffrey Maymon, and Randall H. McGuire
1999   Feathered, Horned, and Antlered Serpents: Mesoamerican Connections with the Southwest and Southeast. In *Great Towns and Regional Polities in the Prehistoric American Southwest and Southeast*, edited by Jill E. Neitzel, pp. 165–182. University of New Mexico Press, Albuquerque.

Cobean, Robert H.
1991   Principales yacimientos de obsidiana en el altiplano central. *Arqueología* 5:9–31.

Cobean, Robert H., and Alba Guadalupe Mastache
1989   The Late Classic and Early Postclassic Chronology of the Tula Region. In *Tula of the Toltecs: Excavations and Survey*, edited by Dan M. Healan, pp. 34–46. University of Iowa Press, Iowa City.

Cobos, Rafael
1998   Chichén Itzá y el Clásico Terminal en las tierras bajas mayas. In *XI simposio de investigaciones arqueológicas en Guatemala, 1997*, edited by Juan Pedro Laporte and Hector Escobedo, pp. 791–801, vol. 2. Museo Nacional de Arqueología y Etnología, Guatemala City.

Codex Borbonicus
1974   *Codex Borbonicus. Bibliothéque de l'Assemblée Nationale, Paris (Y 120)*. Edited with commentary by Karl Anton Nowotny and Jacqueline de Durand-Forest. Akademische Druck- u. Verlagsanstalt, Graz.

Codex Fejéváry-Mayer
1971   *Codex Fejéváry-Mayer, 12014 M. City of Liverpool Museums*. Edited by Cottie A. Burland. Akademische Druck- u. Verlagsanstalt, Graz.

Codex Magliabechiano
1970   *Codex Magliabechiano, CL. XIII.3 (B.R. 232), Biblioteca Nazionale Centrale di Firenze*. Edited by Ferdinand Anders. Akademisch Druck- u. Verlagsanstalt, Graz.

Codex Mexicanus
1952   Codex Mexicanus Nos. 23–24 de la Bibliothèque Nationale de Paris. *Journal de la Société des Américanistes* 41 (Supplement).

Codex Nuttall
1975   *The Codex Nuttall: A Picture Manuscript from Ancient Mexico*. Edited by Zelia Nuttall and Arthur G. Miller. Dover Publications, New York.

Códice Borbónico
1981   *Códice Borbónico: Manuscrito mexicano de la Biblioteca del Palais Bourbon (libro adivinatorio y ritual ilustrado) publicado en facsímil*. Siglo Veintiuno, Mexico City.

Coe, Michael D.
1961   *La Victoria: An Early Site on the Pacific Coast of Guatemala*. Papers, vol. 53. Peabody Museum of Archaeology and Ethnology, Cambridge.
1973   *The Maya Scribe and His World*. The Grolier Club, New York.
1999   *The Maya*. 6th ed. Thames and Hudson, New York.

Coe, Michael D., and Kent V. Flannery
1967   *Early Cultures and Human Ecology in South Coastal Guatemala*. Contributions to Anthropology, vol. 3. Smithsonian Institution, Washington, D.C.

Coe, Sophie D., and Michael D. Coe
1996   *The True History of Chocolate*. Thames and Hudson, New York.

Coggins, Clemency, and Orrin C. Shane (editors)
1984   *Cenote of Sacrifice: Maya Treasures from the Sacred Well at Chichen Itza*. University of Texas Press, Austin.

Cohen, Mark Nathan
1977   *The Food Crisis in Prehistory: Overpopulation and the Origins of Agriculture*. Yale University Press, New Haven.

Columbus, Ferdinand
1959   *The Life of the Admiral Christopher Columbus by his Son Ferdinand*. Translated by Benjamin Keen. Rutgers University Press, New Brunswick.

Conkey, Margaret W., and Christine A. Hastorf (editors)
1990   *The Uses of Style in Archaeology*. Cambridge University Press, New York.

Connor, Judith G.
1983   The Ceramics of Cozumel, Quintana Roo, Mexico. Ph.D. dissertation, Department of Anthropology, University of Arizona.

Contreras Ramírez, José Antonio
1985   *La presencia tarasca en el estado de Guanajuato: Fluctuación de frontera*. Licenciatura thesis, Universidad de Veracruz.

Cook, Scott
1966   The Obsolete "Anti-Market" Mentality: A Critique of the Substantive Approach to Economic Anthropology. *American Anthropologist* 68:323–345.
1982   *Zapotec Stoneworkers: The Dynamics of Rural Simple Commodity Production in Modern Mexican Capitalism*. University Press of America, Lanham, MD.

Cooper, Frederick
1993   Africa and the World Economy. In *Confronting Historical Paradigms*, edited by F. Cooper, A. F. Isaacman, F. E. Mallon, W. Roseberry, and S. J. Stern, pp. 84–186. University of Wisconsin Press, Madison.

Cortés, Hernán
1961   *Cartas de relación de la conquista de México*. Espasa-Calpe Mexicana, Mexico City.

1971   *Letters from Mexico*. Translated by A. R. Pagden. Orion Press, New York.

Costin, Cathy L.
1991   Craft Specialization: Issues in Defining, Documenting, and Explaining the Organization of Production. In *Archaeological Method and Theory*, edited by Michael B. Schiffer, pp. 1–56, vol. 3. University of Arizona, Tucson.

Coto, T. de
1983   *[Thesavrvs verbore]*. Edited by René Acuña. Universidad Autónoma de México, Mexico City.

Covarrubias V., Manuel
1961   Notas para el estudio de la arqueología de la costa de Jalisco. *Eco* 7:4–7.

Cowgill, George L.
1979   Teotihuacan, Internal Militaristic Competition, and the Fall of the Classic Maya. In *Maya Archaeology and Ethnohistory*, edited by Norman Hammond and Gordon R. Willey, pp. 51–62. University of Texas Press, Austin.
1996   Discussion, Special Section: Recent Chronological Research in Central Mexico. *Ancient Mesoamerica* 7:325–332.

Craddock, Paul T.
1995   *Early Metal Mining and Production*. Smithsonian Institution, Washington, D.C.

Craine, Eugene R., and Reginald C. Reindorp
1970   *The Chronicles of Michoacan*. University of Oklahoma Press, Norman.

Cramp, D. C.
1998   Pre-Columbian Beekeeping in the Americas. *American Bee Journal* 138:451–456.

Crespo M., M.
1956   Títulos indígenas de tierras. *Antropología e Historia de Guatemala* 8(2):10–15.

Cruz Antillón, Rafael
1994   *Análisis arqueológico del yacimiento de obsidiana de Sierra de las Navajas, Hidalgo*. Colección Científica, vol. 281. Instituto Nacional de Antropología e Historia, Mexico City.

Cruz Antillón, Rafael, and Alejandro Pastrana
1994   Sierra de Las Navajas, Hidalgo: Nuevas investigaciones sobre la explotación prehispánica de obsidiana. In *Simposio sobre arqueología en el estado de Hidalgo*, edited by E. Fernández Dávila, pp. 31–45. Instituto Nacional de Antropología e Historia, Mexico City.

Culbert, T. Patrick
1988   The Collapse of Classic Maya Civilization. In *The Collapse of Ancient States and Civilizations*, edited by Norman Yoffee and George Cowgill, pp. 69–101. University of Arizona Press, Tucson.

Culebro, Carlos A.
1975   *Monografía histórica de Chiapas, la zona costera de Soconusco a través e su historia*. Editorial Culebro, Huixtla, Mexico.

Curet, L. Antonio, Barbara L. Stark, and Sergio Vásquez Z.
1994   Postclassic Changes in Veracruz, Mexico. *Ancient Mesoamerica* 5:13–32.

Dahlgren, Barbro
1990a   *La grana cochinilla*. Instituto de Investigaciones Antropológicas, Universidad Nacional Autónoma de México, Mexico City.
1990b   *La mixteca: Su cultura e historia prehispánicas*. 2nd ed. Universidad Nacional Autónoma de México, Mexico City.

Dahlin, Bruce H., Anthony P., Andrews, Timothy Beach, C. Bezanilla, Pat Farrell, Sheryl Luzzadder-Beach, and Valery McCormick
1998   Punta Canbalam in Context: A Peripatetic Coastal Site in Northwest Campeche, Mexico. *Ancient Mesoamerica* 9:1–15.

Dandamayev, Muhammed
1996   An Age of Privatization in Ancient Mesopotamia. In *Privatization in the Ancient Near East and Classical World*, edited by Michael Hudson and Baruch A. Levine, pp. 197–222. Peabody Museum Bulletin, vol. 5. Peabody Museum of Archaeology and Ethnology, Harvard University, Cambridge.

Daneels, Anick
1997   Settlement History in the Lower Cotaxtla Basin. In *Olmec to Aztec: Settlement Patterns in the Ancient Gulf Lowlands*, edited by Barbara L. Stark and Philip J. Arnold III, pp. 206–252. University of Arizona Press, Tucson.

Daneels, Anick, and Alejandro Pastrana
1988   Aprovechamiento de la obsidiana del Pico de Orizaba: El caso de la cuenca baja del Jamapa-Cotaxtla. *Arqueología* 4:99–120.

Darling, J., Andrew
1998   Obsidian Distribution and Exchange in the North-Central Frontier of Mesoamerica. Ph.D. dissertation, Department of Anthropology, University of Michigan.

Darras, Véronique
1998   La obsidiana en la *Relación de Michoacán* y en la realidad arqueológica: Del símbolo al uso o del uso de un símbolo. In *Génesis, culturas y espacios en Michoacán*, edited by Véronique Darras, pp. 61–88. Centre d'Études Mexicaines et Centroaméricanes, Mexico City.
1999   *Tecnologías prehispánicas de la obsidiana: Los centros de producción de la región de Zináparo-Prieto, Michoacán*. Cuadernos de Estudios Michoacanos, vol. 9. Centre d'Études Mexicaines et Centroaméricanes, Mexico City.

Davies, Nigel
1968   *Los señoríos independientes del imperio azteca*. Instituto Nacional de Antropología e Historia, Mexico City.
1973   *The Aztecs: A History*. University of Oklahoma, Norman.
1977   *The Toltecs Until the Fall of Tula*. University of Oklahoma Press, Norman.
1978   The Military Organization of the Aztec Empire. In *Mesoamerican Communication Routes and Cultural Contacts*, edited by Thomas A. Lee Jr., and Carlos Navarrete, pp. 223–230. Papers, vol. 40. New World Archaeological Foundation, Provo, UT.
1980   *The Toltec Heritage: From the Fall of Tula to the Rise of Tenochtitlan*. University of Oklahoma Press, Norman.

Davila, Diana Z. de
1975   El proyecto arqueológico Cuauhtinchan y la constatación arqueología de algunos rasgos del mapa de la ruta Chicomoztoc-Cuahtinchan (mapa no. 2). In *XIII Mesa Redonda*, pp. 223–230, vol. 1. Sociedad Mexicana de Antropología, Xalapa, Mexico.

Day, Jane Stevenson
1994   Central Mexican Imagery in Greater Nicoya. In *Mixteca-Puebla: Discoveries and Research in Mesoamerican Art and Archaeology*, edited by H. B. Nicholson and Eloise Quiñones Keber, pp. 235–248. Labyrinthos, Culver City, CA.

Deal, Michael
1988   An Ethnoarchaeological Approach to the Identification

of Maya Domestic Pottery Production. In *Ceramic Ecology Revisited, 1987: The Technology and Socioeconomics of Pottery*, edited by Charles C. Kolb and Louanna Lackey, pp. 111–142. BAR International series, vol. 436. British Archaeological Reports, Oxford.

DeBoer, Warren R.
1985   Pots and Pans Do Not Speak, nor Do They Lie: The Case for Occasional Reductionism. In *Decoding Prehistoric Ceramics*, edited by Ben A. Nelson, pp. 347–358. Southern Illinois University, Carbondale.

Delgado, Agustín
1965   *Archaeological Reconnaissance in the Region of Tehuantepec, Oaxaca, Mexico*. Papers, vol. 18. New World Archaeological Foundation, Provo, UT.

Demarest, Arthur A.
1997   The Vanderbilt Petexbatun Regional Archaeological Project 1989–1994: Overview, History, and Major Results of a Multidisciplinary Study of the Classic Maya Collapse. *Ancient Mesoamerica* 8:209–228.

DeMarrais, Elizabeth, Luis Jaime Castillo, and Timothy Earle
1996   Ideology, Materialization, and Power Strategies. *Current Anthropology* 37:15–31.

De Vos, Jan
1994   *Viven en frontera: La experiencia de los indios de Chiapas*. Historia de los pueblos indigenas de México. Edited by Teresa Rojas Rabiela and Mario Humberto Ruz. CIESAS and INI, Mexico City.

Díaz del Castillo, Bernal
1984   *Historia verdadera de la conquista de la Nueva España*. 6th ed. Espasa-Calpe, Madrid.

Diehl, Richard A.
1981   Tula. In *Archaeology*, edited by Victoria R. Bricker and Jeremy A. Sabloff, pp. 277–295. Supplement to the Handbook of Middle American Indians, vol. 1. University of Texas Press, Austin.
1983   *Tula: The Toltec Capital of Ancient Mexico*. Thames and Hudson, New York.
1993   The Toltec Horizon in Mesoamerica: New Perspectives on an Old Issue. In *Latin American Horizons*, edited by Don S. Rice, pp. 263–294. Dumbarton Oaks, Washington, D.C.

Diehl, Richard A., and Janet Berlo (editors)
1989   *Mesoamerica After the Decline of Teotihuacan, A.D. 700–900*. Dumbarton Oaks, Washington, D.C.

Diehl, Richard A., and Margaret Mandeville
1987   Tula and Wheeled Animal Effigies in Mesoamerica. *Antiquity* 61:239–246.

Digrius, Dawn Mooney, and Marilyn A. Masson
2001   Further Investigations at Structure 1, Caye Coco. In *The Belize Postclassic Project 2000: Investigations at Caye Coco and the Shore Settlements of Progresso Lagoon*, edited by Robert M. Rosenswig and Marilyn A. Masson, pp. 5–26. Occasional Publication, vol. 6. Institute for Mesoamerican Studies, Albany, NY.

Dillon, Brian
1977   *Salinas de los Nueve Cerros, Alta Verapaz, Guatemala: Preliminary Investigations*. Studies in Mesoamerican Art, Archaeology, and Ethnohistory, vol. 2. Ballena Press, Socorro, NM.

DiPeso, Charles C.
1974   *Casas Grandes: Fallen Trading Center of the Gran Chichimeca*. 3 vols. Amerind Foundation, Dragoon, AZ.

Dockall, J. E., and Harry J. Shafer
1993   Testing the Producer-Consumer Model for Santa Rita Corozal, Belize. *Latin American Antiquity* 4:158–179.

Donkin, R. A.
1979   *Agricultural Terracing in the Aboriginal New World*. Viking Fund Publications in Anthropology, vol. 56. University of Arizona Press, Tucson.

Doolittle, William E.
1990   *Canal Irrigation in Prehistoric Mexico: The Sequence of Technological Change*. University of Texas Press, Austin.

Douglas, Mary, and Baron Isherwood
1979   *The World of Goods: Toward an Anthropology of Consumption*. Basic Books, New York.

Dreiss, Meredith L.
1988   *Obsidian at Colha, Belize: A Technological Analysis and Distributional Study Based on Trace Element Data*. Papers of the Colha Project, vol. 4. Texas Archaeological Research Laboratory, University of Texas, San Antonio.
1994   The Shell Artifacts of Colha: The 1983 Season. In *Continuing Archaeology at Colha, Belize*, edited by Thomas R. Hester, Harry J. Shafer, and Jack D. Eaton, pp. 177–200. Studies in Archaeology, vol. 16. Texas Archaeological Research Laboratory, Austin.

Dreiss, Meredith L., and David O. Brown
1989   Obsidian Exchange Patterns in Belize. In *Prehistoric Maya Economies of Belize*, edited by Patricia A. McAnany and Barry L. Isaac, pp. 57–90. Research in Economic Anthropology, Supplement, vol. 4. JAI Press, Greenwich, CT.

Dreiss, Meredith L., K. S. Stryker, David O. Brown, Thomas R. Hester, Michael D. Glascock, and Hector Neff
1993   Expanding the Role of Trace-Element Studies: Obsidian Use in the Late and Terminal Classic Periods at the Lowland Maya Site of Colha, Belize. *Ancient Mesoamerica* 4:271–283.

Drennan, Robert D.
1984a   Long-Distance Transport Costs in Pre-Hispanic Mesoamerica. *American Anthropologist* 86:105–112.
1984b   Long-Distance Movement of Goods in the Mesoamerican Formative and Classic. *American Antiquity* 49:27–43.

Drucker, Philip
1948   Preliminary Notes on an Archaeological Survey of the Chiapas Coast. *Middle American Research Records* 1:151–169.

Dumézil, G.
1973   *The Destiny of a King*. University of Chicago Press, Chicago.

Dunning, Nicholas P., and Jeff K. Kowalski
1994   Lords of the Hills: Classic Maya Settlement Patterns and Political Iconography in the Puuc Region, Mexico. *Ancient Mesoamerica* 5:63–95.

Durán, Fray Diego
1967   *Historia de las Indias de Nueva España*. Translated by Edited by Angel M. Garibay K. 2 vols. Porrúa, Mexico City.
1971   *Book of the Gods and Rites and the Ancient Calendar*. Translated by Fernando Horcasitas and Doris Heyden. University of Oklahoma Press, Norman.
1994   *The History of the Indies of New Spain*. Translated by Doris Heyden. University of Oklahoma Press, Norman.

Du Solier, Wilfrido
1946   Primer fresco mural Huaxteco. *Cuadernos Americanos* 30(6):151–159.

Dyckerhoff, Ursula, and Hans S. Prem
1976   La estratificación social en Huexotzinco. In *Estratificación social en la mesoamérica prehispánica*, edited by

Pedro Carrasco and Johanna Broda, pp. 157–180. Instituto Nacional de Antropología e Historia, Mexico City.

Earle, Timothy K.
1997 *How Chiefs Came to Power: The Political Economy in Prehistory*. Stanford University Press, Stanford.

Easby, Dudley T., Earle R. Caley, and Khosrow Moazed
1967 Axe-Money: Facts and Speculation. *Revista Méxicana de Estudios Antropológicos* 21:107–148.

Eaton, Jack D.
1978 Archaeological Survey of the Yucatán-Campeche Coast. In *Studies in the Archaeology of Coastal Yucatán and Campeche, Mexico*, pp. 1–67. Publication, vol. 46. Middle American Research Institute, Tulane University, New Orleans.

Eaton, Jack D., and Joseph W. Ball
1978 *Studies in the Archaeology of Coastal Yucatán and Campeche, Mexico*. Publication, vol. 46. Middle American Research Institute, Tulane University, New Orleans.

Edmonson, Munro S.
1982 *The Ancient Future of the Itzá: The Book of Chilam Balam of Tizimín*. University of Texas Press, Austin.
1986 *Heaven Born Mérida and Its Destiny: The Book of Chilam Balam of Chumayel*. University of Texas Press, Austin.

Edwards, Clinton R.
1978 Pre-Columbian Maritime Trade in Mesoamerica. In *Mesoamerican Communication Routes and Cultural Contacts*, edited by Thomas A. Jr. Lee and Carlos Navarrete, pp. 199–210. Papers, vol. 40. New World Archaeological Foundation, Provo, UT.

Ekholm, Gordon R.
1942 *Excavations at Guasava, Sinaloa, Mexico*. Anthropological Papers, vol. 38, pt. 2. American Museum of Natural History, New York.

Ekholm, Susanna M.
1969 *Mound 30a and the Early Preclassic Ceramic Sequence of Izapa, Chiapas, Mexico*. Papers, vol. 25. New World Archaeological Foundation, Provo, UT.

Elam, J. Michael
1993 Obsidian Exchange in the Valley of Oaxaca, Mexico, 2500–500 B.P. Ph.D. dissertation, Department of Anthropology, University of Missouri.

Elam, J. Michael, Michael D. Glascock, and Hector Neff
1992 Source Identification and Hydration Dating of Obsidian Artifacts from Oaxaca, Mexico: Preliminary Results. Paper presented at the 28th International Symposium on Archaeometry (Los Angeles).

Elkins, James
1996 Style. In *The Dictionary of Art*, edited by Jane Turner, pp. 876–883, vol. 29. Macmillan and Grove Dictionaries, London and New York.

Elton, Hugh
1996 *Frontiers of the Roman Empire*. Indiana University Press, Bloomington.

Elvin, Mark
1973 *The Pattern of the Chinese Past*. Stanford University Press, Stanford.

Erasmus, Charles J.
1968 Thoughts on Upward Collapse: An Essay on Explanation in Anthropology. *Southwest Journal of Anthropology* 24:170–194.

Escalona Ramos, A.
1946 Algunas ruinas prehispánicas en Quintana Roo. *Boletín de la Sociedad Mexicana de Geografía y Estadística* 61:513–628.

Esparza López, Juan Rodrigo
1999 *Aplicación de las técnicas nucleares PIXE y NAA para el estudio de las redes de comercio de la obsidiana en Tierra Caliente, Michoacán*. Licenciatura thesis, Escuela Nacional de Antropología e Historia, Mexico City.

Evans, Susan T.
1980 Spatial Analysis of Basin of Mexico Settlement: Problems with the Use of the Central Place Model. *American Antiquity* 45:866–875.
1990 The Productivity of Maguey Terrace Agriculture in Central Mexico During the Aztec Period. *Latin American Antiquity* 1:117–132.
1991 Architecture and Authority in an Aztec Village: Form and Function of the Tecpan. In *Land and Politics in the Valley of Mexico: A Two Thousand Year Perspective*, edited by Herbert R. Harvey, pp. 63–92. University of New Mexico Press, Albuquerque.

Evans, Susan Toby, and AnnCorinne Freter
1996 Teotihuacan Valley, Mexico, Postclassic Chronology: Hydration Analysis of Obsidian from Cihuatecpan, an Aztec-Period Village. *Ancient Mesoamerica* 7:267–280.

Ewald, Ursula
1985 *The Mexican Salt Industry, 1560–1980: A Study in Change*. Gustav Fischer Verlag, Stuttgart.

Fahmel Beyer, Bernd
1988 *Mesoamérica Tolteca: Sus cerámicas de comercio principales*. Universidad Nacional Autónoma de México, Mexico City.

Farriss, Nancy M.
1984 *Maya Society Under Colonial Rule: The Collective Enterprise of Survival*. Princeton University Press, Princeton, NJ.

Fauman-Fichman, Ruth
1999 Postclassic Craft Production in Morelos, Mexico: The Cotton Thread Industry in the Provinces. Ph.D. dissertation, Department of Anthropology, University of Pittsburgh.

Fedick, Scott
1991 Chert Production and Consumption Among Classic Period Maya Households. In *Maya Stone Tools*, edited by Thomas R. Hester and Harry J. Shafer, pp. 102–118. Prehistory Press, Madison.

Feinman, Gary M.
1982 Patterns in Ceramic Production and Distribution, Periods Early I through V. In *Monte Alban's Hinterland, Part 1, The Prehispanic Settlement Patterns of the Central and Southern Parts of the Valley of Oaxaca*, edited by Richard E. Blanton, Stephen Kowalewski, Gary M. Feinman, and Jill Appel, pp. 181–206. Memoirs, vol. 15. Museum of Anthropology, University of Michigan, Ann Arbor.
1985 Changes in the Organization of Ceramic Production in Pre-Hispanic Oaxaca, Mexico. In *Decoding Prehistoric Ceramics*, edited by Ben A. Nelson, pp. 195–223. Southern Illinois University Press, Carbondale.
1994 Toward an Archaeology without Polarization: Comments on Contemporary Theory. In *Caciques and Their People: A Volume in Honor of Ronald Spores*, edited by Joyce Marcus and Judith F. Zeitlin, pp. 13–43. Anthropological Papers, vol. 89. Museum of Anthropology, University of Michigan, Ann Arbor.
1997 Thoughts on New Approaches to Combining the Archaeological and Historical Records. In *Journal of Archaeological Method and Theory* 4(3/4):367–377. Special issue: New Approaches to Combining the Ar-

chaeological and Historical Records (S. Kepecs and
M. Kolb, guest editors).

1999a The Changing Structure of Macroregional Mesoamerica: The Classic-Postclassic Transition in the Valley
of Oaxaca. In *World-Systems Theory in Practice: Leadership, Production, and Exchange*, edited by P. Nick
Kardulias, pp. 53–62. Rowman and Littlefield, Lanham,
MD.

1999b Rethinking Our Assumptions: Economic Specialization
at the Household Scale in Ancient Ejutla, Oaxaca, Mexico. In *Pottery and People: Dynamic Interactions*, edited
by James M. Skibo and Gary M. Feinman, pp. 81–98.
University of Utah Press, Salt Lake City.

Feinman, Gary M., Sherman Banker, Reid F. Cooper, Glen B.
Cook, and Linda M. Nicholas

1989 A Technological Perspective on Changes in the Ancient
Oaxacan Grayware Ceramic Tradition: Preliminary
Results. *Journal of Field Archaeology* 16:331–344.

Feinman, Gary M., Stephen A. Kowalewski, and
Richard E. Blanton

1984 Modeling Ceramic Production and Organizational
Change in the Pre-Hispanic Valley of Oaxaca, Mexico.
In *The Many Dimensions of Pottery: Ceramics in Archaeology and Anthropology*, edited by Sander E. van
der Leeuw and Alison C. Pritchard, pp. 295–353. University of Amsterdam, Amsterdam.

Feinman, Gary M., and Linda M. Nicholas

1991 New Perspectives on Prehispanic Highland Mesoamerica: A Macroregional Approach. *Comparative Civilizations Review* 24:13–33.

1992 Pre-Hispanic Interregional Interaction in Southern
Mexico: The Valley of Oaxaca and the Ejutla Valley. In
Resources, Power, and Interregional Interaction, edited
by Edward M. Schortman and Patricia A. Urban, pp.
75–116. Plenum Press, New York.

1993 Shell-Ornament Production at Ejutla: Implications for
Highland-Coastal Interaction in Ancient Oaxaca. *Ancient Mesoamerica* 4:103–119.

Feldman, Lawrence H.

1978 Moving Merchandise in Protohistoric Central
Quauhtemallan. In *Mesoamerican Communication
Routes and Cultural Contacts.*, edited by Thomas A. Lee
Jr. and Carlos Navarrete, pp. 7–17. Papers, vol. 40. New
World Archaeological Foundation, Provo, UT.

1985 *A Tumpline Economy: Production and Distribution
Systems in Sixteenth-Century Eastern Guatemala.*
Labyrinthos, Culver City, CA.

Fernández Tejedo, Isabel

1996 Intercambio sin mercados entre los mayas de las tierras
bajas. In *Temas mesoamericanos*, edited by Sonia Lombardo and Enrique Nalda, pp. 111–134. Instituto Nacional de Antropología e Historia, Mexico City.

Ferriz, H.

1985 Caltonac, a Prehispanic Obsidian-Mining Center in
Eastern Mexico? A Preliminary Report. *Journal of Field
Archaeology* 12:363–370.

Figueira, Thomas J.

1984 Karl Polanyi and Ancient Greek Trade: The Port of
Trade. *Ancient World* 10:15–30.

Fisher, Christopher, Helen P. Pollard, and Charles Frederick

1999 Intensive Agriculture and Socio-Political Development in
the Lake Pátzcuaro Basin, Michoacán, Mexico. *Antiquity* 73:642–649.

Flannery, Kent V.

1968 The Olmec and the Valley of Oaxaca: A Model for Inter-

regional Interaction in Formative Times. In *Dumbarton
Oaks Conference on the Olmec*, edited by Elizabeth
Benson, pp. 79–110. Dumbarton Oaks, Washington,
D.C.

1983 Major Monte Alban V Sites: Zaachila, Xoxocotlan,
Cuilapan, Yagul, and Abasolo. In *The Cloud People:
Divergent Evolution of the Zapotec and Mixtec Civilizations*, edited by Kent V. Flannery and Joyce Marcus,
pp. 290–294. Academic Press, New York.

Flannery, Kent V., and Joyce Marcus (editors)

1983 *The Cloud People: Divergent Evolution of the Zapotec
and Mixtec Civilizations.* Academic Press, New York.

Flores, Teodoro

1946 *Geología minera de la region NE. del estado de Mi-
choacán.* Boletín Instituto Geológico de México, vol. 52.
Universidad Nacional Autónoma de México, Mexico
City.

Florescano, Enrique

1993 *El mito de Quetzalcóatl.* Fondo de Cultura Económica,
Mexico City.

Flores de Aguirrezabal, María Dolores, and César A. Quijada L.

1980 Distribución de objetos de metal en el occidente de México. In *Rutas de intercambio en Mesoamérica y norte de
México: XVI mesa redonda (Saltillo, 1979)*, pp. 83–92,
vol. 2. Sociedad Mexicana de Antropología, Mexico
City.

Ford, Anabel, Fred Stross, Frank Asaro, and Helen V. Michel

1997 Obsidian Procurement and Distribution in the Tikal-
Yaxha Intersite Area of the Central Maya Lowlands.
Ancient Mesoamerica 8:101–110.

Foster, Michael S.

1999 The Aztatlán Tradition of West and Northwest Mexico
and Casas Grandes: Speculations on the Medio Period
Florescence. In *The Casas Grandes World*, edited by
Curtis F. Schaafsma and Carroll L. Riley, pp. 149–163.
University of Utah Press, Salt Lake City.

Fowler, William R., Jr.

1989 *The Cultural Evolution of Ancient Nahua Civilizations:
The Pipil-Nacarao of Central America.* University of
Oklahoma Press, Norman.

1996 Special Section: Recent Chronological Research in
Central Mexico. *Ancient Mesoamerica* 7:215–331.

Fowler, William R., Jane H. Kelley, Frank Asaro, Helen V.
Michel, and Fred H. Stross

1987 The Chipped Stone Industry of Cihuatan and Santa
Maria, El Savador, and Sources of Obsidian for
Cihuatan. *American Antiquity* 52:151–160.

Fox, John W.

1977 Quiché Expansion Processes: Differential Ecological
Growth Bases within an Archaic State. In *Archaeology
and Ethnohistory of the Central Quiche*, edited by
Dwight T. Wallace and Robert M. Carmack, pp. 82–97.
Publication, vol. 1. Institute for Mesoamerican Studies,
Albany, NY.

1978 *Quiché Conquest: Centralism and Regionalism in Highland Guatemalan State Development.* University of New
Mexico Press, Albuquerque.

1980 Lowland to Highland Mexicanization Processes in
Southern Mesoamerica. *American Antiquity* 45:43–
54.

1987 *Maya Postclassic State Formation: Segmentary Lineage
Migration in Advancing Frontiers.* Cambridge University Press, Cambridge.

1989 On the Rise and Fall of Tulans and Maya Segmentary
States. *American Anthropologist* 91:656–681.

1991   The Lords of Light Versus the Lords of Dark: The Post-classic Highland Maya Ballgame. In *The Mesoamerican Ballgame*, edited by Vernon L. Scarborough and David R. Wilcox, pp. 213–238. University of Arizona Press, Tucson.

1994   Political Cosmology among the Quiché Maya. In *Factional Competition and Political Development in the New World*, edited by Elizabeth M. Brumfiel and John W. Fox, pp. 158–170. Cambridge University Press, Cambridge.

Fox, John W., Garrett W. Cook, Arlen F. Chase, and Diane Z. Chase

1996   The Maya State: Centralized or Segmentary? Current Anthropology Forum on Theory in Anthropology. *Current Anthropology* 37:795–830.

Fox, John W., Dwight T. Wallace, and Kenneth L. Brown

1992   The Emergence of the Quiche Elite: The Putun-Palenque Connection. In *Mesoamerican Elites: An Archaeological Assessment*, edited by Diane Z. Chase and Arlen F. Chase, pp. 169–190. University of Oklahoma Press, Norman.

Frank, Andre G.

1966   The Development of Underdevelopment. *Monthly Review* 18(4):17–31.

Frank, Andre G., and Barry K. Gills

1993a   *The World System: Five Hundred Years or Five Thousand?* Routledge, London.

1993b   Rejoinder and Conclusions. In *The World System: Five Hundred Years or Five Thousand?*, edited by Andre G. Frank and Barry K. Gills, pp. 297–307. Routledge, London.

1993c   Introduction to *The World System: Five Hundred Years or Five Thousand?* edited by Andre G. Frank and Barry K. Gills, pp. 3–55. Routledge, London.

Frankenstein, Susan, and Michael J. Rowlands

1978   The Internal Structure and Regional Context of Early Iron Age Society in South-Western Germany. *Bulletin of the Institute of Archaeology* 15:73–112.

Freidel, David A.

1981a   Continuity and Disjunction: Late Postclassic Settlement Patterns in Northern Yucatan. In *Lowland Maya Settlement Patterns*, edited by Wendy Ashmore, pp. 311–332. University of New Mexico Press, Albuquerque.

1981b   The Political Economics of Residential Dispersion Among the Lowland Maya. In *Lowland Maya Settlement Patterns*, edited by Wendy Ashmore, pp. 371–385. University of New Mexico Press, Albuquerque.

1983   Political Systems in Lowland Yucatán: Dynamics and Structure in Maya Settlement. In *Prehistoric Settlement Patterns: Essays in Honor of Gordon R. Willey*, edited by Evon Z. Vogt and Richard M. Leventhal, pp. 375–386. University of New Mexico Press, Albuquerque.

1985   New Light on a Dark Age: A Summary of Major Themes. In *The Lowland Maya Postclassic*, edited by Arlen F. Chase and Prudence M. Rice, pp. 285–310. University of Texas Press, Austin.

1986   Terminal Classic Lowland Maya: Successes, Failures, and Aftermaths. In *Late Lowland Maya Civilization: Classic to Postclassic*, edited by Jeremy A. Sabloff and E. Wyllys Andrews V, pp. 409–432. University of New Mexico Press, Albuquerque.

Freidel, David A., and Jeremy A. Sabloff

1984   *Cozumel: Late Maya Settlement Patterns*. Academic Press, New York.

Freidel, David A., Linda Schele, and Joy Parker

1993   *The Maya Cosmos: Three Thousand Years on the Shaman's Path*. William Morrow, New York.

Freter, AnnCorinne

1993   Obsidian Hydration Dating: Its Past, Present, and Future Application in Mesoamerica. *Ancient Mesoamerica* 4:285–303.

Friedman, Jonathan, and Michael J. Rowlands

1977   Notes Towards an Epigenetic Model of the Evolution of "Civilisation." In *The Evolution of Social Systems*, edited by Jonathan Friedman and Michael J. Rowlands, pp. 201–276. University of Pittsburgh Press, Pittsburgh.

Fuente, Beatriz de la, Silvia Trejo, and Nelly Gutiérrez Solana

1988   *Escultura en piedra de Tula: Catálogo*. Instituto de Investigaciones Estéticas, Universidad Nacional Autónoma de México, Mexico City.

Fuentes y Guzmán, F. A. de

1932–

1933   *Recopilación Florida*. Biblioteca "Goathemala," vols. 6–8. Sociedad de Geografía e Historia, Tipografía Nacional, Guatemala City.

Furst, Jill Leslie

1977   The Tree Birth Tradition in the Mixteca, Mexico. *Journal of Latin American Lore* 3:183–226.

1978   *Codex Vindobonensis Mexicanus I: A Commentary*. Publications, vol. 4. Institute for Mesoamerican Studies, Albany.

1990   Rulership and Ritual: Myth and the Origin of Political Authority in Mixtec Pictorial Manuscripts. In *Circumpacifica: Festschrift für Thomas S. Barthel*, edited by Bruno Illius and Matthias Laubscher, pp. 123–141, vol. 1. Peter Lang, Frankfurt.

1995   *The Natural History of the Soul in Ancient Mexico*. Yale University Press, New Haven.

Gallegos Ruíz, Roberto

1978   *El señor 9 Flor en Zaachila*. Universidad Nacional Autónoma de México, Mexico City.

Gándara V., Manuel

1986   El modo de producción asiático: ¿Explicación marxista del origen del estado? In *Origen y formación del estado en Mesoamérica*, edited by Andrés Medina, Alfredo López Austin, and Mari Carmen Serra Puche, pp. 41–59. Universidad Nacional Autónoma de México, Mexico City.

Gann, Thomas W.

1900   *Mounds in Northern Honduras*. Bureau of American Ethnology, Nineteenth Annual Report, 1897–1898, part 2.

García, Gregorio

1981   *Origen de los indios del Nuevo Mundo: Estudio preliminar de Franklin Pease G. Y*. Fondo de Cultura Económica, Mexico City.

García Alcáraz, Agustín

1976   Estratificación social entre los tarascos prehispánicos. In *Estratificación social en la Mesoamérica prehispánica*, edited by Pedro Carrasco and Johanna Broda, pp. 221–244. Instituto Nacional de Antropología e Historia, Mexico City.

García Chávez, Raúl, J. Michael Elam, Harry B. Iceland, and Michael D. Glascock

1990   INAH Salvage Archaeology Excavation at Azcapotzalco, Mexico. *Ancient Mesoamerica* 1:225–232.

García Cook, Angel

1981   The Historical Importance of Tlaxcala in the Cultural Development of the Central Highlands. In *Archaeology*, edited by Victoria R. Bricker and Jeremy A. Sabloff, pp. 244–276. Supplement to the Handbook of Middle American Indians, vol. 1. University of Texas Press, Austin.

García Cook, Angel, and Beatriz Leonor Merino Carrión
1974   Malacates de Tlaxcala: Intento de una secuencia evolutiva. *Comunicaciones* 11:27–36.
1998   Cantona: Urbe prehispánica en el altiplano central de México. *Latin American Antiquity* 9:191–216.

García García, E. V.
1992   *Reconocimiento arqueológico de las tierras altas centrales de Chimaltenango.* Licenciatura thesis, Department of Arqueología, Escuela de Historia, Universidad de San Carlos de Guatemala.

García Martínez, Bernardo
1987   *Los pueblos de la sierra.* El Colegio de México, Mexico City.

García Payón, José
1933   Unas salinas precortesianas en el estado de México. *Boletín del Museo Nacional de Arqueología, Historia y Etnografía (época 5)* 2(2):49–51.
1965   *Descripción del pueblo de Gueytlalpan (Zacatlan, Jujupango, Matlatlan y Chila, Papantla) por el alcalde mayor Juan de Carrion, 30 de mayo de 1581.* Cuadernos de la Facultad de Filosofía, Letras y Cienceas, vol. 23. Universidad Veracruzana, Jalapa.

Garibay K., Angel M.
1973   *Teogonía e historia de los mexicanos: Tres opúsculos del siglo XVI.* 2nd ed. Porrúa, Mexico City.

Garnesy, Peter, and Peter Saller
1987   *The Roman Empire: Economy, Society, and Culture.* University of California Press, Berkeley.

Garníca Vanegas, M. J.
1997   *La cerámica de la fuente de obsidiana Pachay, Chimaltenango.* Licenciatura thesis, Department of Arqueología, Escuela de Historia, Universidad de San Carlos de Guatemala.

Garza, Mercedes de la, Ana Luisa Izquierdo, Maria del Carmen León, and Tolito Figueroa (editors)
1983   *Relaciones histórico-geográficas de la gobernación de Yucatán,* vols. 1 and 2. Universidad Nacional Autónoma de México, Mexico City.

Gasco, Janine
1989a Economic History of Ocelocalco, a Colonial Soconusco Town. In *Ancient Trade and Tribute: Economies of the Soconusco Region of Mesoamerica,* edited by Barbara Voorhies, pp. 304–325. University of Utah Press, Salt Lake City.
1989b The Colonial Economy in the Province of Soconusco. In *Ancient Trade and Tribute: Economies of the Soconusco Region of Mesoamerica,* edited by Barbara Voorhies, pp. 287–303. University of Utah Press, Salt Lake City.
1989c Una visión de conjunto de la historia demográfica y económica del Soconusco colonial. *Mesoamérica* 18:371–399.
1990   Reconocimiento de pueblos coloniales en la provincia del Soconusco. *Boletín del Consejo de Arqueología (Mexico)* 1990:124–126.
1991a El máximo tributo: El papel del Soconusco como tributario de los Aztecas. In *La economía del antiguo Soconusco, Chiapas,* edited by Barbara Voorhies, pp. 61–113. Translated by Raúl del Moral. Universidad Nacional Autónoma de México and Universidad Autónoma de Chiapas, Mexico City.

1991b La economía colonial en la provincia de Soconusco. In *La economía del antiguo Soconusco, Chiapas,* edited by Barbara Voorhies, pp. 335–353. Translated by Raúl del Moral. Universidad Nacional Autónoma de México and Universidad Autónoma de Chiapas, Mexico City.
1992   Material Culture and Colonial Indian Society in Southern Mesoamerica: The View from Coastal Chiapas, Mexico. *Historical Archaeology* 26:67–74.
1993   Socioeconomic Change within Native Society in Colonial Soconusco, New Spain. In *Ethnohistory and Archaeology: Approaches to Postcontact Change in the Americas,* edited by J. Daniel Rogers and Samuel Wilson, pp. 163–180. Plenum Press, New York.
1996a Cacao and Economic Inequality in Colonial Soconusco, Chiapas, Mexico. *Journal of Anthropological Research* 52:385–409.
1996b Cacao as Commodity in Postclassic Soconusco. Paper presented at the 95th Annual Conference of the American Anthropological Association (San Francisco).
1998a Cacao and Commerce in Postclassic Soconusco: Evidence from the 1997 Field Season. Paper presented at the 63rd Annual Conference of the Society for American Archaeology (Seattle).
1998b *Informe del proyecto, "Las dinámicas del cambio en mesoamérica postclásica: Evidencia del Soconusco."* Manuscript on file, Instituto Nacional de Antropología e Historia, Mexico City.
1999   The Province of Soconusco from Aztec Conquest to Spanish Colonial Rule. Paper presented at the 64th Annual Conference of the Society for American Archaeology (Chicago).
2001   *Informe del proyecto, "La historia de la ocupación de Xoconochco."* Manuscript on file, Instituto Nacional de Antropología e Historia, Mexico City.

Gasco, Janine, and Barbara Voorhies
1989   The Ultimate Tribute: The Role of the Soconusco as an Aztec Tributary. In *Ancient Trade and Tribute: Economies of the Soconusco Region of Mesoamerica,* edited by Barbara Voorhies, pp. 48–94. University of Utah Press, Salt Lake City.

Geertz, Clifford
1966   *Agricultural Involution.* University of California Press, Berkeley.

Gerhard, Peter
1970   A Method of Reconstructing Pre-Columbian Political Boundaries in Central Mexico. *Journal de la Société des Americanistes de Paris* 59:27–41.
1977   Congregaciones de indios en la Nueva España ántes de 1570. *Historia Mexicana* 26:347–395.
1993a *The Southeast Frontier of New Spain.* Rev. ed. University of Oklahoma Press, Norman.
1993b *A Guide to the Historical Geography of New Spain.* Rev. ed. University of Oklahoma Press, Norman.

Gibson, Charles
1964   *The Aztecs Under Spanish Rule: A History of the Indians of the Valley of Mexico, 1519–1810.* Stanford University Press, Stanford.
1971   Structure of the Aztec Empire. In *Archaeology of Northern Mesoamerica,* part 2, edited by Gordon F. Ekholm and Ignacio Bernal, pp. 376–394. Handbook of Middle American Indians vol. 10. University of Texas Press, Austin.

Gilberti, R. P. Fr. Maturino
1975   *Diccionario de la lengua tarasco o de Michoacán (1559).*

Fascimile edition of 1902 publication, Pimentel ed. Balsal Editores, Morelia.

Gillespie, Susan D.
1995 The Role of Ancestor Veneration in Maya Social Identity and Political Authority. Paper presented at the 94th Annual Conference of the American Anthropological Association (Washington, D.C.).
1998 The Aztec Triple Alliance: A Postconquest Tradition. In *Native Traditions in the Postconquest World*, edited by Elizabeth Hill Boone and Tom Cummins, pp. 233–263. Dumbarton Oaks, Washington, D.C.
2000a Rethinking Ancient Maya Social Organization: Replacing "Lineage" with "House." *American Anthropologist* 102:467–484.
2000b Lévi-Strauss: Maison and Société à Maisons. In *Beyond Kinship: Social and Material Reproduction in House Societies*, edited by Rosemary A. Joyce and Susan D. Gillespie, pp. 22–52. University of Pennsylvania Press, Philadelphia.
2000c Maya "Nested Houses": The Ritual Construction of Place. In *Beyond Kinship: Social and Material Reproduction in House Societies*, edited by Rosemary A. Joyse and Susan D. Gillespie, pp. 136–160. University of Pennsylvania Press, Philadelphia.

Gillespie, Susan D., and Rosemary A. Joyce
1997 Gendered Goods: The Symbolism of Maya Hierarchical Exchange Relations. In *Women in Prehistory: North America and Mesoamerica*, edited by Cheryl Claasen and Rosemary A. Joyce, pp. 189–207. University of Pennsylvania Press, Philadelphia.

Gills, Barry K., and Andre G. Frank
1991 5000 Years of World System History: The Cumulation of Accumulation. In *Core/Periphery Relations in Precapitalist Worlds*, edited by Christopher K. Chase-Dunn and Thomas D. Hall, pp. 67–112. Westview, Boulder.
1993 The Cumulation of Accumulation. In *The World System: Five Hundred Years or Five Thousand?*, edited by Andre G. Frank and Barry K. Gills, pp. 81–114. Routledge, London.

Glascock, Michael D., William J. Parry, Thomas H. Charlton, Cynthia L. Otis Charlton, and Hector Neff
1999 Obsidian Sources Supplying the Aztec City-States of Otumba and Tepeapulco. Paper presented at the 64th Annual Conference of the Society for American Archaeology (Chicago).

Gledhill, John, and Mogens Larsen
1982 The Polanyi Paradigm and a Dynamic Analysis of Archaic States. In *Theory and Explanation in Archaeology: The Southamton Conference*, edited by Colin Renfrew, Michael J. Rowlands, and Barbara A. Segraves, pp. 197–229. Academic Press, New York.

Gombrich, Ernst
1968 Style. In *International Encyclopedia of the Social Sciences*, edited by D. L. Sills, pp. 352–361, vol. 15. Macmillan, New York.

González, Carlos Javier, and Bertina Olmedo Vera
1990 *Esculturas Mezcala en el Templo Mayor*. Instituto Nacional de Antropología e Historia, Mexico City.

González, E. T.
1994 Apiarios prehispánicos. *Boletín de la ECAUDY* 20(117):43–57.

Good, Catherine
1995 Salt Production and Commerce in Guerrero, Mexico: An Ethnographic Contribution to Historical Reconstruction. *Ancient Mesoamerica* 6:1–14.

Goody, Jack
1971 *Technology, Tradition, and the State in Africa*. Cambridge University Press, Cambridge.

Gorenstein, Shirley
1973 *Tepexi el Viejo: A Postclassic Fortified Site in the Mixteca-Puebla Region of Mexico*. Transactions, vol. 63, 1. American Philosophical Society, Philadelphia.
1985 *Acambaro: Frontier Settlement on the Tarascan-Aztec Border*. Vanderbilt University Publications in Anthropology, vol. 32. Department of Anthropology, Vanderbilt University, Nashville.

Gorenstein, Shirley, and Helen Perlstein Pollard
1983 *The Tarascan Civilization: A Late Prehispanic Cultural System*. Vanderbilt University Publications in Anthropology, vol. 28. Department of Anthropology, Vanderbilt University, Nashville.

Graham, Elizabeth A.
1987 Terminal Classic to Early Historic Period Vessel Forms from Belize. In *Maya Ceramics*, edited by Prudence M. Rice and Robert J. Sharer, pp. 73–98. BAR International Series, vol. 345. British Archaeological Reports, Oxford.

Graham, Mark Miller
1996 Merchants and Metalwork in Middle America. In *Paths to Central American Prehistory*, edited by Frederick W. Lange, pp. 237–252. University Press of Colorado, Niwot, CO.

Graham, Mark Miller, Vincente Guerrero, and Michael Snarskis
1998 *Jade in Ancient Costa Rica*. Metropolitan Museum of Art, New York.

Gregory, Chris A.
1982 *Gifts and Commodities*. Academic Press, New York.

Grinberg, Dora M.
1989 Tecnologías metalúrgicas tarascas. *Ciencia y Desarrollo* 15(89):37–52.

Grinberg, Dora M., and Francisca Franco V.
1987 Estudio de cuatro cascabeles de falso alambre provenientes de las excavaciones del tren subterráneo de la Ciudad de México. *Antropología y Técnica* 2:143–151.

Grinberg, Dora M., R. E. Rubinovich, and A. A. Gasca
1986 Intentional Production of Bronze in Mesoamerica. In *Precolumbian American Metallurgy: 45th International Congress of Americanists*, pp. 57–65. Banco de La Republica de Colombia, Bogota.

Grube, Nikolai
2000 The City-States of the Maya. In *A Comparative Study of Thirty City-State Cultures*, edited by Mogens Herman Hansen, pp. 547–566. The Royal Danish Academy of Sciences and Letters, Copenhagen.

Gruzinski, Serge
1992 *Painting the Conquest: The Mexican Indians and the European Renaissance*. Translated by Deke Dusinberre. Flammarion, Paris.

Guillemín, Jorge F.
1961 Un entierro señorial en Iximché. *Anales de la Sociedad de Geografía e Historia (Guatemala)* 34:89–105.
1965 *Iximché, capital del antiguo reino Cakquiquel*. Instituto de Antropología e Historia, Guatemala City.
1977 Urbanism and Hierarchy at Iximche'. In *Social Process in Maya Prehistory: Studies in Honour of Sir Eric Thompson*, edited by Norman Hammond, pp. 227–264. Academic Press, New York.

Guzmán V. A., and Lourdes Martínez O. (editors)
　1990　*La validez teórica del concepto Mesoamérica. XIX Mesa Redonda de la Sociedad Mexicana de Antropología.* Instituto Nacional de Antropología e Historia, Mexico City.

Hall, Thomas D., and Christopher Chase-Dunn
　1996　Comparing World-Systems: Concepts and Hypotheses. In *Pre-Columbian World Systems,* edited by Peter N. Peregrine and Gary M. Feinman, pp. 11–26. Monographs in World Archaeology, vol. 26. Prehistory Press, Madison, WI.

Hammond, Norman
　1976　Maya Obsidian Trade in Southern Belize. In *Maya Lithic Studies: Papers from the 1976 Belize Field Symposium,* edited by Thomas R. Hester and Norman Hammond, pp. 71–81. Special Report, vol. 4. Center for Archaeological Research, University of Texas, San Antonio.

Hammond, Norman, M. D. Neivens, and Garman Harbottle
　1984　Trace Element Analysis of Obsidian Artifacts from a Classic Maya Residential Group at Nohmul, Belize. *American Antiquity* 49:815–820.

Hansen, Mogens Herman
　2000a　Introduction: The Concepts of City-State and City-State Culture. In *A Comparative Study of Thirty City-State Cultures,* edited by Mogens Herman Hansen, pp. 11–34. The Royal Danish Academy of Sciences and Letters, Copenhagen.
　2000b　*A Comparative Study of Thirty City-State Cultures.* The Royal Danish Academy of Sciences and Letters, Copenhagen.
　2000c　Conclusion: The Impact of City-State Cultures on World History. In *A Comparative Study of Thirty City-State Cultures,* edited by Mogens Herman Hansen, pp. 597–623. The Royal Danish Academy of Sciences and Letters, Copenhagen.

Harbottle, Garman, and Phil C. Weigand
　1992　Turquoise in Pre-Columbian America. *Scientific American* 266(2):78–85.

Hare, Timothy S., Lisa Montiel, and Michael E. Smith
　n.d.　Prehispanic Settlement Patterns in the Yautepec Valley, Morelos, Mexico. Manuscript in preparation for submission to the *Journal of Field Archaeology.*

Hare, Timothy S., and Michael E. Smith
　1996　A New Postclassic Chronology for Yautepec, Morelos. *Ancient Mesoamerica* 7:281–297.

Harris, Marvin
　1968　*The Rise of Anthropological Theory: A History of Theories of Culture.* Thomas Y. Crowell, New York.

Harris, William V.
　1993　Between Archaic and Modern: Some Current Problems in the History of the Roman Economy. In *The Inscribed Economy: Production and Distribution in the Roman Empire in Light of Instrumentum Domesticum,* edited by William V. Harris, pp. 11–29. Journal of Roman Archaeology, Supplemental Series, vol. 6, Ann Arbor.

Hart, Keith
　1982　On Commoditization. In *From Craft to Industry: The Ethnography of Proto-Industrial Cloth Production,* edited by Esther N. Goody, pp. 38–49. Cambridge University Press, New York.

Harvey, Herbert R.
　1971　Ethnohistory of Guerrero. In *Archaeology of Northern Mesoamerica,* part 2, edited by Gordon F. Ekholm and Ignacio Bernal, pp. 603–18. Handbook of Middle American Indians, vol. 11. University of Texas Press, Austin.

　1984　Aspects of Land Tenure in Ancient Mexico. In *Explorations in Ethnohistory,* edited by H. R. Harvey and Hanns Prem, pp. 83–102. University of New Mexico Press, Albuquerque.

Hassig, Ross
　1985　*Trade, Tribute, and Transportation: The Sixteenth Century Political Economy of the Valley of Mexico.* University of Oklahoma Press, Norman.
　1988　*Aztec Warfare: Imperial Expansion and Political Control.* University of Oklahoma Press, Norman.

Häusler, Alexander
　1981　Zur ältesten Geschichte von Rad und Wagen im nordpontischen Raum. *Ethn/-Arch. Zeitschrift* 2:581–647.
　1994　Archäologische Zeugnisse für Pferd und Wagen in Ost- und Mitteleuropa. In *Die Indogermanen und das Pferd,* edited by B. Hänsel and S. Zimmer, pp. 217–257. Archaeolingua, Budapest.

Hayden, Brian
　1987　Traditional Metate Manufacturing in Guatemala Using Chipped Stone Tools. In *Lithic Studies Among the Contemporary Highland Maya,* edited by Brian Hayden, pp. 8–119. University of Arizona Press, Tucson.

Hayen, H.
　1989　Früheste Nachweise des Wagens und die Entwicklung der Transport-Hilfsmittel: Beiträge zur Transportgeschichte. *Mitteilungen der Berliner Gesellschaft fur Anthropologie, Ethnologie, und Urgeschichte* 10:31–49.
　1991　*Ein Vierradwagen des dritten Jahrtausends v. Chr.- Rekonstruktion und Nachbau.* Isensee, Oldenburg.

Hays-Gilpin, Kelley, and Jane H. Hill
　1999　The Flower World in Material Culture: An Iconographic Complex in the Southwest and Mesoamerica. *Journal of Anthropological Research* 55:1–38.

Healan, Dan M.
　1989　*Tula of the Toltecs: Excavations and Survey.* University of Iowa Press, Iowa City.
　1991a　Proyecto arqueológico en la región Zinapécuaro, Michoacán: Análisis de materiales. *Boletín del Consejo de Arqueología 1990 (Mexico)*:147–148.
　1991b　Investigaciones del asentamiento prehispánico y la explotación de obsidiana en la región de Zinapécuaro, Michoacán. *Boletín del Consejo de Arqueología 1990 (Mexico)*:138–139.
　1993　Local Versus Non-Local Obsidian Exchange at Tula and Its Implications for Post-Formative Mesoamerica. *World Archaeology* 24:449–466.
　1997　Pre-Hispanic Quarrying in the Ucareo-Zinapecuaro Obsidian Source Area. *Ancient Mesoamerica* 8:77–100.
　2000　New Perspectives on Possible Obsidian Trade Between Tula and Chichén Itzá. Paper presented at the Dumbarton Oaks Colloquium "Rethinking Chichén Itzá, Tula, and Tollan" (Washington, D.C.).

Healan, Dan M., Robert H. Cobean, and Richard A. Diehl
　1989　Synthesis and Conclusions. In *Tula of the Toltecs,* edited by Dan M. Healan, pp. 239–252. University of Iowa Press, Iowa City.

Healy, Paul F.
　1980　*The Archaeology of the Rivas Region, Nicaragua.* Wilfred Laurier, Waterloo.

Healy, Paul F., Frank Asaro, Fred H. Stross, and Helen V. Michel
　1996　Precolumbian Obsidian Trade in the Northern Intermediate Area: Elemental Analysis of Artifacts from Honduras and Nicaragua. In *Paths to Central American Prehistory,* edited by Frederick W. Lange, pp. 271–296. University of Colorado Press, Niwot.

Hegmon, Michele
1992   Archaeological Research on Style. *Annual Review of Anthropology* 21:517–536.

Heller, Lynette, and Barbara L. Stark
1998   Classic and Postclassic Obsidian Tool Production and Consumption: A Regional Perspective from the Mixtequilla Region, Veracruz. *Mexicon* 20(6):119–128.

Helms, Mary W.
1993   *Craft and the Kingly Ideal: Art, Trade, and Power*. University of Texas Press, Austin.

Henderson, John S., Ilene Sterns, Anthony Wonderly, and Patricia A. Urban
1979   Archaeological Investigation in the Valle de Naco, Northwestern Honduras: A Preliminary Report. *Journal of Field Archaeology* 6:169–192.

Hendrichs P., Pedro R.
1944–
45   *Por tierras ignotas: Viajes y observaciones en la región del Río Balsas*. 2 vols. Instituto Panamericano de Geografía e Historia, Mexico City.

Hernández, Christine, and Dan M. Healan
1999   The Classic to Postclassic Transition in Northeastern Michoacán, Mexico. Paper presented at the 64th Annual Conference of the Society for American Archaeology (Chicago).

Hernández Rivero, José
1994a   La arqueología de la frontera Tarasco-Mexica: Arquitectura bélica. In *Contribuciones a la arqueología y etnohistoria del Occidente de México*, edited by Eduardo Williams, pp. 115–155. El Colegio de Michoacán, Zamora.
1994b   *Arqueología de la frontera Tarasco-Mexica: Conformación, estrategía y practicas de control*. Licenciatura thesis, Escuela Nacional de Antropología e Historia.
1996   Materiales cerámicos en frontera: Cerámica tarasca y cerámica azteco-chontal. In *Teimpo y territoria en arqueología: El centro norte de México*, edited by Ana María Crespo and Carlos Viramontes, pp. 59–76. Colección Científica, vol. 323. Instituto Nacional de Antropología e Historia, Mexico City.
1998   Tlapicaltepeque: Lindero y cuña occidental del imperial mexica en territorio tarasco. *Actualidades Arqueológicas* 3(17–18):7–10.

Hernández Rivero, José, and Davíd Escobedo Ramírez
1997   *Proyecto de salvamento arqueológico "La Peña," Valle de Bravo, Estado de México, Segunda fase: Resultado preliminares*. Report, Centro INAH en el Estado de México, Toluca.

Herrejón Peredo, Carlos
1978   La pugna entre Mexicas y Tarascos. *Cuadernos de Historia (Toluca)* 1:11–47.

Herrera, Antonio de
1945   *Historia general de los hechos de los castellanos en las Islas y Tierra-Firme de el Mar Oceano*. Vol. 4. Guarania, Buenos Aires.

Hester, Thomas R.
1982   The Maya Lithic Sequence in Northern Belize. In *Archaeology at Colha, Belize: The 1981 Interim Report*, edited by Thomas R. Hester, Harry J. Shafer, and Jack D. Eaton, pp. 39–59. Center for Archaeological Research, University of Texas and Centro Studie Ricerche Ligabue, San Antonio and Venezia.
1985   *Late Classic–Early Postclassic Transitions: Archaeological Investigations at Colha, Belize*. Final Performance Report to the National Endowment for the Humanities Grant RO20534–83 and RO 20755, Center for Archaeological Research, University of Texas, San Antonio.

Hester, Thomas R., R. N. Jack, and Alice Benfer
1973   Trace Element Analyses of Obsidian from Michoacan, Mexico: Preliminary Results. *Contributions of the University of California Archaeology Research Facility* 13:65–133.

Hester, Thomas R., R. N. Jack, and Robert F. Heizer
1972   Trace Element Analysis of Obsidian from the Site of Cholula, Mexico. *Contributions of the University of California Archaeological Research Facility* 16:105–110.

Hester, Thomas R., and Harry J. Shafer
1983   On Obsidian Supply at Colha, Belize. *Current Anthropology* 21:810–811.
1991   Lithics of the Early Postclassic at Colha, Belize. In *Maya Stone Tools: Selected Papers from the Second Maya Lithic Conference*, edited by Thomas R. Hester and Harry J. Shafer, pp. 155–162. Prehistory Press, Madison.
1994   The Ancient Maya Craft Community at Colha, Belize, and Its External Relationships. In *Archaeological Views from the Countryside: Village Communities in Early Complex Societies*, edited by Glenn M. Schwartz and Steven E. Falconer, pp. 48–63. Smithsonian Institution Press, Washington, D.C.

Heyden, Doris
1987   Symbolism of Ceramics from the Templo Mayor. In *The Aztec Templo Mayor*, edited by Elizabeth H. Boone, pp. 109–130. Dumbarton Oaks, Washington, D.C.

Hicks, Frederic
1984   La posición de Temazcalapan en al Triple Alianza. *Estudios de Cultura Náhuatl* 10:235–260.
1986   Prehispanic Background of Colonial Political and Economic Organization in Central Mexico. In *Ethnohistory*, edited by Ronald Spores, pp. 35–54. Supplement to the Handbook of Middle American Indians, vol. 4. University of Texas Press, Austin.
1994a   Cloth in the Political Economy of the Aztec State. In *Economies and Polities in the Aztec Realm*, edited by Mary G. Hodge and Michael E. Smith, pp. 89–111. Institute for Mesoamerican Studies, Albany.
1994b   Alliance and Intervention in Aztec Imperial Expansion. In *Factional Competition and Political Development in the New World*, edited by Elizabeth M. Brumfiel and John W. Fox, pp. 111–116. Cambridge University Press, Cambridge.
1999   The Middle Class in Ancient Central Mexico. *Journal of Anthropological Research* 55:409–427.

Hill, Robert M., II
1984   Chinamit and Molab: Late Postclassic Highland Maya Precursors of Closed Corporate Community. *Estudios de Cultura Maya* 15:301–327.
1996   East Chajoma (Cakchiquel) Political Geography: Ethnohistorical and Archaeological Contributions to the Study of a Late Postclassic Highland Maya Polity. *Ancient Mesoamerica* 7:63–87.

Hill, Robert M., II, and John Monaghan
1987   *Continuities in Highland Maya Social Organization: Ethnohistory in Sacapulas, Guatemala*. University of Pennsylvania Press, Philadelphia.

Hirshman, Amy J., Helen P. Pollard, Hector Neff, and Michael D. Glascock
1999   Emergence of the Tarascan State: Chemical Characterization of Ceramic Sherds from Urichu and Clay Sam-

ples, Lake Pátzcuaro Basin, Michoacán, Mexico. Paper presented at the 64th Annual Conference of the Society for American Archaeology (Chicago).

Hirth, Kenneth G. (editor)

1984   *Trade and Exchange in Early Mesoamerica.* University of New Mexico Press, Albuquerque.

1989   Militarism and Social Organization at Xochicalco, Morelos. In *Mesoamerica After the Decline of Teotihuacan, A.D. 700–900,* edited by Richard Diehl and Janet Berlo, pp. 69–81. Dumbarton Oaks, Washington, D.C.

1998   The Distributional Approach: A New Way to Identify Marketplace Exchange in the Archaeological Record. *Current Anthropology* 39:451–476.

2000   *Archaeological Research at Xochicalco.* 2 vols. University of Utah Press, Salt Lake City.

Hodge, Mary G.

1984   *Aztec City-States.* Memoirs, vol. 18. Museum of Anthropology, University of Michigan, Ann Arbor.

1994   Polities Composing the Aztec Empire's Core. In *Economies and Polities in the Aztec Realm,* edited by Mary G. Hodge and Michael E. Smith, pp. 43–71. Institute for Mesoamerican Studies, Albany.

1996   Political Organization of the Central Provinces. In *Aztec Imperial Strategies,* by Frances F. Berdan, Richard E. Blanton, Elizabeth H. Boone, Mary G. Hodge, Michael E. Smith, and Emily Umberger, pp. 17–45. Dumbarton Oaks, Washington, D.C.

1997   When Is a City-State? Archaeological Measures of Aztec City-States and Aztec City-State Systems. In *The Archaeology of City-States: Cross-Cultural Approaches,* edited by Deborah L. Nichols and Thomas H. Charlton, pp. 209–28. Smithsonian Institution Press, Washington, D.C.

Hodge, Mary G., and Michael E. Smith (editors)

1994   *Economies and Polities in the Aztec Realm.* Institute for Mesoamerican Studies, Albany.

Holm, Olaf

1978   Hachas monedas del Ecuador. In *El hombre y la cultura andina,* pp. 347–361, vol. 1. Editora Lasontey, Lima.

Holmes, William H.

1900   The Obsidian Mines of Hidalgo, Mexico. *American Anthropologist* 2:405–416.

Hosler, Dorothy

1986   The Origins, Technology, and Social Construction of Ancient West Mexican Metallurgy. Ph.D. dissertation, Department of Anthropology, University of California, Santa Barbara.

1988a   Ancient West Mexican Metallurgy: A Technological Chronology. *Journal of Field Archaeology* 15:191–218.

1988b   Ancient West Mexican Metallurgy: South and Central American Origins and West Mexican Transformations. *American Anthropologist* 90:832–855.

1994   *The Sounds and Colors of Power: The Sacred Metallurgical Technology of Ancient West Mexico.* MIT Press, Cambridge.

1997   Unpublished field notes.

1999   Los fuentes de cobre en el Occidente de Mexico. Actas del IV coloquio de Occidentalistas, Guadalajara, Mexico.

2000   Informe final: Reconocimiento de la superfecie para localizar sitios de producción de cobre en la región sureste del cinturón de cobre mexicano. Submitted to and accepted by INAH.

In   Nuevos hallazgos sobre la metalurgia Antigua de
press Guerrero. In *Arqueología del Estado de Guerrero.*

n.d.   Archaeological Implications of New Data from Lead Isotope Studies of Guerrero Cu Ores. In author's possession.

Hosler, Dorothy, Heather Lechtman, and Olaf Holm

1990   *Axe-Monies and Their Relatives.* Dumbarton Oaks Studies in Pre-Columbian Art and Archaeology, vol. 30. Dumbarton Oaks, Washington, D.C.

Hosler, Dorothy, and Andrew Macfarlane

1996   Copper Sources, Metal Production, and Metals Trade in Late Postclassic Mesoamerica. *Science* 273:1819–1824.

Hosler, Dorothy and Guy Stresser-Péan

1992   The Huastec Region: A Second Locus for the Production of Bronze Alloys in Ancient Mesoamerica. *Science* 257: 1215–1220.

Hosseini, Hamid

1995   Understanding the Market Mechanism Before Adam Smith: Economic Thought in Medieval Islam. *History of Political Economy* 27:539–561.

Houston, Stephen, David Stuart, and J. Robertson

1998   Disharmony in Maya Hieroglyphic Writing: Linguistic Change and Continuity in Classic Society. In *Anatomía de una civilización: Aproximaciones interdisciplinarias a la cultura maya,* edited by Andrés Ciudad Ruiz, Yolanda Fernández Marquínez, José Miguel García Campillo, María Josefa Iglesias Ponce de León, Alfonso Lacadena García-Gallo, and Luis T. Sanz Castro, pp. 275–296. Sociedad Española de Estudios Mayas, Madrid.

Hunt, Eva

1978   The Provenience and Contents of the Porfirio Díaz and Fernández Leal Codices: Some New Data and Analysis. *American Antiquity* 43:673–690.

Isaac, Barry L.

1983   Aztec Warfare: Goals and Battlefield Comportment. *Ethnology* 22:121–131.

1986   Notes on Obsidian, the Pochteca, and the Position of Tlatelolco in the Aztec Empire. In *Economic Aspects of Highland Central Mexico,* edited by Barry L. Isaac, pp. 319–343. Research in Economic Anthropology, Supplement, vol. 2. JAI Press, Greenwich, CT.

1993a   AMP, HH, and OD: Some Comments. In *Economic Aspects of Water Management in the Prehispanic New World,* edited by Vernon L. Scarborough and Barry L. Isaac, pp. 429–471. Research in Economic Anthropology, Supplement, vol. 7. JAI Press, Greenwich, CT.

1993b   Retrospective on the Formalist-Substantivist Debate. *Research in Economic Anthropology* 14:213–233.

Izquierdo, Ana Luisa

1997   *Acalán y la Chontalpa en el siglo XVI: Su geografía política.* Universidad Nacional Autónoma de México, Mexico City.

Jack, R. N., Thomas R. Hester, and Robert F. Heizer

1972   Geologic Sources of Archaeological Obsidian from Sites in Northern and Central Veracruz, Mexico. *Contributions of the University of California Archaeological Research Facility* 16:117–122.

Jansen, Maarten

1982   *Huisi Tacu: Estudio interpretativo de un libro mixteco antiguo: codex vindobonensis mexicanus I.* Centrum voor Studie en Documentatie van Latijns Amerika, Amsterdam.

1988   The Art of Writing in Ancient Mexico: An Ethno-Iconological Perspective. *Visible Religion; Annual for Religious Iconography* 6:86–113.

1989   Nombres históricos e identidad étnica en los códices mixtecos. *Revista Europea de Estudios Latinoamericanos y del Caribe* 47:65–87.

1994   *La gran familia de los reyes mixtecos: Libro explicativo de los códices llamados Egerton y Becker II.* Akademis-che Druck-und Verlagsanstalt, Fondo de Cultura Económica, Vienna, Mexico City.

Jansen, Maarten, and Margarita Gaxiola (editors)
1978 *Primera Mesa Redonda de estudios mixtecos: Síntesis de las ponencias.* Estudios de Antropología e Historia, vol. 15. Instituto Nacional de Antropología e Historia, Centro de Oaxaca, Oaxaca.

Jiménez Moreno, Wigberto
1948 Historia antigua de la zona Tarasca. In *El Occidente de México (Cuarta Mesa Redonda).* Sociedad Mexicana de Antropología, Mexico City.
1962 Estudios mixtecos. In *Vocabulario en lengua mixteca por Fray Francisco de Alvarado. Reproducción facsimilar con un estudio de Wigberto Jiménez Moreno y un apéndice con un vocabulario sacado del arte en lengua mixteca de Fray Antonio de los Reyes,* pp. 10–105. Instituto Nacional Indigenista and Instituto Nacional de Antropología e Historia, Mexico City.
1970 Mesoamerica Before the Toltecs. In *Ancient Oaxaca,* edited by John Paddock, pp. 1–82. Stanford University Press, Stanford.

Johnson, Nicholas
1994 Las líneas rojas desvanecidas en el Lienzo de Tlapiltepec: Una red de pruebas. In *Códices y documentos sobre México: Primer simposio,* edited by Constanza Vega Sosa, pp. 117–144. Instituto Nacional de Antropología e Historia, Mexico City.
1997 The Route from the Mixteca Alta into Southern Puebla on the Lienzo de Tlapiltepec. In *Códices y documentos sobre México:Segundo simposio,* edited by Salvador Rueda Smithers, Constanza Vega Sosa, and Rodrigo Martínez Baracs, pp. 233–268, vol. 1. Instituto Nacional de Antropología e Historia and Consejo Nacional para la Cultura y las Artes, Mexico City.

Jones, Grant D.
1989 *Maya Resistance to Spanish Rule: Time and History on a Colonial Frontier.* University of New Mexico Press, Albuquerque.
1999 *The Conquest of the Last Maya Kingdom.* Stanford University Press, Stanford.

Josserand, Judy Kathryn
1983 Mixtec Dialect History: Proto-Mixtec and Modern Mixtec Text. Ph.D. dissertation, Department of Anthropology, Tulane University.

Joyce, Arthur A., J. Michael Elam, Michael D. Glascock, Hector Neff, and Marcus Winter
1995 Exchange Implications of Obsidian Source Analysis from the Lower Rio Verde Valley, Oaxaca, Mexico. *Latin American Antiquity* 6:3–15.

Joyce, Rosemary A.
1996 Social Dynamics of Exchange: Changing Patterns in the Honduran Archaeological Record. In *Chieftains, Power, and Trade: Regional Interaction in the Intermediate Area of the Americas,* edited by C. H. Langebaek and F. Cardenas-Arroyo, pp. 31–46. Departamento de Antropología, Universidad de los Andes, Bogota.
1999 Social Dimensions of Pre-Classic Burials. In *Social Patterns in Pre-Classic Mesoamerica,* edited by David C. Grove and Rosemary A. Joyce, pp. 15–47. Dumbarton Oaks, Washington, D.C.
2000a *Gender and Power in Prehispanic Mesoamerica.* University of Texas Press, Austin.
2000b High Culture, Mesoamerican Civilization, and the Classic Maya Tradition. In *Order, Legitimacy, and Wealth in Ancient States,* edited by Janet Richards and Mary van

Buren, pp. 64–76. Cambridge University Press, New York.

Joyce, Rosemary A., and Susan D. Gillespie (editors)
2000 *Beyond Kinship: Social and Material Reproduction in House Societies.* University of Pennsylvania Press, Philadelphia.

Just, Bryan
2000 Concordances of Time: In Extenso Almanacs in the Madrid and Borgia Group Codices. *Human Mosaic* (Tulane University) 33:7–16.
n.d. In-Extenso Almanacs and Cross-Referencing in the Madrid Codex. Paper presented at the workshop "Current Research on the Madrid Codex: Issues of Provenience and Dating," organized by Gabrielle Vail and Victoria R. Bricker (Tulane University, June 22–24, 2001).

Justeson, John S., and George A. Broadwell
1996 Language and Languages in Mesoamerica. In *The Legacy of Mesoamerica: History and Culture of a Native American Civilization,* edited by Robert M. Carmack, Janine Gasco, and Gary H. Gossen, pp. 379–406. Prentice-Hall, Englewood Cliffs, NJ.

Kaufman, Terence
1976 Archaeological and Linguistic Correlations in Mayaland and Associated Areas of Meso-America. *World Archaeology* 8:101–118.

Kehoe, Alice B.
1998 *The Land of Prehistory: A Critical History of American Archaeology.* Routledge, London.

Kellenbenz, Hermann
1974 Rural Industries in the West from the End of the Middle Ages to the Eighteenth Century. In *Essays in European Economic History, 1500–1800,* edited by P. Earle, pp. 45–88. Clarendon Press, Oxford.

Kelley, J. Charles
1990 The Classic Epoch in the Chalchihuites Culture of the State of Zacatecas. In *La época clásica: Nuevos hallazgos, nuevas ideas,* edited by A. Cárdos de Méndez, pp. 11–14. Museo Nacional de Antropología, Instituto Nacional de Antropología e Historia, Mexico City.
1995 Trade Goods, Traders, and Status in Northwestern Greater Mesoamerica. In *The Gran Chichimeca: Essays on the Archaeology and Ethnohistory of Northern Mesoamerica,* edited by Jonathan E. Reyman, pp. 102–145. Avebury, Brookfield, VT.
2000 The Aztatlán Mercantile System: Mobile Traders and the Northwestward Expansion of Mesoamerican Civilization. In *Greater Mesoamerica: The Archaeology of West and Northwest Mexico,* edited by Michael S. Foster and Shirley Gorenstein, pp. 137–154. University of Utah Press, Salt Lake City.

Kelly, Isabel T.
1947 *Excavations at Apatzingan, Michoacan.* Viking Fund Publications in Anthropology, vol. 7. Viking Fund, New York.
1949 *The Archaeology of the Autlán-Tuxcacuesco Area of Jalisco.* Vol. 2. University of California Press, Berkeley.
1980 *Ceramic Sequence in Colima: Capacha, an Early Phase.* Anthropological Papers, vol. 37. University of Arizona Press, Tucson.
1985 Some Gold and Silver Artifacts from Colima. In *The Archaeology of West and Northwest Mesoamerica,* edited by Michael S. Foster and Phil G. Weigand, pp. 153–179. Westview Press, Boulder.

Kennett, Douglas, and Barbara Voorhies
1996 Oxygen Isotopic Analysis of Archaeological Shells to Detect Seasonal Use of Wetlands on the Southern Pacific

Coast of Mexico. *Journal of Archaeological Science* 23:689–704.

Kenoyer, Jonathan M.
1998   *Ancient Cities of the Indus Valley Civilization*. Oxford University Press, New York.

Kepecs, Susan
1997   Native Yucatán and Spanish Influence: The Archaeology and History of Chikinchel. *Journal of Archaeological Method and Theory* 4(3–4):307–330.
1998   Diachronic Ceramic Evidence and Its Social Implications in the Chikinchel Region, Northeast Yucatan, Mexico. *Ancient Mesoamerica* 9:121–136.
1999   The Political Economy of Chikinchel, Yucatán, Mexico: A Diachronic Analysis from the Prehispanic Era through the Age of Spanish Administration. Ph.D. dissertation, Department of Anthropology, University of Wisconsin.
2000   Chichén Itzá, Tula, and the Epiclassic/Early Postclassic Mesamerican World System. Paper presented at "Rethinking Chichén Itzá, Tula, and Tollan," a colloquium at Dumbarton Oaks, organized by C. K. Graham and J. K. Kowalski, March.

Kepecs, Susan, Gary M. Feinman, and Sylviane Boucher
1994   Chichen Itza and Its Hinterland: A World-Systems Perspective. *Ancient Mesoamerica* 5:141–158.

Kepecs, Susan, and Tomás Gallareta Negrón
1995   Una visión diacrónica de Chikinchel y Cupul, noreste de Yucatán, Mexico. In *Memorias del Segundo Congreso Internacional de Mayistas, Mérida, Yucatán*, pp. 275–293. Instituto de Investigaciones Filológicas, Centro Estudios Mayas, Universidad Nacional Autónoma de México, Mexico City.

Kindon, A., and S. Connell
1999   Xunantunich Obsidian: From Bloodletting to Shaving. Paper presented at the 64th Annual Conference of the Society for American Archaeology (Chicago).

Kirchhoff, Paul
1943   Mesoamérica: Sus límites geográficas, composición étnica, y caracteres culturales. *Acta Americana* 1:92–107.
1952   Mesoamerica: Its Geografical Limits, Ethnic Composition, and Cultural Characteristics. In *Heritage of Conquest*, edited by Sol Tax, pp. 17–30. Free Press, New York.

Kirchhoff, Paul, Lina Odena Güemes, and Luis Reyes García (editors)
1976   *Historia tolteca-chichimeca*. Instituto Nacional de Antropología e Historia, Mexico City.

Klein, Cecelia F.
2000   The Devil and the Skirt: An Iconographic Inquiry into the Pre-Hispanic Nature of the Tzitzimime. *Ancient Mesoamerica* 11:1–26.

Knab, Tim
1980   Lenguas del Soconusco, Pipil y Náhuatl de Huehuetán. *Estudios de Cultura Náhuatl* 14:375–378.
1983   En que lengua hablaban los tepalcates Teotihuacanos? (no era náhuatl). *Revista Mexicana de Estudios Antropológicos* 29:145–158.

Kohl, Philip L.
1978   The Balance of Trade in Southwestern Asia in the Mid-Third Millennium B.C. *Current Anthropology* 19:463–492.
1987   The Use and Abuse of World Systems Theory: The Case of the Pristine West Asian State. *Advances in Archaeological Method and Theory* 11:1–36.
1989   The Use and Abuse of World Systems Theory: The Case of the "Pristine" West Asian State. In *Archaeological Thought in America*, edited by C. C. Lamberg-Karlovsky, pp. 218–240. Cambridge University Press, Cambridge.
1992   The Transcaucasion "Periphery" in the Bronze Age: A Preliminary Formulation. In *Resources, Power, and Interregional Interaction*, edited by Edward M. Schortman and Patricia A. Urban, pp. 117–138. Plenum Press, New York.

Köhler, Ulrich
1978   Reflections on Zinacantan's Role in Aztec Trade with the Soconusco. In *Mesoamerican Communication Routes and Cultural Contacts*, edited by Thomas A. Lee Jr. and Carlos Navarrete, pp. 67–73. Papers, vol. 40. New World Archaeological Foundation, Provo, UT.

König, Viola
1979   *Inhaltliche Analyse und Interpretation von Codex Egerton*. Beitrage zur Mittelamerikanischen Völkerkunde, vol. XV. Hamburgischen Museum für Völkerkunde, Hamburg.
1984   Der Lienzo Seler II und seine Stellung innerhalf der Coixtlahuaca-Gruppe. *Baessler-Archiv* 32:229–320.

Kopytoff, Igor
1987   The Internal African Frontier: The Making of African Political Culture. In *The African Frontier: The Reproduction of Traditional African Societies*, edited by Igor Kopytoff, pp. 3–84. Indiana University Press, Bloomington.

Kowalewski, Stephen A.
1982   The Evolution of Primate Regional Systems. *Comparative Urban Research* 9:60–78.
1983   Monte Albán V Settlement Patterns in the Valley of Oaxaca. In *The Cloud People: Divergent Evolution of the Zapotec and Mixtec Civilizations*, edited by Kent V. Flannery and Joyce Marcus, pp. 285–289. Academic Press, New York.
1990   The Evolution of Complexity in the Valley of Oaxaca. *Annual Review of Anthropology* 19:39–58.

Kowalski, Jeff Karl
2000   What's Toltec and What's Maya at Uxmal and Chichén Itzá? Merging Mayan and Mesoamerican Worldviews and World Systems in Terminal Classic/Early Postclassic Yucatán. Paper presented at the Dumbarton Oaks Colloquium "Rethinking Chichén Itzá, Tula, and Tollan" (Washington, D.C.).

Kowalski, Jeff Karl, and Nicholas P. Dunning
1999   The Architecture of Uxmal: The Symbolics of Statemaking at a Puuc Maya Regional Capital. In *Mesoamerican Architecture as a Cultural Symbol*, edited by Jeff Karl Kowalski, pp. 274–297. Oxford University Press, New York.

Kraft, John C., and Stanley E. Aschenbrenner
1977   Paleogeographic Reconstructions in the Methoni Embayment in Greece. *Journal of Field Archaeology* 4:19–44.

Krickeberg, W.
1969   *Felsbilder Mexico: Felsplastic und Felsbilder bei den Kulturvölkern Altament OO*. Dietrich Reimer Verlag, Berlin.

Krochock, Ruth J.
1998   The Development of Political Rhetoric at Chichén Itzá, Yucatán, Mexico. Ph.D. dissertation, Department of Anthropology Southern Methodist University.

Kroeber, Alfred L.

1931 The Culture-Area and Age-Area Concepts of Clark Wissler. In *Methods in Social Science*, edited by S. Rice, pp. 248–265. University of Chicago Press, Chicago.

1939 *Cultural and Natural Areas of Native North America.* Publications in American Archaeology and Ethnology, vol. 38. University of California, Berkeley.

Kubler, George

1979 Towards a Reductive Theory of Visual Style. In *The Concept of Style*, edited by Berel Lang, pp. 119–127. University of Pennsylvania Press, Philadelphia.

Kuhrt, Amalie

1998 The Old Assyrian Merchants. In *Trade, Traders, and the Ancient City*, edited by Helen M. Parkins and Christopher Smith, pp. 16–30. Routledge, London.

Kuper, Adam

1982 Lineage Theory: A Critical Retrospect. *Annual Review of Anthropology* 11:71–95.

Lagunas, Fray Juan Baptista de

1983 *Arte y diccionario con otras obras en lengua michuacana.* Edited by J. Benedict Warren. FIMAX Publicistas Editores, Morelia.

Landa, Diego de

1941 *Landa's Relación de las Cosas de Yucatan.* Translated by Alfred M. Tozzer. Papers, vol. 18. Peabody Museum, Harvard University, Cambridge.

Lange, Frederick W.

1984 The Greater Nicoya Archaeological Subarea. In *The Archaeology of Lower Central America*, edited by Frederick W. Lange and Doris Stone, pp. 165–194. University of New Mexico Press, Albuquerque.

1986 Central America and the Southwest: A Comparison of Mesoamerica's Two Peripheries. In *Research and Reflections in Archaeology and History: Essays in Honor of Doris Stone*, edited by E. Wyllys Andrews V, pp. 159–177. Publications, vol. 57. Middle American Research Institute, Tulane University, New Orleans.

1988 *Costa Rican Art and Archaeology.* University of Colorado, Boulder.

1993 *Precolumbian Jade: New Geological and Cultural Interpretations.* University of Utah Press, Salt Lake City.

Lange, Frederick W., and Doris Stone (editors)

1984 *The Archaeology of Lower Central America.* University of New Mexico Press, Albuquerque.

Larsen, Mogens T.

1976 *The Old Assyrian City-State and Its Colonies.* Akademisk Forlag, Copenhagen.

1987 Commercial Networks in the Ancient Near East. In *Centre and Periphery in the Ancient World*, edited by M. Rowlands, M. T. Larsen and K. Kristiansen, pp. 47–56. Cambridge University Press, Cambridge.

Leach, Edmund R.

1961 *Pul Eliya: A Village in Ceylon: A Study of Land Tenure.* Cambridge University Press, Cambridge.

Lechtman, Heather, and Sabine Klein

1999 On the Production of Copper-arsenic Alloys by Cosmelting: Modern Experiment and Ancient Practice. *Journal of Archaeological Science* 26(5):497–526.

Lee, Thomas A., Jr.

1978 The Historical Routes of Tabasco and Northern Chiapas and Their Relationship to Early Cultural Developments in Central Chiapas. In *Mesoamerican Communication Routes and Cultural Contacts*, edited by Thomas A. Lee Jr., and Carlos Navarrete, pp. 49–66.

Papers, vol. 40. New World Archaeological Foundation, Provo, UT.

Lee, Thomas A., Jr., and Carlos Navarrete (editors)

1978 *Mesoamerican Communication Routes and Cultural Contacts.* Papers, vol. 40. New World Archaeological Foundation, Provo, UT.

Lefond, Stanley J.

1969 *Handbook of World Salt Resources.* Plenum Press, New York.

Leibsohn, Dana

1994 Primers for Memory: Cartographic Histories and Nahua Identity. In *Writing Without Words: Alternative Literacies in Mesoamerica and the Andes*, edited by Elizabeth Hill Boone and Walter D. Mignolo, pp. 161–187. Duke University Press, Durham.

Le Roy Ladurie, Emmanuel

1972 *The Peasants of Languedoc.* University of Illinois Press, Urbana.

Lesure, Richard G.

1997 Early Formative Platforms at Paso de la Amada, Chiapas, Mexico. *Latin American Antiquity* 8:217–236.

Leventhal, Richard M.

1983 Household Groups and Classic Maya Religion. In *Prehistoric Settlement Patterns: Essays in Honor of Gordon R. Willey*, edited by Evon Z. Vogt and Richard M. Leventhal, pp. 55–76. University of New Mexico Press, Albuquerque.

Lévi-Strauss, Claude

1982 *The Way of Masks.* University of Washington Press, Seattle.

1983 *The Way of Masks.* Jonathan Cape, London.

1987 *Anthropology and Myth: Lectures, 1951–1982.* Blackwell, Oxford.

Lewenstein, Suzanne, and Michael D. Glascock

1997 Presencia del altiplano en la región de Comalcalco. *Los Investigadores de la Cultura Maya (Campeche, Mexico)* 5:205–211.

Lind, Michael D.

1987 *The Sociocultural Dimensions of Mixtec Ceramics.* Vanderbilt University Publications in Anthropology, vol. 33. Department of Anthropology, Vanderbilt University, Nashville.

1994 Cholula and Mixteca Polychromes: Two Mixteca-Puebla Regional Sub-Styles. In *Mixteca-Puebla: Discoveries and Research in Mesoamerican Art and Archaeology*, edited by H. B. Nicholson and Eloise Quiñones Keber, pp. 79–100. Labyrinthos, Culver City, CA.

2000 Mixtec City-States and Mixtec City-State Culture. In *A Comparative Study of Thirty City-State Cultures*, edited by Mogens Herman Hansen, pp. 567–580. The Royal Danish Academy of Sciences and Letters, Copenhagen.

n.d. The Great City Square: Government in Ancient Cholula. *Notas Mesoamericanas.*

Lister, Robert H.

1949 *Excavations at Cojumatlan, Michoacan, Mexico.* University of New Mexico Publications in Anthropology, vol. 5. University of New Mexico, Albuquerque.

Litvak King, Jaime

1968 Excavaciones de rescate en la presa de La Villita. *Boletín del Instituto Nacional de Antropología e Historia* 31:28–30.

1971 *Cihuatlan y Tepecoacuilco: Provincias tributarias de México en el siglo XVI.* Universidad Nacional Autónoma de México, Mexico City.

Lockhart, James
1992 *The Nahuas After the Conquest: A Social and Cultural History of the Indians of Central Mexico, Sixteenth Through Eighteenth Centuries.* Stanford University Press, Stanford.

Long, Richard
1919 The Date of Maya Ruins at Santa Rita, British Honduras. *Man* 19:59–61.

López, Raúl Avila
1991 *Chinampas de Iztapalapa, D.F.* Colección Científica, vol. 225. Instituto Nacional de Antropología e Historia, Mexico City.

López, Robert, Dorothy Hosler, and Dante Moran.
1999 Coastal and Inland Pb Isotope Groups of Pb Paleocene Cu Ores from the Río Balsas Basin, Guerrero State. Paper presented at the American Geophysical Union Annual Meeting, San Francisco, December.

López Aguilar, Fernando, and R. Nieto Calleja
1989 Yacimientos y talleres de obsidiana en Otumba. In *La obsidian en Mesoamérica*, edited by Margarita Gaxiola G., and John E. Clark, pp. 199–203. Instituto Nacional de Antropología e Historia, Mexico City.

López Aguilar, Fernando, R. Nieto Calleja, and Robert H. Cobean
1989 Producción de obsidiana en la Sierra de las Navajas, Hidalgo. In *La obsidian en mesoamérica*, edited by Margarita Gaxiola G., and John E. Clark, pp. 193–198. Instituto Nacional de Antropología e Historia, Mexico City.

López Austin, Alfredo
1976 El fundamento mágico-religioso de poder. *Estudios de Cultura Náhuatl* 12:197–240.
1988 *Human Body and Ideology: Concepts of the Ancient Nahuas.* Translated by Bernard R. Ortiz de Montellano and Themla Ortiz de Montellano. 2 vols. University of Utah Press, Salt Lake City.
1993 *The Myths of the Possum: Pathways of Mesoamerican Mythology.* University of New Mexico Press, Albuquerque.
1994 *Tamoachan y Tlalocan.* Fondo de Cultura Económica, Mexico City.

López de Gómara, Francisco
1987 *La conquista de México.* Translated and edited by José Luis de Rojas. Hermanos García Noblejas, Madrid.

López Luján, Leonardo
1994 *The Offerings of the Templo Mayor of Tenochtitlan.* Translated by Bernard R. Ortiz de Montellano and Themla Ortiz de Montellano. University Press of Colorado, Niwot.

Lorinczi, G. I., and J. C. Miranda V.
1978 Geology of the Massive Sulfide Deposits of Campo Morado, Guerrero, Mexico. *Economic Geology* 73:180–191.

Lothrop, Samuel K.
1924 *Tulum, An Archaeological Study of the East Coast of Yucatan.* Publication, vol. 335. Carnegie Institute of Washington, Washington, D.C.
1926 *Pottery of Costa Rica and Nicaragua.* Contributions, vol. 8. Museum of the American Indian (Heye Foundation), New York.
1927 The Word "Maya" and the Fourth Voyage of Columbus. *Indian Notes* 4(4):350–363.
1933 *Atitlán: An Archaeological Study of Archaeological Remains on the Borders of Lake Atitlán, Guatemala.* Publication, vol. 444. Carnegie Institute of Washington, Washington, D.C.
1936 *Zacualpa: A Study of Ancient Quiché Artifacts.* Publication, vol. 472. Carnegie Institute of Washington, Washington, D.C.
1942 The Sigua: Southernmost Aztec Outpost. In *Proceedings of the Eighth American Scientific Congress*, pp. 109–116, vol. 2. U.S. Government, Department of State, Washington, D.C.
1952 *Metals from the Cenote of Sacrifice, Chichen Itza, Yucatan.* Memoirs, vol. 10, 2. Peabody Museum, Cambridge, MA.
1966 Archaeology of Lower Central America. In *Archaeological Frontiers and External Connections*, edited by Gordon F. Ekholm and Gordon R. Willey, pp. 180–208. Handbook of Middle American Indians, vol. 4. University of Texas Press, Austin.

Love, Bruce
1994 *The Paris Codex: Handbook for a Maya Priest.* University of Texas Press, Austin.

Lowe, Gareth W., Thomas A. Lee, and Eduardo Martínez Espinosa
1982 *Izapa: An Introduction to the Ruins and Monuments.* Papers, vol. 31. New World Archaeological Foundation, Provo, UT.

McAnany, Patricia A.
1991 Structure and Dynamics of Intercommunity Exchange. In *Maya Stone Tools: Selected Papers From the Second Maya Lithic Conference*, edited by Thomas R. Hester and Harry J. Shafer, pp. 271–293. Prehistory Press, Madison, WI.
1993 The Economics of Social Power and Wealth Among Eighth Century Maya Households. In *Lowland Maya Civilization in the Eighth Century A.D.*, edited by Jeremy A. Sabloff and John S. Henderson, pp. 65–89. Dumbarton Oaks, Washington, D.C.
1994 Operation 2033: Horizontal Exposure of a Terminal Classic Platform. In *Continuing Archaeology at Colha, Belize*, edited by Thomas R. Hester, Harry J. Shafer and Jack D. Eaton, pp. 79–89. Studies in Archaeology, vol. 16. Texas Archaeological Research Laboratory, University of Texas, Austin.
1995 *Living With the Ancestors: Kinship and Kingship in Ancient Maya Society.* University of Texas Press, Austin.

McAnany, Patricia A., Ben S. Thomas, Steven Morandi, Polly A. Peterson, and Eleanor Harrison
n.d. Praise the Ajaw and Pass the Kakaw: Xibun Maya and the Political Economy of Cacao. In *Ancient Maya Political Economies*, edited by Marilyn A. Masson and David A. Freidel. Altamira Press, Walnut Creek, CA.

McCafferty, Geoffrey G.
1994 The Mixteca-Puebla Stylistic Tradition at Early Postclassic Cholula. In *Mixteca-Puebla: Discoveries and Research in Mesoamerican Art and Archaeology*, edited by H.B. Nicholson and Eloise Quiñones Keber, pp. 53–78. Labyrinthos, Culver City, CA.
1996a Reinterpreting the Great Pyramid of Cholula. *Ancient Mesoamerica* 7:1–18.
1996b The Ceramics and Chronology of Cholula, Mexico. *Ancient Mesoamerica* 7:299–324.

Macdonald, C. (editor)
1987 *De la hutte au palais: Sociétés "à maisons" en Asie du Sud-Est insulaire.* Editions du Centre National de la Recherche Scientifique, Paris.

McGuire, Randall H.
1989 The Greater Southwest as a Periphery of Mesoamerica. In *Centre and Periphery: Comparative Studies in Ar-*

chaeology, edited by Timothy C. Champion, pp. 40–66. Unwin Hyman, London.

Macías, Martha C.

1990 La metalurgia en el México prehispánico: Oaxaca, tierra de orfebres. In *Mesoamérica y norte de México, siglo IX–XII*, edited by Federica Sodi Miranda, pp. 179–193, vol. 1. Instituto Nacional de Antropología e Historia, Mexico City.

Macías G., Angelina

1989 La cuenca de Cuitzeo. In *Historia general de Michoacán*, pp. 171–190, vol. 1. Gobierno de Michoacán, Morelia, Mexico.

1990 *Huandacareo: Lugar de juicios, tribunal*. Colección Científica, vol. 222. Instituto Nacional de Antropología e Historia, Mexico City.

McKillop, Heather I.

1995a Underwater Archaeology, Salt Production, and Coastal Maya Trade at Stingray Lagoon, Belize. *Latin American Antiquity* 6:214–228.

1995b The Role of Northern Ambergris Caye in Maya Obsidian Trade: Evidence from Visual Sourcing and Blade Technology. In *Maya Maritime Trade, Settlement, and Population on Ambergris Caye, Belize*, edited by Thomas H. Guderjan and James F. Garber, pp. 163–174. Maya Research Program and Labyrinthos, Lancaster, CA.

1996 Ancient Maya Trading Ports and the Integration of Long-Distance and Regional Economies: Wild Cane Cay in South-Coastal Belize. *Ancient Mesoamerica* 7:49–62.

2001 Ports of Trade. In *Archaeology of Ancient Mexico and Central America: An Encyclopedia*, edited by Susan Evans and David Webster, pp. 596–597. Garland, New York.

McKillop, Heather, and Paul Healy (editors)

1989 *Coastal Maya Trade*. Occasional Papers in Anthropology, vol. 8. Trent University, Peterborough.

MacKinnon, J. Jefferson

1989 Coastal Maya Trade Routes in Southern Belize. In *Coastal Maya Trade*, edited by Heather McKillop and Paul Healy, pp. 111–122. Occasional Papers in Anthropology, vol. 8. Trent University, Peterborough.

MacKinnon, J. Jefferson, and Susan Kepecs

1989 Prehispanic Saltmaking in Belize: New Evidence. *American Antiquity* 54:522–533.

MacKinnon, J. Jefferson, Susan Kepecs, Gary Walters, and E. M. May

1989 Coastal Trade and Procurement Sites in Southern Belize: Implications for Yucatecan Salt Production and Circum-Peninsular Trade, edited by Heather McKillop and Paul Healy. In *Memorias del Segundo Coloquio de Mayistas, Campeche, México, agosto 1987*, pp. 703–716, vol. 1. Universidad Nacional Autónoma de México, Mexico City.

MacNeish, Richard S., Frederick A. Peterson, and Kent V. Flannery

1970 *Ceramics*. Vol. 3 of *The Prehistory of the Tehuacan Valley*. University of Texas Press, Austin.

McQuown, Norman A.

1964 Los orígenes y la diferenciación de los mayas según se infiere del estudio comparativo de las lenguas mayanas. In *Desarrollo cultural de los mayas*, edited by Evon A. Vogt and A. Ruz, pp. 49–80. Seminario de Cultura Maya, Universidad Nacional Autónoma de México, Mexico City.

Maguire, Susan

2001 Soconusco Postclassic Project Obsidian Analysis. Manuscript on file, Department of Anthropology, State University of New York at Buffalo.

Maldonado Cárdenas, Rubén

1980 *Ofrendas asociados a entierros del Infiernillo en el Balsas: Estudio y experimentación con tres métodos de taxonomía numérica*. Colección Científica, vol. 91. Instituto Nacional de Antropología e Historia, Mexico City.

Maldonado Jiménez, Druzo

1990 *Cuauhnahuac y Huaxtepec: Tlalhuicas y xochimilcas en el Morelos prehispánico*. Centro Regional de Investigaciones Multidisciplinarias, Universidad Nacional Autónoma de México, Cuernavaca.

Mallon, Florencia

1993 Dialogs Among the Fragments: Retrospect and Prospect. In *Confronting Historical Paradigms*, edited by F. Cooper, A. F. Isaacman, F. E. Mallon, W. Roseberry, and S. J. Stern, pp. 370–401. University of Wisconsin Press, Madison.

Mann, Michael

1986 *The Sources of Social Power*, vol. 1, *A History of Power from the Beginning to A.D. 1760*. Cambridge University Press, New York.

Marcus, Joyce

1983a The Conquest Slabs of Building J, Monte Alban. In *The Cloud People: Divergent Evolution of the Zapotec and Mixtec Civilizations*, edited by Kent V. Flannery and Joyce Marcus, pp. 106–108. Academic Press, New York.

1983b Stone Monuments and Tomb Murals of Monte Alban IIIa. In *The Cloud People: Divergent Evolution of the Zapotec and Mixtec Civilizations*, edited by Kent V. Flannery and Joyce Marcus, pp. 137–143. Academic Press, New York.

1983c Changing Patterns of Stone Monuments after the Fall of Monte Alban, A.D. 600–900. In *The Cloud People: Divergent Evolution of the Zapotec and Mixtec Civilizations*, edited by Kent V. Flannery and Joyce Marcus, pp. 191–196. Academic Press, New York.

1983d The Reconstructed Chronology of the Later Zapotec Rulers, A.D. 1415–1563. In *The Cloud People: Divergent Evolution of the Zapotec and Mixtec Civilizations*, edited by Kent V. Flannery and Joyce Marcus, pp. 301–308. Academic Press, New York.

1983e Aztec Military Campaigns Against the Zapotecs: The Documentary Evidence. In *The Cloud People: Divergent Evolution of the Zapotec and Mixtec Civilizations*, edited by Kent V. Flannery and Joyce Marcus, pp. 314–318. Academic Press, New York.

1983f Zapotec Religion. In *The Cloud People: Divergent Evolution of the Zapotec and Mixtec Civilizations*, edited by Kent V. Flannery and Joyce Marcus, pp. 345–351. Academic Press, New York.

1989 From Centralized Systems to City-States: Possible Models for the Epiclassic. In *Mesoamerica After the Decline of Teotihuacan, A.D. 700–900*, edited by Richard A. Diehl and Janet C. Berlo, pp. 201–208. Dumbarton Oaks, Washington, D.C.

1992a *Mesoamerican Writing Systems: Propaganda, Myth, and History in Four Ancient Civilizations*. Princeton University Press, Princeton.

1992b Political Fluctuations in Mesoamerica: Dynamic Cycles of Mesoamerican States. *National Geographic Research* 8:392–411.

1993 Ancient Maya Political Organization. In *Lowland Maya Civilization in the Eighth Century A.D.*, edited by Jeremy A. Sabloff and John S. Henderson, pp. 111–184. Dumbarton Oaks, Washington, D.C.

1998   The Peaks and Valleys of Ancient States: An Extension of the Dynamic Model. In *Archaic States*, edited by Gary M. Feinman and Joyce Marcus, pp. 59–94. School of American Research Press, Santa Fe, NM.

Marcus, Joyce, and Kent V. Flannery

1983   An Introduction to the Late Postclassic. In *The Cloud People: Divergent Evolution of the Zapotec and Mixtec Civilizations*, edited by Kent V. Flannery and Joyce Marcus, pp. 217–226. Academic Press, New York.

Marquina, Ignacio

1964   *Arquitectura prehispánica*. 2nd ed. Instituto Nacional de Antropología e Historia, Mexico City.

Martínez, Hildeberto

1984   *Tepeaca en el siglo XVI*. Ediciones de la Casas Chata, Mexico City.

Mason, Roger D.

1980   Economic and Social Organization of an Aztec Provincial Center: Archaeological Research at Coatlan Viejo, Morelos, Mexico. Ph.D. dissertation, Department of Anthropology, University of Texas.

Massey, Virginia K., and D. Gentry Steele

1997   A Maya Skull Pit from the Terminal Classic Period, Colha, Belize. In *Bones of the Maya: Studies of Ancient Skeletons*, edited by Stephen L. Whittington and David M. Reed, pp. 62–77. Smithsonian Institution Press, Washington, D.C.

Masson, Marilyn A.

1997   Cultural Transformation at the Maya Postclassic Community of Laguna de On, Belize. *Latin American Antiquity* 8:293–316.

1999a   Postclassic Maya Communities at Progresso Lagoon and Laguna Seca, Northern Belize. *Journal of Field Archaeology* 26:285–306.

1999b   Postclassic Maya Ritual and Laguna de On Island, Belize. *Ancient Mesoamerica* 10:51–68.

2000a   *In the Realm of Nachan Kan: Postclassic Maya Archaeology at Laguna de On, Belize*. University Press of Colorado, Niwot.

2000b   Segmentary Political Cycles and Elite Migration Myths in the Postclassic Archaeology of Northern Belize. In *The Past and Present Maya: Essays in Honor of Robert M. Carmack*, edited by John Weeks, pp. 89–103. Labyrinthos Press, Lancaster, CA.

2000c   Postclassic Political and Economic Development in the Chetumal Province: Eastablishing a Chronological Framework. Report posted at www.famsi.org. Foundation for the Advancement of Mesoamerican Studies, Inc.

2002   Postclassic Maya Community Economy and the Mercantile Transformation in Northeastern Belize. In *Ancient Maya Political Economies*, edited by Marilyn A. Masson and David A. Freidel. Altamira Press, Walnut Creek, CA.

n.d.a   Type-Variety Analysis of Terminal Classic through Late Postclassic Ceramics at Caye Coco, Progresso, Belize. In *The Belize Postclassic Project 2001: Expansion of Temporal Investigations at Progresso Lagoon*, edited by Marilyn A. Masson and Robert M. Rosenswig. Occasional Publication, vol. 7. Institute for Mesoamerican Studies, Albany, NY.

n.d.b   Changing Patterns of Ceramic Stylistic Diversity in the Pre-Hispanic Maya Lowlands. (Submitted to *Acta Archaeologia*.)

n.d.c   Laguna de On and Caye Coco: Economic Differentiation at Two Postclassic Island Communities in Northern Belize. In *The Social Implications of Ancient Maya Rural Complexity*, edited by Gyles Iannone and Samuel V. Connell. Institute of Archaeology, University of California Press, Los Angeles.

Masson, Marilyn A., and Shirley Boteler Mock

n.d.   Transformations in Ceramic Economies from the Terminal Classic to Postclassic Periods at Lagoon Sites of Northern Belize. In *The Terminal Classic in the Maya Lowlands: Collapse, Transition, and Transformation*, edited by Don S. Rice and Prudence M. Rice. Westview Press, Boulder.

Masson, Marilyn A., and Henry Chaya

2000   Obsidian Trade Connections at the Postclassic Maya Site of Laguna de On, Belize. *Lithic Technology* 25:125–134.

Masson, Marilyn A., and Dawn Mooney Digrius

2001   Further Investigations at Structure 1 (Subop 6), Caye Coco. In *The Belize Postclassic Project 2000: Investigations at Caye Coco and the Shore Settlements of Progresso Lagoon*, edited by Robert M. Rosenswig and Marilyn A. Masson, pp. 5–26. Occasional Publication, vol. 6. Institute for Mesoamerican Studies, Albany, NY.

Masson, Marilyn A., and Robert M. Rosenswig (editors)

1998a   *Belize Postclassic Project 1997: Laguna de On, Progresso Lagoon, and Laguna Seca*. Occasional Publication, vol. 2. Institute for Mesoamerican Studies, Albany, NY.

1998b   *The Belize Postclassic Project: Report of the 1996 Investigations at Laguna de On Island*. Occasional Publication No. 1, Institute for Mesoamerican Studies, Albany, NY.

1999   *The Belize Postclassic Project 1998: Investigations at Progreso Lagoon*. Occasional Publication No. 3, Institute for Mesoamerican Studies, Albany, NY.

n.d.   Postclassic Maya Ceramic Chronology of Caye Coco, Belize. Manuscript in preparation.

Matheny, Raymond T.

1970   *The Ceramics of Aguacatal, Campeche, Mexico*. Papers, vol. 27. New World Archaeological Foundation, Provo, UT.

Mathien, Frances J., and Randall H. McGuire (editors)

1986   *Ripples in the Chichimec Sea: New Considerations of Southwestern-Mesoamerican Interactions*. Southern Illinois University Press, Carbondale.

Matos Moctezuma, Eduardo

1974   *Proyecto Tula (primera parte)*. Colección Científica, vol. 15. Instituto Nacional de Antropología e Historia, Mexico City.

1989   *The Aztecs*. Rizzoli, New York.

Matrícula de Tributos

1980   *Matrícula de Tributos (Códice de Moctezuma)*. Edited by Frances F. Berdan and Jacqueline de Durand-Forest. Akademische Druck u Verlagsanstalt, Graz.

Mayhew, Anne, Walter C. Neale, and David W. Tandy

1985   Markets in the Ancient Near East: A Challenge to Silver's Argument and Use of Evidence. *Journal of Economic History* 45:127–134.

Mazeau, Daniel

2000a   Excavations at Structure 2 and Structure 3, Caye Coco. In *Belize Postclassic Project 1999: Continuing Investigations at Progresso Lagoon and Laguna Seca*, edited by Robert M. Rosenswig and Marilyn A. Masson, pp. 7–20. Occasional Publication, vol. 5. Institute for Mesoamerican Studies, Albany, NY.

2000b   Subop 30: A Cemetery Near Structure 2, Caye Coco. In

Belize Postclassic Project 1999: Continuing Investigations at Progreso Lagoon and Laguna Seca, edited by Robert M. Rosenswig and Marilyn A. Masson, pp. 21–30. Occasional Publication, vol. 5. Institute for Mesoamerican Studies, Albany, NY.

2000c Terminal Classic and Postclassic Obsidian Exchange and Production in the Maya Lowlands. M.A. thesis, Department of Anthropology, State University of New York at Buffalo.

Medellín Zeñil, Alfonso

1952 *Exploraciones de Quauhtochco, Temporada I.* Gobierno del Estado de Veracruz y Instituto Nacional de Antropología e Historia, Jalapa.

1960 *Cerámicas del Totonacapan.* Universidad Veracruzana, Jalapa.

Medina, Jose Torbidio

1912 Monedas usadas por los indios de América al momento del descubrimiento. In *Actas del 17th Congreso Internacional de Americanistas*, pp. 556–567.

Meighan, Clement W.

1960 Prehistoric Copper Objects from Western Mexico. *Science* 131:1534.

1969 Cultural Similarities between Western Mexico and Andean Regions. *Mesoamerican Studies* 4:11–25.

1974 Prehistory of West Mexico. *Science* 184:1254–1261.

1976 *The Archaeology of Amapa, Nayarit.* Institute of Archaeology, University of California, Los Angeles.

1999 The Mexican West Coast and the Hohokam Region. In *The Casas Grandes World*, edited by Curtis F. Schaafsma and Carroll L. Riley, pp. 206–212. University of Utah Press, Salt Lake City.

Meighan, Clement W., and Leonardo J. Foote

1968 *Excavations at Tizapan El Alto, Jalisco.* Latin American Studies. Latin American Center, University of California, Los Angeles.

Melgarejo Vivanco, José Luis

1970 *Los lienzos de Tuxpan.* Editorial la Estampa Mexicana, Mexico City.

Mendieta, Gerónimo de

1971 *Historia Eclesiástica Indiana.* Porrúa, Mexico City.

Mendizábal, Miguel Othón de

1926 "El lienzo de Jucutacato." Su verdadera significación. Museo Nacional de Arqueología, Historia y Etnografía, Mexico City.

1946 Influencia de la sal en la distribución geográfica de los grupos indígenas de México. *Obras Completas* II:181–340.

Metcalfe, S. E., F. A. Street-Perrott, R. B. Brown, P. E. Hales, R. A. Perrott, and F. M. Steininger

1989 Late Holocene Human Impact on Lake Basins in Central Mexico. *Geoarchaeology* 4:119–141.

Metcalfe, Sara E., F. Alayne Street-Perrott, R. Alan Perrott, and Douglas D. Harkness

1991 Palaeolimnology of the Upper Lerma Basin, Central Mexico: A Record of Climatic Change and Anthropogenic Disturbance Since 11600 yr BP. *Journal of Paleolimnology* 5:197–218.

Michaels, George H.

1987 A Description of Early Postclassic Lithic Technology at Colha, Belize. M.A. thesis, Department of Anthropology, Texas A&M University.

1994 The Postclassic at Colha, Belize: A Summary Overview and Directions for Future Research. In *Continuing Archaeology at Colha, Belize*, edited by Thomas R. Hester, Harry J. Shafer, and Jack D. Eaton, pp. 129–136. Stud-

ies in Archaeology, vol. 16. Texas Archaeological Research Laboratory, University of Texas, Austin.

Michaels, George H., and Harry J. Shafer

1994 Excavations at Operation 2037 and 2040. In *Continuing Archaeology at Colha, Belize*, edited by Thomas R. Hester, Harry J. Shafer, and Jack D. Eaton, pp. 117–129. Studies in Archaeology, vol. 16. Texas Archaeological Research Laboratory, University of Texas, Austin.

Michelet, Dominique

1995 La zona occidental en el Posclásico. In *Historia antigua de México.* Vol. 3, *El horizonte Posclásico y algunos aspectos intelectuales de las culturas mesoamericanas*, edited by Linda Manzanilla and Leonardo López Luján, pp. 153–188. Instituto Nacional de Antropología e Historia, Mexico City.

Michels, Joseph W.

1979 *The Kaminaljuyu Chiefdom.* Pennsylvania State University Press, University Park.

Migeon, Gérald

1998 El poblamiento de Malpaís de Zacapu y de sus alrededores, del Clásico al Posclásico. In *Génesis, culturas, y espacios en Michoacán*, edited by Véronique Darras, pp. 35–45. Centre D'Études Mexicanes et Centroaméricanes, Mexico City.

Mikesell, Marvin W.

1961 *Northern Morocco: A Cultural Geography.* University of California Publications in Geography, vol. 14. University of California, Berkeley.

Milbrath, Susan

1999 *Star Gods of the Maya: Astronomy in Art, Folklore, and Calendars.* University of Texas Press, Austin.

Miles, Susanna W.

1957 The Sixteenth-Century Pokom-Maya: A Documentary Analysis of Social Structure and Archaeological Setting. *Transactions of the American Philosophical Society* 47:731–781.

Miller, Arthur G.

1974 The Iconography of the Painting in the Temple of the Diving God, Tulum, Quintana Roo, Mexico: The Twisted Cords. In *Mesoamerican Archaeology: New Approaches*, edited by Norman Hammond, pp. 167–186. University of Texas Press, Austin.

1982 *At the Edge of the Sea: Mural Painting at Tancah-Tulum, Quintana Roo, Mexico.* Dumbarton Oaks, Washington, D.C.

1985 The Postclassic Sequence of Tancah and Tulum, Quintana Roo, Mexico. In *The Lowland Maya Postclassic*, edited by Arlen F. Chase and Prudence M. Rice, pp. 31–49. University of Texas Press, Austin.

1986 From the Maya Margins: Images of Postclassic Power Politics. In *Late Lowland Maya Civilization: Classic to Postclassic*, edited by Jeremy A. Sabloff and E. Wyllys Andrews, pp. 199–222. University of New Mexico Press, Albuquerque.

Miller, Daniel

1995 Consumption and Commodities. *Annual Review of Anthropology* 24:141–161.

Miller, Edward, and John Hatcher

1978 *Medieval England: Rural Society and Economic Change, 1086–1348.* Longman, New York.

Miller, Virginia E.

1999 The Skull Rack in Mesoamerica. In *Mesoamerican Architecture as a Cultural Symbol*, edited by Jeff Karl Kowaslki, pp. 340–360. Oxford University Press, New York.

Millon, René

1955   When Money Grew on Trees: A Study of Cacao in Ancient Mesoamerica. Ph.D. dissertation, Department of
Anthropology, Colombia University.

1988   The Last Years of Teotihuacan Dominance. In *The Collapse of Ancient States and Civilizations*, edited by Norman Yoffee and George L. Cowgill, pp. 102–164.
University of Arizona Press, Tucson.

Minc, Leah D., Mary G. Hodge, and James Blackman

1994   Stylistic and Spatial Variability in Early Aztec Ceramics:
Insights into Pre-imperial Exchange Systems. In
Economies and Polities in the Aztec Realm, edited by
Mary G. Hodge and Michael E. Smith, pp. 133–173.
Institute for Mesoamerican Studies, Albany.

Mock, Shirley Boteler

1994a   The Northern River Lagoon Site (NRL): Late to Terminal Classic Maya Settlement, Saltmaking, and Survival
on the Northern Belize Coast. Ph.D. dissertation, Department of Anthropology, University of Texas.

1994b   Yucatecan Presence in Northern Belize Postclassic Ceramics at Colha. In *Continuing Archaeology at Colha,
Belize*, edited by Thomas R. Hester, Harry J. Shafer, and
Jack D. Eaton, pp. 9–16. Studies in Archaeology, vol.
16. Texas Archaeological Research Laboratory, University of Texas, Austin.

Moholy-Nagy, Hattula

1997   Middens, Construction Fill, and Offerings: Evidence for
the Organization of Classic Period Craft Production at
Tikal, Guatemala. *Journal of Field Archaeology*
24:293–314.

Moholy-Nagy, Hattula, and J. M. Ladd

1992   Objects of Stone, Shell, and Bone. In *Artifacts from the
Cenote of Sacrifice, Chichen Itza, Yucatan*, edited by
Clemency Chase Coggins, pp. 99–152. Memoirs of the
Peabody Museum of Archaeology and Ethnology, vol.
10, 3. Harvard University, Cambridge.

Moholy-Nagy, Hattula, and Fred W. Nelson

1990   New Data on Sources of Obsidian Artifacts at Tikal,
Guatemala. *Ancient Mesoamerica* 1:71–80.

Monaghan, John

1990a   Performance and the Structure of the Mixtec Codices.
Ancient Mesoamerica 1:133–140.

1990b   Reciprocity, Redistribution, and the Transaction of
Value in the Mesoamerican Fiesta. *American Ethnologist* 17:758–774.

1995   *The Covenants with Earth and Rain: Exchange, Sacrifice, and Revelation in Mixtec Sociality*. University of
Oklahoma Press, Norman.

1998   The Person, Destiny, and the Construction of Difference
in Mesoamerica. *RES* 33:137–146.

Motolinía, Fray Toribio de

1941   *Historia de los indios de Nueva España*. Editorial Salvador Chavez Hayhoe, Mexico City.

1950   *History of the Indians of New Spain*. Translated by Elizabeth A. Foster. The Cortés Society, Berkeley.

Mountjoy, Joseph B.

1982   *Proyecto Tomatlán de salvamento arqueológico*.
Instituto Nacional de Antropología e Historia, Mexico
City.

2000   Prehispanic Cultural Development Along the Southern
Coast of West Mexico. In *Greater Mesoamerica: The
Archaeology of West and Northwest Mexico*, edited by
Michael S. Foster and Shirley Gorenstein, pp. 81–106.
University of Utah Press, Salt Lake City.

Mountjoy, Joseph B., and Luis Torres M.

1985   The Production and Use of Prehispanic Metal Artifacts
in the Central Coastal Area of Jalisco, Mexico. In *The
Archaeology of West and Northwest Mesoamerica*, edited by Michael S. Foster and Phil G. Weigand, pp. 133–
152. Westview Press, Boulder.

Muller, Jon

1997   *Mississippian Political Economy*. Plenum, New York.

Multhauf, Robert P.

1978   *Neptune's Gift: A History of Common Salt*. Johns Hopkins University Press, Baltimore.

Muñoz Camargo, Diego

1984   *Descripción de la ciudad y provincia de Tlaxcala*. Edited
by René Acuña. Universidad Nacional Autónoma de
México, Mexico City.

Murra, John V.

1975   *Formaciones económicas y políticas del mundo andino*.
Instituto de Estudios Peruanos, Lima.

Nash, Michael A.

1980   An Analysis of a Debitage Collection from Colha, Belize.
In *The Colha Project: Second Season, 1980 Interim Re-
port*, edited by Thomas R. Hester, Jack D. Eaton, and
Harry J. Shafer, pp. 333–352. Center for Archaeological
Research, University of Texas and Centro Studie
Ricerche Ligabue, San Antonio and Venezia.

Navarrete, Carlos

1966   *The Chiapanec History and Culture*. Papers, vol. 23.
New World Archaeological Foundation, Provo, UT.

1975   Nueva información sobre la lengua Nahuatl en Chiapas.
Anales de Antropología 12:273–282.

1976   Algunas influencias mexicanas en el área maya meridional durante el Posclásico tardío. *Estudios de la Cultura
Náhuatl* 12:345–382.

1978   The Prehispanic System of Communications between
Chiapas and Tabasco. In *Mesoamerican Communication Routes and Cultural Contacts*, edited by Thomas A.
Lee Jr. and Carlos Navarrete, pp. 75–106. Papers, vol.
40. New World Archaeological Foundation, Provo, UT.

1996   Elementos arqueológicos de mexicanización en las tierras altas mayas. In *Temas mesoamericanos*, edited by
Sonia Lombardo and Enrique Nalda, pp. 305–342. Instituto Nacional de Antropología e Historia, Mexico
City.

Neale, Walter C.

1971   Monetization, Commercialization, Market Orientation,
and Market Dependence. In *Studies in Economic Anthropology*, edited by George Dalton, pp. 25–29. Anthropological Studies, vol. 7. American Anthropological
Association, Washington, D.C.

Neely, James A., S. Christopher Caran, and Frances Ramírez
Sorsensen

1997   The Prehispanic and Colonial Saltworks of the Tehuacan Valley and Vicinity, Southern Puebla, Mexico. Paper
presented at the 62nd Annual Conference of the Society
for American Archaeology (Nashville).

Neff, Hector, and Ronald L. Bishop

1988   Plumbate Origins and Development. *American Antiquity* 53:486–504.

Neff, Hector, Ronald L. Bishop, Edward B. Sisson, Michael D.
Glascock, and Penny R. Sisson

1994   Neutron Activation Analysis of Late Postclassic Polychrome Pottery from Central Mexico. In *Mixteca-
Puebla: Discoveries and Research in Mesoamerican Art
and Archaeology*, edited by H. B. Nicholson and Eloise

Quiñones Keber, pp. 117–141. Labyrinthos, Culver City, CA.

Neff, Hector, and Michael D. Glascock
1999 *Compositional Analysis of Ceramics and Raw Materials from the Lake Pátzcuaro Basin, Mexico.* Report on file, Missouri University Research Reactor, Columbia, MO.

Neivens, M., Garman Harbottle, and J. B. Kimberlin
1983 Trace Element Analysis of Obsidian Artifacts from Northern Belize. In *Archaeological Excavations in Northern Belize, Central America*, edited by Raymond V. Sidrys, pp. 321–339. Monograph, vol. 17. Institute of Archaeology, University of California, Los Angeles.

Nelson, Ben A.
1990 Observaciones acerca de la presencia tolteca en La Quemada, Zacatecas. In *Mesoamérica y norte de México, siglo IX–XII*, edited by Federica Sodi Miranda, pp. 487–519. Instituto Nacional de Antropología e Historia, Mexico City.
n.d. Aggregation, Warfare, and the Spread of the Mesoamerican Tradition. In *The Archaeology of Regional Interaction: Religion, Warfare, and Exchange Across the American Southwest*, edited by Michelle Hegmon. University of Colorado Press, Boulder.

Nelson, Fred W., Jr.
1985 Summary of the Results of Analysis of Obsidian Artifacts from the Maya Lowlands. *Scanning Electron Microscopy* 2:631–649.
1989 Rutas de intercambio de obsidiana en el norte de la península de Yucatán. In *La obsidiana en mesoamérica*, edited by Margarita Gaxiola G. and John E. Clark, pp. 363–368. Instituto Nacional de Antropología e Historia, Mexico City.
1997 Appendix 3: Trace Element Analysis by X-ray Fluorescence of Obsidian Artifacts from Dzibilchaltún, Komchén, and the Mirador Group, Yucatán. In *Maya Stone Tools of Dzibilchaltún, Yucatán, and Becán and Chicanná, Campeche*, edited by Irwin Rovner and Suzanne M. Lewenstein, pp. 152–161. Publication, vol. 65. Middle American Research Institute, Tulane University.

Nelson, Fred W., Jr., K. K. Nielson, N. F. Mangelson, M. W. Hill, and Raymond T. Matheny
1977 Preliminary Studies of the Trace Element Composition of Obsidian Artifacts from Northern Campeche. *American Antiquity* 43:209–225.

Nelson, Fred W., Jr., David A. Phillips Jr., and Alfredo Barrera Rubio
1983 Trace Element Analysis of Obsidian Artifacts from the Northern Maya Lowlands. In *Investigations at Edzná, Campeche, Mexico*, vol. 1, part 1, *The Hydraulic System*, edited by Raymond T. Matheny, Deanne L. Gurr, Donald W. Forsyth, and F. Richard Hauk. Papers, vol. 46. New World Archaeological Foundation, Provo, UT.

Nelson, Fred W., Jr., Raymond V. Sidrys, and R. D. Holmes
1978 Trace Element Analysis by X-Ray Fluorescence of Obsidian Artifacts from Guatemala and Belize. In *Excavations at Seibal, Department of Peten, Guatemala, Artifacts*, edited by Gordon R. Willey, pp. 153–161. Memoirs, vol. 14. Peabody Museum, Harvard University, Cambridge.

Netting, Robert McC.
1968 *Hill Farmers of Nigeria: Cultural Ecology of the Jos Plateau.* University of Washington Press, Seattle.
1993 *Smallholders, Householders: Farm Families and the Ecology of Intensive, Sustainable Agriculture.* Stanford University Press, Stanford.

Nichols, Deborah L.
1994 The Organization of Provincial Craft Production and the Aztec City-State of Otumba. In *Economies and Polities in the Aztec Realm*, edited by Mary G. Hodge and Michael E. Smith, pp. 175–193. Institute for Mesoamerican Studies, Albany.

Nichols, Deborah L., and Thomas H. Charlton
1996 The Postclassic Occupation at Otumba: A Chronological Assessment. *Ancient Mesoamerica* 7:231–244.
1997 *The Archaeology of City-States: Cross-Cultural Approaches.* Smithsonian Institution Press, Washington, D.C.

Nicholson, H. B.
1957 Topiltzin Quetzalcoatl of Tollan: A Problem in Mesoamerican Ethnohistory. Ph.D. dissertation, Department of Anthropology, Harvard University.
1959 The Chapultepec Cliff Sculpture of Motecuhzoma Xocoyotzin. *El México Antiguo* 9:379–444.
1960 The Mixteca-Puebla Concept in Mesoamerican Archaeology: A Re-examination. In *Men and Cultures: Selected Papers from the Fifth International Congress of Anthropological and Ethnological Sciences*, edited by Anthony F. C. Wallace, pp. 612–617. University of Pennsylvania Press, Philadelphia.
1966 The Problem of the Provenience of the Member of the "Codex Borgia Group": A Summary. In *Suma antropológica en homenaje a Robert J. Weitlaner*, edited by Antonio Pompa y Pompa, pp. 145–158. Instituto Nacional de Antropología e Historia, Mexico City.
1967 The Royal Headband of the Tlaxcalteca. *Revista Mexicana de Estudios Antropológicos* 21:71–106.
1971 Religion in Pre-Hispanic Central Mexico. In *Archaeology of Northern Mesoamerica*, part 1, edited by Gordon F. Ekholm and Ignacio Bernal, pp. 395–446. Handbook of Middle American Indians, vol. 10. University of Texas Press, Austin.
1978 The Deity 9 Wind "Ehecatl-Quetzalcoatl" in the Mixteca Pictorials. *Journal of Latin American Lore* 4:61–92.
1982 The Mixteca-Puebla Concept Revisited. In *The Art and Iconography of Late Post-Classic Central Mexico*, edited by Elizabeth H. Boone, pp. 227–254. Dumbarton Oaks, Washington, D.C.
1991 The Octli Cult in Late Pre-Hispanic Central Mexico. In *To Change Place: Aztec Ceremonial Landscapes*, edited by Davíd Carrasco, pp. 158–187. University Press of Colorado, Niwot.
1994 The Eagle Claw/Tied Double Maize Ear Motif: The Cholula Polychrome Ceramic Tradition and Some Members of the Codex Borgia Group. In *Mixteca-Puebla: Discoveries and Research in Mesoamerican Art and Archaeology*, edited by H. B. Nicholson and Eloise Quiñones Keber, pp. 101–116. Labyrinthos, Culver City, CA.
1996 Mixteca-Puebla. In *The Dictionary of Art*, pp. 739–741, vol. 21. Grove Press, New York.
2000 The Iconography of the Feathered Serpent in Late Postclassic Central Mexico. In *Mesoamerica's Classic Heritage: From Teotihuacan to the Aztecs*, edited by Davíd Carrasco, Lindsay Jones, and Scott Sessions, pp. 145–164. University Press of Colorado, Niwot.
2001 *Topiltzin Quetzalcoatl: The Once and Future Lord of the Toltecs.* University Press of Colorado, Boulder.

Nicholson, H. B., and Eloise Quiñones Keber
1983   *Art of Aztec Mexico: Treasures of Tenochtitlan.* National Gallery of Art, Washington, D.C.
1994a *Mixteca-Puebla: Discoveries and Research in Mesoamerican Art and Archaeology.* Labyrinthos, Culver City, CA.
1994b Introduction. In *Mixteca-Puebla: Discoveries and Research in Mesoamerican Art and Archaeology,* edited by H. B. Nicholson and Eloise Quiñones Keber, pp. vii–xv. Labyrinthos, Culver City, CA.

Noguera, Eduardo
1954   *La cerámica de Cholula.* Editorial Guaranía, Mexico City.
1975   *La cerámica arqueológica de mesoamérica.* 2nd ed. Instituto Nacional de Antropología e Historia, Mexico City.

Norris, Susan
n.d.   The Aztec-Period Obsidian Industries of Morelos, Mexico: Production and Exchange. Ph.D. dissertation, Department of Anthropology, Harvard University.

Nowotny, Karl Anton
1961   *Tlacuilolli: Die mexicanischen Bilderhandschriften, Stil und Inhalt, mit einem Katalog der CodeX-Borgia-Gruppe.* Verlag Gebr. Mann, Berlin.

Ochoa S., Alvaro, and Gerardo Sánchez D. (editors)
1985   *Relaciones y Memorias de la Provincia de Michoacán, 1579–1581.* Universidad Michoacana, Ayuntamiento de Morelia, Morelia.

Ochoa, Lorenzo, and Ernesto Vargas
1987   Xicalango, puerto chontal de intercambio: Mito y realidad. *Anales de Antropología* 24:95–114.

Odena Güemes, Lina
1994   El señorío de Tepeticpac: Arribo y origen de sus fundadores según fuentes escritas y pictográficas. In *Códices y documentos sobre México: Primer simposio,* edited by Constanza Vega, pp. 211–222. Instituto Nacional de Antropología e Historia, Mexico City.

Offner, Jerome A.
1981   On the Inapplicability of "Oriental Despotism" and the "Asiatic Mode of Production" to the Aztecs of Texcoco. *American Antiquity* 46:43–61.

O'Hara, Sarah L.
1993   Historical Evidence of Fluctuations in the Level of Lake Pátzcuaro, Michoacán, Over the Last Six Hundred Years. *The Geographical Journal* 59:51–62.

O'Hara, Sarah L., and Sarah E. Metcalfe
1997   The Climate of Mexico Since the Aztec Period. *Quaternary International* 43/44:25–31.

O'Hara, Sarah L., Sarah E. Metcalfe, and F. Alayne Street-Perrott
1994   On the Arid Margin: The Relationship Between Climate, Humans, and the Environment: A Review of Evidence from the Highlands of Central Mexico. *Chemosphere* 29:965–981.

O'Hara, Sarah L., Alayne Street-Perrott, and Timothy Burt
1993   Accelerated Soil Erosion Around a Mexican Highland Lake Caused by Prehispanic Agriculture. *Nature* 362:48–51.

Okoshi, Tsubasa
1994   Ecab: Una revisión de la geografía política de una provincia Maya Canul. In *Memorias del Primer Congreso Internacional de Mayistas,* pp. 280–287. Instituto de Investigaciones Filológicas, Centro Estudios Mayas, Universidad Nacional Autónoma de México, Mexico City.
1995   Revisión crítica de la organización política de la provincia de Ah Canul en vísperas de la invasión española. In *Memorias del Segundo Congreso Internacional de Mayistas, Mérida, Yucatán,* pp. 60–69. Instituto de Investigaciones Filológicas, Centro Estudios Mayas, Universidad Nacional Autónoma de México, Mexico City.

Okoshi, Tsubasa, and Sergio A. Quezada
1988   Tzucab y Cuchcabal: Dos términos para entender la organización territorial de los Mayas Yucatecos del tiempo de la invasión española: El caso de la llamada provincia de los Cupul. In *Etnoarqueología: Coloquio Bosch-Gimpera,* edited by Yoko Sugiura Yamamoto and Mari Carmen Serra Puche, pp. 363–370. Universidad Nacional Autónoma de México, Mexico City.

Oland, Maxine
1998   Lithic Raw Material Sources at the Southern End of the Freshwater Creek Drainage. In *The Belize Postclassic Project 1997: Laguna de On, Progresso Lagoon, and Laguna Seca,* edited by Marilyn A. Masson and Robert M. Rosenswig, pp. 163–176. Occasional Publication, vol. 2. Institute for Mesoamerican Studies, Albany, NY.
1999   Lithic Raw Material Sources at the Southern End of the Freshwater Creek Drainage: A View from Laguna de On, Belize. *Lithic Technology* 24:91–110.
2000a Lithic Tool and Debitage Analysis from Caye Coco, Progresso Op 7, and Laguna Seca. In *Belize Postclassic Project 1999: Continuing Investigations at Progresso Lagoon and Laguna Seca,* edited by Robert M. Rosenswig and Marilyn A. Masson, pp. 133–140. Occasional Publication, vol. 5. Institute for Mesoamerican Studies, Albany, NY.
2000b Off-Mound Excavations on the North Shore of Caye Coco, Subop 13. In *Belize Postclassic Project 1999: Continuing Investigations at Progresso Lagoon and Laguna Seca,* edited by Robert M. Rosenswig and Marilyn A. Masson, pp. 7–25. Occasional Publication, vol. 5. Institute for Mesoamerican Studies, Albany, NY.

Oland, Maxine, Heather Ambrose, Jessica Oppenheimer, and Amanda Vellia
2000   Lithic Raw Material Use During the Postclassic: Evidence from Subops 18, 18a, and 18b, Caye Coco. In *Belize Postclassic Project 1999: Continuing Investigations at Progresso Lagoon and Laguna Seca,* edited by Robert M. Rosenswig and Marilyn A. Masson, pp. 141–144. Occasional Publication, vol. 5. Institute for Mesoamerican Studies, Albany, NY.

Olivera, Mercedes
1970   La importancia religiosa de Cholula. In *Proyecto Cholula,* edited by Ignacio Marquina, pp. 211–242. Instituto Nacional de Antropología e Historia, Mexico City.
1976   El despotismo tributario en la región de Cuauhtinchan-Tepeaca. In *Estratificación social en la mesoamérica prehispánica,* edited by Pedro Carrasco and Johanna Broda, pp. 181–206. Instituto Nacional de Antropología e Historia, Mexico City.

Olson, Jan Marie
2001   Unequal Consumption: A Study of Domestic Wealth Differentials in Three Late Postclassic Mexican Communities. Ph.D. dissertation, Department of Anthropology, University at Albany, SUNY.

Olson, Jan Marie, Michael E. Smith, and Elizabeth DiPippo
1999   Ceramic Figurines and Domestic Ritual at Late Postclassic Sites in Morelos, Mexico. Paper presented at the 1999 Annual Meeting of the Society for American Archaeology (Chicago).

O'Mack, Scott
 1991 Yacatecuhtli and Ehecatl-Quetzalcoatl: Earth Divers in Aztec Central Mexico. *Ethnohistory* 38:1–33.

Orellana, Sandra L.
 1995 *Ethnohistory of the Pacific Coast.* Labyrinthos, Lancaster, CA.

Otis Charlton, Cynthia
 1993 Obsidian as Jewelry: Lapidary Production in Aztec Otumba, Mexico. *Ancient Mesoamerica* 4:231–243.
 1994 Plebians and Patricians: Contrasting Patterns of Production and Distribution in the Aztec Figurine and Lapidary Industries. In *Economies and Polities in the Aztec Realm*, edited by Mary G. Hodge and Michael E. Smith, pp. 195–219. Institute for Mesoamerican Studies, Albany.

Oudijk, Michel R.
 1998a The Genealogy of Zaachila. In *The Shadow of Monte Albán: Politics and Historiography in Postclassic Oaxaca, Mexico*, by Maarten Jansen, Peter Kröfges, and Michel R. Oudijk, pp. 13–36. Research School CNWS, Leiden University, Leiden.
 1998b The Geneaology of San Lucas Quiaviní. In *The Shadow of Monte Albán: Politics and Historiography in Postclassic Oaxaca, Mexico*, by Maarten Jansen, Peter Kröfges, and Michel R. Oudijk, pp. 123–133. Research School CNWS, Leiden University, Leiden.
 2000 *Historiography of the Bènizàa: The Postclassic and Early Colonial Periods (1000–1600 A.D.).* CNWS Publications, vol. 84. Research School of CNWS, Leiden University, Leiden.

Oviedo y Valdés, Gonzalo Fernández de
 1853 *Historia general y natural de las Indias.* Imprenta de la Reál Academia de la Historia, Madrid.

Paddock, John
 1982 The Mixteca-Puebla Style in the Valley of Oaxaca. In *Aspects of the Mixteca-Puebla Style and Mixtec and Central Mexican Culture in Southern Mesoamerica*, edited by Jennifer S. H. Brown and E. Wyllys Andrews V, pp. 3–6. Occasional Papers, vol. 4. Middle American Research Institute, Tulane University, New Orleans.
 1983 *Lord Five Flower's Family: Rulers of Zaachila and Cuilapan.* Vanderbilt University Publications in Anthropology, vol. 24. Department of Anthropology, Vanderbilt University, Nashville.

Pailes, R., and Joseph Whitecotton
 1979 The Greater Southwest and Mesoamerican "World" System: An Exploratory Model of Frontier Relationships. In *The Frontier: Comparative Studies*, edited by William Savage and Stephen Thompson, pp. 105–121, vol. 2. University of Oklahoma Press, Norman.

Pailles, Maricruz
 1980 *Pampa El Pajón, An Early Estuarine Site, Chiapas, Mexico.* Papers, vol. 44. New World Archaeological Foundation, Provo, UT.

Paredes, Carlos S.
 1976 *El tributo indígena en la región del Lago de Pátzcuaro, siglo XIV.* Licenciatura thesis, Facultad de Filosofía y Letras, Colegio de Historia, Universidad Nacional Autónoma de México.

Pareyon Moreno, Eduardo
 1972 Las pirámides de doble escalera. In *Religión en Mesoamérica: XII Mesa Redonda, Sociedad Mexicana de Antropología*, edited by Jaime Litvak King and Noemí Castillo Tejero, pp. 117–126. Sociedad Mexicana de Antropología, Mexico City.

Parmenter, Ross
 1982 *Four Lienzos of the Coixtlahuaca Valley.* Studies in Pre-Columbian Art and Archaeology, vol. 26. Dumbarton Oaks, Washington, D.C.

Parsons, Jeffrey R.
 1970 An Archaeological Evaluation of the Códice Xolotl. *American Antiquity* 35:431–439.
 1976 The Role of Chinampa Agriculture in the Food Supply of Aztec Tenochtitlan. In *Cultural Change and Continuity: Essays in Honor of James B. Griffin*, edited by Charles Cleland, pp. 233–257. Academic Press, New York.
 1991 Political Implications of Prehispanic Chinampa Agriculture in the Valley of Mexico. In *Land and Politics in the Valley of Mexico: A Two-Thousand-Year Perspective*, edited by Herbert R. Harvey, pp. 17–42. University of New Mexico Press, Albuquerque.
 1994 Late Postclassic Salt Production and Consumption in the Valley of Mexico: Some Insights from Nexquipayac. In *Economies and Polities in the Aztec Realm*, edited by Mary G. Hodge and Michael E. Smith, pp. 257–290. Institute for Mesoamerican Studies, Albany.

Parsons, Lee A.
 1967–
 69 *Bilbao, Guatemala: An Archaeological Study of Pacific Coast Cotzumalhuapa Region.* Publications in Anthropology, vols. 11, 12. Milwaukee Public Museum, Milwaukee.

Parsons, Lee A., and Barbara J. Price
 1971 Mesoamerican Trade and Its Role in the Emergence of Civilization. In *Observations on the Emergence of Civilization in Mesoamerica*, edited by Robert Heizer and John Graham, pp. 169–195. Contributions, vol. 11. University of California Archaeological Research Facility, Berkeley.

Paso y Troncoso, Francisco del
 1905 *Papeles de Nueva España.* 2nd series ed., 7 vols. Sucesor de Rivadeneyra, Madrid.
 1939 *Papeles de Nueva España*, vol. V and VI. Sucesor de Rivadeneyra, Madrid.

Paso y Troncoso, Francisco del (editor)
 1939–
 1942 *Epistolario de Nueva España (1505–1818).* 16 vols. Biblioteca Histórica Mexicana de Obras Inéditas, Segunda serie. Antigua Librería Robredo, Mexico City.

Pastrana, Alejandro
 1990 Proyecto yacimientos de obsidiana. *Boletín del Consejo de Arqueología* (Mexico) 1990:190–195.
 1991 Los yacimientos de obsidiana del oriente de Querétaro. In *Querétaro prehispánico*, edited by Ana María Crespo and Rosa Brambila, pp. 11–30. Colección Científica, vol. 238. Instituto Nacional de Antropología e Historia, Mexico City.
 1992 Proyecto yacimientos de obsidiana. *Boletín del Consejo de Arqueología 1991* (Mexico):219–221.
 1998 *La explotación azteca de la obsidiana en la Sierra de las Navajas.* Colección Científica, vol. 383. Instituto Nacional de Antropología e Historia, Mexico City.

Peacock, D. P. S.
 1982 *Pottery in the Roman World: An Ethnoarchaeological Approach.* Longman, New York.

Pearson, M. N.
 1991 Merchants and States. In *The Political Economy of Merchant Empires*, edited by James D. Tracy, pp. 41–116. Cambridge University Press, New York.

Pendergast, David M.
1962 Metal Artifacts from Amapa, Nayarit, Mexico. *American Antiquity* 27:370–379.
1981 Lamanai, Belize: Summary of Excavation Results, 1974–1980. *Journal of Field Archaeology* 8:29–53.
1985 Lamanai, Belize: An Updated View. In *The Lowland Maya Postclassic*, edited by Arlen Chase and Prudence Rice, pp. 91–103. University of Texas Press, Austin.
1986 Stability Through Change: Lamanai, Belize from the Ninth to the Seventeenth Century. In *Late Lowland Maya Civilization: Classic to Postclassic*, edited by Jeremy A. Sabloff and E. Wyllys Andrews V, pp. 223–250. University of New Mexico Press, Albuquerque.
1991 The Southern Maya Lowlands Contact Experience: The View from Lamanai, Belize. In *The Spanish Borderlands in Pan-American Perspective*, edited by David H. Thomas, pp. 337–354. Columbian Consequences, vol. 3. Smithsonian Institution Press, Washington, D.C.

Peraza Lope, Carlos
1993 *Estudio y secuencia del material cerámico de San Gervasio, Cozumel.* Licenciatura thesis, Department of Anthropology, Universidad Autónoma de Yucatán.
1998 Mayapán: Ciudad-capital del posclásico. *Arqueología Mexicana* 2:48–53.

Peraza Lope, Carlos, Pedro Delgado Kú, Bárbara Escamilla Ojeda, and Mario Garrido Euán
1998 Trabajos de conservación arquitectónica en Mayapán, Yucatán, México. Paper presented at the Fourth Congreso Internacional de Mayistas (Antigua, Guatemala).

Peraza Lope, Carlos, M. Garrido Euán, P. Delgado Kú, B. Escamilla Ojeda, M. Lira Chim, and C. García Ayala
1996 *Trabajos de mantenimiento y conservación arquitectónica en Mayapán, Yucatán: Informe de la temporada 1996.* Manuscript on file, Instituto Nacional de Antropología e Historia, Merida, Mexico.

Peregrine, Peter N., and Gary M. Feinman (editors)
1996 *Pre-Columbian World Systems.* Prehistory Press, Madison, WI.

Pérez Romero, José Alberto
1988 *Algunas consideraciones sobre el cacao en el norte de la península Yucatán.* Licenciatura thesis, Department of Anthropology, Universidad Autónoma de Yucatán.

Peterson, David A., and Thomas B. MacDougall
1974 *Guiengola: A Fortified Site in the Isthmus of Tehuantepec.* Vanderbilt University Publications in Anthropology, vol. 10. Department of Anthropology, Vanderbilt University, Nashville.

Pijoan, Carmen María, and Josefina Mansilla Lory
1997 Evidence for Human Sacrifice, Bone Modification, and Cannibalism in Ancient Mexico. In *Troubled Times: Violence and Warfare in the Past*, edited by Debra L. Martin and David W. Frayer, pp. 217–240. Gordon and Breach, Amsterdam.

Piña Chán, Román
1960 Algunos sitios arqueológicos de Oaxaca y Guerrero. *Revista Mexicana de Estudios Antropológicos* 16:65–76.
1978 Commerce in the Yucatan Peninsula: The Conquest and Colonial Period. In *Mesoamerican Communication Routes and Cultural Contacts*, edited by Thomas A. Lee Jr. and Carlos Navarrete, pp. 37–48. Papers, vol. 40. New World Archaeological Foundation, Provo, UT.

Plattner, Stuart
1989 Markets and Marketplaces. In *Economic Anthropology*, edited by Stuart Plattner, pp. 171–208. Stanford University Press, Stanford.

Pogue, Joseph E.
1974 *Turquoise.* Rio Grande Press, Glorieta, NM.

Pohl, John M. D.
1994a Weaving and Gift Exchange in the Mixtec Codices. In *Cloth and Curing: Continuity and Exchange in Oaxaca*, edited by Grace Johnson and Douglas Sharon, pp. 3–14. Museum Papers, vol. 32. San Diego Museum of Man, San Diego.
1994b Mexican Codices, Maps, and Lienzos as Social Contracts. In *Writing Without Words: Alternative Literacies in Mesoamerica and the Andes*, edited by Elizabeth Hill Boone and Walter D. Mignolo, pp. 137–160. Duke University Press, Durham.
1994c *The Politics of Symbolism in the Mixtec Codices.* Vanderbilt University Publications in Anthropology, vol. 46. Department of Anthropology, Vanderbilt University, Nashville.
1994d Codex Zouche-Nuttall: Notebook for the Third Mixtec Pictographic Writing Workshop. Manuscript on file, Department of Art History, University of Texas, Austin.
1995 Codex Vindobonensis: Notebook for the Fourth Mixtec Pictographic Writing Workshop. Manuscript on file, Department of Art History, University of Texas, Austin.
1996 Codex Bodley: Notebook for the Fifth Mixtec Pictographic Writing Workshop. Manuscript on file, Department of Art History, University of Texas, Austin.
1998a Themes of Drunkenness, Violence, and Factionalism in Tlaxcalan Altar Paintings. *Res: Anthropology and Aesthetics* 33:184–207.
1998b Codex Selden: Notebook for the Seventh Mixtec Pictographic Writing Workshop. Manuscript on file, Department of Art History, University of Texas, Austin.
1999 The Lintel Paintings of Mitla and the Function of the Mitla Palaces. In *Mesoamerican Architecture as a Cultural Symbol*, edited by Jeff Karl Kowalski, pp. 176–197. Oxford University Press, New York.
2001 Chichimecatlalli: Strategies for Cultural and Commercial Exchange between Mexico and the American Southwest, 1100–1521. In *The Road to Aztlan: Art from a Mythic Homeland*, edited by Virginia M. Fields and Victor Zamudio-Taylor, pp. 86–101. Los Angeles County Museum of Art, Los Angeles.

Pohl, John M. D., and Bruce E. Byland
1994 The Mixteca-Puebla Style and Early Postclassic Socio-Political Interaction. In *Mixteca-Puebla: Discoveries and Research in Mesoamerican Art and Archaeology*, edited by H. B. Nicholson and Eloise Quiñones Keber, pp. 189–200. Labyrinthos, Culver City, CA.

Pohl, John M. D., John Monaghan, and Laura R. Stiver
1997 Religion, Economy, and Factionalism in Mixtec Boundary Zones. In *Códices y documentos sobre México: Segundo simposio*, edited by Salvador Rueda Smithers, Constanza Vega Sosa, and Rodrigo Martínez Baracs, pp. 205–232, vol. 1. Instituto Nacional de Antropología e Historia, Mexico City.

Pohl, John M. D., and Marcus Winter
n.d. The Carved Bones of the Tenango Cave. Unpublished manuscript in author's possession.

Polanyi, Karl
1957 *The Great Transformation.* Beacon Press, Boston.

1963   Ports of Trade in Early Societies. *Journal of Economic History* 23:30–45.

1977   *The Livelihood of Man.* Academic Press, New York.

Polanyi, Karl, Conrad M. Arensburg, and Harry W. Pearson (editors)

1957   *Trade and Market in the Early Empires.* Henry Regnery Co., Chicago.

Pollard, Helen P.

1972   Prehispanic Urbanism at Tzintzuntzan, Michoacán. Ph.D. dissertation, Department of Anthropology, Columbia University. University Microfilms, Ann Arbor, MI.

1977   An Analysis of Urban Zoning and Planning in Prehispanic Tzintzuntzan. *Proceedings of the American Philosophical Society* 121:46–69.

1980   Central Places and Cities: A Consideration of the Protohistoric Tarascan State. *American Antiquity* 45:677–696.

1982   Ecological Variation and Economic Exchange in the Tarascan State. *American Ethnologist* 9:250–268.

1987   The Political Economy of Prehispanic Tarascan Metallurgy. *American Antiquity* 52:741–752.

1993   *Tariacuri's Legacy: The Prehispanic Tarascan State.* University of Oklahoma Press, Norman.

1995   Estudio del surgimiento del estado tarasco: Investigaciones recientes. In *Arqueología del occidente y norte de México,* edited by Eduardo Williams and Phil C. Weigand, pp. 29–63. El Colegio de Michoacán, Zamora.

1997   Recent Research in West Mexican Archaeology. *Journal of Archaeological Research* 5:345–384.

2000   Tarascan External Relationships. In *Greater Mesoamerica: The Archaeology of West and Northwest Mexico,* edited by M. Foster and S. Gorenstein, pp. 71–80. University of Utah Press, Salt Lake City.

Pollard, Helen P., and Laura Cahue

1999   Mortuary Patterns of Regional Elites in the Lake Pátzcuaro Basin of Western Mexico. *Latin American Antiquity* 10:259–280.

Pollard, Helen P., Michael Glascock, and Michael Rizo

1998   Preliminary Analysis of Obsidian Sources from the Lake Pátzcuaro Basin: The Urichu, Xaracuaro, and Pareo Polities. Paper presented at the 21st Annual Conference of Midwest Mesoamericanists (Michigan State University, East Lansing).

Pollard, Helen P., and Shirley Gorenstein

1980   Agrarian Potential, Population, and the Tarascan State. *Science* 209:272–277.

Pollard, Helen P., Amy Hirshman, Hector Neff, and Michael D. Glascock

2001   Las elites, el intercambio de bienes y el surgimiento del área nuclear tarasca: Análisis de la cerámica de la cuenca de Pátzcuaro. In *Estudios cerámicos en el occidente y norte de México,* edited by Eduardo Williams and Phil C. Weigand, pp. 289–309. El Colegio de Michoacán and Instituto Michoacano de Cultura, Morelia.

Pollard, Helen P., and Thomas A. Vogel

1994a   Late Postclassic Imperial Expansion and Economic Exchange Within the Tarascan Domain. In *Economies and Polities in the Aztec Realm,* edited by Mary G. Hodge and Michael E. Smith, pp. 447–470. Institute for Mesoamerican Studies, Albany, NY.

1994b   Implicaciones políticas y económicas del intercambio de obsidiana del estado tarasco. In *Arqueología del occi-*

dente de México, edited by Eduardo Williams and R. Novella, pp. 159–182. Colegio de Michoacán, Zamora.

Pollock, Harry E. D.

1936   *Round Structures of Aboriginal Middle America.* Publication, vol. 471. Carnegie Institution of Washington, Washington, D.C.

1962   Introduction. In *Mayapán, Yucatan, Mexico,* by Harry E. D. Pollock, Ralph L. Roys, Tatiana Proskouriakoff, and A. Ledyard Smith, pp. 1–24. Publication, vol. 619. Carnegie Institution of Washington, Washington, D.C.

1980   *The Puuc: An Architectural Survey of the Hill Country of Yucatan and Northern Campeche, Mexico.* Memoirs, vol. 19. Peabody Museum of Archaeology and Ethnology, Harvard University, Cambridge.

Pollock, Harry E. D., Ralph L. Roys, Tatiana Proskouriakoff, and A. Ledyard Smith

1962   *Mayapán, Yucatan, Mexico.* Publication, vol. 619. Carnegie Institution of Washington, Washington, D.C.

Pope, Kevin O.

1987   The Ecology and Economy of the Formative-Classic Transition along the Ulua River, Honduras. In *Interaction on the Southeast Mesoamerican Frontier,* edited by E. J. Robinson, pp. 95–128, BAR, International Series vol. 327. British Archaeological Reports, Oxford.

Popenoe de Hatch, Marion

1997   *Kaminaljuyú/San Jorge: Evidencia arqueológica de la actividad económica en el valle de Guatemala 300 a.C. a 300 d.C.* Universidad del Valle de Guatemala, Guatemala City.

1998   Los k'iche's-kaquchikeles en el altiplano central de Guatemala: Evidencia arqueológica del periodo clásico. *Mesoamérica* 35:93–115.

Proskouriakoff, Tatiana

1955   The Death of a Civilization. *Scientific American* 192(5):82–88.

1962a   Civic and Religious Structures of Mayapán. In *Mayapán, Yucatan, Mexico,* by Harry E. D. Pollock, Ralph L. Roys, Tatiana Proskouriakoff, and A. Ledyard Smith, pp. 87–164. Publications, vol. 619. Carnegie Institution of Washington, Washington, D.C.

1962b   The Artifacts of Mayapán. In *Mayapán, Yucatan, Mexico,* by Harry E. D. Pollock, Ralph L. Roys, Tatiana Proskouriakoff, and A. Ledyard Smith, pp. 321–442. Publication, vol. 619. Carnegie Institution of Washington, Washington, D.C.

Prown, Jules

1980   Style as Evidence. *Winterthur Portfolio* 15(3):197–210.

Quezada, Sergio

1993   *Pueblos y caciques Yucatecos, 1550–1580.* El Colegio de México, Mexico City.

Quezada Ramírez, María Noemí

1972   *Las matlatzincas: Época prehispánica y época colonial hasta 1650.* Serie Investigaciones, vol. 22. Instituto Nacional de Antropología e Historia, Mexico City.

Quiñones Keber, Eloise

1994   The Codex Style: Which Codex? Which Style? In *Mixteca-Puebla: Discoveries and Research in Mesoamerican Art and Archaeology,* edited by H. B. Nicholson and Eloise Quiñones Keber, pp. 143–152. Labyrinthos, Culver City, CA.

1995   *Codex Telleriano-Remensis: Ritual, Divination, and History in a Pictorial Aztec Manuscript.* University of Texas Press, Austin.

Quirarte, Jacinto

1975 The Wall Paintings of Santa Rita, Corozal. *National Studies* (Belize) 3(4):5–29.

1982 The Santa Rita Murals: A Review. In *Aspects of the Mixteca-Puebla Style and Mixtec and Central Mexican Culture in Southern Mesoamerica*, edited by Doris Stone, pp. 43–57. Occasional Papers, vol. 4. Middle American Research Institute, New Orleans.

Ramírez Urrea, Susana, and Rosario Acosta Nieva

1997 Inhumación de cráneos humanos: Un hallazgo en el occidente de México. *Journal de la Société des Américanistes* 83:251–265.

Ramsey, James R.

1975 An Analysis of Mixtec Minor Art, with a Catalogue. Ph.D. dissertation, Department of Latin American Studies, Tulane University, New Orleans.

1982 An Examination of Mixtec Iconography. In *Aspects of the Mixteca-Puebla Style and Mixtec and Central Mexican Culture in Southern Mesoamerica*, edited by Jennifer S. H. Brown and E. Wyllys Andrews V, pp. 33–42. Occasional Papers, vol. 4. Middle American Research Institute, Tulane University, New Orleans.

Rands, Robert L., Ronald L. Bishop, and Jeremy A. Sabloff

1982 Maya Fine Paste Ceramics: An Archaeological Perspective. In *Analyses of Fine Paste Ceramics*, edited by Jeremy A. Sabloff, pp. 315–343. Memoirs, vol. 15, 2. Peabody Museum, Harvard University, Cambridge, MA.

Rathje, William

1975 Last Tango at Mayapán: A Tentative Trajectory of Production-Distribution Systems. In *Ancient Civilization and Trade*, edited by Jeremy A. Sabloff and C. C. Lamberg-Karlovsky, pp. 409–448. University of New Mexico Press, Albuquerque.

Rathje, William L., David A. Gregory, and Frederick M. Wiseman

1978 Trade Models and Archaeological Problems: Classic Maya Examples. In *Mesoamerican Communication Routes and Culture Contact*, edited by Thomas A. Lee Jr. and Carlos Navarrete, pp. 147–175. Papers, vol. 40. New World Archaeological Foundation, Provo, UT.

Rathje, William L., and Jeffrey A. Sabloff

1975 Theoretical Background: General Models and Questions. In *A Study of Changing Pre-Columbian Commercial Systems: The 1972–73 Seasons at Cozumel, Mexico*, edited by Jeffrey A. Sabloff and William L. Rathje, pp. 6–28. Monographs, vol. 3. Peabody Museum, Harvard University, Cambridge.

Ravesloot, J. C., Jeffrey S. Dean, and Michael S. Foster

1995 A New Perspective on the Casas Grandes Tree-Ring Dates. In *The Gran Chichimeca: Essays on the Archaeology and Ethnohistory of Northern Mesoamerica*, edited by Jonathan E. Reyman, pp. 240–251. Avebury, Brookfield, VT.

Recinos, A.

1957 *Crónicas indígenas de Guatemala*. Editorial Universitaria, Guatemala City.

Recinos, A., and D. Goetz

1953 *Annals of the Cakchiques and Title of the Lords of Totonicapán*. University of Oklahoma Press, Norman.

Reents-Budet, Dorie

1994 *Painting the Maya Universe: Royal Ceramics of the Classic Period*. Duke University Press, Durham, NC.

Reinhold, Manfred

1981 *Arqueología de Valle de Bravo, México*. Biblioteca Enciclopédica del Estado de México. Estado de México, Toluca.

Relación de Michoacán

1956 *Relación de las ceremonias y ritos y población y gobierno de Michoacán: Reproducción facsimilar del ms. IV de El Escorial, Madrid*. Aguilar Publicistas, Madrid.

1980 *Relación de Michoacán: Versión paleográfica, separación de textos, ordenación coloquial, estudio preliminar y notas de F. Miranda*. Estudios Michoacanos, vol. 5. Fimax, Morelia.

Relación de Zacatula

1945 Relación de Zacatula, 1580 (edited by Robert H. Barlow). *Tlalocan* 2:258–268.

Remesal, Antonio de

1932 *Historial general de las Indias occidentales y particular de la gobernación de Chiapa y Guatemala*, vol. 1. Biblioteca "Goathemala" de la Sociedad de Geografía e Historia, vol. 4.

1964 *Historia general de las Indias occidentales y particular de la gobernación de Chiapa y Guatemala*, vol. 1, vol. 175. Biblioteca de Autores Españoles, Madrid.

Renger, Johannes

1995 On Economic Structures in Ancient Mesopotamia. *Orientalia* 63:157–208.

Restall, Matthew

1997 *The Maya World: Yucatec Culture and Society, 1550–1850*. Stanford University Press, Stanford.

1998 *Maya Conquistador*. Beacon, Boston.

Revere, Robert B.

1957 "No Man's Coast": Ports of Trade in the Eastern Mediterranean. In *Trade and Market in Early Empires*, edited by Karl Polanyi, Conrad M. Arensberg, and Harry W. Pearson, pp. 38–63. Free Press, Glencoe, IL.

Reyes García, Luis

1961 Documentos nahoas sobre el estado de Chiapas. In *Los mayas del sur y sus relaciones con los nahuas meridionales (Octavo Mesa Redonda)*, pp. 167–194. Sociedad Mexicana de Antropología, Mexico City.

1977 *Cuauhtinchan del siglo XII al XVI: Formación y desarrollo histórico de un señorío prehispánico*. Franz Steiner, Wiesbaden.

Rice, Don S.

1986 The Peten Postclassic: A Settlement Perspective. In *Late Lowland Maya Civilization: Classic to Postclassic*, edited by Jeremy A. Sabloff and E. Wyllys Andrews V, pp. 301–344. University of New Mexico Press, Albuquerque.

Rice, Don S., Prudence M. Rice, and Timothy Pugh

1998 Settlement Continuity and Change in the Central Peten Lakes Region: The Case of Zacpeten. In *Anatomía de una civilización: Aproximaciones interdisciplinarias a la cultura maya*, edited by Andrés Ciudad Ruiz, Yolanda Fernández Marquínez, José Miguel García Campillo, María Josefa Iglesias Ponce de León, Alfonso Lacadena García-Gallo, and Luis T. Sanz Castro, pp. 207–252. Publication, vol. 4. Sociedad Española de Estudios Mayas, Madrid.

Rice, Prudence M.

1980 Peten Postclassic Pottery Production and Exchange: A View from Macanché. In *Models and Methods in Regional Exchange*, edited by Robert E. Fry. SAA Papers, vol. 1. Society for American Archaeology, Washington, D.C.

1986 The Peten Postclassic: Perspectives from the Central Peten Lakes. In *Late Lowland Maya Civilization: Classic to Postclassic*, edited by Jeremy A. Sabloff and E. Wyllys Andrews V, pp. 251–300. University of New Mexico Press, Albuquerque.

1987a *Macanché Island, El Peten, Guatemala: Excavations, Pottery, and Artifacts.* University of Florida Press, Gainesville.

1987b Economic Change in the Lowland Maya Late Classic Period. In *Specialization, Exchange, and Complex Societies,* edited by Elizabeth M. Brumfiel and Timothy K. Earle, pp. 76–85. Cambridge University Press, New York.

1991 Specialization, Standardization, and Diversity: A Retrospective. In *The Ceramic Legacy of Anna O. Shepard,* edited by Ronald L. Bishop and Frederick W. Lange, pp. 257–279. University Press of Colorado, Niwot.

Rice, Prudence M., Helen V. Michel, Frank Asaro, and
Fred Stross

1985 Provenience Analysis of Obsidian from the Central Peten Lake Region, Guatemala. *American Antiquity* 50:591–604.

Ridder, R. de

1993 The Assumed Marriage of a Quiche Ruler to Two Daughters of Motechuzoma. *Mexicon* 15:12–17.

Riese, Berthold

1982 Eine mexikanische Gottheit im Venuskapitel der Maya-handschrift Codex Dresdensis. *Bulletin de la Société Suisse des Américanistes* 46:37–39.

Rincón Mautner, Carlos

1994 A Reconstruction of the History of San Miguel Tulancingo, Coixtlahuaca, Mexico from Indigenous Painted Sources. *Texas Notes* 64:1–18.

Ringle, William M., and George J. Bey III

2001 Postclassic and Terminal Classic Courts of the Northern Maya Lowlands. In *Royal Courts of the Ancient Maya,* vol. 2, *Data and Case Studies,* edited by Takeshi Inomata and Stephen D. Houston, pp. 266–307. Westview, Boulder.

Ringle, William M., Tomás Gallareta Negrón, and
George J. Bey III

1998 The Return of Quetzalcoatl: Evidence for the Spread of a World Religion During the Epiclassic Period. *Ancient Mesoamerica* 9:183–232.

Rivera Dorado, Miguel

1995 Las tierras bajas de la zona maya en el posclásico. In *Historia antigua de México,* vol. 3, *El horizonte posclásico y algunos aspectos intelectuales de las culturas mesoamericanas,* edited by Linda Manzanilla and Leonardo López Luján, pp. 121–152. Instituto Nacional de Antropología e Historia, Mexico City.

Robertson, Donald

1959 *Mexican Manuscript Painting of the Early Colonial Period: The Metropolitan Schools.* Yale University Press, New Haven.

1963 The Style of the Borgia Group of Mexican Pre-Conquest Manuscripts. In *Latin American Art and the Baroque Period in Europe: Studies in Western Art,* edited by Millard Meiss et al., pp. 148–164. Acts of the Twentieth International Congress of the History of Art, vol. 3. Princeton University Press, Princeton.

1966 Mixtec Religious Manuscripts. In *Ancient Oaxaca,* edited by John Paddock, pp. 298–312. Stanford University Press, Stanford.

1970 The Tulum Murals: The International Style of the Late Post-Classic. In *Verhandlungen del XXXVIII Internationalen Amerikanisten-Kongres, Stuttgart-München, 1968,* pp. 77–88, vol. 2. Kommissionsverlag Klaus Renner, München.

Robinson, Eugenia J.

1990 *Reconocimiento de los municipios de Alotenango y Sumpango, Sacatepéquez.* Centro de Investigaciones Regionales de Mesoamérica, Antigua, Guatemala.

Robles Castellanos, Fernando

1986 Cronología cerámica de El Meco. In *Excavaciones arqueológicas en El Meco, Quintana Roo, 1977,* edited by Antonio P. Andrews and Fernando Robles Castellanos, pp. 77–130. Colección Científica, Instituto Nacional de Antropología e Historia, Mexico City.

1987 La secuencia cerámica preliminar de Isla Cerritos, costa centro-norte de Yucatán. In *Maya Ceramics: Papers from the 1985 Maya Ceramic Conference,* edited by Prudence M. Rice and Robert J. Sharer, pp. 99–120. BAR International Series, vol. 345. British Archaeological Reports, Oxford.

1990 *La secuencia cerámica de la región de Coba, Quintana Roo.* Instituto Nacional de Antropología e Historia, Mexico City.

Robles Castellanos, Fernando, and E. Wyllys Andrews V

1986 A Review and Synthesis of Recent Postclassic Archaeology in Northern Yucatan. In *Late Lowland Maya Civilization: Classic to Postclassic,* edited by Jeremy A. Sabloff and E. Wyllys Andrews V, pp. 53–98. University of New Mexico Press, Albuquerque.

Roddick, Andrew

2000 Investigations in the Vicinity of Structure 6, Caye Coco. In *Belize Postclassic Project 1999: Investigations at Progresso Lagoon and Laguna Seca,* edited by Robert M. Rosenswig and Marilyn A. Masson, pp. 60–74. Occasional Publication, vol. 5. Institute for Mesoamerican Studies, Albany, NY.

Rojas, Gabriel de

1927 Relación de Cholula. *Revista Mexicana de Estudios Históricos* 1:155–169.

Rojas, José Luis de

1986 *México Tenochtitlan: Economía e sociedad en el siglo XVI.* Fondo de Cultura Económica, Mexico City.

1993 *A cada uno lo suyo: El tributo indígena en la Nueva España en el siglo XVI.* El Colegio de Michoacán, Zamora.

1998 *La moneda indígena y sus usos en la Nueva España en el siglo XVI.* Centro de Investigaciones y Estudios Superiores en Antropología Social, Mexico City.

Rojas Rabiela, Teresa

1985 La tecnología agrícola mesoamericana en el siglo XVI. In *Historia de la agricultura: Epoca prehispánica–siglo XVI,* edited by Teresa Rojas Rabiela and William T. Sanders, vol. 1. Instituto Nacional de Antropología e Historia, Mexico City.

Romero R., María Eugenia, and Susana Gurrola B.

1995 Los sitios en las márgenes de la Laguna de Yalahau y Santa Rosa, desde el punto de vista del estudio de la navegación como sistema. In *Memorias del Segundo Congreso Internacional de Mayistas,* pp. 458–476. Centro de Estudios Mayas, Universidad Nacional Autónoma de México, Mexico City.

Root, William C.

1962 Report on the Metal Objects from Mayapán. In *Mayapán, Yucatan, Mexico,* by Harry E. D. Pollock, Ralph L. Roys, Tatiana Proskouriakoff, and A. Ledyard Smith, pp. 391–400. Publication, vol. 619. Carnegie Institution of Washington, Washington, D.C.

1969 Metal Artifacts from Chiapa de Corzo, Chiapas, Mexico. In *The Artifacts of Chiapa de Corzo, Chiapas, Mexico,* edited by Thomas A. Lee, Jr., pp. 203–207. Papers, vol. 26. New World Archaeological Foundation, Provo, UT.

Roseberry, William
1989   Peasants and the World. In *Economic Anthropology*, edited by Stuart Plattner, pp. 108–126. Stanford University Press, Stanford.

Rosenswig, Robert M.
1998   Burying the Dead at Laguna de On: Summary of Mortuary Remains from the 1991, 1996, and 1997 Seasons. In *The Belize Postclassic Project 1997: Laguna de On, Progresso Lagoon, Laguna Seca*, edited by Marilyn A. Masson and Robert M. Rosenswig, pp. 149–156. Occasional Publication, vol. 2. Institute for Mesoamerican Studies, Albany, NY.

Rosenswig, Robert M., and Marilyn A. Masson (editors)
2000   *The Belize Postclassic Project 1999: Continuing Investigations at Progreso Lagoon and Laguna Seca*. Occasional Publication, vol. 5. Institute for Mesoamerican Studies, Albany, NY.

Rosenswig, Robert M., and Thomas W. Stafford Jr.
1998   Archaic Component Beneath a Postclassic Terrace at Subop 19, Laguna de On Island. In *The Belize Postclassic Project 1997: Laguna de On, Progresso Lagoon, and Laguna Seca*, edited by Marilyn A. Masson and Robert M. Rosenswig, pp. 81–89. Occasional Publication, vol. 2. Institute for Mesoamerican Studies, Albany, NY.

Roskamp, Hans
1998   *La historiografía indígena de Michoacán: El lienzo de Jucutacato y los títulos de Carapan*. Research School CNWS, Leiden University, Leiden.

Rovner, Irwin
1989   Patrones anómalos en la importación de obsidiana en el centro de las tierras bajas mayas. In *La obsidiana en Mesoamérica*, edited by Margarita Gaxiola G., and John E. Clark, pp. 369–373. Instituto Nacional de Antropología e Historia, Mexico City.

Rowe, John H.
1962   Stages and Periods in Archaeological Interpretation. *Southwestern Journal of Anthropology* 18:40–54.

Rowlands, Michael, Mogens T. Larsen, and Kristian Kristiansen (editors)
1987   *Centre and Periphery in the Ancient World*. Cambridge University Press, Cambridge.

Roys, Ralph L.
1939   *The Titles of Ebtun*. Carnegie Institution of Washington, Washington, D.C.
1943   *The Indian Background of Colonial Yucatán*. Publication, vol. 548. Carnegie Institution of Washington, Washington, D.C.
1957   *The Political Geography of the Yucatan Maya*. Publication, vol. 613. Carnegie Institution of Washington, Washington, D.C.
1962   Literary Sources for the History of Mayapán. In *Mayapán, Yucatan, Mexico*, by Harry E. D. Pollock, Ralph L. Roys, Tatiana Proskouriakoff, and A. Ledyard Smith, pp. 25–86. Publication, vol. 619. Carnegie Institution of Washington, Washington, D.C.
1972   *The Indian Background of Colonial Yucatan*. University of Oklahoma Press, Norman.
1973   *The Book of Chilam Balam of Chumayel*. University of Oklahoma Press, Norman.

Rubín de la Borbolla, Daniel F.
1944   Orfebrería tarasca. *Cuadernos Americanos* 3(3):127–138.

Sabloff, Jeremy A., and E. Wyllys Andrews (editors)
1986   *Late Lowland Maya Civilization: Classic to Postclassic*. University of New Mexico Press, Albuquerque.

Sabloff, Jeremy A., and William L. Rathje
1975a   The Rise of a Maya Merchant Class. *Scientific American* 233(4):72–82.
1975b   *A Study of Changing Pre-Columbian Commercial Systems: The 1972–73 Seasons at Cozumel, Mexico: Preliminary Report*. Monographs, vol. 3. Peabody Museum of Archaeology and History, Harvard University, Cambridge.

Sabloff, Jeremy A., and Gordon R. Willey
1967   The Collapse of Maya Civilization in the Southern Lowlands: A Consideration of History and Process. *Southwest Journal of Anthropology* 23:311–336.

Sahagún, Fray Bernardino de
1950–
82   *Florentine Codex, General History of the Things of New Spain*. 12 books. Translated and edited by Arthur J. O. Anderson and Charles E. Dibble. School of American Research and the University of Utah Press, Santa Fe and Salt Lake City.
1975   *Historia general de las cosas de Nueva España*. Anotaciones y apéndices por Padre A. Ma. Garibay K. Editorial Porrúa, Mexico City.
1993   *Psalmodia Christians: Christian Psalmody*. Translated by Arthur J. O. Anderson. University of Utah Press, Salt Lake City.

Salgado González, Silvia
1996   Social Change in a Region of Granada, Pacific Nicaragua (1000 B.C.–1522 A.D.). Ph.D. dissertation, Department of Anthropology, State University of New York, Albany.

Sánchez Vázquez, María de Jesús
1984   *Zacatenco: Una unidad productora de sal en la ribera noroccidental del Lago de Texcoco*. Licenciatura thesis, Department of Arqueología, Escuela Nacional de Antropología e Historia, Mexico City.

Sanders, William T.
1956   The Central Mexican Symbiotic Region: A Study in Prehistoric Settlement Patterns. In *Prehistoric Settlement Patterns in the New World*, edited by Gordon R. Willey, pp. 115–27. Viking Fund Publications in Anthropology, vol. 23. Wenner-Gren Foundation for Anthropological Research, New York.
1960   *Prehistoric Ceramics and Settlement Patterns in Quintana Roo, Mexico*. Contributions to American Anthropology and History, no. 60, Publication, vol. 606. Carnegie Institute of Washington, Washington, D.C.
1992   Ranking and Stratification in Prehispanic Mesoamerica. In *Mesoamerican Elites: An Archaeological Assessment*, edited by Diane A. Chase and Arlen F. Chase, pp. 278–291. University of Oklahoma Press, Norman.

Sanders, William T., and Deborah L. Nichols
1988   Ecological Theory and Cultural Evolution in the Valley of Oaxaca. *Current Anthropology* 29:33–80.

Sanders, William T., Jeffrey R. Parsons, and Robert S. Santley
1979   *The Basin of Mexico: Ecological Processes in the Evolution of a Civilization*. Academic Press, New York.

Sanders, William T., and Barbara J. Price
1968   *Mesoamerica: The Evolution of a Civilization*. Random House, New York.

Sanders, William T., and Robert S. Santley
1983   A Tale of Three Cities: Energetics and Urbanization in Pre-Hispanic Central Mexico. In *Prehistoric Settlement Patterns: Essays in Honor of Gordon R . Willey*, edited by Evon Z. Vogt and Richard Leventhal, pp. 243–291. University of New Mexico Press, Albuquerque.

Santley, Robert S.
  1983   Obsidan Trade and Teotihuacan Influence in Meso-
          america. In *Highland-Lowland Interaction in Meso-
          america: Interdisciplinary Approaches*, edited by Arthur
          G. Miller, pp. 69–124. Dumbarton Oaks, Washington,
          D.C.
  1984   Obsidian Exchange, Economic Stratification, and the
          Evolution of Complex Society in the Basin of Mexico. In
          Trade and Exchange in Early Mesoamerica, edited by
          Kenneth G. Hirth, pp. 43–86. University of New Mexico
          Press, Albuquerque.
  1989   Economic Imperialism, Obsidian Exchange, and Teoti-
          huacan Influence in Mesoamerica. In *La obsidiana en
          Mesoamérica*, edited by Margarita Gaxiola G. and John
          E. Clark, pp. 321–329. Instituto Nacional de
          Antropología e Historia, Mexico City.
Santley, Robert S., Ponciano Ortiz Ceballos, Thomas W. Killion,
Phillip J. Arnold III, and Janet M. Kerley
  1984   *Final Report of the Matacapan Archaeological Project:
          The 1982 Season*. Research Paper, vol. 15. Latin Ameri-
          can Institute, University of New Mexico, Albuquerque.
Saravia E., A., and J. R. Guarchaj
  1996   *Poopol Wuuj = Popol Vuh: K'ichee'-español*. Editorial
          Piedra Santa, Guatemala City.
Sauer, Carl O.
  1966   *The Early Spanish Main*. University of California Press,
          Berkeley.
Sauerländer, Willibald
  1983   From Stilus to Style: Reflections on the Fate of a Notion.
          Art History 6:253–270.
Saville, Marshall H.
  1920   *The Goldsmith's Art in Ancient Mexico*. Indian Notes
          and Monographs, vol. 7. Museum of the American In-
          dian, Heye Foundation, New York.
  1922   *Turquoise Mosaic Art in Ancient Mexico*. Indian Notes
          and Monographs, vol. 8. Museum of the American In-
          dian, Heye Foundation, New York.
Schaafsma, Curtis F., and Carroll L. Riley (editors)
  1999a   *The Casas Grandes World*. University of Utah Press, Salt
          Lake City.
  1999b   The Casas Grandes World: Analysis and Conclusion. In
          The Casas Grandes World, edited by Curtis F. Schaaf-
          sma and Carroll L. Riley, pp. 237–249. University of
          Utah Press, Salt Lake City.
Schele, Linda, and David Freidel
  1990   *A Forest of Kings: The Untold Story of the Ancient
          Maya*. William Morrow, New York.
Schele, Linda, and Peter Mathews
  1998   *The Code of Kings: The Language of Seven Sacred
          Maya Temples and Tombs*. Simon and Schuster, New
          York.
Schneider, David M.
  1984   *A Critique of the Study of Kinship*. University of Michi-
          gan Press, Ann Arbor.
Schneider, Jane
  1977   Was There a Precapitalist World-System? *Peasant Stud-
          ies* 6(1):20–29.
  1991   Was There a Precapitalist World-System? In *Core/
          Periphery Relations in Precapitalist Worlds*, edited by
          Christopher Chase-Dunn and Thomas Hall, pp. 45–66.
          Westview Press, Boulder.
Scholes, Frances V., and Eleanor B. Adams
  1957   *Información sobre los tributos que los indios pagaban a
          Moctezuma, año de 1554*. Documentos para la Historia
          de México Colonial, vol. 4. Porrúa, Mexico City.

Scholes, Frances V., and Ralph L. Roys
  1948   *The Maya Chontal Indians of Acalan-Tixchel*. Publica-
          tion, vol. 560. Carnegie Institution of Washington,
          Washington, D.C.
  1968   *The Maya Chontal Indians of Acalan-Tixchel: A
          Contribution to the History and Ethnography of the
          Yucatan Peninsula*. University of Oklahoma Press,
          Norman.
Schöndube B., Otto
  1974   *Tamazula-Tuxpán-Zapotlán: Pueblos de la frontera
          septentrional de la antigua Colima*. Edited by J. M.
          Muriá. Escuela Nacional de Antropología e Historia,
          Mexico City.
  1980a   La tradición de las tumbas de tiro. In *Historia de Jalisco*,
          pp. 171–212, vol. 1. Gobierno de Jalisco, Unidad Edito-
          rial, Guadalajara.
  1980b   La nueva tradición. In *Historia de Jalisco*, pp. 213–258,
          vol. 1. Gobierno de Jalisco, Unidad Editorial, Guadala-
          jara.
Schortman, Edward M., and Patricia A. Urban
  1992a   The Political Value of Imports. In *Resources, Power, and
          Interregional Interaction*, edited by Edward M. Schort-
          man and Patricia A. Urban, pp. 153–156. Plenum Press,
          New York.
  1992b   Current Trends in Interaction Research. In *Resources,
          Power, and Interregional Interaction*, edited by Edward
          M. Schortman and Patricia A. Urban, pp. 235–255.
          Plenum Press, New York.
  1994   Living on the Edge: Core/Periphery Relations in Ancient
          Southeastern Mesoamerica. *Current Anthropology*
          35:401–413.
  1996   Actions at a Distance, Impacts at Home: Prestige Good
          Theory and a Pre-Columbian Polity in Southeastern
          Mesoamerica. In *Pre-Columbian World Systems*, edited
          by Peter N. Peregrine and Gary M. Feinman, pp. 97–
          114. Prehistory Press, Madison, WI.
Schortman, Edward, Patricia Urban, Wendy Ashmore, and
Julie Benyo
  1986   Interregional Interaction in the Southeast Maya Periph-
          ery: The Santa Barbara Project 1983–84 Seasons. *Jour-
          nal of Field Archaeology* 13:259–272.
Schumann, Otto
  1969   El Tuzanteco y su posición dentro de la familia mayense.
          *Anales del Instituto Nacional de Antropología e Histo-
          ria (época 7a)* 1:139–148.
Seler, Eduard
  1887   Der Codex Borgia un die verwandten aztekischen Bilder-
          schriften. *Zeitschrift für Ethnologie* 19:105–114.
  1902–
  1923   *Gesammelte Abhandlungen zur amerikanischen Sprach-
          und Alterthumskunde*. 5 vols. A. Asher, Berlin.
  1904–
  1909   *Codex Borgia: Eine altmexikanische Bilderschrift der
          Bibliothek der Congregatio de Propaganda Fide*. 3 vols.
          Gebr. Unger, Berlin.
  1963   *Comentarios al Códice Borgia*. 2 and fascimile vols.
          Fondo de Cultura Económica, Mexico City.
  1990–
  1998   *Collected Works in Mesoamerican Linguistics and Ar-
          chaeology*. Edited by Frank E. Comparato. 6 vols.
          Labyrinthos, Culver City, CA.
Serna, Jacinto de la
  1987   Manual de ministros de indios para el conocimiento de
          sus idolatrías y extirpación de ellas. In *El alma encan-
          tada*, edited by Fernando Benítez. Anales del Museo

Nacional de México, Instituto Nacional Indigenista, Fondo de Cultura Económica, Mexico City.

Shadow, Robert D., and María J. Rodríguez V.
1995   Historical Panorama of Anthropological Perspectives on Aztec Slavery. In *Arqueología del norte y del occidente de México: Homenaje al Doctor J. Charles Kelley*, edited by Barbro Dahlgren de Jordán and María de los Dolores Soto de Arechavaleta, pp. 299–323. Universidad Nacional Autónoma de México, Mexico City.

Shafer, Harry J.
1979   A Technological Study of Two Maya Lithic Workshops at Colha, Belize. In *The Colha Project, 1979: A Collection of Interim Papers*, edited by Thomas R. Hester, pp. 28–78. Center for Archaeological Research, University of Texas, San Antonio.

Shapiro, Meyer
1959   Style. In *Anthropology Today: An Encyclopedic Inventory*, edited by A. L. Kroeber, pp. 287–312. University of Chicago Press, Chicago.

Sharer, Robert J.
1984   Lower Central America as Seen from Mesoamerica. In *The Archaeology of Lower Central America*, edited by Frederick W. Lange and Doris Stone, pp. 63–84. University of New Mexico Press, Albuquerque.
1994   *The Ancient Maya*. 5th ed. Stanford University Press, Stanford.

Sheets, Payson, Kenneth G. Hirth, Frederick Lange, Frederick Stross, Fred Asaro, and Helen Michel
1990   Obsidian Sources and Elemental Analysis of Artifacts in Southern Mesoamerica and the Northern Intermediate Areas. *American Antiquity* 55:144–158.

Shepard, Anna O.
1948   *Plumbate, a Mesoamerican Trade Ware*. Publication, vol. 573. Carnegie Institution of Washington, Washington, D.C.
1951   Ceramic Technology. *Carnegie Institution of Washington Yearbook* 50:241–244.
1964   Ceramic Development of the Lowland and Highland Maya. *35th International Congress of Americanists*, vol. 1, pp. 518–520. Mexico City.
1974   *Ceramics for the Archaeologist*. Carnegie Institution of Washington, Publication No. 609, 2nd reprint by the Kirkby Lithographic Company, Washington, D.C.

Shook, Edwin M.
1965   Archaeological Survey of the Pacific Coast of Guatemala. In *Archaeology of Southern Mesoamerica*, part 1, edited by Gordon R. Willey, pp. 180–194. Handbook of Middle American Indians, vol. 2. University of Texas Press, Austin.

Sidrys, Raymond V.
1977a   Mass-Distance Measures for the Maya Obsidian Trade. In *Exchange Systems in Prehistory*, edited by Timothy K. Earle and Jonathon E. Ericson, pp. 91–108. Academic Press, New York.
1977b   Trace-Element Analysis of Obsidian Artifacts from Portezuelo, Mexico. *Journal of New World Archaeology* 2:47–51.
1983   *Archaeological Excavations in Northern Belize, Central America*. Monograph, vol. 17. Institute of Archaeology, University of California Press, Los Angeles.

Sierra Sosa, Telma
1998   Xcambó: Centro adminstrativo y puerto de comercio del clásico maya. Paper presented at the Fourth Congreso Internacional de Mayistas, Antigua, Guatemala.

Silver, Morris
1983   Karl Polanyi and Markets in the Ancient Near East: The Challenge of the Evidence. *Journal of Economic History* 43:795–829.
1985   *Economic Structures of the Ancient Near East*. Croom Helm, London.

Silverstein, Jay E.
1999   Reconstructing the Aztec-Tarascan Frontier: New Data from Northern Guerrero. Paper presented at the 1999 Annual Conference of the Society for American Archaeology (Chicago).
2000   A Study of the Late Postclassic Aztec-Tarascan Frontier in Northern Guerrero, Mexico: The Oztuma-Cutzamala Project. Ph.D. dissertation, Department of Anthropology, Pennsylvania State University.
2001   Aztec Imperialism at Oztuma, Guerrero: Aztec-Chontal Relations During the Late Postclassic and Early Colonial Periods. *Ancient Mesoamerica* 12:1–30.

Simmons, M. P., and G. F. Brem
1979   The Analysis and Distribution of Volcanic Ash-Tempered Pottery in the Lowland Maya Area. *American Antiquity* 44:79–91.

Sisson, Edward B.
1973   *First Annual Report of the Coxcatlan Project*. Tehuacan Reports, vol. 3. R. S. Peabody Foundation for Archaeology, Andover.
1983   Recent Work on the Borgia Group Codices. *Current Anthropology* 24:653–656.

Sisson, Edward B., and T. Gerald Lilly
1994a   A Codex-style Mural from Tehuacan Viejo, Puebla, Mexico. *Ancient Mesoamerica* 5:33–44.
1994b   The Mural of the Chimales and the Codex Borgia. In *Mixteca-Puebla: Discoveries and Research in Mesoamerican Art and Archaeology*, edited by H. B. Nicholson and Eloise Quiñones Keber, pp. 25–44. Labyrinthos, Lancaster, CA.

Smith, A. Ledyard
1955   *Archaeological Reconnaissance in Central Guatemala*. Publication, vol. 608. Carnegie Institution of Washingon, Washington, D.C.
1962   Residential and Associated Structures at Mayapán. In *Mayapán, Yucatan, Mexico*, by Harry Pollock, Ralph L. Roys, Tatiana Proskouriakoff, and A. Ledyard Smith, pp. 154–320. Publication, vol. 619. Carnegie Institution of Washington, Washington, D.C.

Smith, Carol A.
1976a   Analyzing Regional Social Systems. In *Regional Analysis*, vol. 2, *Social Systems*, edited by Carol A. Smith, pp. 3–20. Academic Press, New York.
1976b   Regional Economic Systems: Linking Geographic Models and Socioeconomic Problems. In *Regional Analysis*, vol. 1, *Economic Systems*, edited by Carol A. Smith, pp. 3–67. Academic Press, New York.
1976c   Exchange Systems and the Spatial Distribution of Elites: The Organization of Stratification in Agrarian Societies. In *Regional Analysis*, vol. 2, *Social Systems*, edited by Carol A. Smith, pp. 309–374. Academic Press, New York.
1982   Modern and Premodern Urban Primacy. *Comparative Urban Research* 9:79–96.

Smith, Mary Elizabeth
1973a   *Picture Writing from Ancient Southern Mexico: Mixtec Place Signs and Maps*. University of Oklahoma Press, Norman.

1973b The Relationship between Mixtec Manuscript Painting and the Mixtec Language: A Study of Some Personal Names in Codices Muro and Sánchez Solís. In *Mesoamerican Writing Systems*, edited by Elizabeth P. Benson, pp. 47–98. Dumbarton Oaks, Washington, D.C.

1979 Codex Becker II: A Manuscript from the Mixteca Baja? *Archiv für Völkerkunde* 33:29–43.

1998 *The Codex López Ruiz: A Lost Mixtec Pictorial Manuscript*. Vanderbilt University Publications in Anthropology, vol. 51. Department of Anthropology, Vanderbilt University, Nashville.

Smith, Mary Elizabeth, and Ross Parmenter

1991 *The Codex Tulane*. Publication, vol. 61. Middle American Research Institute, Tulane University, New Orleans.

Smith, Michael E.

1979 The Aztec Marketing System and Settlement Pattern in the Valley of Mexico: A Central Place Analysis. *American Antiquity* 44:110–125.

1980 The Role of the Marketing System in Aztec Society and Economy: Response to Evans. *American Antiquity* 45:876–883.

1984 The Aztlan Migrations of the Nahuatl Chronicles: Myth or History? *Ethnohistory* 31:153–186.

1986 The Role of Social Stratification in the Aztec Empire: A View From the Provinces. *American Anthropologist* 88:70–91.

1987a Archaeology and the Aztec Economy: The Social Scientific Use of Archaeological Data. *Social Science History* 11:237–259.

1987b Household Possessions and Wealth in Agrarian States: Implications for Archaeology. *Journal of Anthropological Archaeology* 6:297–335.

1990 Long-Distance Trade Under the Aztec Empire: The Archaeological Evidence. *Ancient Mesoamerica* 1:153–169.

1992a *Archaeological Research at Aztec-Period Rural Sites in Morelos, Mexico*, vol. 1, *Excavations and Architecture/ Investigaciones arqueológicas en sitios rurales de la época azteca en Morelos*, tomo 1, *Excavaciones y arquitectura*. University of Pittsburgh Memoirs in Latin American Archaeology, vol. 4. University of Pittsburgh, Pittsburgh.

1992b Rhythms of Change in Postclassic Central Mexico: Archaeology, Ethnohistory, and the Braudellian Model. In *Annales, Archaeology, and Ethnohistory*, edited by A. Bernard Knapp, pp. 51–74. Cambridge University Press, New York.

1994a Social Complexity in the Aztec Countryside. In *Archaeological Views from the Countryside: Village Communities in Early Complex Societies*, edited by Glenn Schwartz and Steven Falconer, pp. 143–159. Smithsonian Institution Press, Washington, D.C.

1994b Economies and Polities in Aztec-period Morelos: Ethnohistoric Introduction. In *Economies and Polities in the Aztec Realm*, edited by Mary G. Hodge and Michael E. Smith, pp. 313–348. Institute for Mesoamerican Studies, Albany, N.Y.

1996a *The Aztecs*. Blackwell Publishers, Oxford.

1996b The Strategic Provinces. In *Aztec Imperial Strategies*, by Frances F. Berdan, Richard E. Blanton, Elizabeth H. Boone, Mary G. Hodge, Michael E. Smith, and Emily Umberger, pp. 137–150. Dumbarton Oaks, Washington, D.C.

1997a Life in the Provinces of the Aztec Empire. *Scientific American* 277(3):56–63.

1997b City Planning: Aztec City Planning. In *Encyclopaedia of the History of Non-Western Science, Technology, and Medicine*, edited by Helaine Selin, pp. 200–202. Kluwer Academic Publishers, Dordrecht.

1999 Comment on Hirth's "Distribution Approach." *Current Anthropology* 40:528–530.

2000 Aztec City-State Culture. In *City-State Cultures in World History*, edited by Mogens Herman Hansen. The Royal Danish Academy of Sciences and Letters, Copenhagen.

2001a Trade and Exchange. In *The Oxford Encyclopedia of Mesoamerican Cultures: The Civilizations of Mexico and Central America*, edited by Davíd Carrasco, pp. 254–257, vol. 3. Oxford University Press, New York.

2001b The Mixteca-Puebla Style. In *The Archaeology of Mexico and Central America: An Enyclopedia*, edited by Susan T. Evans and David L. Webster, pp. 481–482. Garland, New York.

2001c The Aztec Empire and the Mesoamerican World System. In *Empires: Perspectives from Archaeology and History*, edited by Susan E. Alcock, Terence N. D'Altroy, Kathleen D. Morrison, and Carla M. Sinopoli, pp. 128–154. Cambridge University Press, New York.

2002 Domestic Ritual at Aztec Provincial Sites in Morelos. In *Domestic Ritual in Ancient Mesoamerica*, edited by Patricia Plunket, pp. 93–114. Institute of Archaeology, UCLA, Los Angeles.

2003 *Tlahuica Ceramics: The Aztec-Period Ceramics of Morelos, Mexico*. IMS Monographs, vol. 13. Institute for Mesoamerican Studies, Albany, N.Y. In press.

Smith, Michael E., and Frances F. Berdan

1996a Introduction. In *Aztec Imperial Strategies*, by Frances F. Berdan, Richard E. Blanton, Elizabeth H. Boone, Mary G. Hodge, Michael E. Smith, and Emily Umberger, pp. 1–9. Dumbarton Oaks, Washington, D.C.

1996b Appendix 4: Province Descriptions. In *Aztec Imperial Strategies*, by Frances F. Berdan, Richard E. Blanton, Elizabeth H. Boone, Mary G. Hodge, Michael E. Smith, and Emily Umberger, pp. 265–349. Dumbarton Oaks, Washington, D.C.

2000 The Postclassic Mesoamerican World System. *Current Anthropology* 41:283–286.

Smith, Michael E., and John F. Doershuk

1991 Late Postclassic Chronology in Western Morelos, Mexico. *Latin American Antiquity* 2:291–310.

Smith, Michael E., Timothy S. Hare, and Lea Pickard

1996 Yautepec City-States in the Mesoamerican World System. Paper presented at the 95th Annual Meeting of the American Anthropological Association (San Francisco).

Smith, Michael E., and Cynthia M. Heath-Smith

1980 Waves of Influence in Postclassic Mesoamerica? A Critique of the Mixteca-Puebla Concept. *Anthropology* 4:15–50.

1994 Rural Economy in Late Postclassic Morelos: An Archaeological Study. In *Economies and Polities in the Aztec Realm*, edited by Mary G. Hodge and Michael E. Smith, pp. 349–376. Institute for Mesoamerican Studies, Albany, N.Y.

Smith, Michael E., Cynthia Heath-Smith, Ronald Kohler, Joan Odess, Sharon Spanogle, and Timothy Sullivan

1994 The Size of the Aztec City of Yautepec: Urban Survey in Central Mexico. *Ancient Mesoamerica* 5:1–11.

Smith, Michael E., Cynthia Heath-Smith, and Lisa Montiel

1999 Excavations of Aztec Urban Houses at Yautepec, Mexico. *Latin American Antiquity* 10:133–150.

Smith, Michael E., and Kenneth G. Hirth
  1988   The Development of Prehispanic Cotton-Spinning Technology in Western Morelos, Mexico. *Journal of Field Archaeology* 15:349–358.

Smith, Michael E., and Lisa Montiel
  2001   The Archaeological Study of Empires and Imperialism in Pre-Hispanic Central Mexico. *Journal of Anthropological Archaeology* 20:245–284.

Smith, Michael E., Hector Neff, and Ruth Fauman-Fichman
  1999   Ceramic Imports at Yautepec and Their Implications for Aztec Exchange Systems. Paper presented at the 1999 Annual Meeting of the Society for American Archaeology (Chicago).

Smith, Michael E., and T. Jeffrey Price
  1994   Aztec-Period Agricultural Terraces in Morelos, Mexico: Evidence for Household-Level Agricultural Intensification. *Journal of Field Archaeology* 21:169–179.

Smith, Michael E., Jerrel H. Sorensen, and Philip K. Hopke
  1984   Obsidian Exchange in Postclassic Central Mexico: New Data from Morelos. Paper presented at the International Symposium on Archaeometry (Washington, D.C.).

Smith, Michael E., Jennifer Wharton, and Jan Marie Olson
  n.d.   Aztec Feasts, Rituals, and Markets: Political Uses of Ceramic Vessels in a Commercial Economy. In Pots as Political Tools: The Culinary Equipment of Early Imperial States in Comparative Perspective, edited by Tamara Bray. Unpublished manuscript.

Smith, Robert E.
  1958   The Place of Fine Orange Pottery in Mesoamerican Archaeology. *American Antiquity* 24:151–160.
  1971   *The Pottery of Mayapán.* Papers, vol. 66. Peabody Museum of Archaeology and Ethnology, Cambridge.

Snell, Daniel C.
  1997   Appendix: Theories of Ancient Economies and Societies. In *Life in the Ancient Near East, 3100–332 BCE,* edited by Daniel C. Snell, pp. 145–158. Yale University Press, New Haven.

Solís, Felipe
  2001   Tiempo Mesoamericana, VIII: Postclásico Tardío (1200/1300–1521 d.C.). *Arqueología Mexicana* 9(50):20–29.

Sorensen, Jerrel H.
  1988   Rural Chipped Stone Technology in Late Postclassic Morelos, Mexico. Paper presented at the 1988 Annual Meeting of the American Anthropological Association (Phoenix).

Sorensen, Jerrel H., Kenneth G. Hirth, and Stephen M. Ferguson
  1989   The Contents of Seven Obsidian Workshops Around Xochicalco, Morelos. In *La obsidiana en Mesoamérica,* edited by Margarita Gaxiola G. and John E. Clark, pp. 269–276. Instituto Nacional de Antropología e Historia, Mexico City.

Soustelle, Jacques
  1961   *Daily Life of the Aztecs on the Eve of the Spanish Conquest.* Stanford University Press, Stanford.

Spence, Michael W.
  1981   Obsidian Production and the State in Teotihuacan. *American Antiquity* 46:769–788.
  1984   Craft Production and Early Polity in Teotihuacan. In *Trade and Exchange in Early Mesoamerica,* edited by Keneth G. Hirth, pp. 87–114. University of New Mexico Press, Albuquerque.
  1985   Specialized Production in Rural Aztec Society: Obsidian Workshops of the Teotihuacan Valley. In *Contributions to the Archaeology and Ethnohistory of Greater Mesoamerica,* edited by William J. Folan, pp. 76–125. Southern Illinois University Press, Carbondale.

Spence, Michael W., and Jeffrey R. Parsons
  1972   Prehispanic Obsidian Exploitation in Central Mexico: A Preliminary Synthesis. In *Miscellaneous Studies in Mexican Prehistory,* edited by Michael W. Spence, Jeffrey R. Parsons, and Mary H. Parsons, pp. 1–33. Anthropological Papers, vol. 45. University of Michigan, Museum of Anthropology, Ann Arbor.

Spores, Ronald
  1965   The Zapotec and Mixtec at Spanish Conquest. In *Archaeology of Southern Mesoamerica,* part 2, edited by Gordon R. Willey, pp. 962–987. Handbook of Middle American Indians, vol. 3. University of Texas Press, Austin.
  1967   *The Mixtec Kings and Their People.* University of Oklahoma Press, Norman.
  1974   Marital Alliances in the Political Integration of Mixtec Kingdoms. *American Anthropologist* 76:297–311.
  1984   *The Mixtecs in Ancient and Colonial Times.* University of Oklahoma Press, Norman.
  1993   Tututepec: A Postclassic-Period Mixtec Conquest State. *Ancient Mesoamerica* 4:167–174.

Spranz, Bodo
  1973   *Los dioses en los códices mexicanos del grupo Borgia: Una investigación iconográfica.* Translated by María Martínez Peñaloza. Fondo de Cultura Económica, Mexico City.

Stark, Barbara J.
  1990   The Gulf Coast and the Central Highlands of Mexico: Alternative Models for Interaction. *Research in Economic Anthropology* 12:243–285.

Stark, Barbara L., Lynette Heller, and Michael A. Ohnersorgen
  1998   People with Cloth: Mesoamerican Economic Change from the Perspective of Cotton in South-Central Veracruz. *Latin American Antiquity* 9:7–36.

Stein, Gil J.
  1998   World System Theory and Alternative Modes of Interaction in the Archaeology of Culture Contact. In *Studies in Culture Contact: Interaction, Culture Change, and Archaeology,* edited by James G. Cusick, pp. 220–255. Occasional Paper, vol. 25. Center for Archaeological Investigations, Southern Illinois University, Carbondale.

Stern, Steve J.
  1993a Africa, Latin America, and the Splintering of Historical Knowledge: From Fragmentation to Reverberation. In *Confronting Historical Paradigms,* edited by Frederick Cooper, Allen F. Isaacman, Florencia E. Mallon, William Roseberry, and Steve J. Stern, pp. 23–83. University of Wisconsin Press, Madison.
  1993b Feudalism, Capitalism, and the World-System in the Perspective of Latin America and the Caribbean. In *Confronting Historical Paradigms,* edited by Frederick Cooper, Allen F. Isaacman, Florencia E. Mallon, William Roseberry, and Steve J. Stern, pp. 23–83. University of Wisconsin Press, Madison.

Stiver, Laura R., Michael D. Glascock, and Hector Neff
  1994   *Socioeconomic and Historical Implications of Obsidian Source Analysis from Dos Pilas, Petexbatun Region, Guatemala,* Manuscript on file, Department of Anthropology, Vanderbilt University, Nashville.

Stocker, Terrence L., and Robert H. Cobean
  1984   Preliminary Report on the Obsidian Mines at Pico de Orizaba, Veracruz. In *Prehistoric Quarries and Lithic Production,* edited by Jonathon E. Ericson and Barbara A. Purdy, pp. 83–95. Cambridge University Press, Cambridge.

Stone, Doris

1982 Cultural Radiations from the Central and Southern Highlands of Mexico into Costa Rica. In *Aspects of the Mixteca-Puebla Style and Mixtec and Central Mexican Culture in Southern Mesoamerica*, edited by Doris Stone, pp. 61–70. Occasional Papers, vol. 4. Middle American Research Institute, New Orleans.

Storey, Glenn R.

1999 Archaeology and Roman Society: Integrating Textual and Archaeological Data. *Journal of Archaeological Research* 7:203–248.

Street-Perrott, F. A., R. A. Perrott, and D. D. Harkness

1989 Anthropogenic Soil Erosion Around Lake Pátzcuaro, Michoacán, Mexico, During the Preclassic and Late Postclassic-Hispanic Periods. *American Antiquity* 54:759–765.

Stresser-Péan, Guy

1995 *El códice de Xicotepec: Estudio e interpretación.* Gobierno del Estado de Puebla, Centro Francés de Estudios Mexicanos y Centroamericanos, Fondo de Cultura Económica, Mexico City.

Stronach, David

1994 Village to Metropolis: Nineveh and the Beginnings of Urbanism in Northern Mesopotamia. In *Nuovo fondazioninel vicino oriente antico: Realtà e ideologia*, edited by S. Mazzoni, pp. 85–114, Pisa.

Suárez, Jorge A.

1983 *The Mesoamerican Indian Languages.* Cambridge University Press, New York.

Suárez Díez, Lourdes

1997 El comercio de la concha en el mundo prehispánico de Occidente. *Trace* 31:7–21.

Subrahmanyam, Sanjay

1990 Introduction. In *Merchants, Markets, and the State in Early Modern India*, edited by Sanjay Subrahmanyam, pp. 1–17. Oxford University Press, Delhi.

Suhler, C., and David Freidel

1998 Life and Death in the Maya War Zone. *Archaeology* 51(3):28–34.

Suma de Visitas

1905 *Suma de visitas de pueblos por orden alfabética.* Edited by Francisco del Paso y Troncoso. Papeles de Nueva España, vol. 1. Sucesores de Rivadeneyra, Madrid.

Swaney, James A.

2002 Karl Polanyi. In *The Oxford Encyclopedia of Economic History*, edited by Joel Mokyr. Oxford University Press, New York (in press).

Sweetman, Rosemary

1974 Prehistoric Pottery from Coastal Sinaloa and Nayarit, Mexico. In *The Archaeology of West Mexico*, edited by Betty Bell, pp. 68–82. Sociedad de Estudios Avanzados del Occidente de México, Ajijic, Jalisco.

Taggart, James

1983 *Nahuat Myth and Social Structure.* University of Texas Press, Austin.

Taube, Karl A.

1989 Ritual Humor in Classic Maya Religion. In *Word and Image in Mayan Culture*, edited by William Hanks and Don S. Rice, pp. 351–382. University of Utah Press, Salt Lake City.

1992 *The Major Gods of Ancient Yucatan.* Studies in Pre-Columbian Art and Archaeology, vol. 32. Dumbarton Oaks, Washington, D.C.

1993 The Bilimek Pulque Vessel: Starlore, Calendrics, and Cosmology of Late Postclassic Central Mexico. *Ancient Mesoamerica* 4:1–15.

2000 The Turquoise Hearth: Fire, Self Sacrifice, and the Central Mexican Cult of War. In *Mesoamerica's Classic Heritage: From Teotihuacan to the Aztecs*, edited by Davíd Carrasco, Lindsay Jones, and Scott Sessions, pp. 269–340. University Press of Colorado, Niwot.

2001 The Breath of Life: The Symbolism of Wind in Mesoamerica and the American Southwest. In *The Road to Aztlan: Art from a Mythic Homeland*, edited by Virginia M. Fields and Victor Zamudio-Taylor, pp. 86–101. Los Angeles County Museum of Art, Los Angeles.

Taube, Karl A., and Bonnie L. Bade

1991 *An Appearance of Xiuhtechutli in the Dresden Venus Pages.* Research Reports on Ancient Maya Writing, vol. 24. Center for Maya Research, Washington, D.C.

Taube, Karl A., and Tomás Gallareta Negrón

1988 Survey and Reconnaissance in the Ruinas de San Angel Region, Quintana Roo, Mexico. In *Preliminary Report of the 1988 San Angel Survey Project*, submitted to the National Geographic Society, Washington, D.C.

Tedlock, Barbara

1989 Review of *Continuities in Highland Maya Social Organization: Ethnohistory in Sacapulas, Guatemala* by R. M. Hill II and J. Monaghan. *American Anthropologist* 91:498–499.

Terraciano, Kevin

1994 Ñudzahui History: Mixtec Writing and Culture in Colonial Oaxaca. Ph.D. dissertation, Department of Anthropology, UCLA.

Thirsk, Joan

1961 Industries in the Countryside. In *Essays in the Economic and Social History of Tudor and Stuart England, in Honor of R. H. Tawney*, edited by F. J. Fisher, pp. 70–88. Cambridge University Press, Cambridge.

Thomas, Nicholas

1991 *Entangled Objects: Exchange, Material Culture, and Colonialism in the Pacific.* Harvard University Press, Cambridge.

Thomas, Norman D.

1974 *The Linguistic, Geographic, and Demographic Position of the Zoque of Southern Mexico.* Papers, vol. 36. New World Archaeological Foundation, Provo, UT.

Thompson, J. Eric

1943 A Trial Survey of the Southern Maya Area. *American Antiquity* 9:106–134.

1945 A Survey of the Northern Maya Area. *American Antiquity* 11:2–24.

1948 An Archaeological Reconaissance in the Cotzumalhuapa Region, Escuintla, Guatemala. *Contributions to American Anthropology and History*, no. 40, pp. 1–94. Carnegie Institution of Washington, Washington, D.C.

1951 Canoes and Navigation of the Maya and Their Neighbors. *Journal of the Royal Anthropological Institute (London)* 79:69–78.

1954 *The Rise and Fall of Maya Civilization.* University of Oklahoma Press, Norman.

1957 Deities Portrayed on Censers at Mayapán. *Current Reports* (Carnegie Institute of Washington) 40:599–628.

1966 *The Rise and Fall of Maya Civilization.* Rev. ed. University of Oklahoma Press, Norman.

1970 *Maya History and Religion.* University of Oklahoma Press, Norman.

1972 *A Commentary on the Dresden Codex.* American Philosophical Society, Philadelphia.

1977 A Proposal for Constituting a Maya Subgroup, Cultural and Linguistic, in the Petén and Adjacent Regions. In

Anthropology and History in Yucatan, edited by Grant Jones, pp. 3–42. University of Texas Press, Austin.

Thouvenot, Marc
1982   *Chalchihuitl: Le jade chez les Aztèques.* Institut d'Ethnologie, Paris.

Torquemada, Juan de
1969   *Monarquía indiana.* 3 vols. Porrúa, Mexico City.
1986   *Monarquía indiana.* 3 vols. Porrúa, Mexico City.

Torres M., Luis, and Francisca Franco V.
1989   La orfebrería prehispánica en el Golfo de México y el tesoro del pescador. In *Orfebrería prehispánica*, edited by Carlos Aguilar, Beatriz Barba, Román Piña Chán, Luis Torres Montes, Francisca Franco and Guillermo Ahuja, pp. 217–270. Corporación Industrial Sanluis, Mexico City.

Tourtellot, Gair, and Jeremy A. Sabloff
1972   Exchange Systems Among the Ancient Maya. *American Antiquity* 37:126–135.

Tozzer, Alfred M.
1941   *Landa's* Relación de las Cosas de Yucatán: *A Translation.* Papers, vol. 18. Peabody Museum, Cambridge.
1957   *Chichen Itza and Its Cenote of Sacrifice: A Comparative Study of Contemporaneous Maya and Toltec.* Memoirs, vols. 11–12. 2 vols. Peabody Museum, Harvard University, Cambridge.

Trigger, Bruce G.
1989   *A History of Archaeological Thought.* Cambridge University Press, Cambridge.
1993   *Early Civilizations: Ancient Egypt in Context.* The American University in Cairo Press, Cairo.

Troike, Nancy
n.d.   Untitled manuscript on file. Instituto de Investigaciones Antropológicas, Universidad Nacional Autónoma de México, Mexico City.

Trombold, Charles D.
1990   A Reconsideration of Chronology for the La Quemada Portion of the Northern Mesoamerican Frontier. *American Antiquity* 55:308–324.

Trombold, Charles D., J. F. Luhr, T. Hasenaka, and Michael D. Glascock
1993   Chemical Characteristics of Obsidian from Archaeological Sites in Western Mexico and the Tequila Source Area: Implication for Regional and Pan-American Interaction within the Northern Mesoamerican Periphery. *Ancient Mesoamerica* 4:255–270.

Turok, Marta
1996   Xiuhquilitl, nocheztli y tixinda: Tintes del México Antiguo. *Arqueología Mexicana* 3(17):26–33.

Turok, Marta, et al.
1988   *El caracol púrpura: Una tradición milenaria en Oaxaca.* Dirección General de Culturas Populares, Mexico City.

Umberger, Emily
1996   Aztec Presence and Material Remains in the Outer Provinces. In *Aztec Imperial Strategies*, by Frances F. Berdan, Richard E. Blanton, Elizabeth H. Boone, Mary G. Hodge, Michael E. Smith, and Emily Umberger, pp. 151–180. Dumbarton Oaks, Washington, D.C.

Umberger, Emily, and Cecilia Klein
1993   Aztec Art and Imperial Expansion. In *Latin American Horizons*, edited by Don S. Rice, pp. 295–336. Dumbarton Oaks, Washington, D.C.

Uruñuela, Gabriela, Patricia Plunket, Gilda Hernández, and Juan Albaitero
1997   Biconical God Figurines from Cholula and the Codex Borgia. *Latin American Antiquity* 8:63–70.

Vail, Gabriel
1988   *The Archaeology of Coastal Belize.* BAR International Series, vol. 463. British Archaeological Reports, Oxford.

Vaillant, George C.
1938   A Correlation of Archaeological and Historical Sequences in the Valley of Mexico. *American Anthropologist* 40:535–573.
1940   Patterns in Middle American Archaeology. In *The Maya and Their Neighbors*, edited by Clarence L. Hay, pp. 295–305. Appleton-Century, New York.

Valdez, Francisco, and Catherine Liot
1994   La cuenca de Sayula: Yacimientos de sal en la frontera oeste del estado tarasco. In *El Michoacán antiguo*, edited by Brigitte Boehm de Lameiros, pp. 285–305. El Colegio de Michoacán, Zamora, Mexico.

Valdez, Francisco, Catherine Liot, Rosario Acosta, and Jean Pierre Emphoux
1996   The Sayula Basin: Lifeways and Salt-Flats of Central Jalisco. *Ancient Mesoamerica* 7:171–186.

Valdez, Francisco, Catherine Liot, and Otto Schondube
1996   Los recursos naturales y su uso en las cuencas lacustres del sur de Jalisco: El caso de Sayula. In *Las cuencas del occidente de México*, edited by Eduardo Williams and Phil C. Weigand, pp. 325–366. El Colegio de Michoacán, Zamora.

Van De Mieroop, Marc
1999   *The Ancient Mesopotamian City.* Oxford University Press, Oxford.

van Doesburg, Bas, and Olivier van Buren
n.d.   The Origin of the "Lienzo de Tulancingo." Unpublished manuscript on file.

van Zantwijk, Rudolf
1963   Los últimos reductos de la lengua náhuatl en los altos de Chiapas. *Tlalocan* 4(4):179–184.

Vargas Pacheco, Ernesto
1994   Síntesis de la historia prehispánica de los Mayas Chontales de Tabasco-Campeche. In *América indígena, historia prehispánica*, pp. 15–61, vols. 1–2. Instituto de Investigaciones Antropológicas, Universidad Nacional Autónoma de México, Mexico City.

Vega Sosa, Constanza, and Roberto Cervantes-Delgado (editors)
1986   *Arqueología y etnohistoria del estado de Guerrero.* Instituto Nacional de Antropología e Historia, Mexico City.

Videjko, Mikhail
1995   Großsiedlungen der Tripol'e-Kultur in der Ukraine. *Eurasia Antiqua* 1:45–80.

Villacorta C., J. Antonio, and Carlos A. Villacorta
1977   *Códices mayas.* 2nd ed. Tipografía Nacional, Guatemala City.

Vivó, Jorge A.
1942   Geografía lingüística y política prehispánica de Chiapas y secuencia histórica de sus pobladores. *Revista Geográfica del Instituto Panamericano de Geografía e Historia* (Mexico) 2:121–156.

von Hagen, Victor W.
1944   *The Aztec and Maya Papermakers.* J. J. Augustin, New York.

von Winning, Hasso
1976   Escenas rituales en la cerámica policroma de Nayarit. In *Actas del XLI Congreso Internacional de Americanistas*, pp. 387–400, vol. 2. Instituto Nacional de Antropología e Historia, Mexico City.
1977   Rituals Depicted on Polychrome Ceramics from Nayarit. In *Pre-Columbian Art History: Selected Read-*

ings, edited by Alana Cordy-Collins and Jean Stern, pp. 121–134. Peek Publications, Palo Alto.

Voorhies, Barbara

1989a An Introduction to the Soconusco and Its Prehistory. In *Ancient Trade and Tribute: Economies of the Soconusco Region of Mesoamerica*, edited by Barbara Voorhies, pp. 1–18. University of Utah Press, Salt Lake City.

1989b Whither the King's Traders: Reevaluating Fifteenth-Century Xoconochco as a Port of Trade. In *Ancient Trade and Tribute: Economies of the Soconusco Region of Mesoamerica*, edited by Barbara Voorhies, pp. 21–47. University of Utah Press, Salt Lake City.

1989c A Model of the Pre-Aztec Political System of the Soconusco. In *Ancient Trade and Tribute: Economies of the Soconusco Region of Mesoamerica*, edited by Barbara Voorhies, pp. 95–129. University of Utah Press, Salt Lake City.

1989d Textile Production. In *Ancient Trade and Tribute: Economies of the Soconusco Region of Mesoamerica*, edited by Barbara Voorhies, pp. 194–214. University of Utah Press, Salt Lake City.

1989e Settlement Patterns in the Western Soconusco: Methods of Site Recovery and Dating Results. In *New Frontiers in the Archaeology of the Pacific Coast of Southern Mesoamerica*, edited by Frederick Bové and Lynette Heller, pp. 103–124. Anthropological Research Papers, vol. 39. Arizona State University, Tempe.

1989f *Final Report to the National Geographic Society, Grant #3689–87.* Pertaining to survey and excavations at Tlacuactero.

1989g *Ancient Trade and Tribute: Economies of the Soconusco Region of Mesoamerica.* University of Utah Press, Salt Lake City.

1991a La producción textil. In *La economía del antiguo Soconusco, Chiapas*, edited by Barbara Voorhies, pp. 227–250. Translated by Raúl del Moral. Universidad Nacional Autónoma de México and Universidad Autónoma de Chiapas, Mexico City.

1991b Un modelo del sistema política pre-Azteca del Soconusco. In *La economía del antiguo Soconusco, Chiapas*, edited by Barbara Voorhies, pp. 115–153. Translated by Raúl del Moral. Universidad Nacional Autónoma de México and Universidad Autónoma de Chiapas, Mexico City.

Voorhies, Barbara, and Janine Gasco

1984 El periodo posclásico tardio de Acepetahua, Chiapas, Mexico. In *Investigaciones recientes en el area maya*, pp. 431–438, vol. 1. Sociedad Mexicana de Antropología, San Cristóbal de las Casas, Mexico.

2002 *Postclassic Soconusco Society: The Late Postclassic History of the Coast of Chiapas, Mexico.* IMS Monographs. Institute for Mesoamerican Studies, Albany (in press).

Voorhies, Barbara, and Douglas Kennett

1995 Buried Sites on the Soconusco Coastal Plain, Chiapas, Mexico. *Journal of Field Archaeology* 22:65–79.

Walker, Deborah

1990 Cerros Revisited: Ceramic Indicators of Terminal Classic and Postclassic Settlement and Pilgrimage in Northern Belize. Ph.D. dissertation, Department of Anthropology, Southern Methodist University.

Wallerstein, Immanuel

1974 *The Modern World-System: Capitalist Agriculture and the Origins of the European World-Economy in the Sixteenth Century.* Academic Press, New York.

1976 A World-System Perspective on the Social Sciences. *British Journal of Sociology* 27:345–352.

1979 *The Capitalist World-Economy.* Cambridge University Press, London.

1982 World-Systems Analysis: Theoretical and Interpretive Issues. In *World-Systems Analysis: Theory and Methodology*, edited by Terrance K. Hopkins and Immanuel Wallerstein, pp. 91–103. Explorations in the World-Economy, Publications of the Fernand Braudel Center, vol. 1. Sage, Beverly Hills.

Wallrath, Matthew

1967 *Excavations in the Tehuantepec Region, Mexico.* Transactions of the American Philosophical Society, vol. 57 (2). American Philosophical Society, Philadelphia.

Warren, J. Benedict

1968 Minas de cobre de Michoacán, 1533. *Anales de Museo Michoacano* 6:35–52.

1977 *La conquista de Michoacán.* Fimax Publicistas, Morelia.

1985 *The Conquest of Michoacan: The Spanish Domination of the Tarascan Kingdom in Western Mexico, 1521–1530.* University of Oklahoma Press, Norman.

Wauchope, Robert

1949 Las edades de Utatlán e Iximché. *Antropología e Historia de Guatemala* 1(1):10–22.

1970 Protohistoric Pottery of the Guatemalan Highlands. In *Monographs and Papers in Maya Archaeology*, edited by William R. Bullard, pp. 89–244. Papers, vol. 61. Peabody Museum, Harvard University, Cambridge.

1975 *Zacualpa, El Quiche, Guatemala: An Ancient Provincial Center of the Highland Maya.* Publication, vol. 39. Middle American Research Institute, Tulane University, New Orleans.

Weaver, Muriel Porter

1993 *The Aztecs, Maya, and Their Predecessors: Archaeology of Mesoamerica.* 3rd ed. Academic Press, San Diego.

Webb, Malcolm C.

1964 The Post-Classic Decline of the Peten Maya: An Interpretation in Light of a General Theory of State Society. Ph.D. dissertation, Department of Anthropology, Harvard University.

1978 The Significance of the "Epiclassic" Period in Mesoamerican Prehistory. In *Cultural Continuity in Mesoamerica*, edited by David L. Browman, pp. 155–178. Mouton, The Hague.

Webster, David

1994 Comment on Living on the Edge: Core/Periphery Relations in Ancient Southeastern Mesoamerica. *Current Anthropology* 35:419–420.

Weigand, Phil C.

1985 Considerations on the Archaeology and Ethnohistory of the Mexicanos, Tequales, Coras, Huicholes, and Caxcans of Nayarit, Jalisco, and Zacatecas. In *Contributions to the Archaeology and Ethnohistory of Greater Mesoamerica*, edited by William J. Folan, pp. 126–187. Southern Illinois University Press, Carbondale.

1990 The Teuchtitlán Tradition of Western Mesoamerica. In *La época clásica: Nuevos hallazgos, nuevas ideas*, edited by A. Cárdos de Méndez, pp. 25–54. Instituto Nacional de Antropología e Historia, Mexico City.

1993 The Political Organization of the Trans-Tarascan Zone of Western Mesoamerica on the Eve of the Spanish Conquest. In *Culture and Contact: Charles C. Di Peso's Gran Chichimeca*, edited by Anne I. Woosley and John C. Ravesloot, pp. 191–217. University of New Mexico Press, Albuquerque.

Weigand, Phil C., and Garman Harbottle
1993   The Role of Turquoise in the Ancient Mesoamerican Trade Structure. In *The American Southwest and Mesoamerica: Systems of Prehistoric Exchange*, edited by Jonathon Ericson and Timothy G. Baugh, pp. 159–177. Plenum Press, New York.

Weigand, Phil C., Garman Harbottle, and Edward V. Sayre
1977   Turquoise Sources and Source Analysis: Mesoamerica and the Southwestern U.S.A. In *Exchange Systems in Prehistory*, edited by Timothy K. Earle and Jonathon E. Ericson, pp. 15–34. Academic Press, New York.

Weigand, Phil C., and Acelia G. de Weigand
1996   *Tenamaxtli y Guaxicar: Las raíces profundos de la rebelión de Nueva Galicia.* El Colegio de Michoacán, Zamora.

Weitlaner, Robert J.
1947   Exploración arqueológica en Guerrero, in El occidente de México. Pp. 77–85. Sociedad Mexicana de Antropología, Cuarta Reunion de Mesa Redonda, Mexico City.

Welsh, W. B. M.
1988   *An Analysis of Classic Lowland Maya Burials.* BAR International Series, vol. S409. British Archaeological Reports, Oxford.

West, Robert C.
1961   Aboriginal Sea Navigation Between Middle and South America. *American Anthropologist* 63:133–135.

Whitecotton, Joseph
1977   *The Zapotecs: Princes, Priests, and Peasants.* University of Oklahoma Press, Norman.
1990   *Zapotec Elite Ethnohistory: Pictorial Genealogies from Eastern Oaxaca.* Vanderbilt University Publications in Anthropology, vol. 39. Department of Anthropology, Vanderbilt University, Nashville.

Whitecotton, Joseph W., and Richard A. Pailes
1986   New World Precolumbian World Systems. In *Ripples in the Chichimec Sea: New Considerations of Southwestern-Mesoamerican Interactions*, edited by Frances Joan Mathien and Randall H. McGuire, pp. 183–203. Southern Illinois University Press, Carbondale.

Whitmore, Thomas M., and Barbara J. Williams
1998   Famine Vulnerability in the Contact-Era Basin of Mexico: A Simulation. *Ancient Mesoamerica* 9:83–98.

Whittaker, Gordon
1986   The Mexican Names of Three Venus Gods in the Dresden Codex. *Mexicon* 8(3):56–60.

Whittington, Stephen L., and David M. Reed
1994   Los esqueletos de Iximché. In *VII Simposio de investigaciones arqueológicas en Guatemala*, edited by Juan Pedro Laporte and Hector L. Escobedo, pp. 23–28. Museo Nacional de Arqueología y Etnología, Guatemala City.

Whorf, Benjamin L.
1943   *Loan Words in Ancient Mexico.* Philological and Documentary Studies I, Publication, vol. 11. Middle American Research Institute, Tulane University, New Orleans.

Willey, Gordon R., William R. Bullard, John Glass, and James Gifford
1965   *Prehistoric Maya Settlements in the Belize Valley.* Papers, vol. 54. Peabody Museum, Cambridge.

Willey, Gordon R., and Philip Phillips
1955   Method and Theory in American Archaeology, II: Historical-Developmental Interpretation. *American Anthropologist* 57:723–819.
1958   *Method and Theory in American Archaeology.* University of Chicago Press, Chicago.

Willey, Gordon R., and Jeremy A. Sabloff
1993   *A History of American Archaeology.* 3rd ed. W. H. Freeman, San Francisco.

Williams, Barbara J.
1989   Contact Period Rural Overpopulation in the Basin of Mexico: Carrying-Capacity Models Tested with Documentary Data. *American Antiquity* 54:715–732.

Williams, Eduardo
1999   The Ethnoarchaeology of Salt Production at Lake Cuitzeo, Michoacan, Mexico. *Latin American Antiquity* 10:400–414.

Williams, Eduardo, and Phil C. Weigand
1996   *Las cuencas del occidente de México: Época prehispánica.* Colección Memorias. El Colegio de Michoacán, Zamora, Mexico.

Williams-Beck, Lorraine
1998   *El dominio de los batabob: El área Puuc occidental campechana.* Universidad Autónoma de Campeche/Secretaría de Educación Pública, Campeche.

Winter, Marcus C.
1985   Los altos de Oaxaca. In *Historia de la agricultura: Época prehispánica–siglo XVI*, edited by Teresa Rojas Rabiela and William T. Sanders, pp. 77–124, vol. 2. Instituto Nacional de Antropología e Historia, Mexico City.
1989   La obsidiana en Oaxaca prehispánica. In *La obsidiana en Mesoamérica*, edited by Margarita Gaxiola G. and John E. Clark, pp. 345–361. Instituto Nacional de Antropología e Historia, Mexico City.

Wissler, Clark
1914   Material Cultures of the North American Indians. *American Anthropologist* 16:447–505.
1927   The Culture Area Concept in Social Anthropology. *American Journal of Sociology* 32:881–891.

Wittfogel, Karl A.
1957   *Oriental Depotism: A Comparative Study of Total Power.* Yale University Press, New Haven.

Wobst, H. Martin
1999   Style in Archaeology and Archaeologists in Style. In *Material Meanings: Critical Approaches to the Interpretation of Material Culture*, edited by Elizabeth S. Chilton, pp. 118–132. University of Utah Press, Salt Lake City.

Wolf, Eric R.
1951   The Social Organization of Mecca and the Origins of Islam. *Southwestern Journal of Anthropology* 7:329–356.
1982   *Europe and the People Without History.* University of California Press, Berkeley.

Wonderly, Anthony
1985   The Land of Ulua: Postclassic Research in the Naco and Sula Valleys, Honduras. In *The Lowland Maya Postclassic*, edited by Arlen F. Chase and Prudence Rice, pp. 254–269. University of Texas Press, Austin.
1986   Naco, Honduras: Some Aspects of a Late Precolumbian Community on the Eastern Maya Frontier. In *The Southeast Maya Periphery*, edited by Patricia A. Urban and Edward M. Schortman, pp. 313–332. University of Texas Press, Austin.

Woodbury, Richard B., and James A. Neely
1972   Water Control Systems in the Tehuacan Valley. In *Chronology and Irrigation*, edited by Richard S. MacNeish and Frederick Johnson, pp. 81–161. Prehistory of

the Tehuacan Valley, vol. 4. University of Texas Press, Austin.

Woodbury, Richard B., and Aubrey S. Trik
1953 *The Ruins of Zaculeu, Guatemala.* 2 vols. William Byrd Press, Richmond, VA.

Wright, Barton
1994 *Clowns of the Hopi: Tradition Keepers and Delight Makers.* Northland, Flagstaff.

Wurster, Wolfgang W. (editor)
2000 *El sitio maya de Topoxté: Investigaciones en una isla del lago Yaxhá, Petén, Guatemala.* Materialien zur Allgemeinen und Vergleichenden Archäologie, vol. 57. Verlage Philipp von Zabern, Mainz.

Wyllie, Cherra
1994 How to Make an Aztec Book: An Investigation into the Manufacture of Central Mexican Codices. M.A. thesis, Department of Anthropology, Yale University.

Ximénez, Fray Francisco
1999 *Historia de la provincia de San Vicente de Chiapa y Guatemala de la orden de predicadores*, vol. 1. Consejo Estatal para la Cultura y las Artes de Chiapas, Tuxtla Gutierrez.

Yoneda, Keiko
1981 *Los mapas de Cuauhtinchan y la historia cartográfica prehispánica.* Archivo General de la Nación, Mexico City.

Zeitlin, Judith F., and Robert N. Zeitlin
1990 Arqueología y época prehispánica en el sur del Istmo de Tehuantepec. In *Lecturas históricas del estado de Oaxaca*, edited by Marcus C. Winter, pp. 393–454. Epoca Prehispánica, vol. 1. Instituto Nacional de Antropología e Historia, Mexico City.

Zeitlin, Robert N.
1982 Toward a More Comprehensive Model of Interregional Commodity Distribution: Political Variables and Prehistoric Obsidian Procurement in Mesoamerica. *American Antiquity* 47:260–275.

Zorita, Alonso de
1963 *Life and Labor in Ancient Mexico: The Brief and Summary Relation of the Lords of New Spain.* Translated by Benjamin Keen. Rutgers University Press, New Brunswick.

Index

Abu-Lughod, Janet L., 18, 19, 25, 67, 314
Acalan region, 110
Acámbaro, 82, 89
Acapetahua, 51–52, 53, 289, 294, 295
Acatlan, 127, 245–46, 320n3
Acazacatlan, 75
accumulation, and world-systems theory, 16–17
Achiutla, 244
Acolhua city-states, 240
Acolman, 101
Adams, Robert McC., 11–12, 307
adaptionist approach, to Postclassic Aztec economy, 10
affluent production zones: and Chikinchel as regional case study, 259–68; Postclassic Mesoamerican world system and concept of, 24, 26–28, 95
agriculture: and economic change in Morelos region, 250, 251; intensity of and population growth in Postclassic Mesoamerica, 6, 96, 309; and population increase in Basin of Mexico, 241; and population increase in Jalisco region, 56; and resources of Soconusco, 293. *See also* cacao; diet; land-tenure systems and land use
Ahuatlan province, 76
Ahuitzotl, 74
Alahuiztlan, 87, 127, 129
Alexander, Rani T., 42
almanacs, and divinatory codices, 215, 217
Altun Ha, 163
altepetl, 59, 74-75. *See also* city-states
Amapa, 161
American Museum of Natural History, 204–205
Anales de Cuauhtitlan, 174
Andes, and metalworking, 163. *See also* Peru
Andrews, Anthony P., 324n7
Andrews, E. Wyllys, IV, 10
annals history, and codices, 208–209
Apatzingan, 153, 164
Apoala, 245
Appadurai, Arjun, 117, 122
Araró, 128
archaeology: and central Mexican influence in highland Guatemala, 297–98; and consumption levels of obsidian artifacts, 155–56; and documentation of market exchange, 101, 102; and economic change in Morelos, 249–51; and economic patterns in northern Belize,

269–81; and economic value of commodities, 118, 120–22; and international trade centers, 109, 111; and long-distance trade networks in Soconusco, 296; and material record of Chikinchel, 261–63; and world-systems theory, 15
architecture, and central Mexican influence on highland Maya, 298. *See also* double temple; fortresses; pyramids; skull platforms
art: and concept of style in history of, 186; Tarascan and Mesoamerican heritage of Postclassic Mexico, 85–86. *See also* mural paintings; polychrome pottery; Postclassic international symbol set
astronomy, and interpretations of symbolism in Maya mural paintings, 200
Atemajác, 57
Aterio, 84
Atotonilco el Grande, 76
Aubin Manuscript No. 20, 214
authority, and political structure of Tarascan empire, 80–81
axes, as form of money, 123, 167–69, 170–71, 316
Ayala site (Nicaragua), 139
Ayotlan, 174
Ayutla, 53
Azcapotzalco, 58, 101, 139
Aztatlan Trade System, 55–56, 57
Aztec Black-on-orange ceramics, 255
Aztecs and Aztec empire: and borders of eastern empire, 73–77, 79–80; and border with Tarascan empire, 87–90, 112; and central Mexican influence on K'iche'an society, 302; and city-states in Basin of Mexico and Morelos, 58–60; codices and information networks, 184, 185, 207–21; and conquest of Morelos, 250; and conquest of Soconusco, 282, 287, 295–96; and exchange circuits, 30; factionalism and rise of in central and southern Mexico, 65–66; and international trade centers, 110–11; and mural paintings, 188; place of in Postclassic Mesoamerican world system, 67–72; and Postclassic international symbol set, 192–93; royal ideology and political organization of, 212–13; and small polities of Postclassic period, 6, 36; and social class of merchants, 103; and style zones, 31; and system of tribute, 69, 105, 267; and Tarascan empire, 79–80, 87–90; views of Postclassic economy of, 10–11; and warfare, 38. *See also*

Eastern Nahua; Nahuatl language; Tenochtitlan; Teotihuacan; Texcoco; Tlacopan; Triple Alliance

Ball, Joseph W., 194
Balsas Basin, 80, 84, 87, 88, 161, 234
Bandera, 43
bark paper and bark beaters, 253
Barlow, Robert H., 73
Barrett, Elinore M., 166
Basin of Mexico: as affluent production zone, 28; agricultural intensification and population growth in, 6, 96, 315; and Aztec city-states, 58–60; and chronology of Postclassic period, 5; evolution of as core zone, 238–42; and iconography in Morelos, 256; and long-distance trade, 104; and trade with Morelos, 255
batabils, and Late Postclassic Maya, 41–42
Belize, northern: as affluent production zone, 28, 269; and economic patterns, 269–81; and luxury goods, 10; Maya and political organization in, 40–44; and metalworking, 163, 169; and obsidian, 141; and regional exchange, 316; as resource-extraction zone, 29. *See also* Chetumal
bells, and metal artifacts, 124, 162, 165, 166, 167, 170
Beltrán, Ulises, 78, 81, 82
Berdan, Frances F., 4, 13, 19, 89, 208
Bernard (Guerrero), 164
Bey, George J., 266, 320n4
Bezelao (god), 204–205, 206
Binford, Lewis R., 15
Blanton, Richard E., 7, 37
Blom, Frans, 319n1–2
Boone, Elizabeth H., 182, 184, 192
borders: of Aztec and Tarascan empires, 38, 87–90; of eastern Aztec empire, 73–77. *See also* political organization; spatial structure
Borhegyi, Stephan F., 8, 297
Boserupian model, of population pressure, 6
Brand, Donald D., 56
Braswell, Geoffrey E., 36, 185
Braudel, Fernand, 16, 267, 268, 316
Bray, Warwick, 163, 164, 169
Bricker, Victoria R., 220
bronze, and metalworking, 124, 164, 166, 167, 255. *See also* metals and metallurgy